SEATTLE IN THE

Seattle 1921-1940

FROM BOOM TO BUST

Richard C. Berner

Charles Press
Seattle, Washington

Printed and Bound in the United States of America

Library of Congress Cataloging-in-Publication Data
(Revised for vol. 2)

Berner, Richard C.
Seattle in the 20th century.

Cover title.
Includes bibliographical references and indexes.
Contents: v. 1. Seattle, 1900-1920 -- v. 2. Seattle, 1921-1940.
1. Seattle (Wash.)--History. I. Title.
F899.S457B47 1991 979.7'772 91-74159
ISBN 0-9629889-1-X (v. 2 : acid-free paper)

Published by Charles Press
3616 East Cherry Street
Seattle, WA 98122

ISBN: 0-9629889-1-X

This book is printed on pH neutral, acid-free paper.

Contents

List of Photographs

Abbreviations Used

AFL	American Federation of Labor
City Light	Seattle Lighting Department
CIO	Congress of Industrial Organizations
CBI	Commonwealth Builders, Inc.
PSP&L	Puget Sound Power and Light Company
P-I	*Seattle Post-Intelligencer*
Times	*Seattle Times*
Star	*Seattle Star*
UR	*Seattle Union Record*
UCL	Unemployed Citizens' League
WCF	Washington Commonwealth Federation
WOAP	Washington Old Age Pension Union

List of Charts, Maps, and Tables

Acknowledgments

As with the research on *Seattle, 1900-1920: From Boomtown, Urban Turbulence, to Restoration*, the author is indebted to many people and services. The superb collections of the University Archives and Manuscripts Division have been indispensable. Division head Karyl Winn, and her staff, provided excellent service. Gary Lundell led me to English Department records of critical value, bearing on the Hughes-Jameses rivalry. As to the new facility, it is a marked improvement over the one I vacated, though it also lacks adequate processing space—a handicap that ultimately affects the user.

Glenda Pearson, head of the Newspaper and Microforms Section, and her assistant Terry Kato, continue to offer an array of services, not the least of which is trouble-shooting on their technical equipment, most of which is outmoded and/or poorly designed for research use. Holdings of the Special Collections Division's scrapbooks and notable weekly and monthly newspapers like the *Argus*, *Town Crier*, and *Municipal News*, plus its photographic collection, have been of inestimable value. The author is indebted to Carla Rickerson and Richard Engeman for their assistance.

I have appreciated the help of City Archivist Scott Cline, Seattle Public Schools' Archivist Eleanor Toews, the staff of the Seattle Public Library's History Division for accessing the Chamber of Commere minutebooks, and Jo Ann Fenton of the Library's Art Division for assistance in selecting suitable photographs. Rick Caldwell and Carolyn Marr of the Museum of History and Industry provided comparable help in selecting photographs. Once again Dave Freeh of City Light lent his invaluable assistance in locating appropriate photographs. Finding an appropriate harbor photograph proved more troublesome than expected, but that indefatiguable "Now and Then" photographic historian Paul Dorpat led me to the collection of Walker and Associates in Tukwila, where the cover illustration and other candidates were found. Dorpat's other advice benefited the author greatly.

Outside the Seattle area Desmond Taylor, of the University of Puget Sound Library, guided me with dispatch to the Homer T. Bone papers in their collection. Within five minutes I found precisely the documentation I was looking for—it found its way to chapter 29. Robert E. Ficken—biographer of Rufus Woods—led me to the Woods papers at the *Wenatchee World*, where Wilfred Woods so warmly welcomed us. The Woods correspondence also was woven into the complex chapter 29.

The late Jesse Epstein, Fayette Krause, and Miner Baker read early versions of the manuscript. Their respective critiques guided me in making revisions. Hu Blonk and Baker, as student leaders at the UW in 1935, provided background on the anti-militarism controversy of that year.

Permission from the *Seattle Times* to reproduce the photograph of Dave Beck and Joe Ryan with the accompanying text is appreciated, as is the permission granted by the University of Washington Press for use of the charts appearing in Calvin F. Schmid's *Social Trends in Seattle*.

My veteran friend and former library colleague Gerald J. Oppenheimer, generously provided the kind of editorial services that would have benefited me in the production of volume one. If there is a surviving colon or semi-colon in the text it is there because he allowed it. Being no grammarian, I was putty in his hands. He also demanded clarification where needed. If any cloudiness remains it is no fault of his.

As to textual criticism, who could have asked for more than having the University of Idaho's Professor Carlos A. Schwantes's help? To acknowledge his generosity in providing both a sharp critique of the final draft and warm praise, is to understate my appreciation.

That the New Deal specialist and FDR biographer, Professor Frank Freidel of Harvard University, has found time from his busy schedule to warmly commend this volume to an audience outside the Pacific Northwest is most gratifying.

To Margaret Savage—whose special expertise in computerization is but a sideline to her career as a physiologist—I am particularly grateful.

This volume is dedicated to Murray Morgan, who has done more than anyone to excite interest in Pacific Northwest history, and to Robert E. Burke, whose professional collaboration over the years has led to the production of this history.

Preface

This second volume of *Seattle in the Twentieth Century* covers a period in the city's history that, surprisingly, has received little formal attention. One measure of this inattention is reflected in the relatively few journal articles appearing in *Pacific Northwest Quarterly*, the main vehicle for scholarly articles on the region's history. Perhaps a half dozen are cited for the period 1921-1940. For the period 1900-1920, probably two dozen articles are cited. Yet the archival documentation is far more abundant for the later period. Fortunately, however, some excellent theses and dissertations—based largely on these archival materials—have been written. I have doubly benefited from having worked directly with most of the authors. Their studies have been true building blocks, making possible a more comprehensive work such as mine. In some cases, archival sources, relative to their special studies, were subsequently added to the holdings of the University of Washington Libraries' Archives and Manuscripts Division. Although these graduate students did not benefit from those additions, I have. That is the nature of archival documentation—it continues to get collected. I expect my own work to be superseded—the fate of most historians.

As the reader might not appreciate how dependent I have been on these graduate studies, the following is a list of those that were most heavily used.

Albert A. Acena. *The Washington Commonwealth Federation: Reform Politics and the Popular Front*. 1975.

Bruce D. Blumell. *The Development of Public Assistance in the State of Washington During the Great Depression*. 1973.

Robert L. Cole. *The Democratic Party in Washington State, 1919-1933: Barometer of Social Change*. 1972.

Jonathan Dembo. *A History of the Washington State Labor Movement, 1885-1935*. 1978.

Wesley A. Dick. *Visions of Abundance: the Public Power Crusade in the Era of J.D. Ross and the New Deal*. 1973.

William J. Dickson. *Labor in Municipal Politics: a Study of Labor's Political Activities in Seattle*. 1928.

Albert F. Gunns. *Civil Liberties and Crisis: the Status of Civil Liberties in the Pacific Northwest, 1917-1940*. 1971.

Margaret A. Hall. *A History of Women Faculty at the University of Washington, 1896-1970*. 1984.

John A. Hogan. *The Decline of Self-Help and Growth of Radicalism Among Seattle's Unemployed*. 1934.

George Michael Jones. *Longshore Unionism on Puget Sound: Seattle-Tacoma Comparison*. 1957.

Fayette F. Krause. *Democratic Party Politics in the State of Washington During the New Deal, 1932-1940*. 1971.

George T. Melton. *The State Grange and the Development of Water Power Resources in Washington*. 1954.

William H. Mullins. *San Francisco and Seattle During the Hoover Years of the Great Depression: 1929-1933*. 1975.

Bryce E. Nelson. *Good Schools: the Development of Public Schooling in Seattle, 1901-1922*. 1981.

Mary Joan O'Connell. *The Seattle Union Record, 1918-1928: a Pioneer Labor Daily*. 1964.

Lee F. Pendergrass. *Urban Reform and Voluntary Association: a Case Study of the Seattle Municipal League*. 1972.

Robert Bedford Pitts. *Organized Labor and the Negro*. 1941.

Herbert Clay Prouty. *Seattle's A.F. of L.-C.I.O. War of the Warehousemen*. 1938.

Douglas R. Pullen. *The Administration of Washington State Governor Louis F. Hart, 1919-1925*. 1974.

George W. Scott. *The New Order of Cincinnatus*. 1966.

Sarah Ellen Sharbach. *Louise Olivereau and the Seattle Radical Community, 1917-1923*. 1986.

William Thomas White. *A History of Railroad Workers in the Pacific Northwest, 1883-1934*. 1981.

Authors of all graduate studies written before the 1960s had no access to archival materials, except for the personal papers still in possession of the principals. Few of these graduate students were in the history department. They were pursuing topics of contemporary interest, usually labor relations, issues generated by the Great Depression, and the conflict between private and public ownership of electrical utilities. Their accounts—and those of others who are cited elsewhere in the book—usually bear a character akin to that of a "participant observer". They are to be valued for that characteristic. Today, one kind of primary source documentation available to these graduate students—personal interviews of participants—is misleadingly termed, "oral history". While a valuable ingredient of documentation, interviews are but one part, and they are also the least reliable, due to the greater problem of authentication. Textual sources of the traditional archival type remain the most trustworthy, particularly those least tampered with before transfer to archival custody.

Some dissertations listed above have been published. They are listed in both sections of the bibliography, under "Books" and "Theses and Dissertations". These authors are Bruce Blumell, Jonathan Dembo, Albert Gunns, and Bryce Nelson. That of William Mullins was expanded to include two other West Coast cities, Los Angeles, and Portland.

Archival sources—embracing manuscript collections—at the University of Washington Libraries constitute the most critical body of source materials for this history. From 1960 to the present, these materials have been collected, more often than not, with complete record series intact. This has been particularly true of records of corporate bodies, whose records often have been transferred directly from their storage areas without, apparently, the intervention of a records management program. Personal papers of recent origin also have come, typically intact, to the manuscript collection. From this process, the documentation is not only abundant, but, in being relatively tamper-free, it is also more dependable. Coupled with this program has been a basic collecting strategy, collecting extensively in any given subject field. Its purpose has been to document, substantially, all relevant sides of a controversial issue. An example is that of private versus public ownership of electrical utilities. As the reader will observe, the key relevant records are those of the Seattle Lighting Department, Puget Sound Power and Light Company, the law firm of Houghton, Cluck and Coughlin, plus the personal papers of Guy C. Myers, Robert W. Beck, and Arthur B. Langlie. For the politics of the 1930s the personal papers of the New Order of Cincinnatus's leaders, activists in the Washington Commonwealth Federation, and the politically involved labor unions, provide a solid documentary basis in support of research.

Volume 1 made clear the character of the city's institutional fabric. For those who have not read the first volume, the "Overview" establishes the linkage between the two periods. As noted in the "Conclusion" of Volume 1, the period from 1900 to 1940 is of a piece. World War II transformed the Seattle metropolitan region, as it did other metropolitan areas on the Pacific Coast. Their economies and demography became more fully integrated with that of the nation as a whole during the war. That period is to be dealt with in subsequent volumes.

A word about the Endnotes. They often contain information that considerably expands upon the text. The reader is urged to give them notice at some stage in coursing through the volume.

Richard C. Berner
June 1992

Looking west-northwest from 2nd Avenue and Cherry Street, Olympic range in background, 1926.
Seattle Public Library. Photograph 11686

Seattle Public Library. Photograph 20784.

Looking northeast from Elliott Bay toward north end of Lake Washngton, Mt. Baker and North Cascades, 1952. This panorama had changed very little before 1960.

Looking southeast from Elliott Bay toward Mt. Rainier, 1956. Except for the Alaska Viaduct astraddle Railroad Avenue, and the Todd Shipyard where Hooverville had been before 1940, this panorama also was unchanged since 1940.

Seattle Public Library, Photograph 21634.

Overview

The first volume of *Seattle in the Twentieth Century* concluded on two key subjects—the aftermath of the February 1919 General Strike, and consequences flowing from the City's purchase of the street railway from Stone and Webster's Puget Sound Traction, Light, and Power Company. This purchase became linked with the City's acquisition of the Skagit River damsite over the objections of the same company.

Two major results of the General Strike were the triumph of the open shop movement and loss of political influence on the part of organized labor. In the boomtown atmosphere, charged by the Klondike gold rush in 1897, labor unions revived. Just as responsive on the part of the Seattle Manufacturers' Association was the creation of an open shop movement. After steering a somewhat neutral course until 1910, the Seattle Chamber of Commerce joined the open shop forces. Out of this coalition the Seattle Employers' Association was formed. It not only fought unionization directly, but it also coerced employers who signed union contracts into breaking those contracts. The teamsters' strike of 1913-1914, followed by large-scale strikes on the waterfront among the laundry and shipyard workers, lumber workers, and meat packers, in 1916 and 1917, brought more employers into line. The formerly neutral Municipal League moved to-

View of metropolitan area looking southeast, 1935. Wooded peninsula near top left marks Seward Park, and beyond it is southern tip of Mercer Island and south end of Lake Washington, where town of Renton is visible. Vacant area at bottom of picture is Denny Regrade.

Walker and Associates, Tukwila. Negative Seattle 662.

ward opposition to unions. The League became more actively opposed once war was declared, especially after the Central Labor Council telegraphed its objections to the declaration, to President Wilson. For the League, dissent would not be tolerated.

Organized labor had been a vital force in the coalition of reform groups that had included the League, the Ministerial Federation, the Federation of Women's Clubs, the State Grange, and the Farmers' Union. It became isolated while gaining organizational strength during the war, due to the labor shortage. At war's end a shipyard workers' strike began. This strike led directly to the General Strike. The open shop movement, which had never flagged, took on fresh life as the public became disenchanted with unions. The city's own open shop movement merged with that forming nationwide under the "American Plan". In Seattle, the Associated Industries of Seattle took the place of the Seattle Employers' Association as the true open shop vehicle. The Seattle Chamber of Commerce worked closely with the AIS. The open shop movement emerged triumphant. Workplace conditions were returned to employer control, to be tempered, primarily, by market place economics, not by a counter-force based on organized labor's participation.

To sustain whatever political influence could yet be mustered, the Central Labor Council joined with disenchanted Democrats, the State Federation of Labor, Grangers, and railway unions in the National Farmer-Labor Party, for the 1920 general election. The defeat that came meant the practical end of organized labor's political effectiveness—not to be revived until 1934 and, then, under federal protection. This political refurbishing will be covered in abundant detail in the chapters to follow. Chapter 1 opens with the depoliticization of organized labor.

Central to the necessarily-long chapter 2, is the many-faceted street railway purchase. At issue throughout the period is how the debt to the Stone and Webster Management Corporation would be paid off—from street railway revenues or from the general fund. Puget Sound Power and Light Company (minus the former traction component) was this Boston-based holding company's utility, operating in western Washington. PSP&L wanted to block the Skagit River damming project of the City's Lighting Department—"City Light". Its strategy was to link the street railway debt obligations to its ultimate re-acquisition of the Skagit site, then of City Light. It chose to do this by using the debt as its leverage instrument. City Light, under leadership of

James D. Ross, in turn sought acquisition of the company's property. Intruding into this conflict was the suspicion of fraud and bribery surrounding the railway's purchase. Two investigations (1921 and 1923) turned up insufficient validating evidence. But, when Mayor Frank Edwards fired Ross on the eve of the March 10, 1931 election, the suspicion of fraud and bribery seemed confirmed by most voters. Edwards was recalled in July. PSP&L's general manager, Alton Leonard, was brought back to Boston, and replaced by Frank McLaughlin. The timing was propitious for the company because voters had approved Initiative 1 in 1930, granting county and sub-county districts the power to form their own electrical utilities, by acquisition of the electrical properties of the private companies through condemnation or negotiation. Because of the breadth of its operations, which included its attempts to monopolize all prospective water power sites in western Washington, PSP&L had encountered rural opposition in the form of the State Grange. The Grange had led the fight, over legislative opposition, to the initiative noted above, the "Grange Power District Act". The municipal utilities, of Seattle and Tacoma joined with the State Grange in coalition against PSP&L and other private utilities in the state. In the course of the 1930s, all of these parties would engage in a political tussle of monumental significance for the future, involving the Columbia River Basin development. However, at this stage—1940—the street railway debt crisis would finally be resolved, and with it, the rehabilitation of the railway. Capping the account of these events is chapter 29, "Financial Crisis: Taking the Street Railway Out of it".

The Great Depression of the 1930s re-introduced political reform, locally, as well as nationally. Local politics merged, inseparably, with state and federal politics, as efforts were made to deal with unprecedented, chronic, mass unemployment and relief. The catalyst for reform in Seattle was the Unemployed Citizens' League, a self-help group that, in the course of meeting basic needs throughout the city, became a political force. The UCL was soon superseded by the Commonwealth Builders, Inc., and the CBI, by the Washington Commonwealth Federation (WCF). Political strength was concentrated in the counties of King, Pierce, Snohomish, and Whatcom. In seeking control of the state Democratic Party and relief policies of the State administration, the WCF was found promoting the "New Deal" policies in opposition to those of Governor Martin's administration. The "Martin Democrats" despaired of dealing with relief and unemployment, conceding that ultimate responsibility lay with the individual and family, not with failure of the general economy.

The core of this reform coalition was found in the labor movement. Labor had become reactivated as a political force during the 1934 coastwide waterfront strike. This watershed strike split the labor movement, as the AFL encountered rank-and-file unionism, which formed around the International Longshoremen's and Warehousemen's Union. AFL power lay in the Teamsters' Union, under the dynamic leadership of Dave Beck. Business leaders, who once opposed Beck, allied with him when the alternative appeared worse. The policies, which they fostered, led to price and production controls, and restricted fresh entry into any business line that was under jurisdiction of the trade group. These developments are dealt with in considerable detail.

Civil liberties, which were seriously eroded during the Great War, received little attention from the population-at-large between the wars. Concentration was upon freeing political prisoners left over from the period of "federalized vigilantism" and the 1920 "Red Scare". A second target of civil libertarians became repeal of the anti-syndicalism law that was passed by the 1919 state legislature. First amendment rights—the base upon which all other constitutional rights are exercised—were never secured judicial protections during this period. This issue, and related civil rights matters are dealt with in some detail.

These political developments occurred within the context of the economy and the city's population mix. The dynamic element of the economy was the waterborne commerce that opened, once the Panama Canal became truly operational, after the war. Markets in the Gulf, the Atlantic Seaboard, United Kingdom, and Europe, at last, were found. Pacific Rim trade remained the backbone of this commerce. It expanded far beyond pre-war range. The silk trade with Japan was the mainstay of the Rim's foreign commerce. That with Alaska continued to grow apace, as did commerce with California, spurred by petroleum consumption for both household and automobile fuel. British Columbia commerce resumed its pre-war course. The "Mosquito Fleet" carried the Puget Sound Basin's trade, accounting for a steadily increasing proportion of the overall, waterborne commerce. When the Depression hit, this commerce went into a tailspin—that with Japan practically disappeared.

Seattle remained primarily a jobbing, wholesaling, and retailing city, heavily into transshipment and all the functions associated with it. Manufacturing declined sharply after the 1920-1921 depression, as shipbuilding abruptly fell off. By all measures, manufacturing steadily declined from 1919 to 1940. The Boeing Airplane Company lay on the southern outskirts of Seattle, and, although it drew upon the city's labor pool, it usually employed less than 1,000 workers at any one time, until war contracts expanded its work force from 1939 on. Building construction continued active until about 1931, when it practically stopped altogether, not picking up until 1939, when the National Housing Act contributed federal money for the Yesler Housing Project and other housing construction in the region.

Population growth leveled off during the 1920s. In 1920, Seattle held 315,312 people. The city's numbers increased to only 365,583 by 1930, and it added a measly 2,719 during the Depression decade. The pre-war composition remained much the same, although those of Japanese origin—the largest non-Caucasian element—declined in number after 1930. Filipinos became the new element. However, due to their employment as migratory labor, their numbers are difficult to measure. Probably, they rarely exceeded 2,000 persons at any one time, and they were predominantly male.

Incongruously, the arts, live theater, parks, playgrounds, and the boulevard system fared better during the Depression years under the New Deal, than in the more prosperous 1920s. Nellie Cornish found tough sledding for her Cornish School, while that operation, nevertheless, continued to provide the catalytic spark for much of the city's cultural life. The school interacted with other art groups, through the cross-membership of its few patrons from the business community, and by supplying cadre to other artistic enterprises, such as the Seattle Repertory Playhouse. The Seattle Fine Arts Society sustained itself by modest membership growth, though not by an innovative program, during the 1920s. Not until Richard and Margaret Fuller donated money for construction of the Seattle Art Museum, at Volunteer Park in 1931, was a more solid base laid for art collecting and patronizing of local artists. Yet, it was federal money of the Federal Art Project that kept local artists alive during the late 1930s. From that funding, and the patronage of a paltry few benefactors, was spawned the "Northwest School" of painters. Their full blooming would come after the war.

Parks, playgrounds, and the boulevard system that had been designed by the Olmsted Brothers in 1903, and which achieved its most significant growth by 1912, had been allowed to decay during the 1920s. As with the arts, federal money brought forth their needed rehabilitation, as funds were supplied from the Work Projects Administration and the Civilian Conservation Corps.

The public school system had to respond to new demands placed upon it by a law requiring attendance through age 18, and by new curriculum. The latter meant technical preparation for white collar employment in the burgeoning bureaucratic structures of modern business and government, the training for professional occupations in engineering, medicine, science, and other fields requiring specialized training beyond the high school level. How to afford the necessary expenditures, in face of the unrelenting opposition to taxation? That issue is dealt with in considerable detail.

The origins of the conservation movement, and of organized mountaineering, were touched upon in volume 1. In this second volume, the conservation movement—which is closely linked with mountaineering—continues to focus upon the development of, and access to, the Snoqualmie Pass area, as well as to Mt. Rainier National Park. It comes of age in the controversy leading to formation of the Olympic National Park. This controversy directly involved the Mountaineers club and the Federation of Women's Clubs, as they worked with conservation groups in the East, in lobbying through the legislation. Attention is directed at how the local conservationists were involved in the park legislation. By 1960 the "conservation" movement is broadened in its perspective, as its leaders expand their intellectual horizons in the face of accelerated deforestation, resource depletion, industrial pollution, and exponential population growth on the planet. The concepts, "ecology" and "eco-systems", become the mode for analyzing the human impact on the earth's environment, and for assessing what should be done to assure survival of the species. These post-1940 developments will be covered in the following volumes.

The period, 1900-1940, represents an integrated institutional fabric that is irreparably torn by the impact of World War II. Seattle and other Pacific Coast cities finally became integrated with those urban complexes to the East. Aircraft production expanded prodigiously, providing the city with its long-sought manufacturing base, based upon a new technology. Shipbuilding resumed during the war, but it would tail off, afterward. Waterborne commerce was inevitably spurred by the war, but port activity declined thereafter, despite feeble attempts at modernization. Portland became the leading Pacific Northwest port, and Tacoma's exports exceeded Seattle's. Seattle's port activity did not pick up until after Japan's innovation of containerized cargo was adopted as the model for port renovation, and administrative reorganization. To accommodate containerized cargo, labor-management peace had to be declared first. It came in 1960. That is part of a later story.

Indicative of the city's integration into the national pattern was the expansion of its non-Caucasian population. During the decade of the 1940s, the number of African Americans increased from 3,789 in 1940 to 15,666 in 1950. They became the largest non-Caucasian component of the city's population. Seattle's experience was essentially paralleled by other Pacific Coast cities, as rural Blacks migrated, nationwide, to the cities, where they could find employment. Other non-Caucasian groups increased more slowly, the Japanese, not until after 1950. This decade witnessed an addition of 100,000 people to the city. King County's population expanded from 504,980 in 1940, to 732,992 in 1950, and 935,014 in 1960. The real push to areas outside the city would not occur until the 1950s decade, most dramatically, to the east side of Lake Washington, as the Mercer Island Bridge facilitated that movement. As the rich farm lands in the Kent-Auburn area became steadily taxed out of existence—by being taxed on the basis of non-agricultural uses—that region became urbanized, after 1960. These developments, too, are part of a later account.

The volume is organized in five parts. Part I is a political history of the 1920s. It begins where volume I leaves off—the depoliticization of organized labor. Most of the subsequent sections deal with the politics of the public ownership of utilities, as City Light and PSP&L square off. Part V is a political history of the 1930s. The key elements in this depression decade are the politics of unemployment and relief, the revival of political activism on the part of organized labor, and resolution of the street railway debt to Stone and Webster. The latter issue becomes linked with the Columbia River Basin projects, as the State Grange joins forces with the municipal utilities against the coalition of private utilities of Washington and Oregon. Parts II and III portray the economic setting and the population framework within which the political history takes place. Part IV provides a topical synthesis for major subjects that are dealt with in passing, in the larger context of the political history These topics are public education, the cultural scene, civil liberties, and the conservation movement.

Part I

A Political History of the 1920s

1

Labor in Turmoil

The *Union Record,* Target of Right and Left

In the aftermath of the General Strike of February 1919, the open shop movement emerged triumphant in Seattle. At the national level, of the many dramatic postwar strikes, it was the 1919 steel strike that signalled the end of assertive unionism, when the steel workers' union lost its momentous strike against the twelve-hour day and brutal working conditions. Seattle's strike culminated in the final alienation of organized labor from a middle class reform coalition, of which it had been a vital part before war was declared in April 1917. Stress had been growing within that coalition, following a rash of strikes during 1916.

The city's open shop movement had begun at the turn of the century. It had coalesced in 1913 under the leadership of the Employers' Association of Seattle. The Seattle Chamber of Commerce worked closely with the association. During the month after the strike the Employers' Association was replaced by the Associated Industries of Seattle. It became the labor relations arm of the Chamber of Commerce. The developments noted above are covered in detail in the closing chapters of volume one of this history.

Seeking political redress, the leadership of the Seattle Central Labor Council (CLC) and the Washington State Federation of Labor (WSFL) turned to a promising, but failed attempt at third party political action in the 1920 election. They found themselves harassed by radical remnants on the left and by the

Associated Industries on the right. Now that the formal open shop campaign of the latter, apparently, had been called off, the easiest target in the labor movement was the *Union Record (UR)*. The *UR* had converted from a weekly to a daily newspaper in 1918. It operated under the auspices of the CLC, and was the nation's first trade union daily. Its three competitors were the *Seattle Times*, the *Seattle Post-Intelligencer*, and the *Seattle Star*. The radicals wanted control over it, and the Associated Industries wanted to silence Seattle labor's nominal voice.[1]

The advertising boycott of the *UR*, which the Associated Industries had organized after the General Strike, continued. Deprived of such normal newspaper revenue as that earned from advertisements by department stores, theaters, dairies, banks, and other businesses, the *UR* was suffering. As if lost advertising revenues were not sufficiently damaging, paper stock had to be purchased on the spot market, where it cost about one cent more per pound than the market price. Because of the *UR*'s shaky condition bank loans could not be obtained by publisher Harry Ault. Borrowing from loan sharks provided the needed funding. Wages of some $25,000 hung heavy overhead—these had been incurred to defend Ault, Frank Rust, Anna Louise Strong and George Listman from sedition charges as a result of their urging restraint in judging fault over the Centralia Massacre. It did not help that the charges finally had been dropped; the expense remained. One thing had become clear during the months since the General Strike, and that was the desire on the part of the other three major daily newspapers to drive the *UR* out of business. With backing of the business community they seemed to be succeeding. The newspapers counted upon a public traumatized by nationwide strikes, and police actions against suspected radicals, pumped up by them during the war and aftermath of the General Strike. Even the moderate Municipal League remained distrustful of the labor movement's leaders since the General Strike. The League never had been quite at ease with organized labor, even less so now.[2]

Harry Ault just dug in and prepared for the next round. He decided that the paper should expand to keep up with the growth of its circulation from about 13,000 in 1918 to 80,000 at the time of the 1919 General Strike. The *UR*'s one press was insufficient and there was not space enough for staff. A new press was purchased and space was obtained by purchase of the Steel Building at First Avenue and Stewart Street. The *UR* would move there in April 1921. Before that transition was made, however, the radicals, who wanted to take over the *UR*, had to be subdued. The metal trades sections in the CLC, in which the radicals predominated, had lost a large proportion of their membership as the shipyards closed and the postwar repression and depression took its toll. Having lost in their attempts to take control of the CLC after the General Strike, the radicals took aim at the *UR*.[3]

Ault had been a prime mover in the formation of many of the labor-prompted enterprises, some of which had been spawned from strikes: the Mutual Laundry and the Cooperative Food Products Association. Some were established to serve other worker needs, like the Trades Union Savings and Loan Association, Padilla Bay Land Development Corporation, five theaters operated by the Workers Union Theaters (the Class A, Star, Colonial, Florence, and Joy) for showing labor-oriented movies, and other enterprises that Ault hoped would show ways of ameliorating the worst features of unrestrained capitalism. He and other CLC leaders, who had similarly invested in these enterprises, were called "labor-capitalists" by the radicals and were accused of making profits at the expense of the rank and file. The *Union Record* was chief among these ventures, many on the verge of failing. The *UR* was teetering on the edge, unable to sell its preferred stock so essential to its growth.[4]

In June 1920 the radicals, who remained in the CLC, joined with the anti-Ault conservatives to get an investigating committee appointed to look into possible conflicts of interest. The radicals dominated the committee; one was a dismissed staffer of the *UR*, lying in wait. After the November elections the committee began its work by establishing a Labor Legal Bureau composed of two of the radicals, Paul Mohr and the ex-*UR* staffer William McNally, and a nominal conservative, Jean Stovel. They hired George Vanderveer and Mark Litchman to act as prosecuting attorneys, in effect. The *UR* itself soon became factionalized; some of the radicals were fired, some for incompetence, some for propagandizing. Leaks flowed to the attorneys from the *UR* staff. One staffer, Bert Coleman, deserted to the arch-enemy, the *Business Chronicle*, where his anti-labor series upset even the Chamber of Commerce. In the view of many in the Chamber, Coleman's series depicted Seattle as a "Bolshevik community" just as the publicity effects of the General Strike were "dying down". While such characterization was alright for "local consumption" the Chamber thought it "damaging" in the East. It decided to take the matter up with colleague and publisher Edwin Selvin, who was also a member of the Chamber's labor relations committee.[5]

The committee investigating the *UR* issued its report on February 2, 1921. It recommended that no time paid for by the *UR* should be used for any other purpose; that regular monthly meetings of the *UR* staff be held to receive employee suggestions; that an appeal procedure should be set up to assure management response; and that no one working in labor-owned firms should be allowed to earn a majority of his income from such sources. These recommendations alienated the anti-Ault labor conservatives who then joined with AFL loyalists led by feisty James Duncan in the CLC to support Ault. (In opposition to AFL leadership and that of WSFL president William Short, Duncan advocated a third political party. He had run for Congress on the Farmer-Labor ticket in 1920; and he was the leading proponent of industrial unionism in the state labor movement.)[6]

Meanwhile, the support that was to be expected from the WSFL was not immediately forthcoming because its leadership had been preoccupied with the 1921 legislative session. This was quickly followed by their involvement in a miners' strike that began in mid-March, when the coal operators refused to abide by terms set by the National Bituminous Coal Commission. The strike, involving about 2,300 miners, would last two years, and result in destruction of the union. A month after the miners' strike began, the Pacific Coast Seamen's Union struck against a wage reduction. Their strike was lost by early June. In both cases, the state Supreme Court enjoined the unions from picketing. But when the radicals charged WSFL president, William Short, of "suspicious" dealing, he also became active in Ault's behalf. Several of the unions then recalled their radical delegates, sending conservatives in their place. (Duncan was even recalled by the Machinists' Local 79.) This proved insufficient, however, as the committee report was accepted at the March 23 meeting by a vote of 100 to 94, with 153 abstaining—mainly those from among the Duncanites who remained suspicious of the labor-capitalists.[7]

To stall implementation of the recommendations, Ault and Rust provided a complete record of their holdings, and Ault promised to have his name removed from any stationery or printed matter of the firms with which he was associated. These actions drew in the support that was missing at the above meeting. Ault then moved on March 30 that the vote of March 24 be reconsidered. The result was 123 against the resolutions and only 102 in favor. When Gompers was then asked to pass judgment on the March 24 resolutions, he pronounced them unconstitutional on the ground that the CLC had no jurisdiction over its members' outside business interests.[8]

Having gained support from the AFL conservatives, against whom he had always done battle in the past, ex-"red" Socialist Ault then published an editorial on April 2 declaring that: "We will fight to the ultimate limit every attempt to turn this paper to either the I.W.W. or the Communist party." When staffers Harvey O'Connor and Mary Chamberlain asked for reinstatement of two ex-staffers in late May, Ault refused, adding that the *UR* "had suffered so much from the activities of members of the News Writers' Union [that the union should let us] get out a newspaper instead of continuing the controversy."[9]

Finally, by October, Ault could telegraph Saul Haas in Washington, D.C., that his control of the *UR* had been reestablished: "The wobbly [*sic*] element was decisively beaten and the Central Labor Council . . . [is] now operating with sessions closed to all but delegates [pledged to AFL loyalty]. Wobbly influence continually declining in city and state." To do this, however, Ault had had to depend upon conservatives in the CLC who would stifle all opposition to their own control by 1925, with the Teamsters leading the way.[10]

As the labor-capitalist issue receded, Ault then futilely resumed his campaign to put the newspaper on a firm financial footing without depending on advertising revenues, and after losing support of the radical unions. The paper was reduced in size. Loans from the Labor Temple Association had been sustaining the paper, but that could not continue indefinitely, despite its being the "friendly banker". A request for a $2.00 per capita tax failed to get the required two-thirds majority from the CLC. Letters went out to the various locals pleading for help. None was forthcoming. Typical was the letter to Local 131 of the Carpenters Union. The *UR* needed $15,000 now and $10,000 more within 60 days to meet obligations incurred by additions and removal to the new building: "The paper itself is operating on its earnings . . . But we are trying to carry on a million dollar business with an investment of only eighty-five thousand dollars—and it can't be done." Bear in mind that most locals were losing members during the depression and some were disbanding altogether. Some funds were also being drained off to support the striking miners. It was not a propitious time to be raising money. However, if the *UR* was to remain the voice of labor, the time to be aggressive about it was "now" . . . or never.[11]

Hard times continued for the *UR* until it finally ceased publication in 1928. Indicative of its tightening straits—owing $30,000 in October 1923—is Ault's report to Roger Baldwin, secretary of the American Fund for Public Service (which had lent money to the *UR* in the past): "[I am trying to arrange to have the *UR*] taken out of local trade union politics so that it may speak out for free speech and a free press." Labor politics at the time was reflected in the denial by the Labor Temple Association of the Labor Temple as a speech-site for radicals. William Dunne, "Mother" Bloor, and Oscar Ameringer, editor of the *Oklahoma Leader*, were denied access to the Temple. By 1924, Short, unhappy with the amount of space the WSFL was getting in the *UR*, decided to start WSFL's own newspaper, the *Labor News*. The handwriting was on the wall. Between 1928 and January 1930, when the *Vanguard* began publication under auspices of the Seattle Labor College, the city was without a voice for organized labor.[12]

Unemployment, 1921-1922

In December 1920 the Chamber of Commerce estimated that 6,000 were unemployed, including 2,500 ex-service men. Its Labor Relations Committee expected the problem to worsen during the winter; consequently, three committees were appointed: one to deal with the problem of homeless men; another to seek out work; and a third to have employers identify married women whose husbands were employed, with the intention of laying wives off. On labor's side the *Union Record* reported that unions were planning to donate $40,000 to help relieve the plight of the unemployed. These union resources were further strained when relief to the miners began once they went out on strike in March 1921.[1]

In dealing with unemployment, the Chamber seemed to have only counted "men". To fill this void the unemployed decided in February to form an Unemployed Association. It approached farmers, fishermen, grocers, and the general public. The Granges of nearby Woodinville, Sunnydale, and Bothell promised truckloads of produce. And while the Legislature was busily passing an anti-alien land bill that was directed at Japanese farmers, these same farmers donated 33 sacks of beets, 88 of carrots, 40 of parsnips, and 220 sacks of potatoes which were transferred to charitable institutions for distribution. The *UR* reported that in the first week of March "hundreds" had been fed by the Unemployed Association at the newspaper's new plant, where the main floor had been converted into a huge dining hall. Five hundred reportedly were fed on Friday, alone. By early April the association claimed that 150 tons of produce, fish, groceries, and wood had been distributed; and that, "Fifty families were being taken care of daily, and more than 4,500 needy families have been helped." An average of five children appeared daily at the association to be shoed for school. The association asked for agricultural tools to cultivate the several acres of land that had been donated . . . and tents to house the cultivators. Not until April 1922 did the Unemployed Veterans Club serve its last meal, but to a "packed" house. For the past two months the Red Cross had given $2,000 to sustain the feeding program, until spring, when it was decided the unemployed could take care of themselves. The *UR* charged its motive was to keep soldiers and sailors out of sight as they begged handouts.[2]

The Civil Service Commission joined in the spirit of giving by firing twenty-five aliens from the street railway system because "it had a long list of eligible men . . . which has never been the case before." By February, the situation had become so desperate that the Mayor's committee on the unemployed was pressured to consider even using public buildings to house the jobless and homeless . . . but to no effect.[3]

Unemployment was so pandemic nationally that President Harding—as President Hoover would do in August 1932—called for a conference in the fall to deal with it. The Seattle Chamber of Commerce and Commercial Club urged him to fund "reclamation construction" throughout the West. Eastern Washington is the region the chamber had foremost in mind. Toward fall's end Captain J.S. Gibson, president of the Waterfront Employers' Union and serving as "regional director of the unemployed" for the president's commission, was requesting a conference of the region's mayors to deal with the problem. In the eyes of the Municipal League Gibson's employers group had worked out a "harmonious" relationship with waterfront employees . . . but only after a bitter strike that re-established practically absolute employer control which would last until 1934.[4]

By October 1921, the Social Welfare League reported that 2,000 families and 10,000 individuals were being cared for, and that at least $45,000 would be needed by the League in fall, alone. It claimed that 12,000 people were unemployed—probably only men were counted, since women remained an uncertain quantity of the "permanent" work force.[5]

By December the United States Labor Department could report that Seattle's 12% rise in unemployed numbers placed it higher than 31 other industrial cities. Shipbuilding was considered to be at a standstill, and lumbering 65% below normal. Employment in municipal and harbor work seemed promising, and construction was becoming "fairly active". But unemployment remained so acute at the end of the year that M.G. Johnson undertook a diking action by establishing the Millionair Club in January 1922 to provide employment services and his own cafeteria-style feeding station. Woodchopping was the major source of employment the club provided, much of it on logged-off lands near the town of Houghton on the east side of Lake Washington. Sleeping accommodations were provided in the town's abandoned school house. By March 1922, soup kitchens also were being operated by the Volunteers of America, Salvation Army, and the Unemployed Veterans' Club.[6]

Employer Insurgency and Strikes, 1921-1922

Indicative of the latitude for maneuver that employers felt they now had was the action taken by the Master Builders' Association in March 1921. Although private contractors working on publicly funded construction were required to pay a minimum wage, they were paying less than scale. The MBA defended this violation of the law, protesting that the minimum wage was higher than the prevailing scale, and by paying it the "return to normalcy" would be retarded. The association was supported by the Chamber of Commerce, Associated Industries, the Seattle Clearing House Association, and other employer groups.[1]

Further indication of the trend in employer insurgency was a lockout of Everett longshoremen by the Weyerhaeuser Company. The company's personnel director, W.H. Boner, vowed to destroy the union-controlled list system. "We are going to clear out the waterfront and form a bosses organization with the brass check system." To help Weyerhaeuser, Seattle's Waterfront Employers' Union supplied longshoremen from its own hiring halls until the union agreed to abandon its list system.[2]

Inspired by these employers actions the First National Bank cut wages by 20% and eliminated its program of giving bimonthly bonuses. This, as a matter of course, was a unilateral act since no union stood in the way.[3]

When the Washington Coal Operators' Association declined to abide by the national agreement worked out by the National Bituminous Coal Commission and the United Mine Workers, and cut wages, instead, by 26%, the miners struck. They had won a ten-month long strike in 1920, so they believed they had a chance to win this one. Unions all over the state contributed to their support throughout the strike, but it was lost two long years later when the open shop was re-established. Regular caravans left Tacoma and Seattle carrying food and other donations to the miner families in the Green river region, Newcastle, and at Wilkeson and Carbonado. As many as a hundred cars made the relief expedition almost weekly in 1921. Money also was contributed, funneled largely through the State Federation of Labor. At the national level, when the 1921 agreement ran out in March 1922, a nationwide miners' strike began, fusing with the lockout/strike in the Washington coal fields.[4]

The miners' union accused shipping magnate, Frank Waterhouse, of trying to break the union by limiting work to two days a week, and by huge imports of coal from British Columbia and Utah mines where open shop conditions prevailed. Waterhouse, who founded the Associated Industries of Seattle, was in the process of establishing the open shop on the waterfront as well. And, although the Chamber of Commerce would complain by August that the imports of "foreign" coal caused higher coal prices, it was considered to be worth it if the open shop could be established; after that, it expected prices to fall. The Chamber accepted at face value the mine owners' promise of "fair treatment" of the workers. The state Supreme Court helped the owners along by ruling in favor of a permanent injunction against picketing, overruling Superior Court judge Austin Griffiths. Like old times! The union did not revive until the 1930s.[5]

The miners and their families were particularly hurt because their modest homes were owned by the companies. It followed that the companies would choose to evict them. An unwilling Sheriff Starwich, dutifully began serving eviction notices in September. Solidarity among the miners and their families was symbolized by the "colonies" they established to cope with the shelter problem. Most noteworthy of the colonies was that established at Morganville on land sold to the union by Timothy Morgan to house the evicted miners. The first anniversary of the lockout was celebrated there.[6]

As to the strikebreakers who were imported from Montana and Utah, they were largely unskilled, and the accidents that followed in the Issaquah mines discouraged their extensive recruitment. In February 1922, the Pacific Coast Coal Company closed its Franklin mine due to the heavy losses resulting from the use of unskilled labor.[7]

In the fishing industry the Alaska Packers Association threatened a wage cut in early March. The cut was rejected by the Alaska Fishermen's Union ten days later.[8]

The Typographers Union, Local 202, began a desultory strike on May 1. When the newspaper publishers and job printers sought a wage reduction in the face of deteriorating business conditions, the union first asked to see their books to determine whether a "fair wage" had been paid since the war. The publishers refused. The union suggested arbitration, which was agreed to, but was not taken seriously by the employers. By July 10 the arbitrators had met fourteen times without result. Strikes continued at five major job printers. Meanwhile, the Newspaper Publishers' Association had established a training school in Spokane for strikebreakers. The unions countered by forming a Pacific Northwest Printers Defense League. But no agreement for a 1921 scale was reached, so by the end of the year a scale for 1922 became the goal. The employers continued operations unabated in 1922 as they had in 1921. The union seemed not to matter.[9]

Symptomatic of the fear of union decay in the face of employer insurgency was the concern of Seattle meat cutters. The union's local secretary, Joe Hoffman, claimed that Japanese meat cutters "are a menace to conditions in the meat industry" by their acceptance of lower pay. To deal with this desperate situation he proposed organizing a Japanese local "if necessary". It became Branch 2 of Local 81, with workers in at least a dozen shops. Hoffman urged people to patronize them if no White butchers are in the area being served. A growing acceptance of "legitimacy" for Japanese workers, however, seemed to be growing. By March 1922 the Central Labor Council congratulated Japanese unionists for cooperating with Whites in "sustaining American conditions". Japanese locals had been established for boot and shoe workers, sign painters, barbers, and the meat cutters—to which Joe Hoffman pointed with pride.[10]

Nevertheless, continued unrest in labor relations finally unsettled the Chamber of Commerce by September 1921—two months after the great maritime strike, and as rumblings of a railroad strike began circulating. At the Chamber's September 21 meeting it resolved "to furnish evidence to the world that Seattle actually is solving her labor problem and is moreover a safe place in which to live and invest money." The Chamber's model—to which it proudly pointed—was that established on the waterfront under the leadership of Frank Waterhouse and Frank Foisie. These were essentially company union conditions. It rewarded Waterhouse by electing him its president for 1922, even as he became involved in a well-publicized financial controversy in which Daniel Kelleher, of the Seattle National Bank, openly accused him of crying because he had made a bad investment in the Vulcan Manufacturing Company and was trying to get out from under by claiming he had been defrauded—a claim that Judge James Ronald refused to accept while ordering the sale of the company's stock to partially satisfy the bank's claim. Initially, federal Judge Jeremiah Neterer denied his bankruptcy appeal because of his "scandalous accusations" against the two banks pursuing him, but by the end of March the judge allowed his bankruptcy plea.[11]

One union, however, flourished during this period of general union decay. The Teamsters went from strength to strength, claiming 100% membership in their trades. It kept abreast of the changing technology introduced by the internal combustion engine, organizing in tandem those business firms that substituted motor driven trucks for horse drawn vehicles. Local 174, the Auto Truck Drivers, headed by Harry Dail, could boast of forcing the Jewel Tea Company into bankruptcy for not recognizing the union. A strike against the Barton Packing Company was in progress. Teamster leadership suffered no taint of radicalism either. Other unions, in fact, came to them for help and, reportedly, usually got it. Behind this unique union success lay the organizing genius of a newcomer, Dave Beck.[12]

Local 174 was the catalyst for teamster organization in Seattle. Other specialized locals were spun off from it as soon as they could prove sufficient membership; Beck's Laundry and Dye Works Drivers was one of them. Teamster membership in the city grew from 400 in 1910 to 3,500 in 1918, 4,000 in 1920, 5,000 by 1929, falling, early in the Great Depression, to 3,500 in 1931. A crucial factor in this growth was the encompassing of the over-the-road truckers; elsewhere in the nation Teamster unions concentrated on their local areas, and operated independently from their International office. While this local Teamster autonomy satisfied the ambitions of the strongest West Coast local, San Francisco's Local 85, it opened the door to organizing the over-the-road truckers in Seattle. As Donald Garnel points out, in his book on the Teamsters, there were reasons. In the San Francisco area agricultural produce was hauled almost exclusively, and it was being hauled by drivers on the rural periphery, mainly to the railroads; truckers and the railroads were symbiotically related. And outside truckers did not compete with those in the city. Not so in Seattle.[13]

Here, the Teamsters wanted to take business from the railroads, broaden its base, and make it strategically stronger than its San Francisco counterpart, while becoming financially stronger in the process. In Seattle, local teamsters often invested their savings in long-haul rigs, becoming owner-operators at the same time. Local 174 organized these truckers in tandem as they expanded and hired drivers in the expansion process. Garnel contends that "most of these early line drivers lived in Seattle and worked for Seattle-based concerns." Local drivers also found job opportunities with firms that handled both lines of hauling, long and local alike. He also points out that, whereas San Francisco's Teamsters and employers had enjoyed harmonious relations since about 1901, this was not the case in Seattle; consequently, aggressive organizing tactics were followed in Seattle.[14]

The Teamsters were not entirely alone in maintaining their strength, however. The Culinary Workers Union resisted an attempt by the Seattle Caterers' Association to break the union. In early October 1921 the Association ordered its members to break their union contracts and to reduce wages immediately instead of giving the required thirty days warning notice. More than 2,300 culinary workers were affected by the lockout/strike which followed. The association leaders were the Chauncey Wright chain, and six other cafes and cafeterias . . . too few to hold the other members in line. By the end of the month more than a hundred restaurants were displaying the union house-card, and they objected to the coercive techniques employed by the association. The strike was won.[15]

The Associated Industries did not always get its way with fellow employers. When the Retail Clerks Union, Local 174, decided to organize the grocery clerks they found an ally in the Retail Grocers' Association. The latter favored this action, overriding opposition of the Associated Industries, because they could use the union to help enforce uniform closing hours.[16]

Through the last week in September and all of October 1921 hung the threat of a nationwide railway strike as a result of the wage cut of 12.5% that the Railroad Labor Board announced on July 1. This was followed by a further 10% reduction planned by the railroad executives whose lines had been returned to them by the federal government after the war, under terms of the Esch-Cummins Transportation Act of 1920. The Board was under jurisdiction of the Federal Railroad Administration, an agency established during the war to deal with the transportation crisis. Its first administrator, William McAdoo, had headed off a general railroad strike in 1917 by granting wage increases to the non-operating employees, establishing the eight-hour day, and encouraging union organizing among the non-operating employees. (The four railroad brotherhoods had organized the operating employees already.) According to W. Thomas White, in his dissertation on the railroad workers in the Pacific Northwest, under McAdoo's protective umbrella, both operating and non-operating employees were brought into the bargaining process, with the AFL's shopmen and maintenance-of-way workers joining the four railroad brotherhoods in negotiations. These conditions lasted during McAdoo's tenure which ended in November 1918. A railroad management representative, Walter D. Hines, replaced McAdoo. Hines's policies: "no" to general wage increases, elimination of overtime pay, and returning the roads to private ownership and operation, now that the war was over. The unions and pro-labor congressmen sought to prevent the latter, and got behind the Plumb Plan that would combine government ownership with private operation. According to White the Plumb Plan attracted considerable support throughout the Northwest, and this is borne out for Seattle by the emphasis given to it by the *Union Record,* and statewide by the Triple Alliance, when it organized for the 1920 election.[17]

The Esch-Cummins Transportation Act established the Railway Labor Board in order to deal with labor grievances. It included three members each from the railroads, labor, and the public. Yet, it could barely contain the wildcat strikes and threats of strikes occurring with increasing frequency. Most notable was the switchmen's strike in 1920 which affected lumber shipments particularly. White summarizes: "The policies of compromise and delay on such demands by Hines and the Railway Labor Board [for wage increases] did not compensate for the rising cost of living and only intensified labor unrest." Against this backdrop the climactic Shopmen's Strike of 1922 unfolded.[18]

During the last week of September strike ballots were being counted in Chicago, headquarters of the various railroad brotherhoods. Acting independently of the other brotherhoods, ninety per cent of the Trainmen voted in favor of strike action. Voting by the firemen, the switchmen, and engineers occurred the next week. A strike deadline of October 30 was set. Later in the month, the shopmen declared they would not join the strike if it were to take place because their president claimed he had no guarantee from the four brotherhoods that they would stand by the shopmen after they had won their demands.[19]

In event of a strike at least 5,000 Seattle workers would be involved, including checkers and clerks on the waterfront. Eighty-seven per cent of these workers had voted for strike action. An estimated 500,000 railway workers, nationally, would be involved in such a strike . . . uneasy, though, haunted by the failed Pullman strike of 1894 in which federal troops supplemented the local constabulary and the employers' private armed forces.[20]

On October 30 the Railway Labor Board (RLB) entered negotiations to head off the strike by ordering the election of representatives to negotiate. Indicative of employer intransigence, the Pennsylvania Railroad refused such initiative outright, claiming such intervention would lead to the closed shop, to sympathetic strikes, and limitation of output. Locally, the *Union Record* charged that the wage cuts were demanded to enable the executives to pay dividends and interest on their watered stock, and that the cost of living—the ostensible reason for the reductions—had not appreciably dropped. The union leadership shared this opinion.[21]

With the strike deadline approaching, the RLB called a meeting of the brotherhoods on the 27th, under the watchful eyes of the Justice Department, which was looking for evidence of indictable actions, should the strike ensue. The Board made clear that the Justice Department would take action, and that Attorney General Harry Daugherty was planning to request an injunction and to take any other more forceful measures, should that be necessary. He regarded such a strike to be illegal on its face. For its part the RLB would enforce only the earlier wage reduction of 12.5% and would deny the extra 10% demanded by the railroad executives . . . until one year, at least, had elapsed. By this timely intervention the strike was called off . . . for the moment, anyway.[22]

Then, in a series of decisions in the spring of 1922, the RLB lowered the wages of non-operating employees. The shopmen countered with their own demands: wage increases to bring their's in line with their counterparts in other industries, restoration of overtime pay for Sunday and holiday work, abolition of contracting out shop work, and correcting the pro-management bias of the RLB. Shopmen and other non-operating employees walked out on July 1. By mid-July, *Labor* claimed 600,000 workers were on strike. Soon, according to White, seniority became the key issue as strikebreakers filled an increasing number of the vacated positions. Lists of workers who were considered undesirable were systematically compiled by the railroads to eliminate dissenters from future employment.[23]

With the nationwide coal strike in progress, and the successful employment of the local constabulary, National Guards, and armed forces of the mine owners in breaking that bitter strike, the tone was set for the Harding administration to act in the shopmen's strike. The President called a special session of Congress on August 18 to deal with the crisis. This was shortly followed by his authorization for injunctive action to be taken by Attorney General Daugherty. Daugherty requested a sweeping injunction from Judge James Wilkerson in Chicago. Wilkerson complied by banning union leaders from "picketing, or in any manner, word of mouth, or interviews encouraging any person to leave the employ of the railroad." This was all the railroad owners wanted. White reports that the outcome in the Northwest was "The Hill and Harriman Lines simply recruited new men, accepted a selected few repentent strikers, and established their own company unions."[24]

The Great Maritime Strike of 1921

By the end of the war the United States Shipping Board had received 2311 steel and wooden ships; more were still under contract for completion. At the beginning of 1921, the Board was operating 1109 steel ships, and it had laid up another 520. Some urgency also was felt in dealing with a $15 million monthly operating deficit. Somehow, these ships had to be sold to private parties at a time of depression. Also, the Board's ships were not state-of-the-art; motor ships were replacing steamships. There were few takers. Meanwhile the Shipping Board leased some of its vessels, and operated others. President Harding even tried to push through a ship subsidy bill in 1922 as a means of sustaining and developing an American merchant marine, but he failed. In this setting the "great maritime strike" of 1921 unfolded.[1]

Rumors of coming wage cuts in the maritime trades were rampant in April. At the national level the Shipping Board was expected to slash wages by 15% on the ships it controlled. And, at a general marine labor conference on April 27, the unions indicated they would not accept the cut. Also at issue was the LaFollette Seaman's Act of 1915, which attempted to set standards of marine safety and to eliminate the traditionally tyrannical authority of ship officers over their workers. Its terms were expected to be evaded . . . at the hands of a federal corporation, no less. The private shipowners, through their American Shipowners' Association, were said to insist on at least a 35% reduction . . . and to ignore the LaFollette Seaman's Act as well.[2]

That the Shipping Board was already girding for a showdown was foreshadowed when the Pacific Coast Steamship Company's *S.S. Governor* was rammed and sunk in Puget Sound on April 1 by a Shipping Board vessel. The latter's crew was non-union and inexperienced. The ship's captain was so displeased with the crew that he fired it upon reaching Vancouver, but the board refused him the opportunity of hiring union men in their place. As to the company, it took the sinking of their ship seriously and filed a damage suit against the federal government.[3]

Locally, the Waterfront Employers' Union reportedly was planning to eliminate about 800 longshoremen from its employment register. This would be in response to a substantial loss of port business to Tacoma, Vancouver, and Portland. An increase in wharfage fees charged by the Port of Seattle to match that on the private docks contributed to this plight. Portland's 10% lower rail shipping rate, set by the Interstate Commerce Commission, also was a factor. Indicative of the slump was the claim of the International Longshoremens' Association, Local 38-12, that until recently it had furnished work for 3,300 members, but by mid-April it could not place even 500 men. The union reported that with the "bottom [falling] out of the port business" men have migrated to these other ports.[4]

The Port of Seattle—which had earlier established the lowest wharfage fees on the Pacific Coast under the influence of commissioner Robert Bridges—also reneged on another of Bridges-originated policies when it began hiring from the employers' hiring hall, bypassing the union's by using the "preferred list" of the commission. Commissioner George Lamping promised to investigate, and if this practice exists, he "will not tolerate it". Early in May, Traffic Manager W.J. Muirhead promised to deal with these "charges of discrimination". With the Port veering towards agreement with the private owners, and no longer setting a standard, the anti-union policies of the private wharf, warehouse, and shipping owners also were reinforced. When the nationwide seamen's lockout/strike began on May 1, it affected the Seattle waterfront.[5]

Two thousand men struck when the three major shipping employers—the Shipping Board, the Pacific Coast Steamship Company, and the Alaska Steamship Company—announced their wage cut and the lockout of union members. Their efforts to erode the LaFollette Seaman's Act would soon become apparent.[6]

The backbone of the strikers was the Marine Engineers Beneficial Association (MEBA) due to the fact that their skills and experience were essential to the operation of the ship. Workers in other ship departments could more readily be replaced by more casual labor. The Shipping Board informed MEBA that it planned a 15% wage cut. The Alaska Steamship Company informed the Marine Cooks and Stewards Union that wages would be slashed by $10 per month, overtime pay to be ended, and that open shop conditions would prevail. Against the longshoremen the Waterfront Employers' Union reinstituted the "card rustling" system wherein an employee's employment history was recorded, including evidence of union activity . . . which could provide grounds for discrimination.[7]

With serious consequences portending, President Harding appointed an arbitration board shortly after the strike began. Included on the Board were Secretary of Labor, J.J. Davis, and Admiral W.S. Benson of the Shipping Board. Its failure would soon be reported by president W.S. Brown of the Marine Engineers Benevolent Association, May 11.[8]

Ships were manned by strikebreakers recruited by the Shipping Board and the private companies. MEBA officers claimed that "Negroes, Filipinos, Great Lakes non-union seamen, and scabs picked up on the streets of coast cities compose the crew." Extensive use of "Orientals" (but not Japanese) unable to understand English threatened the standard set by the Seamens' Act, which required that 75% of the crew must be so qualified. Chinese crew members on some ships even struck upon their arrival in Hongkong. Affidavits were produced in early June indicating that the Shipping Board had been hiring strikebreakers, shipping them to Seattle and housing them at the Butler Hotel. The strike ran its six-week course.[9]

A temporary injunction against picketing was obtained in mid-May from the federal court by local United States Attorney Robert Saunders. When the shipowners had Saunders apply for a permanent injunction on June 8, federal Judge Neterer—whose lack of sympathy for unions was a matter of record—rebuked Saunders for trying to blame the unions for all the violence that was occurring. Neterer also accepted as valid defense attorney George Turner's argument that since unions were not corporations, they could not be enjoined.[10]

MEBA, stimulated by the lack of any progress in negotiations with the Shipping Board, and expecting something worse from the private shipowners, reopened negotiations on June 9. This had the twofold effect of driving officials of local Admiral and Alaska lines to get their former employees back to work before the Shipping Board settled. Rumors were floated that engineers on the East Coast and Gulf were returning to work. Then MEBA confirmed the rumors by signing an agreement with the Board on the 14th, thus ending the biggest merchant marine strike up to then by a resounding defeat of the unions.[11]

But this was only the beginning of such losses. When the agreement expired at the end of the year, the Shipping Board first pressed the private shipowners not to reduce wages further, then, in its own eliptical language, it adopted a scale that "was substantially in line with those promulgated by the private owners." This meant by the Board's estimate, a wage reduction of 15 to 25 per cent. In its annual report of 1922 the Board concluded: "The board's policy was generally commended by the private steamship interests". What else was expected? The Shipping Board had been used by them as their cutting edge to break the unions, from which they did not recover until the mid-1930s.[12]

Marine stewards had a different fate. James H. Roston, who had been instrumental in breaking the 1916 longshoremen's strike by furnishing Blacks as strikebreakers, approached owners of the Alaska Steamship Company and the Pacific Coast Steamship Company with a proposal. He would recruit and supply them with Black stewards to replace striking Whites and strikebreaking Black women, whom the latter company employed. His organization, the Colored Marine Employees Benevolent Association, would remain aloof from unions. Agreement was reached with the companies, and Roston established offices in both Seattle and San Francisco. Grievance machinery was set up, particularly to adjudicate charges of discrimination against the stewards by their White superior stewards. Until his death in 1924 Roston personally intervened by appealing directly to the owners when he judged that the charges were valid; reportedly, he usually won. The Association, formally organized in May 1922 after his post-strike negotiations and preparations, lasted until the 1934 maritime strike.[13]

As to the longshoremen, their union was neutralized in part by the help of the Shipping Board. In its annual report of 1922, the Board reported in unmistakable words that its policy "in dealing with longshore labor in the principal ports has been one of cooperation with the private steamship lines generally, which involved the working out with the longshoremen's organization wages and working conditions . . ." When negotiations began in September, there was no strike in Seattle or at any other Pacific Coast port because the stevedoring companies had already firmly established their control of the waterfront. Under the intellectual leadership of University of Washington lecturer, Frank Foisie, a system had been in place for the "decasualization" of longshore labor. The union hall was simply bypassed and a hiring hall run by the employers supplied the workers—the so-called "fink hall" of the "Blue Book Union". In Foisie's words: "Decasualization involves . . . limiting the number of men eligible to work in a port and to distribute the work among the eligibles . . . [These are] Reserve men—those men who work through a central dispatching hall for all employers as needed . . . The kernel of the problem is the 'reserve' of labor

Paul Dorpat, from Jim Faber's collection used in his *Steamer's Wake*

Part of the waterfront where the 1921 maritime strike took place. Colman Dock is indicated by the tower at its end. To its right is that of the Alaska Steamship Company. On horizon is the Olympic Mountain Range. Taken from Smith Tower, 1932.

needed in each port . . . The crux of the difficulty is to maintain an adequate reserve yet avoid a surplus." Before the marine strike began, the employers' hiring hall had 1420 men registered; this was soon reduced to 600. In 1922 there were 722 registered, 693 in 1923, remaining in the 600 range throughout the 1920s. By 1933 only 525 were registered.[14]

One curious event occurring during the strike affected Alaska. By early May it was reported that Alaska's supplies were running low. This news brought forth a mixed reaction: the Chamber of Commerce wanted to send a relief ship to the affected cities, but so did the Seafarers' Council. The latter offered to man the relief ship free if the shipowners would forego any profits on the operation, making it a genuine relief expedition. The Chamber, apparently wanting to use the occasion to embarrass the unions, rejected this proposal, preferring that of the shipowners—the use of federally-supplied naval reservists. Finally, the Shipping Board sent one of its own ships.[15]

Bruce Nelson reports that after the failure of the 1921 strike—for which Andrew Furuseth, head of the ISU, was severely criticized for his narrow craft sectarianism that found him opposing alliances with longshoremen and other marine workers—"large numbers of seamen and longshoremen left the AFL unions to join the Wobblies." These workers became the nucleus for the Communist Party's Marine Workers Industrial Union in the early 1930s, and of the Unemployed Citizens' League's waterfront local in 1933.[16]

The Labor Movement in Transition: Near-Stagnation

At the national level structural changes were occurring in the economy that affected the conditions of work in the cities. Since the Civil War the expansion of the railroad network had largely driven the growth of the economy. Advancing technology had altered the conditions of work as machine tools gradually displaced many skilled worker functions, and made possible the extensive introduction of less-skilled and unskilled workers (from the immigrant labor supply), and women into the work force. Scientific management rationalized these changes, incorporating as managers many skilled workers who had been displaced. Clerical and service functions expanded as every aspect of production and transportation was brought under more exact scrutiny and control. Mass or continuous line production came to typify modern industry. The automotive industry displaced railroads as the economy's driving force, and it became the prototype for mass production. Immigration, which had come to a near standstill during the war, was slowed to a trickle after passage of the 1924 Immigration Act. By then, there was less need for fresh infusions to the labor supply. The emigration of farmers to the cities contributed to the oversupply as they were displaced by machinery and the burden of debt. The decade, 1919-1929, witnessed the slowest capital investment in manufacturing since the Civil War (3.2% annual growth). Yet, productivity in manufacturing grew by two-thirds—and comparably in mining as well. Despite this improved productivity, however, Gabriel Kolko notes that profitability fell from a high of 43.2% of value in 1921 to 35.6% by 1929. This decline impelled employers to cut labor costs by introduction of new technology and to fight off unionization.[1]

The year 1922 saw the final crushing of union activism. Montgomery writes: "Each union stood alone during the brutal strikes of 1922. No fewer than 1,613,000 men and women struck that year. That number was even greater than the strike turnout of 1916, but the moods surrounding the two strike waves could hardly have been more different." During the former, optimism and hope prevailed. "But 1922 was a year of grimly determined defensive warfare for strikers and was followed by an abrupt decline in strike activity . . . Strikes were not numerous, but they were huge . . . City streets, flophouses, and shantytowns teemed with unemployed. All strikers knew that there were many workers eager for employment at the lowered wages the strikers were resisting."[2]

Montgomery notes that heretofore the railway and miners' unions had stood "in the forefront of a postwar 'progressive bloc' in the labor movement." (For Seattle and its environs the metal trades unions—embracing the shipyard workers—should be added.) This bloc was anathema to AFL conservatives, led by Samuel Gompers. The employers' anti-union crusade had won its war by 1922, and in the process paved the way for Gompers' triumph. At the AFL's Portland convention in 1923 the "progressives"—pressing for some version of industrial unionism that would reflect the changes that had occurred in the economy—were finally suppressed. By then union membership had declined by 25% from its high in 1920. The International Association of Machinists' membership had fallen 70% nationwide, and "transportation" by 25%. In Washington, the miners' union had been destroyed, as had any semblance of a lumber workers union, and the waterfront workers had to certify through a company union. The existing AFL crafts sought only protection of their jobs. Contrariwise, only the Teamsters responded to the changes occurring in transportation by organizing along industrial lines—without saying so, perhaps without awareness of their drift. Their development, referred to above, will be more fully covered below.[3]

The labor movement in the state and city did not suffer the kind of organized violence inflicted by paramilitary action of vigilantes and citizens' committees which were usually reinforced by local constabularies, the National Guard—even the Army in the West Virginia coal miners' strike—and by the courts as typified in the East and Midwest. Local employer organizations were nevertheless effective in combating labor activism in city and state, as we have seen above. This activism also was suppressed within the "movement" itself—movement without momentum. Some local detail will illustrate.

President William Short of the State Federation of Labor expressed his relief to fellow officer Charles P. Taylor in August 1923: "Things are getting a whole lot better in our State Labor Movement . . . and improving steadily. Altho [*sic*] Paddy Morris and his little coterie still hang on at the Tacoma Central Labor

Council and the red bunch are still quite in evidence in the Seattle Council altho your friend Jimmie Duncan declined to run for re-election last month and has gone into business for himself in some machine shop. I think we will have the situation at Seattle cleaned up before long and this will lead to a cleanup, also at Tacoma. With exception of the Central Councils at Seattle and Tacoma they have no hold anywhere."[4]

Timidity about starting any fresh organizing is what characterized the leadership of organized labor in state and city until 1933, once the activists had been forced out. When Homer T. Bone (counsel for the Port of Tacoma, and State Representative of the Farmer-Labor Party) asked Short to look into the possibility of organizing the Tacoma "drug store clerks" in September 1923 his answer was: "However, our experience with all retail clerks organizations . . . has been that they never want to organize until they want something real badly [and then they abandon the organization once they get satisfied.] . . . There isn't a town in the state that has been effective and that has effectively functioned for any length of time . . . it is an awful job to keep them alive." One month later Short reported to D. D'Alessandro, president of the Hod Carriers Union: "Our State Federation of Labor . . . has been limited in its activities by lack of support from locals who reap the full benefit of its accomplishments, and a great deal more could be accomplished in this state were we given the support of all the local unions." He urged D'Alessandro to get his locals in Seattle and Tacoma to re-affiliate. Short sent similar letters to other international union officers. On the 8-hour day issue in 1925, Short responded that the federation would not be able to initiate any action—the federation "can not handle local organization work which should be handled by the local movement itself." And, fearful of jurisdictional disputes within the movement, Short wrote to Frank Cotterill about the federation's "long-standing agreement that each organization will keep out of the other's jurisdiction, unless invited in." In fact, the only effective organizing work was being done by the Teamsters under Dave Beck's driving leadership. The Teamsters came to dominate the Seattle Central Labor Council by 1925.[5]

Only the prod of Section 7(a) of the National Recovery Act of 1933 revived active organizing. Not until September 1933 did a committee in the Seattle Central Labor Council—for "Promoting an Organizing Campaign"—finally recommend: "The most important activity that can be engaged in at the present time is organizing the unorganized . . ." Yet, one can understandably wonder, in the light of what follows, whether the latter would have taken place if it had not been for the pressure of left-wing union activism centered on the waterfronts of Seattle and its sister coastal cities, and in the mass-production industries of the Midwest and Eastern regions of the nation.[6]

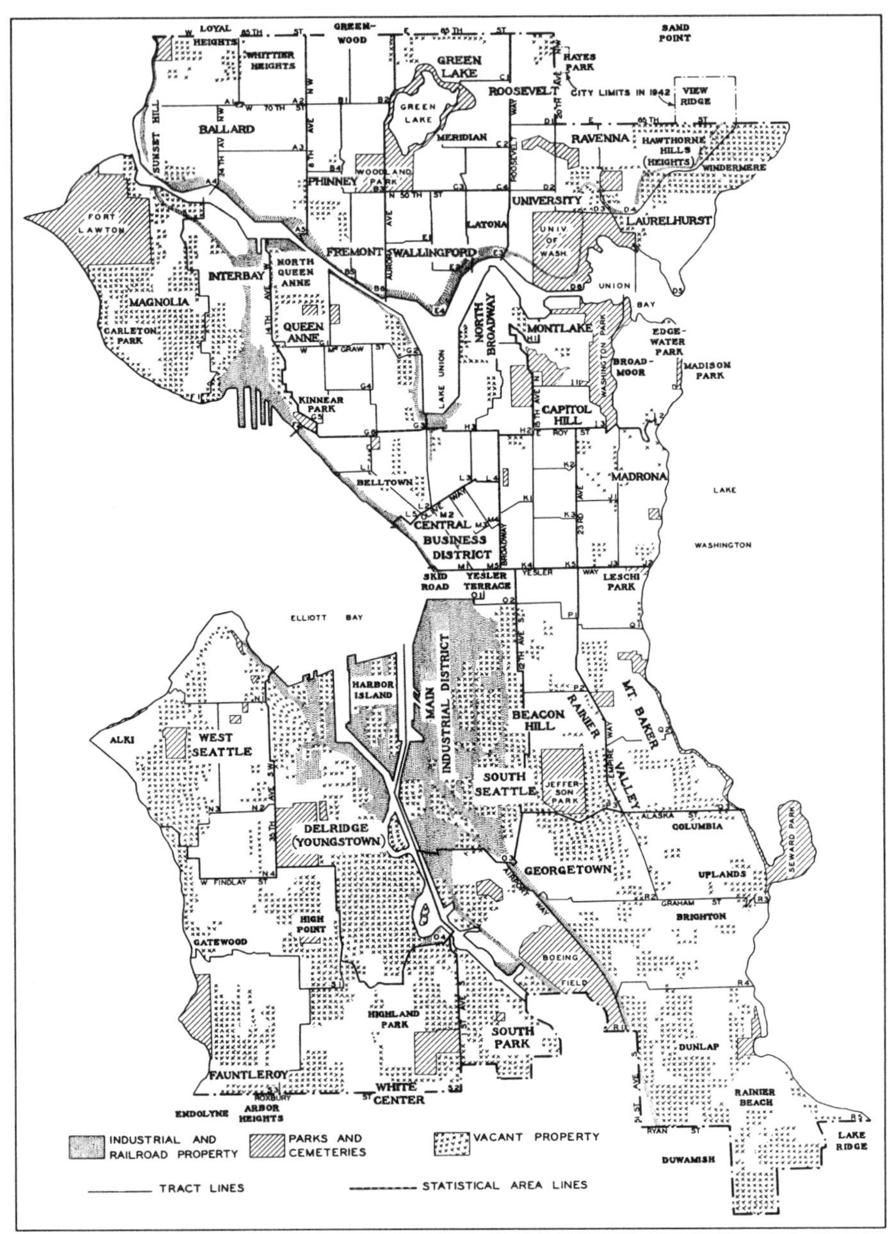

From Calvin Schmid, *Social Trends in Seattle*

Base Map Showing Major Land Use Patterns, Census Tracts and Names of Districts, Seattle, 1942

2

Politics in General

Legislature and City, 1921

In its attack on home rule and municipal ownership, the 1921 Legislature resembled that of 1915. And the initiatives and referenda drives protesting much of the legislation also became reminiscent of the aftermath of the 1915 session. One bill that had widespread popular support, however, was the Anti-Alien Land Act, which was directed at the Japanese. Unlike some acts, this one did not have a referendum clause attached to it, so it was not subjected to a referendum campaign. Several others were overturned by the electorate in 1922.

The Anti-Alien Land Act was the outgrowth of fears generated primarily by and among farmers and owners of rural land in the state. In Seattle, anti-Japanese sentiment was long-centered in the trade unions and among produce merchants who competed with the Japanese. Racial hostility in the city remained latent, but the propaganda would find susceptible elements there when the barrage hit. Much of the local propaganda originated in California where anti-Japanese sentiment was most vehement and highly organized among nativist groups, farmer and labor organizations which joined together in the Asiatic Exclusion League before World War I. They headed the movement for Japanese exclusion, and sought to ally all three Pacific Coast states in the campaign. The League's efforts were rewarded in 1913 by passage by the California legislature, of an Anti-Alien Land Act. It proved ineffectual. The war diverted attention from the issue until 1919, when the older forces were joined by the powerful American Legion. In Washington, as elsewhere, the Legion moved quickly against aliens in general, against anything it could tag as radical ("Bolsheviks" and IWWs), and against foreign threats as they saw or fantasized them. Tensions in the Pacific Rim—the Siberian invasion by U.S. troops and the rise of Japanese naval power—were played upon by the Legion. It claimed Japanese land ownership here was but an entering wedge of the mother country. In Washington, there was little outright ownership, but by 1920 Japanese farmers leased or rented 699 farms spread over 25,340 acres. This number was slightly more than double that of 1910; it represented only 1.1% of the total number of farms in the state, and an even smaller acreage. These farms were concentrated in the merged valleys of the Green, White, Duwamish, and Puyallup rivers between Tacoma and Seattle, often located on marginal lands that they had made arable on the eastern shores of Lake Washington, and east of the Cascades in the Yakima area (including lands on the Yakima Indian Reservation). The produce from the former area supplied the Seattle-Tacoma metropolitan region and was being shipped to Midwest markets, as well. The urban Japanese population was not yet in the target zone of the propagandists.[1]

The *Star*, continuing its hyper-Americanism of the war years, led the propaganda barrage and was joined by the *Argus* and *Times* (the *P-I* and *Union Record* remained neutral, the latter because open shoppers were leading the campaign). The newly formed Anti-Japanese League started an unsuccessful initiative campaign in 1920 that would have prohibited land acquisition by aliens ineligible for citizenship, and also taken away rights of alien parents to act as guardians of their American-born children. Giving vent and focus to all these activities were the Japanese immigration hearings held in Seattle and Tacoma in July and August 1920, chaired by Washington's Congressman, Albert Johnson (co-author of the 1924 Immigration Act).

Although most people seemed relatively indifferent to the restrictive legislation being undertaken by the 1921 state legislature, they were receptive to the propaganda when it flooded the state. The only group that publicly opposed the Anti-Alien Land Act as it was being lobbied was the Chamber of Commerce, both Seattle's and Tacoma's, because of commercial ties with the Japan trade. Some farmers who rented to Japanese and who profited by the increase in their rent revenues also added their voice of opposition, but their number was insignificant. The Seattle Central Labor Council and the State Federation of Labor plus the State Grange stood on the sidelines. The American Legion was credited as the primary force behind the lobbying efforts, joining with other veterans organizations in trying to promote "back-to-the-farm" opportunities for their constituents in the middle of the postwar depression.

The bill (sponsored by King County's Representatives, Adam Beeler and J.T. Jones) passed the House 71 to 19 and the Senate 36 to 2. Governor Hart signed it on March 8, 1921. The law was challenged in the courts, and subterfuges were used to evade it, until another such act was passed in 1923 to plug the loopholes. The latter resulted in a sharp decline in the Japanese farm population and reduced productivity and quality of the farms they left behind.

The general tax on real and personal property had borne the burden for the increasing expenses of state and local government and public schools as they faced up to accelerated urbanization and its attendant expenses. By 1920 about 70% of these governmental and public schools expenses were paid by property taxes. Intangible wealth in the form of credits, mortgages, and interest were excluded from taxation; this form of income accompanied urbanization. As these expenses increased, property taxes continued to increase, and so did the pressure of owners of land, buildings, and other forms of real property to resist further taxation. A forty-mill tax limitation became their top agenda item. The real heart of the problem, if a limit were to be imposed on property taxes, was how and what revenue sources could be tapped to meet the expenses formerly paid from property taxes. Complicating the tax situation further was the variability in property tax assessments from county to county; assessors, being elected officials, were subject to pressure from every imaginable interest group, and uniformity of assessments was not their highest priority.[2]

As early as 1907, the state tax commissioners favored moderate taxation of intangible property, but the Senate rejected their advice on the ground that investment capital would bypass the state. Antagonism between the tax commissioners and the Senate continued, and in 1913 the Senate removed the commissioners from the Board of Equalization, thereby eliminating them from influence on statewide assessments. Then, finally, that august body eliminated the Tax Commission in 1917, replacing it with a single tax commissioner. Abuses followed, making even more critical the need for tax reform because tax levies had been increasing alarmingly . . . for those who paid them. Levies jumped from $43,255,284 in 1917 to $72,352,887 by 1920; school taxes alone rose by 40%. The State's portion of the tax-pie increased from 20% in 1920 to 24% in 1924; the rest went to local governments and schools. School and local governmental deficiencies were regularly met by special legislation instead of employing a budgeting process that would match expected expenditures with anticipated revenues.[3]

When a former tax commissioner, T.D. Rockwell of King County, offered a bill in 1919 to amend the constitution by including intangible property in the list of taxables, the Senate rejected it on the same grounds as before. With governmental expenses continuing to rise, just as the economy was sliding into a depression, Governor Louis F. Hart aimed first to reorganize state government by enacting an administrative code, thereby reducing the cost of government and the need for more taxes. Hart also requested the legislature to look for alternative sources of revenue, specifying a rise in inheritance taxes, a motor vehicle fuel tax to be used for highway construction, a higher fish tax, and a special millage tax to be used for building construction on the state's college and university campuses. When Senator Rockwell introduced a bill that included a state income tax and a gross sales tax, the Federated Industries of Washington successfully led the fight against it.[4]

In desperation to find alternative revenue sources Governor Hart sponsored and lobbied vigorously for a poll-tax bill, and got it. By including an "emergency" clause in the bill it was protected from referendum action in the view of the Supreme Court. The bill levied an annual head tax of $5.00 on all persons between ages 21 and 50. Disfranchisement, however, was not included as a penalty for non-payment. Neither were appropriations made for its collection, but employers were held liable for its deduction from paychecks as well as requiring proof of payment from their employees. County sheriffs were authorized to seize property in lieu of payment, if necessary. Despite its regressive and backward looking character, the measure enjoyed surprisingly more support than might be expected from present day perspective. There was resistance to its enforcement by Sheriff Starwich, along with other county sheriffs. They threatened to drag their feet when it came to collecting the tax because no funds had been provided for their collection. At the annual peace officers' convention held in January 1922 they passed a resolution urging its repeal. For the same reason King County assessor Frank Hull threatened to resign. While organized labor opposed the tax as a piece of class legislation, the Chamber of Commerce supported it for that very reason. The Municipal League looked upon it as an efficient means of collecting taxes until something better was devised. Hart then decided to channel receipts from the poll tax into the veterans' bonus fund instead of using the revenue to meet the more enduring problems.[5]

The poll tax was easily evaded. Protests soon mounted, including an initiative campaign. Former legislative supporters of the tax joined the opposition, including House Speaker Mark Reed, when it became clear that people would not cooperate in its enforcement. At the 1922 state Republican Party convention Hart admitted its failure. Reed moved that it be repealed, and a big majority agreed. Repeal came in the 1923 legislative session. By then, pressure to limit property taxes came nearer passage when the forty-mill limitation was proposed for the first time. That part of the tax story will be continued later in context.[6]

To gain a fuller appreciation of the temper of this legislature, two items that were barely defeated are worth noting. One would have denied Port authorities the power to raise taxes for their support. Another would have given the legislature control over city budgets; it was killed by filibuster. These measures were designed to hamper municipal ownership and to drive down taxes. Although failing to pass these bills, these forces did succeed in passing a Certificate of Necessity bill, H.B. 174, like the one passed in 1915. It, like that in 1915, would be subjected to a referendum campaign. Among other bills of this character that would be subjected to voter action in November 1922 were:

> a bill requiring compulsory registration of political party affiliation (Referendum 14);
>
> a bill requiring candidates to support their party's platform (Referendum 15).

Of a different character was an issue which opposed rich and poor, in this case, poorer school districts of the rural areas wanting equality with the richer urban school districts. On this public education front an attempt was made by the Washington Education Association, in concert with the Grange, to achieve a greater measure of equality in funding by raising the State's proportion from 20 mills to 30, while continuing the county contribution at the 10 mills level. (Not until 1920 had the State's contribution been raised to 20 mills.) WEA's executive secretary, Arthur L. Marsh, feared the worst by February 1921, noting that " . . . certain influential members of the legislature are threatening to cut $1,000,000 from the state school fund." When defeat came, it was no surprise. An initiative campaign was then set in motion to gain equality of funding between rich and poor districts, rural and urban—Initiative 46; it too would be on the November 1922 ballot.[7]

The actions of the 1921 legislature and the initiative and

referenda that spun off it for voter action in November 1922 should be seen in context. The most explosive issue related to public ownership of utilities. Associated with this was the desire of the private utilities to avoid regulation while they were simultaneously in the process of a merger movement that continued through the 1920s, not to be brought under some degree of control until the New Deal legislation was passed to regulate holding companies. Stone and Webster was an utilities holding company, owned and operated out of Boston. It would be derisively referred to as the "Boston syndicate". As described in detail in volume one of this history, one of its subsidiaries was Seattle-based, Puget Sound Power and Light Company (PSP&L). In western Washington, PSP&L purchased thirty independent power companies, while the Spokane-based Washington Water Power Company acquired sixty-three firms in eastern Washington. As these mergers progressed they were linked by intertie-lines into a huge power grid that enabled the companies to transmit power that was surplus in one part of the grid to any part that was experiencing a shortage. (The original H.B. 174 would have turned over all the remaining water power sites in the state to them.) While they practiced this kind of power exchange among themselves, they tried to prevent municipally owned operations from doing the same thing . . . by legislation primarily. H.B. 174, which they had lobbied for, denied municipally owned utilities the right to sell power outside their corporate jurisdictions. It also made it practically impossible for cities to acquire the property of existing private utilities serving their jurisdiction, by requiring the filing of a certificate of necessity and convenience with the Public Service Commission, which had historically favored the private utilities. In 1911, the municipally owned utilities had been exempted from control by the Commission. The private companies wanted to bring them under commission control because of their ability to control the commission. Before turning to the outcome of this piece of legislation, it is well to outline the context in which the issue would be decided.[8]

In a special issue of the Annals of the American Academy of Political and Social Science of 1925, devoted to "Giant Power", Gifford Pinchot wrote in the introduction that "the development of the network of interconnected electric lines is so rapid that a delay of even five years in establishing effective public control will bring the states and the nation face to face with the immediate threat of an overwhelming and almost uncontrollable electric monopoly . . . The question is whether we shall regulate [the industry] or whether it shall regulate us." Given the tight time-frame in which to bring about this conclusion, the industry resorted to nationwide lobbying. Writing in part from the data issuing forth from the Federal Trade Commission's ongoing investigation of the industry, Edward Logan wrote in a 1929 issue of the Annals that the utility lobby had been making the "most extensive use on record of the indirect method of lobbying." He outlined its creation of special lobbying committees under leadership of the Public Utilities Joint Committee in the District of Columbia. The latter collaborated with public utility information bureaus in 28 states in issuing propaganda and in organizing campaigns against public ownership, as well as fighting for favorable legislation. One such state was Washington.[9]

In western Washington, Stone and Webster bore a negative image even within the business community that was traceable to the company's high rates compared to those of the municipally owned utilities in Seattle and Tacoma, and to the suspicion of fraud and bribery hanging over the selling of its street railway system to the City in 1919. A means of counteracting this negative public opinion of the Stone and Webster operations was begun in 1918 when a "customer-ownership policy" was inaugurated. It was the first issue of local power securities offered to regional buyers. A stock issue of $2,850,000 was sold to citizens in more than two hundred communities throughout the state . . . the beginnings of a constituency based on a vested interest in PSP&L. In May 1922, the company announced its reservation for Puget Sound district buyers of part of a cumulative prior preference stock of a $1,600,000 issue bearing 7% interest. Another part was reserved for the company's employees, and it was oversubscribed within three days. By the end of 1923 the corporation had about 5,000 securities holders within the state. The *Times* boasted that "there are now 300 or more companies with similar policies", and that over 200 communities in the state are represented as preferred stock holders. Quite a constituency, well placed.[10]

Another vital instrument in developing an ideological commitment among the general public, became the Voters' Information League which was established by Puget Sound Power and Light in 1921, although this fact did not become known for certain until the Federal Trade Commission began its investigations of the utilities industry in 1928. The league's operations will be encountered throughout this period. Abetting the VIL was the Washington Committee on Public Utility Information which was established in January 1923 in preparation for the 1923 legislative session; its director was E.H. Thomas, with headquarters in the Henry Building.[11]

Municipal ownership advocates, inspired by the success of the "Ontario Plan" wherein publicly owned power was distributed throughout the province at uniform or "postage stamp" rates, the public ownership proponents in the state formed the Super Power League of Washington with city councilman Oliver Erickson its head. While he wanted outright ownership of all electrical utilities, J.D. Ross and Homer T. Bone simply wanted to link the municipal plants of Tacoma and Seattle with rural power districts by means of tie-lines. Ross wanted to be able to sell surplus power all along the southern route of the Skagit power transmission lines in order to reduce Seattle rates and those of the cities and towns that bought the power, thereby creating a reservoir of voter support for municipal ownership. Tacoma's vulnerability became apparent in 1921, when the power for which Tacoma Light and Power contracted was denied it—the contracting party was a Stone and Webster subsidiary. This prompted Tacoma to sign an intertie agreement with Seattle City Light in early 1922. When Tacoma completed its Lake Cushman plant in 1923, it intertied directly with Seattle and with Aberdeen also. As Seattle City Light moved ahead with its Skagit project, it too would have surplus power to sell. The enormous potential of the Skagit project worried not only Stone and Webster but the entire private utility industry. To impede its completion became a matter of highest priority.[12]

When H.B. 174 reached Governor Hart it included a certificate of necessity clause and a section that would have placed municipal utilities under control of the Public Works Department (replacing the Public Service Commission). Attorney James Haight of the Municipal League headed a committee to protest the bill awaiting Hart's signature. He claimed that the bill would "impair" if not "destroy the city's light and power projects and tend to monopolization of the state's water power resources." Strong objection was made to repealing the 1911 law which exempted municipally owned utilities from regulation by the Public Service Commission. Such utilities would be restricted from extending their services in competition with a private utility already serving the area unless the commission approved by issuing a certificate of necessity. City Counsel Walter Meier (who would soon join Puget Sound Power and Light) traced the history of public service commissions for the benefit of Hart, showing how they had changed from instruments for regulating private corporations to tools of private interests to check the development of municipal ownership. The governor was persuaded by these protests to veto the section placing control under the state commission, but he allowed to stand the clause requiring the filing of a certificate of necessity. This issue would be fought over all through the 1920s.[13]

Quickly, Mayor Hugh Caldwell urged citizens to join in a referendum campaign to repeal the act on the ground that by allowing Stone and Webster to monopolize hydro sites, the city itself would be restricted in its development by hampering of City Light's own expansion. The Municipal League, organized labor, and other traditional supporters of municipal ownership, combined under James Haight's leadership to collect the needed signatures. They were not long in coming, averaging about 500 a day in Seattle. As Referendum 12 it, too, would appear on the November 1922 ballot.[14]

Electric Power, Public Ownership, and the Federal Water Power Act of 1920

During the period covered by volume one of this history we have seen how the issue of public versus private ownership of electrical utilities unfolded locally. Municipal ownership of these utilities by the municipalities of Seattle and Tacoma was unique compared to the privatization occurring in the rest of the country. In these two cities publicly owned utilities were successfully competing with the subsidiaries of Stone and Webster Management Corporation, a Boston holding company closely associated with General Electric. David E. Nye, in his *Electrifying America,* has considered the social consequences of the nation's electrification from 1880 to 1940, beginning with the "explosive growth" of streetcars extending from the 1890s to about 1915. By 1902 there were more than 800 street railway companies, in the building of which General Electric and Westinghouse played a "central role"—becoming a duopoly—in developing the electrical generating plants required to power the railways. Their expansion stimulated real estate development outward from the central cities, as promoters appealed to the "growing middle class and skilled workers". Seattle's experience was described as a "microcosm in the macrocosm" in the first volume. In Seattle, the very surge in numbers of its population—from 80,671 in 1900 to 237,000 by 1910—became the basis of the city's public ownership movement, as these newcomers unrelentingly pressed for extensions of basic electrical services. Stone and

Webster had resisted such extensions, allowing its Puget Sound Traction, Power and Light subsidiary (PSP&L's predecessor) to neglect its sadly depreciated street railway, and to concentrate its electrical services upon its nucleus of commercial and industrial customers, while simultaneously acting to block the City's acquisition of water power sites.[1]

By 1920 street railways nationwide were clearly losing out to automotive transportation. (In Seattle, Puget Sound Traction, Power, and Light had gleefully relieved itself of its street railway by selling it to the City in 1919; it had proved increasingly unprofitable, a fate being experienced in most municipalities.) But, while street railways were no longer providing profitable investment opportunities, the electrical industry steadily opened fresh ones. Advances in electrical technology spurred investment elsewhere. Thomas Cochran judges that from 1900 to 1930 "electrical equipment, including central power stations, urban and suburban lighting, and electrical communication absorbed more capital than any other type of industry and rivalled railroad investment of the late nineteenth century in its relative share of the gross national product." The very scale of these operations required concomitantly large scale financing of the type afforded by emergent investment banking houses like J.P. Morgan; Lee, Higginson; and Kidder, Peabody. Ownership of utility company stocks led General Electric and Westinghouse (having previously pooled their patents in 1895) to move into marketing of electricity through their effective control of many utilities. When so many of the stocks later proved unmarketable, General Electric created a holding company in 1905—Electric Bond and Share—as a means of stabilizing the industry by its financial management and provision of engineering advice to the utilities over which it exercized control merely by owning but a minority share of any utility's stock. "This dominance was maintained by several institutions that linked utility mangers, investors, and representatives of the duopoly", according to Nye. The National Electric Light Association became the umbrella trade association to give effect to this institutional constellation. The Federal Water Power Act of 1920 set the stage on which the public ownership of electrical utilities battles would be fought during the next two decades. An examination of the congressional contest leading to its enactment is essential to an understanding of the fight between these forces that took place in Seattle and Washington state.[2]

Through the political power that correspondingly had accrued to this special interest grouping, federal legislation became actively sought for control of the nation's water power resources—a federal grant of outright ownership became its goal. Although the final legislation fell short of its goal, the legislation, on balance, nevertheless favored private development. One of the last acts of the Wilson administration was the Federal Water Power Act of 1920. But the issue had been joined in 1914. Soon after Wilson took the presidential office, Georgia's Congressman William Adamson introduced a bill that would have given Congress the power to issue 50-year-lease water permits on public lands and on navigable streams outside federal land ownership to applicants without charge. In addition, federal regulation would be at the discretion of the Secretary of War. The leases would have become permanent ones in practice. Adamson had heard testimony only from three private power interests: the Alabama Power Company, Muscle Shoals Hydro-Electric Power Company, and Hugh Cooper who was in charge of the Keokuk dam, a private power project on the Mississippi River. When Congressman William Kent of California alerted Wilson to the significance of this bill, the president convened the committee to get modifications. It was so radically modified that not even Adamson voted for it, although it did pass, with 188 members abstaining. The conservationist congressmen quickly followed this bill with another, the Ferris Bill for regulating leases within the public domain; it also passed. Both bills headed to the Senate where, according to Judson King, the Adamson bill's text was deleted and language comparable to Adamson's original was inserted; this became the Shields Bill. The Ferris Bill suffered the same fate. No further action took place before the convening of the next congressional session in 1916 when pressure was being generated for war preparedness. When Shields reintroduced his bill in the guise of a war preparation measure and specified the need to develop Muscle Shoals by private utilities, practically granting perpetual leases, the conservationist senators attacked the bill on grounds that there would be no water power sites left for government use should the Shields Bill pass. But pass it did. Then it went to the House, where it became deadlocked in conference committee, dying in that session as well.[3]

Three days after war was declared, Shields reintroduced his bill, secured its passage again, and it headed to another deadlock in the House in mid-December. Wilson was persuaded by Kent to hold a series of conferences on it, resulting in the creation of a special House committee to develop a bill within certain policy guidelines set by Wilson. The "Wilson Bill" emerged from this committee. Federal jurisdiction over all hydroelectric power on navigable rivers was to be established by it, public preference in dam building was provided in case of conflict, water usage would be charged for, the federal government would be permitted to develop sites on its own initiative, and a 50-year lease limit was included. The bill passed on June 28, 1918, with 174 abstentions. Then it went to the Senate where serious opposition was expected.

It took five months to emerge from the Senate and it closely resembled the House bill except for a definition on stream navigability. The southeastern, states rights group of congressmen—who were also against public ownership in any form—agreed to define navigability as being able to run a motorboat upstream in the stream's natural state, and rejected the idea of navigability that resulted from stream improvements such as dams. When the House passed the bill and sent it to the Senate, Senator Robert LaFollette began a memorable filibuster on the day of scheduled adjournment, March 4, 1919. When it became clear to Vice-President Marshall that the filibuster would continue indefinitely, he simply adjourned the Senate, thereby terminating action. During the special session of Congress, called for May 19, the Wilson Bill was reintroduced and was passed on July 1. In the Senate, it was submitted to the Commerce Committee, under Washington Senator Wesley Jones's chairmanship. (He had replaced the Democrat, Senator Shields, when the Republicans became the majority party.) The bill passed the Senate and was sent to conference committee, from where it emerged as the Federal Water Power Act of 1920. By the end of May it had passed both houses.

What was in it after so long and controversial a career? As outlined by Judson King, it contained in its compromise provisions the following: federal authority over all navigable rivers, including improved ones; a public preference clause to give public bodies preference over private ones in case of conflict; permission for the federal government to build dams at its own initiative; a measure to eliminate watered stock by limiting the issuance of securities; and a measure to set rates only on the basis of actual expenditures on promotion and construction.

While the above listing were all favorable to public ownership proponents there were other features favoring private power interests. These were: 50-year leases that had the effect of being perpetual, by reason of a recapture clause; the Federal Power Commission would not have independent agency status because—as Senator Norris charged—it was composed of political appointees (the secretaries of War, Interior, and Agriculture); charges for use by private utilities was to be based on commission expenses and administrative costs, and not on the value of the use; a provision for temporary stream use was included that King guessed would prove troublesome. Wilson signed the bill on June 10 to the applause of the private utility lobby, and to the disappointment of the conservationists in Congress who believed too much had been conceded to the private power interests. But, King concluded, "There would be no more alienation of the title to power sites. The door was left open for public development." As to the first claim, King claimed too much if we judge from the actions of the 1921 Washington state legislature when it tried unsuccessfully to give control of all remaining water power sites to the private utilities. Whether this act would have sustained constitutional interpretation under the Water Power Act is moot, but the intentions were clear; so too the effectiveness of the private utility lobby. By this time both Seattle and Tacoma had acquired valuable water power sites on the Skagit and Skokomish rivers. Would this be all that public ownership forces could achieve? And what about the presumed limitations on watered stock? In the light of the 1929 Crash, watered stock contributed significantly to the stock market crisis, so these limitations seem to have been fanciful.

"Conservation" as a concept among conservationists carried different meanings. One that was ascendant in the period between the wars is typified by the views of Gifford Pinchot and articulated by the United States Forest Service of which he was the founding father. This group's primary concern was to prevent private monopolization of the nation's natural resources, particularly its forests and waters. To the degree that the federal government withdrew these resources from private entry, they ideally would be managed on a stewardship basis by technical "experts". Presumably, such experts inherently would be politically neutral, acting in the mode of Thorstein Veblen's engineers, preoccupied with the manipulation of "matter of fact" data. Technocrats in the purest sense of the word! Conservation in the sense represented by this group would find expression in the fight over the Bone Bill in the 1923 legislative session and Initiative 52 in the 1924 election. At issue was the threatened monopolization of the state's water power sites.[4]

Another constellation was forming among conservationists. Following the lead of John Muir, these were environmentalists whose thinking was being defined in ecological terms, in which humankind is viewed as but a part of the planet's larger ecosystem. Foremost in this group at the national level were Aldo Leopold and Bob Marshall. Locally, Irving Clark, as chair of the Mountaineers National Parks Committee, articulated its propositions, as we shall see in chapter 15 on the conservation movement.[5]

"Electrifying America" . . . and Seattle

Electrification in the United States before 1910 had been keyed to commercial and industrial users, not toward exploiting the potential of the domestic market. Commercial and street lighting preoccupied investment in the field as a wary people were being introduced to the wonders of electricity during the two decades before the turn of the century. By 1900, street railways had become electrified across the country—along with the merging of myriad unprofitable lines that stretched to serve areas lying outside the original city cores. Central electrical power stations—usually fired by coal—displaced decentralized ones, driving down the costs, finally appealing to potential industrial and commercial customers in the process. However, the cost of ten cents a kilowatt hour in 1897 had to drop precipitously if a larger market were to be served, particularly the domestic one. Leading also toward cost reduction in general was the expanding network of transmission lines already serving industrial and commercial customers. By 1910, the cost of extending transmission lines to homes had also declined since the basic lines needed only to be added onto for domestic consumption. Nevertheless, domestic uses at this early stage did find a market, though exclusively among the upper classes who could afford the expensive products: electric light bulbs, electric irons and fans, washing machines. Advertisements typically displayed exotic uses by fashionably attired women. Only one home in seven had electricity in 1910 (by 1930 this figure grew to seven in ten). Eighty-five percent of the electrified homes lay in the urban and suburban areas. Rural electrification remained a distant dream.[1]

Utilities had not wired most homes by 1910. The war postponed the process somewhat, but the early 1920s witnessed the takeoff for full scale development of the domestic market. One million residential customers were added in 1920; by 1924 two million more were being added annually. By 1930 most urban and suburban homes were wired, and use of appliances—from gadgets to more durable goods—was becoming common. Advertising turned to the mass marketing of home electrification, displacing door-to-door salesmen. Model homes, demonstrating the marvels of electrification, became a nationwide growth industry. Appliance invention and manufacturing required relatively small investment, thereby stimulating entry of small firms like Hotpoint. Once this market was pioneered, the duopoly of General Electric and Westinghouse bought the pioneering companies along with their patents, then turned their own well equipped laboratories toward product improvement. Since many of the products being introduced—vacuum cleaners, electric stoves, radios, washing machines, and refrigerators—required large investment for the home owner or renter, installment buying became the chief mode of purchase (as it also typified automobile buying). "Consumerism" was birthing in its contemporary sense.[2]

Seattle's own lighting department reflected the national trend. City Light reported in 1922 that it had about 68,000 customers compared to about 22,000 for Puget Sound Power and Light Company (although each sold about the same amount of current). While the company possessed the greater part of the downtown business, the City had most of the residential customers. Given this preponderence of residential customers for City Light, it is understandable that the domestic market would be foremost in its marketing strategy. It could report that 2,500 electric ranges had been hooked up to its lines in 1922 and that six new apartment houses had signed on for lighting and service. By the end of 1926, 11,127 ranges had been connected to the City's system, 3,406 during that year alone. Through its own demonstration outlet in the County-City Building it had sold 2,776 ranges. PSP&L operated a comparable demonstration unit. The combined PSP&L and City Light hookups brought "cooking electrically" to an estimated one out of six homes in Seattle. City Light's range load was doubling every two years. The trend was clear: City Light counted 14,679 ranges at the end of 1927; by 1930 the number grew to 23,405—two customers in seven were thought to be cooking electrically. In its 1930 annual report City Light boasted, "Seattle has more electric ranges in use than any other city in America, irrespective of population." (This estimate must have included PSP&L's sales as well.) By then it could also claim that water heaters were selling big—12,000 on the City's lines alone. Cumulatively, the effect demonstrated to J.D. Ross that 1930 marked the best year of the department's operations. He credited this to the "increase in use of current for domestic and commercial lighting purposes." The latter was keyed in large part to outdoor advertising lighting and to spread of improved interior commercial lighting.[3]

Electrified refrigeration was just becoming popular by 1930, but all through the 1920s light electric appliances, from toasters to radios, came into their own as they became affordable to the lower middle class and blue collar families. Seattle was no exception—appliance stores, including radio specialty shops, popped up downtown and in the neighborhood commercial districts.

With this as background we can turn once again to the continuing contest between City Light and Puget Sound Power and Light.

The Public Ownership Fight: PSP&L Links Street Railway Rescue With Acquisition of City Light

Against the backdrop of the national scene, J.D. Ross reported in mid-May, 1921 to newly elected mayor, Hugh Caldwell, that the Lake Union Steam Plant supplied the bulk of the electricity needed by City Light's 63,000 customers, and that it had furnished 46.9% of the total kilowatt hours for the entire system in 1919. Given this slight energy base, it is understandable that Ross would be transfixed by the Skagit project. Without it, City Light would be unable to compete with PSP&L as it expanded its operations through merger deals and interties throughout western Washington. He feared also the demise of Tacoma's municipal plant and the prospect for future public ownership of hydroelectric projects, particularly in light of the recent legislative fight that had almost opened the door for acquisition of most, if not practically all, waterpower sites in the state to the private companies. At the end of the year, when now-Councilman and former ally, R.H. Thomson, proposed another dam on the Cedar, Ross wrote his objections to Caldwell. It would divert funds from the Skagit project at a time when the City was having trouble selling its bonds in a slumping market.[1]

As to the bond sales, Ross critiqued for Caldwell an article appearing in the *Public Service Magazine*, October 1920, "Municipal Electric Plant Proves Burden". Ross claimed this was one of similar recent articles inspired to prevent the sale of municipal light and power bonds in general. The author of this particular piece charged that the taxpayers were losing $125,000 annually, that the City was paying twice the proper amount for street lights, that more than $3 million had been thrown away on the Cedar River dam, and that the steam plant was too expensive to operate, particularly when the private company has offered to sell its surplus power to the City. Ross, indignantly, informed Caldwell that City Light had operated at a net gain, plowing back the proceeds from the depreciation fund into construction, extensions, and paying off bonds according to strict guidelines set by the State Auditor; that loss of tax revenues had been more than compensated for by the savings resulting from low rates, rates the private company had been forced to meet, thereby benefiting its own customers although less directly; and that the Dam cost only $2,371,859.94! Ross added that the private corporation must usually pay 2 to 3% more in interest on its bonds because of "inferior security", thereby adding to the cost of any power purchases from the Company. In addition, what makes it so difficult for the private companies to compete against the municipals is that they must pay commissions, they pay on watered stock, and they pay their subsidiaries for construction, operation and financing that represent costs to be met. Ross cited "cost plus 10%" as the charge by the construction company. He concluded that Seattle's very success "calls forth this attack apparently to hurt us on the bond market." The terms and tone of this debate would run throughout the period. In Caldwell, Ross had a sympathetic ear and he was making the most of it. In the scenario portrayed in the following paragraphs the main elements are conveyed.[2]

Mayor Caldwell, suspecting fraud and bribery, had promised an investigation of the street railway purchase from Stone and Webster. Furthermore, he believed the street railway debt would be used by the company to take over City Light. A series of lawsuits were proceeding through the state courts contesting whether the City's general fund was subject to levy for interest and principal payments on the bonds. Or were only the railway's revenues to be used for this purpose? Caldwell insisted on the latter interpretation, arguing that for the City to guarantee payment would simply be a gift to the company.[3]

For its part the company found it impossible to market its bonds as long as the Grand Jury investigation was underway and the outcome in doubt. PSP&L board chairman, F.W. Pratt, responding to a request from PSP&L's general manager, Alton W. Leonard, for suggestions on how to take over operation of both the street railway and the Lighting Department, advised him that public ownership was not the real issue. He would first negotiate a management contract with the City to operate the system, then lease it. But, if he could get the City in that kind of negotiating position he would make, "[s]uch a trade contingent on satisfactory arrangement on municipal lighting plant."[4]

As to the Grand Jury investigation, Leonard anxiously telegraphed Pratt that the City was laying the foundation for returning the property to the company and abrogating the contract. The Mayor's special attorney was trying to prove "constructive fraud" with that end in view, but he was having trouble coming up with sufficient evidence. Relieved, Leonard reported ten days later, on the last day of January, that the jury had found no evidence of corruption, only "slack business methods of City administration." He followed up this report, ". . . we think it a happy outcome that they at least found trade sweet and clean as we have always maintained." Leonard did express concern whether PSP&L might have to guarantee the bonds in case of the City's default. The company's attorney, J.B. Howe, quieted this anxiety by assuring Pratt that if the City defaults ". . . [we can enforce payment by] compelling levy of a tax." On this issue the Chamber of Commerce was found wanting, for in its October 19, 1920 meeting it reiterated its opposition to using taxation to pay for the purchase. Where it would wind up was anyone's guess at this stage, for just at this time the Chamber was preoccupied with its tax reduction campaign. As to Caldwell's threat of repudiation, Howe reported, "People generally [are] not taking kindly to [it]."[5]

In the wake of Leonard's heartening reports on the Grand Jury investigation, Pratt euphorically asked Leonard to supply him with complete information on the Municipal Street Railway and the Lighting Department with an eye to a takeover; also the carfare to be charged. Along with the latter he requested ammunition to use in "combatting fallacious statements which may be published about [the] impossibility of making the system pay its way even with higher fares." Pratt followed on February 10, telling Leonard that the Seattle "mess is making it impossible to market the utility bonds without some sort of guarantee on our part . . . [In case of default] we, of course share in the general calamity . . . I do not intend to imply [regarding operation of the street railway] . . . that we would take the street railway unless we got the light and power."[6]

Early in May, Leonard wrote Pratt that a company study of the Skagit project showed it "badly from an economic standpoint". He inquired further, "Do you see any objection to putting the situation up frankly to a few people in Seattle . . . including possibly two or three members of the city council, one or two newspaper officials and perhaps some representatives from the Chamber of Commerce?" He continued, "There is yet a possibility that work will be stopped . . . if it can be at this time [and if not] in your opinion [is it] better to let them go ahead and spend the money?"[7]

The Chamber of Commerce's Skagit Committee soon issued its report in June claiming that the Cedar River water was sufficient to meet Seattle's needs. Ross was invited to discuss it. He refused, asking the Chamber "what about future needs?", and he castigated that body for remaining silent when the 1921 Legislature tried to "turn over all the water power in western Washington to Stone and Webster." What remained of that bill was the "Certificate of Necessity" provision which was then being threatened with reversal by a referendum drive . . . as had happened previously in 1916 with comparable legislation favoring the private power companies.[8]

City Light continued to face impediments in pursuing construction of the Skagit dams. Number one was the Gorge dam, which was to be a temporary wood-crib dam that would be replaced by a masonry affair after the other two dams had been completed. Completion of the Gorge dam was expected by late 1923 or early 1924. The project as a whole was intended to use the same water three times over. The Chamber's strategy coincided with that of the PSP&L in obstructing this goal and in confining the "yardstick" competition it would offer.

In July, the Chamber's Skagit Committee urged a halt to construction "until a more definite and conclusive plan . . . can be . . . given to the people . . . before continuing a project that [might cost $50 or $60 million.]" The Chamber moved to confer with civic organizations "to bring pressure on the City Council." While reporting that twelve organizations had joined it in the demand that construction be stopped, one that refused to go along was the Municipal League. Another was the Seattle chapter of the American Association of Engineers.[9]

The League called a meeting to respond to the Chamber's invitation and chose to reinvestigate the matter on its own instead of accepting the Chamber's verdict. It sponsored a tour of the Skagit site, and reported in its favor in late July, expressing its satisfaction with the progress thus far. The League would continue to sponsor Skagit tours throughout the 1920s, usually at times when the Chamber of Commerce and *Seattle Times* were blasting the Skagit project. As to the engineers, they urged completion of the Gorge dam "at the earliest possible date."[10]

Undaunted, the opponents next attacked in October the "secret" manner by which the Skagit bonds were disposed of, charging "fraud and collusion". The *Times* recommended a grand jury investigation, but Prosecuting Attorney Malcolm

Douglas, who normally sided with the newspaper and the Chamber, proved a stickler on the law this time by claiming no evidence had been presented to his office indicating that a crime had been committed. As to J.D. Ross, none of these tactics of public ownership opponents was new or unexpected. He had been long convinced that most corruption in city politics in general could be traced to the influence of the private utilities with their franchise holdings . . . these tactics he saw as part of the overall strategy to defeat public ownership nationwide.[11]

A succession of naggings followed one another in 1922 before the November 7 election would decide by referenda and initiative the fate of some of the most objectionable bills passed by the 1921 Legislature. In mid-April, PSP&L tried unsuccessfully to convince the City Council that it should rescind City Light's 25% reduction of rates for off-peak power to industrial users. On May 1, the Skagit project's chief engineer, Carl Uhden, came under fire from the local chapter of the American Association of Engineers for filling important positions with "men he had imported from other states." And they charged him further with mismanagement, a charge that had gone unanswered since its submission in mid-March. Whether a Skagit tour by some 50 members in June assuaged their distress is uncertain. Then Councilman Fitzgerald got the Council to pass a resolution authorizing negotiations with Henry Ford "for the purpose of securing his assistance and interest in the development of the Skagit River project on the basis of a lease." Ford, who had grown a halo even among workers for lifting their wages above existing levels in the automotive industry, was just then enmeshed in negotiations for the development of Muscle Shoals; this had prompted Fitzgerald to initiate the resolution. But even the *Union Record* liked the idea, just out of admiration of Ford for having broken the wage barrier. The *Star* claimed it was "a smoke screen to allow the Company to take over [the Skagit project] at a crucial moment" when Ford would opt-out for Muscle Shoals. Mayor Caldwell called the resolution absurd before he left office, and incoming mayor, Edwin Brown, credited both his predecessor and Skagit project chief engineer, Carl Uhden, for keeping the project going when suspension was threatened. Brown viewed the Skagit project as the means for making Seattle a "center for industry". He asked the Municipal League to arrange a Skagit tour for interested citizens, which the League did in June. Nothing came of Fitzgerald's resolution, but it helped keep the pressure on.[12]

In all of this unfolding series of strategems the actions of

Fitzgerald should not be slighted. For example, in February, as he was campaigning for re-election to the Council, he proclaimed in a flier, that he wanted to put the street railway on a "paying basis", and, failing that, either lease it along with a guarantee of bond payments by the City, or "return [it] to private ownership to be decided by vote of the people." His message closely paralleled the thinking of PSP&L. His Ford-resolution should be seen in this connection. He, also, would be linked by an affidavit, filed in 1923, with having facilitated the clouded street railway purchase. His record in the City Council showed him consistently in opposition to City Light.[13]

The *Post-Intelligencer*, next, began attacking City Engineer Arthur Dimock who had worked closely and cooperatively with Ross ever since he succeeded R.H. Thomson in 1912. Although the Municipal League defended Dimock against charges that he refused to implement personnel and budget cuts that the *P-I* had been pressing for, Mayor Brown decided to remove him in late July. Brown then replaced him with James Blackwell who was then employed by Stone and Webster. The City Council approved. The *Municipal News* insisted that it was Dimock's commitment to the Skagit project before a "business survey" could be made, that was the underlying reason for his dismissal. Blackwell had been a "severe critic" of the project and wanted it delayed until such a survey could be made.[14]

At its end the *Times* predictably chipped in, as it continued a practically uninterrupted campaign of harassment of City light on the Skagit project. In a late September editorial Clarence Blethen asked "$4,000,000 more for the Skagit? Why? Let's not hurry!" He continued the obvious: that no kilowatts had yet been produced despite "roseate promises . . . Before we sink any more money there, let's see whether those promises are to be fulfilled—and if not, why not! [Rates would be cheaper now] if we had let the Skagit alone."[15]

City Politics, 1921-1922

Conservative forces in the city were led by the Chamber of Commerce and the Voters' Information League (VIL). They joined to force tax reduction, to reduce the scope and size of city and county government, to oppose labor unions, and to oppose public ownership. The Chamber even favored limiting the voting on bond issues and "other public indebtedness" to property owners.[1]

The VIL was organized by Stone and Webster. Operating

through its Puget Sound Power and Light subsidiary, the corporation proclaimed that it would obtain "Official Records and Facts relating to Public TAXATION and EXPENDITURES . . . and make them known to the voters . . . with the ultimate OBJECT of REDUCING TAXES."

Both the *Times* and the, now, Hearst-owned *Post-Intelligencer*, backed these organizations. The Chamber complimented the *P-I* for its educational articles on taxation, as it had earlier the King County Taxation Bureau for bringing about a 20% tax reduction in the county. And the *P-I* even claimed credit for organizing the Tax Reduction Council which was really established by the VIL, once its initial focus became taxation. The big difference between the *P-I*, under its new ownership, and the *Times* lay in their respective attitudes toward public ownership of utilities. Under the leadership of Scott Bone, the former had opposed public ownership as strenuously as the *Times*, dating back to their collaboration in promoting the failed Harbor Island development under a private leasehold, sweetened by special concessions. The *P-I* switched sides under Hearst ownership, joining with the *Star* and the, now flagging, *Union Record* in supporting public ownership.[2]

The VIL brought together fifty civic and social organizations to form the Tax Reduction Council (TRC) in July 1921. The VIL cancelled its own meetings for the next two months so that its members could give undivided attention to the TRC. First targets were school expenditures and pay of city employees. The VIL issued a bulletin series to push its arguments. The one issued on September 1 complained of indifference on the part of City department heads to TRC's insistence "to use the pruning knife to employees . . . This organization is going to bring pressure . . . This must include the public utilities as well." But the public school system bore the brunt of the initial attack.[3]

Former state tax commissioner, Clark Jackson, reported to the Chamber that Seattle's annual per pupil cost was $71.72, compared to Portland's $59.54 and San Francisco's $58.68. He also estimated that 36.5% of King County's taxes went for schools. All this was fodder for the tax reduction forces, who also militated against the educational policies of Superintendent Frank B. Cooper. Reflected in this relatively high per pupil cost was a 30:1 teacher-pupil ratio (approvingly citing 45:1 for Minneapolis), Cooper's promotion of extra-curricular activities, remedial schools, relatively higher teacher salaries, and his program of social services—the latter included a school physician and visiting nurses staff, coupled with free clinics. When Oliver McGilvra filed a taxpayer's suit against the free clinics and the state Supreme Court held in his favor, Cooper considered reclassifying the nurses as inspectors. As to the 30:1 ratio, Cooper took pride in the fact that 21% of elementary school students continued into the high school grades—a relatively high figure for the time.[4]

When the School Board responded to these pressures by establishing a one-dollar laboratory fee for scientific courses, and a fifty-cent fee for girls sewing classes, a taxpayers suit was instituted against these fees by W.W. Ballantyne in September.[5]

To keep the pressure on, the Chamber urged appointment of a school survey commission in July "to prepare for the future conduct of the school system", but this was hardly a beginning. Still euphoric from the war, and in a period when former army officers were still being addressed by their military titles, the Chamber's Military Affairs Committee recommended that military training be introduced into the high schools. A Major Cleary explained the details to the membership, pointing to three coastal cities where it had been instituted: Oakland, San Francisco, and Los Angeles. Only Walla Walla has such a program in the Northwest, he complained. Physical Education credit was being offered, and a minimum of 100 boys over age 14 must register to justify the expense to the Army in supplying personnel, uniforms, and equipment. When the plan was presented to Cooper, who had resisted such a program even during the war, it marked the beginning of his last battle. The headline of the *Union Record*'s February 6, 1922 issue ran: "Seattle Mothers Fight Militarism in Schools".[6]

Quickly, the opposition rallied to Cooper's defense: the League of Women Voters, Women's Legislative Council, the North End Progressive Club, the Commonwealth Club, and the Central Labor Council. At the School Board's February 11 meeting Ebenezer Shorrock led the fight for military training and when he was unable to get even the dependable conservative, E.L. Blaine, to favor it, he succeeded in postponing a vote. When the proposal appeared to be lost the Chamber withdrew it before the next meeting, rather than risk the embarassment of a vote. It was clear that costs were not the only matter at issue, that, in concentrating on them, the tax reduction forces could eventually control educational policies in train. A weary Cooper, tired of fighting these conservative forces, seeing the gradual undermining of his socially sensitive policies by the tax reductionists, finally resigned in March after pioneering a nationally recognized public school program that had become the envy of most major cities.[7]

With Cooper gone, the Chamber returned to the fray. A

Captain E.D. Colvin and a Frank Fretwell were accused by the *Union Record* of browbeating the School Board into acceptance of militarism in the curriculum over the opposition of Board member E.L. Blaine and Councilman Warren Lane. Councilman Philip Tindall and Captain (later a Congressman) Ralph Horr spoke in favor, but most must have become unsettled by Fretwell's assertion that his opponents would be guilty of treason if this were 1917! The pacifists won out this time . . . we were not at war, it seemed to all but a Dickensian—named Fretwell.[8]

In preparation for the May city election, the conservatives, led by former Secretary of the Interior, Richard A. Ballinger, formed the Washington Union League Club. In part, this move was to get the Associated Industries out of direct political action. A letter was mailed on League letterhead February 21, 1922 by Moritz Thomsen (of the Albers Milling Company), chairman of the Seattle Political Campaign Fund, aiming to collect $50,000. In it, Thomsen claimed that the League had been formed as a "clearing house" for several civic and business organizations for "directing how and for whom moneys contributed for election purposes shall be spent." This would make these campaigns "less expensive and more effective." In a related letter, president Ballinger contended that this campaign is needed to "obviate the practical abolition of political parties . . . through the introduction of the primary system of nominating candidates." Clearly, there were larger strategic objectives than the mere winning of the city election. The list of signers of the articles of incorporation reads like a list of Associated Industries membership. Its founder Frank Waterhouse, Judge George Donworth, department store owner D.E. Frederick, Reverend Mark A. Matthews, Great Northern's L.C. Gilman, and theater owner George Danz, typified others on the list.[9]

As to the immediate issue, Thomsen pronounced in early March "we must deny to our public utilities the right to levy taxes for their operation." His target was the Erickson three-cent fare bill that would be voted upon. But other utilities might be affected as well if denied this right—the Port of Seattle and the street railway. Erickson contemplated that any deficit would be made up by a subsidy that somehow would not obligate the City to pay off the bonded indebtedness to Stone and Webster. The Union League candidates were Walter Meier for mayor, and E.L.Blaine, E.B. Cox, and Henry Hall for city council.[10]

Meier was heavily favored to win in the April 1922 primary and in the May runoff, but he was roundly defeated instead. The finalists were to be advertising-dentist and former Socialist Edwin J. "Doc" Brown and State Senator Dan Landon. The Municipal League disappointedly attributed Meier's defeat to the doubt, held by a majority of the voters, of his professed innocence in the streetcar deal; to his overconfidence; and to his close association with Associated Industries people (by being the Union League's candidate). It surely did not help his candidacy to be found also opposing additional bond issues for the Skagit project while nominally supporting the project.[11]

While events were moving toward the fight outlined above, the big debate centered on the street railway—Erickson's 3-cent fare proposal and whether or not the City was obligated to pay off the railway bonds from the general fund or from the revenues earned by the railway. PSP&L had appealed from the state Supreme Court ruling of April 29, 1922 that the general fund could not be so used. Successively, the Circuit Court and the United States Supreme Court upheld the state court.[12]

It was in this setting that the voters would decide the fare issue. Brown favored a 5-cent fare, but so did Landon; and both stood firm behind the Skagit project. Landon drew support from the Central Labor Council and the State Federation of Labor whose leadership distrusted Brown for attracting Associated Industries backing. Alfred Lundin—president of the Municipal League, and a future head of the Chamber of Commerce as well as a soon-to-be defeated mayoral candidate—opposed the three-cent fare because he thought it would only benefit Stone and Webster, based on Erickson's contention that any deficit would be made up by taxes. The Chamber of Commerce also opposed it for the reasons put by Lundin. Its members were alarmed to find that "one-fifth of Seattle's taxes is paid by the three thousand members of the Seattle Chamber . . ."[13]

As it turned out, Brown won by almost 12,000 votes, and the 3-cent fare proposition (Proposition A) lost by almost 25,000 votes. Two women won the most votes in the Council race: Bertha K. Landes drew in excess of 55,000 votes, while Kathryn Miracle attracted more than 33,000, and the well-known conservative, E.L. Blaine, won the third opening with more than 25,000 votes. Miracle would prove a diligent advocate of City Light, even leading trips to the Skagit to show its progress and future potential, and campaigning hard for defeat of the Certificate of Necessity bill (Referendum 12). Landes (also from the University district from where her husband pursued a faculty career as head of the University of Washington's Geology Department) supported the Skagit project, but she was more interested in some of the moral issues surrounding vice and prohibition enforcement, areas where Brown would later prove vulnerable.[14]

With Mayor Caldwell being unable to provide the Grand

Jury with evidence showing actual fraud, Stone and Webster looked forward to selling its railway bonds, but the company had to contend with the matter of guaranteeing payment in event of default by the City. Believing it was doing the company a favor, the *Times* early in 1921 had even urged default so as to return the street railway to the company with a more favorable franchise than before. This caused PSP&L's attorney, James B. Howe, to consider suing the *Times* or, at least, to dissuade Clarence Blethen from pursuing that line—thanks, but no thanks. The real question was: Would the company or the City be responsible? As we have just seen above, the company certainly did not want the role because it would then be placed in that which the City now occupied. How to get the City to assume responsibilty? From the general fund? Not if Samuel Asia and thirteen other taxpayers could prevent it.[15]

Signalling the annual crises of the future, the City had been forced to issue warrants to its street railway employees to spare money for meeting the first of its semi-annual interest payments on September 1, 1921. Choosing to avert a disastrous default that would hurt not only the publicly owned enterprises, but would affect the entire city, the Seattle Central Clearing House agreed to authorize the city's banks to honor the warrants. And when the annual bond redemption payment came due on March 1, 1922, warrants were again resorted to. When interest-paying time came again in September 1922, the Clearing House refused its authorization, and a default was narrowly avoided by the employees accepting postponment of their July wages. Seeing a precedent in the making, the Fourteen Taxpayers decided to sue the City in early January 1921.[16]

The City had transferred $83,000 from the general fund to the street railway fund in December 1920, treating the transfer as only a temporary loan; consequently, it did not violate the City charter in the Corporation Counsel's opinion. The Fourteen Taxpayers thought otherwise, and sued. In Judge James Ronald's Superior Court they lost and promptly appealed to the state Supreme Court. They amended their suit on appeal, seeking to enjoin the City from using the general fund for expenditures on operations and maintenance. On April 29, 1922 the latter court reversed the lower court's decision, declaring that the general fund could not be tapped for operations and maintenance expenses, and that revenues could only be used for interest and redemption payments on the bonds. These court actions put a decided crimp in Stone and Webster's attempts to market the bonds since the general fund could not be used to guarantee payment. This meant the company was stuck with them because it would not act as guarantor either.[17]

While these suits were wending their course through the courts the City experienced the election in spring 1922, referred to above. It turned on the street car-fare issue. Councilman Erickson had pushed a three-cent fare bill through the Council for inclusion on the May ballot. Mayoral candidate Edwin J. Brown campaigned hard against the Erickson bill, arguing for a five-cent fare. Erickson's bill would have forced the City to use the general fund to make up the expected deficit. The Supreme Court's action, on April 29, would have prevented this recourse without a direct popular vote. This court decision helped undermine Erickson's bill. It was resoundingly defeated, and with Brown elected, a five-cent fare was temporarily tried. Subsequently, the original fare of ten cents (and three for a quarter) was reinstituted.[18]

There really was no way out for the street railway. Sympathetically, PSP&L's Alton Leonard wrote a memorandum in late May assessing the predicament: "The system by increasing its net revenue nearly $400,000 despite the loss of 14,000,000 pay passengers has done exceedingly well. The fundamental trouble with the carlines is that they have no friends, no voice with which to reach the public. The mayor has been a critic; the council have been destructive rather than constructive; the newspapers have been critical rather than helpful, and largely because they do not understand the problem . . . [The public is denied the information they are entitled to have] . . . The lines . . . will become . . . [the] waif of municipal politics." Not only was Leonard prophetic, but he would act to make it so, as well.[19]

While PSP&L's legal counsel was appealing through the federal courts, he nevertheless viewed these developments optimistically in May. Howe saw difficulty for the City in marketing its Lighting Department bonds, except at prohibitively high interest rates, due to the fact that the general fund would be out of reach. He saw the company's earning capacity improving at this prospect.[20]

These court actions also caused Howe to advise his superiors, in December 1922, to start a suit to prevent the City from pursuing the Skagit project. He asserted, "I believe that the fight in Washington is going to be over the market instead of over water power and that the development of the Skagit is the greatest cloud on the horizon affecting our prosperity." Indeed, the Skagit River provided the best hydroelectric power site then under construction in the state.[21]

What had emerged from these conflicts over the plight of the Municipal Street Railway were the following. For one thing, the system was being operated more efficiently than it had under the private company. Yet, it could not use tax revenues to meet operations and maintenance expenses, and it had to pay off its bonded indebtedness from its own revenues. While the contract did not have such a clause, Howe, nevertheless, remained confident that the general fund could ultimately be tapped to spare the City financial embarassment and to assure investors that Seattle was really a safe place in which to invest. To avoid default on bond payments, it had to postpone paying operations and maintenance expenses and/or issue pay warrants annually. Sometimes, the Clearing House would cooperate, sometimes not. The railway also had to borrow from other City funds to help meet the bonded debt obligation. (Later, the City would be hailed into court on the intra-City loans by John von Herberg.) The railway was thereby prevented from selling bonds due in part to its instablity, in part to its lack of a guarantor for them, and in part to the unending litigation.

For its part, the Puget Sound Power and Light Company sought to link the street railway's fate to that of the Lighting Department. It wanted the property of the latter, and it was particularly concerned about the Skagit project. The company was undecided about whether to try and block the construction outright or to hold back, satisfied that the Lighting Department's bonded indebtedness would become so great that default would surely follow. Then the company could pick up the pieces. The company's officers were well aware how near the margin of capacity J.D. Ross was operating. Not until Mayor Landes's term of office was A.W. Leonard able to link City Light outright to the railway's finances, but the company and its allies—chiefly the Chamber of Commerce, and the *Times*—did their level best to obstruct the Skagit development. They argued all through the twenties that City Light was operating at a loss, was incredibly extravagant, was about to cave in under its bonded indebtedness, and that J.D. Ross was building a political machine, just like any city boss.

The company, without apparent priming, could also count upon Councilman Oliver Erickson to aid its cause, expecting him to simply pursue his political ambitions and his personal vendetta against Ross. Ever since 1911, Erickson had resented Ross's challenge to leadership of the municipal ownership forces, having forced rate reductions over Ross's opposition, having pushed for rehabilitation of the Cedar dam operation over Ross's objections, offering alternatives to the Skagit project, and interfering with administration of the Lighting Department in general. Coupled with his desire to control the Lighting Department was his persistent efforts to reduce street car fares and to take over the independent Seattle, Renton and Southern Street Railway on unfavorable terms. By urging lower rates in general, he sought to broaden his popular appeal. He misjudged, and in being thwarted, concentrated all of his pent up frustration on J.D. Ross from about 1924 on, a year which saw rejection by his own public ownership forces of his sweeping public ownership bill in favor of support for the alternative Bone Bill. His rejection by the city's voters of his bid to become mayor must also have been unsettling.

Voters Reject Handiwork of 1921 Legislature

The November 1922 election resembled that of 1916 when the voters overwhelmingly rejected key legislation that came before them as initiatives and referenda. The 1921 legislature passed bills like those of its 1915 predecessor which were so unpopular that voters took direct action through initiative petitions and referenda. The one exception was rejection of Initiative 46, relating to public school financing—the "30-10" measure; it will be given special attention below.

Initiative 40, the poll tax law, met defeat by a vote of 86,317 to 24,285. While the Seattle Chamber of Commerce favored it, so too did the Municipal League's taxation committee on the ground that it should stand until a substitute could be found. A majority of its members, however, opposed the measure.[1]

Referendum 12—the Certificate of Necessity Bill (H.B. 174)—like its 1915 version, was rejected 154,905 to 64,800, thereby reaffirming sentiment for public ownership of utilities. Referendum 14, requiring compulsory registration of political party membership, lost 164,004 to 69,593, as, similarly, did its brother, Referendum 15, requiring loyalty to a party's platform. Referendum 13, which would have prohibited compulsory health examinations in the schools (and thereby represented a school expense item), also was decisively defeated.[2]

Initiative 46 deserves special attention for its bearing on the running question of "equality of education", and continuing failure throughout this period to provide poorer school districts with funding that approximated richer ones, like that of Seattle. Though it would be hard to persuade Seattle school administrators and their underpaid, overworked, teachers that they belonged to the enviable richer class, they nevertheless did, when compared to those in rural areas. The Washington Education Association's executive secretary, Arthur Marsh, pointed out that Seattle would ". . . lose (contribute) by application of '30-10' . . . Seattle would receive back $1.04 of the total apportionment for every dollar paid into the state fund; but the average district would receive back $1.12 . . . so of course Seattle is below average . . . [getting] back less under 30-10 than she pays in." For its part, the Municipal League opposed the initiative, favoring local levies instead of a statewide tax, and choosing to wait until the "20-10" law of 1920 be tested first as to its effectiveness. The Chamber of Commerce, doing all in its power to reduce contributions of its constituency to school revenues in general, opposed the initiative. In this, its associates supported the campaign of the "Federated Taxpayers League" in flooding the state with opposition speakers. Noah Showalter, president of the State Normal School at Cheney, credited the League with the measure's defeat, by striking fear among voters by spreading false information. State P.T.A. president, Mrs. Victor Malstrom, reminded those who were not yet persuaded otherwise that poor districts have little taxable property to assess—unlike the cities. She cited Jay Thomas of the Voters Information League as the organizer of the opposition, with his corps of full-time workers—those to whom Showalter pointed his accusing finger. Not so Marsh, who claimed, ". . . we were double-crossed by the nominal generalissimo of education [State Superintendent, Josephine C. Preston] . . . Up to the time when she went into the camp of the opposition we had an even break to win . . . If we had had her leadership . . . we could have won, hands down." The fact that the P.T.A, women's clubs in general, the State Federation of Labor, trade unions in general, and the State Grange all supported Initiative 46 lends credibility to Marsh's claim of solid support.[3]

The ultimate aim of the tax reduction forces was to limit the tax on real property while continuing to avoid impositions on intangible property, then imposing sales and excise taxes to compensate for the loss in revenue formerly provided by real property taxes. As to the prospect of a graduated income tax it could always be challenged on constitutional grounds, should one be enacted—it would be in the early-1930s, and be declared unconstitutional. The irony is that the school system was expected to supply the pool of skilled labor so essential to the functioning of industry and commerce, yet business organizations consistently opposed adequate funding . . . and do, to this day.

The Legislature and the City, 1923

The central issue on which the 1923 Legislature focused was a familiar one: public ownership of utilities. Should public ownership be halted before its continued expansion would convert the national economy from a capitalistic to a socialistic or communistic economy as the private utilities contended? Or should there be a mixing of the two, coupled with regulation that would keep the private utilities honest and produce lower rates that would in turn promote industrial development? Or should the private utilities have it all to themselves by self-regulation as to their securities structures, rates, and general policy and decision making relative to the market: Who is to be served, and who to be denied service? In brief, should the private utilities be granted immunity from public action by being granted the status of a "natural monopoly" . . . in the language of most economics textbooks of the period?

Girding for the legislative session that began in January, the private power companies formed the Washington Committee on Public Utility Information, headed by a former employee of Puget Sound Power and Light, E.H. Thomas. Its primary objective was to block legislation that would allow municipally owned utilities to sell power outside their corporate limits . . . knowing that the Super Power League intended to introduce such legislation on behalf of the public ownership forces. City Light's J.D. Ross threatened an initiative campaign if no such legislation was passed.[1]

Just how significant this local issue was nationally is indicated from testimony given in the later Federal Trade Commission hearings. A report of the Public Policy Committee of the National Electric Light Association stated:

> The Seattle situation is of national importance. Seattle has the second largest municipal plant in the country. Its rates are continually cited as lower than those charged by privately owned plants . . . At a time when active proposals are being made to extend the activities of Government in business in other localities, the claim of successful results of such policy in Seattle is dangerous and requires refutation.[2]

PSP&L had authorized up to $150,000 toward this campaign, and had, since 1921, been subsidizing the work of the

Voters Information League whose pamphlets were distributed to substantially all households in the city. And for good reason—in their competitive area, the PSP&L had had to meet each successive rate reduction of City Light. If Seattle were allowed to sell Skagit power to Bellingham, for example, PSP&L would be forced to reduce its rates from the present 10 cents per kwh, which was about twice that which City Light's customers were paying. PSP&L rates were $8.98 in Seattle for a five-room house using 518 kwh per month, $17.80 in Bellingham, $18.55 in Puyallup, and a whopping $32.50 in Aberdeen where the Company was fighting the citizens who wanted their own plant for obvious reasons. Rates, in fact, were based on high valuation of the utility's property, while a lower one was used for tax purposes. For this reason State Representative Homer T. Bone had introduced legislation in 1923 that would require the same valuation for both rate fixing and taxation. It passed the House overwhelmingly, but was bottled up by committee in the Senate.[3]

The three leaders of the Super Power League were Oliver Erickson, J.D. Ross, and Bone. Councilman Ralph Nichols was its executive secretary. Bone was legal counsel for the Port of Tacoma and a State Representative from the Farmer-Labor Party. In 1922 a split occurred in the League between the more radical forces led by its president, Erickson, who wanted complete ownership of public utilities and a national electric power network. The more dissident farmers and some labor organizations supported Erickson. Ross and Bone preferred a more modest scheme, one that would build upon the basic municipally owned tie-line of Seattle and Tacoma by linking it up with distribution systems of rural power districts that would be established on a county-by-county basis. Ross had in mind a linking up of Yakima and Walla Walla with the power station at Cedar Falls, and Aberdeen with Tacoma at its Lake Cushman plant. He was over-optimistic about sentiment in the former two cities, but judged Aberdeen correctly. (The *Star* credited Ross for swinging Aberdeen voters to approve a bond issue in November for building their own dam on the Wynooche River.) The majority in the League supported Ross and Bone; this included a majority in the State Grange and the more conservative labor organizations.[4]

This settled, Bone introduced his bill which would allow the municipals to sell power outside their corporate boundaries. Debate on the Bone Bill ran throughout January, with PSP&L spokesman, Norwood Brockett, contending that Seattle and Tacoma, by controlling the power, would discriminate against other cities which also wanted industries that might compete with their own, and rural forces would have to contend with corrupt city politicians and bureaucrats. Perhaps the most telling argument was a double-barrelled one keyed to the rural populace—that the costs of the Skagit project would be passed on to them, and that Tacoma and City Light would dominate the rural districts. Another effective slant—one that was regularly employed in the debate over public ownership—was that property would be removed from the tax rolls, and the taxpayer would wind up subsidizing the municipals . . ." do not be deceived by their lower rates." These arguments would prove damaging.[5]

Then, on February 3, House Speaker, Mark Reed, introduced House Bill 126. This bill would have empowered the Public Service Commission to license public utilities, placing such utilities under Commission jurisdiction; a 5% tax on gross sales by the public plants was added. (Reed would tell Ross in 1925 that his original proposal was for a general 5% tax on power sold outside the city limits.) However, the Reed Bill still allowed sale of power outside the corporate boundaries of the cities that had the power to sell. The Bone Bill was voted down on February 15, 57 to 38, with 7 of 17 King County votes cast against it. The Reed Bill passed the House 57 to 38 with 13 of the 17 King County Representatives voting against it.[6]

In the Senate, W.W. Conner, chair of the Public Utilities Committee, amended the bill by trying to place the municipals under jurisdiction of the new Public Works Department, and to distribute 50% of the tax receipts to the counties in which the power was sold. Reed objected and threatened that no power bill would pass with such amendments, and that if they were not eliminated the Bone Bill would confront them as an initiative in 1924. Reed won, then tacked on a referendum clause that would submit his bill to popular vote in the 1924 general election. I.M. Krutz, chairman of the State Republican Party, claimed that Reed wanted to challenge Wesley Jones for his Senate seat in 1924. He wrote Jones:

> I know this from the Stone and Webster people. Reed, as you know, is their man, it was he who introduced the resolution in the legislature to submit to a vote of the people the question of Seattle being allowed to sell electric juice outside the city limits. This was just what the Stone and Webster people desired. It gave them two years in which to buy the electric plants of all the cities so that if the one Bill should be passed by a subsequent legislature, the electric people would have no place to dispose of their surplus juice.

> . . . By the time Seattle and Tacoma are authorized to sell their surplus juice, Stone and Webster will own all the plants in the state and competition in rates will be impossible . . . [Krutz then interviewed his local S&W manager about Reed's candidacy] He was quite frank in saying Reed would be a candidate. I asked what was the matter with Jones. 'Why . . . You know, Krutz, Jones is against us.'[7]

In fact, Stone and Webster had already acquired nine plants in January: in Wenatchee, Vashon, Arlington, Edmonds, Stanwood, Elma, Montesano, Port Townsend, and South Bend. In the southwest it purchased the North Coast Power Company, with its operations in Vancouver, Kelso, Chehalis, Tenino, and Kalama. *P-I* political correspondent J. Newton Colver noted in January 1924 that agitation for public ownership was driving the private companies to increase their investments. (They also issued public announcements to that effect, like one in January, that PSP&L was planning to spend $1 million on its largest plant, that on the White River. Two previous proclamations had been issued in November in the same vein.)[8]

Regarding Reed's motives, Reed's biographer, Robert Ficken, and Douglas Pullen, historian of the Hart governorship, find Krutz was off the mark. Neither author says anything about Reed's senatorial aspirations; so we don't know for sure whether that was merely Krutz's fantasy, born of his pro-Jones sympathies. They concentrate instead on his resistance to pressure among his many supporters for him to succeed Hart. Even Bone volunteered support if Reed chose to run, because Bone was convinced Reed was fair and was not a tool of the power trust. Ross was similarly disposed, and he had a good nose for smelling out such influence, rarely giving anyone the benefit of the doubt. Also, Reed knew from long legislative experience that the old Public Service Commission had consistently supported private corporations over competing public bodies, and that the new Public Works Commission would do similarly. That is why he resisted Senator Conner's attempted amendments. Furthermore, in April 1924, Reed rejected his own bill. The *P-I*'s Colver quoted Reed as advocating "State ownership of all water powers in the state is the ultimate and inevitable solution for the whole problem . . . I think the cities should be permitted to sell their surplus outside their city limits." The *P-I* column head read: "Mark Reed To Drop Fight For His Power Bill." For its part, the state Republican Party abstained from endorsing any power plank.[9]

Reed's initial ambivalence about his bill, followed by his rejection of it, seems to have been conditioned, one, by his concern over the removal of property from the tax rolls as municipals took over the water power sites and were able to assert right-of-way for their transmission lines; and two, by his knowledge of private utility political influence, and their desire to tie up as many water power sites as possible in order to control the terms of competition. It appears that he regarded the private utilities as the worst evil. Whether he also concluded that the secondary benefits resulting from cheaper rates would spin off as accelerated economic development, is not clear. His role was crucial, however.[10]

The public power forces began gathering broad support in the initiative campaign that would get underway in spring 1924. When the Super Power League met in December 1923 to agree on a strategy, Oliver Erickson submitted his proposal for outright state ownership of electric utilities, while the Grange proposed only an interconnection of rural districts with Seattle and Tacoma facilities. Because of the constitutional limit of $400,000 on bonded indebtedness, Erickson had corporation counsel Kennedy draft a bill modelled on the port district and local improvement district legislation by providing for creation of public utility districts.[11]

An attempted compromise was next considered in a second conference in January, but not before Seattle Municipal League representatives walked out, after failing to get support for their proposal for direct legislative action in the 1925 session. Agreement came on submitting both the Erickson and Bone bills for initiative action. At this point the two initiatives became entangled in Erickson's bid to displace Edwin Brown as mayor, with Erickson accusing Brown with responsiblity for the cost overruns, delays, and inefficiencies on the Skagit project. Since Brown was himself considered an outspoken public power advocate, this contest threatened the initiative campaign. Erickson's defeat in the February primaries, however, affected support for his bill; on March 24 he withdrew his proposal so that the League could concentrate attention on only one bill.[12]

The Bone Bill (Initiative 52) offered the widest voter appeal because of its more modest provisions. Support came from the Women's Legislative Council, the Pierce County Republican Women's Club, the state Democratic Party, as well as from traditional sources, such as the State Federation of Labor, Seattle Central Labor Council, and the Municipal League. Grange support had faded by the end of 1923 as divisions within it caused

Grange Master A.S. Goss to withdraw any formal endorsement. And the Western Progressive Farmers, which had split from the Grange, still favored the original Erickson proposal. In this connection the *P-I* accused the "private monopoly of now seeking to align the farmer vote against the cities", as the *P-I* endorsed the Bone Bill initiative and rigorously opposed the Reed Bill.[13]

When the initiative signature drive finally got underway in May 1924, the private power organization countered by circulating petitions in downtown Seattle urging people not to sign. Signed-petitions also mysteriously disappeared from the private offices of some supporters in late May. Then, in late June, an over-zealous friend of PSP&L's Norwood Brockett, Louis Benedetti, was arrested for paying two men $8.00 a day to obtain signatures on some petitions, then destroying them, and inserting fraudulent names on others so that they would be disqualified. Benedetti was co-proprietor of the Men's Exchange, a downtown card room, and he also was a member of Local 46 of the Electrical Workers Union (reputedly, a PSP&L bastion), which opposed Initiative 52, and which was censuring work on the Skagit project. Testimony was presented to Justice of the Peace, C.C. Dalton, after which he initially proclaimed the seriousness of the crime as striking at the foundations of civic life if left unpunished. Eight days later he fined Beneditti a modest $250, claiming he was only a tool of "higher-ups". Also helping the private utility forces, the City Clerk allowed copyists employed by PSP&L to copy signatures from the petitions so that signers could be intimidated into withdrawing. To effect this program Secretary of State, Grant Hinkle, cooperated by extending for one month the time allowed for withdrawals. Despite these obstacles, sufficient signatures were acquired and the initiative was approved on July 18 as Initiative 52.[14]

Indicative of the extent to which private power propaganda had entered the public school system was the action of State Superintendent Josephine Corliss Preston. Her office mailed anti-Bone Bill materials to the public schools and distributed a pro-private utility pamphlet to them, as well.[15]

Within the public ownership ranks Mayor Brown caused a furor. While attending the national convention of the Democratic Party in June in the company of Stone and Webster's Robert Whiting, Brown underwent a conversion of sorts. As will be noted in the following section, Brown had acquired evidence that fraud and bribery had been perpetrated by PSTP&L in the sale of its traction operation to the City for $15 million. While he hoped personally to benefit from any prospective rebate, Brown was undoubtedly open to anything the company might offer. While in New York with Whiting he showed the evidence to one or more attorneys there who claimed he did not have a case. But the evidence was at least embarassing to the company. Upon his return to the city, Brown announced a substitute statewide power plan that called for state "control", but not ownership. He also withdrew from the race for the Democratic nomination for governor—not surprising, because the party was so weak that hardly anyone of its candidates won office before 1932. Brown, though a hound for publicity, had never displayed a longing for martyrdom.[16]

Broad opposition against Initiative 52 was predictably mobilized among businessmen by using ideological arguments, largely. Citizens Associations were organized throughout the state by Alpheus Byers of the Voters' Information League and head of the Seattle Citizens Association. Testifying before the Federal Trade Commission in 1928, E.T. Steel, of Stone and Webster, indicated that after he had informed the National Electric Light Association of the campaign being waged for the Bone Bill, the NELA proposed: "What our people need to do in Washington . . . is to organize through various organizations other than public utility groups a definite campaign against the proposed agitation . . . my experience leads me to believe that we should always be the aggressors and lay out our plans for future electrical development." In November 1923, Steel wrote the NELA that it must help with financial assistance and with publicity men, claiming, "Probably 90% of the newspapers in the state will oppose State ownership, and a lot of good work could be done by these papers . . ." A.W. Leonard hired W.B. Henderson and a Mr. Wood to prepare articles which were distributed to the newspapers after visiting each one to assess its leanings. The *P-I*'s Colver reported in January that the National Electric Light Association had sent propagandists into the state to begin "the fight for their lives"; they were just coming off a successful anti-public ownership campaign in California. Before it was over, the Washington Committee on Public Utilities Information had spent about $175,000, including about $100,000 from PSP&L.[17]

Charges against the initiative as being socialistic or communistic were common. The Manufacturers Association of Washington contended that, "Public operation develops political machines!", furthermore, efficiency of "public management is questionable". Big play was given in rural areas to the notion that the cities were inherently sources of corrupt political machines that would inevitably extend their menacing tentacles around the farmers. In Spokane, fear was expressed that Seattle would benefit at Spokane's expense. Spokane judge, legislator, and attorney for the Washington Water Power Company, F.T. Post, had earlier in the year insisted, "We fear the principle of socialism . . . I am forced to believe that about 75% of Seattle must be socialistic." On election day, November 4, the *Union Record* reported that fashionably dressed women paraded around polling places pleading for free enterprise and the American Way.[18]

They had done their job well. Initiative 52 lost by 80,000 votes, 217,393 to 139,492. The rural areas voted heaviest in opposition: by 2 to 1 in Yakima, by 3 to 1 in Walla Walla county. Favorable voting occurred in Seattle and in Tacoma, and that was about all. The Reed bill (Referendum 3) lost by an even greater margin, 208,809 to 99,450. However, Mark Reed looked at the results differently, contending that since both his bill and Bone's were for public ownership, if totaled, they showed a 40,000 vote majority favoring sale of surplus power by municipal utilities outside their corporate limits.[19]

As a post-mortem on the campaign, J.D. Ross wrote the Public Ownership League of America's director, Carl Thompson, that defeat was not all that bad, because the wording of the Bone Bill initiative had led many to believe that "the whole State would have expected Seattle [and Tacoma] to build [power lines] to them and finance their distribution." Ross also reported that Reed "promises his help to get the [new] bill through [the 1925 Legislature]." That bill provided a 5% tax paid by the consumer, and had been drawn up by Ross. Nothing came of it, because of the Legislature's preoccupying fight with incoming governor, Everett lumberman Roland Hartley, a declared enemy of Reed's. (Reed had been a leader of labor reform legislation that Hartley bitterly opposed.)[20]

The Street Railway: Charges of Fraud

Nagging suspicions of fraud and bribery in the purchase of the Municipal Street Railway from Stone and Webster plagued the City's politics. The key informant in the investigation by the City Council's Efficiency Committee was Emil V. Minich. He had worked for the Puget Sound Traction, Light and Power Company and its predecessor, the Seattle Electric Company, since 1906. Starting as a motorman, he moved up in the organization, being transferred in 1913 to the Secret Service Department to understudy that operation, eventually to become its head. This unit was responsible for investigating employees, particularly with respect to any union activities, and to infiltrate labor organizations by use of agents, some of whom even became union officers. One such man was Robert Whiting who became business agent of the Jitney Drivers' Union, and a member of the Central Labor Council while on the company payroll. The company was alleged to have furnished him with four Ford automobiles for use as jitneys. He succeeded in breaking up the union by getting into a row with the union's attorney, W.R. Crawford. He also struck up a friendship with Harry Bolton and Robert Hesketh while on the labor council. Bolton and Hesketh were also on the City Council.

In his capacity as head of the Secret Service, Minich also allegedly paid off various officers in the trainmens' union to lobby the trainmen in support of the purchase, playing upon the fear of a trainmen's strike, should the purchase fall through. In his affidavit Minich claimed Whiting was transferred to work directly under A.W. Leonard after his jitney union demolition work. His job was to influence wavering members of the City Council, in particular, Bolton and Hesketh. A third target was Councilman Cecil Fitzgerald.

Thomas Murphine, as a Progressive Party member in the state legislature, was alleged to have been successfully lobbied by Leonard. Murphine's closest friend in the legislature was Ole Hanson—soon to be elected Seattle's mayor in the spring of 1918. As mayor he would appoint Murphine superintendent of public utilities after the purchase was consummated. For his part Murphine would also employ Whiting for a time, apparently while Whiting also was on the company's payroll. Addressing the shipyard workers' transportation problem, Mayor Hanson quickly proposed purchase of the street railway from Stone and Webster. The price offered came from Leonard through Murphine, according to Minich's affidavit. Leonard, allegedly, then instructed Minich to use his department in every way to effect the purchase. The advisory vote of the citizenry in the November general election overwhelmingly approved the purchase.[1]

After the state Supreme Court approved the City's purchase of the railway the final say lay with the City Council, as the April 1, 1919 date for transfer of the property drew near. According to Minich, on that date, following Council approval, Leonard instructed Whiting to have $1,000 transferred to Bolton's bank account, which happened to be shared with Whiting. Bolton also lived in Whiting's house, was hard up for money, and Whiting expressed to Minich his dismay at Leonard's stinginess, when Bolton ought to be getting $200,000 in his opinion. Whiting is then alleged to have invited Minich to witness the transfer of the $1,000 to Bolton's account at the Seattle National Bank. During this entire period, Hesketh, Bolton, and Murphine were alleged to have been "daily" visitors to Whiting's office. Another $500 was reportedly given to J.A. Stevenson, business agent of the trainmen's union, for his role.

Minich concluded his affidavit, sworn before G. Wright Arnold, by observing that Whiting owned a yacht with Fitzgerald, on which the latter, Hesketh, and Bolton were entertained to change their vote from opposition to one favoring purchase.[2]

Most of this information came to public attention by front page newspaper coverage during hearings conducted by the City Council's Efficiency Committee in October 1924. The main body of information lacking was that naming the names of union leaders who were alleged, in Minich's affidavit, to have been bought off. Meanwhile, committee chair, Ralph Nichols, was interested in turning up evidence of Brown's possible connections to vice and graft practiced by the Police Department. (Mayor Brown had reversed acting mayor Bertha Landes's dismissal of William Severyns as Chief, after returning from the Democratic Party's national convention. Consequently, no further efforts were made to clean up the department.) Enter Nichols.

A.E. Bodimer was called to testify on October 15. In his testimony Minich was referred to, inasmuch as Bodimer had worked under Minich at the PSTP&L, and he had met Whiting through Minich when the latter was working for Whiting. Bodimer had also been a campaign worker for Brown in the 1922 mayoral race. In September 1922, Bodimer was asked by Brown to get friendly with Whiting because the latter had evidence that he and Minich had prepared to reopen the matter of the street railway purchase. (Minich had been dismissed by A.W. Leonard in 1922, and Whiting seemed about to be discharged.) Bodimer, in attaining friendly access to Whiting, was told by Whiting that he would sell the evidence—which remained in Minich's possession, apparently—to Brown for $25,000. (Whiting at this time seemed to be acting as a mediary, not yet a holder of the evidence.) In a meeting with Whiting, Brown displayed $27,000, the source of which he later refused to divulge to the committee. The money seems not to have exchanged hands at the time, but from the confused testimony it seemed the evidence was turned over to Brown by Minich. But, also, it is reasonable to assume that Whiting had shown it to Leonard beforehand, for Whiting remained with the Stone and Webster organization as a lobbyist and as head of the system's stage services. When later asked by the committee whether Whiting had copied the evidence, Brown unabashedly said he supposed so.[3]

In the hearing process, parallel information was produced indicating that Minich had been hired by Brown to produce evidence that fraud and bribery had been employed by Stone and Webster in their sale of the street railway to the City. If this could be done, Brown expected to take a commission of about $2,000,000 from the anticipated $9,000,000 rebate. He even requested Corporation Counsel, T.J.L. Kennedy, to draw up an ordinance that would authorize a three-way split, indicating that he would "have to take care of the investigators and the attorneys." Kennedy informed Brown that it was his job to do the prosecuting, but that he would first have to have the evidence. To this Brown replied there was yet a "missing link"—which he expected Minich and Bodimer to supply. The running newspaper accounts of the hearings also show that Brown, acting upon Minich's information, instructed him to renew his friendship with Whiting by supplying him with whiskey via Police Chief William Severyns. The chief vehemently denied the accusation.[4]

When Minich told Whiting of Brown's intention to force a rewriting of the purchase contract by proving wrong-doing, Whiting is alleged, in Minich's affidavit, to have claimed that he was already receiving $600 to $700 a month from PSP&L, "and would not go with us unless he knew exactly what he was to get." It was at this point that Brown allegedly offered $25,000 to Whiting from a special cash fund, once it became apparent that a contingency fee might be earned, should the original contract be rewritten.[5]

Brown seems to have been using both Minich and Bodimer to get at the same information that was by then in Whiting's possession. Upon getting the information Minich had to offer, including receipts of the transactions, Brown showed the material to attorney O.B. Thorgrimson, Mark Matthews, and businessman Laurence Colman. And he claimed to have informed councilmen Blaine, Erickson, and Fitzgerald of the Minich affidavit, asking them if 25% of the money to be saved the City was a reasonable fee. Blaine is reported to have said "yes", Erickson 5%, and Fitzgerald "whatever is necessary." Bolton, when asked about the $1,000, claimed it was a loan. It would be practically impossible to prove otherwise. Brown was then accused by

Minich's assistant (Bodimer, presumably) of having turned over the evidence to PSP&L representatives.[6]

When Brown was hailed before the Efficiency Committee, he charged that the Council had virtually destroyed all hope of proving fraud by forcing "premature disclosure". Brown was in turn accused of being only personally interested in the fee he expected to earn for having coordinated the investigation. Ostensibly disappointed in the weakness of the evidence gathered, Brown called off his own investigation—but not without it becoming linked with the 1924 election campaign.[7]

Apart from the publicity given once more to the appearance of fraud and bribery in the City's purchase of Stone and Webster's Seattle traction property, nothing concrete resulted from the investigation. Threatened impeachment of Brown quickly subsided, even in the face of potentially damaging evidence then being turned up by the Civil Service Commission. Perhaps most people believed the charges of fraud and bribery to be true, but clearly the charges could never be proven in court for lack of documentation from the company's files.[8]

Mayor Brown's sincerity in pursuing PSP&L for the City's benefit in the matter of its sale of the street railway is called into question in another respect. Despite having knowledge of what was already public—that Bolton had been living in Whiting's home, and that Whiting was a known lobbyist for Stone and Webster, Brown appointed Bolton to a vacancy on the Civil Service Commission in September 1924. (Bolton, though a co-habitant of Whiting's, innocently disowned any such knowledge of Whiting's employment.) Commission chairman, Frank Boyle, testified that Brown regularly interfered in commission deliberations, holding meetings with Bolton and the other commissioner, Donna Baker, but excluding Boyle. Boyle was then consistently overuled, 2 to 1, once Brown and the two commissioners had decided upon the action to be taken on any matter. This mayoral interference was a clear violation of the city charter and would have been grounds alone for filing impeachment proceedings.[9]

That Nichols did not choose to follow this line might have been due to Brown's counterattack on Nichols's legislative record which Brown claimed showed Nichols not to be a municipal ownership purist. Whether these charges were valid or not, they certainly affected Nichols in his position as secretary of the Super Power League, just at the height of the Initiative 52 campaign.[10]

This was not Brown's only counterattack. On October 23, as the evidence against Brown was mounting, the mayor announced that he had just named his own investigating committee of thirty-one, which read like a blue book of the city's business and civic leaders. Not surprisingly, Nichols charged Brown with trying to create a "smoke screen". After the November election the chairman of this phantom committee, Judge George Donworth, resigned, claiming the committee had no legal standing. The other members followed suit.[11]

As to Whiting's role in all of these proceedings it seems that he was loyal to Leonard and Stone and Webster interests throughout. Minich seems to have had all of the remaining evidence not yet in possession of the company; Whiting was the logical choice to work with Minich in acquiring it. Whiting, having accompanied Brown to the June Democratic convention, and with Brown, Whiting at least witnessed the discussion between the mayor and the unnamed lawyer in New York. Also he was at one time in possession of the evidence for the purpose of copying it. To believe that Leonard was not being kept informed all along is not credible in the face of the public testimony. If there was any more evidence outstanding, apart from the copy of Minich's affidavit in the papers of Homer T. Bone, that might prove fraud and bribery, it never came to light after this time. It is from the circumstantial evidence the reader must decide.

City Politics: City Manager vs. Charter Revisionists, 1923-1926—Who Won, Lost?

After the Municipal League decided not to press for inclusion of a city manager proposition in the spring 1922 election, it published a series of articles on the beauties of city managerships, citing examples of successes from around the country. The League campaigned and publicized its plan throughout 1922 and 1923, declaring in February 1923, upon public release of its completed report, that it was "The most important report ever issued to the League" for consideration by its membership.[1]

It began setting the stage for voter action in a January 1924 editorial written for the *Municipal News* by William Anderson of the University of Minnesota. Anderson declared that the city manager issue is now "at a stage at which a definite crystallation of public opinion in its favor should be attempted." The writer saw Seattle's progress barred by "excessive taxation". It followed that "efforts must be made to prevent improvident bond issues [like those for a civic auditorium and the Montlake Bridge]." Anderson saw the finances of the Municipal Street

Railway as posing the most serious problem, one that was brought to a head in mid-1924 when the banks refused to cash warrants to pay railway wages. This action forced an end to the 5-cent fare experiment and brought a return of the ten-cent/ three-for-a-quarter fare in June 1924. He saw the excessive payment prescribed in the contract with Stone and Webster, combined with the run-down condition of the equipment and facilities at the time of purchase, as posing an almost insurmountable problem that was further complicated by competition from increasing use of privately operated automobiles whose drivers were being generously provided with well-paved streets running on flat terrain. He found inevitable the outlay for rebuilding the lines, and applauded the labor saving measure by which 45 one-man cars were substituted for two-man cars. Anderson concluded that the only way to find a solution was conversion of city government to a city manager form so that politicization of these issues would be minimized, and conflicts between a weak mayor and strong council could be eliminated by the substitution of clear "lines of responsibility" resulting from elimination of the mayor's office and introduction of businesslike efficiency. Not considered as an alternative was the lengthening of the existing two-year term for mayor, an action that would have strengthened the office somewhat.[2]

Prospects for voter acceptance of a city manager plan seemed to be improving, although the Municipal League's advice in the March 1924 city election was by no means adhered to. Bond issues were approved for the Montlake Bridge, for purchase of land from the United States Shipping Board that had been the site of the Skinner and Eddy Plant Number Two, and for improvement of the West Waterway. But that for a civic auditorium was satisfyingly voted down. It might have been hard to judge which issues were "improvident". Also, the League's recommendation for mayor, Alfred Lundin, lost to incumbent Edwin Brown by 5,000 votes. Brown was considered too tolerant of vice and was downgraded for not carrying out any of his campaign promises. Lundin, being a leader in the Chamber of Commerce, was the business candidate, who viewed the Skagit project as the main issue. He would conduct an investigation of the "delays" in its prosecution, and he saw "a real necessity for a change in the administration . . . Not a kilowatt of power has actually been sold." His voice echoed both the Chamber and the *Times*. Surprisingly, he found support also from municipal ownership leader and just-defeated mayoral candidate, Oliver Erickson, who looked upon the Skagit project as a "mess" (he had persistently opposed Ross's single-minded focus on the

Skagit). The League's James Lawler took exception to endorsement of Lundin, claiming that any mayor, not just Brown, would be accused of laxity in enforcing the prohibition laws and those against vice, but since Brown was an "out and out champion of municipal ownership" he should be supported. This particular stand of the League contributed to J.D. Ross's later suspicion of the city manager amendment when it aimed to bring his operation under a director for light and water. As to Lundin and the Skagit issue, the League had an unequivocal record of support for the progress of that project and had consistently backed Ross and chief engineer Uhden when the Chamber and *Times* untiringly continued their attack on municipal ownership on principle alone.[3]

When Brown went East to attend the Democratic Party's National Convention, in June 1924, acting mayor, Bertha Landes, moved quickly. In line with the League's views on efficiency, she got the Council to act on her recommendation to establish a City Planning Commission in place of the ineffective Zoning Commission. Next, she chose June 18 as "Power Day" to reaffirm the city's commitment to the "policy of municipal ownership", and to endorse Initiative 52 (the Bone Bill) and to promote petition-signing on its behalf. Each action was consistent with League ideas. Short-lived though her action was in firing Police Chief William Severyns for "alleged incompetence", it lasted long enough to earn twenty new police positions, six prowler cars for hotter pursuit, and it allowed acting chief, Claude Bannick, time to establish a special vice squad that enthusiastically arrested many for violations of gambling and prohibition ordinances.[4]

The *Star*, as noted previously, would later make much of Brown's sharing a room at the convention with Robert Whiting. It correlated this room-sharing with Brown's opposition to constructing the Diablo dam before first building a masonry dam below the Gorge crib dam. Altogether, the ground was being readied for the League's campaign for the city manager amendment to the city's charter—the Police Department would be taken out of politics, the Lighting Department would be politically neutralized and brought under stricter business management, the street railway system probably could be run more efficiently to meet its debt obligations and pay its employees directly in dollars instead of warrants that were frequently discounted, and costs of government could be reduced in the process. At least the taxpayers allegedly would get what they paid for.[5]

While doubts mounted about Mayor Brown's commitment

to the Lighting Department's Skagit project, and suspicions sprouted about his dedication to enforcement of the law against the illegal liquor traffic, the Municipal League decided to submit its city manager plan as an amendment to the City's charter. The City Council approved it for the March 10, 1925 ballot.

The Municipal League's city manager amendment had received the endorsement of many leading citizens, many of whom we have encountered in other contexts, including David E. Skinner, Oliver Erickson, Laurence Colman, Professor Frank Laube, A.H. Dimock, lumberman A.S. Kerry, Reverend Mark Matthews, real estate man Vincent Miller, influential Drs. Otis Lamson and Park Weed Willis, Chamber of Commerce leader Willard Rhodes, architects Charles Bebb and Carl Gould, the Waterfront Employers' Association's Frank Foisie—a good cross-section of the business and professional classes, but poor representation from the blue-collar ranks. The *Times* led the opposition with a series of front page editorials, as it warmed up to the election. On March 3, its editorial claimed: "City Manager Plan Worse Than Nothing". On the 4th: "Council Clique, Not Superman, Would Run Affairs of Seattle", complaining there would be no executive department, no one to exercise veto power. On the 5th: "City Manager Only Rubber Stamp For Same Old Council". On the 7th: "This Hard-Headed Business Executive Is A Pleasant Myth". On the 9th: "Big Taxpayers Warn Of Fake Manager Plan", listing thirty-eight of them under the heading: "Seattle's Leading Citizens Issue Statement Against Giving Authority To One Man". The amendment was defeated on March 10 by 4,472 votes (26,942 to 22,470). The *Times* headline greeted the result: "Manager Plan Beaten . . . Real Charter Offered", followed by a comment that citizens had endorsed "*Times* plan" instead, and that the "businesmen group" will now turn their attention to charter revision. The *Times*'s meaning would become clearer in the months ahead.[6]

The League, disheartened but not bowed, doggedly set about its educational task. In early May 1925 the League gained the cooperation of the Woman's City Club in pursuing the "same goals". The *Municipal News* even inserted a few columns, regularly called, "Woman's City Club News". Then, in early July, the League introduced its modified charter amendment draft for criticism, and in early September offered it for comment, finally submitting it to the City Council for acceptance to appear on the March 9, 1926 ballot. In answering its own question, "What is the City Manager Plan?", its spokesmen used the private corporation analogy, contending: "it is the private corporation form of organization applied to government." (This aura around the corporation showed brightly in the mid-1920s, before the 1929 Crash tarnished it.) Continuing the analogy: the Council would simply appoint a general manager, just like a corporation's Board of Directors appointing someone to carry out the board's general directives. Approval or disapproval would be done in a prescribed manner, and the city manager be retained or dismissed according to protocol. As to the specific plan for Seattle, the city manager would be the chief executive officer, being appointed by the Council. The Council would also appoint the comptroller and corporation counsel, it would have power to name the Civil Service Commission, and it would have power to consolidate city departments, with the heads of each reporting to the manager. The Council would elect a Mayor from its own membership to serve primarily as the City's ceremonial head.[7]

While this reasoning, using the corporate model, should have appealed to business leaders, even to have flattered them with such expression of confidence in the modern corporation, it did not. The *Times* reported another body was working on a document of its own: the Freeholders Charter Revision Committee, chaired by Thomas G. Hammond. Their chosen vehicle was the Seattle Civic Federation, whose roster read like a combination of the Chamber and Associated Industries officers and members, so extensive was cross-membership. When the League's president, Harold Preston, got wind of a movement toward wholesale charter revision by an elected board of freeholders, he invited cooperation in the League's charter amendment efforts. None was forthcoming, although the *Times* coyly hinted that the revisionists were sympathetic to the city manager idea. Instead, the Freeholders Charter Revision Committee submitted its proposal to the Council for an election of fifteen freeholders, to be placed on the same ballot. The *Times* masqueraded its proposal as embodying the city manager concept, while remaining vague about any potential differences there might be.[8]

In late September, the *Times* indicated the general character of the Revisionists' aims. While opposing the League's plan, the Revisionists preferred some type of city manager function, but being careful, did not spell out the details. Reportedly, these men wanted to enlarge the Council and change the methods of electing its membership, returning to a ward or district system. Also, Council members should receive only "a nominal salary, thus shutting out the politician and attracting the business men to Council seats." Hammond announced the beginning of an initiative petition campaign, as a backup, in case the Council refused to place their measure on the same ballot as the city manager plan. Meanwhile the Revisionists would continue to lobby the Council for a favorable decision, before the required 20,000 signatures were obtained. Jockeying got underway.[9]

Despite the Revisionists challenging the legality of the amendment, the Council approved the League's measure and submitted it to the Corporation Counsel for drafting into appropriate language but, when it came up for final approval in the first week of October, it was tabled for further discussion, because Ralph Nichols, primed by J.D. Ross, objected to placing the water and light departments together. The Revisionists' request also was tabled because it contained nothing specific as to its content, being merely a proposal to elect fifteen freeholders who would produce a charter within sixty days.[10]

After this temporary withdrawal of both proposals by the Council for further study, the League's amendment was re-accepted, with Landes, Hesketh, Blaine, Tindall, Moore, and Erickson voting in the majority. Nichols continued to oppose on grounds that the water and light departments should be independent. Nichols was undoubtedly influenced by J.D. Ross, who had just established a City Light Patrons Club to oppose the amendment, mistakenly believing it to be "sponsored by private power interests to cripple the municipal system", according to the *Star*. As an alternative, Ross suggested taking the municipal utilities out of politics by appointing a board of five commissioners. Charter revision committee member, the Reverend Mark Matthews, endorsed Ross's proposal, apparently expecting his parishioner, Ross, to join forces. Ross needed no encouragement, once he saw the hand of the "power trust" behind the League's amendment.[11]

The Council, failing to get any specifics about the character of the revision, instructed the Revisionists that they must enlist support through the initiative route. Their real intent would not be registered until after the winter 1926 election, during charter revision time and after defeat of the city manager plan.[12]

Debate in Council continued through most of October. Then, two original opponents of the League's proposal, Hesketh and Blaine, joined Erickson, Landes, Moore, and Tindall in a 6 to 3 vote to re-accept the amendment for inclusion on the March ballot. John Carroll remained steadfastly the leader of the Revisionist forces, Campbell continued undecided, and Nichols remained faithful to J.D. Ross. Ross had argued before the Council that the League's amendment would make it impossible to retain control over purchases of machinery and materials for construction, and the department's "duties" would be spread over any departments that the manager might choose. (In fact, City Light had been doing most of its own engineering work, although the Engineering Department was supposed to do it, but it had deferred to Ross.)[13]

Two weeks later, on November 3, "unexpectedly", without waiting for the Revisionists' petition drive to end, Councilman Carroll's resolution, placing the charter revision on the ballot, was accepted by Erickson, Moore, Campbell, and Tindall, giving him a majority. Only Landes and Nichols voted against acceptance. Landes remained an unwavering supporter of city managership. Nichols had misgivings about the Revisionists.[14]

A last-ditch effort was finally made by the League's James Haight to force the charter revision measure off the ballot. Fearing, with good reason, that attention was being diverted from the city manager proposal, he began a referendum petition drive to collect 8,000 signatures by December 5. His effort fell short; so both measures would finally appear on the ballot.[15]

Coloring the atmosphere in November was a move by the State Chamber of Commerce to get a bill passed that would require voter approval of any bond issue for an additional power unit or plant, and "would bring the Skagit under the '50 per cent' law which now only applies to general obligation bond issues", according to the *P-I*. Whether this was timed to thwart Ross's application for $4,000,000 for Diablo construction is not clear, but the timing did coincide. Here, the "power trust's" influence was unmistakable; not so with the city manager plan of the Municipal League. Ross's suspicions, usually well-founded, must have been very trying to long-time loyal supporters of municipal ownership in the League. Tensions would persist.[16]

No sooner was Haight's signature campaign ended, than another impeachment campaign was started for removal of Mayor Brown for failing to enforce the laws against vice, gambling and the liquor traffic. Councilman Nichols's Efficiency Committee had been holding hearings on police protection of these activities. And a grand jury investigation was turning up evidence showing the mayor's unwillingness to enforce the laws against these evils. Rumors began circulating out of the grand jury room that impeachment proceedings against Brown might begin. To counter this potentiality, Brown " . . . crossed his fingers and gave an order to stop gambling." This stunt probably influenced the Council less than the nearness of the spring 1926 election when it voted 6 to 3 not to impeach him. These facts about Brown's administration had been public knowledge even before his re-election. It was not yet clear how much more of the same kind of information was needed to cross the threshold of voter tolerance.[17]

On January 9, the first day of filing for election to the Board of Freeholders, a Freeholders Charter Revision Committee bloc of fifteen filed as nominees. Included were committee chair, Thomas Hammond, Frank Waterhouse, Roy Kinnear, Walter Meier, Nathan Eckstein, Moritz Thomsen—all Associated Industries leaders—five other businessmen, and, incongruously, labor leaders Harry Ault and Charles Doyle. Twenty-nine filed before the day was done.[18]

Before the late February primaries, a sensational bootlegging trial would preempt the headlines—and would further implicate "Doc" Brown in providing police protection to vice operators. This was the trial of ex-police captain Roy Olmstead.

Prohibition Mixes In: The Olmstead Trial and "Doc" Brown

Before the city's primary election in late February 1926, following on the heels of the climax in December 1925 between those fighting for a city manager form of government and those trying to undermine those efforts, there came the trial of Roy Olmstead, "king of the rum runners". This trial would add substance to charges that Mayor Brown had ties with the underworld through his police department. The trial also would see use of evidence gained by wiretapping that was later upheld as valid by the United States Supreme Court. From mid-January through all of February, the five-week long trial captured the headlines and much of the newspaper space as George F. Vanderveer prepared Olmstead's defense by laying the foundation for appeal to the nation's highest court. Every day the trial played to a packed court to watch Vanderveer embarass the federal agents and Judge Jeremiah Neterer for his questionable rulings on evidence and instructions to the jury. The city's social elite would even be paraded before the court for having been heavy customers of elite clubs serving them liquor and escaping police action, while the more vulnerable joints in the skid road area suffered raids as frequently as publicity seemed to require. Sentencing of Olmstead and his co-defendants would occur on election day, March 9.[1]

Olmstead had joined the police department in 1906, and apparently distinguished himself, if testimony of his superiors is to be trusted. In any case, he learned the workings of the department, established friendships among fellow officers that would endure after he left the force, and he undoubtedly established contacts with illicit operators in the skid road area who paid for police protection, while he made contacts among the more elite establishments uptown. He also impressed the court when appearing there as an articulate and trustworthy spokesman in cases in which his testimony was relevant. Norman Clark concludes that Olmstead soon recognized that the prestige he had acquired in this process could be sold and that passage of the Volstead Act in 1920 gave him an irresistible opportunity to do so. While still on the force he began rumrunning, specializing in it to the exclusion of the multitude of other vice rackets usually linked with bootlegging. He was soon caught in the act on March 22, 1920, was dismissed from the force, pleaded guilty and was fined $500. He then went about improving his organization and became one of the most popular figures on the streets of Seattle, a sort of folk-hero, in fact. An elaborate bureaucracy was developed by him to run liquor in from Canada on such a scale that by 1924 he began specializing in the wholesale end of the operation. Olmstead evaded the Canadian tax on liquor bound for the United States by loading two to four thousand cases of liquor and clearing the cargo for Mexico instead. The liquor then would be transported to D'Arcy Island where Olmstead had cajoled the local leprosy station keeper into letting him run the cache to West Waterway on fast boats during stormy nights when enforcement agents were discouraged from venturing out. From West Waterway the liquor was trucked into the city. At one destination point, the Lenora Garage (at 2110 First Avenue), agent William Whitney arrested seven men with 81 cases. One was an ex-policeman, and a motorcycle policeman who was already on the scene underwent investigation for his presence. (Whitney was infuriated when Chief Severyns cleared the latter.) The *P-I* judged that Olmstead was using the garage as a warehouse. Severyns had been granted freedom by Brown to reorganize the police department within Brown's own guidelines. Indicative of the line followed was the transfer of Captain Claude Bannick—a known straight-arrow law enforcer—to Ballard. This removed any threat to Olmstead's operations downtown. Brown also reduced the size of the special detail unit and replaced its director with George Comstock, a policeman who was found to be selling liquor in 1916 that had been seized and warehoused as contraband. Not stopping at that, Roy's brother, Ralph Olmstead, was assigned to the Chinatown district where he would be in close proximity with brother Roy's operations. Having the mayor as a close friend and putative ally, clearly, was a vital part of Olmstead's organization. So ineffective had prohibition enforcement become in the city that one of Senator Wesley Jones's informants reported that most King County Republicans favored abolition of the prohibition office in the city because it was "a disgrace and the talk of the whole town." (Jones had appointed the incumbents and was an avid prohibitionist himself.)[2]

Whitney was not to be easily deterred from following evidence of "Doc" Brown's apparent complicity, however. In October 1924, his agents seized one of Olmstead's boats with 784 cases aboard and quickly filed charges for customs evasion. From the growing body of evidence, much of which was becoming common knowledge from newspaper coverage alone, Whitney raided Olmstead's Mount Baker home in November, disrupted a party being entertained by reading children's bedtime stories over Olmstead's radio station, and collected organizational files. It was the latter that provided the basis for indicting Olmstead. A federal grand jury indicted him and ninety others on January 19, 1925 for evading the Prohibition Act.[3]

Some sense of the climate of opinion that the trial was generating can be gleaned from the *P-I*'s front page headlines and column heads in early February. On February 2, (the day Bertha Landes named her mayoral campaign committee): "DEFENSE TO ASK RUM BUYER INDICTMENTS", followed by one column head, "Whispering Voices To Be Target", and another two column article headed, "Boeing Testifies He Bought Liquor" (a full-length photograph of William E. Boeing accompanied the article). Reference here is to the wiretap evidence that was transcribed from short-hand notes and compiled into "The Book of Jobs" that was used throughout the trial by the federal prosecutors to refresh the memory of their witnesses while Vanderveer was denied access, except to the exact quotations recited by the prosecution.[4]

On February 3 the *P-I*'s headline ran, "POLICE AGAIN LINKED TO RUM RING". The column head detailed, "Sergeant Norton named by tapped wire". Also tagged were George Comstock and George Reynolds. Page 2 was given over to the trial, topped by a headline, "CONFESSIONS OF FOUR OLMSTED [sic] DEFENDANTS GIVEN TO JURY". Earl Corwin, a prohibition agent, told how both police and federal agents stood by while liquor was delivered at various dropoff points. His testimony paralleled that of agent Richard Fryant since he was allowed to read it from the "Book". Vanderveer fruitlessly pointed out that it was the Book's testimony, not Corwin's. He had been reprimanded the day before, not for a racial slur but for disrespecting the court, when he pleaded for a "fair, decent, white man's chance to test this stool"—referring to Fryant.[5]

The *P-I* kept its focus on the trial. On February 9, its headline ran, "CLUBMEN TESTIFY TO BUYING LIQUOR". The accompanying article indicated that Frederick Struve, William McMicken, R.E. Downs (steward of the Seattle Golf and Country Club), and Charles Bancke (steward of the Arctic Club) will testify. Finally, on February 20, the trial concluded with Judge Neterer's instructions to the jury: "JUDGE THINKS OLMSTED [sic] GUILTY HE TELLS JURY IN GIVING CHARGE". A page 2 column was headed, "Nation Waits for Verdict".[6]

In the course of the trial testimony repeatedly associated Mayor Brown with these nefarious doings. At one point, when things were going badly, Olmstead counseled his forces to just "take things easy and look after our best customers until Doc gets back." "Doc" could only have been the mayor. Folk-hero status for Olmstead could not rub off on Brown. He had become more vulnerable, and Vanderveer's tactics did not help, as in the testimony of Fryant and H.G. Behnemann. The latter had been a special investigator for Councilman Ralph Nichols's "vice" committee. Vanderveer charged him with conspiring with Fryant after having had a falling out with Brown; Vanderveer accused him of having given Fryant the idea to wiretap. During the ensuing mayoral campaign, United States Attorney Thomas Revelle took to the stump, charging that $70,000 in graft was collected each month and that 500 policemen were being used to "spy upon officials and to tip off advance information on pending public raids." Revelle later was accredited with Brown's defeat. This was only partly true, for Landes was well organized and campaigned hard with her "Flying Squadron", concentrating not only on law enforcement, where Brown was particularly vulnerable, but also on the city manager plan which Brown stridently opposed. When she won the primaries by a mere 1,072 votes, the *P-I*'s page 2 headline read: "Primary Vote Interpreted As Victory For City Manager".[7]

As the two mayoral candidates headed into the runoff election on March 9, Landes invaded Brown's downtown territory, speaking before a "record downtown crowd" of about 1,500 in which men represented about 85% of the total. She emphasized continued Skagit development, improvement of city hospitals, "and the like", but also appointment of a new police chief and department reorganization. Brown, for his part, attacked Nichols's "domination" of the City Council and he hit the city manager plan. Brown threatened to abolish the Dry Squad and promote its lead man, George Comstock, while lauding Chief Severyns and promising to send to the penitentiary those officials whom Revelle might name. As to the downtown precincts—six in all—Prosecuting Attorney, Ewing Colvin, assigned guards to prevent the kind of "wholesale election frauds in the primaries [from being repeated]."[8]

With this setting before us we can examine the election itself more fully.

Landes Challenges Brown; Charter Fight Continues

It was against the backdrop of the Olmstead trial that the next stage was played in the heated fight between the city manager advocates and Charter Revisionists. Landes's commitment to the city manager amendment, combined with her moral indignation at Brown's tolerance policies, if not his outright corruption, convinced her and her strong supporters that she should run for Mayor. Brown also was suspect now on City Light and the Skagit project for his opposition to proceeding with the Diablo dam. She could count among her loyalists the Municipal League, the various women's clubs, and those from her base in the city's North End where the North End Progressive Club dominated politics. She had an unblemished record in supporting municipal ownership of utilities, in particular, supporting Skagit priority. On the last day for filing she decided to make the run.[1]

To organize for her campaign, the Municipal League established a speakers bureau, the Committee of 100, headed by J.Y.C. Kellogg. (One of her campaign managers was Dick Faris who would become Frank Edwards's campaign manager in 1928, when Edwards would challenge Landes in her re-election bid.) League vice-president, Lewis Schwellenbach, led off, charging that the Freeholders plan was bound to fail because the Associated Industries and Labor factions on the Charter Revision Committee would never be able to agree on the terms for a charter; the charter would fail to win voter support for that reason. All this, he contended, was just to sidetrack the city manager plan. This argument proved largely correct. Probably, the prominent representation of labor leaders Harry Ault, Charles Doyle, and Frank Cotterill on the charter revision committee is to be accounted for by the threat, as they saw it, to civil service employees under the proposed city manager system. For its part, the Civil Service League's spokesmen claimed city managership and civil service were incompatible.[2]

While Brown was clearly the one to beat, it was not clear who could do it. While the *Argus* applauded Landes for her strong showing on the Council, it feared Seattle might be stigmatized by "petticoat rule". Consequently, Corporation Counsel Thomas Kennedy drew the weekly's support—though it conceded anyone who could beat Brown would do. For his part, Kennedy accused Brown of "being hand in glove with Stone and Webster", which was a charge that from his official position he felt he could substantiate. Landes's stand on the issues had already been established by her Council work. Brown's base of support came from a nucleus of civil service employees, the skid road areas and parts South—the blue-collar neighborhoods. A victory for Brown was viewed by some as his stepping stone to the United States Senate seat occupied by Wesley Jones, who was losing favor for his key role in the farce of prohibition enforcement. Results of the February primary were promising for Landes. She ran slightly ahead of Brown, 25,762 to 24,672, while Kennedy trailed with 20,208. For Council, Tindall, Hesketh, and Campbell won out. Only Campbell was shaky on the city manager issue.[3]

As the final election loomed ahead, the *Star* accused Brown of having not only a utility lobbyist (Robert Whiting) for a roommate at the Democratic Party's national convention, but that several others had been seen coming and going from his office since then . . . until attention was directed at this unexpected sight. These visits had now stopped, the *Star* reported. In this line, the newspaper pointed out that Brown had postponed Ross's reappointment for six months, until Landes got the Council to force him to act. He had also opposed Ross and a special investigation commission of the Council's in early 1925 that had recommended concentration on building the Diablo and postponing the building of a masonry dam at the Gorge site. To what extent these actions registered on City Light backers is undetermined, but they must have been a factor in the events to follow.[4]

For its part, the Revisionist's committee charged in a full-page advertisement, on March 6, "Seattle's Gravest Danger And The Way Out", that the city manager plan was autocratic in conception, whereas the "Commission of Fifteen Freeholders, chosen as representatives of all the people and compelled to report back to the people [was democratic]." The *Argus* even proclaimed they ". . . are the best . . . that could possibly be assembled under one organization." The Committee of 100, for its part, reminded voters that as to any freeholders who might be elected, no one knew who they might be, and the result of their deliberations equally were unknown.[5]

Perhaps, of decisive importance, given his well-orchestrated following, was the position of J.D. Ross. Ross felt seriously threatened in his power base by the placement of an intermediary between his office and the Board of Public Works and the general loss of other controls over the Lighting Department programs. Furthermore, he was convinced that the League's plan was inspired by the "power trust" . . . that Oliver Erickson also was implicated by reason of his "hatred" of Ross. So sure was he of his assessment that Ross distributed to voters, on a postcard, a message urging them to reject the city manager amendment and vote instead for freeholders who were known supporters of City Light and its Skagit project. When the time was ripe, later, the *Times* would turn this piece of postcard propaganda against Ross when the latter turned against the Freeholders' Charter.[6]

When election returns came in Landes had won over Brown by about 6,000 votes, 48,700 to 42,802. The *P-I* prematurely announced victory for the city manager proposition; however tabulation errors were found showing its defeat by a mere 111 votes, 36,709 to 36,598. (The demand for a recount went finally to the state Supreme Court before being denied.) In contrast, the Charter Revision measure carried by over 4,000 votes, 33,033 to 28,331. It seems clear that the city manager plan would have carried if the charter revision had not confused the issue. Many voters believed that they had to choose between the two measures, but this was not the case. Ross's influence was without doubt a decisive factor. The Municipal League's M.H. Van Nuys attributed defeat to the organized opposition of civil service employees and to the deliberate campaign of confusion that opponents of the amendment carried on from the start. William Dickson, in his 1928 study of the election, wrote: "It is generally conceded that the organized action of the municipal employees defeated the manager plan . . ."[7]

For Council, Tindall, Hesketh, and Campbell were reelected. They were joined by Otto Case, a Ross man. The next stage in the battle was now set: a charter had to be written within sixty days, and then a date had to be set for voting on it. The latter would prove the toughest issue.[8]

In the week after the election and the Revisionists' victory, the Municipal League tried to influence the Freeholders Committee, suggesting that they structure the government reorganization around a city manager. Walter F. Meier, of PSP&L, was elected chairman of the Freeholders (he had declared for placing all utilities under a business manager earlier in the campaign). The *Argus* also urged the Freeholders to consider the city manager form of government in its deliberations. Ambiguity was stirred around the terms "city manager" and "business manager". The Freeholders then fleshed out what only had been hinted at previously. Upon completion of its work, Meier wrote: "Business Rule Is Aim of Charter". Continuing, he described the role of the business manager as that of controlling all business functions of the government, except the police department. Meier claimed: "At the last two city elections the charter amendment sponsored by the Municipal League was defeated largely because it did not adequately safeguard the financial interest of the city . . ."

In countering George F. Cotterill's charge (his brother Frank was the only Freeholder not to sign the document) that the charter was directed against the City's utilities, Meier detoured the argument by claiming that the professional politician would be eliminated by the low salary commanded—$600 annual salary, two regular Council meetings per month, and $10 expense money to attend each meeting. The Freeholders' document provided for the nomination of two City Council candidates from each of seven districts and subjected to citywide vote—a new version of the ward system. (The ward system had been abolished in 1910.) The mayor's office would be retained but without veto power, thereby removing "a cause for constant controversy", according to William H. Curry, who wrote a series of flattering articles for the *Times*. All bond issues would be subjected to popular vote, reducing the Council's power in this respect. Utility rates would be fixed by the Board of Public Works in Olympia. Tindall charged that the corporations were behind these provisions, speaking through their representatives on the committee—the private utility, the gas company, the railroads, the telephone company, and others.

The *Times* hailed the charter revision as a "Splendid Document", while complaining in May that the Council was deliberately delaying a vote on it. The *Argus*, having given token advocacy of the city manager idea, then joined the *Times* in support, each advocating government by a business and professional elite. The *Municipal News* prophesied that voting might be delayed until November, because the existing ordinances required a waiting period of 45 days after the Council submitted the charter to vote. This would put it into the summer months, an inappropriate time for voting.[9]

As though directed to fulfill Tindall's speculation about corporate control of the document, J. F. Douglas, manager of the Metropolitan Building Company, was named chairman of a campaign finance committee. He enlisted $500 support each from various well-known business leaders, among them A.W. Leonard, Horace Henry, Charles Frye, H. Schoenfeld, Nathan Eckstein, Willard Rhodes, James Hoge, Frank Waterhouse, and L.C. Gilman.[10]

Opposition quickly took shape. Ross and his City Light Patrons Club and Friends of City Light fell in line now that the enemy was clearly sighted. The Friends published a leaflet accusing Stone and Webster of trying to undermine City Light, then absorbing it. The leaflet went on, criticizing the corrupting ward system, guaranteeing extortionate rates for the telephone company, protecting the Metropolitan Building Company from paying its fair share of taxes, of protecting the gas company from quality regulation, of protecting certain railroads from the expense of eliminating dangerous crossings, and finally, of limiting the Skagit development.[11]

The Municipal League denounced it for failing to protect the city's utilities and their development, for eliminating the possibility of establishing a municipally owned telephone system, for dividing authority for operating utilities, and for returning to the ward system which had previously proved so corrupt. The Central Labor Council declared unanimously against it. Included in opposition were Freeholders Ault, Doyle, and Frank Cotterill. The CLC declared that the charter threatened the city's utilities, and that it was detrimental to the wage earner and small home owner. Mayor Landes opposed it for enlarging the mayor's powers, and those of the comptroller and treasurer—"sandwiched in between them [was] a business manager whose powers would be practically nil, if the others chose to combine against him." She spoke from Council experience.[12]

Even Alfred H. Lundin, the Chamber of Commerce's recent mayoral candidate, spoke out against the proposed charter, contesting Reginald Parsons, the Seattle Civic Federation's president, in one of a series of articles run by the *Star*. He focused his criticism on the police department provisions, which he saw as protecting a chief from removal by Mayor or Council. Parsons took the "Yes" side in this series, with the "No" side taken by different parties. Ross also was a sparring mate.[13]

As the campaign headed toward the November 4 election

Corporation Counsel Thomas Kennedy, responding to a request from Tindall for a legal opinion, ruled that under the charter, the Council would not be allowed to issue utility bonds on its own authority, that a vote of the people would be required. The *P-I* emphasized this argument in its front page editorial of November 2: "Proposed Charter Is A Leap In The Dark". On November 1, the *P-I* chose to emphasize James Haight's view that the "Charter Held Foe Of City's Power Plant". For its part, the *Times*, in devoting an entire page of its November 1 issue to an extra-large graph with accompanying argument under: "City of Seattle—Department of Lighting", then proceeded to show its "alarming" bonded indebtedness "without corresponding increase in revenue". By emphasizing this bit on City Light, the *Times* must have seemed to lend credence to the opinion that it was really the City's power plant the Revisionists were aiming at—as well as popular government. In that same issue the *Times* produced a facsimile of Ross's March election postcard favoring the Freeholders and opposing the League's amendment. When Ross caught wind of this he countered with an advertisement in the same issue to dispel the effect of this embarassing reminder.[14]

So blatant was the Seattle Civic Federation's grab for unlimited power for its constituents that the voters roundly rejected the proposed charter by more than 10,000 votes, 30,900 to 20,291. The voter turnout was 44% less than in the March election which sent the city manager plan to defeat. In its epitaph on the election, the *Times* opined: "The opposition centered its attack on the alleged lack of of a provision authorizing the City Council to issue bonds for public utilities extensions without a vote of the people."[15]

Serious questions remain though. Did proponents expect such an extreme document as their charter to win? There was no mistaking its intent to favor the downtown business elite and returning the city government to the way it was run before the reforms made since 1910, and since the flourishing of City Light and the Port of Seattle. The Municipal Street Railway would remain an embarassment to municipal ownership, in the eyes of outsiders, particularly to bond investors, but Seattlelites knew well the shadow of corruption that hung over negotiations for the system's purchase from Stone and Webster during the war. Stone and Webster was still the evil "Boston syndicate" to most of the city's population. Recent public relations efforts of its Seattle subsidiary had not removed this shadow. "Stone and Webster" conjured an almost wholly negative image, probably less so for its Puget Sound Power and Light—due to its recent extensive securities sales to Washington residents and to the personal popularity of its suave Alton W. Leonard. Down the line, the railway's bonded indebtedness would be used as a lever to get hold of City Light . . . soon in fact.

One thing for sure, though, was that the Revisionists had defeated the Municipal League's city manager plan. What did they see in city managership that they disliked so much? Probably, they preferred the existing system which they were experienced at affecting to one that might not prove as malleable. A case in point was growing friction between Ross and municipal ownership supporters on the Council which might be exploited. Certainly, the proposed charter revision would offer them maximum opportunity for influence. But, simple defeat of city managership was probably sufficient in the Revisionists' eyes, suggesting why they simply shot for the moon with their charter revision. Why not? If so, they suckered Ross into helping them out. The League, for its part, could easily have substituted Ross's suggestion for a board of engineers to supervise the utilities, without jeopardizing their vision of unified responsibility. This would have dispelled Ross's suspicions about the influence of the power trust—usually he was justified, though not this time.

Stone and Webster would now turn to another strategem, this time drawing Mayor Landes into their web.

Mayor Bertha Landes Begins

Landes's victory gave her a mandate to reorganize the police department, coming as it did in the wake of revelations, over several months, of police department corruption, peaking with the sentencing of Roy Olmstead on the eve of the March 9, 1926 election. She acted immediately, replacing Chief Severyns with William H. Searing, charging him with the job of restoring lost morale and clearing up the "moral situation". Searing quickly relieved vice squad head, Lieutenant George Comstock, and Captain E.L. Hedges of their responsibilities because they were under federal indictment in the liquor cases.[1]

By September 1926, the *Argus* gave her high marks: Crime was on the decrease, with ". . . the organized gangsters [finding] softer spots for their work", and for doubling the amount of fines collected under Mayor Brown before he left office in June. The gambling, liquor, and vice operators only moved outside the city where "Roadhouses are running wide open." Following

Museum of History and Industry

Mayor Bertha K. Landes (1926-28) enjoying Will Rogers's wit upon presenting him with an anchor (!) to the city.

up on this migration, "Doc" Brown decided to run for King County Prosecuting Attorney while his sidekick, Severyns, decided to run for sheriff—apparently sensing a market for the kind of protective services they were experienced at offering. Brown's candidacy could hardly have been taken seriously, and Severyns encountered notoriously honest and efficient Claude Bannick at a time when the electorate was ready for him. Bannick won easily.[2]

Bannick worked "wonders" in enforcing the law, so effective in fact that he drove the same operators who had fled Seattle to the county's outskirts, into Snohomish County, "where anything and everything goes." Not content with this accomplishment, Bannick intruded on Searing's Seattle jurisdiction, closing up some "resorts" there, and bringing charges against some members of the City's police force— it seems that Searing believed prostitution could not be wiped out while Bannick thought it was at least worth a try. Bannick was accused of trying to "show up" the Seattle police department after having served effectively as Acting Mayor Landes's chief in 1925 when Mayor Brown was in New York attending the Democratic Party convention. He had anticipated being named her chief.[3]

But Searing had his internal problems. For example, Harry Chadwick of the *Argus* charged the Council with not cooperating with the reorganized department when it approved relicencing two card rooms that were known for gambling violations. Despairingly, Chadwick bitingly contended that this sort of behavior of councilmen will continue as long membership on that body remains "attractive to men who have to make a living." He seemed still bitter—being an elitist—about the defeat of the charter revisionists' attempt to foist an elitist form of government on the city.[4]

While the police department absorbed Mayor Landes's earliest attention and responded to her reforms, it was the Municipal Street Railway and the Lighting Department that would preoccupy her administration.

Landes Takes Her Turn at Resolving the Street Railway Crisis

Like original sin, misfortunes of the Municipal Street Railway continued to plague the city's politics. The highly inflated purchase price of $15,000,000 burdened the system with the problem of paying $833,000 annually on its interest and bond redemption obligations in the face of insufficient revenue. The system was periodically forced to pay its employees with warrants which were in turn discounted by the banks, and were even refused payment entirely by the Seattle Clearing House Association from time to time. Loans from other City departments were made in time to meet the March 1 deadline (usually from the Lighting Department). Also at issue was whether the general tax revenues were subject to levy for payment—thus far the courts had ruled against access to them. However, even the Chamber of Commerce opposed use of the general fund for this purpose because it would have meant an unwanted tax increase.[1]

In addition, the *Times* and anti-municipal ownership forces, generally, exploited this local predicament to the hilt in the national securities market. They wanted to make it difficult to sell City Light bonds by pointing to the treacherous condition of the street railway, blaming it all on the failure of municipal ownership. Some indication of what was next in the cards came in early December 1926 from D.C. Barnes, a vice-president of Stone and Webster. In an interview with the *Star's* John W. Nelson, Barnes claimed that the public utility business was a monopoly and that Stone and Webster would like to have it. "Puget Sound Power and Light would like to take over the street railway, light and power, uniting them into one operating company." Barnes wanted city governments to stay out of business, and he applauded the Seattle Central Clearing House for having refused to cash the most recent issue of street railway warrants. All that was needed for a Stone and Webster bailout was a "favorable franchise". This appears to have been the first public declaration of Stone and Webster's ultimate goal.[2]

In early December, when the Clearing House refused to cash the warrants, Mayor Landes and Councilman Blaine got Ross to agree to a loan from City Light to pay railway employees. The Council fully supported them, the majority believing Stone and Webster to be behind the crisis. Landes also talked with many businessmen about their cashing the warrants. Rhodes Department Store agreed to cash $130,000 worth, but there were few other takers. She also got the Council to pass an ordinance, increasing the interest rate paid by banks on City deposits from 2% to 2.5% in order to improve the revenue picture for the future. Rumors began floating that the Clearing House was planning to seek an injunction against the City Light loan.[3]

At the beginning of 1927, as if to reassure people of her steadfast commitment to the Skagit project, she reappointed Ross to another three-year term as superintendent of the Lighting Department. To emphasize her purpose, she replaced Blackwell as City Engineer, appointing W. Chester Morse to that position. Morse had been one of the three engineers who surveyed the Skagit project in 1925. They concluded their investigation by agreeing with Ross that the Diablo dam should be the next step. Morse reaffirmed this opinion.[4]

The lines seem to be clearly forming when, on January 7, theater magnate, John Von Herberg, who had purchased bonds worth over $100,000 with some of his millions, filed a court suit to compel the City to pay street railway operating and maintenance expenses before paying interest and bond redemption costs. He contended in his suit that the street railway was insolvent and that it was illegal for the City to use any other City funds to bail out the railway. The effect of this action would cause default on the bonds and reduce the City's bond market rating. It would affect City Light's bond sales as well. It would also require tapping the general revenue fund for payment.[5]

Councilman Campbell claimed the Voters Information League was preparing a report to "show that the utilities are in a deplorable condition, incompetently, and extravagantly managed and heavily over-loaded with bonded indebtedness." He predicted Puget Sound Power and Light would step forward as savior. Steps along this line were being taken, beginning with a PSP&L suit on January 12 to restrain both the City and Von Herberg from having bond redemption payments postponed until operating expenses had been paid.[6]

To get the City out of this unending predicament, Mayor Landes began discussions with PSP&L's A.W. Leonard to renegotiate the original contract, with a view to reducing the annual payments by extending the redemption period. Unknown to her, the Mayor had really been primed to initiate this request by Leonard himself, working through a Seattle-based financial agent, Calvin H. Hagan. Correspondence between Hagan and Leonard began on this issue in early September 1926 concerning possible refinancing of the railway. Hagan, typing his own letters because he did not trust his secretary, advised ". . . it would be worth a great deal to you to be in a position of having the City come to you with the request to refund the debt . . . at that time you would have the whip hand and could force an amicable adjustment of all matters in dispute." Hagan then wrote Mayor Landes, emphasizing "the liability of the general fund for any failure of the City." Even earlier, in December 1925, Hagan had spoken to Council Finance Committee chairman, E.L. Blaine. He reported to Leonard that Blaine said he would not propose a refunding bill for action by the Legislature unless he was sure Leonard would not oppose it. He continued, "I have gotten the matter started from the right source—the Mayor." On December 16, Leonard responded, "We will be glad . . . to cooperate in any way consistent with the Company's interest." On the same day Board chairman, Frederick Pratt, cautioned Leonard, "While I would like to see money raised through taxation for the purpose of supporting the railway, it is a rather dangerous thing to initiate, because it might later be applied to the Lighting Department." The Company's Norwood Brockett added his voice of caution later in December, reporting that the City Light supporters on the Council are seeking a bond issue to refund the railway, but "I am of the opinion that the legislation they seek is more for the benefit of the Light Plant than the railway system."[7]

On December 15, Leonard notified Boston that Mayor Landes is trying to assure payment and wants another conference "at our early convenience on question reducing annual bond payments." If negotiations fail, Leonard advised ". . . we think Company should institute suit in Federal Court immediately to enjoin city from using any street railway revenues . . . for any purpose than payment of principle and interest then payable [on March 1]." With this opening, Leonard went to Boston to discuss matters with Stone and Webster. He wired Landes on January 21, "I find our directors are conversant with Seattle railway situation and are willing to cooperate. Expect to arrive Seattle about February first and will submit a plan."[8]

By terms of the plan the debt period would be extended by eight years, thereby reducing the annual payment from $833,000 to only $500,000. A joker clause was included as a rider—City Light's charges to the railway for purchases of power from City Light would have to be reduced from one-cent per kilowatt hour to one-half that in order to save the railway $200,000 in expenses. He was now in a position to link the Municipal Street Railway's plight with the future of City Light by forcing a financial crisis upon the latter, and then coming to the rescue on the Company's terms. The end seemed in sight. Quickly, complications surfaced.[9]

As he explained the plan to Landes on February 3, Leonard patronizingly advised "We feel that if we assist the City to the extent of $1,000 per day . . . it is only fair to the thousands of street railway patrons that the City itself should do everything possible to secure increased earnings . . . A revision in the rate of 1 [cent] per kilowatt hour . . . would seem fully justified by the fact that the Lighting Department has recently [contracted] . . . to furnish a private industry in Seattle at 3.42 mills per kilowatt hour . . . a rate of 1/2 [cent] per kilowatt hour for street railway operation is comparable with the above rate of 3.42 mills . . ."[10]

At first, the Council agreed with Landes that this seemed to be a solution. This was before Ross had been consulted. Ross claimed that City Light would be selling at a loss at that rate, and furthermore, PSP&L was losing industrial customers to City Light because of the latter's new lower industrial rates, and that Leonard was using this tactic to force City Light to raise these rates. Leonard insisted on linking the rider with the proposed new contract. Many Council members decided after listening to Ross to take offense at Leonard's audacious attempt to set City policy. They resisted.[11]

Two law suits further complicated the matter: the one filed

by Von Herberg, the second by the Fourteen Taxpayers organization (S. Asia, et al) to prevent payment of the debt out of the general fund. As to the former suit, Leonard wired Pratt, "We are satisfied [the Von Herberg suit] is an attempt to entangle Company in State Court suit." As to the Fourteen Taxpayers suit, Leonard wired, "Our proposition to Mayor . . . was well received . . . but fourteen taxpayers organization are opposing same and suggest prohibitive conditions . . ." To deal with objections from the Fourteen Taxpayers and the Building Owners' Association Leonard had the Company's attorney, James B. Howe, draft a legislative bill giving Stone and Webster prior claim over all others, invalidating the original contract. The latter feature found resistance from Corporation Counsel, Kennedy, because he still suspected fraud in that transaction. By the second week in February, the Council began to sour on the proposal altogether and stated a preferance for refunding the outstanding $10 million in bonds and in replacing them with utility bonds extending over a longer period. It drafted a bill to that effect.[12]

Wearily, at the end of February, Leonard wired Stone and Webster, "Have been unable to get Mayor to accept clause making debt a general obligation in getting validating legislation from Legislature." The whole confusing bundle of offers and court suits would drag on into the next mayoral administration before giving way to other alternatives as the effects of the Great Depression set in.[13]

With the March 1 payment deadline approaching, the Council approved a $600,000 loan from the City Light fund. It also asked for dismissal of Von Herberg's suit on grounds that the payment made his case moot. Von Herberg tried unsuccessfully to obstruct this action by charging it was in violation of the court's restraining order.[14]

While this shadow-boxing was transpiring the Council's enabling bill for refunding went to the State Legislature, where it was approved as H.B. 120 in the House, 66 to 1. The Senate tied it up in committee, for which the *P-I* charged the "Company" with responsibilty. Landes blamed defeat on the fact that it "would have permitted the refunding of city light bonds along with water and street car bonds"—echoing Norwood Brockett's reservations. As a result of this defeat, the only alternative open to the City seemed to be Stone and Webster's extension plan, tied with the rate reduction for City Light sales of power to the railway.[15]

Prospects for acceptance loomed as more of a possibility

when City Light supporter Ralph Nichols was defeated by conservative A. Lou Cohen. The Nichols coalition had included Tindall, Moore, Case, and Campbell; it had produced the defeated refunding bill. The new majority coalition would consist of Cohen, Erickson, Hesketh, Blaine, and Carroll, with Erickson replacing Tindall as Utilities Committee chairman, and Carroll replacing Moore as president. Under Erickson on this crucial committee were Cohen, Hesketh, Blaine, Otto Case, and Campbell. Tempering this committee's work would be Erickson's enduring personal vendetta with Ross.[16]

By mid-May, Street Railway superintendent, D.W. Henderson, could report that the system was now on a "paying basis". Indeed, Leonard, himself, had confessed to Pratt early 1926, when the latter had an opportunity to sell some of City of Seattle bonds, "Believe physical condition of Street Railway property better today than when acquired by city." Revenue was another matter, however; and that was not addressed.[17]

Meanwhile the two suits were awaiting federal circuit court action. At last, in early November 1927, Judge F.S. Dietrich dismissed both suits, claiming in the one that PSP&L could not claim payment default because it had been paid; and in the other that Von Herberg was in no position to instruct the City on how to pay its debts. While this appeared to give some relief, Mayor Landes declared that the street car problem will not go away until more people leave their automobiles at home.[18]

Von Herberg, unwilling to let matters stand, began an appeal process. The immediate result of this was postponement of the purchase of new cars for the system because the bonds to pay for them could not be marketed while the suit was in process. With the next March 1 deadline for payment not far off, the Street Railway went on a warrant basis again on December 25 to meet its payroll. In early January 1928, railway employees began having trouble cashing their warrants, so another loan from City Light was revived, adding $550,000 from some "idle" construction bond funds to be made available at the end of the month.[19]

Meanwhile, Von Herberg's appeal was on file, and Leonard continued to insist on his rider, just as the city headed into another mayoral election.

Not to be lost sight of in the turmoil surrounding the street railway, was the Skagit project. Landes had declared in June 1927 that "We must carry forward the Skagit development without interruption." This meant pursuing the Diablo dam construction as top priority. But the continued problem of sand and gravel entering the Gorge tunnel intake caused a modification to which Ross agreed. This involved the transfer of funds intended for powerhouse construction to building an Ambursen type of masonry dam (hollow, with reinforced concrete) below the Gorge dam as soon as possible. This was to be pursued concurrently with Diablo construction, if implemented.[20]

Erickson soon showed his hand in July by pushing through funding for enlarging the Cedar Falls dam without consulting Ross or Morse. Now Tindall joined with Erickson, ostensibly, to meet current demand for more power. But, in addition to the Cedar project, Erickson pressed for the construction of a dam at the Hanging Rock site on the Skagit before proceeding further on the Diablo. To imagine Ross's annoyance would not be far-fetched; and for Ross to suspect the hand of the "power trust" in all this would not be surprising, either. But Erickson did not require priming by the power trust to oppose Ross—he had been doing so since 1911, and seemed, really, to want to dominate in all utilities issues, having found Ross as his main obstacle. Early in his council career he was thought by Ross to have the governorship in his sights. If true, he failed; and he was rejected by the voters in 1924, when he ran for mayor. As mayor, he could have fired Ross and emerge the dominant force in public ownership politics. As matters now stood, he could be depended upon to fight Ross on the Skagit under his own steam—he did not need the Company's help in doing so. The goal of each was essentially the same—they only differed in their respective approaches and motives.[21]

In November, the *P-I*'s L.E. Hill began a series of articles on City Light's present and future debt obligations, now that the Council had approved a $12,500,000 bond issue that would bring its debt to $38,450,000. He asked, "How much more will have to be spent to perfect the whole system?" In exploring the financial picture, Hill drew attention to accusations made in the past by the *Times* and PSP&L spokesmen that City Light was failing, but that each time the accusers had to eat their words because a profit was always shown. Now, A.W. Leonard was predicting that 1932 would see yet another City Light "crisis" with its payments on its bonds exceeding its revenue, and that PSP&L would have to come to the rescue by taking over the utility. To this, Ross had countered that Leonard was only trying to discredit the sale of the recent issue of $4,000,000 worth of Lighting Department bonds. In fact, for the first time City Light bonds were being sold to non-local buyers, with Dean Witter offering the highest bid of 4.933% effective interest—"by far the best terms ever offered on City Light bonds." Hill concluded his financial analysis," the record of the past twenty-two years seems to warrant the most hopeful expectations." Turning to the City Council's role, Hill found its "interference with executive functions [as having] reached its zenith. Most of the councilmen are said to imagine themselves superior in judgment or learning to the ablest hydroelectric engineers. [Consequently, they have meddled] in the most intimate details [of City Light operations]."[22]

Into this debate stepped Landes, recommending at a public meeting that a board of engineers might best preside over City Light. Then a Ross-dependable, Councilman Campbell, recommended in late November that a board of businessmen and engineers be appointed to advise on all utilities as Los Angeles does. Not surprisingly, Erickson backed Campbell, and suggested yet another Skagit survey and reversal of the decision not to build at Hanging Rock. While the survey proposal was defeated, Hanging Rock was debated all through December. After six weeks of investigation on its own, the Municipal League declared its opposition to Hanging Rock and agreed with past engineering decisions about Skagit priorities. Morse had informed the League that Hanging Rock dam would produce power at a cost of $100 per horsepower, compared to $25 at Diablo, a persuasive comparison.[23]

Mayoral Politics, 1928: Foul Play?

The mayoral race of 1928 was staged in a setting in which the two perennial issues, the street railway system and City Light's Skagit project, were reaching still another climax—once again linked together by A.W. Leonard's deft maneuvering. Out of the race there would emerge victorious a political unknown, Frank Edwards, owner of the Winter Garden Theater, at Fourth Avenue near Pike Street, holder of no public office, past or present, only rarely appearing in public, but backed by record-breaking campaign funds. He won. How come? An analysis of the campaign, as it unfolded, will suggest some reasons, though by no means all. Edwards's actions after his election do suggest some more definitive answers than would be revealed during the campaign itself.

Landes launched her re-election campaign with a ringing speech before an audience of 300 at the Gowman Hotel. She charged that a "bitter campaign against municipal ownership of public utilities [is being waged] and Seattle is one of the storm centers." At this time the Federal Trade Commission's investigation of the nation's electrical utilities was getting underway. But, before this, in early December, it was publicly revealed that sixteen anti-public ownership monographs had been distributed throughout the Seattle public school system through the good offices of school superintendent, S.E. Fleming. These were signed by Clare Kellogg Tripp, executive director of the Washington Industries Education Bureau, and by the Puget Sound Power and Light Company. Tripp explained that they had been distributed throughout the state by the state school superintendent's office and by superintendents of county and municipal school systems. Fleming added that he had ordered another 300 copies, contending that they were not propaganda. This was part of the campaign to which Landes was referring.[1]

Besides siding with Ross for completion of Diablo Dam, Landes persisted in seeking a solution to the endlessly nettlesome street railway problem and pushing through a city-county hospital plan. The latter was given top priority by the *Argus*, claiming that the region's hospital situation was "pathetic". That staunchly conservative political weekly considered the names of the 300 men and women supporters to be ". . . the most representative list of backers that the editor . . . has ever seen in connection with the candidacy of any person for office in this city . . . [indicating satisfaction] with the manner in which she has conducted the business of this city." Editor Harry Chadwick had been observing and commenting on the city's politics since before the turn of the century, always Republican, outspoken against corruption and demogoguery, elitist, though rarely reactionary, and preferring men over women for political office, all other things being equal.[2]

Mayoral candidates began lining up. There was the popular City Light supporter, Councilman Philip Tindall, who was expected to pull a large bloc of votes. Landes's predecessor, "Doc" Brown decided to make another try, even though tarnished in much the same way as the erstwhile comeback artist, Hiram Gill, of the century's second decade. A. Lou Cohen who had ousted Ralph Nichols from the Council in the last election, became a contender. He charged Landes with responsibility for the jail escape of killer William Hickman (who soon was apprehended in Portland, thereby depriving him of an issue), since he dared not openly attack Landes on the municipal ownership issue, although he was a known opponent on that score. Two less widely known candidates were Port Commissioner Dr. W.T. Christensen and Clifford Clark. Then there was Frank Edwards, an unknown politico, who had been campaigning, according to

Landes, for the past eight months. He already had doorbellers working the precincts and was being portrayed on billboards throughout the city, at untold expense. William Dickson, in writing a masters' thesis on the heels of the election, concluded that "[A] clique in the Civil Service League . . . [was] busy planning Edwards' campaign four months before the public had ever heard of him. They not only planned his campaign but induced him to run."[3]

A voter registration drive paralleled the filing. By the close of the drive, 114,273 voters were registered, surpassing the 1926 record by 4,000. What followed was one of the most unusual mayoral campaigns—and probably one of the most suspect—in the city's history.[4]

As the February 27 primary election approached, "betting" favored Landes, with Brown only slightly behind. Both Edwards and Tindall were basing their campaigns on the notion that either of them stood a better chance of beating Landes in the runoff than Brown. While Tindall accused Edwards of having a slush fund, he could not cut into Edwards's following which was coming from somewhere.[5]

Edwards was running third, according to the odds-makers. He had, reportedly, made "inroads among [Landes's] women supporters." His women's vote gatherers were Mrs. J.M. Thatcher, former president of the Women's Republican Club, and Mrs. Edith Gaddis. They organized doorbellers to canvass in Landes's strongholds, and seemed to be making headway. Also, the novelty of a woman mayoral candidate was not carrying over from 1926. As the *P-I* noted, women "lacked the fervor" for Landes that had carried her to victory in 1926.[6]

Edwards was not only capturing critical support among women, but he was managing very well among civil service employees, getting support from the politicized Civil Service League, and using younger members of the Police Department as active campaigners. Police Chief Searing, whom Landes had appointed in place of the allegedly corrupt Severyns, observed a "movement among the younger members of the Police Department [to gain] control of the Police Relief and Pension Board", then force his removal if they got control. Such use of civil service employees in political campaigns was illegal, but that made no difference to Edwards. He seemed confident that he could get away with the tactic, there being little chance that his election would be taken from him for such violations. In this context an important factor to bear in mind was the legacy from the "city manager vs. charter revision" fight. Landes had actively supported the city manager plan, while the civil service employees figured decisively in its defeat. They were similarly aligned here. (In 1931 Edwards would lose their support . . . as will be related below.)[7]

In a lengthy internal memorandum, written by Norwood Brockett for the information of his fellow PSP&L executives, he drew special attention to the Civil Service League's influence. Altogether, he noted there were about 6,500 civil service employees, of which 2,000 were street railway personnel. The latter had quickly gained wage increases, once the City took over the railway, making them the highest paid on the Coast. Similarly, police and firemen had extracted big pay increases. Police were suspected of taking payoffs from bootleggers, houses of prostitution, and racketeers to improve on their legitimate earnings. Brockett estimated that this nucleus formed the basis of a bloc vote of 30,000 to 40,000, when relatives and friends were added in. The League opposed Landes because her reforms affected them negatively—replacing the allegedly corrupt ex-Police Chief Severyns, replacing the Fire Marshall and Water Department superintendent, all of which disrupted the going system. One of Police Chief Searing's first acts had been to relieve Lieutenant George Comstock and Captain E.L. Hedges of their responsibilities because they were under indictment for violation of the prohibition laws. She had also promised and obtained economies in City management.[8]

Not only had Landes drawn well-known business and professional leaders to her cause, but even Teamsters' leader Harry Dail spoke on her behalf on Radio Station KJR. Her campaign manager was none other than Alfred Lundin who had been the Chamber of Commerce's mayoral candidate in 1924. After the primaries she would attract an even more impressive following.[9]

Heading into the primaries the *Argus* warned voters not to follow the advice of the "underground wireless" which told them to vote for Edwards in order to fend off Brown. When the primaries results came in, Landes ran true to form, winning by a margin of 3,149 votes, but not, as expected, over Brown, but over Edwards instead. She received 28,183 votes, Edwards 25,034, Brown 22,515, and Tindall trailed badly with only 8,966. Could a bloc of votes be transferred from the losers to Landes to head off Edwards? Much seemed to hinge on whether Brown would decide to be a "sticker" candidate.[10]

Landes immediately challenged Edwards to a series of "joint meetings". Edwards failed to respond, but, as he would state on the last day of the campaign, he would "[keep] out of sight". She challenged him to reveal the source of his campaign funds, but to no avail, and she accused him of having already promised jobs. Then the streetcar men's union endorsed Edwards—another bloc of civil service employees. Betting now favored Edwards, as he was expected to draw a lot of Brown's vote, if not Brown's outright endorsement.[11]

Landes continued to pick up support though. Former mayor Hugh Caldwell credited her with being one of the best mayors in the last twenty years, "if not the best". She spoke to one large downtown noon audience in which men outnumbered women, reportedly, by 4 to 1—and a favorable audience at that. Landes spent the last week campaigning by radio, and was quoted as worrying about the "welfare of our municipal institutions" if Edwards is elected.[12]

The one radio talk by Edwards was not even given by him, but by a stand-in, Edwards claiming that his voice had cracked—but he was forced to acknowledge this only after the switch was discovered. Much newspaper play was made of this, with the *Star* asking on a front-page editorial, "Who Would Be Mayor Under Edwards?" In the editorial text it was noted that an ex-policeman involved in the liquor protection racket, George Reynolds, was encamped, and he was known to be an "expert collector of campaign funds". Others were listed as having served in the department "from time to time". Other police "gold braid" were noted as having had "soft downtown berths" under Brown. Dick Faris, a former employee in the County Elections Department, and other county employees who were on the way up, were in the Edwards camp, according to the *Star*. He had also been co-manager of Mayor Landes's 1926 campaign against Doc Brown. Mrs. Faris would allege during her divorce proceedings after the election that booze parties at campaign headquarters were a regular affair. As for Edwards's last week, he had nothing planned except visits to "200 industrial centers" in line with his "plan for an industrial foundation"—which the *Times* found somewhat mystical.[13]

On the 6th, Brown finally announced that he would not run as a sticker candidate, and he attacked Edwards for "using a scandalous amount of money to buy the office of mayor [and] at heart he is not for Seattle's wonderful utilities." He concluded that Edwards was unfit. Tindall came out for Landes, accompanied by Christensen. So the hoped-for bloc of also-rans came into the Landes fold after all. Would it make a difference? It seemed like frosting on the cake even before the *Times* declared for Landes.[14]

On the same day the *Times*, in an editorial, wrote "Mr. Edwards momentary leadership in the mayoralty race is due to a unique process of deception . . . Not one reason is urged against the re-election of Mayor Landes. [His campaign workers can only claim] she is a woman . . . It is a sad reflection upon Seattle's sense of decency and appreciation that such a campaign against a capable executive should have made any headway at all . . . Mayor Landes should be re-elected." Just the previous day the *Star* had similarly noted in an editorial that many will oppose Landes because she is a woman. The Central Labor Council next fell into line. Altogether, she had the support of all three major daily newspapers (the *Union Record* was folding). There were endorsements from leading business and professional men (but none from Stone and Webster officials) and from important segments of organized labor . . . unparalleled in the city's political history. Betting was now swinging to Landes.[15]

Finally, on the 10th, expenses for the primary were filed; by Edwards within only ten minutes of the deadline. He reported $15,326, which was at least $10,000 more than the record amount spent by Lundin in 1924. Landes reported $4,708. Lundin was furious, claiming that at least $50,000 had been spent, and in support noted that the 35 billboards were not listed, nor were the amounts paid to campaign workers. Lacking in his report was any mention of the expense incurred for producing a film showing Edwards admiring the Skagit project. When asked about this by reporters, he simply referred them to his "committee". As to City Light, Edwards claimed that Ross was the only one for sure whom he would re-appoint.[16]

After seeing the reports of campaign expenses, Prosecuting Attorney Ewing Colvin, charged Edwards with "a clear violation of the law" and ordered his manager, Dick Faris, to appear before him at 9:00 AM Monday, the day before the election . . . and Edwards too, if he would. Edwards's attorneys, A. Scott Bullitt and two others, advised him not to appear. For his part, Faris admitted that expenses were, indeed, much more than reported, but he contended that the billboards had been donated by "friends of Edwards", along with other expenses.[17]

The betting continued to favor Landes, even more so now that a moral component had been introduced on election eve. At this time Brown helped by openly accusing "Seattle police and firemen [of a] united attempt to secure control of the civil government of this city [by running Edwards for mayor]." And if there had been any misreading of the *P-I*'s sympathies until now there would be no longer. It came out for Landes.[18]

Edwards emerged from hiding on election eve, addressing an audience of 3,000 at the Masonic Temple in the Greenwood district, where, significantly, men outnumbered women by 8 to 1, according to the *P-I*.[19]

Then, in what the *P-I* described as the "most hectic campaign in Seattle's history", Edwards won in a landslide, mustering a majority of more than 16,000 votes, 54,535 to Landes's 37,113.[20]

While chauvinism of men and women against women holding elected public office was undoubtedly a critical factor in her defeat, this chauvinism was multi-faceted. For one thing, Landes had demonstrated that she was a good executive, a principled and outspoken fighter for clean and efficient government and for municipal ownership of public utilities. But these are not qualities which women were expected to have in those days. She might have seemed out of place, in the view of the many men and women who voted for Edwards. That she was slurred badly for being a woman was a good campaign tactic, one that lent itself to doorbeller pitches, and it was undoubtedly used. She was as good or better than any man who had been mayor, and that was a factor that Edwards campaign workers undoubtedly played upon . . . nice women did not run for public office because politics was inherently dirty. Julia Budlong, writing in the *Nation*, concluded that Edwards ran only on the sex issue: "[Seattle] did not like being teased about its mayor."[21]

If she had not been outspokenly in favor of municipal ownership of utilities, would Edwards have been raised from obscurity to be run against her? The fact that he had no public record had to figure in bringing him to public attention by his financial backers. Who were they? Could the Civil Service League muster all the financial support needed? It could, if those accustomed to making payoffs under previous administrations came through, and there is little doubt that they did, judging from the newspaper reporting.

Edwards did not speak out on any issues, avoiding the hot street railway topic. And he identified with the Skagit project in the vaguest way simply by saying he would re-appoint Ross, thereby implying that he supported City Light. If Stone and Webster were paying the bills, as was later charged, they were careful not to have him oppose the municipal utilities because they enjoyed widespread support, and had he done so, his suspected backers would have become clearly known. However, if it was the Boston syndicate, not even the *Times* seemed to know . . . or it was being unusually coy.

As a propaganda piece that must have been a factor in the final days was a four-page tabloid item headed: "EDWARDS MAYORALTY MESSAGE". Then followed a vicious anti-feminist attack in the form of an open letter: "A Message for Her Honor, the Mayor . . . To Mrs. Bertha K. Landis, Mayor of Seattle: [According to the newspapers you have written me] numerous letters inviting me to explain to you why I am a candidate for Mayor . . . You assume that the office was created especially for you and you for the office . . . You have invited me to appear with you on theatre stages to answer the question that is encased in your bosom. There are many reasons why I should not appear with you to protect myself against your insidious barrage. It is manifestly hard for any man to make debate with a hostile or infuriated woman."[22]

Then he attacked her handling of the police department—not acting on information to enforce the prohibition statutes, allowing the murderer Hickman to escape town when his presence was known, and of demoralizing the department.

He concluded the letter incoherently: "If you were a man, Mayor Landes, . . . that if you were ignorant of the vice conditions you were worse than a dolt; if you admitted your knowledge—that you were unfit to occupy the chair for which you think you have a divine franchise."

On page four, Edwards tried to give lie to the charge that he was backed by the "power trust" and to question Landes's devotion to City Light by accusing her of knuckling down to Leonard when she agreed to reduce the power rate that the street railway was charged by City Light.

Not content with this attack, Edwards charged in a four-page pamphlet that, "Dean and Bertha Landes are getting rich at public expense. What is the public getting?"[23]

Who paid the bulk of the expenses? It had to be a well-heeled source, as there was no evidence produced to show that it came from grassroots fund raising, apart from civil service employees. Edwards's later firing of J.D. Ross in 1931, following visits to Stone and Webster's Boston offices, seemed to point the finger toward that party, but he really needed to make those visits at least to negotiate any settlement of the street railway debt. However, given the history of that firm's involvement in the city's politics, its involvement in Edwards's election would not be out of character. Its low profile throughout the election seems suspicious. Could this have been due to the fact that so many of Landes's declared supporters had traditionally opposed municipal ownership, and City Light in particular? A large proportion of the electorate still suspected that fraud and bribery were involved in the sale of the street railway system under duress of wartime necessity. And they would be reminded annually of the exorbitant debt obligation when time came to make interest and redemption payments. Yet, if Stone and Webster did provide financial aid, it is noteworthy that Edwards drew heaviest voter support from southern Seattle areas where those mayors who were most closely linked with police protection of vice, gambling, and the liquor trade had traditionally given their favors. Chief Searing had cut out that racket, and there were police officers who were anxious to have it restored.

Apart from direct funding, the Civil Service League played a critical role. To give Edwards name familiarity among civil service employees, the League's September 1927 journal featured an editorial by Edwards: "FIRE PREVENTION"—a motherhood statement drawn from the experience of a theater owner. In the March 1928 issue of the journal appeared an advertisement paid for by the "Friends of Frank Edwards": "FRANK EDWARDS", [photograph]: "This is the Man you want for Mayor", followed by: "To My friends in the Civil Service: I shall do my part in protecting the principle of municipal ownership of public utilities, as well as the proper financing and operation of the same." League president Dan Boyle figured weightily in Edwards's campaign and he was rewarded with a departmental headship after the election. One thing was clear to Edwards: if he was to win, he could not take a stand against City Light. And furthermore, he had to openly support the department and Ross, at least to remove suspicion that he had the backing of the power trust.[24]

William Dickson, while crediting the CSL with primary responsibility for his election, suggests that his effective use of the radio compensated for his lack of newspaper support. He also suggested that because Mayor Landes had suppressed vice and police corruption below normal standards, vice could not be made an issue, as it had in her campaign against Brown. Edwards's strength lay in South Seattle, Georgetown, downtown, and Queen Anne; he lost in the University district by only slightly more than 1,000 votes and the vote was evenly split on Capitol Hill. In the Central Labor Council, a strong minority had resisted the CLC's endorsement of Landes. These were the Street Carmen's Union, the Electrical Workers Union (where PSP&L had many former and current employees) and the Soft Drink

Dispensers. They had tried to get the CLC to censure David Levine and Charles Doyle for their role in securing the council's Landes endorsement.[25]

After the election, Stone and Webster's mischievous intervention in Seattle's politics, through its local PSP&L subsidiary, became more evident as the Federal Trade Commission hearings had come to focus on the state of Washington. Both the *Star* and *P-I* reported almost daily in April the revelations of nefarious "power trust" propaganda. Striking cartoons emphasized their narratives. Although the local citizenry had already known about the invasion of the public school system by private utility propaganda through Clare Tripp's Washington Industrial Education Bureau and of its subsidization by PSP&L, the hearings brought out more lurid details. The *Times* defended the private utilities' propaganda by contending that it was needed to counteract radical and socialist attacks on them.[26]

What many already suspected about the Voters' Information League was verified as well. It had been subsidized by PSP&L all along, and although Leonard would admit to this, he implied the portion was much less than the reported 75%. The Municipal League would later determine that the proportion was 89%. G.C. Congdon, an Ohio engineer, had been hired by Leonard to fabricate "disinterested" investigations of City Light that were reported in VIL bulletins, showing that the municipal venture was losing money, was creating a bonded indebtedness that would bankrupt the city, was costing taxpayers by hidden subsidies, and it was removing otherwise taxable property from the tax rolls.[27]

Edwards's subsequent actions as mayor would lead viewers to see that reorganization of City Light was a prime goal which could not be done overnight . . . at least, not without risking the public wrath—in light of the suspicions aroused by the Landes forces and other candidates during the campaign. When he finally acted "overnight", he did lose it all. Yet, if Ross and City Light were Edwards's ultimate target, Ross did not seem to suspect this, if a letter he wrote to a friend, R.L. McDonald, on March 7, 1930 is to be taken at face value. In it, Ross said ". . . Edwards has worked with City Light. I would say that he has always done so and he has always taken a considerable interest in our work, cooperating to the fullest degree." Given Ross's tendency to see the Power Trust lurking behind much of the evil in politics, Edwards seemed to be given a clean bill of health. Did Ross misjudge? As we trace the course of the Edwards administration, an answer may come forth.[28]

Mayor Frank Edwards Begins

Edwards began by asking for resignations from all of Landes's appointees except Ross and Fire Chief George Mantor. The latter had established a remarkable record for reducing the number and extent of the city's fires, and had acquired a constituency among the business community in the process. City Engineer W. Chester Morse had resigned before Edwards had made his request, fully expecting to be replaced; he was, by W.D. Barkhuff, an engineer with little record to show for it. Former chief of police, William Severyns, who, Landes had decided, was too corrupt for her taste, was nominated to replace Murray Grant as head of the Water Department. In Barkhuff's former position as head of Streets and Sewers, a campaign worker, Daniel Boyle was named. He had been president of the Civil Service League for the past two years, and had been in the department since 1921. Police Lieutenant Louis Forbes was elevated to Police Chief.[1]

Such appointments had been expected, but they had to muster majorities in the City Council before the nominees could rest easy in their positions. The *P-I* accused Edwards of paying off political debts . . . nothing new. It predicted a fight against the Barkhuff and Boyle nominations. Barkhuff, because he had had no experience in electrical engineering and very limited general engineering experience to draw on. When the *P-I* found traditional City Light supporters Erickson, Blaine, and Tindall backing the nomination, it accused them in a page-one editorial of being "parties to a colossal blunder." The *P-I*, here, seemed oblivious to Erickson's well-known hostility to Ross, and to his continual harassment of Ross in the latter's concentration on the Skagit project. Erickson would find in Edwards a means of destroying Ross, but, in the attempt, wound up writing his own political death certificate. Given the approval, already, by Carroll, Cohen, and Hesketh, Barkhuff's appointment was assured by a 6 to 2 vote; and Boyle's followed in the wake by a 7 to 1 vote.[2]

Serious opposition was registered to Severyns' nomination, but it did not last long either. However, all through July the Council haggled over the nomination of Richard Sweet as Superintendent of Utilities. Edwards gave up and named George Avery to the position, with Council approval.[3]

While the Council and Edwards were wrestling over administrative appointments, the street railway's debt obligations were bubbling to the surface. Mayor Landes was filling out her last days in office when the *Times* issued a front page editorial on April 1, accusing the Council of having done nothing to solve the debt problem, for having made no provisions to acquire new equipment, nor making needed extensions, nor paving between tracks. It urged purchase of more motor buses. It pointed to a rescue attempt in-the-making, in the form of a citizens committee, which styled itself as the Traffic Research Commission, headed by hardware store owner, Fred Ernst, and composed of other businessmen. It would issue its report and recommendations in January 1929. The editorial writer could not resist taking a closing swing at the Skagit project . . . like a conditioned reflex.[4]

For her part, still-Mayor Landes touted the city's utilities for their successes despite propaganda to the contrary. This propaganda, she claimed, had caused postponement of major improvements in the street railway and the purchase of new cars. She defended the street railway for never having defaulted, for having made significant improvements in the face of insufficient ridership, and she contended that it was still better than railways in most cities. The system was making the best of a bad contract, having to set aside 1 1/4 cents of each 8 1/3 cents fare for bond redemption. She objected to the argument against City Light for paying no taxes, by pointing out that its surplus is transferred to the general fund where it draws 2% interest, or about $80,000 annually. She added that it is self-sustaining, and not dependent upon taxes. She could have added that the low electric rates charged by City Light had forced the private utility to charge lower rates than it would have in the absence of City Light competition, and that this more than compensated taxpayers for the loss of otherwise taxable property.[5]

As the annual street railway crisis-time loomed ahead in fall, Councilman Blaine looked for a way out, short of another loan from City Light ($100,000 was still owed from the last one). And, as to warrants, the banks had resisted clearing them. Hanging fire were the court suits filed by Von Herberg and Puget Sound Power and Light. In mid-November the Circuit Court finally ruled that the latter had no prior claim on gross earnings of the system, and that the debt was against the system, not against the city as a whole. Nevertheless, Von Herberg decided to press his argument for prior claim in the superior court. So the issue continued to complicate the railway's future, impeding any long range planning. Whether this was intended by the contesting party is unclear, but the result was the same.[6]

Concurrent with the circuit court decision was action by the voters in approving a bond issue of $1.5 million for purchase of new cars, extensions, and improvements. Also, a petition was approved to seek authorization from the state legislature for a special annual levy of 2 mills to pay for operation and maintenance expenses. By these measures avoidance of the annual crisis was expected. The Legislature would begin sessions in January.[7]

Solution seemed in sight. The Traffic Research Commission heralded the new year by submitting its report to Mayor Edwards. The commission had been organized and financed by retail merchants, central district property owners, and the Clearing House Association two years earlier, after meetings with Mayor Landes, the Council, engineers, and others about the purchase of 200 new cars. This opening broadened into a system study when it was learned that the depreciation reserve fund had to be used to pay off the bonded indebtedness, instead of using it to replace worn-out equipment. The commission recommended the purchase of the Rainier Valley lines, construction of a subway from Westlake Avenue to Broadway along the route of Pike or Pine streets, also a subway under the canal at Fremont Avenue. As to the contract with Stone and Webster, the commission recommended its extension to thirty years.[8]

Ross, in light of the report, then withdrew his opposition to a rate reduction for electricity provided to the railway and met with Edwards and Avery to work out a reasonable reduction. This move was followed quickly by Von Herberg in superior court, where he attacked the validity of the Street Railway contract and claimed that the system was insolvent . . . always a part of his suits. His injunction was intended to prevent the City from taking any money out of other utility funds and transferring it to to the railway fund. This would teeter the system on the brink, which would have satisfied Von Herberg. But Judge Calvin Hall refused to grant the injunction. Von Herberg would appeal to the state Supreme Court which would have the last word; the system would remain stalled in its tracks.[9]

With his appointments now in place, Edwards had Avery draft a bill to allow the City to levy a tax of 2 1/2 mills to aid the street railway. At news of this, the *Star* instigated a public "outcry" over the proposed legislation, forcing the Council to transfer $200,000 from the Water Fund to the Street Railway Fund. For all practical purposes the proposed millage bill was defeated. This was not the end of the story however. As the legislative session was drawing to a close, the House unanimously approved a bill to allow refunding of the remaining $9 million debt. Such a bill had been offered in the previous legislature but was defeated by the private utility lobby, according to the *P-I*, because it would have extended the opportunity to City Light as well. The current piece was limited to the railway debt.[10]

Now, given his legislative mandate, Edwards devised a refunding plan that would pay off the debt in cash and aim for a 2% discount in the process. This would be done by floating a $10 million bond issue. To this, PSP&L's Leonard said: "Yes, we want to act to the benefit of Seattle as well as to our own stockholders . . . We have the plan under advisement." Edwards then went to Boston in early June for the negotiations, and concluded what seemed a "virtual agreement". Upon Edwards's and Leonard's return, Leonard announced: "What will be done depends on future negotiations between the City and the bondholders." In October, Leonard launched the idea of a two-year moratorium on the payments, but discussions became stymied in Council as the decade drew to a close.[11]

Out of this street railway crisis, as it lurched toward the March 1 payment deadline, only two elements remained alive: the Von Herberg suit, and the prospect of a moratorium. The report and recommendations of the Transit Research Commission carried no ripple-effect after initially startling the citizenry. Nothing, either, came from the tentative discussions between Edwards, Avery, and Ross regarding a reduction of the rates charged by the Lighting Department for electricity used by the railway. At best, this issue would remain on the back-burner, although PSP&L offered to supply power to the street railway for 1 cent a kilowatt hour, 1⁄4 cent less than City Light was charging. Of course, this would have taken away a major customer. The offer was refused. The legislative mandate authorizing refunding, similarly, hung for later action, should it be needed.[12]

Leonard soon found an opportunity to directly attack City Light and reported to Stone and Webster, on December 3, that he had met with Edwards, and had frankly talked ". . . about the activities of the Lighting Department employees in securing signatures to the Grange power district petition and told him it would be impossible to cooperate with him on street railway bond payment extension situation . . . if another department under his full control was trying to jeopardize our property in other places of no interest to City of Seattle. He agreed to take question up at once . . . but our check shows no helpful result as far as we are concerned. I have another appointment with the Mayor as soon as he returns."[13]

Meanwhile the Von Herberg suit was wending its long course. It had a two-fold effect: it held up bidding on $1.5 worth of City Light bonds, and the Municipal Street Railway was prevented from sending payment to Stone and Webster until it was settled. It was scheduled for hearing in early February 1929 in Judge James T. Ronald's court. The judge dismissed the suit, thereby relieving the pressure temporarily, although Von Herberg was still considering an appeal to the state Supreme Court.[14]

Erickson vs. Ross—Who's in Control?

Erickson's feud with Ross reached a new stage with the Edwards's administration, due in part to the confidence that Erickson developed in mayoral support for undermining Ross's authority. While the arguments over Edwards's nominations ran their tentative course, Erickson instigated, with Edwards's approval, the appointment of Lars Jorgensen, of the Constant Angle Arch Dam Company of San Francisco, as consulting engineer on the Skagit project. Erickson followed with a proposal to conduct a whole new survey of the City's power development problems; Hanging Rock dam was sandwiched in. As a final touch, Erickson could not resist renewing a request for lower residential rates, taking as his cue the preferential commercial and industrial rates City Light was awarding to take that line of business from the private company . . . and succeeding. This latter group of customers could use off-peak power, which would have been lost if not used.[1]

Despite Erickson's efforts to make life miserable for Ross, the year ended in celebration. On December 1, 1928 none other than Thomas A. Edison pressed a switch at his home in West Orange, New Jersey, lighting up Seattle's new downtown street lighting system. "Enormous crowds", "Ohs", and "Ahs" were expressed when out of the dimmed streets a "great white way" popped into view, in the "flash of an eye". Traffic was "unmanageable" as horns honked and bells clanged. Ross managed the celebration, but not the traffic, apparently. And he put Edwards on center stage.[2]

The war on the Skagit front seemed to be going Ross's way at the beginning of the year, starting as it did with the announcement that laying the foundation for the Diablo Dam had been completed. Raising it on the foundation to its full height would be comparatively easy, and the Skagit Valley residents, seemingly, would be free of flood threat. Councilman Otto Case

Seattle City Light

A recent scene of Diablo Dam, showing the tramway incline near center and powerhouse on left. Construction began in 1928, but delays in powerhouse construction caused the city to wait until 5 October 1936 to receive electricity.

resumed efforts, stalled by Erickson, to have construction begin on the power house. Ross had wanted the dam and powerhouse construction to be done in tandem but Erickson opposed this strategy as head of the Council's Utilities Committee when his Hanging Rock dam proposal was rejected in Council. As matters stood, the water impounded behind Diablo would have to be shunted past the power house site to the Gorge powerhouse until the Diablo powerhouse was completed . . . at least a year after completion of the dam. This would represent a waste of potential energy for which Erickson was primarily responsible.[3]

The feud between Ross and Erickson, begun in 1911, had been out in the open since the dispute over tactics surrounding the 1924 presentation of the Bone Bill. It did not help their relationship that Ross accused him of selling out to the private power interests—Erickson had always been considered an unqualified advocate of public ownership. For his part, Ross had privately expressed the view that Erickson wanted to dominate the city's politics and was contesting Ross for that honor.[4]

Seattle City Light

"The Great White Way." On 1 December 1928, Thomas A. Edison pressed a switch at his home in West Orange, New Jersey that turned on Seattle's new street lighting system. Traffic was "unmanageable" as horns honked and bells clanged. Scene is looking south on Second Avenue. Smith Tower in background.

No sooner was the Diablo announcement made, than rumors began circulating of a rift between Edwards and Ross. A couple of months earlier Edwards had called Ross to task for allowing trees to be mutilated in residential areas to allow free passage of wires. Now, Ross was accused of "giving" some obsolete light standards (surplused by the new ones on the "great white way") to Charles Thomsen for his role in landing contracts with the St. Marks Cathedral and the Northern Life Tower. Edwards demanded and got their return from an embarassed Thomsen. Ross also had gotten in hot water in December for issuing a letter to employees urging them to boycott the Bon Marche because it had contracted with the private company for its electricity. He was castigated from all sides for this rough patronage politicking.[5]

An inkling that all was not smooth sailing on the Skagit was indicated in late December when City Engineer, Barkhuff, overuled Ross on the matter of powerhouse generators. Ross wanted two with a capacity of 60,000 kilowatts each, while

Barkhuff chose two with only 45,000 kilowatts capacity. Ross was planning for their ultimate use upon completion of Ruby Dam, while Barkhuff looked only to tapping the Diablo reservoir.[6]

In this setting, Edwards conferred with councilmen Erickson and Blaine in mid-February about conducting an "efficiency" probe. Ross was not invited. With Erickson's support, Edwards proposed hiring an "efficiency engineer" to investigate the Lighting Department first, then others later. Edwards and Barkhuff then took off to the Skagit for an inspection. Blaine soon followed—after the city election—with an ordinance proposal authorizing a survey of City departments by Lybrand, Ross Brothers, and Montgomery, an accounting firm. The survey would be conducted under mayoral supervision. Unanimous approval was forthcoming.[7]

Off-setting this unsettling trend came a report from the State auditors, who had been working with Comptroller Harry Carroll on the City Light books. They determined that the Lighting Department had earned a profit of $992,305 in 1928, and that gross revenues had reached $4,872,686. From this largesse, bonds worth $786,000 had been redeemed, along with payments of $1,329,001 in interest.[8]

Upon receiving this news, Erickson assailed Ross for inefficiency and waste, to which Ross countered with charges of councilmanic interference as he pointed to the unnecessary expenses incurred at Cedar Falls which the Municipal League had condemned in a report the previous week. Erickson bore responsibility for the Cedar expenses. Undeterred by these reports, Erickson claimed City Light was losing money and would have to raise rates to make up the deficit—an echo of charges regularly made by the *Times* and PSP&L. Before the month of March was ended, Erickson introduced an ordinance to add a $5 million bond issue to the Skagit burden, contending that it was needed because of alleged cost overuns on the Diablo and extensions on others. It was rejected. On the same March 29 Mayor Edwards's survey team began its work while Erickson provided background effects by charging that the Gorge plant was "overmanned". A busy day it must have been.[9]

Ross-dependable, Councilman Otto Case contended that Erickson's tactics were designed to create a climate for a takeover of City Light by Puget Sound Power and Light . . . but leaders of each power operation already had publicly proclaimed their intent to absorb the other. This was war![10]

It wasn't long before Erickson once again introduced another Hanging Rock dam ordinance. However, even his onetime "echo", Warren Lane, opposed the measure (Lane had been appointed to Council in December to replace Hesketh, who had resigned). He joined with Case and Tindall to defeat it.[11]

In his flailings to undermine Ross's authority, Erickson took an even more foolish step as Utilities Committee chairman that the Mayor, himself, would countermand, though only after critical damage had been done to Erickson's career. On April 15, 1929 the Utilities Committee laid off 75 employees from the Skagit payroll without consulting Ross. These were workers engaged mainly in maintenance of the Skagit railroad which was in a state of dangerous disrepair as a result of heavy use to meet the project deadlines. Barkhuff was inspired to investigate, and Edwards sought "disinterested advice". H.L. O'Neill, business agent and secretary of the electrical workers Local 77, claimed this action was inspired as part of a "wage controversy pending between the union and the Puget Sound Power and Light Company." The *Star* reported a "public outcry" against the cut. To offset objections, Erickson then introduced a bill for $35,000 to employ contract labor to do the work, but it would not re-employ those laid off—this would also remove the workers from Ross's control. Minor accidents occurred. Barkhuff's survey of the railroad bed convinced him that all the workers were indeed needed, and Edwards put him in charge to see that the repairs and renovations were completed before something tragic happened, and to escape any onus for delaying the Skagit work. This fracas paved the way for Erickson's final undoing. He had overreached himself in his apparent obsession to undo Ross.[12]

Just as the furor over the Skagit layoffs was at crescendo, the Municipal League issued a voluminous report of its City Light Committee which fully endorsed Ross's policies. The committee drew upon the recent State audit to verify some of its conclusions, but it also had kept a running account over the years of councilmanic injection into City Light administration. Debate on the report ran all through May, both within the League and in the newspapers. Within the League, the final vote on the report was held up by the opposition of five members to the inclusion of references about the Voters Information League, information that had been brought out in the Federal Trade Commission hearings. VIL references were included in the final report as it passed with only those five opposing votes. The League, as noted above, estimated that the VIL was 89% supported by PSP&L, and not the lower 75% figure. It also concluded that an "energy commission" be appointed to plan future development.[13]

Rumors began circulating about Mayor Edwards's efficiency committee. A preliminary report was presented to the Municipal League in which a reorganization was outlined that would establish a business manager for the Lighting Department to take charge of operations and sales. Other divisions would be established for construction and technical work . . . not calculated to amuse Ross, but, then, he had seen this sort of thing before and had survived.[14]

In the middle of these climactic days, the Municipal League entertained itself by inviting Ross to debate PSP&L's Norwood Brockett. In the course of the debate, defending himself against his being held responsible for the inflated cost of the Gorge plant, Ross reminded the overflow audience that he and City Engineer Dimock had been overruled by Mayor Hanson in accepting a contract offer from Grant, Smith and Company to start the project in March 1918. Had it been accepted, the cost would have been about $10 million, and the project would have been completed earlier. Hanson tried to rebut Ross from his settlement at San Clemente, where former superintendent of public utilities, Thomas Murphine, had joined Hanson. The Board of Public Works minutebooks bore out Ross's defense.[15]

Erickson had not helped himself in retaining chairmanship of the powerful Utilities Committee by his recent actions, and the March election did not favor him—Lane and Campbell had been defeated by Robert Harlin and George Hill. The committee had been dominated by him, in combination with Moore and Blaine. Now a coalition was forming against him, combining Carroll, Hill, Cohen, and Harlin in their support of former committee chairman Philip Tindall. Tindall won out.[16]

With Erickson now diminished, Edwards took the limelight in June, first with his annual message, followed in July with presentation of a budget that promised a $1,000,000 reduction—if only Council would approve. In the annual message he asked for a ten-year master plan for public improvements that also aimed to reduce taxes. He urged a 2% tax on gross receipts of the light and water departments to counter the ritual charges by the private utilities about property being removed from the tax rolls. He wanted a slow-down in local improvements (the second Denny regrading was in progess). He requested an ordinance, that the *Times* claimed, would give him "virtually absolute jurisdiction over departmental budget estimates." He recommended a bureau to attract industry. These were the highlights. The *Star* questioned authorship, while Case objected right off against the 2% tax on the utility revenues. But overall a warm reception greeted the mayor on his message. Not so on his budget.[17]

To pay for street lighting, the Council added $125,000 to the City Light budget. It also added $32,000 by instituting a 44-hour week for all city employees, except police, firemen, and street railway trainmen. Altogether, the Council added over $2,000,000 to the mayor's budget. Erickson, Moore, and Blaine opposed all increases. As Edwards vetoed the pay increases the *Times* mounted a taxpayers' revolt, urging community clubs to organize protests, and proclaiming, "Budget Outrage Leads To Protests Of Civic Groups". More calmly, the *P-I* reminded readers that the budget was still lower than that for 1929 by 1.5 mills (36 instead of 37.5 mills). The Council won out and the revolt came to naught.[18]

Getting back to work in late September 1929, Blaine, as Finance Committee chairman, led the Council to press Edwards for reports from his "efficiency engineers", threatening to cut off the committee's appropriation if none was forthcoming immediately. Edwards had previously promised to have it ready within a few days. The Council was repeatedly stalled until the first of the year, when some reports dribbled in, providing the occasion for a meeting with the mayor. Even the *Times* complained of the delay in getting all of them in for review. Finally, at the end of January they were submitted in full, and greeted uniformly by the press complaint that they contained nothing that had not surfaced previously . . . So, why the aura of "secrecy"?[19]

While the budget contest was running down in fall, Edwards announced the possibility of a two-year moratorium being declared by PSP&L on the annual street railway payments. A meeting in early December between the Council and company representatives ended in stalemate, but approval was finally granted on the 10th. Edwards was reported to be looking forward to developing a refinancing plan. Only the enduring Von Herberg suit seemed to lie in the way.[20]

Edwards, Re-elected, Seeks Government Reorganization: Confronts Ross Machine

As the March 1930 City election approached, there was relatively little tension in the air. The Municipal Street Railway was off the hook for two years now that a moratorium had given it reprieve. The report of Lybrand, Ross, and Montgomery had proved less than sensational, but its suggestion of government reorganization caused some stir. And although there was an undercurrent of uneasiness about Edwards's relationship to City Light nothing climactic had happened—Edwards had even rescued the Skagit railroad from Erickson's scuttling tactics. Vigorous campaigning on the Grange District Power Bill had not yet heated up . . . it would though.

In this setting, Otto Case decided to challenge Edwards anyway by charging the Board of Public Works with "gross inefficiency" in letting "politics" control its purchasing and contracting practices, and for neglecting to reappoint Ross. He predicted that Ross would be fired within six months, even if reappointed now. In the face of these attacks on its decision-making the board, nevertheless, overruled Barkhuff on the generators order, yielding to Ross's preference for larger ones, and ordering two with 83,000 kilowatts capacity. It was no surprise that Edwards won in another landslide, polling 54,488 to Case's 36,059 votes. Two known supporters of the mayor were newly elected to Council: James Scavotto and University of Washington political scientist, Frank J. Laube; they replaced Lou Cohen and veteran William Hickman Moore. Councilman Carroll won re-election. All three were sympathetic to what was known about Edwards's reorganization plans.[1]

The week after the election saw Utilities Committee chairman, Tindall, introduce two ordinances; one, to extend city services, and another to pave the way for acquisition of Puget Sound Power and Light's Seattle plant. Case followed shortly with a resolution to submit to popular vote a charter amendment to give the Lighting Department control over its construction projects. Case's resolution came on the heels of a *Star* article blasting Erickson for having held up construction of the powerhouse and the further delay in ordering the machinery, since the powerhouse had to be designed around the machinery. This charter amendment would become entangled with Edwards's reorganization plans once they were announced. A chain of events would unfold that converted the city into a veritable battleground.[2]

Erickson's cup of woes overflowed on June 1, when 76,000,000 gallons of water leaked from the Cedar Falls dam and followed its original course by way of Christmas Creek to Snoqualmie Falls. So much for Erickson's persistent efforts at sealing the dam by a clay-puddling process that had never proved effective, an effort that Ross had been opposing for more than a decade. Bitter drink.[3]

While the lame-duck councilmen were treading water before their exit, come June, Mayor Edwards became concerned about the water quality in the Cedar reservoir. Then the University's Dean of Forestry, Hugo Winkenwerder, had drawn attention to the logging being done in the watershed by the Pacific States Logging Company because silt and debris were sliding into the lake, affecting its water quality. If not halted, the entire slope would be laid bare, making the problem even more acute. The mayor decided to investigate and agreed with the dean that logging must cease. The United States Forest Service increased the tension by asking for bids on forests above the clearcut. Because of its advantage, only Pacific States was expected to bid—it had been logging the area for thirteen years without having gone through the required competitive bid process. In mid-May, Edwards arranged a meeting among company representatives, the district forest head, and Governor Roland Hartley to see if a compromise could be worked out. One was—it allowed further cutting in the Rex River district watershed and closed the other sections temporarily. This was followed by a court suit filed by the City against the company. The suit would drag on for a year, with the company being generously supplied with information from City files by none other than Councilman Erickson. The *Star* would scorch him for his part in the company's victory when Erickson came up for re-election in March 1931.[4]

Edwards drew attention to watershed problems in his annual message, urging prevention of further logging there. He also asked for the rebuilding of Railroad Avenue to facilitate traffic flow and waterfront access, and reduce the number of switchings required. A planning department was recommended to replace the commission. He revived his plea for a limit on bond issues, along with limits on local improvements, and once again, a 2% tax on gross revenues of the water and lighting departments. No reference was made to reorganization except for a request to act upon the reports of his efficiency experts.[5]

On the following day he vetoed an ordinance of the expired Council authorizing a steamplant for City Light at Spokane Street near the West Waterway. Ross had wanted this, but Edwards opted for an addition to the Lake Union plant instead. Edwards was also, understandably, a bit peeved because Ross had not discussed his request with the mayor before asking the Council to act on it.[6]

The Mayor's July budget message was now awaited with some anxiety because it would necessarily be specific in areas where his annual message was not. It was. He asked that the

Lighting Department be organized into three divisions; one for Business, one for Engineering, a third for Operations. The Inside Construction position would be eliminated in the process, and with it a Ross veteran, William McKeen. Significantly, he would eliminate the department's private telephone line and switchboard that had been installed to prevent leaking of information to the rival company, and to facilitate responses to emergencies and customer requests. Not satisfied with these bits of advice, he then asked for abolition of thirty-three positions in the department, along with another forty-one in other departments. These actions could not have endeared him to the Civil Service League, the organization that was mainly responsible for his 1928 election. Loss of civil service worker support could be crucial, particularly, in confronting Ross. Ross was a favorite among them.[7]

As to the Street Railway, he would place it under an assistant superintendant of public utilities and eliminate two managerial positions as part of the change.[8]

The only opposition expected to these requests related to these two departments.

In the middle of all this, Ross relieved some of the growing tension by shining the spotlight on the Diablo Dam in late August, 1930. The ceremony celebrating its completion was attended by about 400, arriving by automobile, bus, and rail. All that was needed now was the long-delayed powerhouse. Finally, in December, the contract for its completion was let to the John Ward Construction Company of Tacoma, the builder of Tacoma's Cushman Powerhouse. Ward agreed to give Seattle workers hiring preference, to take a Seattle engineer in as a partner, and to move his headquarters to Seattle as part of the bargain. Also signifying a sense of permanence for the Lighting Department was the letting of a contract for construction of a new office building for the department at Third Avenue and Madison Street.[9]

An inkling of things to come was foreshadowed in October, when Ross and the new City Engineer, R.H. Thomson (Barkhuff had been killed in an automobile accident), tilted over jurisdiction on transmission line construction. Then Thomson ordered seven new Fords from non-City Light customers over Ross's objections. Ross believed in the patronage system.[10]

As to the Municipal Street Railway, the mayor's Transit Committee reported in October that unlike the situation when the railway had a virtual transportation monopoly purchased, there was now competition from 90,000 automobiles and 400 taxis. This resulted in loading the cost of operation upon the shoulders of those who could least afford it, the patrons, while using the general fund to make improvements that benefited the competing automobile transportation. "In the nature of the public utility business it is impossible to repay capital costs . . . without direct assistance from outside sources." It continued, claiming that political pressures had obstructed operations on the basis of sound business practices, and reminded the mayor that wages were the highest on the Coast. It concluded that the system, while given reprieve by the recent moratorium, was really "insolvent". For this reason the general fund must be tapped and operation must be by a commission that was free of political influence.[11]

In this setting, A.W. Leonard met with Mayor Edwards about refinancing and reported to Boston that the mayor ". . . is very anxious to beat Tindall and Case to any political credit that may be gained through securing our bonds at a discount and the Mayor is very anxious also to secure some price from us on these bonds but . . . I do not see how we can make any firm price on our bonds . . . I think most City officials are in favor of accepting [the proposal of C.W. McNear and Company of Chicago] with slight modifications [but opposition to it has been developing]." The McNear proposition grew out of the Transit Committee's report and included two elements that led to bitter controversy. One was the installation of a commission independent of Council or citizen control. The other was use of the general fund to pay for deficits. In early January the *Star* criticized Erickson for sponsoring an ordinance that would contract with McNear for a loan of $12 million at 6% interest without going through the required bidding process. It was rejected, but not without the public taking note of Erickson's growing wildness. This matter hung fire while controvery heated up on the Skagit front.[12]

On the heels of the succesful compaign leading to voter approval of the Grange's District Power Bill in November, the newly organized Municipal Utilities Protective League presented a charter amendment proposal to the Council on January 5 that would give the Lighting Department control over its own construction projects. The Council had earlier rejected Councilman Case's offering. The League also began a referendum campaign to guarantee its inclusion on the March 10 ballot, in case the Council rejected its proposal. Friends of City Light pitched in, claiming that the department had lost about one million dollars over the past twelve years because of the separation. (This contention was contrary to Ross's previous statement that his department had been doing most of its own construction with permission of the City Engineer in whose office jurisdiction resided.) The threat of a successful referendum drive caused the Council to approve the charter amendment proposal. It would be on the ballot.[13]

Adding credence to the petitioners' arguments, City Engineer Thomson overruled Ross on construction of the powerhouse, opting for a two-story building instead of the single-story one that Ross wanted. Ross contended that $50,000 would be added to construction costs.[14]

In the background, the State Legislature was in session, and it was feeling vindictive for being overruled by the voters on the Grange Power Bill in November. The 1929 Legislature had forced into being the first use of the initiative procedure when the Senate rejected the bill by a 20 to 17 vote. Spitefully, House Bill 17 would levy a 5% tax on municipal utilities, and, as in the previous legislative session, place them under control of the state commission. It went to the Senate as S.B. 24. Edwards and the Council president, Erickson, travelled to Olympia to argue against the bills, on the ground that the legislation would destroy municipal enterprises.[15]

As the city campaign warmed up, *Star* reporter, Jack Hall, saw the election as "Erickson vs. Ross", and if Erickson wins the election, Edwards would take his cue and fire Ross. On February 6, Erickson launched his campaign by issuing thousands of pamphlets attacking Ross. Hall accused him of going over to the power trust. As the primaries approached, the *Star* urged voters to support former councilman Ralph Nichols, Otto Case, and a newcomer, V.C. Webster . . . and "no" on Erickson. Webster had been active in North End community clubs, a Ross bastion and was unmistakably pro-City Light. On the 24th, only 23,000 voters appeared at the polls. Erickson ran fifth, behind Case, Nichols, Blaine, and Webster. To assure his defeat in the finals, the *Star* ran a series outlining the cost to the city of Erickson's obstructions of Ross's policies.[16]

Meanwhile, the charter amendment proposition was not faring well. Both the *Times* and *P-I* opposed it. The influential Municipal League thought it added doubly to operations costs and opposed it. The spreading depression made voters even more penurious, or at least more hesitant to approve a measure that seemed only to add to the tax burden . . . although convincing evidence was brought forward to show it would reduce costs. Ross felt it was doomed on election eve. Then, out of the night, came Mayor Edwards's announcement that Ross was fired for inefficiency and incompetence.[17]

Intended for release in the morning of election day, so that Ross could not respond, Ross and Frank Fitts of the Municipal Utilities Protective League, learned of it on election eve and notified the *Star*. The *Star* promptly ran a special edition of the spectacular news, declaring "Mayor Edwards, in resorting to this trick . . . classifies himself as a one-night stand politician." Voters turned out in droves, supporting the charter amendment by 27,893 to 25,911 votes . . . a measure that had been tabbed for certain defeat by a 2 to 1 margin. The *P-I* claimed "The City Light Ticket Is Victorious". Nichols, Case, and Webster were elected, while Blaine and Erickson went down to defeat.[18]

Harry Chadwick, of the *Argus*, commented, "It is impossible to tell the public for a quarter of a century that a man is able, efficient, and everything that is desired in a public official and then brand him as inefficient on the eve of an election and get away with it." Now Edwards was faced with a new issue, his very political survival . . . a recall was being quickly mounted by the charter amendment sponsor, the Municipal Utilities Protective League, under the leadership of Frank Fitts and former University of Washington student body president, Marion Zioncheck.[19]

Frank Fitts told William Sparks, a historian of City Light, that Edwards was taunted at an election eve party by a group of business men that Edwards had less political power than Ross, and to show them who was boss, Edwards fired Ross. While this specific charge may or not be true, the tension over political power between Ross and Edwards is indisputable. The mayor's firing was only a question of time and political courage. His timing was so bad that it threw him off the mark. He would wind up the target as the recall drive gathered steam.[20]

Fitts recalled for Sparks that after midnight of election day, League (MUPL) officers and representatives of social organizations and homeowners' clubs of the city met to decide on a strategy for the recall campaign. Fitts reported that "they were so eager to get him (Edwards) that we had promises from those people to get something over 200,000 signatures . . . we needed only 24,000." MUPL president Zioncheck asserted "The recall petitions will present to the people a clear-cut issue between City Light and the Power Trust." One thing on which the petitioners were certain was that Mayor Frank Edwards was a tool of the power trust. The populace had been primed to think so by the well-publicised hearings of the Federal Trade Commission investigations and by collapsing utilities holding companies. Whether the mayor was such a tool has never been proved.[21]

Inasmuch as the recall campaign merged with the unprecedented unemployment, brought about by the spreading Depression, it is instructive to see how the local authorities began dealing with unemployment and relief, particularly as organized protests were mounted. Mayor Edwards proved less than innovative. Before turning to Edwards's measures for dealing with political unrest, it will help our perspective to survey the statewide political scene.

3

Political Parties at the State Level

The Republican Party in Disarray, 1924-1932

Seattle did not exist in a political vacuum. Its governance, its enterprises, its public school system, its utilities, its law courts, were all affected by how the state government responded to the city's problems and pressure groups. To examine the relationships that developed, it is instructive to look at the structure and behavior of the major political parties during the latter 1920s, and at early attempts to deal with the consequences of the Great Depression. From 1932 through 1940 the interconnectedness of state and municipal governments is made clear merely by explaining how measures were developed and applied to deal with relief, mass unemployment, implementation of the public utility districts' power initiative of 1930 (in relation to the City's own electrical utility), and labor relations. We can begin by examining the state's dominant political party before 1932: the Republican Party.

Facing no serious opposition from the Democratic Party in the state, and fearing nothing more by way of desertions to a vanishing Farmer-Labor Party, the state Republican Party could fight bitterly within its own ranks and still control the state's political offices and policies. Roland Hill Hartley, having run for governor twice before 1924, won on his third try, defeating Edward French in the primaries by a slight 1,769 votes. (Ten candidates ran; each of the top six garnered more than 20,000 votes; Hartley won with only about 25% of the total cast.) Hartley won in five urban counties: King, Spokane, Whatcom, Snohomish, and Yakima, though he carried fewer voters in King and Snohomish counties than he had in 1920, when he lost to Louis Hart by about 8,500 votes. The contest had been bitterly fought against the forces surrounding retiring governor Hart. They failed to coalesce on one anti-Hartley candidate, thereby making his election possible. The Hart "machine" included practically all holders of major state elective offices: secretary of state, attorney general, land commissioner, state treasurer, superintendent of public instruction, and state auditor. All of them had been long in office, each with attendant patronage and special constituencies.

At least one office held a potential challenger to the governorship itself, Land Commissioner Clark V. Savidge. Another powerful figure in the Hart camp was lumberman and House Speaker, Mark E. Reed. He was believed by Hartley to also have gubernatorial ambitions, and he had been one among those few lumbermen who conceded to compromise in the 1917 lumber strike. Outside the more purely political arena lurked University of Washington president, Henry Suzzallo, who appeared to have high political ambitions beyond those pursued simply on behalf of the university as he moblized its Alumni Association scattered over the state. (Suzzallo had also been instrumental, as head of the wartime State Defense Council, in settling the 1917 lumber strike by establishing the eight-hour day and introducing more civilized living conditions in the logging camps, over the bitter protests of lumbermen like Hartley.) But Suzzallo represented merely a personal target among the education forces; Hartley aimed at the entire public education system because tax revenues went mostly to it. Though tax reduction and government minimization were his ostensible aims, his clear objective became the elimination of any potential opposition to his highly personalized rule of the party and the state. To do so, he had to find a way of developing an overall strategy that would join his populist attack on "special interests"—the "cement lobby", timber interests, and education forces. He succeeded with apparently satanical glee, though the intra-party brawling did allow an opening for the building of the state's Democratic Party.[1]

A second opening was provided at the national level by enforcement of the prohibition amendment throughout the 1920s, accompanied, after the October 1929 stock market crash, by the spread of economic depression. Senator Wesley L. Jones became the focus of intra-party strife at this political level, ultimately also to the benefit of the Democratic Party.

Governor Hartley would occupy center stage throughout the later 1920s, interrupted occasionally when scandals erupted over prohibition enforcement, embarassing Senator Jones through the abusive and sometimes illegal tactics used by his appointed enforcement agents. Hartley, confident of winning against lame Democratic opposition, had remained non-committal about specific policies he would impose; and he continued to withold information after his election. His inaugural address, though, strongly suggested finally what he had in store. Highway construction should slow to pay-as-you-go pace. Public education was costing too much and should be made more efficient. A state board of tax commissioners should be appointed by the governor. A lay board should replace the State Board of Higher Education and draw up a plan to coordinate higher education in the state. He attacked the proposed child labor amendment to the federal constitution alleging it to be bolshevist inspired—children over age 14 should work to contribute to the family welfare in his view. Then, ten days into the legislative session Hartley called it together, requesting that they end their session on February 14, 1925, that it should appropriate sufficient funds for one year of operation only, and that he would call an extraordinary session in November, when he would then present it with a legislative program based on a "business" survey of state operations that he would conduct during the interim. The legislature acquiesced, but not without a fight on some issues, only one of which became serious, in part for its hint of future infighting. This was Hartley's veto of a "seed wheat bill" (H.B. 40), by which farmers could borrow money from a seed wheat fund. After a mean battle in the House which saw Reed leading the Hartley forces—a Speaker's traditional role—it overrode his veto, but in the Senate he held his forces together sufficient to sustain his veto. The legislature adjourned after passing his tax commission bill.[2]

No systematic survey was conducted, only an impressionistic one by the Governor himself. He consulted with none of the elected state officials, not even the various department heads, ostensibly because they would only act to protect their turf. In the course of conducting it, he issued an order forbidding any state institution to spend any of its 1925 appropriation until he had completed the survey. Then he would grant permission on a case-by-case basis. Meanwhile he alienated in vilifying language those who favored child welfare measures, land reclamation in the arid eastern part of the state, and education forces. Upon assembly of the legislature, November 10, he told them that only minor economies could be made in state government proper; therefore, attention should be focused on those agencies and institutions costing most: "Education leads them all . . . [it] is the biggest business in the State . . . and the most neglected in so far as business thought, business planning and business management are concerned . . . I am contending for more education for less money." This finished, he then singled out Henry Suzzallo for going over his head to lobby throughout the state for more funds for the University of Washington. He insisted that this kind of activity cease, and that each governing board at the state's institutions of higher learning be replaced by a single lay board whose members would be appointed by the governor. Returning to the state's common schools he urged abolition of the elective office of state superintendent, replacing it also with an appointive board with control over the entire public educational system. Then he launched an attack on the "cement crowd" (now referred to as the "highway lobby"), next the land reclamationists, demanding repeal of the state's reclamation laws. Was there any group he had not yet threatened?[3]

Reed saw Hartley aiming for complete domination of the state's political and governmental machinery. Triggering Reed's formation of a coalition of anti-Hartley Representatives was the attempt of E.F. Banker (a Democrat from Okanogan) to transfer reclamation from the governor's control by placing it under the state land commissioner. When the Hartley forces attacked the proposal, Reed countered by defending the Banker Bill as the means for saving the state's reclamation program. Then he turned to education, alleging that Hartley was making it a "football of politics". When Hartley vetoed the Banker Bill after it had passed overwhelmingly in both houses, his veto was sustained by the required votes. This signified governmental stalemate, due to the pro-Hartley minority which normally was large enough to thwart the majority's opposition to Hartley. Reed then gathered together the sixty-two House supporters of the Banker Bill to agree on a legislative program. He chaired the executive committee, which drew up a thirteen-point report opposing all of the Hartley initiatives. A substitute reclamation measure was soon passed with full cooperation of the Hartley forces in the House, falsely conveying a sense of pacification.[4]

The Governor broke water, just as the Senate was preparing to vote on the substitute bill, by attacking, before a joint legislative session, the conduct of state timber sales. Since school funding partly depended upon income from such sales, Hartley could simultaneously hit lumberman Reed, Land Commissioner Savidge, and funding of public education which was not getting full value from sale of state timber lands—fraud and incompetence were charged. Reed contended: "The whole timber controversy was a smoke screen raised by the governor to hide destructive designs on the educational system and reclamation policies of the state." Hartley, nevertheless, renewed his appeal to place the educational system under a single lay governing board, a measure that Hartley's opponents claimed would create a political machine that would destroy the system. Hartley's intemperate address, including personal accusations directed at Reed and Savidge, before the joint session, inflamed even some of his own supporters who voted with the majority in formally censuring the Governor, 60 to 32. The Senate quickly followed the House action with its own censure vote. Capitalizing on this momentum Reed then moved to reconsider the Governor's vetoes of the school bills—they were overridden. After adjournment of this extraordinary session the two forces—pro- and anti-Hartley—headed into the 1926 fall election, each arguing its case around the state.[5]

Hartley's mere threat to circumvent the legislature and create a superboard for education on his own authority kept in line all the various officers, regents, and trustees at the state's institutions of higher learning, except those at the University of Washington. President E.O. Holland of Washington State College and that school's regents were active in the Hartley camp, because Suzzallo and the University Alumni Association consistently out-lobbied WSC in competition for the limited funds available. One WSC regent, Duncan Dunn, had managed Hartley's 1924 campaign, and he was a Representative from Yakima. In this capacity Dunn had led the fight against the university's budget requests. For this, Suzzallo attacked him in Yakima before an Alumni Association meeting in April 1925. Suzzallo's personal arrogance and elitism did not endear him to people outside of Seattle, and he lacked a populist-demagogic style that Hartley applied with such zest and effectiveness. The alumni also were closely identified with the anti-Hartley majority in the legislature. These factors only reinforced the general alliance of the southwestern and eastern counties against the wealthiest, most urbanized county, King County. This all added up to a recipe for conflict.[6]

To get at Suzzallo, Hartley soon saw that he had to change the composition of the UW regents, all of whom were Suzzallo supporters. Two vacancies in March 1926 enabled him to seat two Hartley men, each a lumberman. At the end of the month, he ordered all five institutions not to spend their appropriations on ground that they had been enacted irregularly. Only the UW resisted the order. (At the Cheney Normal School, President Noah Showalter resigned.) Hartley then dismissed two UW regents for "misconduct" on May 5, replacing them with two more Hartley lumbermen. Speaking before an audience of 2,000 at Seattle's largest auditorium on that same day, he claimed there was a fight in this state over "whether the educational institutions of the State of Washington are going to run the state, or if the State of Washington is going to run its educational institutions; whether or not we are going to receive a fair price for state owned timber or permit a small, selfish group to hide behind an educational barrage and enrich themselves at the expense of the school funds . . ." With "concentrated invective" he singled out Reed, the *P-I*, Representative Pliny Allen, Alumni Association secretary Matthew Hill, some others, and Suzzallo. While drawing cheers in mentioning these names and special interests, only Suzzallo's carried audience support. That evening the Republican Constitutional Government League met at the Olympic Hotel to consider whether to mount a recall movement. Instead, they chose a lesser alternative, to send a delegation to meet with the governor. Hartley expressed willingness, but as the time for the meeting neared, three-fourth's of the delegation had dropped out of "Cox's Army" (so named after its leader, E.B. Cox). The "conference" lasted but ten uneventful minutes, while the attorney general upheld the governor's authority in dismissing the two UW regents.[7]

With the UW regents now numbering 4 Hartley men against 3 Suzzallo followers the stage seemed set for Hartley's next move, but in June the regents reappointed Suzzallo for one year. The state Supreme Court then upheld the attorney general's view on the governor's power to remove regents for "misconduct". Although much politicking carried forward throughout the summer, no further action on the UW took place apart from a running dispute over control of Alumni Association files. Then, on October 4, the regents abruptly dismissed Suzzallo, after accepting his budget but two days earlier. Alvah H.B. Jordan, president of the Board of Regents, defended the decision, charging that Suzzallo was a de facto head of an anti-Hartley organization, pointing to supporting evidence found in the Alumni Association records.[8]

A Hartley recall campaign was quickly mounted. Time was

crucial because the recall forces were centered, inevitably, in Seattle, against which there was a traditional sectional opposition. However widely unpopular was Suzzallo's firing, the recall movement would quickly lose steam on so narrow an issue. Only three weeks earlier the Hartley forces had held their own conference at the state Republican Party's convention. There, too, it had become clear that anti-Hartley opposition was Seattle-centered. The *Times* and *P-I* led the widespread newspaper assault on Hartley, but the tone elsewhere was more moderate. Much time was spent framing formal charges since Hartley had just won Supreme Court support. The petition, which was finally accepted by the Secretary of State, vaguely charged the Governor with misfeasance, malfeasance, and violation of his oath of office. With voter enthusiasm waning, and with 97,576 valid signatures required, time was running out fast. The Hartley forces did not sit on their hands, as they countered with an anti-recall campaign, calling into question the weak charges and the expense of a special election that seemed to center on one personality and the university, neither of which was widely popular, certainly not in the rural counties . . . emphatically not in eastern Washington. Reed, himself, stood aside from the recall campaign, having earlier disapproved the recall legislation in principle. Other House leaders of the majority also did not participate. By February the campaign leaders gave up. By then, also, the legislature had been in session since early January, facing a more subdued Hartley. More significant, though, was a growing moderation between the two factions in the House which Albert Gunns attributes to the recognition "that Hartley opponents might well find themselves on the severed end of the party lifeline if they persisted in their vehement assaults on the governor." An underlying motivation also was the need for party unity as it prepared for the 1928 general election. Moving legislative matters along in this direction, Hartley proposed a number of "pork barrel" measures to draw under his wing some wavering members of the majority. By the end of the 1927 session near-harmony prevailed.[9]

Calm, however, was short-lived. Hartley cut the highway budget, particularly in those counties where his support had been weakest. Then he fired the man he had appointed as state Highway Engineer, replacing him with Samuel J. Humes (a future Seattle City Councilman and son of turn-of-the-century mayor Thomas J. Humes). Humes then proceeded to fire four officials after two others had resigned. Battle then broke out in the highway commission, with the governor and Humes running roughshod over the other members, Hartley naming himself chairman and Humes secretary. Two highway commissions emerged from this melee, with the attorney general disallowing Hartley's. Soon the highway lobby entered the fray against the governor—$21,000,000 was at stake. Hartley responded by attacking the "cement crowd". In commission meeting the internal dispute erupted in a near-fight, with Hartley ordering the opposing assistant engineer to be thrown out of the meeting by Humes—done with dispatch! The anti-Hartley newspapers had a field day portraying this political sideshow. Meanwhile the Supreme Court was considering which of the two disputants was the legal body, and citing Humes for contempt for refusing to turn over commission records—for which Humes was threatened with imprisonment. By attrition this farce also dissolved while a parallel dispute in the Capitol Commission ran its longer course. It too provided carnival entertainment, making a mockery of politics and government, while the Governor played to the audience statewide with petty bickering over completion of the new capitol building that emerged as "the battle of the cuspidors". All of these elements merged into the 1928 election.[10]

Anti-Hartley forces in the party once again formed behind Edward French, but this time the number of candidates was kept down so as to prevent Hartley from another victory with only 25% of the vote. While saving Seattle and King County (where about 1/3 of the total vote was located) for the last week, Hartley took his campaign to the rest of the state. Gunns reports: "Onto a truck he loaded various pieces of furniture taken from the new capitol building and, with a large number of 'Hartley candidates', stumped the state demonstrating to the voters in sideshow fashion the extravagance and waste being purveyed upon the people by his opponents. The star attraction of the Hartley museum of capitol curiosities was a sixty-seven pound hammered brass cuspidor . . . Several other articles, such as an ornamental chair from the Senate chamber and a hatrack of disputed price, were also presented to the public view." The sober French, and the strict prohibition enforcer Sheriff Claude Bannick, were no match against such a colorful performer. Hartley won the primary, carrying 23 counties (8 of the 12 counties bordering Puget Sound) to French's 16, and winning King County by about 3,500 votes.[11]

French declared for the Democrat, A. Scott Bullitt; so, too, did many normally Republican newspapers, including the *Times*. Desertions to the once obscure Democratic Party became apparent in the runoff: Bullitt gathered a phenomenal—for a

Democrat—214,334 votes while Hartley won with 281,991. Republican infighting would continue throughout next four years. Hartley gave no recognition to the spreading economic depression, seeing no role for government in dealing with it, feeling that private enterprise alone was up to the task of reviving the economy. By the time the 1932 election rolled around he must have appeared to be so out of touch with reality that it came as no surprise when Lieutenant Governor, John A. Gellatly, handily defeated him in the primary, 119,015 votes to 68,718. However, the Depression had taken its toll on the Republican Party in general, even in the state of Washington. The conservative Democrat from Cheney, Clarence D. Martin, became governor after his two liberal opponents could not agree that one of them should not run if a liberal were to be elected.[12]

State Democratic Party After 1924

While the demise of the Farmer-Labor Party in the state seemed assured after the 1924 election despite its running ahead of the Democratic Party (LaFollette got 30% of the vote, Davis, 10%, Coolidge, 52%), as a national party it had no sustaining apparatus, and LaFollette's Progressive Party could not survive his death in 1925. The Democratic Party had the national organization, although in the state it had only seven members in the legislature. In total votes its ineffectiveness was obvious—in the 1928 gubernatorial primary, its candidates mustered a mere 39,000 votes compared to 250,000 for the Republicans. This was not promising as a base on which to build strength even against a Republican Party that was bitterly divided between pro- and anti-Hartley factions. Also, the Democratic Party had been unable to pick up a solid urban vote. In part, this was due to its domination by old line Democrats who were protective of business interests, cool to organized labor, and hesitant to develop any issues which would distinguish it from the Republican Party. (The Washington State Federation of Labor concentrated upon the Republican primaries to assert whatever political influence it could muster, while ignoring the Democratic Party. State Senator George F. Christensen was the party's national committeeman, and he along with Democratic Party Representative E.F. Banker, supported Hartley—a measure of the party's conservatism.) The Republican Party's gubernatorial candidate, Ben Hill, had run behind Hartley in every city in 1924, though running far ahead of the Farmer-Labor Party candidate, 30% to 10%. To challenge the conservative party leadership, strength had to be built in the urban counties. To do this, an issue or set of issues had to be singled out that would distinguish the party from the Republicans, and new, if not young or ambitious politicos, had to make their presence felt and encouraged to participate. Two such men came to the fore in 1926: A. Scott Bullitt and Stephen F. Chadwick.[1]

Chadwick was a Seattle attorney and son of state Supreme Court Justice Stephen James Chadwick, who, in turn, was the son of Oregon's seventh governor. Descended from the Tylers of Virginia (young Stephen took pride in having a President of the United States among his ancestors), a states' rights stance came naturally to him, along with a distaste for federal bureaucracy and the expenses of governing. He classed himself as a true Jeffersonian. Bullitt also was a Seattle lawyer. He had been active in Kentucky Democratic Party politics before migrating to the city and marrying Dorothy Stimson. Hers was a family of long-standing in the nation's forest industry—migrating from Michigan to the Pacific Coast, one branch setting up the Stimson Mill Company in Ballard in the 1890s, then branching out into real estate after the turn of the century, and acquiring a substantial interest in the Metropolitan Building Company in the process. While Chadwick could ride a good distance on his family's name, Bullitt needed a sponsor in the party. James M. Geraghty of Spokane was the man, the most influential person on the State Central Committee. Bullitt had come to his attention as early as 1924, more recently for having debated prohibitionist leader George F. Cotterill on the unhappy experiences being inflicted upon the nation by the Volstead Act. The party leadership was so indifferent to its fate that they considered not holding a state convention in 1926. Geraghty, having found an issue on which the party could challenge the Republicans, and in Bullitt an oracle, pressed for a convention, and got one. Geraghty aimed to put up Bullitt as the party's senatorial candidate, and he wanted to build support for Governor Alfred E. Smith, come the 1928 presidential election.[2]

Geraghty maneuvered Bullitt to the position of permanent chairman of the state convention. It was unusually well-attended and harmonious, paving the way for the fall election. After it, Bullitt and Cotterill met when the latter returned from Europe, only to learn that the Anti-Saloon League had registered him into the senate race, which he interpreted as a maneuver to assure its man's—Senator Jones's—re-election. Cotterill withdrew, leaving Bullitt free to run. Run he did. So did Chadwick in his race for Congress. Each easily won his primary race by focusing on the failures of prohibition—Chadwick, contending that liquor traffic was a matter for the states to decide individually; Bullitt, urging that state prohibition laws should have preference when stronger than the federal law. In the runoff Bullitt stung Jones on his extremism on prohibition, and he covered the state thoroughly. He and Chadwick had a sound truck cavorting in the streets of Seattle daily during the last weeks of the campaign. A Senate committee hearing, inquiring into the source of Bullitt's campaign funding—which Jones promoted, suspecting a liquor conspiracy—backfired in Bullitt's favor. Chadwick ran an openly "wet" campaign against incumbent John F. Miller. He also benefited from labor support, without courting it—so bad was Miller's anti-labor voting record. Bullitt, though probably not expecting to win, gathered strength in every county, and improved on the showing of the 1920 Democratic candidate by getting 47% of the vote, compared with the previous 18%. It was Jones's toughest race. Chadwick lost by only 1,543 votes. Both had done well in the cities where party strength was most needed.[3]

To keep alive his prospects for major political office Bullitt, with the unreserved backing of Geraghty, quietly decided to run for governor in 1928. Supreme Court Justice Chadwick also wanted to run, confident that he could capture dissident Republicans and independents. National committeeman, Senator George Christensen, however, distrusted Chadwick, speculating that if elected he would give half the administrative appointments to his Republican friends. With Geraghty's backing, Bullitt was named keynote speaker at the state convention. After his address, Bullitt graciously invited Chadwick to speak for his gubernatorial candidacy, having announced it but three days earlier. When Bullitt later declared his own candidacy, he campaigned in the primaries against Hartley while ignoring Chadwick. Young Steve, to keep alive his own prospects, ran his father's campaign, portraying him as an elder statesman who in turn had long supported Alfred Smith as the party's presidential candidate, and would unite wets and drys, Catholic and Protestant behind him. While the press and voters largely ignored the Democratic primary, Bullitt, with endorsement from the State Federation of Labor, handily defeated Chadwick, 20,739 to 13,804. The balance of the 39,000 who voted in the party primary went to two "dry" candidates, the veteran George Cotterill and Grange-backed C.L. McKenzie. Cotterill went on to establish a Democrats for Hoover Committee, while Senator Clarence Dill, who was one of two non-Smith supporters in the state delegation to the party's national convention, refused to support Smith in the runoff. Hartley's primary opponent, E.L. French, swung to Bullitt's side, so bitter was his primary fight with the governor. The *Times*, still rankled at Henry Suzzallo's 1926 firing, also backed Bullitt. But, given the party's general weakness, and the overwhelming vote for Hoover over Smith (335,000 to 156,000), he lost to the governor, 281,991 to 214,334. His vote was an 8% improvement over Ben Hill's 31% in 1924. Robert Cole concludes in his study of the Democratic Party in the 1920s that "Bullitt lost the election by not succeeding in attracting a significant urban bloc of votes, where he had hoped to obtain his greatest following."[4]

The 1930 General Election: Repeal and Public Power

The stage for the state's general election in the fall of 1930 was set by the movement for repeal of prohibition and by the State Grange for its Public Utility District Initiative—Initiative 1.

The Republican Party met in May in Bellingham amid growing distaste for the passage in early 1929 of Senator Wesley L. Jones's bill to make even stricter the penalties for violating prohibition laws. Among their number, even steadfast "drys" were becoming disenchanted with prohibition in face of the mounting violence among the liquor traffic operators and assorted abuses being inflicted by enforcement agents against offenders and the general public. Roy Olmstead, himself, had supplied federal officials with a "bribe list" in October 1929. This issue absorbed the convention's attention, while the Grange initiative was largely ignored due to the traditional opposition of the party to public ownership. With King County party chairman, Ralph Horr, mobilizing the wet votes a repeal plank won, 456 votes to 448. Adding force to this action was the grand jury's indictment—acting on Olmstead's evidence—the following week, of enforcement agents Roy Lyle and William Whitney, wiretapper R.L. Fryant, and C.T. McKinney. They were charged with bribery and cooperation with bootleggers. Justice Department investigations quickly followed, accompanied by sensational newspaper coverage through the summer. In Norman Clark's words: "Seattle was treated to the spectacle of spies spying on the spies", as Al Hubbard of Olmstead trial fame—a notorious slicker who operated freely among both bootleggers and agents—was assigned the job of collecting the evidence. As an insider he must have seemed uniquely qualified.[1]

The Republican Party's adoption of a repeal plank forced

the Democrats to rethink their strategy in time for the state party's June convention. At a February meeting of the State Central Committee, the party had favored Scott Bullitt's proposal to accept the prohibition amendment, but to modify its enforcement policies by limiting federal authority to interstate and international traffic. No resolution was made relative to the Grange initiative. The Republican Party's action, combined with the revelations from the federal investigation, forced a showdown within the party. The dry forces, led by Senator Dill, Wenatchee Congressman Samuel Hill, and George Cotterill, urged bypassing of the prohibition issue. The King County contingent, led by Bullitt, Stephen F. Chadwick, party chairman George E. Ryan, and the Seattle Democratic Women, overwhelmed the drys, adopting a repeal plank by a vote of 182 to 25 at its county convention on June 15. To assuage the dry Grangers, the King County Democrats also had endorsed the Grange power initiative. When the state party convention got underway on June 28, the Grange initiative emerged as the first agenda item.[2]

However, Spokane's Edith Dolan Riley (as vice chairwoman of the State Central Committee and in control by proxy of Spokane County's 46 votes) became a factor. For one, she bitterly opposed Dill for his desertion to Hoover in 1928 on the dry issue. Riley regarded the Grange power district "initiative measure [to be] of the most Communistic and confiscatory nature." For his part, Governor Franklin D. Roosevelt, at Dill's request, had announced in favor of the Grange measure on May 24. Riley, herself, had been in correspondence with the governor about interim party organization and strategy since the 1928 defeat. Being also a stern party regular (unlike Dill), she also reminded fellow Democrats that the Grange was a "Republican organization". Taking Bullitt to one side, she explained her position; Bullitt was persuaded to accept rejection of Initiative 1 in order to save the repeal plank. The party, however, remained deeply divided between rural and urban, wet and dry. The party remained so weak that news of its proceedings were easily pushed from newspaper attention as the trial of Lyle, Whitney, et al preempted space. Instead, political focus was upon the Republican primary in Seattle where dry-Congressman John F. Miller was being challenged by Ralph Horr, leader of the wet Republicans. Horr, with the help of Chadwick's old files (he had nearly beaten Miller in 1926) won, 32,400 to 28,672. He would be a shoo-in come November.[3]

With the Democratic Party so weak that Republican candidates often went unchallenged or offered only token opposition, voter attention shifted to the Grange Public Utility District initiative. To place this issue in perspective, it is well to trace its origins in 1928. After defeat of the Bone Bill in 1924, the Grange embarked on an educational campaign to pull together the rural vote which had then opposed the bill. About 47% of the state's farmers were using electricity, but they were paying exorbitant rates, so they should have been susceptible to Grange arguments, particularly in light of the sensational exposure by the Federal Trade Commission of private utilities' propaganda and political tactics. In 1928, the Grange executive board assigned Homer T. Bone, former Seattle city councilman W.D. Lane, and former Seattle corporation counsel James Bradford the task of drafting a suitable bill for an initiative signature campaign, which, if successful, could be presented to the 1929 state legislature for action. Campaign headquarters were in the Railway Exchange Building in Seattle. According to campaign chairman Fred Chamberlain the office was raided regularly by employees of Puget Sound Power and Light. Petitions were stolen, names were copied from them, the originals were kept, and copies were returned; the latter were useless. Nevertheless, 60,000 signatures were gathered by the end of the year. Although neither legislative branch wanted to act on the initiative, the state constitution required that initiative measures be given first priority—this was the first initiative ever faced by the Legislature. After hearings in January, the Senate rejected the bill by a vote of 20 to 17 with no objections to it being raised from the floor. This defeat meant that a referendum campaign would have to be waged, bringing us to 1930.[4]

When it began, the private power companies, as in the past, reduced rates. Much was made of this, but, when it was discovered that PSP&L was paying taxes in Puyallup on a valuation of only $15,000 while claiming a valuation of $400,000 for rate making, Chamberlain had a field day (a revaluation of $178,000 for tax purposes was quickly done). The FTC revelations also helped. Both the *P-I* and *Star* supported the initiative, while the *Times* opposed it. The night before the election, PSP&L hired four hundred people to distribute its opposition circulars, warning voters that City Light would be absorbed if the measure passed. This scare tactic must have been a key factor affecting Seattle voters; it lost by 16,000 votes in the city. Contrary to the voting pattern on the 1924 Bone Bill, the rural vote tipped the the scale statewide as the initiative won, 152,487 to 130,901. Of the 360,087 who voted (a turnout of 64.3%), only 283,388 voted on the bill (78.7% of those who voted). It was a rural victory, for the fifteen cities with over 10,000 population voted against it by a margin of 7,746 votes; it did receive majorities, however, in Spokane, Yakima, Pierce and Thurston counties. As to Seattle's showing, Elliott Marple attached importance to PSP&L's popularity among Seattle's business community and to the fact that about 18,000 of its Washington stockholders lived in the city.[5]

Heading Into the 1932 Election

Soon after the 1930 election, preparations for the 1932 general election got underway. Rivalry between Bullitt and the young Chadwick ran deeper than Judge Chadwick's loss of the party's gubernatorial nomination to Bullitt in 1928 would suggest. While Chadwick remained fixed on prohibition repeal and avoided concern for the manifest economic ills—including the public power challenge to the collapsing private utilities' holding companies—Bullitt had moved beyond that. Senator Dill, with Governor Roosevelt's support, kept the public power issue alive after passage in 1930 of the Grange District Power Initiative. Bullitt, who had been working closely with Dill before the 1928 election, also came out for public power. They were joined by King County Democratic Party Chairman, Lewis B. Schwellenbach, who announced his candidacy for the governorship at the party's Jefferson Day banquet April 14, 1931. Dill claimed then that power and the economy would be the main issues, softpedaling prohibition. (On the latter even Senator Jones, along with Dill and George Cotterill, had announced satisfaction with a referendum on the issue, should one be held.) Roosevelt wired his congratulations to the King County affliliate for its stand on the power issue. The conservative faction in the party, led by Edith Dolan Riley, in the eastern part of the state, and Chadwick in the western part, tried unsuccessfully to keep the focus on prohibition. They found national party chairman, John J. Raskob, more attractive than Roosevelt because of his conservatism and his political intimacy with Alfred E. Smith. They, as a counterforce, aimed to downplay economic issues, though considering the status of the economy, this proved impossible. As the drift toward Roosevelt (FDR) continued among the King and Pierce County Democrats, Chadwick became more of an embittered outsider. Riley was soon to discover how far the push to FDR had expanded statewide, and to find herself on the party's periphery. The State Central Committee, by December 1931, had decided to make Washington state the first to declare for FDR, encouraged by the visit of his personal emissary, James A. Farley. The state convention in Seattle overrode attempts by the conservatives to prevent a Roosevelt instruction. On February 6, Washington's Democrats were the first to declare for FDR. Bullitt, for his part, was too ill to attend the convention, and he succumbed to cancer on April 10.[1]

Delegates to the national convention went there fully committed to FDR, to abolition of the 2/3 rule, for Senator Thomas Walsh as Permanent Chairman (over Raskob), and for outright repeal of the prohibition amendment (instead of resubmission to the voters). Its 16 votes contributed to victory on all these issues. After the convention, for the first time, the Democratic Party had no trouble arousing enthusiasm, now finding candidates anxious to run for practically all open offices. The sweet smell of victory was in the air, and those who had previously refused to test the wind direction, came forward in droves to run for office, including those who had run on the Farmer-Labor ticket in 1924. One of these was Homer T. Bone who had the temerity to run in 1928 in the Republican primary against one of its stalwarts, Albert Johnson, losing by a mere 2,000 votes . . . on the strength of his public power advocacy. Both the *Times* and *P-I* favored the old line Democrats like Chadwick as against interlopers and what they considered opportunists, like Bone, whose candidacy meant advocacy of economic reform. The *Star* welcomed the new faces. Both filed for the Senate race. Chadwick continued to emphasize prohibition repeal, but he added public works to deal with unemployment, and he promised to protect the District Power Bill from legislative tampering. He, also, tended to ride along on his family's reputation—safe, respectable Democrats. He admitted to Robert Cole that he did little personal campaigning outside the Puget Sound area, the area with the highest concentration of votes, claiming lack of finances. Friends were expected to pick up support elsewhere. It did not happen for him. Bone had been attracted by the progressivism of FDR on the power issue; but he also was digusted with the indifference of the Republican Party to the need for economic reform. This, with the gubernatorial campaign, was the most crucial in the state. Bone, carrying on a statewide campaign, defeated Chadwick 98,094 to 47,817 votes, carrying King County 36,946 to 14,957, Pierce County 19,685 to 2,516, but predictably, more narrowly in Spokane, 8,286 to 6,297. Chadwick then swung his support to Senator Wesley Jones in November, so bitter was he about loss to the "radical" opportunist, Bone.[2]

The gubernatorial race found three strong candidates running for the Democratic Party's nomination. One, William Pemberton, had retired from the state Supreme Court, and had supported LaFollette in 1924. Another liberal was Lewis B. Schwellenbach, a Seattle attorney, an ex-president of the Municipal League, and known to have backing of organized labor. The third candidate was Clarence D. Martin, a wealthy miller and banker from Cheney, who had been chairman of the State Central Committee. He was favored by James Geraghty. The deepening depression focused their attention. Pemberton attacked the business community for its responsibility for the depression; he advocated extensive federal and state measures for relief and public works. Schwellenbach vied with Pemberton in western Washington for the liberal vote, recommending tax reduction and a four-point program in support of cooperative enterprise. (Probably he was inspired by the self-help and cooperative programs being forged by the Unemployed Citizens' League in Seattle. He remained attracted by the "production for use" concept until its defeat as an initiative measure in 1936.) Martin kept out of this competition for the vote of liberals and the disaffected. Martin won with about one-third of the votes, receiving 67,168 votes to Pemberton's 57,124, and Schwellenbach's 55,094 votes—reminiscent of Hartley's 1924 primary victory when he won by receiving a mere 25% of the Republican vote. This would mean a conservative Democratic Party administration if Martin could win the runoff.[3]

Heading into the November general election, the Republicans had finally coalesced against the now-ineffectual incumbent, Governor Roland Hartley, giving the nomination to Lieutenant Governor John A. Gellatly of Wenatchee by 119,015 votes to Hartley's 68,718. Senator Jones had defeated former state Supreme Court Justice, Adam Beeler, who had made Jones's prohibition policies the focus of attack. Jones would face not only continued criticism along this line—for which he had earned considerable notoriety, most recently from the recent 1930 Lyle and Whitney trials—but he could not avoid being associated also with the party's linkage with the Depression, then three dreary years long, and with the infamous power trust about which Washington voters had become uncommonly familiar. Though Jones sometimes broke ranks with Hoover loyalists by voting for measures aimed at unemployment relief and for more equitable taxation, he could not avoid guilt-by-association with Hoover policies. Bone capitalized on these vulnerablilities, drawing to him support from prominent national leaders, but most critically, from FDR himself, who underscored his defense of public power in a speech in Portland in which he declared for hydroelectric power development of the Columbia River. (Hoover had openly opposed such a development.) Bone received the highest percentage of votes (60%) of any candidate (365,939 to Jones's 197,450), winning in every county. Martin, with 352,215 votes to Gellatly's 207,497, matched FDR's 57% of the vote, losing only Chelan and Skamania counties. (Bone ran ahead of Martin by 8,000 votes in his home county, Pierce, and by 5,000 votes in King County.) Democratic Party candidates won all of the Congressional seats as well. Significantly, in Seattle, Marion Zioncheck rode the crest of his popularity from his leading role in the recall of Mayor Edwards by defeating John F. Miller who had made a comeback in the Republican primaries when he thwarted Ralph Horr's re-election bid. (Horr had unseated Miller in 1930 on the strength of the repeal issue.) This election also witnessed the start of long-term congressional careers for Mon C. Wallgren and Knute Hill, shorter ones for Martin Smith and Wesley Lloyd. Mainstay Sam Hill ran without Republican opposition in the fifth district. Democrats also won a majority of seats in the state legislature—a party "first".[4]

Part II

The Economy, 1921-1940

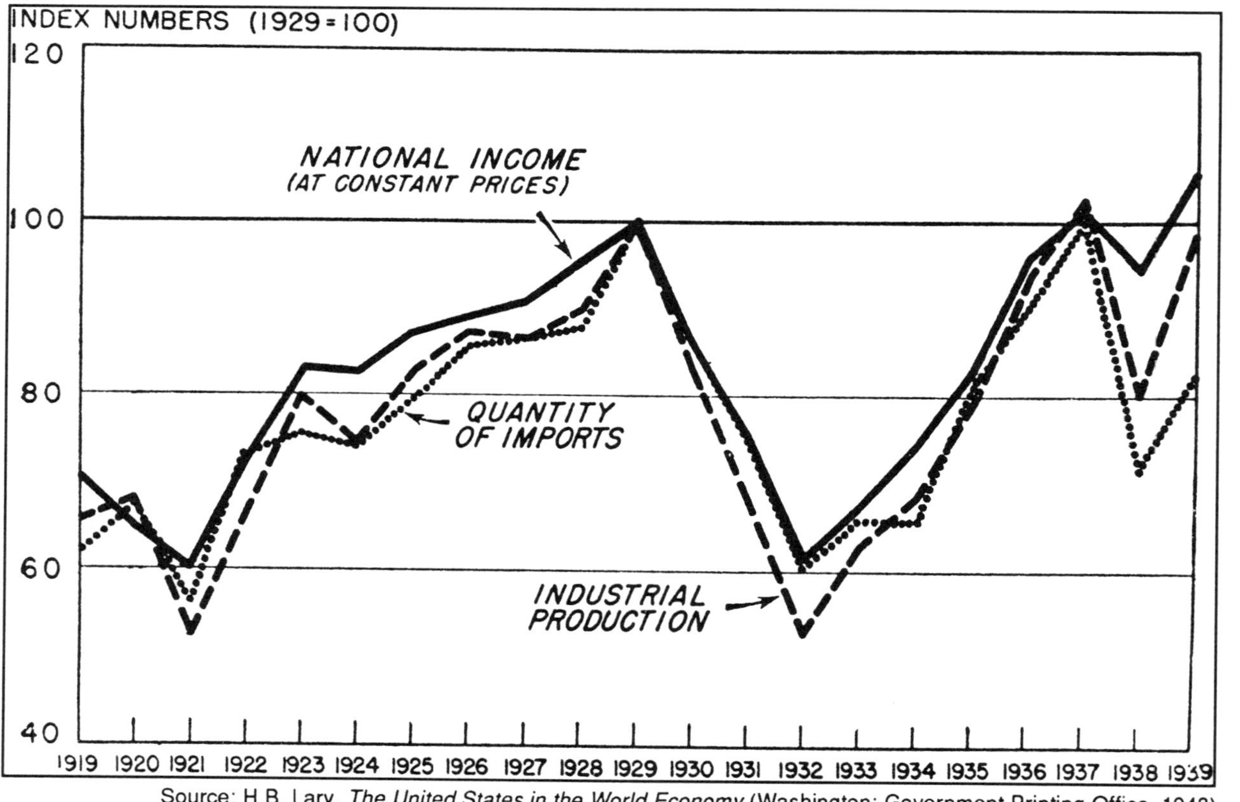

Source: H.B. Lary, *The United States in the World Economy* (Washington: Government Printing Office, 1943)

Indices of quantity of United States imports, national income at constant prices, and physical volume of industrial production, 1919-1939.

4

Waterborne Commerce of the City in the 1920s

By 1916 Seattle had emerged as the leading port on the Pacific Coast. This had been the result, primarily, of the creation of an independent municipal corporation—the Port of Seattle—to own and operate publicly-owned port facilities as a supplement to those of the private companies. Private dock owners, however, treated the Port as competitor because the latter goaded them to lower their rates—as had City Light in its field. The Port served in effect as a performance yardstick. Altogether, there were forty-seven piers and wharves, of which eight belonged to the Port of Seattle. The remainder were owned and operated by the railroads, grain elevators and flouring mills, fish companies, steamship lines; and there were oil company docks, as well as an old coal pier, plus some for general cargo handling. The most modern of these facilities were those recently built by the Port when it became operational soon after 1912. It had the equipment for handling special commodities that no other port on the coast had, explaining Seattle's coastal supremacy. Because of these superior facilities the private owners benefited by catching spinoff business that might not otherwise have come to Seattle. *Railway and Marine News*, speaking for its backers, had consistently railed against expenditures of the Port Commissioners for building such operations for which there was no apparent demand, causing an unwarranted tax burden that discour-

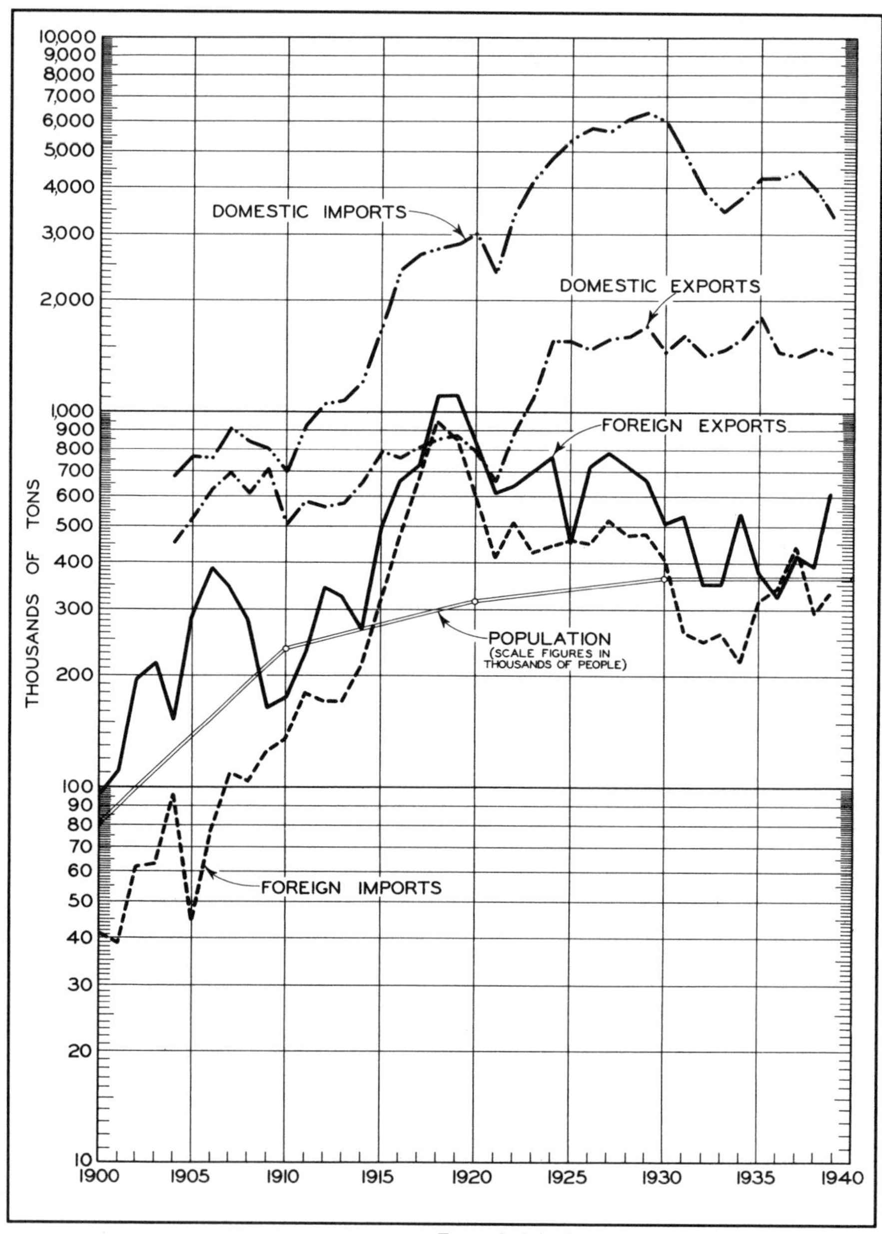

From Calvin Schmid, *Social Trends in Seattle*

Foreign and Domestic Waterborne Commerce, Seattle, 1900 to 1939

aged new investment in the city's economy. Port Commissioner George F. Cotterill contradicted this charge, reminding the public that the Port was self-supporting, had not drawn upon taxes, that its policy was to supplement private facilities, to plan and build ahead of demand, developing new lines of commerce which the reopening of the Panama Canal was expected to stimulate. Symptomatic of opposition to the Port's expansion was the controversy in 1923 over acquisition of waterfront land from the United States Shipping Board that Skinner and Eddy Shipyards' plant number 2 had occupied during its wartime shipbuilding days. Not only the *Times* and Chamber of Commerce, but also the Municipal League opposed the proposition even though the Port could buy it for but a fraction of its value ($600,000 instead of an estimated $2 million). They wanted the land sold to private parties with no strings attached to its future development. (The Port did acquire it after winning voter approval in the May 1923 city election.)[1]

By 1929 there were 142 steamship lines operating out of Seattle. Ninety-eight of these lines ran deep-sea routes; 45 routes were plied by the Mosquito Fleet's 26 steamship companies. One hundred and twenty-two vessels arrived and departed each day. Except for the Mosquito Fleet, during the 1920s the typical size of the ships had increased from about 3,500 tons to 9,000 and 10,000 tons, and in length from about 300-400 feet to more than 500 feet; their capacity correspondingly expanded. In their 1930 annual report the commissioners contended that improvements were required to keep up with demand—that year sheds were built on the huge Pier 40 at Smith's Cove to handle the overflow of canned salmon destined for rail shipment. A sign of the port's relative deterioration (as other ports began following Seattle's example) was the perennial resistance of the railroads to compressing their trackage from eight to four sets of tracks. Their resistance in turn impeded the construction of a seawall that would guarantee a fifty-foot depth at high tide. The railroads also resisted establishment of uniform wharfage rates, preferring to wage a rate war that would force the public docks to operate at a loss, then absorbing them, leaving the railroads free to extort monopoly rates. Not until 1929 did the Port Authorities Association succeed in bringing about uniform wharfage and dockage rates on the Pacific Coast.[2]

Foreign steamship lines numbering thirty-four, operated out of the port in 1922; thirteen operated between the Atlantic and Pacific coasts; eight more ran coastwise service; and another six specialized in the Alaskan trade. Thirty-three Puget Sound and nearby ports were served by the Mosquito Fleet operating out of Seattle; this trade ranged from between 10% and 15% of the total commodity value of port shipping from 1921 to 1932. This fleet had been responsible for the port's early development, leading to Seattle's commercial supremacy on Puget Sound despite the absence of an industrial base that is usually expected to underpin such commerce.[3]

About the time a basic pattern of waterborne commerce had been set for the port as a whole it was altered drastically by the war. Only after the war did the Panama Canal become truly operational for the port, contributing decisively to the future pattern of shipping. Direct trade with the Gulf ports, the Atlantic Seaboard, Great Britain, and Europe, and the east coast of South America opened up. A large proportion of imports from these trading areas entered the city's Alaskan trade. Alaska salmon, in turn, became the main staple of Seattle's exports to the Gulf and Atlantic ports and to Great Britain. Flour and wheat shipments to the latter and to the continent resumed after the war following a promising start before the war. By 1924 apples became a major export to the northern European countries as it had earlier become a staple of trade with the mother country.[4]

The mainstays of the prewar trade were with Alaska, California, the Orient (mainly Japan), Puget Sound ports, and British Columbia. Except for the latter, trade steadily expanded during the 1920s.

The "Oriental" trade with Japan and China exhibited uninterrupted growth: imports were worth $117 million in 1916, $188 million in 1917, and $268 million in 1919. Exports in 1916 totaled $40 million, $123 million in 1917, and $168 million in 1919. Raw silk and silk goods constituted the bulk of the imports; the raw silk was transhipped by rail directly to Hoboken for manufacture. Other major commodities were tea, camphor, porcelain, notions and toys, vegetable oils from Japan, and wood oil, wool, furs and skins from China (whose largest export to Seattle also was raw silk). Most of these commodities were transhipped by rail, fewer by water, to the East. By 1919 the Oriental trade represented 35% of the total value of waterborne commerce; it was 40% of the total in 1920, 43% in 1924, 39% in 1926, dropping to 34% in 1929, and sinking to a mere 16% by 1932 at the bottom of the Great Depression. When this trade became differentiated in 1922 that with Japan showed it peaking at $241 million in 1925, having expanded from a value in 1922 of $180 million. It gradually tapered down to $116 million in 1930, then dropping precipitously to $57 million in 1931, not stopping on its downward course until 1934. That with China rose steadily from $28.5 million in 1922 to $31.8 million in 1928, then falling to $18 million in 1931. Seattle's dominance of the raw silk trade—two times San Francisco's imports of silk, and three times that of New York's in 1927—revived the notion that the city should begin manufacturing finished silk products. Again, to no avail.[5]

A different perspective is provided of the Oriental trade in relation to the total foreign trade. The proportions are: 60% in 1917, 90% in 1920, about 94% from 1922 to 1926; 1929 showed 80% for Japan, and 14% for China. A slight drop in relation to other foreign trading partners was registered in 1932, showing Japan's proportion to be about 50% and China's about 38%. It was in relation to the total of waterborne commerce that its decline is significant—the city needed the domestic market to compensate for the decline of its foreign trade, which had fallen from a 1929 value of $322,252,612 to a value of only $99,409,150 by 1932.[6]

A general overview of the waterborne commerce in the 1920s shows: Imports from the Orient in 1920 accounted for 90% of the total value of foreign imports ($214 million of a total $241 million). Raw silk and silk goods represented 60% of this total, followed by peanut oil ($10.7 million), soy oil ($9 million), peanuts ($6 million), matting ($5.6 million), and braid ($3.3 million). Exports to the Orient in 1920 amounted to $107,745,228, of which raw cotton accounted for almost 40% ($42,230,913), heavy iron and steel for $17.6 million, gold coin for $15.6 million, and copper ingots another $6.6 million. By 1929 imports from Japan were valued at $188,844,474, and from China at $33,812,035, totaling only slightly more than the 1920 figure. In the absence of a commodity breakdown for 1920, that for 1929 is used and will indicate what was specific for each nation.[7] (See TABLE 1.)

TABLE 1

Major imports from Japan, 1929 (Total: $188.8 million)

raw silk	$159,959,596
porcelain	6,379,737
notions & toys	2,729,362
tea	1,620,380
carpets & rugs	1,493,457
matting	1,360,522
glass mfrs	1,267,333

Major imports from China, 1929 (Total: $33.8 million)

raw silk	$14,004,651
wood oil	4,264,585
furs & skins	3,237,155
wool	3,035,898
dried eggs	1,588,702
bristles	965,678

Major exports to Japan, 1929 (Total: $17.75 million)	
autos & trucks (numbering 4,088)	$3,264,993
wheat	2,614,860
cotton, raw	2,336,517
machinery	2,022,650
milk, canned	1,075,744
auto parts & tires	1,318,283
hides	822,342
lumber	600,257

Major exports to China, 1929 (Total: $12.5 million)	
flour	$2,830,661
autos & trucks (numbering 1,762)	1,569,302
ginseng	1,371,150
machinery	1,283,244
milk, canned	845,413
wheat	353,075

Temporarily, the World War disrupted the shipping of rubber and tin from the East Indies and Straits Settlements, all to the advantage of Seattle. In 1917 imports from this area amounted to $45 million of which rubber accounted for $35 million and tin for $7 million. By 1920 trade channels were restored to normal, causing a drop in imports to $7 million, then to $6,500 in 1921!

Trade with India boomed during the war, and a substantial trade continued afterward, based mainly on the importation of jute and jute bags. Although imports from India jumped from $3,698,922 in 1916 to over $12 million in 1917, when normal trading relations were re-established by 1920 the value had dropped to $4,587,197, practically to the 1916 level. Imports declined to between $2.5 and $3 million through the 1920s, finally dropping to $1,550,524 in 1930, and to $488,205 in 1932. Exports to India were modest throughout the 1920s, dropping from just $350,537 only to fall to a slight $46,994 in 1932.

As a percentage of the total value of exports and imports Puget Sound commerce climbed steadily from 5.5% of the total in 1919 to 8.1% in 1920, stabilizing at about 10.5% until 1930 when it crept to 13.3%, then to 15.7% in 1931, and dropping only slightly to 14.3% in 1932, reasserting its relative importance in the port's overall commerce.

Imports from Alaska were mainly of salmon, gold bullion, herring, and furs. Of the total value of Alaska imports in 1922 salmon (canned, cured, and fresh) accounted for $15,707,861, gold for $5,230,623; herring for $2,017,806; and furs $1,716,457. Of this salmon $1,742,706 worth was shipped to Gulf ports, and $5,256,535 of it was exported to the Atlantic Seaboard. (A large but undetermined proportion was shipped by rail. Before the canal came into use, salmon had been shipped by rail to New

York, but it amounted to barely one million dollars in 1916, nothing in 1917 because of wartime railroad restrictions.) Exports to Alaska were mainly tin cans (some of which were manufactured in Seattle from tin slabs imported from the East coast), hardware, machinery, meat, and the whole range of household and personal items totalling $22,152,916 in 1922. By 1929 imports from Alaska amounted to $44,384,069, with salmon accounting for 60% of the total value.

Imports from California expanded as consumption of gasoline, fuel and lubricating oils steadily increased: gasoline as automobiles and trucks displaced horses; and fuel oil as it displaced coal and wood. In 1920 petroleum imports accounted for about $33 million or 56% of the total; sugar ran second (about $5 million throughout the 1920s). Indeed, petroleum imports from California represented 6.5% of the total value of imports in 1920. By 1929 petroleum products totalled about $53 million or about 42% of the total $122,725,779 worth of commodities imported from the Golden State, representing 10% of the total value of all imports. Of the commodities that had become prominent were automobiles and trucks, tires and parts ($7,412,935 all told), canned goods ($3,577,476), cigars and tobacco ($3,910,425), coffee ($4,202,418), and electric and radio manufactures ($6,208,600), and sugar ($4,842,720).

Exports to California in 1920 amounted to $11,000,377, of which flour accounted for about $3 million, and paper for about $1,893,000. By 1929 the total value of exports to California had reached $19,355,390 of which heavy paper accounted for almost $4 million, flour for $2,160,964, canned goods for about $2 million, and lumber for $1,025,613 of the total. A commodity analysis shows some sharp changes: an abrupt decline in exports of canned milk, and sharp increases in exports of heavy paper, seafood, and furniture; salmon and lumber products remained substantial.

Trade with British Columbia had been both general and dependable before the war boomed it out of proportion. In 1913 imports from Seattle's northern neighbor amounted to $2,562,298 (compared with a total of $9.7 million from Alaska). Exports from Seattle totalled $8,378,507 (compared to almost $18 million to Alaska); "merchandise" accounted for slightly more than $5 million of the total. British Columbia exported $12.8 million of commodities to Seattle in 1916 and $22.3 million in 1917, including more than $13 million in gold coin and bullion, scraped together to pay its mounting debts. Returning to a more normal trading pattern in 1920, B.C. exported $12,646,918 worth of commodities to Seattle, including $4.7 million worth of paper and $1,660,832 of coal. Seattle exported commodities to B.C. worth $11,103,851. This was followed in 1921 by slightly more than $8 million in each direction, but coal imports increased to over $2 million as a result of the closure of most of Washington's coal mines due to a lockout/strike that would last for about two years. 1922 saw a drop in Seattle's exports to B.C. to about $6.5 million; imports to $7.2 million. By 1929 exports to B.C. climbed back to almost $9 million while imports fell to $4,956,213. By 1932 imports from B.C. had sunk to $2,968,160 and exports amounted to only $2,581,882 . . . but trade had generally been severely cut as the world hit the economic bottom that year.

Trade with the Atlantic Seaboard began for all practical purposes in 1919 with exports totalling $13,568,152 and imports a modest $150,000. By 1920 these imports climbed to $3.6 million as long-term trading relations were being established; exports fell to $6.8 million. 1921 saw a gradual expansion of both exports and imports to about $10 million each way. By 1924 this trade zoomed: imports ran to $34.5 million and exports to an astounding $46.3 million. This trend continued, with 1926 registering imports valued at $66 million and exports at $63.7 million. The latter figure included $19 million worth of raw silk, $9 million worth of salmon, and $4 million worth of copper. By 1929 exports to the Atlantic Seaboard reached $83.5 million. (See TABLE 2.) By 1932 exports to the East Coast dwindled to $26.4 million; imports to $22.2 million.

TABLE 2

Major Exports to Atlantic Seaboard, 1929 (Total: $83.5 million)		Major Imports from Atlantic Seaboard, 1929 (Total: $60.5 million)	
raw silk	$28,512,222	clothing & dry goods	$11,977,584
salmon	8,275,553	electric & radio mfrs	3,865,720
copper	4,367,961	tin plate	3,337,118
wool	4,017,785	hardware, heavy (mainly pipe fittings & steel items)	9,597,100
porcelain & glassware	3,770,757		
canned goods	3,564,240	hardware & tools	2,873,234
notions & toys	3,019,641	machinery	1,992,793
lumber	2,317,992	oils & grease	1,842,784
zinc	2,190,307	canned goods	1,806,272
furs & skins	2,004,767	drugs & chemicals	1,552,000
		glass & crockery	1,473,752
		soap & powder	1,376,201
		linoleum	1,042,760

Trade with the Gulf of Mexico ports started up in 1921, with imports worth $634,161 and exports valued at $1,076,375 . . . a promising beginning. In 1922 imports from the Gulf jumped to over $3 million, representing a general trade; exports that year ran to $2,471,393 with canned salmon accounting for $1,742,706 of the total, and flour for $300,263, while lumber amounted to $240,809. By 1926 exports to the area totalled $4,275,073, and imports were valued at $6,975,892. 1929 showed how substantial this trade had become: imports had grown to $7,591,968 of which heavy hardware represented $2,643,786 (pipe fittings, $1.86 million), lard compounds and oils $933,532, canned goods almost $1 million, and hardware and tools another $522,722. Exports in 1929, however, fell to $4,216,553 with salmon valued at $2,107,774, canned goods at $552,418, and porcelain and glass at $518,643. Surprisingly, exports in 1932 held up comparatively well, amounting to $3,284,810 of which salmon represented $1,895,112 and canned goods another $458,708. Imports fell from the 1929 high to $4.7 million with corn representing $967,453 of the total and canned goods $951,895; heavy hardware dropped to a bare $350,000, and lard compounds to a modest $280,000 . . . highly volatile.

Use of the Panama Canal also opened up trade with the European continent, and facilitated that with Great Britain. With the latter there was already a substantial trade: exports in 1913 were valued at $2,269,262 and imports at $770,916. When trade resumed in 1919 exports rebounded to a value of $4,729,744 while imports from the mother country were a mere $78,812. Imports expanded to $464,611 in 1920 as exports nearly doubled to $7,772,669. 1922 saw imports almost reach one million dollars with a broad commodity base; but exports dropped to $5,957,439 of which salmon represented a value of $2,095,327, canned fruit and vegetables $910,910, flour $830,424, wheat $622,952, apples $421,714, and lumber $388,701. Apples were finally finding a foreign market, but not yet on the continent. By 1924 a substantial improvement was made in Great Britain's exports to Seattle, shipping $2,465,259 worth of commodities, while receiving Seattle's exports valued at $8,556,989. Imports dropped below the one million figure in 1926, while exports remained stable. By 1929 imports climbed to slightly over the one million dollar mark as exports reached $7,966,924. The latter included $2,555,428 worth of salmon, $2,022,924 of apples, $1,127,574 of wheat, $741,042 of canned fruit, and $591,282 of lumber. The dismal year of 1932 saw imports fall to $156,495 and exports to $3,876,396; but the big staples of the 1920s kept their proportional relationships. (See TABLES 3 and 4.)

TABLE 3
Total Imports & Exports by Major Areas

	Orient %	Local %	Alaska %	Calif. %	Atlantic %	Total Amount $
1920	41	8.0	10.0	12.0	1.7	$588,023,197
1922	48	10.0	10.0	13.0	9.5	498,833,131
1924	43	11.0	9.0	15.0	12.0	664,567,049
1926	39	9.7	10.0	14.0	17.0	754,389,962
1929	34	10.9	9.5	18.4	19.0	771,174,270
1932	16	14.3	15.0	27.0	15.4	308,513,814

TABLE 4
Oriental Trade in Relation to Total Foreign Trade

	Exports to Orient	% of All Exports	Imports from Orient	% of All Imports	Foreign Trade All Countries
1904	$6,543,536	74.0	$1,318,868	22.6	$14,628,354
1909	6,774,798	53.5	21,274,893	87.0	36,809,365
1913	8,172,533	41.0	21,712,894	84.0	45,815,783
1914	6,016,054	41.0	32,018,101	80.0	56,676,716
1917	122,812,254	80.0	187,648,717	60.0	420,950,404
1920	107,745,288	80.0	213,904,806	88.0	376,425,088
1922	21,005,919*	47.0	180,100,724	81.0	266,420,533
	7,003,607**	16.0	28,567,204	13.0	
1924	25,137,857*	45.0	218,204,904	82.0	323,341,836
	14,172,156**	25.0	30,626,424	11.0	
1926	26,950,877*	42.0	220,658,819	82.0	333,264,518
	12,513,507**	20.0	32,082,084	12.0	
1929	17,762,699*	30.0	188,844,474	80.0	322,253,612
	12,547,410**	21.0	33,812,035	14.0	
1932	2,918,547*	17.0	24,084,948	49.8	99,409,150
	2,754,614**	16.0	18,710,935	38.0	

*Japan **China The Port Warden began differentiating the two trading partners in 1929, but the 1932 *Yearbook* of the Port of Seattle differentiates them from 1922 forward.

Active trading with the European continent began in 1920. It was most active with the northern nations: Germany (serving central Europe), Belgium, Holland, Norway, and Sweden. Flour and wheat were the most pressing needs in the war's aftermath: more than 50% of Germany's $182,986 of imports in 1920 were so constituted; of Belgium's $231,165 worth of imports from Seattle $156,000 was wheat; Norway's imports which had never been valued at over $500,000, imported $511,000 worth of flour;

Sweden's $87,110 was almost entirely in flour; and Portugal, which never figured to be a major trading partner, imported $590,000 worth of wheat. Imports from the continent were still slight, although creosote oil from Holland was a big item ($255,000 of its total of $452,070); it would continue to be a major import.

Exports to Germany in 1921 amounted to $898,441 of which flour was about 50% of the total value. Window glass constituted more than 75% of the $519,164 worth of imports from Belgium. Holland's $311,833 worth of exports to the city was chiefly creosote oil. Imports from other continental nations fell under $100,000 in 1921. Belgium's $195,090 worth of imports were mainly in the form of wheat, lard, and salmon. Germany's $898,440 worth of imports were similarly distributed (flour, $436,000; lard, $125,000; salmon, $75,000). And, although Holland's importation of $4,000 worth of apples was small it did represent the first apple imports of the continental nations.

1922 saw a strengthening and broadening of trade. Belgium exported goods worth $450,396 of which glass represented almost the total amount; it received, in turn, commodities worth $382,145, with wheat accounting for about 65% of the total value. (Plate and window glass from the Low Countries, Germany, and Czechoslovakia, through Hamburg, remained a major import through the 1920s.) Germany imported about the same value of general commodities as in 1921, and it exported $763,439 worth of goods of which liquors (!) were the major item ($333,100), followed by about $134,000 worth of glass. In 1924 apples assumed their initial importance, becoming the most valuable export to Germany ($198 million, compared to $182 million worth of wheat, in a total value of $780 million). Holland imported $113 million worth of apples, and $68 million worth of salmon. France's major import from Seattle was in the form of zinc slabs, usually running over 50% of the total value of its imports (totalling $655,000 in 1924, $491,000 in 1926, and $306,000 in 1929, of which the value of zinc slabs dropped to only $109,000 as apples climbed to almost $70,000).

Although Sweden began savoring $10,000 worth of Washington apples in 1924 (compared to wheat valued at $46,000 of a total $81,674), by 1926 they were becoming more popular as witness their $69,000 value, and its doubling to $136,080 in 1929. That year $91,000 worth of cured salmon were also imported. Imports from Sweden were mainly in the form of heavy hardware, steel, and machinery; but the value only substantially exceeded more than $100,000 in 1929 when it reached $189,623.

Importations from Norway consistently were more than those from its Swedish neighbor, growing to a value of $455,760 in 1924, dropping to $330,636 as cement imports fell off, then climbing to $495,192 by 1929. Canned fish products were the major commodities imported from Norway, while cured salmon, apples, and flour were the major exports to that nation—consistently less than $100,000 total value annually.

A highly varied trade was carried on with the Pacific Rim countries of South America, Australia (New Zealand was included in the composite total beginning in 1926), the Philippines, and "Siberia". As to South America, not until 1930 did the Port Warden distinguish the nations making up this composite; and to include these in a "Pacific Rim" grouping is misleading for the breakdown of 1930 imports lists only Argentina, Brazil, Chile, Columbia, Ecuador, and Uruguay. In that year imports totalled $1,152,045 of which coffee from Brazil and Columbia amounted to 60% of the total. Argentina exported about $250,000 of this amount, mainly in the form of beef products and grains. However, coffee was the major import, sometimes over 90% of the total. In 1917 the total value had been $673,707 and about the same in 1919; for 1920 $303,081; for 1922 $762,389; and $1,522,275 in 1929. Exports to the southern hemisphere showed uneven, but gradual growth from a total of $614,911 in 1917; $637,240 in 1919; $1,496,938 in 1920; $743,602 in 1922; $915,060 in 1924; almost $2 million in 1926; and a high of $2,263,812 in 1929. In the latter year apples constituted about 24% ($928,351) of the total, lumber $341,825, flour $295,667, and pears $192,848. Using the 1930 breakdown as an indicator we find Argentina and Brazil taking almost all the apples and pears; Chile most of the lumber; Ecuador most of the flour; Peru bought six airplanes worth $80,000 and lumber valued at $27,537. Small shipments of flour and lumber to Bolivia, of salmon to Guiana, of lumber to Uruguay, of salmon to Venezuela and Trinidad rounded out the export picture.

A modest trade with Australia existed before the war. In 1914 exports amounted to $102,978 (lumber 95%) and imports were valued at $404,911 (butter and meat mainly). The chief exports would consistently be lumber and salmon after the war, while imports varied highly in type from year to year. By 1917 over $200,000 in value passed in both directions; by 1919 imports from that continent rose from $541,354 and exports $258,606 showing a steady growth. Fluctuations in the 1920s altered this pattern. 1921 witnessed a once-ever importation of wool that raised the value of imports to over $2 million, while exports fell from the 1920 figure of $588,567 to $247,134 as the depression of 1920-1921 set in. Exports picked up in 1922, along with the general economy, climbing to $555,216 of which salmon represented $242,633 and lumber $168,522. Imports were worth $222,178 of which rabbit hides were 50% of the total. 1924 saw a deep fall of imports: $21,717, while exports rose to an all-time high of $993,142 and passing the one million mark in 1926, including lumber worth $632,000 and salmon $602,000; imports were valued at only $71,789. Imports in 1929 still had not reached $90,000, while exports remained high at $975,588 of which salmon amounted to $468,636 and lumber $287,237. At the 1932 bottom only $109,091 worth of commodities were exported to Australia and New Zealand, while commodities worth $82,025 were imported.

Although the Philippines were a domestic trading partner until granted Commonwealth status in 1935, these islands are part of the Pacific Rim commerce. Exports to the islands initially bore mainly the character of provisioning the occupying forces, and they did not reach a value of over one million dollars until 1909 ($1,425,589 or about 11% of the total value of the city's exports). Imports were valued at $289,280, but these would climb to over one million dollars by 1913, and exports to $1,761,783. Hemp was the major import from the islands, amounting in 1917 to $4,842,512 of the total value of imports totalling $5,476,451. Exports in 1917 rose to $3,238,704. By 1920 the trading relationship had shown steady growth in both directions: exports worth $6,770,505, of which flour, hardware, and salmon represented about 50% of the total value; and imports $7,439,213. Exports in 1922 showed some recovery from the postwar depression, rising to $3,644,570, of which flour represented $1,193,459 and salmon $557,638 in value, followed by cotton thread ($290,000) and autos ($207,000). Trade during the rest of the 1920s continued to improve, leveling off by 1924, with imports from the islands rising to a high of $5 million in 1926, and exports reaching a high in 1928 of $8,694,253. By then cigars and sugar had become major imports (in 1929: hemp worth $1,072,549, cigars $1,031,318, and sugar $319,037). Exports in 1929 also had changed in emphasis with flour, autos and trucks maintaining leadership, followed by lumber, machinery, and canned milk, each valued at over $1 million. Even 1932 saw exports maintained at a relative high of almost $3 million, and imports at $2.5 million, of which sugar now represented about 50%, cigars falling second in line ($401,336) and hemp to a mere $66,823. Flour remained the leading export ($662,776), followed by canned milk ($555,459), groceries and provisions ($314,840), and machinery (at $304,097). Autos and trucks, parts and tires steadily increased in export value throughout the decade, but the number of units were only 1,090 in 1929 (305 in 1922); in value they ranked second in 1929 at $1,271,935. Just what proportion of these exports went to the armed forces is indeterminate, at least from the Port Warden statistics.

An occasional trade with Siberia existed before the war. In 1905 $558,351 worth of goods were shipped there; this value fell in 1909 to $105,635, and to $46,778 in 1913. It was a one-way trade. The war abruptly interrupted this pattern. In 1916 $711,880 worth of goods (mainly furs and skins) were imported, but $44,667,886 of commodities were exported to support the Russians' war effort. This fell to $7,377,245 in 1917 as a result of the Revolution, but to assist the counter-revolutionary forces, commodities of $23,273,740 value were shipped there in 1919, followed in 1920 with another $1,172,819 worth of commodities. Goods worth $655,673 were imported from there in 1920; and while only $40,375 of imports were brought in in 1922, exports amounted to $713,880, with hardware and tools first ($165,800), followed by machinery ($126,016), and dry goods, clothing, boots and shoes, and a range of domestic items. After a lull in 1924 and 1925 the two-way trade resumed in 1926 in rough balance: exports worth $320,329 and imports $477,711. 1929 saw only $20,000 worth of goods imported from that remote outpost, but $1,086,916 worth were exported there, of which machinery and equipment represented $709,020 in value. By 1932 there was practically no trade, just $4,542 worth of imported crab meat.

The major commodities exported overall during the 1920s were apples, raw cotton, flour, heavy hardware, hardware and tools, lumber, machinery, canned milk, salmon, and wheat. The table below shows the relative importance of each in percentage to total exports, domestic and foreign.[7]

Briefly, apples were exported mainly to the United Kingdom and northern Europe as the market rapidly developed from 1924 on; however, a sizeable market was developed in South America by 1929 ($928,000), almost all of which went to Argentina and Brazil. Raw cotton was exported exclusively to the Orient, with Japan taking almost the entire shipment in 1929. Flour was exported widely to both foreign and domestic markets, with the Orient and United Kingdom being the main foreign customers. The chief domestic consumers were California, the Philippines, and the Atlantic Seaboard. Foreign customers of heavy hardware were the Orient and British Columbia; Alaska was the

	1922		1929	
Commodity	Domestic %	Foreign %	Domestic %	Foreign %
Apples	1.0	1.0	2.3	11.0
Cotton, raw	0.0	7.0	0.0	4.0
Flour	5.5	10.0	3.4	6.0
Hardware, heavy	1.0	2.0	0.5	1.0
Hardware & tools	1.7	1.0	1.0	1.4
Lumber	2.3	8.0	2.2	5.0
Machinery	2.1	4.0	2.3	10.0
Milk, canned	2.6	2.0	1.0	3.4
Salmon	10.0	6.9	6.0	6.0
Wheat	nil	7.7	nil	7.8
Totals	26.2%	49.6%	18.7%	55.6%

main domestic customer. Hardware and tools also found British Columbia a main importer, along with the Orient; Alaska, again, was the chief domestic importer. Lumber, like flour, and salmon, found a wide market. The main foreign importers were the Orient, United Kingdom, and South America. The Atlantic Seaboard, California, Alaska, and the Philippines proved to be large domestic customers, and Hawaii steadily increased its imports.

Machinery represented 2.1% of all domestic exports in 1922, and 4% of foreign exports. Domestic exports remained steady at 2.3% in 1929, climbing to 10% of all foreign exports that year. In both years the Orient and British Columbia absorbed substantially all of the domestic exports of machinery. Canned milk represented 2.6% of domestic exports in 1922, but rose to 3.4% of foreign exports in 1929. The Orient absorbed most to the product in the foreign market in both years, while imports by California, the Atlantic Seaboard, and Gulf states dwindled from the large volumes of 1922.

The salmon market was widely dispersed, finding markets in both highly developed and underdeveloped economies. Exports to domestic markets in 1922 were 10% of all domestic exports, and 6.9% of the foreign, while in 1929 both kinds of exports fell to 6% of the total. In both years the largest foreign customers were the United Kingdom and Australia, with the former taking more than 65% of the total. Domestic buyers in both years were the Atlantic Seaboard, the Gulf states, and California; the Philippines imported little in 1929, while it had been a major importer in 1922. Wheat found no domestic market outside of Hawaii, but it was a major foreign export in both 1922 and 1929; 7.7% and 7.8% respectively. The Orient and the United

Kingdom were the largest buyers. In 1929, when "Orient" is segregated into Japan and China categories, Japan absorbed about $2.6 million of the product, China $353,075 worth, and the United Kingdom $1.1 million of the total wheat export value of $4,642,000.

While net tonnage figures show Seattle's waterborne commerce in decline relative to Portland's (see TABLE 5), the dollar values convey a different impression. Figures, unfortunately, are for customs districts, not for individual ports; but they at least suggest their relative positions.[10]

TABLE 5

Comparison of Seattle With Portland (In 2,000-lb. Tons)

Portland[8]	Foreign Trade	Pacific Coast	Intercoastal	Totals
1920	871,198	1,879,507	161,112	2,911,817
1925	2,128,110	3,540,310	1,944,473	7,612,893
1929	3,977,359	4,675,428	2,436,959	11,089,746
1930	3,663,971	5,022,807	2,738,342	11,425,120
1936				
1939	2,861,461	6,110,409	2,997,209	11,969,079

Seattle[9]				
1920	1,.411,890	Domestic combined:	3,817,171	5,229,061
1925	913,438	" "	6,966,363	7,879,801
1929	1,138,203	" "	8,059,278	9,197,481
1930	911,638	" "	7,450,941	8,362,579
1936	644,300	" "	5,704,148	6,368,448

No compilations are available after those for 1936

Nationally, in terms of rating by dollar value, the San Francisco Bay Customs District ranked third in 1922, behind New York and New Orleans, while the Washington Customs District ranked fourth; Oregon's ranked below twentieth position. Their respective rankings in 1928 were: San Francisco Bay fifth, Washington seventh, Oregon eighteenth.

	San Francisco Bay	Washington	Oregon	Los Angeles
1922	$314,913,342	$308,290,523	$58,814,816	$35,873,914
1923	378,234,000	327,209,118	62,630,250	70,972,002
1924	398,064,853	379,962,387	75,972,375	196,047,522

For 1929: San Francisco fifth, Washington seventh, Oregon nineteenth. A recapitulation of dollar values for 1930 shows the emergence of Los Angeles as a major port:[11]

San Francisco	$366,794,236	(4th nationally)
Washington	291,487,758	(7th ")
Los Angeles	232,033,272	(8th ")
Oregon	79,732,740	(below 20th ")

For major ports within the Pacific Northwest the 1937 *Yearbook* of the Seattle Port Commission provides tonnage figures for the intercoastal trade in 1936 (not repeated for other years). The relative relationships are suggested, at least:[12]

	Eastbound Tonnage	Westbound Tonnage
Seattle	327,219	227,197
Tacoma	283,963	25,937
Everett	245,293	18,479
Bellingham	102,325	negligible
Longview	243,260	negligible
Portland	533,843	190,788

Tacoma, Everett, Bellingham, Longview, and Aberdeen shipped out timber products almost exclusively, although Tacoma's was a more mixed trade that included copper exports as a large component, produced from its nearby smelter at Ruston.

Within the Puget Sound Basin the 1928 *Yearbook* provides dollar values of exports and imports for the major cities for 1927 (again, not repeated):[13]

	Imports	Exports
Seattle	$205,395,663	$60,089,926
Tacoma	18,438,250	42,372,089
Bellingham	718,924	1,946,314
Everett	792,522	2,639,293

5

Manufacturing—1919, 1929, 1939

When Dun and Bradstreet did their study of the city's economy in 1948 they reminded readers that manufacturing relative to the rest of the economy had been fairly stable: employment, for example, had been about 20% of the total for decades. They characterized the city as "a regional distribution and service center with the volume of its business exceeded by Los Angeles and San Francisco among the western cities." The year 1919 marked the high point for manufacturing for the period under study in terms of number of establishments, wage earners, wages paid, index of wage payments (nearly double that paid in 1929), and in value added. The average of value added by manufacture in 1929 was 97.3% of the national average ($3,973 compared to $4,085). Bearing these generalizations in mind we can turn first to the Census of Manufactures of 1920 and 1930 (which record data for 1919 and 1929 respectively). The latter census sometimes did not report some products that were included in the 1919 census: their omission here is due to that and not to an oversight. The following tables provide the focus of the narrative that follows.[1] (See TABLES 6, 7, and 8.)

TABLE 6—Major Product Lines of Manufacture, 1919

	Total Value	Value Added	No. of Employees	Wage Earners
Totals	$274,431,239	$124,780,864	47,074	40,843
Product (Selected)				
Auto repairing	1,687,366	1,040,394	551	388
Brass, copper, bronze	1,380,955	2,541,301	172	133
Brick & terra cotta	2,386,018	319,091	172	151
Bread & bakery	6,817,522	2,541,301	1,055	788
Cars & general shop const, rways	1,615,550	1,030,235	725	662
Clothing, mens	1,381,596	1,011,172	369	302
Clothing, womens	836,707	375,887	231	192
Coffee roastg, grndg	3,297,246	877,720	286	161
Confectnry & ice crm	5,257,504	2,482,345	1,006	745
Copper, tin, sheet metal work	1,392,980	739,922	308	222
Foundry & machine shops, all types	14,153,684	8,513,496	2,777	2,325
Flour milling	29,128,890	3,221,599	790	559
Furniture	967,880	596,381	270	214
Iron & steel frgng	2,934,249	1,247,065	355	305
Lumber & timber	12,737,497	6,035,683	2,375	2,218
" , planing mill	2,083,733	962,796	353	281
Pickles, preserves	1,111,643	371,476	121	85
Printg & publshg, book & job	2,552,383	1,773,180	768	479
Prntg & pub, newsp, prdcls	5,646,748	4,225,755	1,103	483
Shipbldg, wooden	11,093,450	6,882,124	2,553	2,430
Slaughtering, pkg	18,031,098	2,501,691	612	503

TABLE 7—Major Product Lines of Manufacture, 1929

	Total Value	Value Added	No. of Employees	Wage Earners
Totals	$199,810,732	$91,396,947	28,202	23,003
Product (Selected)				
Bread & bakery	10,234,376	5,410,312	1,362	1,187
Canning& presrvg fish, crabs, etc.	1,596,734	381,601	117	96
Coffee & spice	4,931,872	1,518,369	235	154
Confectionary	3,049,119	1,513,829	559	449
Copper, tin, sh.iron	2,177,432	1,281,239	449	375
Electrcl mchnry, etc	1,703,523	817,489	354	272
Feeds (animal & fowl)	7,869,689	1,271,102	282	230
Fndry, machine shp	11,094,680	6,902,916	2,193	1,845
Furniture	3,034,261	1,722,480	792	700
Ice cream	2,218,317	1,074,319	240	219
Lumber & timber	13,887,420	6,233,282	2,496	2,346
Non-ferrous metal alloys, exclg alumn	1,501,410	712,366	205	165
Planing mill prod.	4,074,523	1,685,593	662	573
Prntg & publshg, book & job	4,130,573	3,048,279	839	613
Prntg & publshg, newsp & prdcls	10,497,471	8,170,719	1,632	686
*Flour, grain mill	24,723,153	3,248,506	746	536

*Omitted in Seattle listing, but combined with Tacoma's. Together, the figures are:

30,903,941	4,060,632	933	670

Of their combined total in 1919, Seattle's proportion was 80%. If the same proportion existed in 1929, Seattle flour production would be as estimated above.

TABLE 8—Major Product Lines of Manufacture, 1939

	Total Value	Value Added	No. of Employees	Wage Earners
Totals	$152,748,418	$75,475,413	23,456	20,352
Product (Selected)				
Apparel	6,276,898	2,500,554	1,468	1,376
Bread, etc.	8,145,387	4,664,924	1,299	1,203
Chemicals	6,490,301	2,300,969	325	266
Iron/steel	18,970,059	7,974,973	2,180	1,947
Job printing	2,333,408	1,615,580	438	376
Machinery, non-electrcal	4,686,736	2,741,956	990	881
Newsp pub.	6,391,613	1,880,172	861	525
Meat pkg. whlsle	5,855,272	912,103	275	240
Motor vehicles, bodies, parts	2,086,268	711,122	329	298
Paper, etc.	2,968,348	1,255,823	355	46
Sausages, etc.	1,842,479	368,100	87	77
Saw/veneer/planing mills	8,395,814	3,612,878	1,430	1,351
Shipbldg/reprg	3,453,265	2,395,740	1,031	970
Food & kindred products	21,366,834	7,285,134	1,730	1,541
Furniture & finished products	2,614,569	1,087,706	447	413
Textile mill & other fiber	21,129,747	15,124,433	3,619	3,600
Other industries	91,272,802	44,206,842	13,972	12,114

Some of the commodities listed in the 1919 census were not listed separately in 1929:

Automotive repairing
Cars and general shop construction for steam and electric railways
Clothing, men's and women's
Iron and steel forging
Pickles, preserves and sauces
Shipbuilding, wooden (steel shipbuilding had been lumped with "all industries")

These were all major or significant industries in 1919; so they must have significantly declined by 1929, not to be listed.

Exception would probably have to be made for automotive repairing, for the 1924 *Directory of Manufactures* lists about 175 firms engaged in this line; their number must have increased by 1929 since the automotive industry drove the national economy in the 1920s. Some manufactures do appear in the composite listing for "Seattle-Tacoma Industrial Area", however. These are:

	Total Value	Value Added	No. of Employees	Wage Earners
Clothing, women's	$4,193,791	$2,066,376	1,143	1,034
Meat packg, wholsl	21,116,204	2,741,675	920	727
Ship & boat bldg, steel & wooden	4,861,328	3,090,344	1,395	1,284

Listed in 1929 as a major manufacture in the "Seattle-Tacoma Industrial Area" were:

	Total Value	Value Added	No. of Employees	Wage Earners
Feeds, animal & fowl	$10,939,384	$1,686,141	389	302
Pulp (wd & fibr)	2,198,647	1,202,537	401	378
Structrl & ornmtl iron & steel wrk	2,154,854	1,237,435	448	379

(Pulp manufacture was probably all in Tacoma.)

Despite strong desires and promotional attempts by the Chamber of Commerce, the Seattle Lighting Department, and their supporters, manufacturing between 1919 and 1929 declined by about 27%. The decline of wartime shipbuilding contributed largely to this slump. Yet, statewide during 1923, 172 manufacturing establishments were added to the state's economy, representing a 30 to 40 per cent increase since 1922, though not compensating for the general postwar falloff. Even flour manufacturing, that staple of the waterborne export trade, dropped by about 15%. Foundry work, another major manufacture, also fell comparably, probably due to its partial dependence on the shipbuilding industry. The Chamber of Commerce noted the city's industrial expansion in 1927 from 826 firms in 1923 to 1,157 in 1927. However, the increase in the value of the product was not proportionate: $153 million in 1923; $170 million in 1927. For these years the number of wage earners numbered 17,697 and 20,745, respectively. Three major lines increased production slightly; these were lumber and timber manufacture, planing mill products, and confections and ice cream. Despite the startup of few new firms, 1926 witnessed the upgrading and moving of many old ones. The Boeing Airplane Company was one; by 1928 it was employing about 900 persons as the city's largest manufacturing firm. (The plant lay just outside the city limits.)[2]

Furniture-making increased notably by over 210%, but it still accounted for only about $3 million of the total value. A 50% increase was recorded in the manufacture of "copper, tin, and sheet metal work", but the total value of the product was relatively small. Bread and bakery production showed a significant increase amounting to about 50%, and the total value of the product was relatively important, ranking fourth among manufactures, behind flour milling, lumber and timber, and foundry and machine shop work, and slightly higher than newspaper and periodical publishing.

The main growth industry was publishing: newspaper and periodical publishing, and book and job printing, each, almost doubled in the value of their 1919 products, and their total product value was of major significance, together totalling almost $16 million. Of greater significance, however, was the "value added" factor, which was about 72% of their total value, far higher than that for any other product; labor costs were disproportionately higher than in the other industries.

In terms of value added—which is directly related to numbers of employees—the showing for 1929 is:

	No. of Employees
newspaper and periodical publishing	1,632
foundry and machine shop work	2,193
lumber and timber manufacture	2,496
bread and bakery products	1,362
book and job publishing	839

Next in line in terms of employment, but not in terms of value added are:

furniture manufacture	792
flour and grain products	746
planing mill products	662
confectionary products	559

Together, these firms employed 11,281 men and women, or 40% of the work force engaged in manufacture. Indicated here is small scale manufacturing and a heavy leaning toward light industry.

Special note should be taken of the large waterborne importation of heavy hardware and machinery, hardware and tools, clothing and dry goods, electric and radio manufactures, all of which were relatively insignificant in Seattle's manufacturing economy. These imports supported the wholesaling, jobbing, and retailing commerce of the city. Our examination of the waterborne commerce shows these commodity lines entering the city's exports to Alaska and British Columbia; and, except for clothing, the Oriental trade.

Although several aspects of the economy in the 1930s have already been covered in sections dealing with waterborne commerce and those sections ahead, dealing with unemployment and relief, a comparison of figures from the 1940 census of manufactures with two earlier ones is appropriate, coming as it does before war production distorted the peacetime pattern.

Manufacturing in Seattle, 1919, 1929, 1939

	Total Value	Value Added	No. of Employees	Wage Earners
1919	$274,431,239	$124,780,864	47,074	40,843
1929	199,810,372	91,396,947	28,202	23,003
1939	152,748,418	75,475,413	23,456	20,352

The number of manufacturing establishments in these years were: 1,229 in 1919, 1,219 in 1929, and 1,083 in 1939. The total of factory wages paid in 1939 was $28,742,946, which was 24% of the state's total of $118,326,333.

As with the two previous censuses it is impossible to trace continuity for many series because the composition often will vary from one to the other. Only a gross impression is possible.

Number of Establishments in Above Industries

Apparel	44
Bread & other bakery products, except biscuits, crackers	97
Chemicals & allied products	48
Flour & grain mill products	3
Food & kindred products	87
Furniture & finished lumber products	26
Iron & steel & their products, except machinery	56
Job printing	79
Machinery, except electrical	30
Meat packing, wholesale	3
Motor vehicles, bodies, parts, accesories	14
Newspapers, publishing, printing	13
Paper & allied products	16
Sausages, prepared meats not made in meat packing estabs	9
Saw/veneer/planing/cooperage/ mills	15
Shipbuilding & repairing	16
Textile mill products & other fiber manufacturers	13

6

Manufacturing in Seattle's Hinterland

Manufacturing and warehousing spread more rapidly after the war over the Duwamish delta/flatland area, extending southward from the East and West Waterways. Fed by three railroads entering the city from the south it presented an ideal site in terms of transportation access—later, Highway 99 would feed trucks into this area. Its flatness facilitated low-cost construction and installment of utilities. Also, as an airfield site it was a natural. Much of this property also lay outside the City limits, which meant escape from City taxes. One company which captured the opportunities presented here was the Boeing Airplane Company. It would do so, and then some. William E. Boeing, the City, the University of Washington, and the Chamber of Commerce steadily developed a symbiotic relationship of long standing, though subject to periodic strains on the host whenever the company needed any of a variety of support services. From small beginnings during World War I the company became the backbone of the region's industrial base, displacing forest products from that position.

The company's contribution and relationship to the City are not reflected in census statistics for Seattle because Boeing lay in a protected enclave just outside the southern City limits. A pattern of relationships developed early that became the norm for the future. The City became obligated to extend its utilities out to it. In June 1921, Boeing, acting through John Shorett (attorney for the Commercial Waterway District Number 1), asked the

Chamber of Commerce for help in pressuring the City Council to speed up street paving and for federal money for bridge construction in the West Waterway area. By so doing, Shorett pleaded: "The Waterway has ceased to be a South End project, and is a project now that the Port [of Seattle] should control . . ." He argued, more favorable conditions would spur development of Spokane Street for industrial expansion in general. All of this would make Seattle the national "center for airplane building." Impatiently, Boeing, in reporting an offer from Los Angeles to the Chamber of Commerce, threatened to move there unless better rail service to and from his plant were provided, along with other utilities improvements. He agreed to meet with its committee to develop a strategy for presenting its case to the City Council. In May 1922 the Council responded, authorizing paving West Marginal Way, and "opening a large industrial area and assuring the permanency of the Boeing Airplane industry in Seattle."[1]

Requiring access on its own terms to the nearby King County Airport, Boeing, in 1923, was awarded a temporary permit by the City to test Government ordered planes. The company, with its newly acquired authority, set the tone for future administration of the airport when it ordered the Rushlite-Gray Aviation Company to remove their planes from the field—it soon became "Boeing Field", not condescendingly "King County Municipal Airport". Partly in response to an order from the U.S. Air Corps in 1936 for 299 bombers, the company acquired 28 acres adjacent to the municipal airport—the latter was then being improved with the aid of $492,000 of WPA funds.[2]

Mr. Boeing found in the university a convenient source for trained engineers, providing a steady labor pool to be drawn upon as needed. The precedent became established early, when William Boeing hired two university engineering graduates during the war: Philip Johnson as production manager, and Claire Egtvedt as chief engineer. Boeing felt obligated in turn to occasionally contribute to support the school's facilities, beginning in 1917 with a donation of funds for constructing a wind tunnel. But it was mainly Guggenheim money that led to the construction of the aeronautical engineering building—named appropriately, "Guggenheim Hall".[3]

A tally of aircraft built by Boeing from 1920 to 1940 indicates that 225 planes were built for commercial use, and 1,376 were built for the United States Army, Navy and Marines. (Excluded are some of the 6,981 that were built for the Army from 1935-1945.) Reportedly, 26 planes were built for export in the

1930s; however, they were measured in tonnage figures. China was shipped 12 tons of "airplanes and parts" in 1931, 42 tons in 1932, 120 tons in 1933, 35 tons in 1934, 21 tons in 1935, and 193 tons in 1936. To turn out these planes and parts the company's peak employment in each of the following years was:[4]

1918	337	1924	450	1930	1,026	1936	1,976
1919	282	1925	481	1931	1,207	1937	1,890
1920	173	1926	602	1932	1,655	1938	2,956
1921	240	1927	714	1933	2,264		
1922	549	1928	1,049	1934	1,768		
1923	283	1929	1,491	1935	839		

Reed Hansen, in his study of collective bargaining at the Boeing plant, characterized aircraft production as tied to a "boom and bust cycle". The above figures bear out his observation. Partly for this reason the company developed a policy of extending normal working hours whenever it had a surge of orders, instead of hiring and training new workers, as when the company received an order in 1933 for 224 "battle planes"—the work force then was put on a 12-hour day/7 days a week basis. However, when the company received the order for 13 Model 299 bombers in 1936 it planned to bring its work force up to 1,500, "building the payroll up from the lowest point it has reached in ten years." High turnover, combined with relatively low pay, lack of seniority, and poor working conditions, provided fertile ground for union organizing. Local 751 was chartered by the International Association of Machinists in 1935 as the "Aero Mechanics" union. By 1937 it had signed up enough members to qualify for National Labor Relations Board certification on June 17. Given the volatility in labor relations at that time, and the growing number of aircraft orders, the company signed a union shop agreement with the union. Minimum wages were increased from 25 cents to 62 1/2 cents per hour and from a maximum of 75 cents to $1.00 per hour. Overtime rates and a seniority system were established, along with procedures for settling grievances. This lasted, with modifications, until 1940, when negotiations went to an impasse that brought out a 95% vote in favor of strike action, before the company agreed to arbitration.[5]

7

Other Lines of Economic Activity

Building construction activity is a general indicator of the health of the economy. Its up and down swings project longer term assessments by people of their prospects—whether to invest or not in an office building, an apartment house, a hotel, a hospital, or a family residence means a more durable commitment than does the purchase of an automobile, a washing machine, or a radio.

The facing table, TABLE 9, on building construction in Seattle, derived from the Bureau of Labor Statistics report on building construction in the United States, 1921-1948, gives some initial perspective.[1]

A comparison table, TABLE 10, counting the number of dwelling units authorized for construction in the four major Pacific Northwest cities contributes a regional perspective.

A cursory examination of these two tables shows a fairly sustained investment for all building construction from 1921 through 1930, with the peak being reached in 1928, followed by a modest falloff in 1929 and 1930, before the full impact of the Depression began to sink in. However, there were sharp fluctuations in non-residential construction, while residential construction sustained a fairly steady level of investment, peaking in 1926, but not falling abruptly until 1929, after which it did not regain significant momentum until 1938, when federal funds became available under the 1937 National Housing Act.[2]

TABLE 9—Building Construction in Seattle, 1921-1940

($ rounded to nearest thousand)

	All classes of bldg. (incl. additions)	New non-residential bldg.	New residential bldg.	No. of new family dwelling units
1921	$12,809	$5,496	$5,073	1,961
1922	19,624	8,849	8,716	2,920
1923	22,951	6,805	13,141	2,936
1924	27,212	11,732	12,403	3,676
1925	30,627	7,024	20,133	5,570
1926	13,218	13,905	16,942	5,342
1927	29,070	9,098	16,939	4,505
1928	34,807	12,755	17,785	4,658
1929	29,101	10,540	11,708	3,289
1930	30,356	15,650	11,634	2,583
1931	12,483	6,968	3,487	1,139
1932	3,257	1,773	651	361
1933	1,953	485	404	168
1934	2,318	583	262	150
1935	3,934	1,392	890	251
1936	6,798	2,609	2,196	560
1937	7,183	2,279	2,479	638
1938	8,469	2,292	3,688	1,002
1930	12,701	4,863	5,316	1,305
1940	34,554	23,357	8,373	2,018

Construction of dwelling units peaked in 1925-1926 for all four major Northwest cities. Portland seems to have been the least affected by the postwar depression, sustaining a relatively high level of investment from 1921 through 1926, but these investments started their downward descent sharply in 1927.

Commenting on construction in 1926, the *Journal of Commerce* found construction work at record high levels. Besides the "thousands of houses [and] scores of apartment houses" there had been a number of theaters built, "noticeable for their number and size . . . Rumors of the pending invasion of Seattle by several large department stores and other retail establishments have quickened downtown activity." The retail district continued moving northward, its center becoming the area between Union Street and Stewart Street. Work soon began on the second Denny Regrade north of Stewart which realtor Frank B. Poor touted in 1928 as "destined to become one of the most important business and retail districts in Seattle"—a prophesy that has never borne fruit. All this activity led downtown property own-

TABLE 10—Dwelling Units Authorized for Construction in Four Major Pacific Northwest Cities

	Seattle	Spokane	Tacoma	Portland
1921	1,961	438	843	3,136
1922	1,910	517	862	3,658
1923	1,926	375	861	4,070
1924	2,676	631	1,130	4,809
1925	5,570	716	1,201	4,796
1926	5,342	662	1,790	5,125
1927	4,505	595	769	3,176
1928	4,658	574	822	2,321
1929	3,289	419	515	1,586
1930	2,583	328	347	866
1031	1,139	216	185	539
1932	361	92	78	200
1933	168	81	58	164
1934	150	92	45	142
1935	251	236	47	222
1936	560	296	122	606
1937	638	456	199	1,012
1938	1,002	558	358	760
1939	1,305	698	416	1,234
1940	2,018	822	621	1,764

ers to establish the Associated Central Business Properties, Incorporated. The ACBPI succeeded in getting Second Avenue extended to the railroad depots, and it began pressing for improved street lighting and confronting the tangled traffic mess on Railroad Avenue. The latter would not be addressed until 1933, when the Board of Public Works finally was authorized to open bids for a $1,200,000 project to build a seawall and relocate the railroad tracks; this effort had been at least thirty years in the making.[3]

Such building activity stimulated a demand for labor that exceeded the available supply, thereby encouraging contractors to give in to union pressure for recognition and higher wages. Using 1913 as the base year, wages rose steadily from a 187 index number in 1922 to 248 by 1926. These same workers probably also invested in their own residential construction, thereby contributing to the steady increase overall. That retail trade improved in this setting is no surprise; that of 1925 climbed by 10% over 1924. (Installment buying came into its own during the 1920s, encouraging people to spend beyond their immediate incomes, as though expecting the economic ebullience to continue indefinitely.) Real estate transfers jumped from a figure of $23 million in 1924 to $55.5 million in 1925. Chain store sales in 1926 increased by 13%; department store sales by a more modest 3% over 1925, though wholesale trade declined by 8%. The *Journal of Commerce* boasted that retail and wholesale trade had been the best in history during 1926. For the "first time", according to the *Journal*, six new national chain stores entered Seattle. Also 70 new factories were built in the city (39 were built in Tacoma). The *Journal* noted that apartment house construction in 1928 had been the best "ever known", offsetting the decline in home construction. Office and store building surpassed all previous records, along with an increase in warehouse and factory construction. That year, however, did witness a drop in construction of churches, hospitals, and theaters.[4]

On the eve of the city's descent into economic depression the *Times* listed major construction projects then in progress (its 28 December 1930 issue): Diablo Dam, the Textile Tower, Roosevelt Hotel, Harborview Hospital, the Exchange Building, an extension to the County-City Building, an apartment building at 7th Avenue and Spring, a Ford assembly plant, the Vance Building, the Brooklyn Building, and the West Seattle Bridge (which had just been completed, along with the Washington Athletic Club). Perhaps foreshadowing instability, in mid-summer the Western Hotel chain had announced a major consolidation of twenty hotels in the state. Those in Seattle included: the New Washington, Benjamin Franklin, Camlin Apartment/Hotel, the Meany (to open spring 1931), and the Roosevelt.[5]

Integral to the downtown expansion was the Metropolitan Tract of the University of Washington. The Chamber of Commerce and Commercial Club had long wanted a first class hotel to serve more than the commercial traveler. Other cities were responding to this need, wanting conventions and the tourist trade as well as their standard fare. Both the Chamber and the Metropolitan Building Company thought the Tract ideal for such a project, a 12-story hotel of 609 rooms built around the Metropolitan Theater, horseshoe fashion. With this concurrence in hand, the MBC submitted its proposal to the Board of Regents amidst thunderous fanfare drummed up by the *Times* and *P-I* in May 1921. The catch in the proposal was that once again the MBC requested an extension of the original lease, despite the Regents' record of resistance on this issue. Knowing this, the MBC and Chamber had a backup plan, should the Regents reject the one offered. Rejection came in the face of a hail of protest on the part of the two dailies, so intense that recall of the offending Regents was offered as one way of getting them to say "Yes" to the University's granting an extension from the original 1954 date to 1973. Then, the University would finally be able to take possession of the Metropolitan Theater lot, the hotel site, a power plant location; and an extension of the lease on the temporary buildings from the 1925 date to 1935. The Alumni Association supported the Regents, and the ensuing, spirited public debate served to inform the public of the issues at stake, diverting some of the heat that the two dailies in particular had been directing at the Regents.[6]

When the dust of battle settled, the Chamber and MBC came out with their fall-back plan, to which the business community especially had by then been prepared to respond in a knowing way. In June 1922 the Chamber organized the Community Hotel Corporation, naming as trustees a blue ribbon group which could generate widespread respect and confidence, among them: C.D. Stimson, Horace Henry, J.F. Douglas, Chamber president Frank Waterhouse, iconic Thomas Burke, and ex-Chamber president Willard Rhodes, a department store owner. This corporation contracted with the MBC to build the hotel—now the "Olympic"—then mounted a successful bond subscription drive in July. When bids came in $1,650,000 over the amount subscribed another bond issue was quickly taken up. Construction began February 1924, with lumberman Albert S. Kerry directing the project, determined to meet the November 1 deadline. Neal Hines writes: "Kerry simply drove the hotel into existence." The deadline was met, and Seattle finally had its classy hotel complete with ballroom, sumptuous dining facilities, luxury street level shops, and ready access to the Metropolitan and other theaters, and the retail shopping district. Parallel construction in the tract also went forward, with annexes being built onto the White and Stuart buildings, and across from the Olympic, the Stimson Building was emerging as a link with the Cobb building, the two serving dental and medical practice. The contest between the Regents and Douglas over the "temporary" Arena Building became more embittered during this period, heightened by the 1923 Legislature's concession to regental pressure to protect it in the future, from modifications of the original lease. In the future legislative approval would be required. Douglas won out, finally getting the Regents to classify the building as permanent after certain construction requirements had been met, but it emerged as a garage, not as a "convention hall".[7]

Following soon on these events the MBC formed the Fifth

Avenue Building Company whose objective was to replace the old Hippodrome with an eight-story building—the Skinner Building. To be housed in it were a motion picture theater (the Fifth Avenue Theater in elaborate, exotic Oriental interior design, inside a California style exterior building shell), offices, shops, and studios. Completed in 1926, with all of the associated buildings, Douglas's ambition to make the tract Seattle's "Metropolitan Center" was fulfilled. The White-Henry-Stuart Building, had become "a capital of the lumber industry", and the Stuart Building's eleventh floor found Stuart's very own Carnation Company the only occupant.[8]

At the start of the Depression decade, although building construction seemed promising, residential construction did not. Residential construction—embracing detached single family dwelling units and apartment houses—had been in the doldrums since 1931. The period from 1925 to 1929 had been the high level for this type of construction; 1925 had been the "boom" year. 1931 saw a drop of 16% in residential construction. In 1934 only 159 "family units" were built; a mere 150 permits were issued that year. Not a single permit had been issued for 1933 and 1934 for apartment house construction; only one in 1935, two more in 1936, and one in 1937.[9]

About one-half of all structures had been built before 1917. Practically all of the dwelling units that intermingled with and fringed the original downtown business district were sub-standard, being of unsubstantial wooden frame construction, built before 1910. "Profanity Hill", bordering Jackson Street on the south, Cherry Street on the north, and lying between 12th and 2nd avenues, was an unrelieved slum smack against the police station, city and county government buildings, and the financial section. Cheap hotels and apartment buildings typified the dwelling units in the downtown Yesler district, stretching northward along the hillside above the waterfront to Denny Way. South of Yesler, in the filled-in tideflats, were the shacktowns—"Hoovervilles". Uphill from there toward Beacon Hill was also scattered more sub-standard housing. More of this housing extended onto the Duwamish flats to the edge of West Seattle.[10]

When the Work Projects Administration (WPA) conducted its real property survey for the Seattle Housing Authority during 1939-40, it noted 86,086 "residential structures", containing 124,774 "dwelling units". Of these units 28.5% were classed as sub-standard; 17,437 of them were without private bathing and toilet facilities. The median family income of those living in these units was $771 a year. Of these dwelling units 74,310

(59.6%) were occupied by detached single family units; apartment houses contained 24,071 units (19.3%); businesses with attached units numbered 2,440 (2%); 2-family and 2-deckers accounted for 2,148 units (1.8%); "shacks", another 1,687 units (1.3%). Add 950 houseboats (0.8%) parked along the shores of Lake Washington, Lake Union, and the Duwamish River. Completely converted structures numbered 11,888 (9.5%); 4,141 partially converted ones (3.3%) filled out the picture.[11]

Though dismal, Seattle's housing was nevertheless far better than that in most of the nation's cities. The unrelieved Depression only underscored the need for both low cost housing to replace city slums and revive the construction industry. With this in mind, the Congress passed the National Housing Act (Glass-Steagall Act) in September 1937, establishing the United States Housing Authority. This legislation provided for low-interest 60-year loans to local public agencies to defray the expenses for slum clearance and erection of housing in the vacated area. 90% of the cost would be met from federal funds while local governments had to contribute only 10%. Rent subsidies were included on condition that local agencies contribute an amount equal to 25% of the federal grant. At this time, Jesse Epstein, a research assistant and teaching fellow who specialized in administrative law, was associated with the Bureau of Government Research at the University of Washington. One of his duties was to keep track of federal legislation which might benefit the state and cities. (The Association of Washington Cities was affiliated with the Bureau, assisting towns without resources throughout the state in dealing with their civic problems.)[12]

Although the following account takes the reader into the political history of the period that is dealt with extensively below, it seems more appropriate to continue the outline of construction revival in this economy section. Epstein approached some City Council members to alert them to the opportunity provided by the housing act, hoping the City could act without enabling legislation from the legislature. Councilmen David Levine, John Carroll, and Hugh DeLacy quickly lent their support, while Samuel Humes and Frank Laube opposed. An ordinance drawn up by Epstein was passed in December 1937, creating a Local Advisory Housing Commission; Epstein was named chairman. Carroll proposed and Council approved the loan of $25,000 from the Water Department to begin preparatory work. Ordinance language read: "[T]housands are unemployed in Seattle, among them hundreds of members of the building trades who will share directly in the benefits derived by the whole community from a well conceived local municipal low-cost housing program." Not so fast! The U.S. Housing Authority quickly advised the City that the State Legislature would first have to pass enabling legislation before real work could begin.[13]

While waiting for the legislature to meet in January 1939 the City Council followed its December 1937 ordinance with a resolution in April 1938, declaring its intention to establish a city housing authority in order to qualify for federal funding. On December 19, 1938 the Council sent its request to Congress. Epstein brought the Washington State Planning Council into the picture, earning its approval beforehand to sway the 1939 legislature. Thus prepared, when the legislature did hold hearings, one of the few witnesses appearing before the committee was Epstein, and because of the technicalities involved in preparing the enabling legislation (about which only he was fully informed), he was asked to prepare a bill for creating a housing authority in every city and county, and providing for cooperation with the State in developing their projects. Legislative approval was easily won after all this careful spadework, coupled as it was with the lack of any opposition to such a federal subsidy. The Advisory Commission then submitted its report to Mayor Arthur Langlie and Council on March 13, 1939. With the mayor and council members being kept fully informed at each stage, and given the rationale in the report, the Council established the Seattle Housing Authority which paid back the loan from the Water Department. Langlie then named Epstein director of the SHA's governing board. He became known as the "father of public housing" in Seattle.[14]

Epstein's first priority was to conduct a survey to inventory the city's housing stock, applying to the WPA to undertake the job (noted above). It should be no surprise to learn that "Profanity Hill" became the chosen site for the SHA's initial project—forty-three and one-half acres atop the hill, in the heart of "Japantown", to be named "Yesler Terrace". (The City Council had rejected an alternative site in the Denny Regrade area when adjoining property holders protested.) Most dwellings on the hill had been built between 1895 and 1905; they were a blight upon the whole city, abutting as they did upon the downhill government and financial sections. A few blocks north lay King County's [Harborview] Hospital. From the hill there was cable car access to downtown from as far as Leschi Park on Lake Washington which could be coupled with streetcar transfers south to the industrial and warehouse district, and north to the

Special Collections Division, University of Washington Libraries. Negative No. UW 14037

Example of housing displaced by the Yesler Housing Project on "Profanity Hill". Abutting this housing, at bottom of hill, are the county-city government buildings, police headquarters, and the financial district.

financial, retail, and hotel districts. The area was a slum in which unrelieved poverty, compounded by vice operations, prevailed. Once cleared and rebuilt, Epstein gave first preferance to former residents of the area providing their family income did not exceed the maximum allowed. As a racially mixed neighborhood, it was assumed—as an unarticulated premise—that racial integration would be re-established. (Reputedly, Seattle's was the first integrated public housing project in the country—as Epstein would learn after being appointed Regional Director for the Pacific Coast after the war.)

The size of the contract, providing $3 million initially, enabled Epstein to select five architects instead of just one; each had his own specialty; each also was well connected in the business community, and could be counted upon to swing any wavering support from within it. Spreading contracts around among seven engineers, and four land negotiators, demolition contractors also helped the cause. The Seattle First National Bank, after consulting with eastern bankers, learned the advisability of buying the 10% represented by local bonds, becoming an avid supporter in the process.[15]

Special Collections Division, University of Washington Libraries. Negative No. UW 864

"Yesler Terrace", which replaced the housing pictured opposite. Funding came from the Federal Housing Administration. Completed in 1941, its 690 homes represented the nation's first racially integrated public housing project. Facing west are the Smith Tower, and at top center the domes of the old City Light office building and plant.

8

Seattle and Its Agricultural Hinterland

We have seen how the Mosquito Fleet had sustained Seattle's economic relationships to its hinterland since the 1890s: how it prepared the city for its commercial dominance on the Puget Sound; how this laid the basis for its dominance of the Alaska trade; and from this development, the city's paramount position in the Oriental commerce. Both coastwise shipping and rail transshipping followed in tandem. The former burgeoned, along with that of the Gulf region, the Atlantic Seaboard, the United Kingdom, and Europe, particularly after the war, when full use of the Panama Canal finally became a reality. The Mosquito Fleet, indeed, continued to expand its proportion of shipping even during the depression years: In 1920 its percentage of all shipping was 8.1%, stabilizing at about 10% during the decade, and growing to 13.3% in 1930, to 15.7% in 1932, and dropping slightly in 1933 to 14.3%.[1]

A factor in the city's hinterland relationships that is often overlooked is its meshing with the farming communities lying on the city's periphery. (Tacoma, presumably, would be similarly affected.) Markets in the midwest and northeastern parts of the U.S. were developed primarily by first generation Japanese farmers (Issei) and their offspring (Nisei) during the 1920s and 1930s. Iceberg lettuce and peas were the principal crops. The scale of this trade is indicated by the figures for carload shipments in 1930, when Washington growers shipped 2230 carloads of lettuce; 509 of them for Chicago, another 253 for New York, 118 for Minneapolis, 116 for Philadelphia, 93 for Detroit, 91 for Cleveland, 71 for Milwaukee, 50 for Baltimore, 47 for Boston, and 46 for Washington, D.C. Altogether 56 cities, out of 66 with which the Market News Service had contact, received shipments.[2]

The fact that these crops came to maturity just as regional harvesting ebbed in those markets, was critical. But these markets would never have been developed had it not been for the cultivation of these crops by Japanese farmers in the first place. Despite the enactment of the Anti-Alien Land Law in 1921, and its buttressing by an amendment in 1923 to prevent Japanese parents from acting as guardians for their citizen minors, and the flight of a large proportion of the fearful farmers to the cities and to the homeland, lands were brought under cultivation, particularly the alluvial soils of the White-Green-Puyallup river valleys, and the muck and peat lands spottily exposed when Lake Washington was lowered upon completion of the Chittenden locks in 1917. Rademaker reports the failure of attempts of White farmers to cultivate these crops, as well as the berry crops on Vashon and Bainbridge islands, while Japanese farmers succeeded there also. Japanese farmers were accustomed to techniques of intensive farming, while Whites were not. He points out that the land laws contributed to the development of farm specialization because the Japanese chose truck farming, leaving dairying, orcharding, and grain and hay production to the Whites. The Land Act of 1921 was born during the 1920-1921 depression. When economic conditions improved, pressure from the White farmers subsided; consequently, there was inconsistent enforcement of the law by county prosecutors. As a result, more and more of these lands were brought into production either by Japanese tenant farmers or directly as owners, when second generation Japanese came into their majority as native-born United States citizens.

A further differentiation/specialization was spun from the development of these distant markets. Japanese farmers—aiming at quality controls and associating quality with their brand names—formed cooperatives to carefully prepare the vegetables for market. Actual shipping and warehousing were conceded to the Whites. The latter also performed all the services connected with commission merchandising: from contacts at the local level (in Kent, Auburn, Seattle, Puyallup, Tacoma, and elsewhere in the Sound region) to each of the cities from which distribution took place. The overall result became a web of symbiotic economic relationships that benefited the entire state, one that would not have occurred except for the specialized farming that only the Japanese farmers performed. Indicating the degree of this rapprochement, Rademaker quotes an American Legion officer as favoring what had taken place since enactment of the land laws: "Someone is going to raise vegetables somewhere, and it might as well be in our own locality where we can profit by it through rendering auxiliary service such as furnishing supplies, capital, transportation, land etc., than in California, Mexico, or Florida . . . So let us work WITH the Japanese, not against them."[3]

Not to be overlooked in this portrayal is the continued role they played, along with Italian farmers, in supplying produce for the local markets at the height of the growing season. But California and Mexican crops increased their proportion of the supply even during the local high-season. Off-season, these outside sources dominated the local produce market.

With the expansion of markets for these crops came a demand for more farm labor—small farms grew beyond the capacity of a family to maintain them. Filipino labor primarily filled this need. The Philippine Islands served as the labor pool for the Hawaiian Sugar Planters' Association since 1906. Recruitment was usually under some form of labor contract system with all the attendant abuses known to be associated with it. Of the 112,828 Filipinos recruited by the planters from 1909 to 1931, 18,607 migrated to the West Coast to join the migratory work force there. A sizeable proportion—on the order of 3,000—were recruited in San Francisco to work in the fish canneries of Alaska. A proportion of these ultimately found their way to Seattle, often through Filipino labor contractors who were recruiting from Seattle for the Alaska canneries in southeastern Alaska. Some went directly to Seattle from the California farms and the farming areas in the Willamette Valley in Oregon and the Yakima Valley in eastern Washington. These cannery workers, upon returning to Seattle, then sought work primarily in the farms around Seattle. This migration from Hawaii and directly from the Philippines continued from 1920 until the depression and 1934, when the Tydings-McDuffie Act limited their number to just 50 per year.[4]

The unionization of these Filipino cannery workers in the mid-1930s will be covered below in connection with the jurisdictional disputes between the AFL and CIO unions. Filipinos were employed on farms around Kent, Auburn, Woodinville, South Park, Renton, and Bellevue. In 1930-1931 they had been attacked for driving down wages. Soon they would be found trying to raise them. They had threatened a strike in March 1935 to raise wages, but arbitration with the Japanese Growers' Association, which led to a 47% increase, averted a strike. But Japanese growers were not the only farm operators. When a strike began on April 3, 1937 to raise wages to 35 cents per hour, and 40 cents per hour after eight hours had been worked, the Washington Produce Shippers threatened to break the strike. Making good on this threat, Kent mayor R.E. Woodin led a vigilante attack on Filipino pickets, vowing "not [to] tolerate strikes around here." Wages averaged about 25 cents an hour, with no limit on the number of hours worked in a day. The strike was broken.[5]

9

Women in the Work Force

During the first half of this century dramatic changes were occurring in the sexual composition of the work force. In fact, these modifications merely foretold their accentuation in the last half of the century, just as trends from the turn of the century to 1920 prophesied their gathering momentum during the 1920s. As technological innovation in agriculture drove farm families to cities by the hundreds of thousands, so too in the cities were the technological bases for employment being dramatically altered. Clerical functions were revolutionized by the introduction of the typewriter and successive waves of new office machines—women displaced men in clerical occupations. It was the development of large scale business and the expansion of government at all levels that stimulated inventions and their application in the bureaucracies that mushroomed in tandem. Spread of department stores offered women employment as sales clerks as well as in the store offices. Telecommunication opened a fresh field of employment to which women readily adapted—the "hello girls". (By 1930 95% of telephone operators were women.) The 1920s witnessed a lightening of household chores as electrical appliances were brought into play. Ironically, though, their introduction did not release housebound middle class married women for employment outside the home. It was primarily the middle class families that purchased washing machines, vacuum cleaners, and other durable household goods, designed to lighten domestic labor. As traditionally-hired domestic help found better paying jobs in place of those in the middle and upper class homes they previously serviced, the burden of using the labor saving devices fell to the wife/mother they left behind. These women, more often than not, had some college experience at a time when domestic science was sinking deeper roots into higher education. And, at a time when advertising of electrical products glorified the middle class wife/mother as the torch-bearer of civilization, of high culture—the model homemaker who kept up with the introduction of each new gadget or its modification. Conspicuously!

David Nye describes the irony of it all, observing that in the 1920s women spent between 51 and 64 hours a week in housework, and that studies of a more recent period found no significant change: "Long hours in the home persisted as a result of rising expectations for middle class women, who were exhorted to prepare more varied meals, vacuum the house more often, maintain a larger wardrobe, do laundry more frequently, and spend more time with the children. Electrical conveniences made individual household tasks easier, but their number, frequency, and complexity increased. At the same time, some tasks were displaced from men and children to women." The scale of these changes is only hinted at by the brief remarks above. Nationally, by 1930 gainfully employed women numbered 10,752,116, representing a gain of 2,202,605 or 25.8% since 1920, a rate that surpassed the rate of population growth for women over age 10. During the previous decade the number of gainfully employed women had increased by less than 500,000—a mere 6% rate of increase.[1]

A more detailed look at what was happening for gainfully employed women nationally will at least suggest what was occurring locally. Mary V. Dempsey, in her study on "occupational progress of women" from 1910 to 1930, provides abundant detail from which the author draws for illustration. Women as farm laborers had ranked first in 1910, slipping to sixth by 1920 and 1930, at which time the "servants" category had captured first place. School teachers advanced from fourth to second place by 1930; stenographers and typists from eighth to third place. She writes: "Between 1920 and 1930 the greatest increases occurred among women in professional service and domestic and personal service, in trade, and in the clerical occupations." Between 1910 and 1930 women as "office clerks" (as distinct from stenographers and bookkeepers) expanded as a category to almost 600,000, a gain of 476%. Significantly, with the growth of

TABLE 11—Gainfully Employed Women, 1920, 1930

	1920	1930
Servants	1,012,133	1,634,959
School teachers	635,207	853,967
Stenographers & typists	564,744	775,140
Clerks (except in "stores")	472,163	706,553
Saleswomen and "clerks" in stores	526,718	705,793
Farm laborers	803,209	646,331
Bookkeepers & cashiers	345,746	465,697
Laundresses (not in laundry)	385,874	356,468
Operatives—clothing	265,643	346,751
Trained nurses	143,664	288,737
Farmers (owners & tenants)	265,577	262,645
Housekeepers & stewardesses	204,350	236,363
Telephone operators	178,379	235,259
Waitresses	116,921	231,973
Dressmakers & seamstresses	235,519	157,928
Laundry operatives	72,675	149,414
Cotton mill operatives	149,185	145,683
Nurses (not trained)	132,658	139,576
Boarding/lodging housekeepers	114,740	127,278
Hairdressers & manicurists	33,246	113,194
Retail dealers	78,980	110,166 *
Musicians & music teachers	72,678	79,611
Hotel & restaurant keepers/managers	29,778	57,318

*Omitted are 5 factory operative lines of minimal importance in King County.[5]

ready-made clothing, the number of women in the sewing occupations declined sharply, by 117,108 during the 1920s, while their number increased by 81,108 in clothing factories. Women as factory operatives outnumbered men in 12 manufacturing lines: clothing, silk mills, knitting mills, cigar and tobacco factories, and candy factories.[2]

Dempsey's tables show the distribution of gainfully employed women in major fields for 1920 and 1930, TABLE 11.

While unmarried women continued to far outnumber married women in the non-agricultural work force, married women increased relative to the number of unmarried women. Married women's share of the female part of the work force increased from 21% to 28% during the 1920s. Elyce Rotella, in her study, found that the largest increases among married women was mainly among native-born whites in the age groups 20-44; those in the age 25-44 subgroup accounted for 24% of the total expansion of the female work force from 1920 to 1930. By 1930, she reports, 11 out of every 100 married women were employed in the non-agricultural work force, while 42 of every 100 single women were so employed. Relative to the growth of the married female population as a whole, the rate of gainful employment among married females was 2.4 times greater. Nationwide, as well as in Washington, longer school attendance requirements lowered participation of younger unmarried women among the gainfully employed. Black married women, she reports, showed little change in their participation, and among the oldest and youngest there was a decline in their participation. Working against wider employment of married women was the general bias against employment of both husband and wife, particularly during times of high unemployment. As for teachers, specifically, married teachers were often banned from employment; in Seattle the ban was not lifted until 1947.[3]

The 1940 Population Census provides comparative figures on the sexual composition of the work force in Seattle for the age group, 14 years and older:[4]

	1910	1920	1930	1940
Male	102,395	120,335	130,068	121,921
Female	19,737	33,160	45,354	49,070

For the state as a whole the figures are:

Male	454,248	484,781	587,407	568,119
Female	65,968	92,781	126,603	148,382

In 1940 there were 3,619 men on "public emergency work", while 14,244 were seeking work. (Of the latter, 950 were "new workers".) Corresponding figures for women were 910 on public emergency work and 4,266 seeking work. (Of the latter, 776 were new workers.) Statewide, there were 32,539 men on public emergency work, and 5,407 women. Those seeking work numbered 57,255 men and 13,628 women.

Figures on marital status of employed women in 1940 in Seattle show 16,144 married women and 22,211 single women employed. Of the married women 13,491 lived with their spouses. (There is no indication of the spouses' employment status.) "Widowed or divorced" men numbered 7,669; women numbered 10,715. (See TABLE 12).

TABLE 12—Major Occupations of 43,894 Women in Seattle, 1940*

Occupation		
Professional & semiprofessional		6,173*
Teachers	2,117	
Nurses, trained and student	1,880	
Musicians & music teachers	400	
Social & Welfare workers	229	
Librarians	189	
Artists & art teachers	114	
College presidents, profs, instructors	109	
Authors, editors, reporters	103	
Proprietors, managers, nonfarm officials		2,997*
By industry:		
Manufacturing	158	
Eating & drinking places	378	
Other wholesale & retail trade	822	
Personal services	164	
Clerical, sales & kindred workers		17,139*
Stenographers, typists, secretaries	5,897	
Bookkeepers, accountants, cashiers, ticket agents	2,444	
Other clerical & kindred workers	3,494	
Other saleswomen	3,724	
Operatives & kindred workers		4,590*
By industry:		
Manufacturing		2,162*
Apparel & other fabricated products	981	
Food & kindred products	661	
Paper, paper products, & printing	144	
Non-manufacturing industries & services		684
Domestic service workers		4,597*
Service workers except domestic & protective		7,141*
Waitresses & bartenders	2,487	
Barbers, beauticians, manicurists	1,007	
Servants, except private family	923	
Cooks, except private family	628	
Practical nurses & midwives	417	
Housekeepers, stewardesses, hostesses except private family	392	

*This total and the following subtotals are larger than those from the categories selected for listing here.

10

The Economy in the 1930s

By focusing on the waterborne commerce of the city in the 1930s a general impression of the overall economy can be derived. (See chapters 4 on waterborne commerce; chapters 5-7 on manufacturing and "other lines of economic activity"; chapter 9, "Women in the Work Force"; and chapter 17, for other aspects of the economy in the 1930s.) On the facing page (TABLE 13) a summary of tonnage handled by the port from 1900 to 1936 provides an overview. Between 1904 and 1936 the tonnage increased from 1,378,253 to 6,368,448 tons; but the years from 1923 through 1931 saw more tonnage than in 1936, with the high point reached in 1929, when over 9 million tons were imported and exported. The year 1933 saw a low point that had not been reached since the postwar depression in which only 4,062,981 tons passed over the docks in 1921. This commerce in 1936 represented a steady but gradual increase from the 1933 low that would be interrupted during the 1937-1938 recession, then pick up again in 1939 and continue during the war years, only to resume its secular decline after the war. This secular decline would continue until containerized cargo was introduced in the 1960s, concomitant with a labor-management agreement that ended the years of belligerency that had resumed with the 1934 maritime strike.[1]

With respect to the Pacific Coast maritime shipping industry in general, Gorter and Hildebrand point out that even before 1930 the industry was not attracting new investment; the bitter

YEAR	FOREIGN			TOTAL DOMESTIC			TOTAL COMMERCE FOREIGN AND DOMESTIC		
	IMPORTS	EXPORTS	TOTAL	IMPORTS	EXPORTS	TOTAL	IMPORTS	EXPORTS	TOTAL
1900	41,264	96,484	137,748	...	...	...	...	...	...
1901	38,799	111,442	150,241	...	...	...	...	...	...
1902	61,880	196,828	258,708	...	...	...	...	...	...
1903	62,947	216,826	279,773	...	...	...	...	...	...
1904	97,227	151,643	248,870	677,623	451,760	1,129,383	774,850	603,403	1,378,253
1905	44,560	292,504	337,064	766,613	525,514	1,292,127	811,173	818,018	1,629,191
1906	76,242	387,676	463,918	757,028	627,869	1,384,897	833,270	1,015,545	1,848,815
1907	110,602	343,774	454,376	908,203	693,341	1,601,544	1,018,805	1,037,115	2,055,920
1908	104,336	278,590	382,926	833,728	610,179	1,443,907	938,064	888,769	1,826,833
1909	126,657	163,161	289,818	802,778	712,155	1,514,933	929,435	875,316	1,804,751
1910	135,821	175,462	311,283	693,188	504,231	1,197,419	829,009	679,693	1,508,702
1911	180,180	229,922	410,102	924,896	581,342	1,506,238	1,105,076	811,264	1,916,340
1912	172,252	343,116	515,368	1,048,303	562,135	1,610,438	1,220,555	905,251	2,125,806
1913	172,489	322,287	494,776	1,078,154	573,582	1,651,736	1,250,643	895,869	2,146,512
1914	213,068	267,200	480,268	1,211,200	653,465	1,864,665	1,424,268	920,665	2,344,933
1915	316,066	497,966	814,032	1,690,178	790,270	2,480,448	2,006,244	1,288,236	3,294,480
1916	469,502	656,028	1,125,530	2,419,215	795,658	3,214,873	2,888,717	1,451,686	4,340,403
1917	665,644	719,679	1,385,323	2,655,504	809,800	3,465,304	3,321,148	1,529,479	4,850,627
1918	956,481	1,137,860	2,094,341	2,759,011	850,142	3,609,153	3,715,492	1,988,002	5,703,494
1919	856,802	1,167,186	2,023,988	2,826,895	866,665	3,693,560	3,683,697	2,033,851	5,717,548
1920	599,129	812,761	1,411,890	3,026,916	790,255	3,817,171	3,626,045	1,603,016	5,229,061
1921	412,038	612,308	1,024,346	2,378,752	659,883	3,038,635	2,790,790	1,272,191	4,062,981
1922	510,783	638,832	1,149,615	3,418,643	889,231	4,307,874	3,929,426	1,528,063	5,457,489
1923	426,223	697,194	1,123,417	4,229,156	1,098,624	5,327,780	4,655,379	1,795,818	6,451,197
1924	443,599	761,645	1,205,244	4,852,500	1,560,841	6,413,341	5,296,099	2,322,486	7,618,585
1925	457,961	455,477	913,438	5,410,737	1,555,626	6,966,363	5,868,698	2,011,103	7,879,801
1926	448,252	724,602	1,172,854	5,780,057	1,479,506	7,259,563	6,228,309	2,204,108	8,432,417
1927	515,082	784,044	1,299,126	5,666,953	1,575,965	7,242,918	6,182,035	2,360,009	8,542,044
1928	471,096	721,043	1,192,139	6,124,893	1,590,770	7,715,663	6,595,989	2,311,813	8,907,802
1929	474,787	663,416	1,138,203	6,345,433	1,713,845	8,059,278	6,820,220	2,377,261	9,197,481
1930	406,677	504,961	911,638	6,000,352	1,450,598	7,450,950	6,407,029	1,955,559	8,362,588
1931	261,006	528,363	789,369	4,894,814	1,603,171	6,497,985	5,155,820	2,131,534	7,287,354
1932	247,478	351,079	598,557	3,875,144	1,424,435	5,299,579	4,122,622	1,775,514	5,898,136
1933	259,447	350,649	610,096	3,465,238	1,471,767	4,937,005	3,724,685	1,822,416	5,547,101
1934	217,560	540,792	758,352	3,779,625	1,576,553	5,356,178	3,997,185	2,117,345	6,114,530
1935	317,077	374,837	691,914	4,248,277	1,825,234	6,073,511	4,565,354	2,200,071	6,765,425
1936	343,817	320,483	664,300	4,256,976	1,447,172	5,704,148	4,600,793	1,767,655	6,368,448

Port of Seattle *Yearbook, 1937*

TABLE 13—Summary of Waterborne Commerce at Seattle, 1900-1936, Inclusive: Tons 2,000 Pounds

and unrelenting war between labor and management after unionism revived in 1934 only contributed to the industry's relative and absolute decline. Underscoring investment timidity in Seattle, the Port Commission commented in 1929 that the Port of Seattle once had an excess of facilities, but that they had become inadequate; no new terminals had been built in the last year (when shipping was continuing toward a peak); additional elevators were needed, along with sheds at Pier 40 to house canned salmon. "With the exception of the Salmon Bay Terminal the various operating units are rapidly reaching the limit of possible development." Contributing to this coastwide trend were technological improvements of land-based transportation, both highway and rail. Introduction of oil pipelines provided another alternative to waterborne transport in which labor costs were relatively higher in proportion to overall costs, becoming higher also in the form of unit costs, not to be modified until after 1960.[2]

Seattle's foreign trade dropped sharply for some major trading partners during the Depression, most notably with Japan, with whom the value of imports fell from $57,424,160 in 1931 to a mere $10,752,636 by 1936—despite the showing of an increased import tonnage in these years of 49,264 and 57,501 tons, respectively. Bear in mind that raw silk had been the backbone of that trade, and when combined with transshipment by rail to the east coast, it had provided a solid economic base that never returned. Exports to Japan, except for 1934, showed a steady decline from $5,811,250 in 1931 to $2,609,939 by 1936. Trade with China ran contrary to the overall trend, however: except for a low in 1932, the import tonnage was within the 23,000 to 26,000 range from 1931 to 1936, with a value of over $18 million each in 1931, 1932, 1934, jumping to over $32 million in 1936; the value of exports to China was worth more than $5 million in 1931 and over $4 million in 1936, sagging in the years between. (Airplanes and parts became a major component of exports to China: 12 tons in 1931, 42 tons in 1932, 120 tons in 1933, 35 tons in 1934, 21 tons in 1935, and 193 tons in 1936.)

The value of exports to the United Kingdom also remained relatively high, being worth almost $6 million in 1931, more than that in 1935, and falling to just under $5 million in 1936. Imports from the U.K. steadily grew from a low value in 1932 of $156,495 to $633,713 by 1936. Trade with another major partner, British Columbia, also held up relatively well: exports to B.C. were valued at $4,533,668 in 1931, and revived from the 1932-33 slump to reach $4,963,283 in 1936; and imports climbed steadily from 1931 to 1935, dropping slightly in 1936 ($3 million in 1931 to over $4 million in 1935). Imports from B.C. fluctuated sharply, falling from 144,097 tons in 1932 to 101,521 in 1936, while exports steadily increased, except for 1932 and 1933, from 37,484 tons in 1931 to a high of 57,922 in 1935, then falling to 39,287 in 1936. Overall, however, the city's total foreign commerce recorded a decline in tonnage from 789,369 tons in 1931 to 664,300 tons in 1936, representing a drop in value from $110,599,304 in 1931 to $82,007,155 in 1936. The Japanese trade made the difference.[3]

Domestic commerce showed an overall decline of 847,366 tons as between 1931 and 1936, although the value of it did not show a corresponding drop ($335 million in 1931 and $324 million in 1936). Except for the low years of 1932 and 1933 the Alaska trade remained steady: Exports were valued at $20,805,321 in 1931 and gradually climbed to $33,994,756 by 1936; imports, except for 1932, were valued at $34,410,783 in 1931 and $49,660,525 by 1936. Trade with California, excepting 1932 and 1933, ranged between $92 million in 1931 and $83 million in 1936 for imports, and for exports there was a steady increase, except in 1932, from over $24 million to $34 million for 1931 and 1936, respectively. (Export tonnage fell from 290,943 tons in 1931 to 165,385 in 1936, while import tonnage showed only slight variations above and below 2,225,000 tons.) Trade with the Atlantic Seaboard showed only small variations in terms of value in both directions between 1931 and 1936, although there were relatively wide variations in tonnage. "Local Points"—the Puget Sound Basin—showed a general decline in both exports and imports: exports in 1931 totaled 734,764 tons, declining sharply in 1932 and 1933, picking up in 1934 to 619,996, then rising to 754,159 tons in 1935, only to fall again to 547,194 tons in 1936. The value of these exports saw a practically unrelieved drop from $31,016,998 in 1931 to $17,640,840 in 1936. Imports from Sound ports saw an uninterrupted fall from 2,043,082 tons in 1931 to 1,269,824 tons in 1936; their value reflected this tonnage decline from $39,017,513 in 1931 to $22,570,471 in 1936. It appears from these statistics that the overall secular decline described by Gortner and Hildebrand did not hold as true for Seattle as it seemed for the Pacific Coast in general.[4]

The mainstays of this trade were canned salmon, flour, wheat, apples, and fuel oil and gasoline. Of immense collective value was the continued provisioning of Alaska with everything from household goods and clothing, machinery and hardware, to supplying the canneries. (It was estimated that fish canneries, alone, annually expended $25 million for their operations.) Using 1936 figures a sense of proportion can be gleaned. Almost six million cases of canned salmon were imported from Alaska; they were stored in special sheds (Pier 40 at Smith's Cove added a capacity of 2,000,000 cases in 1930 to what already existed at the other port terminals). Of this total, 1,850,627 cases were shipped by water to the Atlantic Seaboard, 318,949 cases to the United Kingdom, and 284,395 to Gulf ports; most of the rest was shipped by rail to eastern domestic markets. The Atlantic Seaboard took about 40% of the 82,478 tons of flour; California imported over 50% of the 790,900 bushels of wheat, while the Atlantic Seaboard took about 36% of the grain. Of the 1,811,214 boxes of apples exported, over 425,000 went to the Netherlands, 386,000 to France, 352,000 to the United Kingdom, 175,000 to Germany and central Europe. (In 1931 5,500,000 boxes of apples were shipped, the "most ever".) Fuel oil and gasoline remained the far largest imports from California: 822,605 tons of fuel oil; gasoline, another 885,675 tons.[5]

Part III

Population

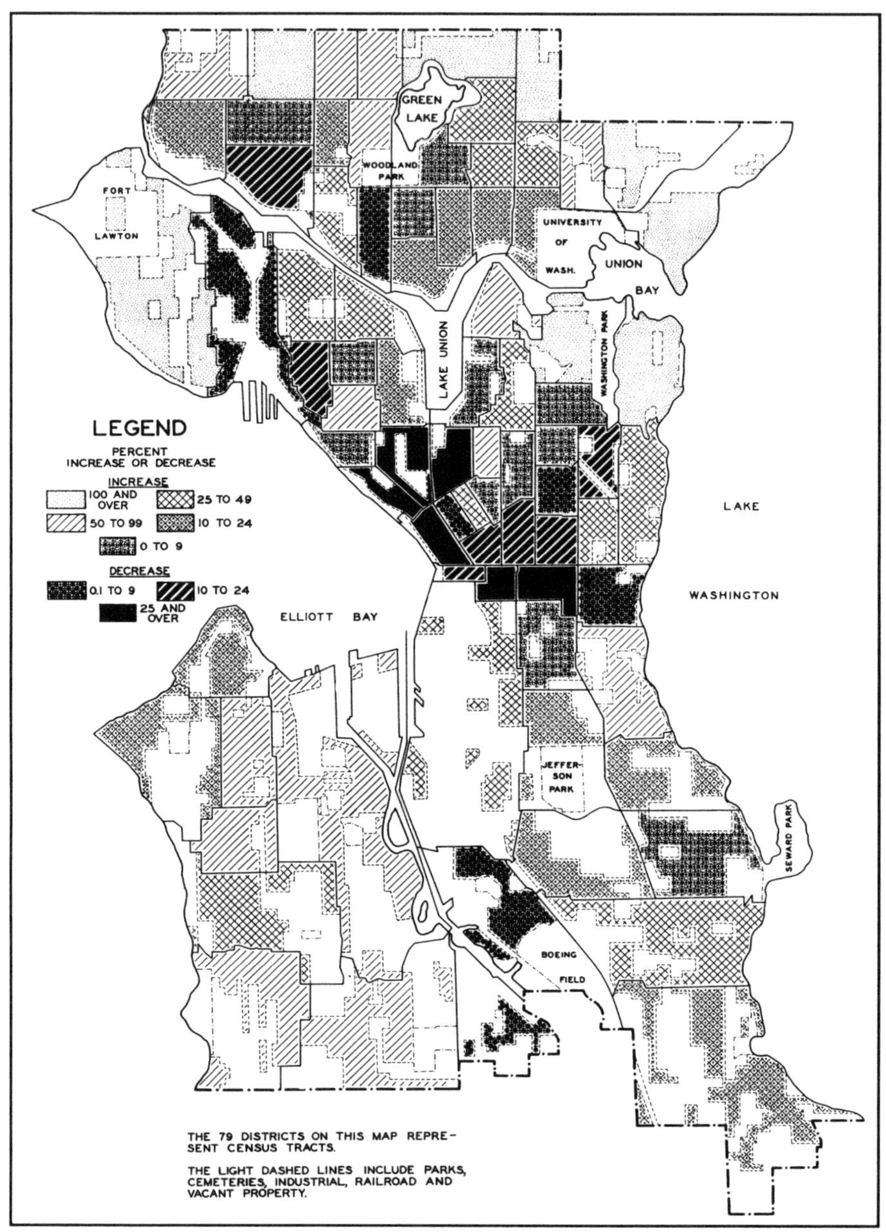

From Calvin Schmid, *Social Trends in Seattle*

Growth and Decline of Population, 1920-1940

11

General Characteristics

Seattle's population in 1920 was 315,312; by 1930 it reached 365,583; however, the city added only 2,719 people during the following decade. Between 1920 and 1930 the total gain of population for the 15 counties making up the Puget Sound Region was 155,919. Of this number, King County's population increased by 74,244 (47.6% of the region's total). Seattle registered 32.2% of this figure (Tacoma represented 6.3%). A marked change occurred in the following decade, with Seattle's population hardly increasing, almost all the growth occurring in King County outside Seattle. Between 1930 and 1940, of the total increase of 92,679 for the 15 counties, 44.7% of it was in King County, almost that of the previous decade. Relative to the state's population growth between 1930 and 1940, the county accounted for 24% of it, while the Puget Sound Region represented 53.6% of the gain statewide.[1]

Focusing upon the "metropolitan district" (encompassing suburbia, and defined mainly as "all adjacent and contiguous minor civil divisions having a density of not less than 150 inhabitants per square mile", plus the city proper)—the increase between 1930 and 1940 was 31,976. The total figure for this area in 1930 was 420,663; in 1940 it was 452,639. The population in the closer-in suburbs in 1930 was 55,080, climbing to 84,337 by 1940, representing a gain of 29,257 since 1930 or 53.1%. This figure contrasted with Seattle's slight 0.7% growth rate. These percentages reflect the declining birth rate during the 1930s depression

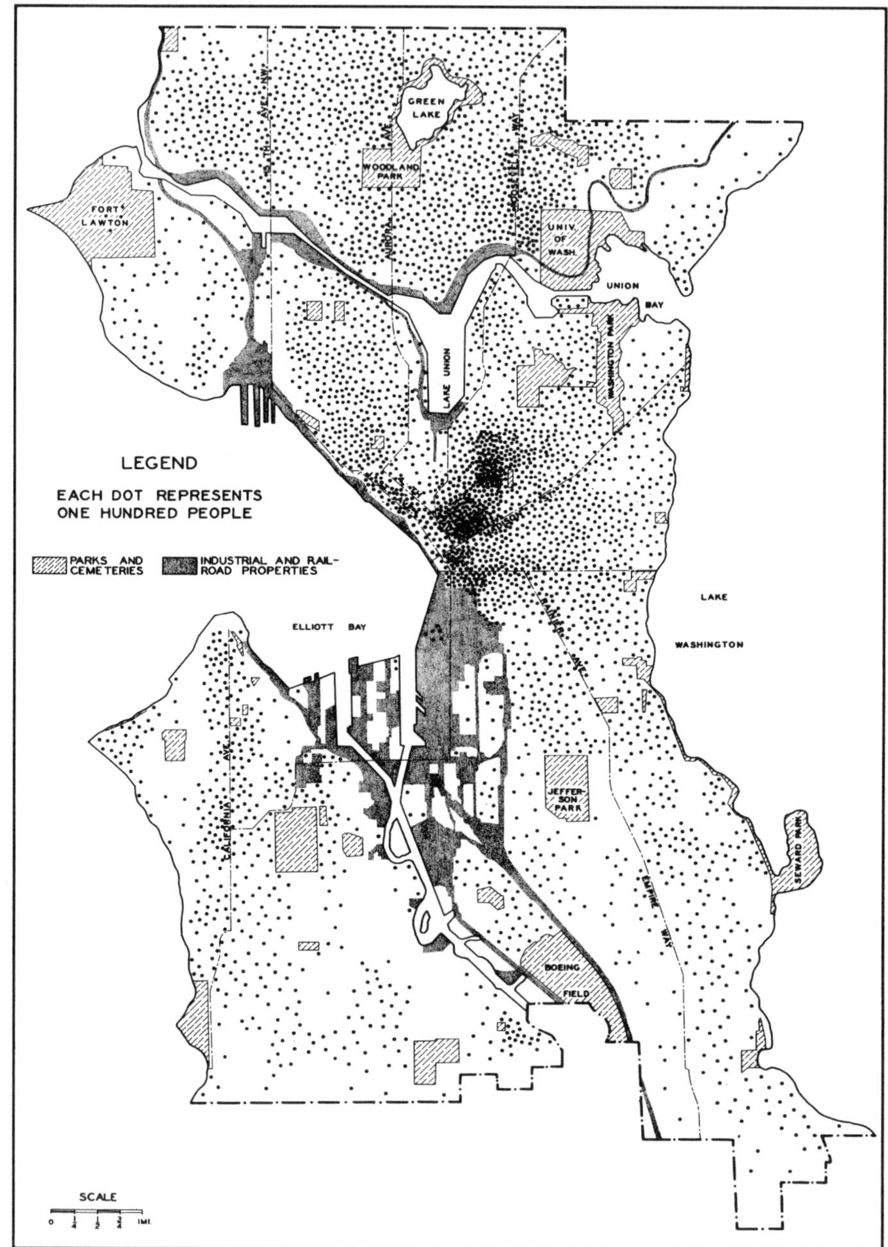

From Calvin Schmid, *Social Trends in Seattle*

Population Density, Seattle, 1940

years, and the migration of desperate people out of the city in search of jobs and with the expectation of being able to eke out an existence by quasi-subsistence farming. Richard White writes that during the 1930s subsistence farming in western Washington increased from 2,339 to 21,869 farms, representing the largest increase for that category of farming in the state; it constituted only a supplement to whatever could be scrounged from other sources. Stimulating this migration was the improvement of transportation, chiefly the automobile, and the networking of county and state roads. Cheaper housing and lower taxes provided added incentives.[2]

Sex and age ratios within the population provide another perspective. The excess of males relative to females steadily declined in Seattle from a ratio in 1900 of 176.7 males to 100 females. By 1920 the ratio was 113.5 to 100; by 1930 it was 103.7 to 100; and 99.3 to 100 in 1940. Seattle, being a commercial, rather than an industrial city, tended to attract a higher proportion of younger females, particularly those from the agricultural sector. The Depression decade interrupted any long term trends. At both ends of the age spectrum its impact is illustrated: Children under age 5 decreased in both relative and absolute numbers; and the age bracket for ages 45 to 64 had changed proportionately from 10.3% in 1890 to 26.5% by 1940, and ages 65 and upward from 1.2% to 8.8% for the same years. These numbers should be borne in mind as we address the politics of unemployment, relief and welfare during the period 1933-1940, when the pension movement gained political momentum.[3]

A look at the ethnic and racial composition of the population gives yet another perspective on the population. Those foreign-born from Canada and Western and Northern Europe continued to predominate, particularly after enactment of the 1924 Immigration Law, which discriminated particularly against those from Eastern and Southern Europe, and Asian countries. In 1940 there were 63,470 foreign-born in Seattle. Of this total, 12,666 were from Canada (20%); 8,436 (13.3%) were from Norway; 7,670 from Sweden (12.1%); 6,065 from England and Wales (9.6%); 3,581 from Germany (5.6%); 3,055 from Italy (4.8%); 2,876 from Japan (4.5%); of the rest, only Scotland, Russia, and Ireland each contributed more than 2,000. Of this total, the number of foreign-born whites was 59,612, compared with 3,858 nonwhites. Among 31 cities of comparable size, Seattle ranked fifth nationally, with 16.8% of its population being foreign-born whites.[4]

The central business part of the city and adjacent area south of Yesler had the highest concentration of foreign-born whites, the lowest percentage of single family dwelling units, and the highest concentration of non-whites. The foreign-born whites living there also were the poorest of their ethnic group. Schmid's maps show that Norwegians and Swedes predominated in this area; but each of the whites from other national origins also had a relatively high proportion of their total number concentrated in this downtown and fringe area. As observed in volume one of this history, foreign-born groups tended to cluster, although only Asians, Jews (mainly "Russians"), African Americans ("Blacks"), and Italians, were concentrated to a higher degree. It appears that the foreign-born whites in the central city were not only poor, but remained so for the large part—being captured in a rim of poverty on which the Great Depression planted a lid after the 1920s failed to gain them entry into the stable force, among the more skilled workers. They represented the more casual work force, as common labor in the building trades, dependent upon seasonal and part-time employment in the maritime trades, upon demand for unskilled laborers in the forest products industry, and agriculture. (Ballard shared a good many of these characteristics also—but the seasonality of the fisheries played a larger part there.) Those among them who found steady work, and who upgraded their skills probably moved outward, paying less attention to ethnic affinity at each stage of their upwardly trek. Probably the poorer whites in this area were first-generation immigrants among whom were those who migrated outward as they gained literacy and job skills. Non-whites who might also have achieved comparable literacy and skills tended to remain in this area due to the array of discriminatory practices facing those who tried to move out. The most successful in migrating out of the area were the Japanese, who moved in the direction of Beacon Hill which also had one of the highest concentrations of Italians.[5]

Among the white minority population groups, Italians and Jews continued to show the highest concentrations. In 1910 there were 3,454 Italians in the city; it is assumed they were almost all foreign-born. The number of foreign-born Italians in 1940 was 3,055. Along with other foreign-born whites they showed one concentration in the central business district, but their numbers were spread mainly south of Yesler and east of 12th Avenue toward Beacon Hill and along the eastern fringe of that hill along Rainier Avenue, and toward Georgetown along the western border. These were the more urban of the Italians. Those still farming were concentrated in the Duwamish-South Park-

Georgetown area toward Boeing Field. Those in this latter area must have worked in the factories and warehouses abounding in this section as well. Overall, males outnumbered females by a ratio of 155.4 to 100, most heavily in the downtown business area—an area where single males predominated in general. The high school districts to which most of the children went to school were Franklin, Broadway, Cleveland, and Garfield.[6]

An index to the concentration of Jews is provided by the distribution of foreign-born Russians—substantially all were Jews. To their number should be added Sephardic Jews, who are not differentiated by Schmid. (Seattle's Sephardic population reputedly was the third largest in the nation, behind that of New York and San Francisco.) In 1940 there were 2,371 foreign-born Russians in the city. Their highest concentration was in the central business district and its southern fringe, in which males far outnumbered females. In 24 census tracts females outnumbered males, and in 13 tracts they were about evenly divided. Overall the ratio was 128 males to 100 females. The main concentration, as with the Jewish population in general, was between Broadway, on the west, to Lake Washington, and between Yesler and Roy Street. This represents a spread outward from their original center, but not a dispersion throughout the city. Garfield High School is where most of the Jewish children matriculated.[7]

12

Seattle's Non-Caucasian Population: General

The 1940 census enumerated 14,201 Non-Caucasians in the city, including 6,975 Japanese, 3,789 Blacks, 1,781 Chinese, 1,392 Filipinos, 222 Native Americans, and 9 Hindus. The Japanese population had declined during the Depression from a high of 8,448 in 1930 as many either returned to the homeland or to California in search of livelihood. Blacks showed a slow, steady increase in numbers, indicating growth by natural processes rather than new migration. Chinese numbers also showed a steady, though modest increase—practically none during the 1930s. 458 Filipinos were counted in 1920, after which they partially filled the demand for seasonal workers. Their numbers can only be considered crude estimates in any case, due to the fact that a high proportion were sojourners and in transit between seasonal jobs. Nominally there were 1,614 in 1930, and 1,392 in 1940.[1]

Apart from the clusters of Blacks in the 23rd Avenue and East Madison Street neighborhood, near East Cherry Street, and around 26th Avenue and Jackson Street area, these non-white minorities remained concentrated in the "Chinatown" section. Blacks and Japanese, as their numbers increased, tended gradually to extend outward from Chinatown—the less-transient Blacks toward the three clusters noted above. Japanese trended away from the crown of "Profanity Hill" toward 18th and Yesler, and also southeasterly in the direction of Beacon Hill.[2]

Both Chinese and Filipinos seemed stuck in Chinatown on the fringes of which the few Native Americans subsisted. In 1929 Filipinos were singled out for information for the director of education of the United YMCA Schools: "[R]oughly three thousand Filipino men enter Seattle yearly, while relatively few stay for any length of time. The group, as a whole, shifts rapidly and is continually going to Alaska and scattering widely in the northwest states in search of employment. During winter, quite a group come to the city where they are crowded into cheap lodging houses . . .All agree that this is a needy group."[3]

A feeling for the social life in Chinatown is portrayed by a Filipino correspondent, Willy Torrin. Before 8 AM Chinatown is "dead". At 10 AM "The crowd begins to form around street corners and in the lobby of the Alps Hotel. By noon King street is like a barrio street in the Philippines . . . Filipino pool halls open, [offering] diversion of pool and cards . . . Labor's latest news is read and discussed . . . Seven o'clock in the evening and . . . the barber shops begin to get busy . . . Jackson street is like Second avenue during a parade. The boys from uptown come downtown to get down to business—lotteries, the card games, the sicoy-sicoy, et al . . . [By 10 PM the] tantalizing music at Rizal Hall . . . the crowd moves around . . . There is pleasure in them thar houses . . . [By 1 AM Rizal Hall closes, but] the Atlas Theatre is open all night." (Rizal Hall, near 6th and King Street, was the effective community center for Filipinos.)[4]

Although Frank Miyamoto describes the Japanese community of the Chinatown-Jackson Street area, his portrayal applies with almost equal relevance to the other non-white components of the population there. "Here, near Fifth and Sixth Avenues on Main and Jackson Streets, is the business center of the Japanese district, consisting of a congeries of shops including everything from barber shops and restaurants to book stores and law offices. The business center is not today what it was in the heyday of the early nineteen-twenties, when Main Street really teemed with the life of the incoming immigrants and prosperous farmers visiting town. Rather is one aware now that the depression has not dealt kindly with the shop-keepers; that the failure of the one community's bank, and the large movements of their population back to Japan, and even more to California, have drained the life-blood out of the community." Picture also the many Chinese restaurants, their small shops catering specifically to Asian diets and cultural tastes, lotteries, gambling hangouts, the growing number of Japanese-owned hotels (which inspired the formation of a Japanese Hotel Owners Association), labor contractor/employment agencies, streets through which policemen walked their beats, some collecting payoffs—picturing these elements conveys a fuller sense of the scene.[5]

An occupational census conducted by the Seattle Japanese Chamber of Commerce in 1935 showed the following

Of the total 2,867 Japanese who were enumerated:

45% were in "Trade" (1,146 males and 146 females)
31% were in "Domestic and Personal Service" (627 males and 259 females)
6% were in "Professional Service" (123 males and 56 females)
6% were in "Manufacturing and Mechanical Industry"(83 men and 73 females)
4% were "Clerical[s]" (91 males and 31 females)
3% were in "Agriculture" (94 males and 2 females)
3% were in "Transportation and Communication" (69 males only)
2% were in "Public Service" (55 males only)

Miyamoto qualifies "Trades" and "Domestic and Personal Service" as practically indistinguishable, because 29% of the latter category includes "hotels, restaurants, barber shops, and laundries". By 1935, of the ten most important occupations among the Japanese 183 worked in hotels, 148 in groceries, 94 in dye works, 64 in public market stands, 57 in produce houses, 57 in gardening, 42 in restaurants, 36 in barber shops, 31 in laundries, and 24 peddled fruit and vegetables.[6]

Gross annual earnings of the Japanese in 1930, by category, show the largest to be:

12 import-export dealers	$7,733,831
100 grocery stores	3,500,000
136 hotels	1,643,250
2 railroad worker contractor[s]	1,530,134
39 American restaurants	1,388,000
10 fish dealers	1,375,300
14 produce houses	1,054,278
61 vegetable markets	910,000
5 cannery contractors	530,132
24 Japanese restaurants	372,500
7 dry-goods stores	284,916
33 laundries	283,125
7 meat markets	121,600

The total investment represented by all 905 Japanese businesses was $7,175,589. Earnings totalled $24,055,494.[7]

Miyamoto, writing in 1939, outlines the center of the Japanese community as running "from Yesler Way to Dearborn, and from First Avenue eastward to Sixteenth, and for all its apparent loss of vigor, it is within this area or on the fringe of it that almost all the important Japanese institutions still tend to be congregated." Extending outward they are intermingled "with the Jews, the Italians and other working-class whites."[8]

Passage of the 1924 Immigration Act affected the proportion of foreign-born to native-born Japanese. With Japanese immigration banned, the proportion of native-born increased—of the 7,874 Japanese in Seattle in 1920 only 1,863 were native-born; of the 8,448 in 1930 4,000 were native-born. Culturally, the effect was to shift emphasis in the community to the well-being and status of the second generation ("Nisei") because their citizenship status enabled them to own property. It is the Nisei who formed the Progressive Citizens League in 1921, which meekly continued until 1925, only to be revived in 1928 to serve as the local chapter of the Japanese American Citizens League, when the JACL was finally established in 1930 under leadership of Seattle Japanese. The JACL was organized "primarily . . . to more closely identify the second generation with American life through their participation in civic activities." A voice for the Seattle Japanese community gave focus to their concerns, beginning in 1928, when James Y. Sakamoto established the *Japanese-American Courier*. It continued publication until the evacuation in 1942.[9]

13

African Americans in the City

We have seen, in volume one, that African Americans—or "Blacks"—were kept at arm's distance by Whites even though their numbers were small. Numbering only 406 in the city in 1900, they became part of the huge population spurt of the ensuing decade, increasing to 2,296 by 1910, and expanding modestly in successive decades: 2,894 in 1920, 3,303 in 1930, and 3,789 in 1940. Joseph S. Jackson, in his study, reported that the Black population peaked at more than 5,000 in 1926 "after the stewards jobs became available." However, by mid-1927 an outward migration set in as jobs did not materialize in the way expected. Fluctuations were traceable to the ups and downs of the Pacific [Coast] Steamship Company, "the largest single employer of Negro labor on the coast." (Details of Black maritime employment is covered below in connection with the 1934 maritime strike.) Since 1910 Blacks remained about 1% of the city's population. For all practical purposes they were excluded from the organized labor movement, though befriended by IWW members of the International Longshoremen's Association, who gained for some a temporary union membership during the war years. Though winning a fine residential neighborhood through the acumen and generosity of William Gross, in the 23rd Avenue and East Madison Street area, restrictive covenants largely confined Blacks to south of Madison Street. Many public establishments discriminated against Blacks. Some theaters restricted their seating (to balconies in Pantages' theaters); some restaurants refused them service; courts consistently denied them civil rights protections. A measure of Black social acceptability is indicated by the attitude expressed by the *Argus*'s sophisticated conservative, Harry Chadwick. He consistently spoke derisively of them, holding them to be genetically inferior, and frequently he sounded the alarm of miscegenation, a worry that he transferred to Asian-White relationships as well. Employment was found primarily in low-paying, menial, temporary, and part-time deadend jobs. In domestic service they were often replaced by Japanese, later by Filipinos, and poorer white immigrants. Yet, despite these obvious disadvantages, Seattle seemed more hospitable to Blacks than almost any other city in the country. To wherever Blacks migrated it seemed the white majority would never allow them escape from the stigma of their original enslavement—as though that condition were self-inflicted, not imposed and policed by the white majority. By perpetuating the social and economic inferiority defined by their original status the white majority had invented their self-fulfilling prophesy for Blacks.[1]

Detailed accounting of the Black population before launching of the *Northwest Enterprise* in 1931 is lacking. We will observe in other sections of this volume that native Japanese and Japanese descendants found a voice in the *Japanese-American Courier,* and the Filipinos through several of their community newspapers. As to the Japanese, they became quickly singled out for attention by Japanophobes on the one hand, and on the other hand by sociologists and historians interested in one aspect or another of their assimilation; consequently, a body of literature and propaganda exists for them that is lacking for urban Blacks in most northern and western cities. We are able to glimpse Black community life in Seattle by profiling some coverage largely given by the *Northwest Enterprise* in the early 1930s. In its makeup, special sections covering Tacoma, Spokane, and Portland were included, along with shorter columns of news from smaller cities and towns in the region. The following offers a Seattle profile.

In the very first issue of the *Enterprise,* January 1, 1931, it was noted: "Colored Waiters Back at Butler Hotel". They had been replaced by a crew of whites in the summer. Also a "colored orchestra" is playing in the hotel's Rose Room. Marian Anderson will give a recital at Reverend Fred Shorter's Plymouth Congregational Church on the 6th. (Shorter was a known defender of minority rights, and would soon be forced from the church, only to establish his own "Church of the People" in the University district.)[2]

The January 8 number reported that the NAACP had found employment for 14. It had stopped discrimination in 4 restaurants, 3 theaters, 2 lake resorts, and at the Ice Arena. Paroles had been gained from Walla Walla for 3 prisoners. Advertising by a roadhouse had been stopped because it "reflected on colored people". (This probably was "Coon Chicken Inn" on then-Bothell Way at the northern edge of the city.) Four radio stations agreed to eliminate "terms that are disagreeable to colored people". And the *Times* agreed to capitalize "N" when using the term Negro; negotiations were in progress with the two other dailies.

On January 22 an account of the 17th annual meeting of the King County Colored Republican Club was presented. The durable ex—publisher of the *Seattle Republican*, Horace R. Cayton, though down on his luck, urged support for the party, "right or wrong". But Cayton was found leading a dissident movement in October, and calling for a meeting on November 7 of all Colored Republican Clubs (women's clubs included) in the state. Cayton presided, but *Enterprise* publisher, William H. Wilson, responded by resigning from the club. In December, Cayton would lose to Newton J. Grafell by a vote of 37 to 11, in the contest for the KCCRC presidency.

Visiting Black entertainers included Paul Robeson, appearing at the Metropolitan Theater on February 18, Stepin' Fetchit at the Fox Paramount during late May, and Roland Hayes, singing at Meany Hall on the University campus, October 22. For December, a "Negro Art Exhibit"—the "Harmon exhibit"—was announced for the Henry Gallery on the University campus.

The October 22 issue noted that "Colored unemployed" will have a place to sleep and have two meals a day at the Welfare Club during fall and winter. On November 19 an East Madison Unemployed Citizens' League local was organized at 2023 East Madison. (The UCLs started as a unique self-help organization in August; its activities are described in detail below.) The paper urged all "Colored citizens" to register at their respective UCL locals. Joseph S. Jackson, executive secretary of the newly established Urban League, and Henry Johnson were instrumental in its formation. The August 18, 1932 issue noted that eleven White members of the East Madison UCL had been ousted for objecting to being served by "colored officers"; other Whites concurred in their ouster. In that same number, the South Side Civic and Improvement Club (organized in January

1932 by Edward Robinson, owner of a drug store at 12th and Jackson) announced the regular serving of one free meal daily at 3 PM; one hundred "colored men" were being served.

In January 1932 the Seattle Urban League held its first annual meeting. In the category "Employment", Jackson reported: employment relief was found for 65 on City projects; the league established a job placement service which registered 498 persons (356 males and 142 females); it made 221 contacts, and placed 117. A sample of the placements made is indicated in its May 1931 report: 10 temporary laborers, 3 housemaids, 1 gardener, 2 porters, 1 extra maid, 1 ranch hand, 1 electrician, 1 painter, and 1 laundress. For the year, it reported cooperation with several social agencies, and received some funding from the Community Chest.[3]

Warming up to the 1932 presidential election, and banking on desertions of Blacks from the "lily-white" Republican policies being perpetuated with a flourish by President Hoover, a King County Colored Democratic Club was organized in August 1932, with N.N. Carter its president. The club had not become active enough to participate in the September primary, but the KCCRC, under Cayton's persevering leadership, helped to nominate 18 of the 21 Republicans who ran. For their active role in the November general election the newly elected county commissioners announced their plans to replace all Republican "colored" employees in the County-City Building with "colored Democratic supporters" to be named by the KCCDC.[4]

Employment and opportunity in the urban setting in general had always been foremost among the problems faced by non-rural Blacks. The Urban League took up this challenge in Seattle in November 1930, as noted above, under the leadership of Joseph S. Jackson. What Whites either took for granted or could accomplish by upgrading their skills, formal knowledge and training, Blacks had yet to achieve in the city. The Urban League's by-laws underscore these basic objectives: ". . . [T]o improve the industrial status of non-white workmen by organization of educational groups, to urge efficiency and teach skills, reliability and honesty on the job, and in cooperation with managements and unions wherever possible, to serve as a resource to improve general efficiency; to form contacts with managements and unions, encourage them to hire their employees on the basis of efficiency and without regard to color; to furnish vocational information . . . in the field of employment . . . [to] conduct health programs . . . [to assist] in landlord-tenant relationships . . .improved housing for non-whites . . . [cooperation] with other social agencies . . . [etc.]." Carrying out this mission, Jackson selected 27 employers for interviews about employment. Twelve were reported in September 1932 to be employing Blacks, ten reported they had once hired Blacks; and five, "never". The League then decided to plan training courses for "chauffeurs, waiters . . ."—aiming not too high in the depth of the Depression.[5]

On the brighter side—but in the shadow of the disturbing trial of the "Scottsboro boys"—attention was directed at the forthcoming Urban League's Negro Achievement KOL radio program, in which Mrs. Burton James (Florence Bean James) would speak about "The Negro and the Stage". Mrs. James, as manager and director of the Seattle Repertory Playhouse, had produced "several Negro plays". (The Negro Repertory Theater is covered below in relation to the Seattle Repertory Playhouse.) The *Enterprise* noted in April 1934 that a record high 21 Blacks had enrolled at the University of Washington—9 had been the previous high. In June it noted the graduation of 16 Black youngsters from Seattle high schools, including 9 from Garfield, 2 from Roosevelt, 1 from Franklin, 1 from O'Dea, and 1 from Queen Anne. Twelve was the earlier high number. On a sour note: Emmett McIver, "an outstanding tennis player from Franklin", was refused admittance to the Seattle Tennis Club because "as a social organization [it] does not admit colored persons."[6]

Blacks at the University of Washington were barely tolerated. Only three Black students at the university is all that the younger Horace Cayton could recall; yet their reception was cool, "ignored" at best. Cayton served as a deputy sheriff, while majoring in sociology, entering the department's graduate program before transferring to the University of Chicago's more hospitable academic setting to study under Robert Park, in 1931. During the late 1930s the three Pitter sisters entered the UW: Maxine in nursing, Constance in speech and drama, Marjorie in business administration. Their experiences are symptomatic of Black reception. (About ten to twenty Black students were registered per quarter between 1935 and 1941.) Maxine was effectively forced out of the School of Nursing, but she switched to sociology upon sympathetic advice from sociologist Robert O'Brien, while accumulating credits to qualify for a nursing major. Unable to find employment in Seattle, she migrated to New York City. Constance, majoring in speech, did practice teaching in the public schools as part of her degree requirement (under Florence James's sponsorship). Applying to the College of Education for admission to teaching, she was sternly advised that Seattle Public Schools would not accept Blacks; therefore, she could not register. But, after confirming that she had already been practice-teaching in the schools, the college let her in, although not without political intervention through the efforts of her politically active parents. Marjorie, upon entering her field, was emphatically told that the College of Economics and Business had not graduated a Black prior to 1935 and did not intend to in the future. She ultimately transferred to Howard University. An exception was made by the college when Clark Kerr taught labor economics: Robert Bedford Pitts earned his master's degree under Kerr's sponsorship in 1941. The sociology department provided a "home" for Blacks. Joseph Sylvester Jackson earned his master's degree there in 1939, while serving as director of the Urban League and acting in the Seattle Repertory Playhouse and the Negro Repertory Theater productions. In forestry, James Johnson became the first Black to earn a degree. His first employment was in Puerto Rico until he returned to stateside when Crown Zellerbach hired him as a forest manager.[7]

Robert Bedford Pitts, in his "Organized Labor and the Negro in Seattle" (1941), dealt with the fields in which Blacks found some stable employment, but in which union opposition was encountered—as seamen, in longshoring, as building service worker, as musician, as cannery worker, as Boeing machinist. Blacks as "seamen"—employees mainly in the stewards departments for two shipping firms—and as longshoremen are dealt with below in connection with the 1934 maritime strike. Before that strike and the onset of the Depression, about 300 men were employed on these ships during the winter, and about 500 during the summer. After that strike the Marine Cooks and Stewards Union admitted Blacks. Hiring was through the union hiring hall and done by rotation; about 300 "Negroes benefited". Pitts estimated that in 1941 about 200 "Negro seamen ship out of the Union hall in Seattle."[8]

Pitts also estimated that between 1920 and 1934 about 40 Blacks were regularly employed as longshoremen, being hired through the employers' hiring hall. Most worked as truckers and on "solid Negro gangs". After the 1934 strike, although Blacks were admitted first to the International Longshoremen's Association, then to its successor, the International Longshoremen's and Warehousemen's Union, the depressed conditions in the maritime trades did not allow much opportunity for entry; consequently, only about "thirty Negroes engaged in longshore work on the Seattle waterfront."[9]

In the building services lines, after the war, Blacks found employment in some hotels (the Butler, Gowman, Grand, Rainier, and New Washington), and at the Bon Marche, MacDougall and Southwick Department Store; and at the National Bank of Commerce. Many were replaced by women and Filipinos during the 1920s and early 1930s. When the AFL rechartered Local 6 of the Building Services Employees Union in 1936, Blacks were finally accorded equal treatment, in part because the preponderance of Filipinos in the union forced equal treatment, irrespective of race. Blacks numbered between 50 and 75 in the union, which overall counted about 4,000 members in 1941. Racial discrimination, however, was continued by most employers, many of whom preferred to employ Asians.[10]

Black musicians, with only one member in Local 76 of the musicians union, applied for and were given a federal union charter in 1917 as Local 493. Their number was small, about fifty; their bargaining power was weak, compared to the approximately 1,200 in Local 76. The latter competed for the same jobs and normally won out in instances of conflict. Blacks enjoyed employment most during the 1920s, even winning a contract from a resistant Park Board to give five park concerts in the mid-1920s. Under these conditions, Blacks found musician jobs primarily to supplement other sources of income. Local 76 was later rechartered as Local 7. With a membership of about 1,000 in 1940 it effectively controlled musician jobs, with Local 493 having but 32 members. Black musicians played mainly in the smaller night clubs in an area radiating from Jackson Street between 12th and 14th avenues, and at dancing parties.[11]

With the issuance of national defense contracts in 1939, the hiring of Blacks came to the fore. Both the Todd Shipyards in Seattle and the Bremerton Naval Yard across the Sound hired some Blacks. At the Boeing plant in Seattle Blacks had never been employed. However, due to the shortage of skilled machinists the company had begun its own apprenticeship training program. It joined forces with the School Board in a training program at the Edison Vocational Training School. In October 1939 a Black applied for admission to the program, but, he was informed, it was against company policy to hire or train Blacks. When a group in the Black community confronted the official about this policy it was informed that all hiring was done through the Aeronautical Mechanics Union, Local 571 of the International Association of Machinists. Blame, thereby, was shifted from the company to the union. Upon approaching officials of the union, the group was informed that the International body did not accept Blacks, due to an oath taken among members that they would never recommend for membership anyone who was not a member of the white race.[12]

Aroused at this demonstrated arrogance of power, a "Committee for the Defense of Negro Labor's Right to Work at Boeings [sic]" was formed in May 1940. The committee met with members of the union's Executive Board on June 10, and succeeded in getting its agreement to submit its recommendation to the membership that Blacks be admitted and that the leader of the Urban League speak to the membership about the situation. At the July 11 union meeting a letter from the Boeing president was read by the Urban League representative in which the company denied that it banned Blacks from employment, but would hire only through the union. The Urban League representative also indicated that Blacks would cooperate with the union in its current negotiations with the company, assuring the audience that Blacks would not become strikebreakers, should a strike occur. By unanimous vote it was decided to admit Blacks into the local and to submit a resolution at the IAM's annual convention to remove the restrictions against Black membership.

At the convention, the resolution was tossed among committees before being finally tabled. Upon return of the local's delegates, one faction charged the other with communistic activities—the one advocating Black admission. The Executive Board then met and rescinded the earlier action taken at the July 11 meeting. The race question then became part of an intra-union struggle in which the threat of CIO affiliation became the key issue. The allegedly communistic officers of the local were ousted; they quickly led a movement among discontented union members to affiliate with the United Automobile Workers Union of the CIO in early 1941. (This action is beyond the coverage of this volume.)

Few Blacks worked in the Alaska fish canneries. Filipinos and Japanese predominated in the work force which was controlled by labor contractors before unionization of the canneries in the mid-1930s. Unionization, which ended the contractors' control, is covered below. Employment for Blacks, however, did open up. Pitts was told by union officials that about forty Blacks were in the union, and the union had won control of the hiring halls.[13]

In the building trades Pitts noted that union rigidities had combined with the general policy followed among contractors of not hiring Blacks as long as white labor was available. Even the few Blacks who were union members were never hired out of the union halls. Most unions in the building trades barred Blacks. In the teamstering trade Pitts judged that only about four Blacks were members in the wide range of Teamster locals. The fact that the union had established closed shop conditions throughout the city meant that only union members were allowed to operate trucks—safely, anyway.[14]

The 1940 Population Census records that of the 170,991 members of the Seattle labor force 1,858 were "Negroes", and 5,242 "other races". White males numbered 116,491, Negro men 1,413, other races 4,017. White women accounted for 47,400 of the work force, Negro women 445, and other races 1,225. Gainfully employed Blacks in the state as a whole numbered only 3,559, other races 12,572, while Whites accounted for 700,370 of the gainfully employed.[15]

Part IV

A Topical Survey

14

Education

The Public School System in the 1920s

The early postwar years for the public school system were understandably transitional in character. The wartime draft showed dramatically the generally poor physical health of the draftees, much of which was attributed to preventable diseases, which, if detected early enough—as in the schools—could have been effectively dealt with. How vulnerable was the population to contagion—a serious concern in the schools—had been sharply conveyed by the wartime influenza epidemic. Low literacy levels of the draftees pointed accusingly at the failure of the nation's educational system, and brought forward in Washington state a law requiring compulsory education for those under age 18. This requirement, in turn, made even more evident that additional permanent facilities had to be built for the overcrowded schools—frame portables had been absorbing the overflow. Pressure would be heaviest on the high schools since children who might have discontinued school for jobs after the eighth grade, now had to continue into the higher grades.[1]

If facilities were woefully inadequate, the pool of qualified teachers was even more so. In the state, only one-half of the teachers met the minimum qualification standards of a high school education plus nine weeks of normal school. Applicants for "temporary certification" flooded the State Superintendent's Office with their pleas. (Not until 1923 did the state legislature pass a certification bill that would, by stages, raise the minimum standard to two years of normal school by 1927.) Dean Frederick E. Bolton of the University of Washington's School of Education pointed to the dilemma: "In the first place teachers must give more for what they are receiving, and in the second place the public must pay more in order to secure the greater skill." He complained that the low pay received by the unqualified teachers lowered that of the qualified, like a Gresham's Law. The other face of this coin favored the Group I cities of Seattle, Tacoma, and Spokane because they drained off the qualified teachers from the poorer districts by paying teachers more. Seattle paid teachers more than they were paid elsewhere in the state. Unhappy tax-reductionists in the city wanted to bring down these higher pay rates (an average, in 1921-22, of $2,025 for elementary, and $2,260 for high school teachers). These same forces—concentrated by business groups in the cohesively organized cities—also resisted any efforts at equalization. Indicative of the recognition finally attained by public education on the positive side, however, was the attitude of organized labor. For the first time, the State Federation of Labor gave a "large place" to education at its 1921 annual convention, following this up by appointing a permanent education committee, and endorsing the "30-10" school equalization bill that the education forces were pushing.[2]

Conceptually, as a goal, the educators and the Seattle School Board agreed to focus curriculum around "Community Life Studies". This program was congruent with that developed by Superintendent Frank Cooper who retired in 1922. His successor, Thomas R. Cole, had understudied and admired Cooper, thereby facilitating the transition. The program was intended to make good citizens as well as healthy ones—a hallmark of Cooper's regime—by introducing them to the workaday world through simulations and direct observation, progressively expanding their geographical and temporal frames of reference through the grades. The program underwent refinement throughout the decade. The Chamber of Commerce and individual firms cooperated through the Washington-Oregon Industries Education Bureau, providing its director, Clare Ketchum Tripp, with "monographs" to support instruction and affording opportunities to tour their facilities. Assistant Superintendent, Samuel Fleming, who headed the newly established Vocational Department, drew heavily upon this freely provided curriculum material, but in doing so he came under fire for officially ordering and distributing private power company propaganda during the 1924 campaign, in which the Bone Power Initiative awaited voter action.[3]

The residue of overage children who had been in the work force on either a part-time or full-time basis had to be accommodated under the new age limit law. Responding to the war-demonstrated shortcomings of schooling for the modern age, the Vocational Department had been created in 1919, offering classes in Evening Extension, and the Part-Time School, as well as the regular day school. (Part-Time or Continuation Schools were introduced to meet the four-hours per week minimum required by law.) Of central concern was correction from the wartime experience, which had illustrated that the labor pool of adequately trained youngsters was too small to fit the needs of industry with its rapidly changing technology, and of commerce with its growing demand for an educated white collar class to perform the clerical and other support operations required to accurately account for, finance, and distribute the products of industry. The public schools had to supply this work force. As the residue of overage youngsters was worked off, a two-track curriculum became firmly established and refined along the way during the 1920s—a vocational and an academic track. Integral to this program was the introduction of intermediate schools for grades 7, 8, and 9—there would be four by the end of the decade—in part, to relieve the pressure on the penurially provided facilities afforded by the elementary and high schools. (Roosevelt and Garfield High Schools, built in 1922 and 1923, respectively, had reached their capacity in only one year; others underwent extensions.)[4]

These junior high schools incorporated a choice of unit study plans more nearly attuned to the child's abilities, but it also resulted in a more homogeneous grouping of students. To reinforce individuality, electives were introduced at this level. Industrial arts for the boys, home economics for the girls became more integral, also, at this level . . . to be reinforced in senior high schools.[5]

A study in 1927-28, by the University of Washington's Sociology Department, of the student population in the Part-Time and Continuation School, showed that most came from families at or below poverty levels, were from broken homes, and that a majority were either foreign-born or were children of foreign-born parents. These students had been forced by their circumstances to seek jobs while still in school, but many dropped out altogether. Responding to this identified need, the Board authorized a broadening of its Continuation School's vocational training program by acquiring land, in 1930, adjacent to Broadway High School, for the Thomas A. Edison Vocational School. Edison would become a veritable showplace for vocational education enthusiasts. During the 1930s, School Board president Dietrich Schmitz and Superintendent Worth McClure placed increasing emphasis on vocational training.[6]

Given the wide range of learning aptitude and interests among children, the Illinois Intelligence Test was conducted by the Research Department of the system to properly place children in the curriculum and within their respective classes. The aim, in part, was to identify those children who might need "preventive teaching" immediately, to avoid more expensive remedial work later, if left undetected. Complementing these tests was the work of the Child Study Department which dealt with exceptional and physically or mentally troubled children.[7]

The System's Medical Department had been headed by Dr. Ira Brown since its origin in 1914. (Brown had apprenticed under William C. Gorgas in combatting yellow fever during the Spanish-American War.) Stemming from regular physical examinations were not only early detection of contagious diseases and correctable defects, but the encouragement of such simple personal hygienic procedures as frequent/regular bathing (which neglectful parents were expected to emulate), and the introduction of a free milk program. After years of urging, Brown finally persuaded the Board to employ trained nurses on a full-time basis at the close of the decade. All of this came under attack, inspired by veteran Board member and banker Ebenezer Shorrock, though led by Carl Croson who had defeated Socialist Richard Winsor in December 1920. Croson contended these social welfare programs properly belonged to state and county jurisdictions. Under Cooper, these programs were conceived as a means to equalize educational opportunity. A committee, set up to study this issue concluded to segregate the "social welfare" and "basic education" expenditures, while postponing elimination of the former for the time being. Their segregation, however, targeted them for regular cuts along the way, under constant pressure from the Tax Reduction Council. Bryce Nelson concludes: "This was the beginning of the end." While economies in the curriculum were effected, nevertheless, most of the social welfare programs of the Cooper era survived through the 1920s.[8]

How to finance the requisite programs and facilities became the most pressing problem for the School Board. The postwar depression contributed to the pain in finding a solution. We have seen above, in the accounting of city politics in 1921, how the TRC, Voters Information League, and the newspapers—particularly Hearst's *P-I*—assigned top priority to cutting taxes by focusing on the school budget, stressing Seattle's comparatively higher per-pupil costs. The TRC, as their medium, focused on classroom instruction and aimed for cuts in all else that seemed peripheral—cutting administrative costs by eliminating positions, raising the pupil-teacher ratio, and reducing teacher salaries. Coupled with efforts to reduce such costs was the drop in the assessed valuation of taxable property in Seattle from $247 million to about $235 million in 1922, thereby reducing further the amount of money allocated to the schools—this in the face of the significant rise in enrollment. Assessed valuation would continue to decline. While "economy" became the cue word of the School Board, voters nevertheless successively approved bond issues to fund the building program—one in 1919 for acquiring land on which to build, then a $2,250,000 one for buildings in 1925, followed by another in 1927 for an additional $2,400,000. The Board then looked forward to one in 1929 for about $5 million, so impressed was it with a surplus in the value of school property over the value of its bonded indebtedness. It seems that the voters would have supported bigger school tax levies if called upon to do so, but that the Board was overly protective of at least part of its perceived constituency, and decided upon a more tight-fisted policy despite the relative prosperous times of the late 1920s. The Board took pride in keeping the tax levy stationary, at 4.32 mills, for each of 1925, 1926, and 1927.[9]

Bryce Nelson writes: "The dominant themes of the 1920s in the Seattle schools were the main themes in other leading urban school districts: an efficiency-minded, hierarchical administration using tools (e.g., testing); a new structure (e.g., junior high schools); an expanded, diversified curriculum (e.g., different tracks, ability grouping); and the popular extracurriculum (e.g., sports, clubs, publications) to operate schools that were enrolling and graduating ever-increasing numbers of students." Cooper's successor, Thomas Cole, being an "administrative progressive", readily adapted to implementation of these changes, beginning with establishment of a Research Department (headed by Fred C. Ayer of the University of Washington) which subjected all aspects of schooling to quantitative analysis. To lay the basis for ability grouping, intelligence testing of elementary school pupils became the rule (Cooper had opposed them). Cole could report that for the period from 1922 to 1929, while attendance increased by 25%, administrative costs fell by 13%. This reflected Seattle's position of 24th in per pupil costs in 1927 among northern cities, and 11th place in percentage spent on instruction. Coupled with these figures was the decision to build junior high schools instead of retaining the neighborhood base of schooling by building more elementary schools—larger schools were more economical to maintain and operate. The junior high schools were to function, according to Cole, as a staging area wherein pupils would sort themselves onto either an academic or vocational track. By 1930 the junior highs accommodated half of the students in grades seven through nine. Class size in high schools was expanded to meet increased enrollment, and the number of classes with less than twenty students was sharply reduced as economy measures. Educational tracks, set earlier, were reinforced along the line.[10]

The Public School System in the 1930s

When Thomas Cole resigned as school superintendent in 1930, little did he know the problems his successor, Worth McClure, would face. It soon became apparent that the onsetting depression was no short term affair. School expenditures of $6,100,000 in 1930 had to be reduced—as property valuations fell so did revenues for school funding; non-payment of taxes carried the same effect. In addition, there was a lid of 5 mills per dollar on the assessed valuation of taxable property. Instruction alone took $4,845,490 of that six million dollars. That cost represented an increase of $8.11 per pupil cost above the 1925-1926 figure of $76.09. Revenue, on the other hand, had fallen by $.63 per-pupil-cost. Under this immediate pressure, McClure reduced general expenditures, by 1934, to $4,400,000, thereby preventing a "serious situation" from getting out of hand, according to School Board president and banker, Dietrich Schmitz. Complicating school funding was the constitutional amendment that voters approved in 1932, limiting tax on real property to 40-mills. Substitute revenue sources were hard to come by when the state Supreme Court ruled the income tax amendment of 1932 unconstitutional. Resort had to be invented: the unpopular sales, and business and occupation taxes. Cuts were made between 1931 and 1935—teacher salaries were reduced by 33% during 1933-34, administrative costs by 30%, capital expenditures by 58%, and books and supplies by 68%.[1]

These reductions did not cut deeply enough to satisfy Board president Schmitz who wrote in 1934 that "All expenditures aside from compensation for teachers and other employees have been reduced to the minimum." Previously some high school teachers had chartered an AFL Teachers union, Local 200. The Board had countered in 1930 with a "yellow-dog contract", naming the AFT, in which membership was forbidden as condition of employment. When the state Supreme Court upheld the contract, some members proceeded to establish the Seattle Teachers League. The League took up the cudgels, criticizing not only the Board for opposing tenure legislation, but also the WEA for "soft-pedalling" on it and on teacher retirement legislation. Through pressure from the Classroom Teachers Association, the Board agreed to restore some of the paycuts—up to 82 1/2 % in September 1935 and 92% in September 1936. The CTA joined the League and remnants of Local 200 in supporting tenure and retirement legislation. Together, as by one voice, they exclaimed displeasure at the WEA's domination by school directors and principals, tracing the WEA's lack of agressiveness on these issues to their overpowering influence. Lending credence to these criticisms, the WEA's Marsh replied to its newly elected president, classroom teacher Frances Reynolds, that he feared tenure would protect teachers to "espouse radicalism". Continuing: "It seems to me that . . . WEA has no apology due for the years of delay we have experienced in coming to this issue of teacher tenure. We had a very earnest and active committee on tenure back in the '20's, but we found ourselves under the reign of an anti-school governor . . . Before his eight-year tenure ended, we were in the depths of the depression. As you know, even retirement, as well as tenure, had to be set aside." He expressed regrets for not having gotten "our rank and file of classroom teachers . . . actively involved before this union movement came about." (Local 200 continued actively recruiting, spurred on by another pay cut in December 1939.)[2]

Reflecting the Depression, high school attendance expanded from 16,981 in 1931 to 18,209 in 1936 as students tended to remain in school, there being no incentive to join the unemployed. Also reflecting the Depression, the falling birth rate and a modest movement to the city's outskirts caused elementary school attendance to fall from 39,645 in 1931 to 34,362 by 1936 and 33,661 in 1938. Junior high school attendance, understandably, peaked in 1934 at 5,170, but then fell by 1936 to 4,794 and 4,986 in 1938. Overall attendance was 62,659 in 1931, steadily declining to 57,855 by 1936, and 51,356 during 1938-39. Between 1931 and 1932 the pupil-teacher ratio decreased slightly as vacancies, with some exceptions, remained unfilled, and some school consolidation took place. In 1933, the ratios had been 32.3 for high schools, 31.9 for junior highs, and 34.8 for grade schools. By 1938, the ratios were 29.0, 27.3, and 32.8 respectively. Toward the end of the decade, school attendance tended to decline, as it had elsewhere in the nation. McClure observed in his 1937-1938 annual report that the drop of 1100 attendees in elementary schools would soon affect high school attendance "unless the city experiences further growth or conditions of reduced employment bring the return of postgraduates for further instruction."[3]

The Depression also revived a public school function that Superintendent Frank Cooper had pioneered earlier in the century—the public schools as a relief agency. Help came from outside the system, from the Parent-Teacher Association's Child Welfare Board in September 1931. Because the district was prohibited by law from directly providing relief (except for milk), the PTA's Welfare Board was organized to pool its resources with other relief agencies. The CWB had spent $300 in 1931. This amount would climb precipitously, as 5,083 needy children were supplied with shoes and clothing between 29 August and 14 September 1932. This was the primary organized relief available for the "many hundreds of children [who] would require food, clothing, and carfare." Without aid, the PTA feared their progress would be interrupted. The Welfare Board organized a drive that netted about $6,900 which was distributed upon application from principals for lunch tickets, free milk and carfare. An equal amount was raised from school faculty, helping to up the total to $18,500. The Welfare Board also became a clearing house for clothing collection and distribution. Reportedly, knowledge of who were the recipients of these services was kept from other pupils. In 1937-1938, the Child Welfare Board even gained the cooperation of the medical and dental societies and the American Red Cross Clinic for service to children "from families with marginal incomes."[4]

Statewide, school forces, despite their combined pressures (though too often divided), along with limited support from the school superintendent's office, failed to get legislation passed to deal with the plight of schools. The tax reductionists were riding high, having won the 40-mills limitation, and divined the failure of the graduated income tax to pass judicial muster. When the voters in 1934 rejected Initiative 94 for improved school funding, the WEA's Arthur Marsh called it a victory for the "Tax Reduction" forces, saving "over four millions of property taxes and Public Education loses three millions of property tax revenues . . . [P]roponents carried the cities [where real estate and property owners were well organized, and propagated misinformation,] while the opposition [was] outnumbered in the counties." He thanked the *P-I* for lining up with the education forces. Credence is lent to Marsh's charge of misinformation by a mimeographed campaign item of the "Community Tax Bureau", which claimed the School Board intended to spend the 3-mills levy on teacher salaries, not as the Board alleged, on construction. That weathervane of professional opinion, the Municipal League, supported Initiative 94, claiming, "In the great greed of tax-spending units for more funds no relief for real property can be hoped for."[5]

School Board election races were not placid affairs in the 1930s. Taking the 1936 campaign as an example, we can observe the depth of ideological commitment felt by participants. Board member James Duncan—once the secretary of the Central Labor Council during the century's first decades, and a long time education advocate—was pushing for the election of two candidates of his persuasion (engineering professor Burt Farquharson and Wilfred Withington). Board president Dietrich Schmitz and fellow member Frank Bayley took this as a challenge to their leadership and organized a joint campaign with American Legionnaire officer Stephen F. Chadwick, its organizer. Their "Bayley-Schmitz For The School Board" letterhead charged: "Our school system is again under attack by self-styled 'liberals'." They were accused of wanting to "turn our schools into propaganda mills to teach their own social and political theories to our children . . . [They] are in the way of all who seek to control our system of education in order to instill un-American theories . . . ."[6]

The School Board's policies during these years was sketched by McClure in 1938: "Emphasis which the Seattle Board of Education is now laying on personal, civic, and occupational fitness in connection with character, education, guidance, curriculum, and vocational improvement programs now being carried on thus seems particularly timely . . . [It is] in line with the best thought of the times." (From the start McClure had looked upon the Edison Vocational School with marked enthusiasm.) Seconding McClure, Dietrich Schmitz took special pride in vocational training. Writing to Benjamin Kizer, chair of the State Planning Council, Schmitz urged "Careful attention should be given to the extension of vocational education [after] surveys to indicate the trades in which employment opportunities exist." He pointed to the success of Edison in placing its graduates (mainly post-high school students)—3/4 during the depth of the depression, and all of them now (October 1937). He encouraged Kizer to consider this in the Council's survey. So impressed was Kizer that he planned the Council's next meeting for Edison. McClure, in his 1938 annual report, expressed pleasure at the "continued validity of the Board's policy of offering skilled vocational training only in those occupations where demonstrated employment needs exist." When national defense orders began flowing in during 1939, there suddenly grew a demand for production and construction workers, foremen, and supervisors. Edison responded by establishing an "Aviation Trades Training Program", as well as courses in other lines. Between August and December 1939, 467 men had been trained and placed in employment, 66 more were enrolled. In June 1940, the State Director of Vocational Education received a request from Boeing to continue the foreman and supervisor training program. It was continued, though Boeing had felt compelled to institute its own training programs as well—Edison's was a useful supplement.[7]

In the area of adult education, the School Board provided 567 free scholarships to "worthy unemployed persons" in 1937-1938, while only nominal fees were charged others. That year also was the third in which school facilities were given over to public forums for "non-partisan discussion of public questions". Just what was considered "non-partisan" is open to question. On February 5, 1936 the Business Manager of the School District, E.B. Holmes, reported that the Milk Dealers Association had managed to force the forum to delete as "controversial" any discussion of the recent rise in milk prices at the Bryant School. (Only recently had the Teamsters joined with the association in fixing prices and controlling entry into the milk business.) In January 1932, prior to the formal public forums program, the Unemployed Citizens' League had been denied use of school facilities by the School Board.[8]

One of the remarkable features of Seattle's educational system—sad and struggling as it was in absolute terms—is that as of 1940, the city ranked first nationally among 31 cities of comparable size in the following categories: median school year completed for those age 25 and older, and for those who had completed four or more years of college. Whether this can be credited to the public school system seems speculative. However, it does provide food for thought about the rest of the country, today as in yesteryear. The public school system—the foundation upon which the nation's very welfare is rooted—was then, and remains short-changed, at every citizen's peril.[9]

Funding of Common Schools in the State

It is obvious that the city's common schools cannot usefully be discussed without reference to their funding from the different levels of government: local, county, state, and federal. Bear in mind also that it is the "school district" that is funded, and not the city or other entity. The following will place the funding of Seattle's public schools in the larger setting.

Parallel with the shift in funding of public welfare from the local level to the state and federal levels was the funding of common schools. Acceleration of the movement of people from farms to the cities during the period made it impossible for the cities' schools even to keep up with their own increased numbers. Coupled with the overcrowding of existing facilities were the demands posed in Washington by the new compulsory education law, and by the need to radically change and adapt the curriculum to meet the demands of a fast-evolving economy. The economy required a higher degree of literacy in the work force to meet the need for advanced education beyond the high school level. Engineers were needed in industry. Scientists were required to expand the frontiers of knowledge on which the engineers and the rest of society depend. Social scientists were in demand to deal with consequences and implications of these changes in the economy and social structure. And, those in the liberal arts were needed to inculcate respect for learning itself, and to sensitize the public to the enriching values of the arts, entertainment, and recreation as "good" in their own right, deserving without questioning their just place in a relentlessly materialistic culture.

A survey of the funding base supporting common schools during the period will provide some perspective. Passing references have been made earlier in sections dealing with education and taxation, but some repetition is necessary for focus. High quality education must respond to societal needs in the broadest sense. This means addressing all problems of society initially through the education system, and subsequently by the individuals whom that system produces—all parts of an ongoing process. Education, throughout our period, absorbed more State tax revenue than any other source, hence its central position in any debates about taxation. It is the politicians who set policy and allocate resources accordingly.

William E. Torget's 1954 study of common school funding in the state provides the detail in the summary which follows. More than half of school expenditures in the 1920s was paid from local sources, from property taxes and from the State's "permanent fund". In 1929/1930 Washington State government provided 26.2% of the funding, the counties 16.1%, and local sources 57.7%. The year 1939/1940 registered the shift toward a larger State role—61.3% from the State, 5.5% from the counties, and 33.2% from local sources. Less than 1% came from federal sources during the period. Torget concluded that Washington State gave more by far to common school education than was true of the national average, and more than any other state for building construction.[1]

In terms of actual dollars collected by the various jurisdictions between 1923 and 1940, local property taxes collected rose steadily from $49,576,000 in 1923 to a high of $67,221,000 in 1930. Then property taxes dropped successively, from $60,738,000 in 1932 to $38,601,000 in 1937, and increased slightly by 1940 to $39,350,000.[2]

State tax collections during the period amounted to $24,159,000 in 1923, $31,847,000 in 1930, falling during 1932-1934, before increasing to $38,975,000 in 1935, to $51,309,000 in 1937, and to $60,487,000 in 1940. During the period 1922 to 1933 the State's share of property taxes ran between 25 and 17 percent—its total exceeded that from all other sources combined. By 1938 the State was receiving only 5% of the property tax revenue, and about the same for the last two years of the decade. The percent of the property tax levied for education, during 1922-1940, ranged between a high of 48.8% in 1932 to a low of 39.8% in 1933. Of this percentage, the school districts gradually increased their proportion from 23.3% in 1922 to a high of 32.4% in 1940. Higher education, state, and county schools divided the remainder.[3]

With the introduction of the retail sales tax and the business and occupation tax, after passage of the 40-mill property tax limitation, and the Supreme Court's invalidation of the income tax, the revenue composition changed radically. The retail sales tax of 2% accounted for $11 million or 21.8% of the total tax revenues in the first full year of its operation, 1936. It was the state's second largest revenue source, second only to the gasoline tax whose revenues increased without interruption during the Depression, accounting for about one-third of the revenue. In 1934 the B&O tax brought in 13% of the total of state revenues, and remained at about that proportion throughout the period. Of other tax sources none averaged as much as 5%.[4]

Torget's table for average county millage rates for 1923-1932 ranks King County fifth, with a levy on property of 70.77 mills, compared with Grays Harbor's high of 77.13 mills, and Pierce County, in second place, with 73.72 mills. (Cowlitz County ranked third, and Kitsap fourth in millage rates levied.) The ranking shifted moderately after passage of the 40-mill limit law. For 1936-1946 Pierce County was high with 50.89 mills; King County second with 49.05 mills; Grays Harbor County third with 45.48 mills. The relative positions among counties changed only moderately throughout the period studied.[5]

During the period 1923-1932, the state contributed $20 to each school district for each child of school age. To encourage districts to establish high schools, the State contributed another $100 annually to each school district for each grade it established above the eighth grade. Counties added another $10 for each child of school age. School districts were limited to assessing property at 10 mills (1%); this could be doubled by popular vote alone. Torget concludes that the flat grants by the state failed to equalize funding for schools because "75% of the property tax revenue was obtained on the local level where assessed valuations relative to need differed considerably. These disparities in assessed valuations necessitated marked differences in tax rates to obtain the necessary school revenue."[6]

The period 1933-1937 saw the State increasing its grants, beginning in 1933. The goal was set to grant 25 cents per pupil per day of actual attendance in the previous year (of a 180 day school year). It was not achieved until 1936 (the State paid only 16 cents per pupil per day in 1934 and 1935). Transportation costs were also met by the State. Counties paid 5 cents per pupil per day in actual attendance during the preceding year. School districts provided the remainder of their budget, but each was limited to a levy of 10 mills unless voters approved a higher levy. Altogether the state's contribution represented about a 40% increase over the earlier period. Nevertheless, equalization among school districts was not achieved, if that was a goal. An equalization bill was passed in 1937, by which a School Equalization Fund was established to compensate districts for shortfalls met in assessing property to the limit allowed. (Differing assessed valuations among counties were not taken into account, however.) Over one-half of the districts needed subsidization in 1937, but $5 million was needed and the equalization fund had only $1 million in it. That was the amount pro-rated.[7]

The University of Washington and the City

The University of Washington faced the same pressures as the common school system: a burgeoning student enrollment and insufficient numbers of teachers to teach them. Though the causes were different, the results were the same. And, as with the expedient use of portables by the city's public schools, the university found itself using indefinitely makeshift temporary buildings erected on campus to meet wartime training demands. Complicating administrative attempts to deal with these problems was the impact of the postwar depression of 1920-1921. During this period most of the university buildings were funded from non-tax sources such as tuition fees, not from the State's general fund. Most were those in progress by 1920: Philosophy Hall in October 1920, Education Hall in 1922, serving as the administration building as well, a Mines Laboratory in 1921 to serve the region's declining coal industry, and a forest products laboratory to serve the state's forest industry. Gifts contributed significantly—to the School of Forestry was added a classroom building funded by Mrs. Agnes H. Anderson (who also was a chief benefactor of the Cornish School). President Suzzallo also persuaded Horace C. Henry to donate his art collection in 1925 and a building to house it. There were other lesser donations of importance. Intending to expand the library's collection to support research, he sent librarian Charles W. Smith to Europe on a buying spree in 1923, then he pushed ahead with construction of a library building in the center of campus, which was ready for occupancy at the time of his dismissal from the presidency.[1]

Within the first postwar biennium, the student enrollment had almost doubled from its prewar size to 4,740. By the end of 1920, the university had spent all its allotted funds and was rescued only by a special emergency legislative appropriation in January 1921. Retrenchment at all levels was required, including the transfer of operations and equipment funds to pay for the increased number of teachers. One of the difficulties imposed on the hiring of new faculty, however, was the diminished pool of qualified candidates. The war had diverted the nation's efforts away from training teachers. Nationwide competition for the relatively few who were qualified inspired localized recruitment and a kind of intellectual inbreeding that reinforced the region's geographical isolation. Precedent for meeting demand for teachers, however, was set by the emergency demands of wartime, when a special sub-faculty category of "Associate" was created in 1918. This rank was below that of the lowest faculty grade of Instructor, that from which one could expect to graduate by "merit" to Assistant Professor, Associate Professor, and Professor. In establishing this position, the Regents declared it to be a temporary one that would make possible the teaching of "elementary" classes. As though fulfilling this emergency mandate after the war, President Suzzallo hired high school teachers and principals, businessmen and contractors, and former university students with only a bachelor's or master's degree. As such, these sub-faculty could not qualify for appointment to faculty ranking no matter how long they served as Associate. The university assumed no obligation to them. Not surprisingly, this rank was one in which women predominated, some for more than a decade, but most served only one to three years. Wide disparities developed in the ranks over the ensuing years. Lecturers were only 12% of all faculty in 1913, but together with the new sub-faculty rank, they constituted 25% of the proportion of teaching staff by 1925. Graduate teaching fellows and assistants grew from 16.5% to 28% by 1925. This growing disproportion, however, was fostered by the administration. It reflected its aim to measure educational effectiveness by lowering unit student costs. How many students registered in any one class became a critical measure of quality, not the substance of the course being taught. This gauge of "efficiency" nicely fitted Suzzallo's temperament, and the temper of the time. In its implementation he met with Regental praise. Although the high turnover in the teaching ranks that followed was inescapable, it is doubtful that the postwar depression would have made a substantial difference, since making "a virtue of necessity" was firmly imbedded already in the minds of Suzzallo, the Regents, and the administration of Governor Louis Hart, who reorganized state government along these lines by his Administrative Reorganization Act of 1921.[2]

Charles M. Gates refers to the period from 1920 to 1925 as one of austerity. A 1925 report to the administration by the Instructors Association—which had been established in 1919 to serve as a unified faculty voice to the administration—found frustrating the lack of opportunities for advancement, at the low pay, and at the negative effect their known-plight had upon the university as a whole ". . . in bidding for new men, [and] . . . in keeping the men now on the staff." It appears that "men" was meant to cover women of faculty rank, inasmuch as the statement continues: "Excellent men and women are now condemned to inferior ranks, either because other nonproductive persons are ahead of them and will never advance, or because it is the fashion to keep them there." In any case, the situation was leading to "mental stagnation." Governor Hartley vetoed salary increases requested by the administration in its 1925-1927 budget. But that was entangled with his feud with Suzzallo, whom he managed to dismiss in 1926 after replacing existing regents with those who would be subservient to him. (This episode is covered above in the section on "The Republican Party in Disarray" in Chapter 3.)[3]

Before turning to the consequences of Suzzallo's dismissal,

it is well to assess the degree to which the university was becoming integrated with the state's economy. One cue is afforded by the College of Forestry. Objectives of the college by 1920 had become more clearly defined. Foremost, they were establishing a forest policy for the State, and promoting a sustained yield policy on privately owned lands before it was too late. Requiring greater outside support in meeting these objectives, the college reorganized its advisory board, composed chiefly of lumbermen and trade association representatives. Henry Schmitz, in his history of the college, attributes much influence to this board in earning industry-wide cooperation. Instrumental in this effort was the introduction of an annual State Forestry Conference, beginning October 1921. Out of the first two conferences emerged a broadening of the curriculum along both technical lines and research in silviculture, forest management and product development. To do this, the college admitted to lacking adequate resources for construction of a classroom building (classes were being conducted in the inhospitable Forest Products Laboratory). Donations of equipment were solicited from the industry as well. A plea for the funding of research professorships and scholarships also was laid on the table. The seeds planted at these conferences led first to the funding of a demonstration forest, in 1924, by Charles Lathrop Pack. The following year, Mrs. Agnes Healy Anderson donated money for construction of a classroom building, to be named after her late husband, lumberman Alfred H. Anderson. In the process of this program-building, new courses were added, including a nation-first, logging engineering, thereby strengthening the college's industrial forestry program. Faculty numbers and enrollment steadily grew in tandem. This success story was not matched by the career of the College of Fisheries.[4]

Steady pressure had been applied since a meeting of the Pacific Fisheries Society—hosted by the University of Washington in 1914—for a fisheries school somewhere in the United States. That the Commissioner of Fisheries, Hugh M. Smith, took the lead is not surprising. However, that local figures of some influence also wanted such a school lent a bias to its ultimate location, should one be established. In close touch with Smith was former Fisheries Bureau investigator, John N. Cobb, who then was editor of Miller Freeman's *Pacific Fisherman*. Freeman added his voice, as did naturalist/zoologist Professor Trevor Kincaid. By this route the nation's first College of Fisheries came into being 2 April 1919. Temporary buildings, surviving the Naval training program, were adapted for teaching and for aspects of the technical programs—fish rearing ponds, and fish technology among them. Cobb, though lacking academic credentials, was named dean, a position he would hold until his death in 1930. Faculty was slim and marked by high turnover. Much of the teaching was done by faculty from related fields—Kincaid was one such contributor. No research program was developed. For this reason, upon Cobb's death, the college was abolished, and a department was established in its place. To head the department, William F. Thompson, a Ph.D. from Stanford, took over the reins, with the intention of developing a research program. Abetting this program was the locating of the International Fisheries Commission on the campus during 1931, due to Thompson's commission membership. When the U.S. Fisheries Bureau built a laboratory a few blocks away, in 1931, Thompson's program could move ahead as he drew upon professional staffers from those two fisheries units as unpaid lecturers in the courses he added to the curriculum. With the university's reorganization in 1935 the department was elevated to school status.[5]

Upon winning Suzzallo's dismissal, Governor Hartley continued to insist upon economy, and that the university must remain out of politics . . . except to be subservient to the governor's office. To insure this, Hartley installed a business manager to supervise fiscal operations. After the acting presidency of Classics Professor David Thomson and the elevation of Dean Lyle Spencer of the College of Journalism to the presidency, the more purely academic affairs were run by a triumvirate that included Spencer, Thomson, and Dean of the Graduate School Frederick M. Padelford. Budget matters were relegated to Thomson; Spencer assumed primary responsibility for public relations; and Padelford directed personnel and academic affairs. The Regents interposed an administrative council that included the four college deans, business manager, the president, and vice president. By duplicating some functions of the triumvirate, the council tended to dilute administration by the triumvirate. These changes were not all bad, to judge from Padelford's assessment. Although he exclaimed Suzzallo's firing was a "shocking violation of academic ethics" he found the recent raises of faculty salaries and promotions had brought "their contentment". However, the Associates did not share in the largess—Gates reports that only one in five were promoted from 1927 to 1932, and about 50% had resigned, while one-third remained at that rank. And since the upper and middle ranks took most of the benefits, there resulted a high turnover among those in the lower faculty ranks, the Lecturers and Assistant Professors. [6]

The years 1927 to 1932 witnessed a building boom on campus, with seven permanent buildings being erected in two phases. In the first phase, a Women's Physical Education Building was occupied in 1927, a Men's Pavilion in 1928, the costs of each to be borne by student fees and profits from intercollegiate athletic events. From 1928 to 1932 two science buildings (Physics and Johnson Hall) and an aeronautical engineering building were built. Negotiations for private funding of the latter—Guggenheim Hall—had been instigated by Suzzallo. The Rockefeller Foundation funded construction of an Oceanography Laboratory. A Law School building named after Dean John T. Condon completed the new building program. The old Science Building was remodeled and renamed Parrington Hall, in honor of the university's first Pulitzer Prize winner. With its renaming, the English Department had found a home, and perhaps a center for the liberal-left politics in the outer world, further honoring the memory of Vernon Louis Parrington, whose *Main Currents of American Thought* became a staple of intellectual life for the next two decades.[7]

Student protests during the decade were few, short-lived, and normally quieted by the administration in quick order at both ends of the period. Compulsory military training met opposition in 1921, when members of the Reserve Officers Training Corps circulated a petition to make ROTC optional for freshmen and sophomores. Officers threatened to flunk signers, and a student leader, Robert Lane, was suspended for two quarters for his part in leading demonstrations. The faculty voted overwhelmingly in favor of retaining ROTC. Later in the year, when students protested the doubling of tuition fees, Suzzallo blocked the use of the YWCA building to women student protesters. It had been estimated that as many as 700 students had been forced to withdraw because of the fee hike, and according to the University Recorder, Edward Stone, about 2,000 potential students from working class and farm families had failed to register, in part from the absence of part-time jobs, as well as the high tuition. At the other end of the decade students protested the dismissal of Assistant Professor Bernhard Stern, distrusting "economy" as the reason for the action. Stern, popular among students, had a reputation of being a Marxist, and he baited religionists with unflattering analogies about ritual practices. President Spencer overrode Dean Padelford's recommendation for probation, insisting "Professor Stern has got to go." His acceptance of a position elsewhere took the steam out of the student protest.[8]

The University of Washington During the Depression Years

President Lyle Spencer, though moving to the presidency from his deanship of the College of Journalism, aspired to broadening student education by making the arts and sciences, not technical training, the hallmark of the university's educational mission. Prompted by the tightening Depression and discouraged by the triviality of many courses, coupled with a trades orientation and duplication/overlap of many offerings, Spencer set up an Educational Research Committee in 1930. In addressing these problems that disturbed Spencer, the committee came up with a reorganization plan that began a short life in 1932. Embraced by a single College of Arts and Sciences were thirty-four departments, employing 283 faculty to teach 4,409 enrolled students. A College of Technology included not only the engineering departments but also forestry, fisheries, mines, pharmacy, and military and naval science. The Law School and Graduate School remained autonomous. Inside the university Dean Winkenwerder, for one, strenuously objected to the "snap judgment" which classified logging engineering as vocational, whereas it had become an integral part of the broader subject of forest economics and had been accepted as such by the U.S. Forest Service. Opposition from outside the university was generated by the Seattle High School Teachers' League which complained that so much emphasis on advanced education bypassed the average citizen who was entitled to admission because the school was tax supported. The League pointed to the high failure rate among students, that only one in three ever graduated, and that in de-emphasizing needed commercial education the university was leaving students in a void, there being no tax supported institution to meet that demand. Spencer relented, reestablishing business administration, pharmacy, forestry, and education as colleges, and restoring offices for a Dean of Men and a Dean of Women.[1]

However, little of substance could be accomplished so long as Hartley remained governor. The 1932 election betokened a change when Clarence D. Martin was elected to that office. Martin had assured voters that, if elected, he would remove Hartley's Regents and would restore the university's former autonomy. Responding to the reminder that as a tax supported institution, the university should open its doors to the citizenry at large, he announced in favor of providing higher education to all high school graduates who chose it. Tuition reduction and lowering of admission requirements were part of the package. He immediately replaced Hartley's Regents and appointed his own, aiming to connect with the Suzzallo legacy, even consulting the former president in the process. When Spencer's resignation became effective June 1933, the university was reeling from the influx of about one thousand more students who faced fewer teachers than the year before. Student/faculty ratios suffered, with the *Daily* insisting that at least 59 new instructors were needed to match staffing at comparable institutions. The Regents communicated their distress to Martin, earning more than a hundred new instructors for 1934-1935, along with restoration of one-half the pay cut inflicted in 1932-1933. Excluded from this restoration was the voiceless sub-faculty. It was this group to whom the nascent AFL Teachers Union, Local 401, appealed inasmuch as the Instructors Association excluded this major component of the teaching force.[2]

The search for a successor to Spencer was handicapped by the school's loss of esteem that Governor Hartley's politicization had brought upon it. Several potential candidates did not even wish to be considered. Finally, once again as in Suzzallo's nomination, Columbia's Nicholas Murray Butler was asked for a list. He came up with eight names, among them Lee Paul Sieg of the University of Pittsburgh. Sieg had established an excellent reputation there as an administrator and for enticing the Westinghouse Corporation to cooperate in developing a graduate program in engineering. Sieg accepted the presidency as a fresh challenge, effective August 1, 1934, succeeding Acting President Hugo Winkenwerder.[3]

Spencer's abortive attempt at reorganization had brought to the surface the university's twofold responsibility—to open its doors to high school graduates regardless of their academic orientation, and to appropriately prepare those who aspired to advanced academic and professional training. Sieg's Pittsburgh experience led him to begin by establishing a "University College", unifying the liberal arts and sciences. In it were schools of art and architecture, fisheries, home economics, music, nursing education, and oceanography, and liberal arts departments, all under a dean, Edward Lauer. Integral to its functioning was provision for general education, which addressed the problem of educational deficiencies among the incoming high school graduates—compensatory education. A general studies department, set up to conduct survey courses, became a central element in this program. Essentially, general studies was for non-majors. It enabled those students who were not yet clearly oriented toward higher education to view the potentiality for expanding their intellectual horizons. Experimentation within this context ensued throughout the period amidst heated internal debate. By 1940 this experimentation led to another comprehensive plan which separated lower and upper division courses, with the former laying the foundation for the latter. How this new program fared takes us beyond the scope of this volume.[4]

From out of the ferment generated by attempts of the administration to reorganize academic programs, from the salary cuts brought on by the Depression, teacher overloads, and overcrowded classrooms, the Instructors Association sought a more administrative role. The new president was more receptive to faculty participation in administration than had been his predecessors. Whether the formation of the Teachers Union in 1934 had anything to do with Sieg's near-collegiality toward the Instructors Association is uncertain, but the union actively recruited among the sub-faculty, and some of the faculty, particularly in the English, psychology, and anthropology departments. (The sub-faculty numbered over 200 of a total faculty of 450 in 1936.) Sieg refused to deal with the union as a body, though he indicated a willingness to meet with members individually. Margaret Hall reports in her study that Sieg wanted the university to speak to the public through one voice, and that union recognition would only confuse the public by the addition of the union's uncontrollable one and "will not be countenanced". Indeed, Sieg saw the sub-faculty as the source of a "great deal of our discontent". For the latter there were reasons—apart from their exclusion from a collegial role in the widest sense, they had no prospect for job security, their low pay (and denial of a pay-restoration granted to the faculty after the earlier pay-cut) kept them servile, making impossible the setting aside of something for retirement, and non-recognition kept them from negotiating a retirement program or any other improvement, except by individual negotiation and through any influence the Instructors Association was willing to muster on their behalf. (These aspects of Sieg's administration bear upon civil liberties, and as such are dealt with in detail in the chapter on "Civil Liberties Between the Wars".)[5]

Sieg, in October 1937, appointed a committee drawn from the faculty, to draft a set of proposals that would integrate the faculty as an official body within the administration. Its report and recommendations were approved by a vote of the full faculty on April 19, 1938. In recognizing its placement administratively below the Regents, the President and academic officers, the General Faculty assumed broad jurisdiction over academic programs. The General Faculty would function through an elected body, the University Senate. Autonomy in faculty relations was granted the colleges. At the end of the period covered by this volume this adminstrative code was just beginning to be implemented. One of its first organizational tasks was to deal with the problem of tenure and academic freedom, for which a committee was appointed in 1940, and whose report was adopted by the Senate in March 1941.[6]

15

The Cultural Scene Between the Wars

Introduction

Leaving to one side the city's part in the nation's burgeoning movie industry and its attendant movie houses, Seattle's art, live-theater, and classical music scene was barely sustained during the 1920s. Reputedly, this was a time of plenty. The Cornish School of Allied Arts supplied most of the original impetus. Partly from its teaching staff and students the 1930s would witness an invigorating cultural life that could hardly have been anticipated during the Depression years. Personalities of the art world and live-theater interacted in an environmental intimacy that sprouted a truly regional cultural expression: a civic theater in the form of the Seattle Repertory Playhouse (SRP), and the emergence of a distinctive group of painters which would become known as the Northwest School. As though underscoring this largely self-contained art community, Burton and Florence Bean James established the SRP in 1928, after teaching drama at the Cornish in the mid-1920s. Mark Tobey, who became the idol and father figure of the Northwest School, taught painting at the Cornish, beginning in 1922, and acted in some of the Jameses' productions. Tobey designed for them the acting-mask mosaic set in the entryway to welcome "Rep" audiences. (The University of Washington bought the property in 1950 after the "blacklisting" of the Jameses, following the hearings of the State's Un-American Activities Committee—the "Canwell Committee".

Later, ironically, it was renamed the Glenn Hughes Playhouse, thereby honoring the Jameses' bitterest antagonist.)[1]

A tiny handful of wealthy patrons performed cultural resuscitations along the way. Art patrons/collectors, were principally the unsalaried University of Washington geologist Dr. Richard E. Fuller, his mother Margaret, and Horace C. Henry. The Fullers funded construction of the Seattle Art Museum (SAM). Henry, a retired railroad builder, provided a temporary home at his Capitol Hill mansion for the SAM's forerunner, the Seattle Fine Arts Society, after he donated his collection to the university along with a gallery to hold it. The Cornish, a mere two blocks away, was kept afloat principally by a lumber-baron widow, Mrs. Agnes H. Anderson. She found critical support from Mrs. C.D. (Harriet) Stimson whose husband's fortune was derived from the Stimson Lumber Mill operations in Ballard, from which some earnings found their way into Seattle real estate in close association with the Metropolitan Building Company—she had introduced Mrs. Anderson to Miss Cornish. Another benefactor was Mrs. Edgar Ames whose husband's fortune was made in wartime shipbuilding at his shipyard adjacent to Harbor Island. All of the above focused their ambitions for fine arts in the city through the Seattle Fine Arts Society.[2]

Indicative of the city's cultural life in transition is a review written by Kenneth Callahan in 1936, in his capacity as an assistant director of the Seattle Art Museum, while his own unique painting style was emerging. He observed, that during the past few years, both painting and sculpting "have been interesting, both in output and in number of people found working in each [field] . . . [Also the] mental attitude of artists has changed a great deal . . . Since 1929 artists, for the greater part, have come to the realization that there is no longer a market for their output. Whereas formerly artists attempted to see, interpret and execute their work and style that conformed to the tastes of the moment, many thereby making a fair living, today the situation is very different . . . [T]here is little actual buying of the art of contemporary artists. As a result, more and more painters are devoting themselves to problems of painting, crafts, and interpretation." From this unsought independence would emerge the Northwest School of which Kenneth and Margaret Callahan, without design, became the intellectual center, Tobey the mythic figure, Morris Graves erratic, self-absorbed, exploitative, on the periphery, and Guy Anderson drawing them all out of the city to La Conner, often enough to see the landscape through his lenses.[3]

The Cornish School

If a cultural catalyst existed in the city most observers would probably accord that honor to the Cornish. Nellie Cornish would travel each year to New York to line up prospective teachers to fill vacancies, to invite guest faculty, to strengthen existing programs, often to begin new ones. Russian emigres proved a ready talent source in ballet, music, and drama. Many of those recruited already were well known among their peers. One, Peter Merenblum, a graduate of the Petrograd Imperial Conservatory, enabled Cornish to reinstate its chamber music course and to reestablish its orchestra. (Some Cornish faculty and students played in the Seattle Symphony, whose first cellist was Koila Levienne.) Merenblum then induced Miss Cornish to enlist his fellow refugee, Levienne, to head up its cello department, and to round out the Cornish Trio. Berthe Poncy Dow of Switzerland, who had been signed on to teach eurythmics, proved also an accomplished pianist whose husband, Wallace Dow, could and did manage eurythmics. Consequently Madame Poncy took over piano teaching. She and Merenblum had been performing to enthusiastic audiences before Levienne arrived, so the trio fell easily in place. Frederick and Nelson Department Store sponsored a regular radio broadcast of their performances. Soon there would be a Merenblum Quartet, peforming up and down the coast, spreading Cornish's reputation in the process. In 1925, Myron Jacobson, a fellow refugee and friend of the two other Russians, joined the faculty to teach opera and piano. He later married Madame Poncy (Walter Dow had departed from her and Cornish earlier). She subsequently joined the piano department at the University of Washington as its head in 1938. One of the last of the Russians to be hired was Alexander Koiransky, who had been on tour with the Moscow Art Theatre, to teach the Stanislawsky approach to drama. He taught for seven years before leaving for Hollywood, then to Berkeley.[1]

The Cornish School's sometime reputation for conservatism was not entirely deserved, if we consider Miss Cornish's recognition first of Mark Tobey, then of Martha Graham. Graham's name had not yet become synonymous with modern dance when she was enlisted by Miss Cornish, though students from "far and near" did know of her and enthusiastically enrolled in her classes, as did some of the faculty. While engaged to teach in the summer of 1930, Martha Graham so impressed "Miss Aunt Nellie" that Miss Cornish decided to sponsor a solo performance at the Metropolitan, drawing in the Seattle branch of the Pro

Musica Society as a co-sponsor. Regularly, Cornish engaged Ellen Van Volkenburg Browne for summers—she, with her husband Maurice, was a founder of the Little Theater movement. "Miss A. N." clearly had an eye for talent, and unique powers of persuasion. But, once on the faculty, she freed them to work their will. Among the avant guardists were even Seattle natives or at least near-natives: dancer Merce Cunningham, composer John Cage, and painter Bill Cumming, youngest of the Northwest School. (Whether Cage could seriously be classed as faculty can best be judged from Cumming's hilarious account, "John Cage and the Cornish Riot" of 1938.)[2]

Cornish's apparent vitality hid its chronic financial distress. The depression of 1920-1921 set the tone for the early years of the decade: loss of pupils, desertion of some faculty for greener pastures, a lean operations budget that restricted the hiring of replacements and guest faculty, and finally the inability of the property owner (the Cornish Realty Company) to continue mortgage payments. The latter crisis led, in 1924, to the formation of the Cornish School Foundation, as a non-profit corporation, to take over the business affairs, leaving Miss Cornish "as director for life" to concentrate on the educational program. From this point on, despite continued financial difficulties, the Cornish took on a fresh life, which she describes as the "golden years".[3]

"Golden" as to its faculty, enrollment, and programs (mainly the weekly Three Arts Program which exposed the public to the Cornish's excellence in music, drama, and dance) . . . but not to its financial condition. While Anna Pavlova paid heed on a visit and praised Cornish to Easterners, and financier Otto Kahn insisted to his surprised Seattle business hosts that he must see the Cornish, Miss Cornish continued having trouble drummming up local support. Niggardly they remained, despite Kahn's admonishing his hosts for not being generous in giving something culturally back to the city from which they derived their wealth. An endowment was needed to make possible long range planning, as well as carrying over faculty and programs from only one year to the next, but no endowment was ever established. Agnes Anderson pulled the Cornish out of a hole in 1929, when she paid off the mortgage. By 1932, at the bottom of the Depression, the board forced an end to the Cornish Trio, a key to the school's fame. Despite these setbacks the school established a touring theater which began in the summer of 1932 with a successful six-week tour through the midwest and southwest, concluding on the Pacific Coast with performances on the campus at Berkeley, then Ashland. Though the board was skeptical that provincial audiences were capable of comprehending live theater, Miss Cornish's confidence proved the board mistaken. Their success probably lent the Jameses some self-assurance when they established the touring Washington State Theatre in the late 1930s.[4]

The Fine Arts Scene, Founding of Seattle Art Museum, and Beginnings of the "Northwest School"

As the main fine arts organization in the city, the Seattle Fine Arts Society promoted what public interest in the fine arts could be stirred up. Its business manager in 1931 commented that from 1906 to 1928 it had been run as a "small club". Contributing to its efforts was the Cornish, with its classes for youngsters, the Music and Arts Foundation, and the West Seattle Art Club, which initiated an annual Katherine Baker award of $100 in 1925 for the "most meritorious painting" in the Northwest Artists' annual exhibit. Reaching out, the SFAS instituted a scholarship in connection with University Extension Division's sponsorship of annual Summer painting classes, conducted by the redoubtable John Butler (he had taught for the society in the prewar years). The University's Walter Isaacs presented a lecture course sponsored by the Society in 1924 and 1925 on the "essentials in art". In the direction of the public schools a biennial exhibit was staged, illustrating the work being done by youngsters in the school's art departments. Joining with the State Federation of Women's Clubs, the Society sponsored a touring exhibit of paintings by state artists. Cooperation with the Cornish was close and continuous throughout the period, resulting in many co-sponsorships of their public offerings. The city's fine arts network remained small and tightly interwoven.[1]

While this evidence of vitality in the art community, along with membership growth in the SFAS itself showed promise, there remained a pinchpenny attitude among those of the social elite on whom support traditionally depends. The annual ball raised much of the sustaining funds for the Society, but when architect Carl F. Gould suggested, in 1927, putting aside $100 for awards in the Northwest Artists' exhibit, the directors patronizingly decided it was "not really needed or wanted by the artists."Also, in this prosperous year of 1927 the board chose to withdraw from the Western Association of Art Museums to save $20 annually. (The Society's indebtedness in 1926 amounted to $2601, down from $4000.) Nellie Cornish, as noted above, also

Special Collections Division, University of Washington Libraries. Negative No. UW 2070

Seattle Art Museum at Volunteer Park. Margaret and Richard Fuller donated $250,000 in 1931 for its construction. In background is view of the University of Washington campus and the "U" District.

heavily dependent on this elite to sustain her school, had encountered the same penuriousness, with notably few exceptions. In her case, Agnes Anderson became her chief benefactor. In the case of the SFAS, it was, first, the generosity of Horace C. Henry, then Margaret Fuller and her son Richard. (Henry also was a Cornish board member.) A small core of dependables among the social elite, in addition to the above, kept alive the fine arts of the city: the Stimson and Baillargeon family branches, Mrs. Edgar (Anne) Ames, Mrs. Horton C. (Anna) Force (who had adopted Kenneth Callahan), and Carl F. Gould, chief among them.[2]

The Society's quarters and gallery moved successively, during the 1920s, from 2028 Third Avenue uptown to Plymouth House at Fifth and Seneca, to the Skinner Building in the University tract, and finally, in 1928, to the Henry mansion near the Cornish School. Henry, as a collector, had a special gallery there, which he vacated upon donating his collection to the University of Washington, along with $100,000 to build the Henry Art Gallery on campus. His donation of paintings was the "first large collection . . . given the public in this state . . . ." Until the Fullers donated $250,000 to the City in 1931 for construction of the Seattle Art Museum at Volunteer Park, the Henry mansion's gallery served as the Society's headquarters.[3]

To staff the new quarters professionally, the Society hired Mildred McLouth of the Los Angeles Art Museum staff. As curator she tried to set a tone for "tolerance" and "open minds" with respect to modern art exhibits, "whether we like them or not." Mrs. McLouth barely lasted one year, being notified in 1928 that her contract would not be renewed. She resigned instead. In replacing her, the directors downgraded the position and were doubly satisfied when they discovered that her replacement could type. In addition, a resident cateress was employed to serve luncheons. Timidity, clearly, marked these hesitant steps toward modernity. Signalling a new direction, however, the SFAS changed its name in 1930 to the Art Institute of Seattle. It began, proclaiming: "[Five galleries will be] turned over to temporary exhibits running the entire gamut of the art field. The Institute holds each year about twelve to fifteen shows of Northwest artists . . . Our specialty is the Oriental field . . . [being] sponsored by the China Club, the Japan Society, the Far East Society, the Oriental Studies Department at the University of Washington, and the Art Institute." These exhibits were circulated to other centers in the region and to schools in the city. Children's and adult classes also received Institute sponsorship.[4]

Upon this foundation the Seattle Art Museum began operation in 1933. Richard Fuller outlined the modest program, beginning with the Fullers' own donation of Oriental art and its Chinese emphasis. Fleshing out the core collection was a small group of American paintings presented in memory of Clarence A. Black, and a "small but important group of American sculpture." It was intended that Occidental art would be represented mainly by facimiles. He hoped to see exhibits monthly, relying on "transient material", which depended upon cooperation with other western art museums. To the Northwest Artists' exhibit would be added an annual exhibit for Northwest printmakers. As topping he added, "We are inviting a local artist each month to have a one-man show of his or her work [to inspire local talent and support modern art]."[5]

This seemingly limited prospectus, nonetheless, underpinned the ambitions of local artists. Assistant director for publicity, Kenneth Callahan—himself a blossoming painter—had just returned from exposure to the Mexican muralists. Cited were Eustace Ziegler, Edgar Forkner, and Walter Isaacs, who in the last two years, have "risen above the local average into definite identity as individuals." But, he continued: "The extremes of modern art have few exponents here [except for] Surrealism [which] is evidenced by no one in these parts and abstraction only by a few painters, chiefly Mark Tobey, Walter Isaacs, James Grunbaum, and Peter Campfermann . . . The real value [of these four] was in helping to plant the seeds of doubt in the minds of the academic laymen and painters . . . ." Isaacs, having studied in France—prior to assuming directorship of the University's School of Art—introduced European styles, French in particular, emphasizing Cezanne. Students and local artists seemed receptive to this instruction. Of special importance in this academic program was Ambrose Patterson. Patterson, an Australian, who had studied in France before World War I, had joined the faculty to impart the cosmopolitan styles of the Occident. Callahan, however, expected something different, expressive of a locale, not of a style.[6]

Thus, two groupings blossomed on the local premises. One, gathered around Fuller, "was variously intrigued by the local Northwest subjects and by Asian art; while the university group might have seemed a little like a Northwest branch of the School of Paris."[7]

Before the 1930s, local artists, apart from their portrait paintings, were heavily into landscape representations, rarely capturing the mood conveyed by the elements making it up. Speaking to this point, Callahan reviewed a 1938 exhibit at SAM of the "American School of Painting", criticizing the artists' work as lacking "in feeling of conviction and sensitivity on the part of these men to ideas, things or objects in nature or the living world." For him, while these painters might satisfy the "Eastern markets", they should not be imitated here. He and a whole group of local artists were establishing their identity. Enmeshed in the Puget Sound environment, they began to capture its somber tones, active skies, its noisy and flambuoyant seabird life, and coastal wetlands habitat. For Mark Tobey and Cumming, particularly, the city's urban scenes of the Pike Place Market and Skid Road habituees received graphic depiction. Oriental influences early colored their thinking and affected their techniques, the result of their immersion by travel to China and Japan and from reading, argument and discussion, to which was added their penchant for painting together for extended periods. Out of this setting the "Northwest School" was spawned. The older among this constellation were Tobey, Callahan, Morris Graves, and Guy Anderson who attracted William Cumming, Fay Chong, George Tsutakawa, Richard Gilkey, Paul Horiuchi, Kamekichi Tokita, Kenjiro Nomura—among "the group of twelve". Sparked by Tobey, together they inspired others.[8]

First of these artists to appear was Tobey. Nellie Cornish, recognizing his teaching prowess as well as his artistry, hired him out of New York in 1922. Tobey assimilated many different styles early in his development and continued to intermingle them throughout his long career. By teaching—and enjoying it—he reached a widening audience, in part, by lectures sponsored by the Seattle Public Library. It should have been no surprise that in 1934 SAM gave Tobey a one-man show. Richard Fuller, already the proud owner of Tobey paintings, as well as some by Graves, promoted contemporary art on principle, but the Oriental influence in the works of these artists, in particular, must have been a satisfying attractant to him.[9]

Yet, despite their many affinities, their individual responses to much they held in common from their environment and philosophical influences, each strived to express his art sharply different from the other. An exception might be Graves's adaptation of Tobey's "white writing" technique to his own subject matter. Apart from that, what could stand more in contrast than Tobey's attention to the microscopic (seeing the universe in the most miniscule of objects through a Bahai mind set) and Anderson's large scale symbolic works? As painting companions, Anderson and Graves were together more rather than less, yet their styles are strikingly contrasted. Tobey's return to the city in 1938 to administer part of the Federal Art Project in Seattle, meant the coalescence of the disparate elements of the nascent Northwest School. After 1940, it became identified as such, and those they inspired became part of the "Northwest Tradition". Martha Kingsbury writes: "That the area's achievements, new as they were, received national acknowledgement in the thirties must have been heartening. In 1933 Seattle provided work for the Museum of Modern Art exhibition . . . Callahan, still in his twenties, was included." Tobey had earlier gained attention; Graves would become the more popular in the East, though Tobey's reputation would broaden more internationally.[10]

National and international attention to the Northwest School came first, and perhaps most critically, through the agencies of Elizabeth Bayley Willis and Nancy Wilson Ross. Marian Willard was introduced to Graves's paintings on one of her Northwest visits (many done while in the Federal Art Project). Willard, through her Willard Gallery in New York, became his agent and also served Tobey in part. The fame of the "School" spreads beyond our period. However, it is worth observing that for many among them, it was the Federal Art Project that sustained them during their critical formative period.[11]

The Seattle Repertory Playhouse

In 1928, Burton and Florence Bean James resigned from the Cornish faculty to start a civic theater. It would become a diverse organization. Plays would be produced, not only in its own house, but beyond, to Seattle school children, then as a touring theater operating under sponsorhip of the State Department of Instruction (once Rockefeller Foundation funding was assured). Prior to these programs, the Jameses had developed a "Negro Theater" which later became part of the Federal Theater Project of the Work Projects Administration. The current liveliness of theater in Seattle owes much to the foundations laid by the Jameses . . . and the Cornish.[1]

A measure of the SRP's success in promoting serious theater is to be found in a December 1933 issue of the *Town Crier,* under a half-page portrait of Florence Bean James: "Keen intelligence, rare insight and understanding, and a tremendous capacity for hard work are three outstanding characteristics of Mrs. James [at the SRP, where she] has established [herself] as one of the outstanding stage directors of the West."[2]

The Jameses' decision to start a theater came from a May 1928 meeting they staged among a group of Cornish students and friends who had acted and worked in their Cornish plays. Their decision was announced in a July *Christian Science Monitor* issue: "The Seattle Repertory Playhouse hopes to maintain a permanent professional acting company capable of building and keeping a repertory of good plays." In Mrs. James's autobiography she concludes that it became really a community theater involving "ethnic groups, intellectuals, artists, labor and young people . . . ." When it opened for the 1928-1929 season, 997 tickets had been sold before a single play had been produced—apparently $5.00 for all six plays was not excessive during this last year of 1920s prosperity. During the first two years, twelve plays were produced after opening with "Juno and the Paycock" at the Metropolitan. Local playwrights found exposure as well. One was Garland Ethel, whose play "In His Image", set in Okanogan County, was given high marks by the *P-I.* A tour to Everett in the second season acquainted them with the notion of a touring theater. Yet they needed a home of their own, if they were to meet expenses. The Met was too expensive, and shopping for alternatives was too diverting. Burton James figured that the University district offered the best potential location as the "cultural center of the city, and [because] it represented a greater purchasing power per person . . . ." They settled upon a building at 41st Avenue and University Way. From their early experience the Jameses decided against trying for a subsidized theater, but they also believed that commercialized theater throughout the country was undermining "sound theatre practices and artistic merit."[3]

In meeting this standard, they staged "Peer Gynt" in 1930-1931—only the fourth time it had been given in the United States. Encouraged by the chorus of rave reviews, they ran the play weeks beyond the original planned dates. "Faust" was the highlight of the 1931-1932 season, attracting over 10,000 people from "thirty towns and cities from four western states." It played in Tacoma and Vancouver as well. Young people were bussed in from around the state. Recognizing its commercial value, the *Times* applauded the Rep for "bringing literally hundreds of visitors from all parts of the Northwest . . . ."[4]

Also in this season the Jameses staged "Uncle Tom's Cabin", unconventionally casting Blacks in the appropriate parts. Audience reception encouraged them next season to perform the Pulitzer Prize winning play by Paul Green, "In Abraham's Bosom". Its setting was in a North Carolina turpentine camp (the nearest approximation in the Northwest would be a pre-World War I logging camp, but without the complicating factor of race relations). Urban League president, Joseph S. Jackson, played Abraham, and his mother also was played by local Black talent, Anne Oliver; all but two parts were played by Blacks. It drew audiences "from up and down the coast, many asking where the actors came from." Heloise Wardall, writing to Mark Tobey in England about the play, commented that within four months the Jameses had "Trained them into a production that I shall never forget . . . [W]hen I was trying to talk about it with Burton afterward I almost was unable to speak . . . How I wished all evening that you could be there." This marked the founding of the "Negro Repertory", for which the Jameses got WPA funding in 1936. The first play given under these auspices was Andre Obey's "Noah", in which Noah is played by a Black. "Stevedore" followed. Set amidst a New Orleans dock strike, entangled with labor racketeering, it included an all-Black cast. Altogether fifteen productions were performed, second in number only to New York City. But when the Jameses tried to stage "Lysistrata" by setting it in Ethiopia—in the context of the Ital-

Special Collections Division, University of Washington Libraries. Negative No. 14053

"Negro Repertory Theatre" was inspired by Florence Bean James as an offspring of the Seattle Repertory Theatre productions, beginning with presentation of "Uncle Tom's Cabin" in 1931-32 season. The Jameses got WPA funding for the NRT in 1936. The scene above is from Paul Green's Pulitzer Prize winning play "In Abraham's Bosom", 1937.

ian invasion of that poor country—the WPA censors cancelled its production despite the promise of a sellout crowd at the Moore Theatre.[5]

Looking to the future for a stable audience, the Jameses decided to expose high school audiences to live theater. Encouraged by their earlier presentation to Seattle school audiences they toured to Aberdeen in November 1936 with "Comedy of Errors". This marked the real beginning of the Washington State Theatre. State Superintendent Noah Showalter was willing to lend his endorsement if the Jameses could get outside funding. Once the Rockefeller Foundation was persuaded of the project's feasibility, it came across with the money and Showalter's office lent its authority. Idaho's Talbot Jennings' "No More Frontiers" was given in the spring of 1937, "Taming of the Shrew" in the fall. 1938 saw productions of Oliver Goldsmith's "She Stoops to Conquer" in the spring of 1938, and Thornton Wilder's "On Stage" in the fall.[6]

By 1938, the Jameses looked upon their theater as "established", but they wanted "[A]n organized audience . . . Our work with the schools comes first . . . We have seen that the theatre is primarily for education . . . Next year the Playhouse will extend its work to two major productions for the Seattle

Special Collections Division, University of Washington Libraries, Negative No. 14054

The Washington State Theatre also was a spinoff of the SRP, once funding was received from the Rockefeller Foundation. The State Department of Public Instruction sponsored this travelling theater group's statewide tour. "No More Frontiers" was written by Idaho's Talbot Jennings.

High Schools . . . Next Fall definite work will begin with the teachers . . . and students of the grade schools of Seattle . . . This work is . . . frankly experimental." As this effort was progressing, they would also approach organized social and religious groups, labor unions, cooperatives, and the Grange in broadening their audience base. Combined with this effort was their introduction of two drama classes—one, a week-end school to attract out-of-towners, was enrolling about 100 by 1940. The other class was a day school.[7]

A strong undercurrent periodically tugged at the Jameses. One came from the *Times*. Another, more serious one, came from the University of Washington in the person of Glenn Hughes, head of the Drama Division of the English Department. In 1930 the Jameses had been appointed to teach a two-hour laboratory course four days a week and to produce some plays in connection with that course. Hughes, also that year, was appointed head of the Drama Division—he had previously served as an instructor of drama, and now had been rehired from Scripps

College. He was told clearly by Dean F.M. Padelford and English Department chairman, Dudley Griffiths, that he was not to produce plays because the Jameses were already producing plays of such high quality that the university would be embarassed to try competing. His mission, he was clearly told, was to teach drama teachers and to offer courses for "cultural purposes".[8]

Hughes, however, irrepressibly, was determined to get into production, one way or another. As member of the SRP's board of directors he persuaded the Jameses to rent him the Playhouse from 1930 to 1932 to expose students to drama as participants. He next cajoled the owner of the district's Egyptian Theatre to allow him to put on plays in the owner's penthouse atop the spanking-new Meany Hotel. As a Rep board member he learned from Samuel Fitz (the SRP's property owner) that the Jameses were behind in their lease payments. Hughes reported this to Griffiths who then wrote to Acting President Hugo Winkenwerder in April 1933, reporting that Fitz had asked Hughes to "consider taking over management of the [Playhouse, making the payments to Fitz]. Hughes would direct it as Head of our Division of Drama and its income would then belong to him . . . ." Hughes, Griffiths continued, wants "the income to be devoted to making the theatre a real community center in which both the University and the community would cooperate. It would give us an auditorium . . . for the cultural development of all students at the University." Winkenwerder was further advised that Law School Dean, Leslie Ayer, would draw up the appropriate papers. The Regents referred the communication to their executive committee for study and recommendations. At its July meeting the Board agreed with its committee that "the University should not associate itself commercially or otherwise with the management of the Seattle Repertory Theatre [sic]." Although the Regents' minutes make no reference to Ayer, Florence James credits him, anyway, with dissuading them from accepting the proposition which certainly would have proved embarassing to the University by the diversion of the income to Hughes personally. Persisting, however, Hughes still aimed for control of the SRP. On October 6, 1937 Hughes wrote to President Sieg (after prompting Fitz on the previous day, on what to say to the Regents), that Fitz was trying to get the Rockefeller Foundation to buy the property and donate it to the university. This deal also fell through (no record of it exists in the Regents' minutes).[9]

During this period Burton James was dismissed from the

university, while Hughes continued unfolding his operations. First, he moved from the Meany's penthouse to its more spacious ballroom until 1935. He then rented a "ramshackle" building near the Playhouse for his "Studio Theatre", opening in late 1934, continuing there for three and one-half years. By then, he had gotten administration approval for construction of the "Showboat Theatre", parked along the university's section of the canal. The theater opened September 22, 1938, with "Charley's Aunt". In contrast to the Jameses challenging repertoire, Hughes had his drama students emulate Broadway productions of the period. In the estimate of Evamarii Johnson, "Hughes was more concerned with popular theatre than with broadening audience's taste in dramatic literature or theatrical production styles." It was now not long before the axe would fall on Mrs. James. She was notified that the Drama Division was to be reorganized in 1938 and that she had too many outside commitments to devote full-time to her teaching assignments; therefore, she was dismissed. Widespread outcry bellowed across campus against the administrative procedure followed. Her dismissal violated an earlier agreement between the Instructors Association and President Sieg. His act was labeled officially as "withdrawal".[10]

Coloring this action was the SRP's presentation in 1936-1937 of two "proletarian" plays, Eugene O'Neill's "Hairy Ape", followed by Clifford Odet's "Waiting for Lefty". While the former ran to mixed reviews "Lefty" caused a real furor among conservatives. Adding to the controversy was Florence James's recent public appearances in which she portrayed the Soviet Union in flattering terms, after her 1934 tour there. She records that the *Times* became so embittered about her public speaking and "Lefty" that the Rep "was never mentioned in the *Times* again and as individuals our names were never printed until the Canwell Committee got into action" in 1947-1948. Then, both the *Times* and Hughes would finally undo the Rep and the Jameses.[11]

The Seattle Symphony and Other Musical Groups

Hardly had the war ended, when the Seattle Symphony was reorganized in 1919, under the lead of banker James D. Hoge. John Spargur returned as conductor, and eighty-five musicians were signed up. Encouraged by both a bountiful fund drive and by the overflow audiences of that season, the orchestra moved its concerts from the Masonic Temple (across from

Broadway High School) to the Meany Auditorium on the University campus. These signs of life, however, were short-lived. The austerity program, inflicted by the postwar recession, forced cancellation of the 1920-1921 season. This fate occurred, despite a "gentlemen's agreement" among Hoge, the *Times*'s Joseph Blethen, and Broussais Beck (an executive of the Bon Marche) to sustain the Symphony. Like the Cornish, the Symphony fell victim to the downswing. Even enlistment of esteemed "Major" J.F. Douglas (head of the Metropolitan Building Company) to persuade the Chamber of Commerce "to call together 40 or 50 citizens to determine what should be done", drew only a lame response—that it "should be supported". (The Chamber at this time was fixed upon a tax reduction drive affecting public schools, the addition of playgrounds, resurfacing of boulevards, and other civic frills.) Failure to shake loose funding through the Chamber diverted Nellie Cornish from her own financial troubles. She viewed the symphony in relation to the school's own future—musical careers for some of her own students. Thus committed, she organized a group of women's clubs presidents to stage a fund drive, but this effort also petered out. The city was to be without a symphony until 1926.[1]

A trial run, in May 1926, initiated by the Musicians' Association and those Cornish stalwarts—Harriet (Mrs. C.D.) Stimson, Mrs. Edgar Ames, and Katherine (Mrs. A.S.) Kerry—engaged Karl Krueger to conduct an improvised orchestra of 65 professional musicians at the Metropolitan. Krueger, reportedly, was amazed at the high quality of these musicians, given the absence of a symphony for the past five years (many of the musicians had been Cornish students). While conducting in Europe, he was offered the conductorship in Seattle. In accepting the offer he made arrangements for the first concert on November 6, 1926. Budding local impressario Cecilia A. Schultz took charge of ticket sales. (She would soon become its manager, then establish her own music and dance series.) Instrumentalists ranged in character from a Russian emigre-concert master, Mischa Levienne (brother of cellist Koila), to local fireman-bassoonist, Harry Nelson. Not only was the concert series sold out, but Krueger put on five "popular concerts" and four children's concerts, complemented by public lectures. Krueger, being committed to exposing audiences to one modern work per concert, juxtaposed Mozart's "Jupiter" and Stravinsky's "Firebird". Enthusiasms grew apace, spiced by an open air presentation of "Aida" before a crowd of 12,000 in the University stadium. As Krueger's local popularity expanded, so too his ambition to reach larger audiences. The first symphony concert of the 1928-1929 season, given at the newish Civic Auditorium, gathered together 6,500, then a city record for a concert.[2]

From this pinnacle came a big fall as the Depression hit, leading to dissension among board members in 1931. Krueger resigned. Spunkily, a publicity campaign was launched during a brief hiatus, and the English conductor Basil Cameron was signed on to give an Easter concert, March 25, 1932. Capitalizing on the enthusiasm generated, a "Save the Symphony" campaign raised enough funds to program a modest 1933-1934 season of five concerts with an orchestra scaled down to 55 members. Conducting the first concert without score, Cameron caught audience fancy, but during the prior two weeks of rehearsals he had gained the musicians' confidence as well—he seemed to know what he was doing. The season closed before an audience of 7,000 in the Civic Auditorium. Cameron agreed to another season, just as another fund drive was mounted to collect $15,000 as financial underpinning in those dark days at the bottom of the Depression. Success was catching on—the 1934-1935 season included six popular concerts for the Civic Auditorium, a series of five Saturday morning concerts exclusively for children at ten cents a head, to be quickly succeeded amid enthusiastic acclaim with another "popular" series. The symphony also gave out-of-town concerts, six nationwide radio broadcasts and four on a Pacific Coast hookup. Cameron and the orchestra earned high praise all around. At the end of the next season, the *Town Crier* reported: "Artistically the Seattle Symphony reached greater heights this year than ever before", when 157,000 were counted for those attending its sixty-nine performances.[3]

All this seemed too good to last. It was. Despite a highly successful 1937-1938 season, capped by an apparently stunning performance of the Beethoven Ninth, a fund drive after that season failed miserably. Cameron was notified, while he was guest-conducting in Europe, that his contract could not be renewed. (This coincided with the 1937-1938 recession to which the sudden cutback in public works funding had contributed.) To replace the relatively expensive Cameron, the Symphony board hired the former director and founder of the Cleveland Symphony, Nicolai Sokoloff. Concerts were downscaled from the elitist Metropolitan to the Music Hall Theater at Seventh Avenue and Olive Street. Successful fund drives followed the 1938-1939 season, enabling Sokoloff to continue through the 1940-1941 season, after which he resigned and was replaced by an English refugee, Thomas Beecham, who was regarded as one of the world's six best conductors.[4]

It is doubtful that the Symphony would have been sustained even on the meager basis outlined above, if Cecilia Schultz had not been bringing artists, opera and dancing groups to the city, and drawing upon the symphony to provide the necessary accompaniment. Even before she contracted with the owners of the Moore Theatre in 1935 to present regular musical series, Schultz had been bringing artists to the city, beginning with "Olympic Matinee Musicales" held in the Spanish Ballroom of the Olympic Hotel in 1928-1929. Inspired by the success of bringing the Chicago Civic Opera here in 1930, a Seattle Civic Opera Association presented "Tannhauser" in 1932, followed by "Lohengrin" in 1933, each being managed through her, and each providing employment for the symphony. In 1934, she staged five concerts at the Civic Auditorium, attracting five thousand per concert, exposing audiences—not for the first time, however—to Sergei Rachmaninoff, Jascha Heifetz, John Charles Thomas, Chaliapin, and the Don Cossacks. Apart from that series she brought in the San Carlo Opera Company for performances of "La Boheme", and her Lawrence Tibbett concert attracted 6,500 admissions. With successes like this to her credit, and the aging Moore needing patronage, a partnership must have been easy to contract. In a kind of celebration in 1935, she turned the Moore over to Nellie Cornish for presentation of "Roadside", a spoof by her "School of the Theatre" graduating class. Once established at the Moore, as the "only woman manager west of Chicago, and one of very few in the United States", she regularly engaged the above-listed performers, added others, and included a Saturday evening "Dance Series" in 1937, highlighted by the Ballet Russe de Monte Carlo. She repeated with this stable of performers as long as each continued to draw the requisite audiences. In 1936, under "Cecilia Schultz Attractions" she even served up a Travelog series for the vicarious traveler.[5]

These were not the only musical fare in town. The Ladies Musical Club continued its artists series, begun at the turn of the century. The Seattle Federation of Women's Clubs also sponsored concerts of a caliber indicated by Rachmaninoff and violinist Efrem Zimbalist. Their concerts were usually held at the Meany Auditorium, where an annual music series also was staged, sponsored by the Associated Women Students of the University. Over the city was scattered a number of other musical clubs, all contributing real vigor at both professional and non-professional levels of participation and appreciation. The audience potential was there, even though adequate funding usually was not.[6]

Parks, Playgrounds, and Boulevards Between the Wars

The City's Park Department has jurisdiction over parks, playgrounds, and boulevards. As a foundation for development the Olmsted plan of 1903 had conceptualized the broad framework within which these civilized amenities would extend in consonance with population growth. One operating premise was to place a park and/or playground within one-half mile of every family. Bond issues from 1909 to 1913 had underpinned the funding for most of the development before 1922. Yet, as the Park Superintendent pointed out in his annual report (the last until 1930): "these improvements have been in use for from ten to fifteen years, and due to wear and tear, are now becoming worn out." Indeed, he estimated that $750,000 would be necessary to put all these facilities in "first class condition". He argued for "permanent structures" to reduce the cost of maintenance, otherwise it would take ten to fifteen years, if only fixed income was to be the funding source.[1]

Eight of the thirty miles of boulevard remained unpaved, while the paved portions had badly deteriorated for lack of maintenence. Green Lake had been closed, due to pollution, for the past few years, finally to reopen in 1922 after a special $10,000 appropriation for its purification was granted by the City Council. At the parks, playgrounds, bathing beaches, and the Woodland Park Zoo all of the utilities had been allowed to deteriorate badly. This was the dark side. As the city emerged from the postwar recession, some new projects got underway—an automobile tourist camp at the northeast end of Green Lake was established; work was started on a second municipal golf course at Jackson Park on the north edge of the city, while at the Jefferson links the addition of a nine-hole course neared completion. The first overnight camp at the end of a three mile hike for both boys and girls was established at Carkeek Park on the shores of the Sound north of the city. Two miles north of Kirkland another camp facility, along sixteen hundred feet of Lake Washington waterfront, was acquired through the bequest of Mrs. Orin B. (Helen) Denny (to be named O.O. Denny Park). Purchase of 130 acres of land also had been made that year for Lincoln Park, extending about a mile along the Sound about two miles south of Alki bathing beach. Enlivening this revival were thirty free band concerts given during the summer at Woodland Park, the Auto Camp, Volunteer Park, Alki Beach, Cowen Park, and at South Park. All told the city could boast of 46 parks, plus the two outside the city, and with few exceptions, there was a park or playfield in every district or neighborhood. Playgrounds numbered twenty-three, four with field houses to be used for recreation during the inclement months, and as community houses all year long. At the bathing beaches (6 fresh water and 2 salt water), free swimming and life saving classes had been operating since 1920.[2]

By 1930, eleven new playfields had been added to the City's stock. Facilities at—now ten—bathing beaches were upgraded with more durable structures, including "modern" bath houses at Madrona, West Green Lake, and Golden Gardens (a newly acquired salt water beach on Ballard's shores), and new field houses at East Green Lake and Rainier Beach had been added to the five existing ones. By 1930 the city could count 34 neighborhood parks, 8 large "recreation parks" (Woodland, Carkeek, Seward, Green Lake, Golden Gardens, and Lincoln parks). Sprinkled among the city blocks were small triangles, squares and the like, garnished often with lush landscaping that flourished in the temperate surroundings.[3]

When the Depression set in, the Parks Department suffered in some ways, but it also benefited in others. Unemployed were put to work, initially with meager City funds, then later with federal dollars. The Civil Works Administration afforded employment during the winter of 1933-1934, followed by work relief projects funded by the Work Projects Administration and Civilian Conservation Corps. An overview of what was accomplished by supply of these bounties is merited. It is doubtful that the City would have accomplished what was done if left to its own devices, even in the best of times—the 1920s.

During the winter months of 1930 the City Council appropriated $15,000 to employ single and married men to clear brush, grub out stumps, grade pathways and the like. Single men were employed through the Volunteers of America, receiving $1.00 per day plus board and room, while married men were paid from $2.75 to $3.25 per day, based on the number of dependents. As economic conditions deteriorated further, the City Council felt compelled to up its ante for unemployment relief to $56,497.47 for the period December 1930 through March 1931; but the rate of pay for married men fell to $2.50 and $3.00, respectively. Since unemployment would not disappear another $89,850 was appropriated in September, but the rate of pay was forced upward (under pressure of the Unemployed Citizens' League and the Central Labor Council) to $4.50 per day so that union wage scales would not suffer. By the end of 1931, little remained of this appropriation. So unremitting was unemployment that in 1932 a recreation center for unemployed men was opened in a large storeroom at 21 Occidental Avenue, providing 195,000 men with some warmth and comfort during the autumn and winter months. (No mention is made of any provisions for unemployed and homeless women.)[4]

During the winter of 1933-1934, the federal administration, goaded by Harry Hopkins, set up the Civilian Works Administration as a temporary measure to assure some means of work relief. By December 1933, 3,000 men were so employed, mainly at Woodland, Seward, and Lincoln parks, each containing stands of old growth forest with downed trees, stumps, and rain forest brush waiting to be cleared for public trail access. State contributions to the program amounted to $21,205. The Civilian Conservation Corps employed about 200 men in camps at Carkeek and O.O.Denny parks outside the city. In September 1934 work was begun on the proposed arboretum in Washington Park when an agreement was struck with the University of Washington to supervise expenditure of federal funds supplied to the Washington Emergency Relief Administration (WERA). Appropriately, the contract went to the Olmsted Brothers, who had designed the original parks, playgrounds, and boulevard system in 1903. Since then successive additions had been made to Washington Park, almost doubling its size to about 750 acres by substantial acquisitions in 1922 and 1930. The firm's John F. Dawson set to work designing the arboretum's layout of almost 750 acres, now the city's finest landscaped jewel. Of equivalent importance in 1934 was the grant of a five-year lease from the Forest Service for use of 45 acres at Snoqualmie Pass for a ski park, combined with expenditure of more CWA funds for building construction. Now the Pass area is known in some circles as "Snoqualmie City". Two new field houses also were built with WERA funds at Montlake and Laurelhurst playfields. After the CWA was discontinued in early 1934, Work Projects Administration funds were put to use continuing the same kind of work relief projects, finally, apparently, even employing women as gardeners at Volunteer Park, and later at Woodland Park's gardens. Quoting from the 1935 annual report: "All construction work in 1935 was done by state and [federal] government relief projects, as no money was allowed in the Park budget for new work." Funds also came from another federal agency, the Public Works Administration, for the Jefferson Park Clubhouse. Construction that year was begun for a golf course on 207 acres of uncleared land in West Seattle, representing the largest single project undertaken by the WPA for the Park Department. It was formally opened May 16, 1940. At Lincoln Park, WPA funds brought forth a swimming pool in 1938. That year the WPA funded even the Park band concerts. The above is but a partial list of federally funded projects benefiting the city and its environs to the present day. Most have been maintained by the City.[5]

In terms of operations, the Jackson Park Golf Course was formally opened in March 1930 at ceremonies witnessed by a crowd of 69,726. Ten bathing beaches accommodated 779,680 people, and for the first time free first aid classes were given. By 1930 playfields numbered 38, while seven of them were equipped with field houses. By special arrangement with the University of Washington, students majoring in physical education were employed without pay as supervisors, a practice that would continue for a few years. That year "attendance in the parks increased tremendously." However, the Superintendent reported in 1932 that parks and boulevards were far below standards for a city of its size—which another year of heavy use made worse. All through the Thirties, park attendance increased "tremendously". Summers were always highlighted by a "Novelty Parade" held during "Fleet Week"; and in 1934 the "Potlatch" festival was revived as in old times, with canoe races, parades, band concerts, contests of all sorts, Indian ceremonials, capped by an open-air performance at Green Lake of "H.M.S. Pinafore".[6]

Conservation and Mountain Recreation Between the Wars

Locally, the conservation movement derived its nourishment from the National Parks Committee of the Mountaineers and the Federation of Women's Clubs, particularly from the latter's Garden Clubs component. Abetting their work in the 1930s, when creation of the Olympic National Park became the primary focus of conservation activity, were Owen A. Tomlinson and Preston Macy, superintendent and assistant superintendent, respectively, of Mt. Rainier National Park.

During the 1920s, two areas commanded primary attention of the Mountaineers. One was facilitating access to Mt. Rainier National Park. The other was the Snoqualmie Pass region, including the trail system radiating from it, northeast toward Stevens Pass, and southward toward the south Cascade Mountains. Being only about forty-five miles from Seattle and accessible by two railroads, the Snoqualmie Pass area invited early attention as a recreation area for urbanites. Of secondary importance, but on the horizon, were concern for protection from commercial exploitation of the Mt. Baker-Mt. Shuksan region, the Glacier Peak "wilderness", and the Goat Rocks area. Irving Clark, chairman of the organization's National Parks Committee, played the key role (over some internal opposition) in facing these issues, but also in alerting members in the mid-1920s to questioning the damming of Lake Chelan and Lake Crescent (near Port Angeles), and to what was at stake in the Northern Pacific Railroad's plan to sell its timber rights for logging between Snoqualmie Pass and Stevens Pass.[1]

For their part, the Mountaineers participated on a volunteer basis with the Forest Service in identifying potential trail routes, then their actual construction. The current result of their efforts and of other volunteer groups is the Cascades section of the Pacific Crest Trail system. Under initiative of the Mountaineers, the pass area also underwent step-by-step development as a ski area, beginning in the early 1920s, when the club leased land to build its ski lodge. Much of the confidence of members in the Forest Service must have stemmed from these early cooperative field operations. During the Olympic National Park controversy in the 1930s this confidence would mightily be tested.[2]

However, access to Mt. Rainier National Park, along with latitude to the concessionaire, preoccupied the Mountaineers (as one of the two primary conservation groups in the 1920s). Setting its stance in November 1920, during the hearings on the Federal Water Power Act, the organization, fearing another Hetch Hetchy, passed a resolution to exclude water power sites from development in national parks and monuments. Soon, its analysis of national parks administration was distributed to members, to other mountaineering clubs, and to the Park Service in late 1922. In process since 1921, it criticized the administration of national parks in general, and singled out the Rainier National Park Company for its "oppressive measures", provoking such an uproar that Horace Albright, Field Director of the National Park Service, called a conference in Seattle for February 19 and 20, 1923 to iron out differences. The report also inspired dissension within the Mountaineers itself. Seattle-based photographer and veteran mountaineer, Asahel Curtis, as chair of the Mt. Rainier Advisory Committee, sent out the invitations, though Arno Cammerer, Director of the service, sent one specifically to the Mountaineers. Under pressure from the club, the Park Company later was thwarted by Superintendent Tomlinson in its attempt to build a tramway in 1928 from the snout of the

Nisqually Glacier to the top of the bluff nearer Paradise Valley, and he agreed to set aside as "wilderness" those areas in the park so designated by the club. Persistent in its apparent belief that the visiting public wanted all the recreational opportunities afforded in the cities, the company was allowed in 1931 to construct a nine-hole golf course in the valley as an "experiment", one that fortunately aborted.[3]

Tied to park administration was transportation access to the mountain. Roads—improved and non-existent—to the various access points had yet to be built, for the most part. The Carbon River entrance could not be approached until the Pierce County Commission completed its part of its bargain to complete the road from the coal town of Carbonado. To approach Longmire, a railroad carried visitors to Ashford, and a Park Company bus shuttled them from there. From the lumber town of Enumclaw was a narrow dirt road leading to the White River entrance. Yakima would not have access over Chinook Pass to the White River entrance until the 1930s. Curtis, in his committee capacity, and the Park administration were fixed upon circling the mountain with a road. Already, there was a West Side branch, forking off the one to Longmire and Paradise. How to connect its end with the one along the Carbon River posed a real problem. Park Superintendent W.H. Peters (Tomlinson's predecessor) looked favorably upon a route passing over the luxuriant meadows of Spray Park to satisfy passersby with a view of spectacular Willis Wall and its towering ice-cap. Curtis favored a low route largely devoid of heavy snows, but one that entailed a tunnel through Ipsut Pass. Luckily, from today's perspective, in 1925, Park Service funding was reallocated to cut out the "impractical" Carbon-Ipsut Pass road.[4]

Access to Mt. Rainier steadily improved during the 1930s, making the area ever more popular, winter as well as summer. These "improvements" had been in progress since at least 1915. For example, in May of 1922 Howard Hanson of the Chamber of Commerce invited Mountaineers president Edmond Meany to lunch to enlist the club in considering plans to form a "Rainier National Park Ski Club". Its purpose would be to aid in developing the mountain as "one of the great public playgrounds of America . . . [with] ski tournaments and contests to be held there at different times of the year, but especially during the summer season." All of these objectives were accomplished by the end of our period. The concessionaire became moderately reined in—though allowed to install a rope ski tow up Alta Vista, a hill rising above Paradise Inn. Yakima gained its access route, and the Lake Tipso area at Chinook Pass was added to the park. A road to connect the Ohanapecosh entrance to that at White River also was completed. The park, with its spacious trails leading to flower-bursting meadows, and to its challenging routes to the summit and satellite peaks, became the mountain playground for the casual visitor, day-hiker, backpacker, climber, and skiing enthusiast. (Serious skiers carried their skis and/or fastened climbers on them to travel up the Muir Glacier as high as 10,000 feet, then, two to three hours later, glided five to six miles downhill at any chosen speed by any combination of routes.)[5]

Looking toward the Snoqualmie Pass area, the Federation of Women's Clubs initiated a "Save a Tree" campaign in 1927 to raise funds to buy a tract of forested land on the western approach to the Pass, near Denny Creek. The Federation wanted a state park there to protect the old growth timber from being harvested by Weyerhaeuser's Snoqualmie Falls Logging Company. Only $3,000 was needed in addition to the $27,000 already raised by late 1927. Success soon crowned their campaign, though dedication of the "Federation Park" waited until June 1934, timed to celebrate the opening of the new transcontinental highway that cut through the Federation's forest. This was but a portent of events to come. A fire in 1938 further reduced its acreage. A selective logging experiment that trespassed on the forest took its toll. In December 1939 a fierce storm blew a number of huge trees across the highway. The Highway Department decided to widen the corridor as a protection for motorists. The Park Department—to which the Federation had donated the forest—then recommended selling the surviving trees and applying the proceeds to some other tract. Not until 1949 would a substitute be found, near Greenwater, on Highway 410. As to the Snoqualmie Pass area, it has been substantially clearcut under the auspices of the Forest Service, Burlington Northern, and the Highway Department.[6]

While Mt. Rainier became the playground for urbanites, pressure increased for creation of a Mt. Olympus National Park. Such pressure had emerged as far back as 1904, when a bill to create an "Elk National Park" was introduced. A Mountaineers summer expedition in 1907 inspired the club to request the State's congressional delegation to introduce legislation for national park status. These efforts were crowned by lame-duck President Theodore Roosevelt's Executive Order establishing a National Monument within the national forest in 1909. The Forest Service's district office and the Olympic National Forest supervisor repeatedly were rebuffed in their efforts to cancel the monument designation before 1911, when a national park bill was introduced by Washington Congressman William Humphrey. Tussle over it ran until May 1915, when President Wilson reduced the monument boundaries by one-half, freeing up the Forest Service's lowland timber for harvesting. Confidence began to wane in the wilderness values entertained by the USFS, occasioning a visit to Seattle by Chief Forester Henry S. Graves to meet with the Mountaineers in order to modify their agitation for a Park by promising them trails. When a Seattle conference that included representatives from the Mountaineers and the Federation of Women's Clubs met in November 1915, it passed a resolution for establishing a national park; to this Asahel Curtis and the Seattle Chamber of Commerce protested. The controversy soon got lost in the legislation leading to creation of the National Park Service in 1916, along with its placement in the Interior Department—thereby establishing a potential alternative to exclusive Forest Service management of the national forests. (All the national parks would have to be carved largely from the national forests.) The 1920s witnessed the Teapot Dome scandal, further tarnishing an Interior Department that seemed inherently susceptible to corruption for having jurisdiction over so much of the public domain. Then was not a propitious time to extend Park Service jurisdiction over national monuments. However, with the election of Franklin D. Roosevelt and his appointment of Harold Ickes to head Interior (Ickes's ambition was to have the Forest Service transferred to Interior), the stage was set for status change.[7]

The range of what follows is narrowed to coverage of local involvement in the movement to establish an Olympic National Park. Ben W. Twight's *Organizational Values and Political Power: the Forest Service Versus the Olympic National Park,* thoroughly covers Forest Service maneuvering throughout the controversy. The USFS's insistence on managing all forest cover on a sustained yield basis—which was premised on the cutting of all timber—proved its undoing. Even the Forest Service's "primitive" areas were planned for cutting in due time, though to be harvested theoretically on a sustained yield basis that, in turn, was based on the notion that the Forest Servce could eventually manage the entire peninsula, including its private land. National concern was led by the Emergency Conservation Committee, operated out of New York by people accustomed to having access to federal level decision makers and legislators. Also, the Forest Service headquarters—because of its broader concerns, which became entwined with bureaucratic politics—repeatedly tried to temper the opposition being generated by the Northwest District office in Portland and the forest supervisor. However headquarters might blunt its field officers' adamancy, in its defense of Forest Service practices that office nevertheless continued to stress its basic "value orientation": "timber primacy, stability, land scarcity, certainty, closed economy, and telic forestry". (The latter relates to establishing permanent, relatively self-contained communities based on exploitation of its forest hinterland, all within a sustained yield program.) Bureaucratic politics, threatening return of the Forest Service to the Interior Department, began at Ickes's prodding in January 1933 and continued throughout the decade. This issue affected the outcome, forcing the Forest Service to make its program more publicly explicit than ever before. In having to do so, wider public support for a national park grew apace—forest preservation below the subalpine level lay outside the service's program. (Its message was communicated in its "Timber Management Plan Policy Statement" of March 15, 1934, which indicated its intention to harvest even within the Monument area if repossessed by the Service.)[8]

Auspiciously, President Roosevelt, by an Executive Order, transferred all National Monuments to Interior jurisdiction in June 1933. The Forest Service did not learn of it until August, too late to contest it. With the National Park Service established as a competing entity on the peninsula, the stage was now set within a new framework. (Modifying Forest Service opposition was Interior Secretary Ickes's control over Public Works Administration funds which the Forest Service needed to tap. To this should be added the crucial factor of FDR's known sympathies favoring a national park.) Preston P. Macy, Assistant Superintendent of Mt. Rainier National Park, was named "acting custodian" of the Monument. From that position, he and Rainier superintendent, Owen A. Tomlinson worked with the Mountaineers' Irving Clark and Mrs. Thomas (Emma) Stimson of the Federation of Women's Clubs, and with other local outdoor groups in mobilizing pro-Park forces.[9]

One week prior to issuance of the Olympic National Forest's "Timber Management Plan" of March 15, 1934, the Mountaineers' trustees instructed its National Parks Committee to oppose all road building and other commercial enterprises in the National Monument. This was followed in June by a resolution recommending Monument preservation as a "wilderness" area, as defined in the recently published "National Plan for American Forestry" (known also as the "Copeland Report"). Vacillating, the trustees decided it was too early "to commit ourselves" to national park status. However, when Clark returned from a September meeting of the Washington State Planning Council, he reported that the State Forester had told him logging would begin on the West side of the national forest (where the heaviest rain forest was located) "in the next year or so". Acting on this information, the club, in October, came out for national park status. The Emergency Conservation Committee's proposal for Mt. Olympus National Park having been issued in early 1934, its recommendations were then incorporated by Washington Congressman Monrad Wallgren into H.R. 7086. The bill would add 400,000 acres to the Monument area, combining them for the park.[10]

Lobbying intensified, with the district foresters doing their best to persuade organizations that industrial and commercial values should be foremost, and that if given a chance, sustained yield forestry would stabilize the peninsular economy, making possible the permanence of existing communities. Operating against their argument was their own admitted overlogging of private holdings, and a landscape pockmarked by ghost towns and logging devastation, sufficient to undermine confidence in any projected Forest Service program. At the level of Washington State administration, Governor Martin lent his opposition, and the Washington State Planning Council followed his cue. Initially the Council opposed a park outright, but when the second Wallgren bill was making its way, drawing the necessary support that made a park highly predictable, it opted for a smaller park. During the course of the first hearings, the Council urged postponement, with Council secretary Ross K. Tiffany complaining to FDR that creating a national park would "bottle up perpetually timber and mineral resources essential to the economy of the Olympic Peninsula." Helping the Council's argument on the recreation side was Asahel Curtis who testified that hiking in the area was declining due to the long distances to be covered and the relentless rainfall. He advocated pushing roads into the interior along with logging to make the upper alpine region more accessible. The first Wallgren bill, though generating support and focusing opinion, failed passage. Wallgren opined to Irving Clark that it would have passed if the state's two senators had backed it (Senators Clarence C. Dill and Homer T. Bone).[11]

By 1936, pro-Park sentiment had grown to such proportions that former Olympic forest supervisor Fred Plumb (then elevated to Assistant Regional Forester) seemed ready to concede defeat. His cause was not helped when the State Planning

Council, observing the gathering momentum, decided to introduce its proposal in December 1936 for a small national park. Wallgren followed by introducing his second bill two months later. When it appeared that further hearings were considered superfluous in light of the ground covered during the first set, Governor Martin succeeded in gaining audience. He and Benjamin Kizer (chair of the Planning Council) presented arguments to reduce the proposed park boundaries to 452,000 acres (about one-half that in the bill) because "there ought to be a limit to the sacrifice asked of the State of Washington." They argued for a sustained yield program.[12]

Meanwhile, local pro-Park forces were mobilized and active, foremost among them Preston Macy and Irving Clark. A note on Macy's mailing list reads, opposite the name of Emma Stimson: "Very favorable and the brains of all Garden Club women of Seattle. Has been given Mrs. Edge's pamphlet [that of the Emergency Conservation Committee] also Northwest Con. [sic] League material. Was Director of Garden Clubs of America for 3 years. Get in touch and give all the facts; she will telegraph and write and also make report to Garden Club of America if requested." Irving Clark, who lobbied for the Mountaineers, claimed that the State Federation of Women's Clubs "has perhaps been more active than any other group in the state in support of the Wallgren bill . . . protesting again[st] the Governor lobbying against the park."[13]

FDR's visit to the peninsula in 1937, as part of his western tour that included Grand Coulee, let it be known that he wanted an expanded boundary that would include rain forest in the main river watersheds. That the bill would pass became a foregone conclusion. Signed into law June 29, 1938, park size was limited to 898,292 acres, though the exact boundaries would be determined by negotiation among the concerned agencies, including the State Planning Council, which wanted to exclude as much of the western forest as possible. Not surprising, FDR got his way, proclaiming inclusion of the Hoh-Bogachiel river corridors. The tussle over boundaries would continue over the next decade as Governor Langlie pressed for park diminution.[14]

When a proposal for a "Cascades Ice Peaks Park" was making the rounds in 1937, the Chamber of Commerce objected because it would cut off access to minerals, grazing, logging, and other commercial development. It supported a continuation of multiple use management, expressing complete confidence in the Forest Service's judicious restraint. When the Mountaineers addressed the same issue in 1939, it adopted a similar tone: "We are absolutely opposed to a Cascades Peaks Park as a National Park . . . The U.S. Forest Service is now completing the Cascade Crest Trail, and it is ideally equipped to administer it for the public, both for industrial development and recreation use." Clearly, the lessons learned of Forest Service obstruction and of its confession to logging of all temperate forest stands during the course of the Olympic National Park fight did not carry over to the Cascades, at least for the time being.[15]

Mountain recreation has operated in tandem with growth of the conservation movement. As accessibility to the mountains improved, more people took to the hills; they added to the conservation constituency year after year. This local conservationist base unmistakeably contributed decisively toward establishment of the Olympic National Park, as it would later to formation of the North Cascades National Park and the Alpine Lakes Wilderness Area. There, on the peninsula, the Forest Service was encountered as an opponent, not as a collaborator. In the Cascades the service was found a friend. Assistant Supervisor of the Snoqualmie National Forest, C.J. Conover, could report in 1937 that 40 miles of new trail construction had been completed along the Cascade Crest Trail, leaving only "unusable" gaps of more "rugged" portions to be completed. Initially, the Snoqualmie "Lodge Country" preoccupied hikers and climbers, but the unexplored backcountry beckoned fresh challenges from the butt-ends of uncompleted trail sections. Veteran climber Joseph Hazard noted the wider use of rope and ice axes as first ascents in the region were made and routes duly noted to guide others.[16]

Responding to the need to impart mountaineering knowledge and techniques to the uninitiated and to the novice, the Mountaineers organized a climbing course in 1935 under the leadership of its reknowned Wolf Bauer. Lectures, demonstrations, and field trips were included this first year, followed by division into elementary and intermediate levels in the second year. The course proved more than one person could handle. Consequently, it was reorganized on a subject basis in 1937 under direction of Lloyd Anderson, with a subject specialist assigned to each topic. Because so much terrain lacked trails and clearly defined routes, woodcraft became an integral part of the course. Attendance began with 19 in 1935, growing to 80 by 1939. Instructees became instructors in the process. It is not surprising that a mountaineering equipment cooperative took root—almost every technical device had to be imported: crampons, pitons, ice axes, and carabiners chief among them. This outfit was the Recreational Equipment Cooperative (now "REI")—its founder, Lloyd Anderson.[17]

Mountaineer Madelene Ryder reported that between 1925 and the late Thirties climbing and skiing had become the "greatest development within the Club in the past ten years." What was true of the club proved even more so to the outside public, as it was drawn to the new sport of skiing. Newspapers gave extensive coverage in their sports and society news pages, often featuring it in their Sunday rotogravure sections, mainly for the pretty scenes sometimes highlighted by skiers shooting off snow cornices above Paradise Valley. Ski clubs sprouted in the Snoqualmie Pass area, the Commonwealth Ski Club, building its lodge in 1931 to join those already there. Club races became a regular weekend affair. Ski instruction gradually found its way to the non-club public when the *Times* initiated its ski school at the pass in the late Thirties. Ski equipment and clothes became normal commercial fare once specialty outlets proved the viability of this sports business. Some Alaska outfitters extended their production into this fancy garment line. By the late 1930s the road to Paradise was kept open, initially, to Narada Falls, from where a shuttle bus would extend their journey, unless the one-mile hike to Paradise was chosen. Finally, private cars could be driven to Paradise itself. Symbolizing progress of the sport was siting of Paradise in 1935 for the national ski championships and the Olympic Games team tryouts. When Stevens Pass opened to winter traffic in the late 1930s, the Mountaineers applied for a cabin permit in 1939, being joined there by the Penguins and the Everett Ski Club. Mt. Baker found its advocate in Bellingham, the Mt. Baker Ski Club. By the end of our period major ski areas numbered four, each drawing weekend and vacation period crowds. Besides club lodges, Paradise Inn provided guest facilities, as did the public lodge at Mt. Baker. (The latter also had small huts with bunks and a wood stove.) Rope tows operated at all locations. Mt. Baker supplemented theirs with a large "toboggan" shaped like a barge that was pulled uphill by a cable that ultimately snapped. Despite its distance from Seattle, Mt. Baker attracted many from the city. Like the region above Paradise its wide open slopes outside the commercial areas proved irresistible to the ski mountaineer, packing skis and knapsack amidst all-encompassing beauty, challenged by the miles of hiking in untracked snow free of people (excepting your chosen few) and the thrill of randomly sailing downhill usually in wide sweeping turns, in contrast to the tighter turns of skiers nowadays—the equipment made the difference in technique.[18]

By the mid-1960s, the Snoqualmie Pass area was nicknamed "Snoqualmie City", but even then there were stands of virgin forest. Now, almost the entire region has been clear cut, done under Forest Service management and by the private land owners (currently, by the Burlington Northern which inherited the Northern Pacific land grant holdings when the huge railroad merger was consummated in the 1970s). As in the fight to establish Olympic National Park, the Forest Service played a key role in trying to defeat the Wilderness bill of 1964, legislation establishing the North Cascades National Park, the Alpine Lakes Wilderness Area, and subsequent "Wilderness" status of selected subregions in the Cascades in the early 1980s. Ben Twight's contention of its "value orientation" toward the Olympic peninsula in the first half of the century would seem comparably unchanged in the Cascades experience. What has made the difference is a public alerted to conservation values as portrayed in ecological terms that place humankind in an ecological setting in which survival of humankind itself is at stake.

16

Civil Liberties Between the Wars

Within Seattle's boundaries those civil liberties that are presumably protected by the Bill of Rights met with less flagrant abuse than they suffered elsewhere in the state. Reviewing in turn many events that have been referred to in other contexts already, we can assess implications for civil liberties resulting from prohibition enforcement, shifting labor relations, and restrictions on freedom of speech and assembly in general.

Throughout the state, prohibition enforcement officers were quickly brought under restraint by being required to obtain search warrants before conducting raids, even for the taking of samples from soft-drink parlors. However, once granted search warrants, federal agents and the City Police Department's Dry Squad frequently used unnecessary force. While no study has yet been made of the pattern of Dry Squad raids or crackdowns, the author's impression from newspaper scanning is that illicit operations conducted by Asians were subjected to disruption—though only temporarily—disproportionate to the number operated by Whites, itself constituting violations of civil rights. We have seen in the Roy Olmstead case that the United States Supreme Court approved the use of wiretap evidence—"whispering wires"—the use of which served to convict Olmstead.[1]

In labor relations, internal dissent within the labor movement itself had been stifled by elimination of known and suspected Communists from officialdom in the Central Labor Council. Indeed, the Associated Industries of Seattle had begun a campaign to eliminate dissent within the labor movement at the time of the General Strike, urging the CLC to "clean house" while it proceeded with its open shop drive. We have seen above how this two-pronged attack led to the subduction not only of labor militancy, but the actual breaking of some unions. The CLC and the State Federation of Labor simply extended the coverage begun by the Associated Industries.[2]

Laws originating as restrictions against radicalism, with which the labor movement itself was inescapably linked by reason of its implied threat to existing industrial and social relations, affected the civil liberties of everyone. These laws inhibited freedom of speech and assembly, and were employable at the whim of state and local authorities. Changing these laws and court rulings involved more formal action on the legislative front. The state Supreme Court, for example, accustomed to supporting the issuance of injunctions by the lower courts, had ruled against the right to peacefully picket, and when an anti-injunction bill was introduced in 1925 that would have substituted the language of the federal Clayton Act to limit injunctive action and protect picketing, it was voted down. In 1928, when the Seattle High School Teachers League joined the AFL as Local 200 and signed up members, the School Board required all teachers to sign "yellow-dog" contracts. The Board was upheld by the state Supreme Court in 1930. Attempts to repeal the criminal syndicalism law of 1919 failed until the last day of the 1937 legislative session, as Senator Mary Farquharson adroitly maneuvered the repeal bill past the Rules Committee to the Senate floor, where it passed 33 votes to 7. Albert Gunns concludes: "In a sense, the repeal of the criminal syndicalism laws marked the end of an era in the fight to protect civil liberties in the Pacific Northwest, an era at least partially conceived in the hysteria and excesses brought on by national crises, first of war, then of economic depression. Elimination of these laws, which punished advocacy rather than action, took from state governments their principal instruments for the repression of dissent and eased the tasks of civil libertarians."[3]

Indeed, First Amendment rights—freedom of speech and assembly—are basic to all the nine other constitutional amendments making up the Bill of Rights. Without their guarantee, the constitution itself would be hollow, without substance. Attacks against civil liberties usually begin with attempts to restrict their exercise. With this in mind, it is well to quickly survey their status during the period.

The Depression very early prompted a rash of public speaking and mass demonstrations. As noted below (chapter 17), Mayor Edwards used police to break up parades, rallies, and public gatherings in 1930 by having mounted police ride roughshod through demonstrators and extract speakers from their podiums even before they had uttered a word. Though not upheld by the judge as a lawful means of arrest, the damage was none the less real as the official actions went unpunished. Attempts to amend the City charter with a "Hyde Park" amendment to permit public speaking without permit failed.[4]

Albert Gunns notes with respect to initiation of deportation of "undesirable" aliens that "patterns of cooperation between government officials and local law enforcement authorities that had been developed during World War I and the Red Scare periods were still in existence . . . ." The immigration authorities were fed candidates by local authorities who made the arrests in dragnet fashion. Indicative, nationally, of the role deportations played in suppressing dissent is seen in Labor Department records, which reported that only one person a year was deported from 1928 to 1930, for those in the "Anarchist and kindred classes" category. Yet, 18 were deported in 1931, 51 in 1932, and 74 in 1933, dropping to 37 altogether in 1934 and 1935, before climbing again to 47 in 1936, then tailing off to none by 1940. In Seattle, a strategem of immigration authorities was to ship Russian deportees by boat to Shanghai from where they were promised transportation to the Soviet Union. Michael Saksagansky became the first test run. Without warrant, without evidence of probable cause, and without access to legal counsel, he was arrested as a suspected Communist agent in February 1931. He denied affiliation, though radical literature was in his possession. This served as justification enough to indicate his advocacy to overthrow the government which hearings only reinforced. Successively, the district court, then the circuit court of appeals upheld the decision. Another case was that of Vladimir Wolck. He arrived in the United States at age fifteen in 1912; by 1931 he still remained unnaturalized. Unemployed, he got odd jobs, and he attended a public meeting on May 10, 1931 in the Seattle headquarters of the Communist Party, when the police crashed in, arresting all in attendance. Five confessed to being aliens; only they were taken into custody. Wolck was one of the five. Not until May 12—after he was subjected to examination by the immigration authorities—was a warrant issued for his arrest (the other four received the same treatment, but his was the test case). A civil liberties/labor attorney, Mark Litchman, took the case (he had handled several deportation cases in 1920 and obtained the release of IWWs from a stockade in Yakima in 1933), wanting to establish rights for aliens to legal representation at each stage of any hearings, and that thoughts alone were not sufficient ground for punishment. The fact that Wolck was not a party member complicated his case, but the district court denied Litchman's application for writ of habeas corpus, and the circuit court upheld the ruling that Wolck was nonetheless "affiliated" within the meaning of the law. A third case was that of Leon Glaser, a delegate from the Tailors' Union to the Central Labor Council. He was arrested by two policemen with warrants in hand, but Litchman prevented a house search. Glaser had been recently named by Policeman Sowoll Jennings, during hearings of Congress's Fish Committee (forerunner of the House Un-American Activities Committee), as a prominent Seattle Communist. Glaser denied membership, but he had been secretary of the Seattle branch of the Friends of the Soviet Union, which was considered by some to be a front of the party. Litchman's protests were overruled by the Immigration Inspector, John F. Boyd, Jr., and a deportation warrant was issued in March 1932. He, like Saksagansky and Wolck, was not actually deported, remaining among the "backlog" of Russian aliens whom the Immigration authorities had stacked up before formal diplomatic relations were established with the Soviet Union.[5]

When it came to abridging first Amendment rights, the University of Washington was second to none. In 1930, assistant professor of sociology, Bernhard Stern, was dismissed, ostensibly for budgetary reasons. But, when compulsory Bible reading in the schools became an issue, he poked fun at the idea. This, coupled with his classroom warmth in expounding Marxism and his collegial combativeness, probably were the real factors influencing his dismissal. Popular with irreverent students, the news sparked student rallies and protests. However, he resigned to take another position before the effective date of his dismissal, making any further action moot. While the Stern case was still warm, while the Supreme Court had just upheld the yellow-dog contract, and while mass demonstrations among the unemployed were becoming more common, the 1931 Legislature passed a loyalty oath law, requiring all employees in state supported schools and institutions of higher learning to sign it. All protest quickly faded at the university after a protest leader, Professor Howard Woolston, signed it.[6]

With the ascendancy of Hitler and the Nazis to power in Germany in 1933, following on the heels of the Japanese invasion of Manchuria, and the sudden increase of military spending by the Roosevelt administration, liberal and left activism added anti-war protests to their political critique. Despite a University ban on political speakers, a non-partisan campus political club, the Thursday Noon Club, had been inviting speakers representing opposing views of an issue. Not until the club sponsored a talk in May 1933 by a former University student, Jesse London Wakefield, was the ban implemented. (Wakefield had been jailed for her part in the the 1931 Harlan County, Kentucky miners strike.) Acting President Hugo Winkenwerder ordered cancellation of her appearance, reportedly for being an "asserted Communist". The clubbers defied his order, attracting a larger than usual audience of 150. The club, having no organization as such, quickly appointed some officers as accommodating targets for disciplinary action. They, and others, were then placed under "indefinite" suspension. One, Selden Menefee, was excluded from graduation. Governor Martin, addressing a Faculty Club meeting the next week, cautioned attendees, "that with times as they are, the University must be careful about permitting speakers on controversial subjects to appear on campus, [that once] economic stress [is relieved] the university may be able to do away with the rule." The club soon changed its name to the Washington Liberal Club, then in January 1934 to the National Student League (NSL), which was joining nationwide with the League for Industrial Democracy (LID) to organize student opposition against the rise of fascism and the growing threat of war. Ammunition was drawn from reports emitting from the ongoing Senate investigation of how the nation became involved in the Great War. Wall Street was being linked to United States participation. Concurrently, the Hearst papers were carrying exposes of communist infiltration of schools, allegedly aiming to cripple national defense and stirring up class and race hatred.[7]

Prior to his ascendancy in October 1934 to the University's presidency, Lee Paul Sieg, as dean of three academic units at the University of Pittsburgh, had been directly involved in suppressing the first anti-war protest there in April 1934 (at many of the nation's campuses protests had been violently put down by police and vigilante groups, but no demonstration was mounted at the UW). Carrying his Pittsburgh experience to the UW Sieg devoted about one-half of his inaugural speech to politics, referring initially to the "troubles which the University has experienced", and obliquely castigating the New Deal "Brain Trust" whose ideas had "hurt" universities. As to the "slogan" of academic freedom, it is a term that has been "abused by a minority of our faculties"—freedom is not "licence". In their public expressions "professors . . . must stick to [their] own field in which [they are expert]." He linked "communism" with opposition to the "compulsory drill" issue, continuing, that "Communism is a complicated theory of the State." Sieg then urged students "to study, to think, to wait awhile", above all, to engage in traditional student activities. Beware of "outside" agencies spreading their propaganda, he added for good measure.[8]

Having set the tone for his administration, Sieg proceeded to lend administration support to formation of a political club befitting his own temperament, the "Pathfinders". Its professed aim was to "blaze a [trail] for a new American empire", along the way building an "effective voting unit" of 500,000 "college men". The ten charter members included the student body president and vice-president, the editor and associate editor of the *University of Washington Daily*, the crew captain, and a former track star, expecting to tap "More that 130 prominent fraternity and independent leaders." Installation festivities at the district's Meany Hotel brought together University administrators and the political elite of the two major political parties. The Pathfinders would find their first mission in disrupting an anti-war demonstration at the November 13 Armistice Day celebration. This followed in the wake of a violent suppression of an anti-war "riot" at UCLA on October 30, which was inflicted in turn on Berkeley students when they organized their sympathy strike. The Pathfinders responded, warning they would "oppose Radical demonstrations". The *Daily* reported: "Pacifists Are Routed At Armistice Services" by the Pathfinders.[9]

The next freedom of speech and assembly test for the University administration came as campus liberals and leftists prepared for their part in the nationwide anti-war demonstrations planned by the NSL and LID on April 12, 1935. The *Daily*'s headline of April 3 announced: "'Strike' Plans Collapse As Administration Bans Use of Campus Buildings . . . [Sieg refuses facilities use by] student liberals to hold a peace assembly on the campus . . . ." The day before the strike, Sieg alerted students to the detestability of war, but that, "we equally detest many other subversive agitations that are abroad in the land. The students should know that this whole movement was originated on the Atlantic seaboard . . . Do you want outsiders to tell you what to do?" While the *Daily* predicted a turnout of 450, the number reported was about 800 who rallied one block off campus, then peacefully paraded through the district. Unlike experiences in New York and Chicago where police and vigilante suppression was common, the demonstration in Seattle came off without incident despite Sieg's worry about potential violence.[10]

It is fruitful to view as a civil rights issue the policy during the Depression of discrimination against employment of women whose pay might constitute a second family income. In county and state government, and at the University of Washington, married women were threatened with dismissal, or officially dismissed, if their's represented a second income. At the latter institution, President Sieg proudly responded to Governor Martin's request that the new president look into the existence of "nepotism" on campus: "This is one of the first questions we raised after we came to the University, and we had already taken steps looking toward correcting this practice at the earliest practicable date." Indeed, the Regents had anticipated some of Sieg's enthusiasm as early as 1928, when that body ruled that "no more wives of faculty men should be added to the faculty or office forces . . . ."[11]

As the Depression deepened in 1931, Vice-President David Thomson requested that all department heads send him their recommendation whether "women whose relatives or husbands are gainfully employed" ought to be continued. Implementation, though slow, began in 1933-1934 when the administration recommended dismissal of those women listed. Under pressure from the Instructors Association, which sought to protect already-married faculty couples, the Regents modified their resolution against dual employment by not making it retroactive. Paralleling the university's actions, the City Council encountered pressure from the Allied Veterans Club as it revived the club's effort to get an amendment to the city charter banning wives from city jobs if their spouses were employed. The Judiciary Committee unanimously approved such action; however, the committee's resolution was tabled by the Council. County Commissioner Don Evans introduced a resolution to ban from employment all married women who were not the sole support of their families. It was further resolved to fill all positions under their control with married men with families. Married nurses at Harborview Hospital were among the first to be laid off.[12]

So preoccupied was President Sieg with eliminating women from faculty ranks in cases of dual employment that he ignored a due process agreement he had made with the Instructors Association in 1934. Affected was Florence Bean James (whose case was discussed above in connection with the Seattle Repertory Playhouse), Lea Puymbroeck Miller, and Teresa McMahon. The Miller case played to newspaper headlines, while testy liberal McMahon's case played out between her and Sieg. Perennially one of the more productive among the faculty, with a national reputation that had gained her a position on the original federal Social Security Board, McMahon had been under pressure to resign because her husband was on the History faculty. She did not budge. Instead, she sounded an alarm in behalf of Miller and the university, proclaiming, "you will have to pay [a price] in terms of national publicity . . . ." Miller, an Instructor in Art, was dismissed on January 4, 1938 because of her marriage in September 1937 to a professor in the Zoology Department. Due process and one-year notice of termination that had been agreed to in 1934 were bypassed by the administration. Both the Instructors Association and the Teachers Union on campus came to her defense (though Miller tried to keep the latter at arms-distance for fear of radical taint), and wide controversy extended to the national level as the broader implications of her case became apparent. Considering that there were only four married couples on the faculty at the time, and the negative attention focused upon the university, the wisdom of Sieg's and the Regents' preoccupation with nepotism is questionable. Concern for the university's welfare seems to have been clouded by their preoccupation with nepotism.[13]

The Puymbroeck Miller case raised as a general issue the question, "Should Wives Work?". "Yes", is Seattle Women's Reply, reported the *Times*. In the 1937 legislative session, Senator Lady Willie Forbus had led a successful attack on a proposed "working wives bill". Soon, however, at the county level the axe fell—the King County Welfare Department head announced in February 1938 that 77 "working wives" will be laid off over the next few weeks.[14]

Any discussion of civil liberties must examine the role and functions of that pre-eminent defender of the Bill of Rights, the American Civil Liberties Union (ACLU). Germinating in Seattle during the war, from attempts of the Anti-Conscription League and assorted labor and radical leaders to protect the right of dissent, the Seattle branch was loosely formed in 1920. Clemens J. France, a founder and former president of the Municipal League and 1920 Senatorial candidate of the Washington State Farmer-Labor Party, was named chairman. Erstwhile labor leader James A. Duncan added his enthusiasm, while several liberals and radicals lent their support from time to time. Already in progress, though, were many IWW cases. The ACLU cooperated with their defense, particularly those who were imprisoned because of their connection with the Centralia Massacre. Pre-occupation with the Centralia prisoners throughout the 1920s, the decline of dissent (non-governmental suppression by civic and war veterans organizations were the most persistent, effective, and practically not documentable, except by circumstantial evidence), combined with its lack of an office base from which it could expound a broader mission than freeing the Centralia prisoners—all of the above acutely circumscribed the ACLU's effectiveness. Albert Gunns adds, from his study of civil liberties in the Northwest, that "The unpopularity of civil liberties cases had much to do with the fact that 'progressive' elements tended to shy away from them." Against this local scene must be placed the general uncertainty of ACLU's very life. Coupled with this was the backlog of federal and state civil liberties violations that had to be dealt with, while defining its mission and priorities for the future. Samuel Walker writes in his recent history on civil liberties and the ACLU: "The ACLU's second priority in the 1920s was to undo the damage of the war years, including the ending of censorship of the mails, amnesty for political prisoners, and repeal of state sedition laws."[15]

Mayor Frank Edwards's repression of mass demonstrations and soapbox speakers in 1930 resuscitated concern for free speech protections. It was Edward Henry, a university law student, who led the unsuccessful drive, noted above, for a "Hyde Park" amendment to the city charter. At this time, Adele Parker had been operating a nominal ACLU bureau—the Washington Conciliation Committee, which had been set up primarily to seek release of the Centralia prisoners. Yet, she was not sympathetic to defending the demonstrators, reportedly, because the Communists had baited the police to start things going. Despite internal bickering between Parker and the UCL's Carl Brannin, who wanted anyone's free speech right defended, the national office was persuaded to set up a branch to address civil rights protections in general. Henry became the choice to head the branch (using Marion Zioncheck's office as headquarters), beginning September 22, 1931. Henry organized a legal committee comprising Zioncheck and George Vanderveer. A first objective was repeal of the criminal syndicalism law . . . not to be accomplished until 1937. Henry was lost to the Seattle branch, however, when Zioncheck was elected to Congress. Henry became his administrative assistant in 1933, thereby leaving the ACLU to limp along in the city.[16]

The anti-radical repressions stemming from the 1934 maritime strike (police raids on the Marine Workers Industrial Union and Communist offices in particular) revived concern. Two church leaders—Raymond E. Attebery and Fred Shorter, joined by Mary and Burt Farquharson, and Irving Clark, Sr.—attempted to revive the aborted branch, but the very same people were simultaneously caught up in organizing the Washington Commonwealth Federation, by itself a time-consuming task. Paul Olson, a recent university graduate in anthropolgy, had taken the organizing initiative in early 1935. He persisted, succeeding later in the year. To the nucleus of Clark, Shorter, Mary Farquharson, and executive secretary Olson, were added union leaders Bert Harman as chairman, and Ed Weston, Joseph S. Jackson of the Urban League, and Joseph B. Harrison of the university's English Department. Once active, the ACLU branch began dealing with issues—investigating use of the National Guard in the 1935 Tacoma lumber strike, obtaining restraining orders to prevent use of the state patrol where peaceful picketing was in progress, and to seek equality in use of public facilities. Fruit from the latter effort came when the ACLU won use of the Civic Auditorium for a mass meeting to be addressed by ACLU president, Harry Ward, who had been a target of Red-baiting. (Rev. Attebery's Grace Methodist congregation would not allow Ward to address it, but Attebery presided at the Civic Auditorium event without incident.)[17]

The ACLU's fight in Seattle for freedom of speech and assembly was but a part of its national focus upon attempts to restrict the kind of mass protests generated by the Depression. First, the public had to be educated as to what basic rights were their due under the Constitution. This at least was accomplished to some degree, although this educational task remains an unending one from generation to generation, from one national crisis to another, during which rationalizations are elaborated by governmental authorities to suppress free speech—always the first step toward totalitarianism. (Roger Baldwin reminded his cohorts from time to time that civil liberties never stay won.) Gunns speculates that schisms within left-liberal circles were quieted by its efforts. A case in point is the coalescence of the AFL and CIO to defeat Initiative 130 in the 1938 election. As for the Seattle branch, it lost Olson in January 1936, when he left for Washington, D.C. (soon to become Congressman John Coffee's assistant). Mary Farquharson and Irving Clark carried on as best they could. As a State Senator, Farquharson managed the repeal of the criminal syndicalism law in 1937, and she also engineered the pardon of the last Centralia prisoner, Ray Becker. ACLU's effective force in the city and state had sharply diminished by the time of Pearl Harbor.[18]

Part V

A Political History of the 1930s

17

Mayor Edwards and the Radicals

At the time when Mayor Edwards fired Ross, Seattle, like the rest of the country, was becoming mired in the "Great Depression"; and similarly, its citizens were not yet convinced that it would not end soon, like those downswings in 1907, 1913-1914, and 1920-1921. Even most of the growing number of unemployed thought so. Their plight was viewed at all levels of government as temporary, to be dealt with locally by charity, and by whatever stratagems of self-help and cooperation might be devised. Volunteerism seems to be the solution. It became part of the problem as the unemployed successively organized self-help and cooperative programs, then became a threatening political force by 1932.[1]

Before the above noted elements took shape, however, Mayor Edwards had shown how he would deal with the agitation soon to be generated by the local Unemployed Council which was affiliated with the National Unemployed Council, an auxiliary of the Communist Party. Even before that organization had been formed in 1930, Edwards had ordered the arrest of 31 demonstrators during the 1929 Armistice Day (November 11) celebrations. These cases were later dropped by police court authorities. When the Unemployed Council organized a demonstration at Second and Yesler on February 26, 1930, Edwards ordered about 100 mounted police to break it up; 8 men and 3 women were arrested. Judge Mitchell Gordon dismissed these cases upon hearing the argument of the International Labor Defense League attorneys. Police Chief Forbes, responding to similar demonstrations in Portland and Vancouver, B.C., had Edwards request a federal investigation. Edwards followed on March 1 by denying a permit for a March 6 demonstration, ordering the police to prevent "any further outbreak of 'Bolshevist or soviet' agencies . . . There will be no bolshevist or soviet uprisings or demonstrations in Seattle while I am mayor."[2]

There were in fact two radical programs set to deal with the growing unemployment problem, nationally and in Seattle. One was social democratic in character, that of the Conference on Progressive Labor Action, being generated from the program of the Seattle Labor College. The College began publication of the *Vanguard* in January 1930. In its own words: "radical yet realistic in its approach to the problems of the producers, independent of trade union bureaucracy, aiming to give the facts . . . to stimulate effective action." It favored industrial unionism, an independent political party of farmers and workers, a 5-day week, old age pensions, workmen's compensation, unemployment insurance—in short, most of the benefits and protections enjoyed by the present generation, who might be ignorant of the fact that they were not the gift of a benevolent business community and a compliant conservative labor bureaucracy acting through a compassionate governing apparatus. Quoting from an article in *Labor Age*, the *Vanguard* identified the other radical group as the genuine Communist Party (CP) which regularly held its street meetings in the skid-road area, appealing to the "lumberjack and the maritime transport worker. Their hall meetings are well attended with a sprinkling of students and a large foreign-born element . . . The response here is slow . . . [T]housands of new workers must be organized without obsolete craft divisions . . . It involves rank and file education along the lines of practical idealism."[3]

Given the tactics and propaganda of the Edwards forces with respect to the unemployed and the growing agitation among those afflicted, it is well to survey this onsetting depression. Then, a look at the kind of propaganda issuing from the Edwards camp will convey its perspective: the linkage of the radical upsurge from ranks of the unemployed with the defenders of public ownership of utilities—which Ross, himself, had come to symbolize.

The Edwards campaign tabloid, *The Seattle Review*, claimed: "The fact that Communists have taken an active part in Seattle municipal politics is most important in that it indicates the strength the revolutionary movement has gained in Seattle . . . They will be ready to strike when they have a trained and disciplined army equal to 5 per cent of the adult population . . . The Reds organized the Unemployed Council in Seattle to exploit the men out of a job." And the Communists are being aided by the "foreign-owned press" (Hearst's *Post-Intelligencer* and the Scripps's *Star*, each of which had been supporters of public ownership of utilities). In two boxes at opposite corners of the front page: "Reds in Plot to Ruin City" and "Red Mayor is Next Step".[4]

The above was published June 19. The same theme was repeated in a special election issue, called *Fair Play*: "Newspaper Conspiracy Exposed" . . . "Ross Selected to be the Martyr in the Hearst-Scripps Political Scheme" . . . "[Their editors are] itinerent [sic] yellow journalists building up circulation and advertising appeal by starting new dog-fights." It continued, "Sane and sober citizens there are who genuinely believe the funds have come from Moscow." Then it speculated that probably some of Senator George Norris's presidential campaign funds might have found their way to the coffers of the Recallers. It volunteered that the money certainly " . . . wasn't supplied by the street car men, the fire laddies, or the boys of the police department out of their idle Surpluses!"—this group had been a major source of Edwards's original support, it will be remembered.[5]

While it is true that the Unemployed Councils in Seattle were affiliated with the National Unemployed Councils of the Communist Party, their strength was exaggerated by the increasingly familiar scare tactics warning of the "Communist Menace", and Red-smearing of all dissident groups, much like the organized labor movement and dissidents were charged as Wobblies in the period of the "Wobbly horrors" (ca. 1915-20). Their weakness at this time is indicated by the ease with which the Unemployed Citizens League (UCL) overtook the Unemployed Councils, initially, when the UCL's began operations in August 1931. Eventually the UCL fell under Communist domination, but at first, both the CP and IWW influence was held in check by social democrats like Hulet Wells and Carl Brannin who believed in working for reform within the political system.[6]

High unemployment rates in Seattle were not unfamiliar before the Great Depression. Outgoing-Mayor, Bertha Landes, reported in her annual report of June 1928 that while Seattle fared better in 1927 than other large cities in the "matter of organized labor" its unemployed rate was 11.3% according to an American Federation of Labor survey. Reportedly only three other cities could boast lower unemployment rates.[7]

In 1930, unemployment in Seattle, based on different statistical sources, was figured at 7%—at a time when such statistics were not systematically compiled. This was 0.4% above the national average. J.H. Shields of the Seattle Public Employment Office noted that the seasonal workers who usually left the city during summer, for the first time were being underemployed, or not at all. From ten to twenty thousand people reportedly were either not working or were working only short hours. Almost one-third of the jobless were heads of families. As the Depression lengthened, more and more blue collar workers and lower paid white collar workers were laid off. Gradually, the traditionally more comfortable middle classes were hit, and as their savings were eaten into, they came to share the fate of the earlier victims who had nothing to fall back upon.[8]

Auguring the future were the shutdown of forty of the 304 lumber mills in the Northwest, and planned reduction of 40% by the rest, come June 1930, the layoff of 1100 employees by the telephone company, another 500 by Frederick and Nelson in June. Lines of men formed outside the Youngstown Steel Plant and at the Ford plant "hoping some worker will drop dead or get fired."[9]

At its 1931 convention, the Washington State Federation of Labor noted the dispiriting picture for those still employed. And in 1932 it reported that "large numbers of workers who have been accustomed to good homes and plenty of everything [are] unable to secure employment. These people are forced to live on what they are able to obtain from the city and county relief stations . . . there will be twice that number this fall and winter." Symptomatic were the unemployed carpenters, meeting at union headquarters in January 1930 to decide what could be done, debating a proposal for unemployment insurance and more radical measures—this, in a conservative union whose business agent would soon succeed in expelling some members for distributing the *Vanguard*. Business Agent, W.R. Bennett, claimed the *Vanguard* was Communist, its distributors within the union were disloyal to the AFL, were sympathetic to the Soviet Union, and were creating dissension by their cacophony.[10]

Also symptomatic were early volunteer efforts at relief . . . before the realization set in that chronic larger scale unemployment would be a permanent feature of industrial society. The Volunteers of America reported that meals served in November 1929 were double the previous year, and were steadily climbing: 20,617 in January 1929 to 29,509 in January 1930.[11]

Wage scales were maintained throughout 1931, but shorter

hours and work-sharing were tactics used to spread the work. However, by the end of 1931 both wages and the value of manufactures had fallen by 35% from the 1929 peak. Despite this decline, William Mullins, in his comparative study of Seattle and San Francisco during the Hoover years, notes that no large plants had failed during the year, that J.C. Penney's had opened a new downtown store, and that Ford had begun construction of an assembly plant. Also, there were about twenty thousand Elks expected with bulging pocketbooks. On the bleak side, some banks had closed, retail sales had dropped by 17.7%, and construction had fallen drastically from a 1930 figure of $30.8 million to a mere $9.4 million in 1931. This abrupt decline in construction activity hit Seattle later than San Francisco and the industry in general, so when it reached Seattle the effect was to almost dry up the local market for timber products, a mainstay of the economy.[12]

Sensing the futility of volunteerism and local charity, the Conference on Progressive Labor Action began pressing in October 1930 for unemployment insurance legislation by the state and federal government. When petitions were presented to the legislature in January 1931, they were ignored, and no ameliorative action of any kind was initiated. The *Vanguard* headline in February read: "Workers, Build Your Own Political Party." In its March editorial, Carl Brannin urged the unemployed to organize because the Armory feeding station will shut down at the end of March—nothing left to fulfill its function.[13]

Port activity reflected the general decline, with a fall of 985,225 tons in total tonnage handled during the year. In detail, domestic imports in 1931 registered a decline of 15% from 1930 (a drop of about 115,000 tons). Domestic experts, however, increased by about 152,000 ton with rises mainly occurring in exports to California, and the Puget Sound basin. Tonnage of foreign imports fell by 35%, but tonnage of foreign exports actually increased slightly, by about 25,000 tons, with the increases being registered only for China and the United Kingdom. The total decline from 1929, in total tonnage, was 1,790,127 tons.[14]

Thus, we see that two factors figured in the movement to recall Mayor Edwards: agitation among the growing number of the unemployed, and the fate of City Light which the firing of J.D. Ross seemed to make vulnerable. The *Times* and Edwards tried to link the two by associating the Recallers' Citizen's Municipal Utilities Protective League with the Communist Party, portraying all actions on behalf of the unemployed as being inspired solely by the Communists.

In the chapters to follow the reader should take note that the public power issue—which figures so large in the politics of the liberal-left in 1931—recedes from prominence during the decade. This shift, in the author's judgment, is due to the contest between the two radical components of the liberal-left in seeking a mass base for their political influence. That political base was sought by focusing upon the politics of unemployment and relief, not upon public power. Consequently, public power did not become radicalized. Instead it became solely the concern of the two major municipals (in Seattle and Tacoma) and the State Grange. J.D. Ross proposed the purchase of Puget Sound Power and Light in 1934, while the Grange fought for establishment of public utility districts as it tried to implement its district power act of 1930. Opponents of public power refrained for the most part from tarnishing the public power advocates with the same kind of "Red" smear, noted in the above paragraphs.

18

Edwards Is Recalled

Edwards's firing of Ross resulted not only in victory for the charter amendment, giving the Lighting Department control of its own engineering, but it set in motion a recall drive by the charter amendment's sponsor, the Citizen's Municipal Utilities Protective League (CMUPL). At midnight, before the polls opened on March 10, 1931, officers of the League, representatives of community clubs known for their support of City Light, and other activists met, as noted above, in a downtown cafe to conduct a strategy meeting. They agreed to launch a petition drive immediately. The climate was indeed favorable because it was widely assumed that Edwards was working hand-in-glove with the "power trust". Wide publicity had been given to the propaganda mill run by the National Electric Light Association, and locally by the PSP&L-funded Voters' Information League. And the utilities industry was in disgrace nationally with collapse of the Insull utilities empire. The steady spread of the depression into the middle classes, undermining their confidence in the economy, added more strength to the recall campaign.[1]

Locally, at Puget Sound Power and Light, when the Engineers Public Service Company took over control, Leonard was retired to become chairman of the company board. He was replaced by J. Frank McLaughlin as president of PSP&L. Leonard resigned his new position within a month, leading some to speculate that the position had never existed. Norwood Brockett was soon let go as well. On May 25, McLaughlin announced that

PSP&L had terminated its contract with Stone and Webster. For whatever reason, it had become clear that efforts were being made to clear away the atmosphere of suspicion clouding the company's halo as a result of both the revelations made before the Federal Trade Commission and the presumed linkage of the company with the Edwards forces.[2]

Although the leaders of the recall campaign wanted to restrict the charges to the firing of Ross, seventeen charges were listed, among them graft, granting of contracts without going through the bidding process, and cronyism. The corporation counsel ruled on March 29 that there were grounds for recall, and by April 28 sufficient signatures had been gathered. They were validated on May 19, and July 13 was selected as the date for the recall election.[3]

In the interim, it was necessary to appoint a replacement for Ross. When the Council acted upon Ross's recommendation and appointed Glen Smith, Edwards removed Smith and named George Roberge, the Secretary of the Board of Public Works. Marion Zioncheck then got the Superior Court to enjoin Roberge from taking office. Temporary resolution was obtained by placing the Lighting Department in charge of the Board. Edwards followed by successively naming five candidates over the next two months, each of whom was rejected by the Council (one was related to the Blethen family). In late March the Council even considered impeachment proceedings against the mayor. Pressure was mounted in late March from the Central Labor Council and Reverend Mark Matthews to get his parishioner Ross reinstated. And, while not directly supporting Edwards, J.W. Maxwell, president of the Clearing House Association, was joined by American Legionnaire leader Stephen F. Chadwick and aspiring-politico John Dore in efforts to head off a divisive recall campaign. Finally, lame-duck councilman Oliver Erickson was able to bring together a majority to support the nomination of W. Chester Morse to replace Ross. The recall campaign, nevertheless, went forward by its own momentum, once the lines had been drawn by the adversaries at the extremes of the spectrum. Edwards could at least count upon the *Times* for support.[4]

To manage his opposition campaign, Edwards formed a Committee of 57 on May 1 under leadership of his political appointees, but he claimed broad support of the business community. The first strategem was to illegally acquire a list of petition signers, to contact them and persuade them to withdraw their names. Upon the filing of a complaint by Zioncheck, the city clerk closed the registration books to Edwards's battery of stenographers who were copying the signatures. This ended the withdrawal effort.[5]

Next, Edwards sought to block the recall in court, but Superior Court Judge James T. Ronald rejected this effort by ruling there were grounds for recall. When Edwards appealed to the state Supreme Court, that court evenly divided on July 2, thereby sustaining Ronald's ruling.[6]

While these strategems were running their course, Edwards was failing to mobilize support from the business community because its leaders feared the destabilizing effects which a bitter civic struggle would have on the already depressed economy. Tourism, for one, was expected to give the local economy a boost those summer days. His cause was damaged early, when Arthur Ritchie resigned as head of the Committee of 57, fearing the consequences for the city in such a divisive battle.[7]

Perhaps, best indicator of the alienation Edwards experienced from among his previous supporters was that represented by the *Argus* as the election date drew near: "Ross might have done better had he been left alone. He might have done worse. The city council might have wrecked the utility but for the watchful eye that Ross has given it . . . All that we know is that we are building up a public utility that, if we complete it as outlined will keep Seattle in a class of low electric power. [Edwards, while promising a business administration, has] appointed his friends to most of the important offices. That is business . . . But on the eve of the election [to have fired a man who had been praised until then for his competency, then turn around and contend the opposite, is not credible]."[8]

It remained for Edwards and the *Times* to link the recall campaign with the "Communist menace". The *Times* issue of April 29 ran a front page column head: "Communist and Fitts Denounce Mayor Edwards", followed by a report that Ross and Fitts were at a meeting at which nineteen-year old Yetta Stromberg, "a widely-known Communist leader" spoke last night at the Seattle Labor College at which the audience was urged to sign recall petitions. (Stromberg was at liberty pending her trial in California under its anti-syndicalism law.)[9]

Edwards, in his fourth radio talk on May 19, declared that "leaders of the Communist movement and foreign-owned newspapers are backing the recall campaign . . . As every resident knows I have resisted every subversive or radical movement which threatened the peace of Seattle." He continued by accusing the *Star* of sending an "emissary" to his office on February 11 who, upon making some "demands", was told "to get out of the office with orders to tell his overlords that Bolshevism had no place in Seattle government." He claimed the *Star*'s attacks on him began then, and "Communism is the root of the present trouble."[10]

Edwards followed up this address by having posted on all City department bulletin boards: "It is indeed unfortunate that Seattle at this particular time [the tourist season] be embroiled in a controversy brought upon our city by the Communists, aided and abetted by the foreign-owned newspapers . . . The unfavorable publicity which has come from the activities of this RED REVOLUTIONARY GROUP must be countenanced to the fullest extent possible . . . ." The *Star*, for its part, claimed that these charges were so absurd as to only add to Edwards's opposition.[11]

That these charges carried little weight with most of the electorate is partly attested to by the return of Ross from New York, where he had been called by Governor Franklin Roosevelt to advise upon the St. Lawrence power project. More than a thousand supporters gathered at the Chamber of Commerce meeting hall for a sentimental, but rousing, welcome-back for their battle-scarred hero. Lewis B. Schwellenbach, a University of Washington regent, and head of the King County Democratic Club, was even able to finally swing the party to support of a public ownership issue.[12]

On July 13, the electorate turned on Edwards, recalling him by a vote of 35,659 to 21,839. Undaunted, he would return for redemption in the February 1932 primaries, to compete with a rising political star, John F. Dore, who would set a new tone in the city's politics while reviving some corruption that many thought to have expired with Bertha Landes's defeat of "Doc" Brown.[13]

With the Recall Election out of the way, and Councilman Robert Harlin elected by the Council to replace Edwards, the City administration could now turn its attention to the acute problem of unemployment and relief measures.

19

Politics of Unemployment and Relief, 1931-1935

The Unemployed Citizens' League

By 1931 it had become clear that unemployment had become a problem that would not go away. A survey sponsored by the Washington Emergency Relief Commission, covering eleven Washington cities in 1934, provided a profile of the unemployed:

> The average unemployed person is a native white male forty-two years of age.
> He is an unskilled worker in the manufacturing and mechanical industries.
> He has been employed at his usual occupation for fifteen years.
> He has not worked at his usual occupation for one year and seven months.
> He has not had any work for over ten months.
> He is married and has 2.34 persons dependent upon him.
> He has received a common school education.
> He has resided in the state for over twenty years.[1]

Extensive unemployment, though cyclic, was not new. Spliced in every year was seasonal unemployment. William S.

Hopkins, writing on seasonal unemployment in the state in 1936, concluded that " . . . seasonality of industrial operations is especially significant in the State of Washington. When it is borne in mind that agriculture, subject to extravagant seasonality, [is] not included in this study, it will become apparent that the whole economic life of the people is vitally influenced by the calendar."[2]

For the period 1929-1932, Hopkins's indices of seasonal employment showed how vulnerable Seattle's industries were to such fluctuations. Marked seasonality was true for saw, planing and shingle mills, iron and steel mills, flour milling, longshoring, general construction, textiles (excepting men's clothing), boat and shipbuilding, foundries and machine shops, fruit, vegetable and fish canning. Some trade lines such as department stores were subject to seasonality. City hotels not only had seasonal variations, but labor turnover was high, running at about 60% during normal times, although it fell to about 35% during the Depression. Consumers' goods industries such as furniture-making and dairy and bakery products were less affected by seasonal variations than those farther removed from the local consumer. Stated differently, lower rates of employment existed for the service industries and trades which dealt with articles "after they have been produced, processed, and transported to the distribution center." When the Depression hit, extractive and heavy industries suffered worst, the effects rippling out to consumer goods lines as purchasing power diminished. For example, in the state there were 58,570 workers employed in iron and steel manufacturing in 1929, but this labor force dropped to 29,540 by 1931. A comparable fall in employment was true of the state's largest industry—logging and wood processing—both carrying comparable effects through loss of purchasing power.[3]

Rates of unemployment for the eleven cities studied for the Washington Emergency Relief Administration showed that Seattle's rate in April 1930 was 11%. It jumped to 26.5% in January 1935. The average for the cities as a group was 11.1% and 25.4%, respectively. For Tacoma the rate was 11.1% and 26.1%, respectively, Everett 7.9% and 28%, Bellingham 9.6% and 23.4%, Aberdeen-Hoquiam 15% and 25.3%. East of the Cascades, Spokane's unemployment rate for these same dates was 12.3% and 26.5%, for Yakima 10.1% and 26.1%, Wenatchee 9.7% and 24%, Walla Walla 9.7% and 26%. Unemployment in Seattle, December 1934, totaled 32,781 (84% males and 16% females). This percentage held true for the cities as a group as well. Nearby Tacoma had 9,788 unemployed, including 86% males and 14%

females. Everett's percentages were comparable for its 2,695 unemployed. Females were normally 24% of the work force, indicating that relatively fewer of them were laid off.[4]

This same study showed that for these cities as a whole more than 50% of the unemployed were forty years of age or older; of these 20% were fifty-five years or older, and 6% were sixty-five or older. It is understandable that agitation for old-age pensions and social security were among the most heated political issues of the 1930s. About 25% of the state's unemployed fell in another node, the twenty to twenty-nine age bracket. The average age for unemployed Seattleites was 42.5 for males and 35.2 for females.[5]

Potter's study found that only 2% of the unemployed were non-white. Unemployed Blacks had the highest rate among the cities studied, 21.7%. This rate compared with 21.2% for native Whites, and 18.5% for foreign-born Whites, of whom Canadians and Scandinavians predominated.[6]

With this information as background, we can better approach the issue of how the city's unemployed began to cope with a problem that was thought to be only of short duration, not a chronic one, not merely a local aberration, but, instead, a national and world-wide dilemma of industrial society. Pitiable efforts at self-help abetted by neighborly compassion gave way to local responses outside the family, to city and county governments, to the state, then the federal government. In Seattle, these efforts took form under the auspices of the Unemployed Citizens' League. Many of its members and leaders would become involved in left-wing politics during the decade, and would do combat with the stodgy AFL and militant Teamsters union as they fought to organize the previously unorganized or revive dormant unions, trying to mold the new unionism into an effective political force.

When Mayor Edwards responded to mounting unemployment, he saw "Red"—the Unemployed Councils that the Communist Party had sprouted in 1930 and thinly spread to major industrial centers. These councils proved ineffectual, though portrayed as a national menace of major proportion. In Seattle, a new organization of volunteers among the unemployed sprang forth with apparent spontaneity, taking over the Unemployed Councils where they existed in the city. This was the Unemployed Citizens' League.[7]

John Hogan worked among the volunteers and leaders of Seattle's Unemployed Citizens' League (UCL) for two years as he did research for his master's thesis at the University of Washington. His, and Arthur Hillman's published dissertation, are the most extensive and authoritative accounts of the rise and fall of the League. Hogan concluded: "The decline of cooperative self-help in Seattle was directly responsible for the radical movement . . . [The] radicalism which existed previous to the decline of the self-help movement was but a ripple alongside the tidal waves of mass protest which followed the passing of the cooperative program." He found the growth of radicalism and the failure of self-help to be "inseparable parts of a process."[8]

The self-help movement in the United States reportedly originated in Seattle. On July 23, 1931, shortly after Mayor Edwards was recalled, Hulet Wells and Carl Brannin called a meeting at the Olympic Heights Clubhouse to address the problem of the Seattle unemployed. Wells was a veteran Socialist of the Norman Thomas stripe who had once served as president of the Seattle Central Labor Council, as well as serving a sentence in the Federal Penitentiary for passing out anti-draft literature before the conscription act actually had been passed. Game, he stood fast in the cause, and wrote a column for *The Unemployed Citizen*, then the *Vanguard*, a monthly newspaper published by the Seattle Labor College (SLC), of which Brannin was head. Each was anti-Communist, and they contested the Communist Party for influence on the radical left.[9]

Originating in 1920, the SLC, in the phrasing of Sarah Sharbach: "was the bridge which spanned the gap between wartime radicalism and the Depression-era agitation and organizing . . . the only vestige of radicalism extant in Seattle in the 1920s." The SLC operating out of the Labor Temple, offered ten-week courses during evenings and weekends—tuition was $2.50. Instructors included the University of Washington's J. Allen Smith and philospher William Savery. Among lecturers were the battle-scarred James Duncan and Reverend Sydney Strong whose pacifism had led to his unceremonious ouster from the Municipal League during the war. Public lectures on controversial issues also were regularly offered. Attorney Mark Litchman who had handled many deportation cases during the "Red Scare" became the SLC's president in 1921, and in this capacity he exposed audiences to Marxism. The SLC broadened its influence further by creating a Workers' Dramatic Club, offering plays three times a week, usually for three-week runs. One instructor was recruited from the Cornish School, Maurice Browne. Proceeds were dedicated to the freeing of political prisoners.[10]

With unemployment spreading and neighbors near starvation, Wells and Brannin put job relief topmost on their agenda.

They dismissed any charity system as degrading. Notable for the lack of radical rhetoric, they recommended a work relief plan for the winter, presented it to the proper authorities, and indicated they would conduct an unemployment survey. To carry out their program, they established district groups ("locals"). Seven locals were quickly formed in south Seattle. The local in Columbia City was established after a fight with the Communist-controlled Unemployed Council there. By October, twenty-one locals were functioning. They were run as autonomous units of the League, and they were largely non-political at this stage. Since some central body had to represent the organization, a Central Federation was formed in August. Hogan writes: "Throughout its history the personnel of the U.C.L. remained what it originally was—a cross section of the working class, predominantly composed of skilled and common laborers."[11]

Meanwhile, since people were near starvation, food relief took priority over work relief, although the latter would remain the long-run goal. Token work relief of $143,729 was provided by the City Council, but as of January 1932, only six to twelve days work had been given to 4,750 men of the 12,000 who had registered. The League fought for and got an hourly wage of $4.50 to avoid undercutting the existing wage scale for the employed. Mayor Robert Harlin did establish a Commission for Improved Employment, in September, under telephone company head, I.F. Dix—he would use the UCL locals to implement his program. Before the commission became active the locals began collecting surplus vegetables and gathering fuel-wood. This self-help program started when the Columbia City local decided to collect wood for the coming fall and winter. Soon, as by an internal logic, this idea would spread to other commodities. Just as wood was cut from scrub timber tracts with permission of the owners, Yakima Valley farmers let the UCL dig potatoes and salvage pears and apples. The fishermen's union made fishing boats available, and so on. By "chiseling" (their own term) they commandeered empty railroad cars, and got the County administration to furnish trucks to supplement what transportation they could pull together from their own resources. By the end of 1931, these efforts had brought in 120,000 barrels of fish, 10,000 cords of firewood, and 8 carloads of potatoes, pears, and apples. All the labor was volunteered. Each local handled its own food program through commissaries—eighteen by the end of 1931. Most also planted their own gardens.[12]

Around each local occurred the growth of "secondary industries": barbers, mechanics, shoe repairing, beauty parlors, tailoring—the germ of a later "production-for-use" program. To prevent eviction of any of the members from their homes for non-payment of rent, the locals would negotiate with the owner, offering free home repair as a substitute for cash; it worked much of the time. An emergency health clinic was set up in the Schaefer Building—possibly the inspiration for Group Health Cooperative (GHC), since some of the members (Jack Cluck, for one) were founders of the GHC.[13]

A parallel program operated under the Women's Division of the Mayor's Commission for Improved Employment. Under former mayor, Bertha Landes, two sewing rooms were equipped in the "Red Cross Building" and "Court Building" to provide work for 255 different women working two days a week for $2.50 per day. "Higher type women" were given preference through a screening process. Registration began late November 1931; by 30 April 1932 three thousand women had signed in. Of this number, 503 had either found "permanent" positions or simply had not returned to work. The Singer Sewing Machine Company lent the machines, the Textile Tower contributed sewing room space, and the Metropolitan Building Company offered office space. Volunteer financial support was contributed by a number of clubs, University of Washington faculty, and the Committee of Business Women. The latter two contributed $1,250 between December 1931 and April 1932. Finished garments were supplied to Firland Sanitarium, to Child Welfare, and to Goodwill for its distribution.[14]

When the Dix Committee failed to find employment for applicants, it turned to direct relief and established the District Relief Organization for that purpose. As we shall see, the UCL was ready at hand for the chore.

The Unemployed Citizens' League Becomes Politicized

On the heels of the UCL's founding, Mayor Harlin, as noted above, appointed a Commission for Improved Employment, in September 1931, chaired by I.F. Dix, vice president of the Pacific Telephone and Telegraph Company—the "Dix Commission". Unable to provide employment, the Commission decided, with winter coming on, to at least provide some form of direct relief, establishing the Direct Relief Organization (DRO) to put County funds to work buying food and supplying logistical support. The problem—besides buying enough food—lay in its distribution. Since the UCL's commissaries, conveniently, were already doing this, they were converted into public agencies. After heated debate about staffing, the DRO agreed to continue the system of local control in which staffing was by unpaid volunteers. Dix, himself, saw the DRO as " . . . deliberately designed as a buffer to prevent direct contact of the unemployed with the government. As large a group as the unemployed would be a political threat if they were dealt with collectively by the county commissioners." This policy also pre-empted any mass action planning contemplated by the UCL leadership. Mass actions became the order of the day in late 1932 when paid managers took over the relief stations, and after the State took over the program in February 1933. The number of families served sprang from 10,143 in March 1932 to 13,652 by June. Serving this number of people, nevertheless, provided political temptation to the commissary managers. The temptation proved irresistable.[1]

John F. Dore, a wealthy criminal lawyer, had earlier enticed the unemployed with a demagogic speech on September 25, 1931 when he announced: "I'm in favor of taking the huge fortunes away from those who stole them from the American workers." In 1934 he would argue the opposite. Although not yet a mayoral candidate he also argued for tax exemptions for homes appraised at less than $4,000, and for a special session of Congress to provide five billion dollars for public works, the very amount that the Hearst newspaper chain was requesting. Hogan reports that Dore's popularity among the unemployed steadily grew in the ensuing months, while his prospective primary opponents were treading water—Mayor Harlin, confident of the labor vote, Edwards still smarting from the recall and concentrating on Ross, and a political unknown, Arthur Ritchie, a former *Star* staffer who was in line for that newspaper's support.[2]

Sensing Dore's appeal to the unemployed, Edwards even sent out packs of smoking tobacco with his card attached; but his tabloid propaganda tiresomely repeated all of the arguments of his defense against recall. (Much of his attack on Ross was ghost-written by Willis T. Batcheller, a one-time City Light engineer and aspirant for the superintendency.) Two factors blunted Harlin's appeal for the labor vote. One was the contest for it between him and candidate Otto Case. The *Argus* believed it was Case's revenge for having been defeated by him in Council when a successor to Edwards was contested. Mayor Harlin lost some labor support by using police to break up meetings in the park near the County-City Building, and then banning them altogether. Dore's rhetoric seemed to offer an alternative for a direct attack on unemployment and the relief problem.[3]

With the labor vote—embracing the unemployed—considered crucial by the contestants, it is not surprising that the two finalists in the mayoral race won because of it. Dore and Harlin won the nomination; Edwards trailed in third place with his hard core of supporters, and Case who, unlike Harlin, was not a trade unionist, ran a poor fourth. The *Times* noted that Harlin's and Edwards's strengths were in the residential neighborhoods, but that the "Dore vote was so large in those precincts he did carry . . . that there was no doubt that he was running away from the field."[4]

After the victory of Dore in the March runoff, the State Federation of Labor judged that labor was attracted by Dore's "impossible" promises and "assisted in the defeat of Brother Harlin"—Dore's victory margin was the largest in the city's history: 72,448 to 41,212. Hogan reports that, "Officially, the League took credit for the elections of [Frank] Fitts and [Roy] Misener, councilmen, and Smith Wilson, port commissioner. Dore, [Austin] Griffiths, and [John B.] Shorett testified to the value of the support of the League." The *Vanguard* estimated the League's voting bloc at 20,000—which indicates that Dore drew heavily from still-employed labor and the threatened middle classes, as well as from the unemployed.[5]

Within the UCL, as its political strength was demonstrated, the influence of both the Communists and the IWW grew among the rank and file. In January, the *Vanguard* reported the injection of Communists into UCL local meetings "using tactics which are calculated to create dissension and break up the organization . . . If communists wish to work with the League in a constructive way there is room for them." These internal tensions would grow as political action bore no fruit. As self-help seemed only to prove the failure of the "system", the radicals would take over, introducing direct mass action techniques as a means of demonstrating the indifference of public officials to the distress caused by the engulfing depression.[6]

After the March election finals, the *Vanguard* took heart, urging the unemployed to "press forward along two lines—industrial and political"—producing their own commodities and getting employment through public works; and nominating and electing their own candidates, even forming their own political party. With other unemployed organizations springing up over the state, plans went forward for a convention at Tacoma, May 29. Four hundred delegates attended, representing 111 branches and 5 county and city federations, plus Alaska. Issuing from the convention was the United Producers League of Washington, aiming to develop an "industrial program" and leaving open "the possibility for united political action in the future." Seen as a threat, the UCL leadership found IWWs prominent as organizers of the other locals and at the Tacoma meeting. We see here the seed that gradually germinated into the "production-for-use" initiative sponsored by the Democratic Party in 1936.[7]

Just as King County Relief head, Charles F. Ernst, was estimating that almost one-third of the state's population was dependent on some form of relief, the American Legion decided to recognize the threat that chronic unemployment posed to the American free enterprise system. Puget Sound Power and Light's Frank McLaughlin, as chairman of the Legion's statewide employment drive, announced on April 19 its "Man-a-block" campaign, claiming it had put 5,000 men to work. After this, the Legion remained quiet on the unemployment issue while concentrating on its "Americanism" ploy. Two weeks later, lame-duck Mayor Harlin also decided to head off the threat that the organized unemployed posed by cooperating with the UCL, making available the Civic Auditorium for a mass meeting of 7,000, for which he and councilmen Webster and Scavotto earned praise from the Municipal League. This probably marked the high point of UCL influence.[8]

Disappointment among the unemployed with Mayor Dore quickly followed his ascendancy. With the Clearing House Association refusing to honor pay vouchers issued by the City in lieu of cash, a financial crisis was posed immediately. Addressing a group of businessmen and professionals, chaired by the Great Northern's, L.C. Gilman at the New Washington Hotel on July 1, the mayor laid the blame on "municipal extravagance", advocating the slashing of wages of City employees in order to get the CHA to redeem the vouchers "which have been flooding Seattle for the last six weeks." Before this receptive audience he contended that business men "have been forced to cut their payrolls and cut them again to meet their tax bills [to pay] for municipal extravagance which strangles business and industry." He mockingly referred to councilmen Fitts and Misener for leading a coalition of six to oppose his proposed cuts, while praising Scavotto, Carroll, and Laube for their support. (Scavotto attempted to instigate an investigation of the obstructionists.) Winkingly, Dore concluded: "How much control I have over the light department, the future will tell"—a clear call upon their sympathies. The *P-I's* front page two-column head ran: "Business Men Cheer, Back Dore's Plans" . . . "Leaders Hail Mayor As Man City Has Awaited 25 Years."[9]

Dore followed quickly by suspending 250 firemen for thirty days, and he threatened those who refused to sign acceptances for voucher payments. Dore ignored the ruling of the Corporation Counsel that waivers signed under duress were illegal. That the firemen lost came as no surprise, but the mayor's manner in forcing the issue clearly indicated the future course of his administration. By late July, the council, by a 5 to 4 vote, approved Dore's cuts, amounting to a reduction of $2,500,000 from the 1932 budget, representing a 9-mill tax drop. In pursuing this course, he would alienate the bloc of votes represented by the civil service employees and organized labor.[10]

While these internal conflicts were moving to a head, Dore and Tacoma's Mayor, M.G. Tennent, recognizing their cities' inability to deal with the unemployment problem, mobilized mayors of other Puget Sound cities to press Governor Hartley to call the legislature into special session to deal with relief. They found legal encouragement also in the state Supreme Court's decision, on July 1, upholding the King County commissioners' implementation of the commissary system. The court contended that "relief measures in excess of [the] legal debt limits [are] necessary to preserve government", averring that it was the "duty" of local officials to execute relief measures. Hartley contemptuously refused them such a meeting, telling them to send him a "written communication" to which he would then respond. This rebuff prompted the Unemployed Citizens' League to threaten a march on Olympia on July 4 to "force the governor to cooperate." In this effort the UCL could count on mayoral support. They actually encouraged the marchers. Eight months later Dore would oppose such a march, even threatening to close the route through Seattle.[11]

"Thousands Will March On Olympia In Jobless Protest" . . . "Unemployed Move Spreads Over the State" . . . "Hartley's Refusal To Meet Mayors Starts Drive"; thus ran the *P-I*'s July 2 headline. It went on to report that M.M. London—executive secretary of the state's unemployed umbrella organization, the United Producers of Washington—expected at least 2,000 from Whatcom County alone. Mayor Tennent added his plea to have the governor set aside gasoline tax revenue for emergency relief, arguing the cities cannot continue indefinitely to operate feeding stations. Rarely have dissidents so enjoyed establishment support—which may have been due also to a wearying distaste for Hartley's detached arrogance as the crisis spread undeterred over the state.[12]

March they did, given this cover of authority. Seattle's UCL went first as the advance party to prepare for the rest. It was forced by City police and state patrolmen to camp at Priest Point State Park for the night. As they gathered on the capitol steps, a bitter fracas broke out inside the marchers' ranks. "Jobless Win Battle With Reds On Steps Of Capitol" . . . "Clash Seen By 5,000" . . . "Fight Was Between Seattle UCL And The Communists", ran the *P-I* headlines, accompanied by photographs. The *P-I* reported that the fight was over the refusal of the UCL and UPW to accept the Communists' demands for a $15 per week dole, plus a $3 supplement for each dependent. The UCL and UPW pressed instead for a moratorium on mortgage payments, adequate food and shelter, a gasoline tax diversion, pay for relief work at the "legal" scale, and repeal of the law authorizing foreclosure after two delinquencies. The opposing groups segregated themselves on the steps, one gathering under a red banner. The *P-I* estimated Communist strength at about 400: "many imported agitators from California and the East." Nevertheless, the haughty governor, who refused an audience with the mayors, met with representatives of the UCL and UPW for three and one-half hours. Nothing came of it, of course. The November general election was not far off.[13]

Upon return from the state capitol, the Seattle Communists set about unseating the social democrats from UCL leadership: Wells, Brannin, John C. Cronin, and Charles Gilbreath (who was in charge of the commissaries). Elected in late August to replace them were chairman W.H. Murray and vice-chairman C.J. Boardman (both, IWWs from the Capitol Hill local), and P.M. Larson, a Communist from the Crown Hill local as executive secretary. Hogan correlated their election with the decline in effectiveness of the self-help program and the introduction of paid managers to run the commissaries. Indicative of the attempts of commissioners Don Evans and Jack Early to undermine the growing political influence of the UCL was their naming W.C. Bickford to head the relief program; he would appear as a leader of the American Vigilantes in a few short months. Riots occurred at some commissaries to protest the employment of the managers with money that had to be diverted from the food supply, and the introduction of "social welfare methods" by which applicants would be subjected to eligibility tests. Logistical support for self-help activities fell off as well. When the November elections came around, both commissioners lost to UCL-supported candidates, "radio speaker" John C. Stevenson and Louis Nash. Between the election and January 1, 1933, the lame-duck commissioners discontinued self-help operations altogether.[14]

Parallel with the onset of the UCL's political decline, was its losses in chiseling successes—also "political", though of a different kind. Reacting to both the political incursions of the UCL and to the takeover by the direct action radicals, business firms withdrew support. Hogan also suggests that begging became tiresomely confrontational, as well as being financially burdensome . . . without apparent end. Small businesses also began complaining about the competition offered from the commissaries. Charges of fraud and racketeering, although unproven, helped undermine the operation—Hogan claims there was both. However, investigators did not know where to look.[15]

Coinciding with the introduction of the new commissary system in August 1932, were two efforts on the part of the business community to deal with the unemployment problem. The first was initiated by President Hoover, aimed at a late August conference in the nation's capital. In preparation fifty "leading Seattle employers" met on August 15 to launch a statewide "staggered work" campaign by calling for a conference on August 19 of the state's "biggest employers." The campaign slogan became "Job security by job sharing"—which chairman O.D. Fisher, head of the Fisher Flouring Mills, claimed was the only way to deal with the unemployment problem. When he and his counterparts from other states met in Washington on the 27th, they agreed on a six-point program, three of which related to credit sources, one to the Reconstruction Finance Corporation's advancement of funds to the railroads, and one to job sharing or work "rationing". If this effort was intended to stimulate investment and get the economy moving, its defeatist tone hardly set the process in motion.[16]

The second effort of the business community came from the Kiwanis Clubs, but it largely underscored how deeply the depression had dropped the populace—the Kiwanis started a campaign to "obtain shoes and clothing for 7,000 needy school children of the city." The UCL threatened a strike on September 19, if this need was not met by the county commissioners, but it proved only a threat.[17]

Mayor Dore, in seeking to undermine the power of the UCL, even tried to prevent the UCL locals from distributing fruit that the unemployed had gathered in the summer. The *Vanguard* labeled him "public enemy number one"—doing the bidding of the bankers. Not until late November would Judge Frater order the release of the fruit to the commissaries. In the months to come, as the Communist-led UCL chose direct action demonstrations at relief stations and organized marches, Dore further showed his mettle to the conservatives he had been

Paul Dorpat

Mayor John F. Dore addressing a gathering of the unemployed, 6 June 1932, in City Hall Park. Pugnacious and demogogic, this boxing ring-appearing platform seems fitting. The banner reads "National Unemployed Council".

courting with his budget cuts: "No one need fear as to the outcome of such demonstrations by the rabble. I'll maintain 'lor' and order if its necessary to kill every person who raises a hand against the constituted authorities."[18]

What Dore seemed not to realize is that the conservatives did not trust him, and that by alienating the organized unemployed, organized labor, and the civil service employees, he had lost his original support without gaining that of the conservatives who would choose one of their own if given the opportunity.

Hooverville and the Unemployed Citizens' League

Hoovervilles sprang up in Seattle, as they had elsewhere, during the Hoover years of the Great Depression. Seattle's most prominent one occupied the site of yard number two of the Skinner and Eddy Shipyards (it had been sold by the U.S. Shipping Board to the Port of Seattle in 1924). Homeless people on the move—scrounging leftover food, discarded utensils and tools, construction debris, remnants of packing cases and other detritus—put together makeshift hovels for protection from the weather and a place in which to use the collectibles . . . simple survival. A city within the city.[1]

Men predominated among the approximately 600 inhabitants there in 1934; only seven women were counted by Donald Roy. About 51 percent of those tallied by Roy had lived intermittently in the community for 13 months or more—"intermittently", because seasonal jobs would be offered in fishing, canneries, logging camps, wheat and fruit harvests. Most wanted to work, but there was little opportunity or none at all. Roy reported, "Hoover's tide-flats bedouins . . . are unemployed unskilled laborers, footloose and fancy free because they cannot find industrial pegs to hang." In terms of prior occupation they were hard for Roy to classify because the unemployed tended to migrate from one kind of unskilled job to another. However, he determined that of the 1020 occupational "mentions", the following predominated: 254 from the timber industries, 210 from railroad labor, 111 from construction work (including many at skilled levels), 122 from mining, 36 from fishing, 81 from farming, 37 from navigation (25 seamen), 37 from kitchen work, 49 from skilled mechanical labor lines, 17 from city trade (white collar, typically), 28 from city transportation (including 16 longshoremen).[2]

The average age of the occupants was estimated at 45.4 years. Caucasians predominated, accounting for about 71 percent of the population. In the "colored" grouping, Roy listed 120 Filipinos, 29 Negroes, and 25 "Mexicans". Filipinos, as a group, were the best educated of all the residents and the most cohesive social unit, judging from Roy's account.[3]

Was this population integrated in any way with the UCL? There would appear every reason to expect a close interaction among their respective constituents, but Roy and the "mayor" of this Hooverville, Jesse Jackson, reported little evidence to this effect. Roy reported, "a passivity in regard to the national politico-economic order", though a leaning toward some form of socialism was detected. "[The residents are] not violently bitter about the present state of affairs, nor [do they] violently agitate for a new system." Of the few Communists, Roy considered them pretty innocuous. Psychic depression, despair, and hopelessness seemed the prevailing mood . . . understandably. Not until April 1941 was this Hooverville demolished . . . replaced by an ocean terminal.[4]

Poor Law Mentality Greets the Great Depression

Before proceeding further, chronologically, a look at the status of welfare administration before 1933 will be helpful.

Nationwide, it was the structure of the poor laws of the nineteenth century that were in place when the Great Depression hit after the stock market crash of October 1929. Modifications had been made in the original poor laws, but the main financial burden had been placed on the counties to provide for indigent poor, the deaf, blind, enfeebled, insane, and children of the helpless poor. Supplementing meager county assistance was private charity of the type rendered by the Community Chest, the Milk Fund, and Salvation Army. According to 1928 figures, 71.6 % of the money spent for local relief in fifteen major cities came from public funds.[1]

In Washington the 1854 act "relating to the support of the poor" survived with only slight modification until the early 1930s. The Board of County Commissioners was assigned the "entire and exclusive superintendence of the poor." Relatives of the poor, however, were made financially responsible, either directly or by being required to pay the county $30 per month regardless of where the relative(s) lived in the state. Failing such support, the county then assumed the burden by contracting out the services needed, or by appointing an agent to assume superintendency. Minors were apprenticed to "some respectable householder." Residence requirements were tacked on to this basic legislation. The Board could also build workhouses, and did so. In a state Supreme Court decision in 1931 (Moss vs. Moss), "poor" was defined as someone who possessed no property, and that relief could be denied to anyone who was not completely destitute. Illustrating the state's abnegation of fiscal responsibility in these matters is the 1913 Mothers' Aid Act which laid that burden upon the county commissioners. That no uniform standards could be applied statewide is obvious, due to the wide variation in taxable property, character of each county, and population numbers among the counties.[2]

By 1921, in Washington, a dozen institutions had been created at the state level to deal with persons in the above noted categories. Then, passage of the Adminstrative Code in 1921 placed public welfare administration under the Department of Business Control, a management body. Aiming at economy, the state's expenditures for institutional care fell below the national average during the 1920s and early 1930s. As in all other states, no provision was made for outdoor relief—the kind of relief program that could meet the problem of mass unemployment. It was assumed that anyone who was unemployed was there by his/her own choice, and not so fated by a failure of the economic system. Bruce Blumell observes, " . . . unemployment relief remained entirely a local concern until well into the depression of the 1930's . . . It is doubtful that any state funds were spent for such purposes anywhere in the country."[3]

The Great Depression caused the nation to confront not only the problem of mass unemployment of a more evident permanent character, but also non-institutional assistance to the aged, in the form of pensions (instead of the poor house). Inability to deal effectively with these two crucial issues led to their politicization. Organization among the afflicted themselves filled the political vacuum. In Seattle, they developed their own leadership, then succumbed to exploitation of their plight by politicians—both compassionate and opportunistic—of the liberal-left who met resistance from fiscal conservatives in both the Democratic and Republican parties. These conservatives fused their fiscal rigidity with fears of political destabilization. Welfare administrators shared many of the attitudes of the conservative politicians who set policy. Some key administrators were businessmen in the early stages, when local relief efforts were being implemented. I.F. Dix and William Shannon are examples whose work will be described below. Such persons were chosen, in part, because there were not yet enough trained social workers available, and, in part, because of confidence that they would not press for fundamental change. Among trained social workers was Charles F. Ernst who became Governor Clarence D. Martin's director of welfare and relief programs from 1933 to 1940. He and Martin shared an underlying conviction that the unemployed were there because of their own failing. Perhaps they were impelled toward this conclusion by the seeming intractability of the unemployment and relief problem by the end of our period. Ernst was selected for his role because of his management of the welfare program in King County—for which he had earned the lasting enmity of the organized unemployed. Ernst, also, would train his own cadre of social workers.

When recognizing that state support of welfare before the depression was pitifully inadequate, compared with the needs to be met, it is easy to imagine the severity of hardship encountered by the needy, once the downturn really set in. Mildred Buck, in her pioneering study for the State Board on Public Welfare, observed that after 1931 state expenditures on welfare declined below the previous 10% level of government expenditures, " . . . not because of a decrease in the need, but because they have been cut more severely than other branches of government." It should not be surprising that the liberal-left became the advocate for those who should have been better served—particularly after their numbers were enormously supplemented by the unemployed. Among the latter were persons who had held responsible white collar positions, as well as blue collar veterans of the work force and of the earlier labor wars. Many among them were articulate and assertive. They filled the existing political vacuum with vigor—as we have witnessed, above, in the career of the Unemployed Citizens' League.[4]

One year passed before President Herbert Hoover finally established a body to deal with relief—thought to be only an emergency; this was the Emergency Relief Organization. Under it, state Unemployment Relief Committees were established to serve as "clearing houses for job opportunities", and to organize local relief. Hoover refused to authorize direct federal relief during the winter of 1931, preferring to stimulate local self-help agencies to help themselves. Finally, though, he allowed the Federal Farm Board to distribute surplus commodities during the winter of 1932; the Red Cross handled their distribution. Congress tried to pass relief bills throughout its 1932 session, and when one providing grants totalling $2.3 billion was passed on July 9, he vetoed it. To meet his objections, Congress passed another bill on July 21, authorizing the Reconstruction Finance Corporation to lend $300,000,000 to the states for both direct and work relief. This money was to be administered according to strict RFC guidelines, and it was to carry over into 1933. Each governor had to prove his state's need before receiving the loan; this meant that each governor in turn had to require means tests down the line. This RFC period would be succeeded by state administrations under the Roosevelt Presidency. In 1934 the "loans" would be rescinded in light of the immense financial burdens at every level of government. Indeed, there was the general feeling at the time that repayment never was intended to be made, but that the loan requirement allowed the President to save face in light of acute opposition to his earlier veto.[5]

With the above as a framework, we can focus on the response in Seattle and King County to the problem of unemployment relief and welfare.

The Politics of Unemployment and Relief, 1932-1935

Loan money from the Reconstruction Finance Corporation began flowing into the state by October 1932, though only for King County. Three more counties were added in November.

The lag time between July 21, when Hoover signed the authorizing bill, and October lay in the need, first, for the conduct of a needs survey. Another critical factor was the refusal of Governor Hartley to admit to the existence of a crisis. Failing to negotiate successfully with Hartley, the RFC's northwest regional representative, Pierce Williams, encouraged individual counties to apply for loans—King County was the first in line. In this role, he also became involved in setting policy as a consequence of having to supervise the implementation of RFC rules and regulations. When the RFC function was succeeded on June 1, 1933 by the Federal Emergency Relief Administration (FERA), he became its field representative. Throughout his terms of office he exercised some control over the the State Emergency Relief Administration (SERA) which was established January 23, 1933—use of federal funds carried with it federal control. SERA and its successor agency would be directed by Charles F. Ernst who had been director of King County relief until he was dismissed by the newly elected commissioners in January. They (John C. Stevenson and Louis Nash) owed their victories to the UCL which had bitterly and ritually attacked Ernst from the beginning for his application of "social work" methods in assessing "need", when it seemed everywhere obvious, and in his role in removing the UCL from control of the commissaries. By the end of November King County had spent its entire $675,000. Governor Hartley finally consented to file applications for King and Pierce counties so that they could receive monies in January and February.[1]

The stage was now set for the interplay of these jurisdictions: federal, state, and county. County boards of commissioners (later, County Welfare Boards) were the conduit through which relief funds were routed. These county boards had first to apply to the state agency in control (SERA, then to the Department of Public Welfare). The state agency set the rules and regulations. For the expenditure of federal monies, the state agency had, in turn, to follow federal guidelines which were in continual process of definition because of the uniqueness of the problems posed by the Great Depression.

Results of the November 1932 general election betokened changes to come, though tempered by conservative protections. Indicative was voter approval of a 40-mill property tax limitation, the effect of which would be felt once the legislature had written a bill to implement the initiative. Both relief and public school funding would be directly affected. Restrictions on taxation severely limited the state's ability to come anywhere near dealing with the scale of the enduring emergency. This ineffectiveness stimulated the growth of radicalism and the splitting of the state's Democratic Party. Newly elected as governor was Clarence D. Martin, a flour miller/banker from Cheney, its most recent mayor, and state chairman of the Democratic Party. The week after his election, Martin announced his intention to seek federal cooperation for a work program to employ as many as possible of the state's estimated 200,000 unemployed/underemployed, once the "city and county relief funds are exhausted"—hardly an inspirational message, if the state's population was expecting the offering of a state-generated program.[2]

As to local efforts at funding Seattle's 1932 relief expenditures, they were 680% higher than those in 1931, averaging $430,000 a month since July, and totaling $3,929,000 for the year. Of this total, $3,539,000 came from the county, including $1,025,000 funneled from the RFC. This scale of expenditures came at a time of sharply declining tax revenues and amidst special efforts of the business community and property holders to reduce these revenues even further, as they mounted an attack on the tax base, first by limiting the property tax, then seeking other means of providing revenue, of which a sales tax carried the most appeal. Costs of these relief expenditures faced the City with a shocking $500,000 deficit; the County, $1 million. With this shock came a shift in public sentiment, moving it away from ameliorative efforts to relieve unemployment distress through private compassion/charity. The new direction pointed toward more protection of taxable property, while shifting the burden to consumers through sales and excise taxes. In effect, taxpayers—or those who could still pay taxes—were trying to protect their principal, after initially paying some interest voluntarily, in hope that that would head off the effects of acute social unrest. That hope was expiring, and with it came a splintering of the traditional political order.[3]

Governor Martin began to address the relief problem by appointing House majority leader Donald McDonald to frame a bill that would set up a conduit through which federal funds could be channeled, and for enforcing "uniform standards of relief in all counties." The bill (H.B. 45) was passed and signed into law January 20, 1933. It established the State Emergency Relief Adminstration (SERA). By it, county commissaries were displaced, and a voucher system was installed. The latter was intended to re-establish normal lines of trade. County Welfare Boards (CWBs) were responsible for home and work relief; they reported directly to SERA. To the annoyance of the UCL, Governor Martin appointed Charles F. Ernst as director. To implement the act, a $10,000,000 bond issue was authorized by the legislature.[4]

One of the operating rules established by Ernst related to determining the needs and resources of relief applicants—a "means test". In its application, this test resulted in the elimination of reportedly 20,000 relief recipients in the state within the first six weeks of operation. Between April 1 and April 14 alone, William D. Shannon, director of King County's CWB, and a consulting engineer for Puget Sound Power and Light Company, cut off food to 227 families, as a result of home visitations. In King County the maximum allowance per person was $1 a week, which possibly might be stretched to cover critical nonfood items as well, if one believed in the efficacy of prayer. Reporting to his superior, Pierce Williams commented that Shannon's attitude seemed "to be that as long as they do not have any disturbance or outbreaks, or organized protest against the amount of the food allowance, it is proof that the allowance is satisfactory." Also, Shannon insisted that those applying for relief do work in partial compensation despite the lack of any such requirement for the receipt of RFC funds. Shannon would remain as County director throughout the RFC period and during the first three months of the WERA/SERA period—until his resignation, September 1, 1933, when he concluded that the "economy of the state was rising, and the relief staff had been materially reduced." Gnatlike, the UCL just as insistently pressed for cash payments instead of vouchers, and it objected to the exclusion of stores that advertised in its newspaper from the CWB's approved list. Grocers also preferred cash. During March, a number of "forced labor strikes" were undertaken under its leadership. However, when the Central Labor Council investigated the charges, its investigators learned, not evidence of their validity, but that the county commissioners were employing reliefers on county work instead of using their permanent employees because of the lower wages paid to the former. That the CLC also insisted upon union wage scales for relief workers is not surprising. The CWB responded by raising the pay scale to "not less than $.45 an hour". Concerning the UCL, Blumell suggests that its control over the commissaries was abolished because they were moving toward "their own economy within the larger economy." In fact this observed tendency soon would emerge as the "production-for-use" platform of the state Democratic Party, and finally as a ballot initiative in 1936.[5]

Newly elected County Commissioner John C. Stevenson, who had been supported by the UCL in his election bid (along with Louis Nash), lent his support to the voucher system and to the pending McDonald Relief Bill, thereby alienating the now Communist-dominated UCL. As for the UCL, it lost its director of food distribution, Charles Gilbreath. He defected to form the Economic Security League, and was trying to dissuade the county commissioners from further recognizing the UCL in its program. For his part, Ernst had been in close touch with Gilbreath since August, when Gilbreath informed him of the takeover of the UCL by the Communists and IWWs from the "so called conservatives". These were UCL centrists: John F. Cronin, Wells, and Brannin who, in turn, countered that Gilbreath had been forced out by "rank and file protest", and that the ESL was a "company union". In early February, the UCL, in an apparent attempt to make its absence felt, refused to cooperate with the county relief board entirely, mainly insisting on cash payments for work, continuation of the self-help program, and fair treatment of single men and women.[6]

To drive home its message opposing implementation of the McDonald "Peonage Relief Bill", the UCL leaders chose direct mass action. On February 14, led by the UCL's waterfront local, about 5,000 unemployed marched in the downtown streets, massing at the relief board's offices at Fourth Avenue and Stewart Street where they demanded a work program guaranteeing at least three days work per week and cash payment of $4.50 per day. Shannon refused any official hearing as he announced a scale ranging from $1 to $4 a week for a family of four. Given this negative response, the marchers reversed direction and headed for the County-City Building. Once in the building, they remained for sixty hours until forcibly removed under orders from Mayor Dore and the newly elected county commissioners who pleaded helplessness for the lack of any county funds. Demonstrators outside the building then paraded uptown and returned to UCL headquarters.[7]

The stage had now been set for a previously postponed hunger march to Olympia that had been planned for early December 1932, then for mid-January. March 1 became the definite date, focusing on the "R.F.C. relief law" and to insist on an adequate relief program. The marchers were met in miserable weather at the outskirts of Olympia by state and local police who were reinforced by members of the American Vigilantes whose leader allegedly was W.C. Bickford of the King County Relief Board. The vigilantes' group had their own instructions to arm themselves with clubs if they could not find firearms, and to "Temper your severity to suit the occasion . . . [remembering] . . . that nothing so swiftly sickens a mob as brutal, stomach-wrenching, soul-sickening force, swiftly, fearlessly and judiciously applied." Their advance barred at the city limits, the marchers were forced to encamp at Priest Point State Park.[8]

The *P-I* reported that Representative Warren G. Magnuson had been instrumental in gaining permission for women and children to sleep in the "old state house", and of having futilely tried to get fellow legislators to provide sleeping quarters for men in the city's vacant stores. The *P-I*, on March 3, reported an estimated 2,000 "Dole marchers on way home", but never referred to the vigilantes. The *Times* edition of March 1 gave no reference to the march, concentrating its attention on the "Bank Holiday". Its March 2 edition gave the march only passing reference and none to the intimidating presence of vigilantes. The *Star* did refer to the vigilantes "only 10 feet away", preventing entry to the city, and that legislators were denied entry to the park where the National Guard officers, city and state police ringed the area.[9]

Upon returning from Olympia, the UCL leaders, agreeing that the hunger march had been a failure, instigated a strike against the county relief program and gained support of the Seattle Central Labor Council through the persuasive powers of durable warrior James Duncan. A committee met with Shannon four weeks into the strike and won agreement that the county wage scale of the aforementioned 45 cents per hour would be paid relief workers instead of vouchers worth only $2.00 per day. Two objectives were won by this action: protecting union pay scales, and satisfying merchants who disliked being paid in vouchers that might be discounted. Blumell speculates that the ranks of the UCL itself probably were thinned by this affirmative action.[10]

Experience with the stopgap RFC program was invaluable for the implementation of the New Deal relief programs. For one, the "unemployables" (those receiving veterans' relief, mothers' aid, old age indigents, and those under special institutional programs) were excluded from coverage by the RFC. This placed the burden for their care on the counties which were deeply in debt and could not float bonds because of their financial instability. What this situation pointed to, in the opinion of Assistant Director of SERA, Arlien Johnson, was the need for an overall state relief agency, a "public welfare" department. In the background yet were the $10,000,000 bond funds awaiting expenditure. When the Federal Emergency Relief Administration program supplanted the RFC's on June 1, how these funds were to be used proved an unending bone of contention between federal administrator Harry P. Hopkins, and the state administration. Potentially, at least, these monies could be used as the state's matching contribution for direct relief which was $3 from the state for every $1 from federal sources.[11]

Following on the heels of Roosevelt's signing of the Federal Emergency Relief Act (May 12), in late May the UCL leaders sent representatives to a conference of unemployed leagues in Chicago, which began by excluding representatives from the Communist-organized Unemployed Leagues, but finally admitting them. Two Washingtonians were elected to the executive board of the federation, Victor Bidwell of the Bellingham People's Council and Richard Harrington of the Seattle UCL—both Communists.[12]

Locally, opinion was being mobilized to free the Scottsboro youths. A National Youth Day was also proclaimed by the newly organized Seattle Federation of Youth Clubs in cooperation with the UCL, on May 30, to protest "imperialist wars"—responding to the Japanese takeover of Manchuria, the wars in South America, and growing tensions in Europe, generated by the rise of the Nazis to power in Germany. Interest in Tom Mooney was revived in the process.

When the federal relief program (FERA) took hold, the state Supreme Court ruled in June—after satisfying itself that a required emergency existed in the form an "incipient insurrection"—that the state's bond funds could be used for work relief, but not for direct relief. The latter pleased Ernst and Martin (the same administrators as those under RFC's program were continued under FERA) because they had public works in mind for those funds. They expected to squeeze direct relief aid from Hopkins, whenever the counties' funds ran dry. Like their counterparts elsewhere, they never seriously considered putting up the "required" State matching money, feeling that Hopkins was soft on relief. As early as mid-July, Hopkins was complaining of the state's non-cooperation and threatened to cut back on direct relief funds. Commissioners from King and other counties expressed fear of the form protests would take if relief was not forthcoming. Pierce Williams reported to Hopkins in early August that Martin was holding off on direct relief expenditures in order to put up matching funds for public works under the new Public Works Administration, whose state director was yet to be appointed at the end of September. As these tensions multiplied among the contending agencies, each with different views of its mission and necessarily short range objectives, the problem of relief would not go away. Winter was approaching, to make even more acute the suffering already being endured. Under Hopkins's prodding the President established the Civil Works Administration (CWA) in November, to provide employment of short duration during the winter months. In combination with this came a state Supreme Court decision finally authorizing exependiture of some of the bond funds also for direct relief. The problem remained, however, because Martin and Ernst held rigidly to their strategy of avoiding such usage. A brazenly unflustered Martin reported to Hopkins on January 24 that the state would need $600,000 direct relief for the rest of January, and for each of the two following months. In the course of the communication he noted that $9 million of the original $10 million of bond money had already been committed to public works, and that he wanted to use the balance as PWA matching money. Hopkins, annoyed, resisted. Pierce Williams pitched in with his criticism of Martin, insisting that Martin would have to come up with two-thirds of the cost. SERA did reduce its relief allocations, but on March 30, Ernst phoned Hopkins to report that the state would be without funds in two days. Admitting defeat, because he realized only the unemployed and unemployables would continue to suffer, while Martin and Ernst continued their plans defiantly, Hopkins consented to giving the state $1,750,000 for the month of April. An additional $8,398,988 was supplied by FERA during the rest of 1934—94% of the total relief expenditures in the state for this period. Five per cent of the balance came from the counties, only one per cent from the state.[13]

The state's work program of the Washington Emergency Relief Administration (WERA) was taken over by the CWA. In King County, 3,500 men immediately were put to work on miscellaneous short term work projects. Before the end of November, 12,700 were so employed. By January, CWA employment in the county reached its maximum of 17,173. Statewide, there were 45,000 CWA workers in February, but that number was systematically reduced to zero by the end of the month as the program was terminated. The CWA experience, nevertheless, proved invaluable at the local level in the opportunities it gave people in developing their own works projects. This exposure would carry over to other public works projects of longer duration in the months and years to come. Also, during its short four-months life the CWA stimulated the UCL to organize a

Relief Workers Protective Association. This group soon would become the Public Workers Union, a key radical component of the Commonwealth Builders, Inc. and its successor, the Washington Commonwealth Federation.[14]

One section of the FERA authorized grants to cooperatives and self-help organizations. When asked about Washington's plans for seeking grant funds supporting these organizations, Ernst, smarting from UCL attacks on his administration, expressed the opinion that while theoretically this might be a good idea, in practice it was infeasible. What had clearly been demonstrated by the career of the UCL is that any organization of the unemployed could not remain politically neutral so long as no progress was being made or demonstrated to relieve unemployment. The carry-over of the poor law mentality into Washington's welfare program of the 1930s made inevitable an enduring politicization of unemployment and relief in general. Radicalization, in train, was inevitable. However, it remained to be seen whether that process could be accomplished within a traditional domestic radical framework embodied in a combination of left-unionism, populism, technocratic ideology, utopianism, and the cooperative movement; or whether that radicalization would become spearheaded by an organization like the CP which took its lead from the Soviet Union's Comintern. If the former, the role of the state administration must be considered among the primary causative agents leading to radicalization. If the latter, then, in future, all domestic liberal-left groupings would become suspected of being under alien influence or control, and they would become vigorously portrayed thenceforth by those fearful of any substantive change toward even social ameliorization.[15]

Blumell concludes that, at this stage, the state's efforts at instituting public works had had "virtually no effect" on the relief rolls, and that the federal government had footed almost the entire bill. Furthermore, "Ernst . . . was prepared to cut back the relief rolls rather than adhere to federal requests to use some of the $10 million for relief."[16]

As the CWA was winding down, Hopkins began reorganizing FERA. By the end of 1934 the new administration was in place in the state, but always within the framework of conflict between Ernst and FERA regional director Pierce Williams over financing and program responsibility. Satisfactory to Ernst and Governor Martin was abolition of the county as the administrative unit, and substituting six district organizations in their place. These administrators served as Ernst's field representatives. The County Welfare Boards, although continuing to function, were deprived of any administrative role. The voucher system which stigmatized the user was replaced with cash payments for work relief. And work relief was paid at a 25% higher rate than direct relief, averaging, statewide, $45 per month for a family of four. Blumell estimates about 80% of the state's relief bill was paid with federal dollars. In June 1934, the direct relief payment was raised from $1.10 per person, each week, to $1.20, to take into account the inflation rate. Work relief from federal sources was taken over by the Work Projects Administration after demise of the stopgap CWA. The surplus commodities program of the federal government supplemented these relief efforts. To spread the work around and to allow as many of the unemployed to sustain their work skills, rotation between work and direct relief became state policy.[17]

Implementation of the above programs was played against the political cacophony generated by the liberal-left forces aiming for control of the state's Democratic Party. A look at the political realignments occurring during this period is instructive.

Political Realignments, 1932-1935: An Overview

Washington had primarily been a one-party state—Republican—for most of its history. During the period of our focus, only 72 Democrats had been elected to the House of Representatives out of a total of 873 for the years from 1914 to 1930. As for the state Senate, a single Democrat occupied it in the 1921, 1923, 1929, and 1931 sessions; none in 1928. In that year only five Democrats were even elected to the House of Representatives, given the state of euphoria for which the national Republican administration claimed full credit.

Democratic Party leadership in the state was conservative, and rural values dominated it. An urban constituency had not yet been formed for the party. For example, National Committeeman, banker George Christensen of Skamania County along the Columbia River, admired Treasury Secretary Andrew Mellon and found Governor Hartley more in harmony with Democratic Party traditions than "some Democrats". He considered Senator Dill a demogogue. As noted above, these views were shared by the state's leading Democrat, state Supreme Court Justice Stephen J. Chadwick who hailed from Colfax and whose father had been Oregon's seventh governor. Young Stephen F. Chadwick of Seattle was following in line, coming about 1,500 votes short of being elected to Congress in 1924, and fully expecting to inherit a Senate spot in 1932 in the anticipated Democratic landslide of that year. His disappointment led him to support Republican incumbent, Wesley Jones. He fell back upon an American Legion career, from where he would try, as its National Commander (1937-1938), to build an anti-New Deal coalition within the Democratic Party, then conclude by running for the Senate in 1940 as a Republican when that effort failed.[1]

Outside the Farmer-Labor Party, which was the second strongest state party in 1920 and 1924, progressive strength lay in the Republican Party, primarily in Pierce, King, and Snohomish counties. These progressive Republicans (along with traditional conservatives like Mark Reed) were rejected by Governor Hartley from any influence upon his personalized, rambunctious administration. The bulk of these progressive Republicans drifted into the Democratic Party after 1932; indeed, Homer T. Bone had been one of them, as well as a Farmer-Labor Party Representative in the state legislature before being elected as a Democrat over Chadwick to the United States Senate in 1932.[2]

Out of this political confusion within the two major parties, some young Republicans would join with some young Democrats and political independents in 1933 and 1934 to form the New Order of Cincinnatus, aiming to clean up Seattle's politics. Beginning as a non-partisan movement, it launched a distinguished political career for Republican Arthur B. Langlie, a short one for David Lockwood, and a judicial career for Frederick G. Hamley that would lead him to a seat on state Supreme Court, then to one on the Ninth District Circuit Court. Nothing comparable happened to its Democrats among them.[3]

Apart from the Cincinnatans, and outside the Democratic and Republican parties, there were two movements, one more clearly defined than the other. The shorter-lived one was Technocracy, the more enduring one was the Commonwealth Builders, Inc. (CBI). Technocracy came to national prominence through the national press attention given its leader, Howard Scott, who claimed he, if given the power, could solve the nation's problems by the simple application of engineering efficiency outside the constraints imposed by the money economy represented by capitalism. After being feted for a few months in late 1932 and early 1933, Scott lost his proto-fascist appeal. However, his place was taken by Harold Loeb's Continental Committee on Technocracy which aimed toward a solution based on a mobilization of the resources of the whole North American continent by a "Plan of Plenty". Like Cincinnatus, Technocracy claimed non-partisanship, but unlike Cincinnatus, it disclaimed politics for fear of contaminating its social engineering program.

When Loeb toured the state in the summer of 1933, he found a Technocracy organization in formation that combined a curious mix of personalities, ranging from socialists like reformist Congregationalist minister Reverend Fred Shorter and the University of Washington's engineering professor F. Burt Farquharson, to politically conservative engineers like Willis T. Batcheller who had been adviser to recalled mayor, Frank Edwards. By January 1933, lawyer Florence Mayne and laundry owners H.A. and Ivan Merrick joined with Farquharson, Batcheller, and an architect, C.A. Merriam, as an executive committee. As disappointment with the New Deal set in, its membership expanded to an estimated 60,000 statewide, at its height. Spreading its influence was its weekly newspaper, *The Western States Technocrat*. In March 1934, this group became the Washington Division of the Continental Committee on Technocracy, with Richard G. Tyler, dean of the University of Washington's College of Engineering, as its president. (Later, he would become president of the Washington Commonwealth Federation and be demoted from the deanship.) The common ground among its members and its common appeal probably can be found in the idea of putting idle land, machines, and labor to work without hampering commercial constraints. This feature was central to Upton Sinclair's plan to End Poverty In California (EPIC), a campaign that heavily influenced current developments in Washington. However, the momentum that was gathering clearly grew from the foundation laid by the UCL. When the latter lost its political base, amidst internal disintegration and the loss of confidence in the New Deal, Technocracy became an attractant.

By June 1934, there were thirty Technocratic clubs in Seattle, and fifteen hundred people collected at its Woodland Park picnic. In the rural areas, Technocracy found fertile ground sown by the Grange-led public power movement. In the 1950s Technocracy signs still abounded in the Puget Sound countryside.[4]

Despite its non-political protestations, but because of the known political proclivities of many of its members, Technocrats were courted. Many drifted into the Commonwealth Builders, Inc., some becoming founding members of that organization in August 1934. Indeed, helping to found the CBI were the Merrick brothers, Farquharson, and Shorter (by then Shorter had been ousted from the Plymouth Congregational Church and had formed his own "Church of the People"). When the CBI platform was written, Tyler contributed to its drafting. Aiming at "production-for-use", its platform seemed to project much of the Technocratic program. And when the CBI endorsed a slate of candidates for the 1934 election, the Technocrats' "mainstay", Florence Mayne, encouraged members to vote their choice. Unlike Cincinnatus, which was right-leaning, Technocrats were left-leaning. The Republican Party would absorb the bulk of Cincinnatans, while the CBI, succeeded by the Washington Commonwealth Federation, absorbed the bulk of the Technocrats and worked within the framework of the Democratic Party. Before the Communist Party's adoption of the Popular Front tactic (anti-fascist, and for collective security), known Communists were kept at arm's distance.[5]

Among the groupings outlined above, the New Order of Cincinnatus (NOOC) would have the earliest impact on Seattle's politics, beginning in 1934. In a leaflet issued in May 1934 the NOOC recounted its aims: " . . . rebirth of political idealism among the younger citizens of America. We believed that the field of local government, especially, was fallow and weed-grown for the want of leaders willing to try their mettle against ignorance and entrenched politicians . . . [T]he major political parties have become nothing but job-hunting cliques, and special interest lobbies . . . Cincinnatans believe that the people want a renaissance in politics . . . Cincinnatus advocates a Spartan-like devotion to honesty, efficiency, and ability in government."[6]

Beginning in September 1933 with about ten men, by spring of 1934 it had gathered into its folds about 500 of "Seattle's finest young men in all fields of endeavors." Membership was limited to men between ages 21 and 35, with allowance up to age 40 for those who had enlisted by age 35. Auxiliary status was later established for older men and for women of any age (women would become active campaigners). One of the earliest objectives in city government was tax reduction of at least 40%, earning for it the "tax dodger" epithet. It sought to counteract the popular impression that it was conservative; indeed, most members seemed to think of themselves as being "liberal" reformers.[7]

Its prime mover and first commander was Ralph Bushnell Potts. He resigned as president of the Consolidated Republican Clubs of King County to develop the NOOC, claiming that his work in the party had been "largely done . . . They are well organized with an intelligent and loyal leadership . . . ." Potts closed his commentary by pointing out difficult times ahead for the taxpayers in light of the "nearly insolvent" cities and counties, which was only compounded by the recent 40-mill tax limit law which had drawn his and other Republican and conservative support in general. At last, being tax-tied, "The only solution is to reduce government to the size of the taxpayers' purse." With this inspirational end in mind, he set up an organizational model that was military in tone, and whose original aspiration was to develop a national organization that bore a contemporary resemblance in spirit to the Fascists in Italy and National Socialists in Germany and Austria. By December 1933, it had 17 divisions in the state, each headed by a captain (majors and colonels of state-rank were above them). In its "state plan" it projected the form of government it aimed to establish following a constitutional convention. Cincinnatus reflected the general shift from concern with unemployment and relief, declaring those problems were both permanent and federal and international in scope. Solutions should be sought at the local level, in its view. Taxation that, in its mind, would impede investment, should be limited on property to 40 mills, and not levied at all on intangible wealth. A state constabulary would be established, and all police offices between state and municipal levels would be eliminated. Age 40 would be the upper limit for employment and the enlistment period would be four years, after completion of a training course in a State Police School, for which purpose one of the Normal Schools would be used.

In implementation, and as a foretaste of the future, was the march of fifty Cincinnatans into the Comptroller's office in early 1934, dressed in white shirts and green and yellow head-pieces (the Roosevelt High School colors, the home district of its leaders), to accompany three who filed as council candidates. Each chose "Cincinnatus" as his middle name—which the office accepted. After the February 1934 primary, some members suggested that everyone stand and salute the commander upon his entry for the evening's meeting, but this thought was quickly vetoed as being too "fascist". Frederick Hamley, in his councilmanic diary for 1933-1936, describes a real tension between the Potts forces, aiming for a nationwide organization of ambiguous character, but bearing his personal proto-fascist stamp, and those like city councilmen Hamley and David Lockwood, who wished to concentrate on local problems. Potts, later, judged the membership to be nominally Republican in sympathy, but being dissatisfied with the party, and "chary of the wilder imagination of the Democrats." For the time being the leadership was content to turn the rascals out, abolish patronage, and bring merit to the city's government and civil service, all of which would contribute to lowering taxes.[8]

Beginning inauspiciously in October 1933, the NOOC attacked and demanded the resignation of King County Commissioner John C. Stevenson (born Stockman and wanted for stock fraud in New York), for resisting attempts to extradite him, and for responsibility for alleged mismanagement in the administration of county relief. Attention gained in this campaign encouraged the leadership to enter the city's primaries in February 1934. Three came forward to run for City Council: David Lockwood, Wellington Rhinehart, and Lloyd Johnson. Only Lockwood survived the primaries, running far behind in sixth place. The *P-I* saw the primary results as victory for the economizers and a "surprising" defeat for the UCL. All three, plus the fiscally conservative incumbent, John E. Carroll, were supported by the Washington Taxpayers Council. Also surviving the primaries were incumbent mayor John Dore and mayoral race finalist Charles Smith, recent head of the King County Republican Club. Smith attracted the traditional business community support for Republican candidates—that which Dore had worked so hard to attract by his economy measures, while alienating organized labor and civil service support. Smith's victory in the runoff was not surprising, considering the circumstances. Lockwood's was, however, because he had no endorsement from the three daily newspapers, had little apparent financial support, and he had to survive charges that one of his publicity writers (Mel Voorhees who later joined the *Star*) was on loan from Puget Sound Power and Light. Voters might have become weary of this revived issue in light of the oppressive depression, and the charge might well have backfired, for Lockwood led all council candidates with a vote total that jumped from 15,294 in the primary to 62,179 in the final, coming within six votes of matching Smith's total.[9]

When Smith assumed office in June, the maritime strike was in progress along the entire Pacific Coast. Outgoing mayor, John Dore, having dealt with the strike from its beginning on May 9, began forging a renewed support from organized labor, through the medium of the Teamsters' Dave Beck. The strike generated the emergence of a new leadership of the International Longshoremen's Association when the old one had become discredited for appearing to having sold out to the Waterfront Employers Association. When a final arbitration award nominally provided equal control of the hiring hall, it proved only an illusion in practice for the employers. New life in the maritime unions would provide a special leftward impetus to the Democratic Party in western Washington as part of the labor constituency of the New Deal coalition.

Mayor Smith was first tested in his new job by his management of the police forces during the course of the strike. Organized labor resurfaced as a political force, just as the political influence of the organized unemployed was declining. For this reason alone, the strike's long-range importance requires special attention. That a strike was in the making was foretold in the context of the early days of the New Deal. The employee representation plan that had been in place on the waterfront since 1921 would not last for long.

20

Labor Movement Revives, Becomes a Political Force Again

The Great Maritime Strike of 1934, a Watershed—From Dore to Smith

1934, nationwide, has been described by Irving Bernstein as one of the most climactic in the nation's labor history. Trade unions had been eclipsed by the postwar open shop movement. Job protection was the primary concern in the AFL crafts, not organizing. As will be described in chapter 22, on the rise of Dave Beck and the Teamsters' Union, only the Teamsters seemed to be organizing actively. The rise of the Teamsters was due to the introduction of the internal combustion engine which was displacing horses with trucks since about 1915. By way of contrast, technological changes that brought about mass production in automotive-related industries produced no serious effort to organize these very industries. Puny attempts, authorized by the AFL headquarters, permitted the temporary formation of federal unions which disintegrated as the individual crafts unions then raided the federal unions, once they made any progress. The AFL craft unions had not even held their own during the 1920s and they had been further decimated by the pre-New Deal depression years.

Only the balm of a generally distributed prosperity—excepting traditional agriculture—kept up wages and expanded living standards during the 1920s. When the National Industrial Recovery Act was passed on June 16, 1933, it included in Title I (which established the National Recovery Administration) a section 7(a) which seemed to be aimed at protecting employees in organizing for collective bargaining through representatives of their own choosing. It was interpreted by labor as a charter to organize workers into legitimate unions that were independent of employer influence. If this interpretation was upheld, company unions and employee representation plans of the 1920s would be outlawed in effect.

Employers, however, chose to interpret a clause that exempted anyone seeking employment from having to join an organization not of his own choosing as a prohibition against unionization.

These conflicting interpretations would lead to extensive and bitter conflicts that would rend the nation, splitting the craft-dominated AFL, giving rise to the Congress of Industrial Organizations, incorporating the latter into the New Deal wing of the Democratic Party, inspiring the National Labor Relations Act, and fomenting concerted employer resistance to application of the act, and its constitutionality, that made previous labor-employer confrontations pale by comparison.

Section 7(a) set off a wave of strikes in 1933, the most since 1922. Basically they were over the right to bargain collectively—union recognition. To deal with this issue, a National Labor Board was set up after the first wave of strikes, but it lacked the means to enforce any mediatory decision it might reach. Regional boards were also established. Early mediatory successes only served to invigorate employer opposition, led by the National Association of Manufacturers and the chambers of commerce, buttressed by local employer associations. When NRA industry codes were drafted, they nearly all were done without independent labor participation, and normally they underwrote some form of company union plan. The crucial test was in the automotive industry because it was the key to any economic resurgence, and it seemed to be reviving. The industry refused to negotiate, but worse, the President refused to accept the broad interpretation of 7(a) that the unions had accepted as their charter—that all workers in a plant would be represented by a bargaining agent favored by a majority of the workers by means of secret vote. Roosevelt accepted, instead, a proportional representation interpretation urged upon him by two of his advisers, NRA administrator Hugh Johnson and Donald Richberg. This set the stage for the contests of 1934. These contests, in turn, would lead, by 1935, to the National Labor Relations Act which grew out of the dispute over interpreting section 7(a). With these developments in the background, we will see how Seattle fitted into the national picture.[1]

There was little reference to labor organizing during the 1934 winter city election campaign. The national Democratic Party administration saw the mayoral candidacy of Charles Smith as a step aimed by the Republicans to regain control of the legislature and the congressional delegation. Under this illusion, the Skagit issue was injected into the campaign when E. Pat Kelly (state director of the Labor and Industries Department) announced that President Roosevelt had assured him funding for the project would be forthcoming, adding, "A vote for Dore is a vote for Roosevelt." Senator Bone added emphasis, informing Ross that FDR had promised $13 million in Public Works Administration funds for the Skagit. City Light's acting superintendent, Glen Smith, was sent to Portland to talk with the regional PWA administrator. Senator Dill chimed in with his Dore endorsement as: "City Light also moved to the top as a major issue." Smith answered by assuring the public that Ross was not in danger, nor was City Light. It was like a ritual dance, and barely as relevant.[2]

The election results gave Smith a majority of more than 15,000 votes. Dore's defeat was credited to the civil service workers who had suffered a 16% pay cut. For his economy measures that kept down taxes, the Municipal League backed Dore. All incumbent council members who were running—Nichols, Levine, and Webster—lost to David Lockwood, James Scavotto, and aged, but politically durable, Judge Austin Griffiths. Not to be overlooked was election of labor leader and adult education advocate James Duncan, to the School Board; and the election of former County Commissioner Jack Early to the Port Commission, replacing commission veteran and former mayor George Cotterill. Meanwhile acute labor unrest was brewing, mainly on the waterfront.[3]

One of the locals of the UCL—that along the waterfront—became the catalyst for a revival of the International Longshoremen's Association, although since 1931 longshoremen had already been drifting back to the ILA. The Marine Workers Industrial Union—like the Lumber Workers Industrial Union, it was affiliated with the Communists' Trade Union Unity League—sought to organize workers by industry instead of by craft. The Communist-dominated *Voice of Action*, however, was found criticizing Captain John Fox of the Masters, Mates, and Pilots Union for seeking just such an industrially based union when he led an effort to form a maritime alliance with the ILA; apparently, this would have thwarted the MWIU. Meanwhile, longshoremen began flocking to the ILA from July onward. And, under the stimulus of Harry Bridges's leadership out of San Francisco, the ILA began drawing up labor provisions under the NRA code for presentation at a code hearing in November. Although the provisions were accepted by NRA administrator Hugh Johnson, they were rejected by President Roosevelt, ostensibly for their impact upon existing treaties and the like. However, these labor provisions became the basis for future ILA demands.[4]

The NRA then proceeded to recognize the company union—the so-called Blue Book union—despite the fact that its numbers had been decimated by movement out to the ILA. Nevertheless, when the Blue Book union met on November 16, the employee representatives on it announced their resignations, adding that the ILA would appoint a negotiating committee. Tacoma veterans of the ILA District 38—where the ILA had been kept breathing during the years since 1921—provided the initial leadership.[5]

Two weeks after the NRA hearings, a coastwise ILA conference was held in Portland at which ILA President Joseph Ryan's acceptance of a government-run hiring hall proposal was rejected, and a committee was appointed to seek negotiations with employers. The latter were supposed to agree to meet by December 10. Failing that, a strike vote was to be taken along the entire coast. Upon failure to get the employers to negotiate, Seattle's Local 38-12 voted 885 to 21 for union recognition and a raise in the pay scale. The MWIU backed the ILA demands. Yet, no strike was called.[6]

In early February, the *Voice of Action* proclaimed that a West Coast longshoremen's strike loomed ahead. The MWIU followed with a strike against the "Andrea Luckenback" in late February; this was followed by another against the "Vermar" in early March. Attempts of the ILA to unload the latter failed. Concurrently, a convention of the ILA was being planned, incorporating unique rank-and-file representation which Bridges was instrumental in getting as a result of a January 1934 tour of coast ports by him and ILA Pacific Coast officer Lee Holman.[7]

The convention, with twenty-four ports represented, was held in San Francisco from February 26 to March 6. It became, in effect, the founding convention of a new union, in the view of

Charles Larrowe. Most significant at this meeting was the decision to form a federation of maritime unions to negotiate with the employers—instead of each craft negotiating independently. Significant also, was the decision to bargain on a coastwise basis, not port-by-port. ILA leaders in the past had used the opposite tactics which the unified waterfront employers exploited, allegedly by paying off the leaders, of whom Ryan was only the most flagrant example. The basic demand was termination of the abusive shape-up system of hiring—the basis for collusion and racketeering—and its replacement by a union-controlled hiring hall.[8]

Waterfront employers also were meeting in San Francisco; so, an ILA committee asked George Creel of the Regional Labor Board to arrange a meeting with them. He reported back their refusal. This report was quickly followed by a telegram to Creel telling him that the holding of an election to choose a bargaining representative was not possible because the maritime industry was not yet covered by an NRA code. Employer intransigence made an election impossible. They would not agree to ending the shape-up, and they insisted on port-by-port negotiations. Their attitude only coalesced the rank-and-file behind Bridges, and drew away support from the regular ILA leadership through which the employers expected to cut a deal, if they failed to break the union at its inception.[9]

At the urging of Ryan, it was agreed to postpone any strike action until FDR had signed the shipping code—expected on March 22. It was also agreed that if the employers did not accept the March 7 demands by the 22nd, a strike would be called for on March 23. By mid-March, in a coastwise referendum, 6,616 longshoremen voted in favor of striking, only 699 opposed. The Seattle Local 38-12 voted 995 to 92 in favor of a strike in the face of the Waterfront Employers Association's claim that longshore labor conditions in Seattle were the best in the country. To circumvent the expected opposition of ILA president Ryan and Lee Holman, Bridges managed to set up a strike committee derived from the rank-and-file. If a strike were to occur, there appeared little likelihood that the regular leaders would be able to get a settlement without rank-and-file participation—unheard of at this time. Bridges was elected chairman of the strike committee, thereby taking control out of the hands of Holman and Pacific Coast District president Bill Lewis, both of whom opposed any strike action. They wired Ryan that only the radicals wanted one. Creel reported to Washington that the shipowners also wanted one, " . . . it would be worth [two or three million] . . . to destroy the union."[10]

Only a letter from President Roosevelt to the ILA leadership in San Francisco, urged upon him by Creel, gained postponement of the strike. Roosevelt quickly appointed a mediation board composed of Assistant Secretary of the Labor Department, San Francisco's Edward McGrady, Seattle's Charles Reynolds, and J.L. Leonard of Los Angeles. This board held meetings in San Francisco March 28-31 and on April 1 the board issued its recommendations: representation elections, joint-venture hiring halls, dispatching to be determined locally, and wages and hours to be fixed by arbitration. Attempts to get agreement on these recommendations were rejected by both parties. When May 7 arrived, strike votes were taken. On May 9, the walkout began along the entire coast.[11]

In Seattle, 1,500 men struck on the first day, May 9. By nightfall, the Waterfront Employers Association realized it was serious, so they began setting up shop to recruit, house, feed, and protect the strikebreakers they intended to bring in, after fencing off the docks against the pickets. Three ships were brought into the harbor to serve as barracks. The strikebreakers were to be transported by boat to their jobs, thereby evading the picket lines that sealed off entry to the docks. Pacific Lighterage busily recruited 200 strikebreakers. Representatives of the steamship lines canvassed the fraternities at the University of Washington, signing up more than 100 students; however Acting President Hugo Winkenwerder and Dean of Men Herbert Condon objected, with Winkenwerder declaring himself "unalterably opposed", and that he would do "everything within [his] power to halt the student action." The companies were denied docking privileges when they tried to pick up the students. The Alaska Steamship Company requested police protection as pickets forced back trucks heading for the docks, but the teamsters were sympathetic and held off until Dave Beck countered by ordering drivers to pass through the lines. The Masters, Mates, and Pilots Union refused to handle cargoes. After the fourth day, the ILA, by convincing longshoremen elsewhere that the fate of the Seattle strike would determine their own, organized a "flying squadron" of about 2,000 reinforcements from Everett and Tacoma to beef up the picket lines because cargoes were still being worked. With this help, strikebreakers were routed out from wherever they were found. Some company guards were dumped into the bay. When more violence seemed imminent, Mayor Dore ordered a carload of police to the Stacy Street pier, but they remained car-bound at the sight of the massed strikers. By nightfall, substantially all strikebreakers were removed. At day's end, four of the employers withdrew the remaining strikebreakers. By May 15, the off-shore unions had joined the strike. That same day, teamsters ceased crossing the picket lines. As more off-shore unions joined the longshoremen, the steamship companies cancelled sailings, and the waterfront employers demanded the governor call out the National Guard. Dore waited for a federal response to his request for federal troops, and Governor Martin instead called for a parley.[12]

Dore refused to ask Governor Martin to call in the National Guard, claiming that the Seattle police were up to the task—but probably because this kind of action might have incited a general strike in the last days of his administration, and at a time when he was renewing his labor backing through linkage with Dave Beck. The *Times* headline blared: "Mob Rushes Todd Docks" . . . "Soviet Rules Seattle, Says Dore". Its article contended the city government has been "replaced by a soviet of longshoremen", and that the employers insist on the open shop as the basis for any settlement. However, the *Times* later intimated on July 1 that many on the police force had sympathized with the strikers, and the *Times* admitted that the strikers did have "a great deal of right and justice on their side" in the beginning.[13]

As the local economy began closing down, with 37 ships standing idle, the Waterfront Employers Association (WEA) then used their familiar tactic of threatening to divert cargo to other ports, hoping to play one off against the other—but times had changed. ILA leadership itself was changing—a de facto maritime federation was being formed under Bridges's leadership, and coastwise bargaining was being strictly adhered to. When Governor Martin tried to mount a mediation meeting for May 15 in Olympia, he invited representatives from the WEA, State Federation of Labor president, James Taylor, Dave Beck, representatives from the Grace Steamship Lines, the McCormick Steamship Line, and representatives from the Ports of Seattle and Tacoma, six longshoremen, but no ILA representative. Jones states that Local 38-12 leaders refused to attend, that they were by then taking their cue from San Francisco. Martin then joined with the two other coastal states governors in asking for federal aid. To this, the Portland Central Labor Council threatened a general strike. The *Times* front page pictured Dave Beck and Joe Ryan as they were deplaning at San Francisco—Beck as Martin's representative—to work towards settlement and to seek general exemption of Alaska shipping. Meanwhile, Seattle's ILA head, Dewey Bennett, looked to San Francisco for his cue.[14]

Into this tense situation the Labor Department quickly sent Edward McGrady to San Francisco. Upon his arrival on the 17th, McGrady met with local businessmen and two mediators whom Roosevelt had appointed to work on the case; he did not meet with any strikers. On the 18th, he asked both sides to fully empower their negotiating committees to make a settlement. The employers agreed, but only on their terms, essentially the status quo plus accommodation of the regular ILA leadership. The San Francisco local rejected McGrady's proposal on the grounds that any agreement would have to be voted upon by the rank-and-file. Such a procedure lay outside McGrady's experience, as well as Ryan's. There would have to be a referendum vote by the entire membership, for one thing. Also, the ILA demanded exclusive union control over the hiring hall and a closed shop, both of which were rejected by the shipowners. In addition, the San Francisco longshoremen insisted that they would remain out until the other marine unions had gotten their settlement as well. Impasse! McGrady only further alienated himself from the strikers' cause when he declared on the 19th that they were being kept on strike by Communists: "A strong radical element within the ranks of the longshoremen seems to want no settlement of this strike . . . The Executive Committee [of the ILA] appears to me to be helpless to do anything with the men they represent, or to combat the radical element . . . ."[15]

The expected arrival of ILA president Joseph Ryan lent confidence that a settlement might be won. He arrived in San Francisco on May 24, announcing that recognition of the ILA was the paramount issue. Ryan met the shipowners' spokesman, Roger Lapham, who promised Ryan—who was a model-ship collector—his choice of any ship model in Lapham's collection if Ryan could wrench a settlement. On the 26th, Ryan dismissed the idea of pursuing the closed shop, and downplayed Bridges's maritime-unity strategy. Bridges then went to the membership and got reaffirmation of the initial strike goals. Ryan went ahead with negotiations anyway, reaching an agreement on the 28th signed by his officers in Seattle, Portland, San Francisco, and Los Angeles and the shipowners' representatives in those cities. The agreement provided for ILA recognition and joint operation of the hiring halls. The employers would be free to choose their

Joe Ryan and Dave Beck arriving in San Francisco to negotiate a settlement of the 1934 coastwise maritime strike. By an unprecedented vote of the rank and file members, their agreement was rejected. The strike redefined labor relations for the next two decades.

MAY 29, 1934. PRICE TWO CENTS

LABOR OFFICIALS HERE

Joseph P. Ryan (left), president of the International Longshoremen's Association, of New York, and Dave Beck of Seattle, Northwest representative of the Teamsters' Union and Gov. Clarence D. Martin's representative at San Francisco mediation meetings, as they alighted from a United Air Lines plane here this morning.

RYAN, HERE, URGES MEN TO ACCEPT COMPROMISE

Majority of Total Ballot by Individuals in Coast Units Will Decide; Ship Operator Favors Acceptance

Joseph P. Ryan of International Longshoremen's Association flies to Seattle to urge strikers to accept the shippers' temporary settlement offer, which concedes I. L. A. recognition but maintains the open shop in hiring workers.

San Francisco strike committee denounces proposal and threatens general coastwide strike of all unions.

The Ferryboatmen's Union walks out on Puget Sound Navigation Company craft, but strikebreakers take their places under heavy police guard. The company says it will maintain uninterrupted service.

All other ferry lines are unaffected by the strike, having agreed to demands for a six-day week and no cut in wages.

District longshoremen resume deadlocked conference at Tacoma on lifting strike ban from vessels plying to ports north of Kuskokwim Bay, Alaska.

While striking longshoremen in all Coast ports were preparing today to vote on a plan proposed by employers which would effect a temporary truce and reopening of the ports, the strike committee of the San Francisco union issued a statement flatly rejecting the plan and threatening a coast-wide strike of all trade unions.

The San Francisco longshoremen have not voted on the peace proposal.

Joseph P. Ryan, International Longshoremen Association's president, who flew here from San Francisco today o urge longshoremen to

(Continued on Page 4, Column 2.)

MRS. SWALE, WIFE

SOUND FERRIES

Reprinted with permission of the *Seattle Times*

men and be responsible for the dispatching records. Wage and hours disputes would be submitted to arbitration. The big difference from the old system seemed to be only the injection of the ILA into the picture—with ample opportunity provided for collusion. Newspapers reported the strike as ended. But not so, if Bridges and his supporters had their way.[16]

When the news reached Seattle, Dave Beck advised the longshoremen to accept it and to forget about the other unions. Ryan set off for the Northwest to see about reversing the opposition he had been facing in the Bay City, encouraged by Beck's support. First, Portland's longshoremen voted down the settlement, then Tacoma's rank-and-file followed suit. While Ryan was in Seattle, San Francisco's longshoremen, acting on McGrady's recommendation for a secret ballot, voted 2,404 to 88 against the agreement. In Seattle, while conferring with Dave Beck, the two of them learned that Mayor Dore and his counterparts in Tacoma and Portland and three smaller cities were planning to use force to open their respective ports. To avert this, Ryan and Beck came up with a proposal that the employers in Seattle accepted. They left then for San Francisco and found the shipowners and the Industrial Association there also ready to accept it.[17]

Meanwhile, in Seattle, attempts to load Alaska-bound ships were being blocked until a truce was worked out on June 9 with participation of the new mayor, Charles Smith. It provided for removal of police from the docks. Their later re-introduction would lead to renewed hostilities and renewal of the embargo.[18]

Meeting in San Francisco Mayor Rossi's office on June 16, to hammer out a formal agreement were thirteen men, but none from the strike committee. Included were T.G. Plant of the shipowners, plus three representatives of the Industrial Association, Ryan and three of his officers, Teamsters Beck, Mike Casey, and John McLaughlin, and the President's mediators. Larrowe records that when Plant asked Ryan whether the longshoremen would accept any agreement the group might forge, Ryan admitted "I don't think so . . . This local has been captured by the radicals and the Communists . . . ." Nevertheless, Ryan contended that he could make any agreement stick. But, when the agreement was ready, all in the mayor's office signed, except the longshoremen at the meeting who contended they could not sign until the membership had ratified it.[19]

Again, it looked like an end to the strike had come. Ryan had even wired McGrady to that effect. Not so, the agreement was rejected. In reality only one more stage in its development was reached—the discrediting of the regular ILA leadership, and defeat of craft union sectarianism, stressing the self-interest of each craft. Ryan did not get his model ship.[20]

Attempts by Mayor Smith to set up arbitration had failed by June 15. He quickly declared that an emergency existed, and he assumed direct control of the police forces. The *Argus* reported police headquarters "became a mobilization camp . . . standing by for riot duty [should strikebreakers be used]." Sheriff Claude Bannick claimed he could pitch in with 500 "special deputies" in case more support might be needed. Chamber of Commerce president Alfred H. Lundin, chairing the Seattle Citizens' Emergency Committee, asserted that Smith had no alternative if he was to reopen the port because the employers could make no more concessions. San Francisco's Industrial Association, which had taken over employer leadership there, lent its voice in the background.[21]

Concurrently, the off-shore unions (Masters, Mates, and Pilots and the Marine Engineers) declared they would not work with inexperienced crews even if the ships got loaded. Then, by a 5 to 4 majority, the City Council repudiated the mayor's police protection policy. At a Municipal League debate civil libertarian Irving Clark, congratulated the Council for its vote, contending that the special police were being paid for by the WEA and the Citizens' Committee of the Chamber of Commerce. Smith ignored the Council majority and proceeded to make preparations to reopen the port. The standard tear gas was supplemented with a new one which linked cannisters to car exhausts to pump out their toxic fumes. Police recaptured bats from the strikers after the strikers had raided a bat-making factory that was supplying the constabulary. Although the Alaska shippers and the Chamber of Commerce reportedly registered "amazement" when the unions declared the truce was no longer in effect on Alaska shipping, it should have surprised no one under the circumstances. During the period June 9 to 21 twenty-five ships had sailed to Alaska.[22]

On June 21 police sent three strikers to the hospital after an attempt to blockade the railroad tracks at Smith's Cove was thwarted. Activity was concentrated at piers 40 and 41 on the Cove, with strikers greasing the rails, cutting phone lines and skirmishing physically and verbally with the police. By the end of June, pickets there had expanded their number to 150, police to 400. On July 3, Smith sent reinforcements to the piers where they forced the pickets back, creating a two-block long "no-man's land" in coordination with the loading of lumber on two ships at Pier 41. Loading by non-strikers would continue.

On the same day, in San Francisco, Mayor Rossi was pursuing the same path, but it was one that would lead first to massive violence on July 5, climaxing in the "Battle of Rincon Hill" and the loss of two lives, injuries to scores, to an incomparable funeral cortege of thousands up Market Street, the beginning of talks about a general strike, then the calling of that strike on July 16. Seattle's situation was made more moderate probably for two primary reasons—its employer organizations were not as solidly organized nor as adamant as those in the Bay City, and the Seattle Teamsters were kept under control by Dave Beck—Mike Casey lost control of his Teamsters, particularly after they, too, were accused of being "a bunch of Reds".[23]

Pressure to reopen shipping to Alaska continued as its "lifeline" link to the northland was played up in the newspapers. The unions agreed to load ships for the Territory at a "neutral" port. Tacoma was named to this honor, but union wages and conditions were conceded by the employers. Tacoma became the center for the Alaska trade at least for the duration of the strike.[24]

While this agreement was being worked out, the Citizens' Emergency Committee pleaded with Governor Martin to send in the National Guard to "drive out the Communists who have swarmed into town . . . to inject terrorism into the strike situation." Committee chair Alfred Lundin complained that ILA membership had sprouted from 1,200 at the strike's beginning to between 12,000 and 15,000. Beck advised the Governor against such action for fear of generating another general strike—which would have damaged Beck's long-range plans as well as radical labor's—keeping in mind the aftermath of Seattle's 1919 General Strike. The Guard was not dispatched; they were not needed. The mayor would soon demonstrate his mettle.[25]

July began with the shooting death of one striker, Shelby Daffon, when sixty strikers rushed guards at the Point Wells oil docks north of the city. Seeing the strike running out of control, the *Times* blamed "the government" for failing to control union leadership. It spread blame further upon the "radicals", and finally expressed dismay at the "breakdown of the old 'Seattle Spirit'." On July 3, a special deputy was even abducted, taken to ILA headquarters, questioned as to "non-union operations" and released. Mayor Smith then ordered the number of pickets be limited to three at Pier 41. At the pier, eighty more strikebreakers were hired, bringing their number to two hundred—five ships were being worked and a seventh train entered the dock. At Tacoma, Alaska-bound ships were being loaded as trucks from Seattle brought in cargo. Shipping seemed trending toward normal as acts of violence became more frequent—beating of a strikebreaker uptown was reported on the 6th, followed by arrest of the assailant. Then a special deputy sheriff, Steve B. Watson, was shot to death during a scuffle with strikers.[26]

With the San Francisco General Strike in progress, with arbitration by the National Longshoremen's Board rejected on the hiring hall issue, and with the pickets now numbering about 1,200, police lines were breached despite their tear gassing. On that same July 18, police up and down the coast began raiding headquarters of the Communist-led Marine Workers Industrial Union and other suspected radical hangouts. Seattle was no exception; it was like the period from 1916 to 1920 when IWW halls and Socialist offices were regularly raided and public gatherings and demonstrations were routinely broken up by the police. Five "Communist leaders" were arrested in Seattle when the MWIU office was raided on two successive days. This led to a counter-attack on police headquarters, from where the attackers retreated to Smith's Cove, merging with the forces in conflict there. Longshoremen from other Puget Sound ports joined in. The *Times* headline on the 19th ran: "28 Reds arrested; Pickets Hampering Work At Smith Cove". Its column noted that the "28" arrestees were gathered from a third raid on Communist headquarters that day "after a morning of more violence." By July 20, the *P-I* counted 35 arrests, "Revealing the amazing part that Soviet agitation has played in Seattle's waterfront strike . . . ." Police also raided headquarters of the Sailors' Union of the Pacific, arresting eleven suspected pickets who were presumed to be Communists. That day saw Mayor Smith assuming direct control of police at Smith's Cove, leading 300 police armed with submachine guns and tear gas apparatus against the strikers. Smith himself fell victim to the gassing. Injuries were heavy on both sides. But, unlike San Francisco's police, Seattle's held their fire, and no lives were lost. That a truce emerged is not surprising.[27]

On July 21, the National Longshoremen's Board requested a coastwise referendum on whether to accept arbitration. With weariness setting in on both sides, and with public impatience growing, voting got underway. Under weight of the once-steadily employed former Blue Book members, Local 38-12 voted 762 to 102 to accept arbitration. Only the Everett local voted against it, 110 to 109; San Francisco's longshoremen voted for it 2,316 to 759. Both parties agreed to resume normal operations on July 29. The arbitration award would be made October 12. The hearings were to provide the arbitrators with the essential historical and technical background to enable them to reach a decision that would have lasting effect. That the testimony of Harry Bridges persuaded them to reach the decision they did is evident.[28]

On the crucial hiring hall issue, the board decided upon a jointly operated hiring hall with expenses of operating it shared equally. But the dispatcher was to be elected by the union, with instructions to equalize earnings as close as possible. This feature would lead in practice to the union's control of the hiring hall. Also, a coastwise contract was awarded, providing a six-hour day, thirty-hour week with time-and-a-half for overtime, and a base pay of 95 cents an hour.[29]

This monumental strike would critically affect future political alignments in Seattle. The role of Dave Beck in the course of the strike has been noted. On the Pacific Coast, he clearly was emerging as the best hope of the conservative elements in the labor movement, bent upon preserving the craft structure of union organization along with its narrowly defined vested interest in job control. With this orientation was allied a distrust of rank-and-file control of the union leadership; referral of leadership decisions to the rank-and-file threatened the union bureaucracy. Beck also became the best hope of employers who not only sought pacification of their labor forces, but also non-governmental regulation of their business competition.

Parallel with Beck's emergence into political prominence, there was occurring a split in the AFL that carried with it national as well as local implications, because the vote of organized labor was becoming crucial. Mayor Dore began courting Beck and the AFL, just as the longshoremen were beginning to radicalize Seattle's politics. The latter would break away from the ILA in 1937, joining the newly formed Congress of Industrial Organizations (CIO) as the International Longshoremen's and Warehousemen's Union—Seattle's branch would be Local 19.

Gradually, the business community largely reconciled itself to the necessity of unions, once their existence was assured under the Wagner Act (the National Labor Relations Act). But, when they had a choice between the AFL and the CIO, they leaned to the former. In Seattle, Dave Beck and his Teamsters spoke for the AFL, so this led them to favor Beck in their dealings. In his respect for keeping contracts and suppressing wildcat strikes, he helped to stabilize the labor force, while using contract enforcement as a tactic for breaking CIO-led strikes. Business leaders also learned that in dealing with Beck they could gain some more purely business objectives as well—price stabilization combined with elimination of "cut-throat competition" being key elements. However, before these elements in the industrial relations mix became more clearly understood—before the CIO established itself in the New Deal coalition—the political elements remained fluid. What had become clear was that organized labor was once more a factor in politics.

Maritime Unions Become Reconciled to Blacks as Fellow Unionists

In waterfront strikes, since 1916, Blacks had been traditionally used as strikebreakers. Asians also had been recruited for this unsavory work. Both groups had been excluded on racial grounds from ILA membership, a practice that was followed also by the Marine Cooks and Stewards Union; consequently, they could be exploited to help break strikes. Exceptions were minor. Blacks never seriously broke the color line either on the part of the union or employers. During the war, Blacks had been admitted to the ILA through the influence of its IWW members, but they lost their jobs during the postwar recession. Many worked the Great Northern and Milwaukee docks during the 1921 strike. From 1921 to 1934, about forty Blacks worked out of the companies' hiring hall. However, even this small number of fruitfully employed Blacks lent stability to the city's Black community, until the full effects of the Depression set in.[1]

As noted above, after the 1921 maritime strike, James Roston, who had organized the Colored Marine Employees Benevolent Association, had contracted with the Alaska Steamship Company and the Pacific Coast Steamship Company to furnish them with Black cooks, stewards, and waiters. Essentially, this was a company union. Grievances were handled personally by Roston himself until his death in 1924. One of the conditions of the contracts required that the employees must refrain from union activity. The two companies contributed to the financial support of the association. In all, an average of 300 Blacks were thusly employed during a year, peaking during the summer at about 500 jobs. Working conditions steadily deteriorated. Graft, gambling, and drinking that often was made compulsory as a condition for taking a job, bred widespread discontent with the association. Nevertheless, during a brief longshore strike in 1932 the CMEBA refused to support it. Instead, its members remained aboard ships to feed strikebreakers. As related above in the section covering the origins of the 1934 maritime strike, by the end of 1933, the company "Blue Book" union had lost control to the revived ILA. This revival lent encouragement to maritime workers all down the line.[2]

When the 1934 strike got underway, some of the CMEBA members were persuaded to support the strike after receiving promises from Marine Cooks and Stewards Union officials that it would open up to Blacks. Strikers threatened to demolish the association offices when it was rumored that its secretary, Harry Duvall, was recruiting strikebreakers. The rumors proved false. Those members who started the strike by working on "scab ships" gradually drifted into the strikers' ranks, with about thirty Blacks joining the MCSU, effectively ending the life of the old association.[3]

Early in the strike, some Blacks acted as strikebreakers along with others, and some University of Washington students, two of whom were killed in a lumber loading accident. But the ILA opened its ranks also to Blacks to minimize their use as strikebreakers. They served on strike committees and did picket line duty. Robert B. Pitts records this as a "turning point in race relations in the longshoremen's union." During the 1936-1937 strike, the employers, being deprived of a source of supply, refrained from recruiting strikebreakers. Pitts reports that of thirty-two new members initiated into the ILWU in 1937, six were Blacks, and that as of 1941, there were about thirty Blacks longshoring in Seattle. The fall-off in maritime activity confined much expansion of the union membership. Pessimistically, Pitts saw "the Negro longshoreman . . . slowly vanishing."[4]

21

Mayor Smith Faces the Clean Government Crowd

The Cincinnatans saw in Mayor Smith's management only a continuation of machine politics, this time by a Republican, no less. They suspected him of being involved in police protection of gambling and the vice operations despite his promise to end the system which Mayor Dore allegedly had installed under his own police chief, L.L. Norton. Smith's chief was W. B. Kirtley, known to be tolerant of conditions that he claimed were beyond his control, given his limited manpower and the intractability of the problem. No administration had done away with police corruption, not even that of Mayor Landes. At least arrests were up, one indication that he was doing better than his predecessor. But, also, Smith's indifference to police corruption was matched by his coolness toward reducing the growing budget deficit. In the mind of the Cincinnatans' councilman, David Lockwood, the two were linked—economies in the police department were not being undertaken because Smith was benefiting from the existing set-up, and there was too much political risk for himself to disturb it.

Lockwood had been stymied in his attempts to investigate purchasing practices, to establish a central garage, to establish a definite tenure for the police chief, freeing the latter from the usual turnover by each new mayor. Almost all mayors seemed to find the chief as an entree to payoffs for the kind of protection police had traditionally provided. These elements became parts of the Cincinnatan platform for the upcoming spring election when three council seats were to be filled. The incumbents, David Levine, Willaim Gaines, and Frank Fitts were given the backing of the Central Labor Council and the newly established Washington Commonwealth Federation. They were combined on a single ticket to prevent the takeover of city government, allegedly, by a "secret organization" (the NOOC) aiming for a "fascist dictatorship". Cincinnatus candidates Arthur Langlie and Frederick Hamley led in the primary, and Mildred Powell, running on the strength of her past presidency of the Parents and Teachers' Association, managed to get the sixth position for the March runoff. She also would receive the endorsement of the NOOC.

This time the NOOC got the support of all three dailies, although the *Star* also endorsed Levine. In an editorial, the *Star* claimed the NOOC no longer aspired to be a state or national party, and that in opposing the proposal of J.D. Ross to purchase the Puget Sound Power and Light Company's city operations, the NOOC nevertheless favored municipal ownership of utilities. In the runoff, Langlie and Hamley led, each with more than 47,000 votes, followed by Powell's 44,333 votes—over 10,000 votes more than Levine's total, less than half his 1932 vote. It was conceded that both he and the conservative Gaines would have run better if they had run as independents. As it turned out, Hamley had also contested Gaines for a short-term seat lasting until the new adminstration took office, so Hamley began his councilmanic work immediately. He was quickly joined by Langlie when Fitts resigned instead of remaining as a "dark horse" until June. Fitts recommended Langlie to fill his vacancy, and the Council concurred. This turn of events placed the three Cincinnatans in a position to begin implementing their program at once.[1]

By dividing responsibilities among them, it was hoped the Council could present the Mayor in June with a budget reduction proposal that he could not override with a veto (six votes were needed). Lockwood resumed the framing of a central purchasing ordinance, a plan for a central garage, and was assigned the job of examining the lighting department's condition in view of Ross's merger proposal. Hamley was assigned the street railway problem; Langlie was given the police department. However, Hamley really took the lead in investigating the police department, meeting with two men on April 11 who informed him that $275,000 was collected in graft annually and divided among the police and public officials. In terms of numbers he was informed that 900 prostitutes were managed by houses that paid $5.00 monthly per woman; and that there were 221 "bootlegging joints". Sheriff Bannick, a former Seattle police chief himself, told Hamley how detectives could be shifted to police duty, and of the obsolescence of many precinct stations. In early May, Chief Kirtley seemed even to agree in general with Bannick's suggestions. Hamley followed up these discussions by doing his own sleuthing, in which he would later engage Lockwood, Langlie, other Cincinnatans, and even Powell.[2]

After the Council met with all department heads and learned that none would offer cuts, each member was assigned a department for investigation to see for themselves. By a 5 to 4 vote, a budget was passed, cutting out 120 positions, mainly in the police and fire departments and in the public schools. Mayor Smith vetoed the budget May 25, promising one of his own soon. With this in mind, he met with Langlie and Hamley on the 29th, promising unspecified reductions, telling them he did not want the NOOC to "pick it to pieces". Hamley, in his diary, reported that Smith was under the impression that he had been elected as a "spender" not as an economizer—Dore had been the "economy mayor".[3]

When the new Council met on June 3, the veto was sustained because of the decisive vote of Powell who objected to the cuts in the public schools program. Somewhat sarcastically, Hamley recorded that Bertha Landes "shook her hands and kissed Mrs. Powell [indicating who was] the force behind the throne." Powell, in the future, would normally follow Hamley's cue—at least in the view of Hamley, but on schools she definitely had her own commitment. For his part, in opposing the proposed budget cuts Councilman Scavotto told a Municipal League audience that the state had contributed only $548,000 of an expected $1 million from gasoline and liquor excise taxes, and that the drop in the assessed valuation of property, when combined with the 40-mill tax limit, reduced revenue from that source by another $75,000. He tallied a revenue loss of $1,125,000 before ending his presentation, but not before reminding listeners that the City had reduced operating costs by 54% during the past five years. However, the Cincinnatans insisted more cuts could be made and turned their focus on the police department, vulnerable because of its notoriety. Budget matters would not be returned to until September.[4]

A *P-I* editorial accused Smith of running a "wide open"

city, for being unwilling to make cuts in departments controlled by his office, and for seeking "the favor of the powerful political machine of the police department." Gambling establishments had taken on fresh life after Smith's election, moving uptown with full confidence in being protected. As noted above, Hamley's sources had reported that an estimated $275,000 in graft was collected annually from the operations of 400 slot machines, 900 prostitutes, and 221 bootlegging businesses (liquor, wine, and beer could not legally be purchased on Sundays). The *Argus* looked back to the days of Hiram Gill for a comparable situation. Admiral T.T. Craven, Commandant of the Thirteenth Naval District, warned that he would place Seattle off-limits, unless the City officials acted. Sharing this view were two organizations which joined to work closely with the Cincinnatans in developing evidence to support reforms in the police department. One was the Clean Government League (CGL), headed by Julius Baldwin. The other organization was the Morals Committee of the Council of Churches, chaired by Dr. Walter Hiltner. In their view, expected reforms would simultaneously reduce City expenses and improve the moral climate of the city.[5]

Reinforcing this vice information from the political and social elite were reports by the district inhabitants and sojourners. The *Philippine-American Chronicle* in its first number carried the headline: "$1,000,000 Payroll Goes to Chinese Gambling Syndicate". The accompanying articles claimed the Chinese "dens" operate openly. In a petition sent to Mayor Smith and the City Council it was charged: "For 25 years [the] Chinese Gambling Syndicate has been the scourge of Chinatown. [Closing down] the 'small fry' overlooked the two largest and up-to-date gambling establishments on the Pacific Coast." They were identified: one was between 669 and 673 King Street; the other, at 221 Washington Street, "is almost a stone's throw from the Police Department, [and can] accommodate from 100 to 300 patrons"—its name, "Tin Yee Society". Editor Frank Alonzo was concerned about the annual fleecing of Filipino cannery workers returning from Alaska, contending that 65% of their earnings were lost to the whole range of these vice operators. He claimed there were 2,000 Filipino residents, and "over 2,000 Filipino lads who are employed in the farms, [a] majority [of whom are] students . . . [who] lose 55% of their payroll."[6]

Late in June, Rev. U.G. Murphy of the CGL presented his evidence to Langlie, but Langlie, upon consulting with the *P-I*'s city hall reporter, Carl Cooper, was persuaded to get more evidence. Cooper suggested that they first determine whether the operations were wide open and above ground. The Cincinnatans and the two organizations had their work cut out for them, but they stuck to it by "slumming" to collect evidence. Soon, having decided they had enough solid evidence, Hamley scheduled hearings before his Efficiency Committee beginning July 10.[7]

Chief Kirtley was first to testify, outlining the organizational structure of his department, and startlingly admitting that no written reports had been made of licensed card room operations, although regular inspections were routine. He admitted that a "liberal construction" of the ordinances was the rule, and that he opposed a "fanatical enforcement of the laws." But, also, access to the suspected gambling spots and "resorts" was difficult due to barred doors, the destruction of which took so much time that patrons and evidence had vanished by the time entrance was gained. Kirtley reported that "large property owners" and "pillars of the church" urged that their renters remain open without abatement "so that they could take enough revenue to pay taxes." Then the chief complained about the endless strikes to which he had had to divert men: the oil tanker strike in January, one by government workers, the timber workers that shut down a dozen mills, and the Teamsters' strike against the Northwest Brewery Company which resulted in the shooting death of one Teamster. He pointed to more strikes to come after the garment workers' strike ends. Altogether, a dismal picture, not offering the Cincinnatans much hope in cutting back the police department.[8]

The chief, when given names and addresses of wide open operations, had done nothing toward closing them down. This so provoked the Cincinnatans that during the hearings, upon receiving word of a wide open operation at Battersby and Smith's card room (near First Avenue and Madison), they charged out of the hearing room with Kirtley in tow. The chief, faced with the evidence, ordered the trashing of the place, in the course of which money was confiscated, but to Hamley's dismay, it never reached the department to be held as evidence.[9]

While the hearings went well, little of concrete reform resulted, except the passing of an ordinance establishing a five-year term for the police chief, ostensibly to take the department out of politics. The Cincinnatans succeeded in January in making staff cuts of sixty positions, and the elimination of three precinct stations, but both positions and stations were soon restored. As to closing down gambling and vice operations, token raids and arrests were made, followed quickly by resumption of operations. Adding to their discouragement, County Prosecuting Attorney Warren Magnuson told only of futility in ever being able to close down the city.[10]

As Mayor Smith headed into the 1936 election, he found himself weakened by desertion of the church-goers for his ineffectiveness in dealing with the vice rackets. They even suspected his direct involvement in the corruption. Also, once Councilman Langlie announced his candidacy, the business groups largely deserted to Langlie. Both of these constituencies had been his key support in the 1934 race against John Dore. Now Dore was back, courting the labor vote, in particular, that of the AFL unions. However, the Teamsters supported Smith in the primary because of his militant actions against their rival maritime unions during the 1934 waterfront strike. The Washington Commonwealth Federation produced Representative Tom Smith as its candidate. All three of Langlie's opponents portrayed him as the candidate of a "secret society", and both Dore's and Smith's supporters tried to link Langlie with fascism, for proclaiming his endorsement by Cincinnatus. Yet the Municipal League endorsed him, as well as the two Cincinnatus candidates for city council, Carlos Zener and Albert Kelley. Langlie won the primary with 21,290 votes against Dore's 15,234—a bare 134 votes more than Smith's.[11]

Dave Beck now began to figure in the campaign. Through his emissary, George Vanderveer, he invited Langlie to pay a visit to discuss the election. Langlie indicated his own office was open from 4:00 to 5:00 in the afternoon. Given this rebuff, and knowing that Dore was seeking and needed labor support, Beck then swung his following to Dore. Tom Smith, with his 14,000 votes, and in part dissuaded by Beck, rejected a move to run as a sticker candidate. This meant that Dore would inherit those votes. Mayor Smith then called upon his backers to support Langlie. Dore next began counteracting his economizing misdeeds of 1932-1934—when he had cut the City's employment rolls and administered wage cuts—by assuring City employees there would be no wage cuts, and that each City unit under his control could elect its own department head. In addition, he promised to appoint Beck's right-hand man, Frank Brewster, as civil service commissioner, to name a Black "to represent the colored people" on the commission, retention of J.D. Ross, and to re-appoint Norton as police chief. The Council race focused upon the labor candidates, Robert Harlin and David Levine, in battle with Zener and Kelley. In the closing days of the campaign, Cincinnatus came in for heightened attack for being secretive and fascist. The campaign concluded with a 90-minute oration by Dore at the Eagles Auditorium which the *Argus* estimated to cost the Cincinnatus candidates more than the votes by which they lost. Dore defeated Langlie, 53,844 to 46,898, while Harlin, Levine, and Frank Laube won the council seats. Langlie even lost in Ballard by 1,730 votes, despite its preponderent Scandinavian composition—a vote that Langlie assumed was his. Also, all five charter amendments passed. One displayed some contempt for the results of the summer's police department investigation—the police force was restored at 571 men, along with the three abolished precinct stations.[12]

Dore could not resist bragging: "I had Democrats and Republicans working for me. I had the small businessmen, and the sportsmen, and 95 per cent of the unemployed and I had union labor and the city employees. All city employees . . . This election means the end of fascist, semi-military organizations and of dictatorship in Seattle . . . ." Instead, Dore would proceed to establish his own boss-version through his alliance with Dave Beck to whom he attributed his victory: "I say I am going to pay back my debt to Dave Beck and the teamsters in the next two years regardless of what happens."[13]

22

The Rise of Dave Beck and the Teamsters

> Certain it is that Dave Beck has warm friends among Seattle bankers and industrialists, some of whom were publicly denouncing the head of the teamsters' union only a year ago . . . The value of Dave Beck's consolidating his political position with employers is apparent.
>
> "The Stroller", in *The Argus*, 10 April, 1937.

In the account of the 1934 longshore strike the prominent role played by Dave Beck was noted. In it he was closely allied with Joe Ryan and the national AFL leadership in protecting the ILA leadership against a rank-and-file uprising led by Harry Bridges. Governor Martin had even sent Beck to a mediation conference in San Francisco as his representative. This early in the New Deal period, Martin had recognized that unionization probably was inevitable, and that, if he had to choose the kind with which he could comfortably ally politically, Beck's model was preferable. A look at its origins is instructive.

After the apparent victory of the truck owners over Local 174 of the Teamsters Union, in May 1914—ending a year-long strike—the Seattle union soon gained contracts with many of the trucking firms that had been kept in line by the Employers' Association during the strike. By the end of 1916, Local 174 had largely unionized the trucking business in the city. Part of the future organizing successes of the union can be attributed to the technological revolution occurring in the teamstering trades and the recognition of its potential consequences by the Seattle Teamster union leadership. Horse-drawn vehicles were being displaced by motor-driven ones. During the war a special Auto Drivers Local 234 was formed in recognition of this change; it was portentous. So, too, was the start of long-haul operations between Seattle and Portland which began when an industrial gas manufacturer in Seattle needed to guarantee regular shipping of its product to Portland. Arrangements were made with a local trucking firm, the already-unionized Herd Transfer Company. This example helped set a pattern for the future as both motorized equipment and roads were steadily improved. Other specialized locals were spun off Local 174, thereby providing the basis for a joint council of teamsters to coordinate their activities—Joint Council No. 28 was born.

Strategically, the teamstering trades occupied the key position in the labor movement because road transportation was essential at the local level in moving commodities to market within the city and its environs. The initiation of over-the-road hauling added further potential to the Teamsters, should the leadership recognize it. This strategic position provided untold opportunities for an aggressive leadership that was willing to engage in craft jurisdictional battles and in selectively organizing the unorganized. To win jurisdictional claims meant that the AFL hierarchy had to be cultivated, while organizing the unorganized carried both the extension of Teamster jurisdiction into trades that seemed but extensions of the teamstering trades, warehousing, for example, and helping established crafts extend their own controls. The latter efforts won allies.[1]

Facilitating entry into trucking was the relatively slight capital outlay. Also, credit often was easily negotiated with truck manufacturers and supply companies. Thus, owner-operators became common in the trade. Many of these owner-operators lived in Seattle and they took on much of the over-the-road hauling, sometimes independently, sometimes carrying cargo of a local drayage company. Introduction of the pneumatic tire, replacing the solid-rubber tire, reinforced this trend, making possible longer distance hauling while including a range of more fragile commodities. As business expanded these operators, who usually had been union members, hired drivers to operate the additional trucks. Seattle's Teamster catalyst, Local 174, seized the opportunity and actively organized these long-haul drivers ("line drivers"). And, unlike the Teamsters in the Bay Area who disowned the line drivers, the Teamsters in Seattle established complementary relations between them and the drayage employees, one element of which was providing employment for these local drivers in over-the-road driving when employment in the city slackened.

Into this setting stepped Dave Beck after the General Strike of 1919. He had been a charter member of the Laundry and Dye Workers Local 566 when it was established in 1917. Returning after the war as a laundry driver, and working on the standard commission basis while buying his truck on easy credit, he became active in the union. His popularity grew from his lively participation in meetings of Joint Council No. 28, leading to his election as its president in 1923. A reorganization of the Seattle Teamsters had been ordered in 1919 when the international leadership discovered that the Seattle Teamsters had violated the union's constitutional prohibition against formation of intermediate bodies above the Joint Council level when it had organized a Puget Sound District Council.[2]

As Joint Council No. 28's president, Beck began repeating the earlier effort because of its inherent tactical logic, if the union was to grow. Small outlying locals were invited to attend Joint Council meetings. Since the Joint Council had the staff and experience that the outlying locals could not afford, the latter drew upon this resource in their organizing efforts. Tactically, for Beck, this expansion strengthened his position when dealing with Seattle firms that had branches outside Seattle, for he insisted that they be unionized throughout their chain or be struck in Seattle. They usually capitulated.

On this basis, the Seattle Joint Council of Teamsters continued to flourish throughout the 1920s while other unions languished. His influence spread over the Teamsters throughout the state. Having larger objectives in mind in the early 1930s, Beck, after being denied entry into Portland by the national Teamster office, proceeded irrepressibly to have the Seattle Joint Council fund his organizing drive in that city. He succeeded there, getting the Portland Joint Council 37 to follow the pattern that he had established in Washington. It would not be long before he would control the Teamsters in all of the western states, and become the dominating force in the AFL in the West.[3]

Within Seattle, Beck had established his control of the Central Labor Council by 1925. With this control there also ended the long-time espousal of industrial unionism by the Council—along with the ejection of known Communists from the SCLC. Beck, through his speeches and in his contract negotiations, became recognized for sharing the profit goals of firms with which he negotiated. If they were to remain profitable and thereby assure employment, competition had to be switched from the standard employer tactic of cutting wages and ignoring working conditions to accepting uniformity in these matters throughout any given product line. Beck gained the support of the State Federation of Labor's president, William Short, who shared these views; Beck's rise to power meant also the decline of James Duncan's—Duncan had been Short's nemesis for being the leader of the industrial unionist forces in the SCLC. Beck also took pride in avoiding strikes, preferring to employ tactics of the business world, in which the goal for any one firm is to monopolize the market for its product line or, failing that, to seek a sharing agreement that would at least limit the competition.[4]

Local 174 had won a renewal of its contract with the Truck Owners' Association in May 1925 by means of arbitration after the TOA had refused to negotiate. A strike had been ordered for May 11. In this same May, the Laundry Owners' Association had refused to negotiate with Beck's Local 566 which was negotiating for both inside and outside laundry workers. Although it took time, Beck emerged victorious in 1926 over one of this most intransigent of open shop groups. As it was Mayor Edwin Brown who had been instrumental in getting the TOA to agree to arbitration in May 1925, it probably was Beck in 1926 who got the mayor, along with the Reverend Mark Matthews, and A.G. Bixby of the *Times*, to pressure the LOA also to agree to arbitration. What emerged in 1926 was a three-year union shop agreement for the outside workers and a four-year one for the inside workers, plus wage increases for each. That the LOA seemed to cave in to these pressures alone is not fully credible, given its past record as a leader in the open shop movement. What seems likely is that Beck had agreed to impair the competitiveness of the Central Labor Council's laundry, the Mutual Laundry, in exchange. The *Vanguard*, in 1931, accused the "Beck clique" of trying to break the Mutual, pointing to its condition as always being on the "verge of bankruptcy". Since removal of two of the clique for allegedly leaking customer information to other laundries, the Mutual's efficiency had improved. Beck also was accused of diverting business away from Mutual. When the SCLC blacklisted the firm, it was viewed as an attempt to restore control to Beck's men. His threat of a strike against the laundry tends to support this contention. The laundry's last manager was Jay Eckert, a Teamster. It closed down in 1932.[5]

When Prohibition was abolished in the 1932 general election, beer could once again be manufactured. This meant also the revival of the Brewery Workers Union, an industrial union. They had claimed jurisdiction over the beer truck drivers before Prohibition when the Teamsters had been weak. According to Jonathan Dembo, only in Washington did the Brewery Workers encounter opposition to their reassertion of jurisdiction. The AFL's executive council had given jurisdiction, in May 1933, to the Teamsters, but Teamster president Dan Tobin would not fund Joint Council No. 28's organizational drive. Beck, therefore, turned to his own resources, first getting the backing of the SCLC. Then he notified all brewery heads who were planning to resume production in the state that the Teamsters had jurisdiction over their drivers. A boycott of Brewery Workers-produced beer followed. In July, he induced the WSFL to expel the Brewery Workers from the federation. The Brewery Workers counter-boycotted. Beck then supplied inside workers to the plants being struck by the Brewery Workers. Consequently, the Teamsters wound up controlling the inside brewery workers, as well as the drivers. This contest would continue through 1937 when the Teamsters would not only emerge victorious, but the state's breweries would wind up being protected from an invasion of their market by California and Midwest beer produced by the Brewery Workers.[6]

The *Argus* kept track of Beck's rise to power, disliking his "dictatorial" methods of running the Teamsters and his use of the union's tactical position in organizing other trades. It frequently commented on the warm welcome extended to him by various industrialists and bankers, particularly after the 1934 ILA strike when his conservative potential was demonstrated. Indicative of his method—as already noted with the brewery workers—was his attempt to gain recognition for the Produce Drivers, Salesmen, and Helpers Union, Local 195, in August 1935. Although Beck disclaimed any price fixing attempt, Jack Weston, president of the Produce Merchants' Association contended that besides recognition, Beck wanted a price committee established to oversee a price schedule modeled upon that established for the cleaning and dyeing business. In the 1936 Auto Mechanics Union strike, in which the Teamsters took control, there was offered the bait of helping the employers to suppress "chiselling competition", a tactic which, the *Argus* noted, had been used in other lines.[7]

As tensions over industrial versus craft unionism grew—paralleled by its personification as "Beck vs. Bridges"—Beck became a featured speaker before business groups, Cincinnatus, the Municipal League, the American Legion, and community clubs. Repeatedly he linked the rise of industrial unions and the Committee for Industrial Organization with radicalism and communism, a theme that had played well during the "Wobbly horrors" only fifteen years ago. To the conservatively inclined, Beck's version of unionization seemed far preferable to that represented by Harry Bridges. Interestingly, the *Argus* was so appalled by the tactics employed by Beck and his rise to power that it became sympathetic to his more "democratic" opposition.[8]

With the rise of the Seattle Teamsters in the background, with signs of rank-and-file unrest within established trade jurisdictions, with the demonstrated power of the organized unemployed as it became allied with worker unrest, with the desertion of progressive Republicans into the Democratic Party, and with the election of many pro-labor legislators, Governor Martin was forced to appease these elements if he intended to stay in power. Indicative of his policy was his veto in the regular 1933 legislative session of a workmen's compensation bill (HB 268) that would have practically eliminated the existing law, and the signing of an alternate bill (HB 35) favored by labor. This action was followed during the special legislative session of 1933-1934 by his signing an anti-injunction bill that outlawed the Yellow-Dog contract and permitted peaceful picketing (HB 28). Another bill established a State Relief Commission with representation of the State Federation of Labor on it. The effect of the latter was to enable WSFL president James Taylor to lobby successfully for payment of union scales in work relief projects, thereby countering criticism that work relief represented a form of "forced labor". Other pro-labor legislation was passed and signed that either had been vetoed successively by Governor Hartley, or had been bottled up by the Republican-controlled legislature. Governor Martin, by nature conservative, found it congenial to ally with the more conservative elements that lay behind the Democratic victory of 1932. Even they supported the pro-labor legislation just referred to.[9]

There is a distinct contrast between the period when earlier unionization reached its peak during World War I and the period being covered here. In the former period, organized labor had relatively little political influence. Indeed the AFL leadership vowed not to authorize strikes during the war—although major strikes in Seattle did occur. With election of Franklin Roosevelt and the semi-protection of collective bargaining by the federal government under Section 7(a) of the NRA, organized labor became politicized once again. Failure to deal with mass unemployment led the unemployed to organize themselves—dramatically in Seattle. These organized unemployed provided an essential spark to the unionization that gathered flame from 1933 on. Many of them were drawn into nascent industrial unions forming in the lumbering industry and along the waterfront. Resistance of the national AFL leadership to meet this challenge led to the rise of the Congress of Industrial Organizations when AFL leadership consistently ruled against its industrial union advocates, represented by the AFL's Committee for Industrial Organization, in jurisdictional disputes. Locally, the *P-I* strike of 1936 and the confrontation between the Teamsters and the ILA over jurisdiction of warehousemen in 1936-1937 portray this interweaving of unionization and local politics.[10]

Not only did the Newspaper Guild emerge victorious, but Beck advanced his position to one of near-impregnability as a result of his libel suits against the *Times* and *P-I* and two of the radio stations. Beck won an out-of-court settlement of a mere $25,000, but circumstantial evidence compiled by William Ames and Roger Simpson, and an article in *Time* magazine for November 29, 1948, point to the fact that no criticism of Beck subsequently appeared in these newspapers. Ames and Simpson report: "The *Times*'s relationship to Beck changed considerably following the 1936 strike . . . Following the strike and the libel suit, no locally written criticism, either editorial or letters to the editor was run between 1937 and 1957." As to the *P-I*, it did run a guest editorial in 1937 attacking Beck. No columns of Westbrook Pegler were run after 1937 that attacked Beck. This absence of normal criticism undoubtedly contributed to Beck's steady accretion of power and respect in the years ahead.[11]

23

The 1936 *P-I* Strike—Teamsters and Maritime Unions in Uneasy Embrace

> [Every time Clarence Blethen] sees a guild member walk past his plant he boosts the salaries of the editorial workers, who are now getting much higher than the guild scale provides.
>
> "The Stroller", in *The Argus*, 19 June, 1937

In August 1936, when the *P-I* fired, for union activity, two of its veteran staffers, photographer Frank Lynch and relatively well-paid columnist Everhardt Armstrong, it was almost without precedent. These men were of the editorial staff, and that staff had never been organized on any newspaper prior to founding of the American Newspaper Guild in December 1933 under the inspiration of Heywood Broun. Earlier, in August, he had warned in his *New York World-Telegram* column that the American Newspaper Publishers' Association was planning to classify reporters and editorial staff as professionals to avoid their inclusion as candidates for unionization in any industry code the publishers might draw up under the NRA.

The Guild had taken its first strike action against the *Newark Ledger* in November 1934, when its owner proclaimed his open hostility to its Guild unit by threatening to fire 50% of his staff after the unit tried to open negotiations. An eighteen-month long strike was settled in the courts against the Guild. At that time, the case of Dean Jennings was pending before the National Labor Relations Board—he had been fired from Hearst's *San Francisco Call-Bulletin* staff for attending a Guild convention. Fearing the power of newspaper publishers, President Roosevelt had intervened by ordering the transfer of the case to the NRA industry code authority which the publishers controlled. Not until August 1935 was a Guild contract signed with a major newspaper publisher, one who was sympathetic to the Guild, in the first place. As to the ANG leadership, it wanted to avoid strikes, particularly against any one of the newspaper chains like that of Hearst or Roy Howard's Scripps-Howard group. The Guild was too weak yet, either for any major confrontation, or to command the kind of respect that FDR seemed to require.[1]

Hearst's attitude toward unions had been made clear in Seattle eleven years earlier, in 1924-1925, when he had tried to break the ultra-conservative Typographers Union, Local 202, but failed. At that time both the *Times* and *Star* had renewed their contracts with the union in March 1924, but the *P-I* held out, despite the tradition of all three signing uniform contracts. After the strike began on May 30, the *P-I* continued publishing by drawing upon non-union typographers trained at the trade school of the Northwest Publishers Association in Spokane. For its part, the union staged an effective boycott, including a "house-to-house" campaign over western Washington to discourage purchase of the *P-I*, and to discourage advertising in it. Not until both parties wearied of achieving their respective goals, was a union shop agreement signed July 24, 1925. However, the union had to accept for membership all those strike-breakers whom the *P-I* had hired during the strike.[2]

Another attempt to break the Typographers Union was made in 1933, this time by all three dailies. The union had been operating on the basis of a 1926 wage scale, and while it accepted a 10% cut, it balked at the demand to abolish seniority rules that had been in effect for thirty-three years. To spread the work, for the past two years, the typographers had been working five-day, thirty-hour weeks; the publishers wanted to reinstate the six-day week. The lockout strategy was coordinated by a Hearst official from San Francisco. Trainees were brought in from Spokane, were paid $9.00 per day, were housed in comfortable hotels in the city, and were protected by "plug-uglies". The lockout lasted for three and one-half weeks, when federal mediator Ernst Marsh, a former president of the Washington State Federation of Labor, succeeded in getting a settlement of sorts. The typographers conceded the "right of priority" on the reserve list, took a 10% pay cut, but retained the five-day week.[3]

Not until Terry Pettus organized a Guild chapter among the *Tacoma Ledger* reporters in November 1935 was the ANG represented in the Northwest. Pettus was then urged by the ANG's national officers to establish a Seattle chapter. From such a base they would then be in a better position to protect members and to move ahead on organizing other chapters. By the time Pettus finally was able to set up a meeting in February with four prospects representing the three dailies, a strike was already in progress against a Hearst newspaper, the *Wisconsin* in Milwaukee. Only the *P-I*'s Forrest Williams attended this first meeting. With the resources of the ANG committed to the Milwaukee strike, the prospect for organizing in Seattle seemed bleak because the probability was high that invitations to negotiate would be rejected outright by any of the three dailies. This kind of impass normally leads to strike action; consequently, timidity marked organizing efforts. However, due to Hearst's widely unpopular tirades against FDR, the *P-I* attracted more attention than either the *Times* or *Star*. This tattoo, rained on FDR, was combined with Hearst's irresponsible red-baiting of many popular figures, and his running a series on the penetration by communism in practically all facets of American life, while praising fascism.[4]

No one from the *Times* had signed with the Guild, while two key people from the *Star* had joined—city editor Charles Daggett, and Fred d'Avila. At the *P-I*, only about a half-dozen had signed up by April, 1936. A catalyst at the *P-I* was then injected, a Hearst "efficiency expert", Bart Guild (that's his real name). He began stirring up resentment against the management by his stealing by-lines from columnists and making his nuisance value felt. In May came a turning point with the reinstatement of ANG chapter chairman, Rex Kelly, to his position on the *Tacoma Times*, and the issuance of a charter to the Seattle group on May 12. Despite attempts to keep the latter news secret for fear of reprisals against members should they become known, the *P-I* learned of the charter from the ANG's *Guild Reporter*. In it, the *P-I* was pictured as intimidating and pressuring its employees. Where was this information coming from?[5]

Next, the *P-I*'s middle management began quizzing those suspected of Guild membership. First to admit it was photographer Jack Heise who quickly was denied any prospect of advancement in the Hearst organization. This admission was followed by that of photography department head, Frank (Slim) Lynch, then, of his colleague Art French. All three were told that Hearst would not tolerate Guild members for long. Without advance notice, Lynch was demoted, replaced as manager by Samuel Sansone who then proceeded to build a case against Lynch, sufficient to sustain his firing. It came on July 6.

Lynch proceeded to the Labor Temple to get sympathy, and was disappointed until he talked with Ed Weston, business agent for the Boilermakers Union and a leftist. Immediately, Weston drafted a resolution with the apolitical Lynch's help to have the Central Labor Council vote whether to request an answer from the *P-I* as to why it should not be placed on the unfair list. The left-wing metal trades section of the CLC sponsored the resolution, presenting it at the July 8 CLC meeting, where the right-wing Teamsters, surprisingly, supported it. A committee was then appointed to seek Lynch's reinstatement and to advise the Guild on how to handle the negotiations from here on. The NLRB was then notified. It in turn requested an explanation from *P-I* publisher, Vaughn Tanner.

While these steps were being taken, drama editor Everhardt Armstrong took over Lynch's job as chief Guild recruiter. He quickly came under management scrutiny. Sharp exchanges followed, then he was fired on July 16. On that day, while the Washington State Federation of Labor convention was in session, evidence of the firings was laid before it. On Beck's motion a committee was appointed to seek a settlement, conditioned upon an agreement that the Guild would not call a strike while negotiations were proceeding—the Guild, anxious as it was to call a strike, would never have been able to carry a strike anyway, given the few activists among them (twenty-two at that time) and the lack of any resources. Nevertheless, the Guild kept pressing for a vote to put the *P-I* on the unfair list—tantamount to calling a strike in this case. The co-publishers, Tanner and Charles Lindeman, refused a request to meet with the Guild committee.

Stalling proceedings within the CLC was uncertainty over the role the Typographers might play in event of a strike—in Milwaukee they had crossed the picket line. When the Typographers protested that they had a contract the representative of the Inland Boatmen's Union claimed they too had one, that they were an industrial union, and would not carry the newsprint needed. In the view of strike historians Ames and Simpson, the

IBU statement challenged Beck to bring the Teamsters to support strike action, inasmuch as these developments transpired against the backdrop of the overall industrial versus craft union contest, wherein Beck was forced to respond each time to the initiative of the industrial unionists.

Hearst's chief labor relations man, Harvey Kelly, then proceeded to blame Beck for these developments, charging him with planning to encircle the plant with pickets. He sought out the heads of the international officers of the printing trades unions, trying to get them to persuade Beck not to block entry of their men to the plant. The *P-I* began preparations for a strike, hauling in supplies of newsprint into a refurbished basement area, and importing company guards. Arrival of the latter at a downtown hotel brought them attention from the Seattle police, who warned them not to start anything—Mayor Dore's first entry on the scene, now that Beck had declared where he stood.[6]

The strike began inauspiciously, on August 13, with about twenty uneasy pickets parading helplessly outside the *P-I* as the staff routinely passed by them to their work inside. This picture soon changed as idle longshoremen, who had been alerted to the possibility that they might be called upon for picket duty, marched up from the waterfront. To their numbers were added those who were mobilized at the nearby Labor Temple. Absent before noon were the Teamsters. Then came word that Harold Hiatt was inside on guard duty. In 1935 he had murdered a teamster during a strike of the Northwest Brewery Company, and although he had been convicted of manslaughter, the state Supreme Court had just overturned his conviction. This news galvanized the Teamsters. The *P-I* was quickly encircled. Hiatt boldly, but foolishly, stepped outside and was attacked by vengeful teamsters while the police stood idly by. What had become apparent was that the Guild strikers had not only the full support of Seattle's organized labor, but that the police were not about to be used to help break the strike. Mayor Dore had proclaimed to the WSFL convention only the month before that he was " . . . going to pay back my debt to Dave Beck and the Teamsters in the next two years regardless of what happens." Dore even joined the pickets in gay comraderie, just to make his point.[7]

With the picket line so effective in preventing entry to the *P-I* building, and the police keeping hands-off, the publishers decided to seek cooperation of the *Times*, hoping to have the *P-I* published by its printers. C.B. Blethen was willing, but when he ordered his typographers to work overtime to set the *P-I*'s type, the Typographers Union's executive committee ordered the *Times* typographers off the job, since the contract permitted the union to specify who could do the work. When word got out that the *P-I* was arranging to print elsewhere, picket lines were set up around both the *Times* and *Star* plants. With these actions the worrisome problem of what the typographers might do was settled—they were now part of the strike.[8]

Before the end of this first day there was more violence, and for the first time in 69 years the *P-I* was not published. Blethen responded by attacking Beck, accusing him of trying to establish a labor dictatorship, of banditry, of ending constitutional government, and of blocking the city's progress by discouraging investment as a result of his antics. These accusations would come to haunt Blethen after the strike ended, for Beck filed a libel suit on August 25 against both the *Times* and *P-I*.[9]

Details of the strike's progress are fully covered in the account by Ames and Simpson, including Hearst's threat to move from the city, to which Dore said good riddance. A Pro-America march of women to Olympia, led by Mrs. Edwin Selvin, sought Governor Martin's authorization for National Guard intervention. A counter-march quickly followed by Guild women supporters led by Senator Mary Farquharson—promoted by a Martin aide in order to place the governor in a position where he could even-handedly profess neutrality.

The Hearst forces underestimated the widespread hostility the publisher had generated. The thought that he might move out even inspired the idea of publishing another labor daily. What seems clear to Ames and Simpson is that Hearst was playing for time, waiting for the November general election results, hoping for a Landon victory, in the aftermath of which he expected to whip the Guild.

When AFL president William Green, who was unsympathetic to the Guild, sought an early settlement by getting the international presidents of the printing trades unions to order their men back to work, their members in Seattle remained recalcitrant, and Beck told Green to hold off until after the election. Instead, Green called a meeting of the AFL Executive Council for a meeting with the printing trades leaders and Kelly. What emerged on October 24 was a proposal that avoided Guild recognition. Upon its receipt in Seattle, opposition telegrams were sent off to Green, along with a resolution from the Central Labor Council urging Green to wait for the election results. Heywood Broun charged the AFL Executive Committee of working " . . .

hand in glove with the Hearst management in an effort to compel acceptance of defeat in the Seattle strike."[10]

An earlier arbitration recommendation by Dore had been rejected by Hearst, but now, to gain time, the Guild, acting partly on Beck's advice, sent Hearst an offer to arbitrate on October 29. With the election only four days away, no answer was received. After the Roosevelt landslide victory, an end came in sight, made even clearer to Hearst when he was informed that he was facing a financial crisis. Yet, an agreement worked out by Beck and another Hearst negotiator was rejected by the *P-I* publishers, thereby returning Kelly as chief negotiator. Lindeman was instructed to meet with the Guild, and upon receiving the go-ahead from Hearst himself, agreement was finally reached. Lindeman agreed to recognize the Guild as bargaining agent. All striking employees were to return without discrimination against them. A forty-hour, six-day week would be installed until March 1, 1937. Wage scales would be in line with the standard set in Milwaukee. And the cases of Lynch and Armstrong were to continue before the NLRB. Armstrong would die before an award was given. The *P-I* resumed publication on November 29.[11]

24

Governor Martin's Unwanted Left-Wing

Seattle's Unemployed Citizens' League had been the catalyst for mobilizing the state's political reform forces—originally, in response to the failure of government at all levels to recognize that unemployment had become a permanent feature of the capitalist economy, so long as it remained the plaything of unconstrained market forces. The UCL's strength was centered in the eastern Puget Sound counties of Pierce, King, Snohomish, and Whatcom. After the state took over the relief program in early 1933, the political influence of the UCL waned and it was displaced by the more broadly based Commonwealth Builders, Inc. (CBI) in 1934. Both the UCL and CBI had been hostile to the Communist Party (CP). Each in turn did its utmost to resist efforts of the CP to infiltrate its membership and take control, but finally the CP did get control of the UCL. While the CBI needed a mass base if its programs were to be legislated, the CP shared that same aspiration. Each appealed to much the same disillusioned citizenry, although the CBI attracted the more moderate elements seeking socio-economic reform by meliorative political means. Suspicion persisted that the CP did not share this political stance, except as an ephemeral measure inspired by opportunism. The CBI might, for example, be seen by observers as but a stepping stone to political power for the CP. The CBI hoped, for its part, to get the now-revitalized Democratic party to adopt its platform. The CP was suspected of aiming to control first the

CBI, then its successor organization, the Washington Commonwealth Federation (WCF). These elements would be played out in the few years to come chiefly over whose responsibility it was to deal with mass unemployment and in developing relief measures to address its consequences.

Measures of the Martin administration tended increasingly to place responsibility upon the individual and family because the state's finances could not provide remedy without appropriate taxes. By the end of Martin's administration one is legitimately led to question whether Martin and Charles Ernst ever abandoned the poor law mentality in dealing with chronic mass unemployment and relief from its consequences. The new 40-mill property tax limit confined local property taxes to a maximum of 15-mills thereby overburdening other forms of taxation, particularly after the state Supreme Court ruled the graduated income tax unconstitutional in 1933. The CBI, then the WCF, insisted that the responsibility lay beyond the control and capacity of the individual and family, and that mass unemployment was an inherent malaise of the capitalist system for which the supporting government apparatus bore responsibility. The CBI and WCF, consequently, pushed for relief measures that more directly addressed the problems of unrelieved mass poverty. That "production-for-use"—as a concept—could absorb so much serious attention on the part of the liberal-left is a measure of discouragement being widely felt with the New Deal policies at this early stage. That it would take the form of a ballot initiative as late as 1936 points to the pervasiveness of that disenchantment. By then it surely was fanciful; and as a propaganda ploy against capitalism there was no chance that it could be taken seriously.[1]

The CBI concentrated on the fall 1934 election in which candidates were to run for state offices, for a United States senate seat, and for congressional offices. Nevertheless, the CBI's Seattle orientation was inevitable—of its 12 local units in October, 11 were in Seattle, the twelfth just across the lake in Kirkland. In August, the CBI's elected officers agreed on a platform, and began publishing the *Washington Commonwealth Builder*. Its executive secretary, Howard Costigan, launched a series of radio talks.[2]

The CBI's platform was drafted by Costigan, Dean Richard Tyler, and the recently defeated gubernatorial candidate, Lewis Schwellenbach. That it bore the imprint of the UCL and the Technocrats is evident. Its centerpiece was a production-for-use program, which included the establishment of farm colonies, acquisition of non-profit factories to employ the unemployed, establishment of state-owned chain stores both to employ the unemployed and to sell the products of this "self-contained" system, payment of workers in scrip to be redeemed at these stores, and the exchange of this system's surplus goods for goods from outside it.[3]

Although failing to get the Democratic Party to adopt its platform, the CBI endorsed a slate of 62 candidates to run in the Democratic Party primaries in September, and got these candidates to agree, if elected, to put a miniature "End Poverty in California" plan into effect in Washington. Two candidates, Mary Farquharson and Kenneth Caplinger, resigned from the Socialist Party to run on the ticket. Another, Adele Parker, probably had been a Socialist. Three candidates had been UCL leaders. For the runoff election, the CBI endorsed 37 of the surviving Democratic candidates. CBI winners included Schwellenbach for United States Senator, Mary Farquharson, Paul Thomas, and James Dailey for the State Senate; and to the House, Parker, Jurie B. Smith, Thomas E. Smith, Mike Smith, and three others who would prove less influential.[4]

In the legislative session to follow, the CBI narrowly failed to elect the House Speaker. This doomed the passage of any bills related to the CBI's production-for-use platform. Indicative of the temper of the legislature was passage in the House, by a 94 to 2 vote, of a measure promoted by the American Legion denying the Communist Party a place on the state ballot. In this vein also was failure to repeal the state's 1919 criminal syndicalism law, by a 72 to 27 vote. On the other hand, with farmer and business support, both the state's agricultural adjustment act and NRA programs were renewed. An attempt by left-wing legislators failed to prevent passage of Governor Martin's bill to create a public welfare department under his direct control. Clearly, the 1935 legislature was dominated by the Martin Democrats who could predictably count on Republican support. Together, they passed the regressive 2% sales tax which the left-wing was able to modify by getting agreement to exempt certain foodstuffs. This coalition of conservative Democrats (mainly from eastern Washington) and Republicans would continue to the present day. Passage of a Grange-sponsored blanket primary law also passed. By it, voters could choose in which party primary they would vote, thereby encouraging cross-over voting.[5]

After the legislative session in March 1935, the CBI held its first convention at the Labor Temple in Seattle. To minimize the appearance of Seattle's domination, four delegates from Everett were seated, and one each from Tacoma and the logging town of

Sultan in the Cascade foothills. While asserting that the CBI would cooperate with any party in implementing its program, it excluded Communists from the meeting. At the local-unit level, however, Communists were able to gain entry. With its attention focused on the state level to broaden its base, the CBI bypassed the Seattle city election of March 1935. Discouraged with their failures in the legislative session, with the conservative city election results (election of Cincinnatans Arthur B. Langlie and Frederick Hamley, and their ally Mildred Powell, plus defeat of labor leader David Levine), and disappointment with the New Deal, the CBI directors called a conference for June. While the CBI members and Technocrats formed the main core, some Democratic Party clubs, farmers, and organized labor also were represented. The latter were inspired to participate after Governor Martin ordered the National Guard to intervene in Tacoma where the lumber strike, then in progress, had erupted in violence. This became the founding meeting for the Washington Commonwealth Federation (WCF).[6]

It is important, here, to stress the independence of the liberal-left from the CP. Most of it would grudgingly cooperate with the CP, knowing full-well the danger that the CP would seek to take over liberal-left issues and organizations, as recently had occurred with the UCL. The liberal-left usually had been characterized by the CP as "social-fascists" before the Popular Front period—before the CP adopted an anti-fascist/pro-New Deal line, and no longer ran a CP political ticket. The liberal-left, while critical of the shortcomings of the New Deal, had nevertheless been supportive members of the coalition that came to make it up after 1935. That coalition included the CIO unions, whose members previously lay outside the scope of the AFL. Both the liberal-left and CP were seeking a mass base for political action from the very same constituencies. The former were doing so within established political parties, supplemented by special shortlived organizations along the way, such as the EPIC in California and the Commonwealth Builders and Washington Commonwealth Federation in Washington. To have conceded anything to the CP on issues which had been staple ones such as civil liberties, unemployment, and relief, just because the CP adopted them as its own, would have meant abdication of liberalism altogether—not something the liberal-left was ever willing to do. That addressing these and related public policy issues hazarded being smeared "RED", was an inevitable consequence, particularly after 1946. The seeds of political reaction were, however, being sown in the mid-1930s.[7]

The WCF's first convention, meeting in Everett in August

1935, drew up a constitution, and participants agreed to meet in October in Tacoma. There, 483 delegates ratified the constitution and approved a platform centered on production-for-use. 298 of the delegates were from four groups, the Washington State Federation of Labor, the CBI, Technocrats, and Democratic Party clubs. Of these, 116 represented organized labor—the largest new ingredient in the coalition. Delegates from Bellamy clubs, the Liberty Party, the Grange, and United Producers of Washington also attended. Cyrus Woodward, a former UCL leader and editor of the *Commonwealth Builder*, was elected president, while Howard Costigan became executive secretary. The CBI remained as a conduit to serve the WCF.[8]

While preparing for an April 1936 convention in Everett, the WCF, to demonstrate its alliance with organized labor, collaborated with the Central Labor Council in the Seattle election. They backed State Representative Thomas (Tom) Smith for mayor, veteran labor candidates Robert Harlin and David Levine for council, and Burt Farquharson and Wilfred Withington for school board. The latter two, being anti-CP WCFer's, to their dismay, were endorsed by the CP. This gave Stephen F. Chadwick's Citizens' Committee opportunity to claim the WCF was only a Communist-front. Still, they received about 23,000 votes each. When Tom Smith lost in the primaries, the WCF and the CLC switched to Dore in the runoff against the Cincinnatus candidate, Councilman Arthur Langlie. Dore, as noted above, would credit his victory over Langlie to the influence of Dave Beck and the Teamsters who controlled the CLC. The two Cincinnatus candidates for council seats also were defeated by Harlin, Levine, and former U of W faculty member Frank Laube. Altogether, the results were encouraging for the WCF as it headed for Everett. However, this left Lockwood, Langlie, Hamley, and Powell as the Cincinnatan votes in the Council, and the conservative Laube as a probable supporter.[9]

One of the problems facing the conveners of the Everett meeting lay in the domination of the Public Workers' Union by the CP. Since neither the WCF leadership nor the CLC wanted anything to do with Communists, if they could help it, they insisted that the PWU delegates be non-Communist. Of the 400 delegates attending, 39 of the 54 representing organized labor were from the Public Workers' Unions (the PWU later became the Workers' Alliance). Only five delegates were from east of the Cascades, and it was not clear whom they represented. At the end of the convention a resolution was passed, rescinding all resolutions passed at the Tacoma convention. According to WCF historian, Albert Acena, the PWU probably played the key role in effecting this change—it opened the door to CP representation while avoiding the issue of its affiliation. Executive board representation also was altered, with the dropping of representatives from the Grange, Veterans, Liberty clubs, pension groups, and United Producers of Washington. Its candidate for governor, John C. Stevenson, had his own pension plan, thereby causing the WCF to exclude pension groups from the board. As to its central program—production-for-use—the WCF decided to stage an initiative drive to get it on the books, giving up on the legislative route.[10]

With the state Democratic Party's 1936 convention coming up in late May, the WCF leaders decided to work through Seattle's liberal Democrats to gain control of the party. At its May 16 meeting of the King County Democratic Party, the WCF's planks for public ownership of natural resources, production-for-use, and for nationalizing banks were adopted, over bitter conservative and moderate opposition. Liberal delegates also prevailed in the party meetings in Kitsap, Whatcom, Snohomish, Pierce, Thurston and Grays Harbor counties. When the delegates moved to Aberdeen the next week, the WCF prepared by getting enough liberal-left delegates elected from King, Pierce, Thurston, Grays Harbor, and Cowlitz counties to control the convention. In most other western counties stinging, divisive fights ensued between the Martin conservatives and the liberal-left, who now laid exclusive claim to being the true New Dealers. The Aberdeen convention saw their replay, but on a statewide scale, in which the Martin Democrats so outnumbered the WCFers that they defeated the application of the WCF's unit voting rule, which would have given control outright to the liberal-left counties. However, from that point on the liberals and leftists controlled, by electing King County Prosecutor, Warren G. Magnuson, as permanent chairman. As keynote speaker, Magnuson, who also was temporary chairman, spoke enthusiastically in favor of production-for-use, while pleading—necessarily, but helplessly—for party-healing in preparation for the general election. His election led to the adoption of the following planks: the public ownership of natural resources, a Townsendite old age pension plan, a production-for-use plan, and condemnation of the sales tax. [11]

The WCF next prepared for its own July convention in Seattle. Of the 460 delegates, 350 were from King County, including 141 from "labor", 97 from WCF affiliates, and 48 from the CBI. Because of Stevenson's control over King County patronage, he won endorsement for his gubernatorial campaign and his own pension plan, now Initiative 115. Costigan set the tone of the meeting by referring to the dangers of fascism as the Spanish Civil War got underway in the wake of Germany's march into the Rhineland, and Italy's conquest of Ethiopia. He also criticized Martin's use of the National Guard in Tacoma during the IWA strike, and use of the state police against strikers in the Roslyn-CleElum coal miners strike, depicting it as foreshadowing fascism. When Zioncheck withdrew from the congressional race, Costigan was quickly nominated for that seat. But when Zioncheck committed suicide on August 7, the WCF withdrew its Costigan nomination, switching to Magnuson, when the latter declared he had Teamster support. At the national convention, Senator Schwellenbach had been expected to introduce the state party's planks, but he demurred, thenceforth incurring the wrath of the WCF.[12]

The 1936 general election was the first run under the blanket primary rule, a fact that probably affected the outcome in the gubernatorial race. Martin won over Stevenson in the primary by about 35,000 votes. The cross-over of Republicans is indicated by the fact that 80.04% of the voters voted for governor in the Democratic primary, while only 19.96% voted for that office in the Republican primary.[13]

After the primary, the Washington State Federation of Labor announced its support of several Democrats, including Martin, and it rejected Initiative 119, the WCF's production-for-use initiative. The Central Labor Council endorsed the entire Democratic slate. The WCF's board met soon after and decided to run its own Initiative 119 campaign. Division followed when Dr. R.G. Bomar, the Technocrats' representative, resigned, complaining of growing Communist influence and because of his disappointment in the endorsement of Magnuson in place of deserving Technocrat/Democrat and founding WCFer, Ivan Merrick.[14]

This period was dominated by the strike against the *P-I* in which Martin resisted the demand to call in the National Guard, as he had done in the lumber strike. This restraint earned Martin the support of the State Federation of Labor. The WCF briefly put up Costigan as a potential third party candidate to run against Martin, but that was nipped in the bud when Costigan joined the Communist Party in October, and thenceforth headed the WCF toward "People's Front Politics", and against any third-party movement. The latter was led by WCF president, Cyrus Woodward, who then resigned from the Federation. He, like R.G. Bomar, who had resigned in August, had wanted a gradual and peaceful transition towards socialism which they felt was the main drift of history. The WCF, thereby, joined the Roosevelt coalition. All WCF-endorsed candidates for state legislature seats were elected, along with four congressional candidates: Magnuson, Martin Smith, John Coffee (brother-in-law of Senator Bone), and Knute Hill. For this the WCF claimed credit. But Initiative 119 was resoundingly defeated, 370,140 to 90,329, being obviously out of synchrony with the times; it probably would have stood a better chance in 1932. Special note should be taken of the absence in WCF campaign literature of concern for the many vital elements taking shape in the public power movement. It seems apparent that the WCF chose to focus on issues on which the Martin administration appeared most vulnerable—unemployment, relief, and soon, old age pensions. City Light's merger proposal and the fire it was drawing remained on the periphery of WCF's visual field. More on this issue will appear below.[15]

25

City Politics and New Unionism, 1936-1938

Dore, Beck and the New Unionism

By the spring of 1937, the American Federation of Labor's Committee for Industrial Organization had become, in fact, a dual constituency within the AFL. Agreements had been struck with the United States Steel Corporation by the Steel Workers Organizing Committee in March. The following month, after sensational sit-down strikes, the United Auto Workers won an agreement with General Motors. Stimulated by these successes, affiliations with the CIO continued to mount. By October 1937, the CIO could claim 32 national and international unions, 600 local industrial unions, and 80 state and city central organizations. A membership of almost 4,000,000 was claimed, a number which exceeded the AFL's crafts membership. This number also represented workers who would not have been organized, had it not been for the pressure of the industrial unionist contingent within the AFL.[1]

In this setting, jurisdictional disputes were inevitable because the industrial unions that were being formed cut across craft lines in each industry. Craft jurisdiction could be asserted even though any given craft previously had been weak, paralyzed for one reason or another, or simply had failed to make the required organizing effort. The character of these disputes was revealed in Seattle, prompted by the efforts of the Seattle

Newspaper Guild's to organize the circulation department's workers at the *Seattle Star*, and in the jurisdictional conflict over warehousemen.

What lent uniqueness to the local situation was the role of the Seattle Teamsters and their alliance with Mayor John F. Dore. Organized labor definitely had become a political force, climaxing a comeback after almost fifteen years in the doldrums. This political reactivation of labor had begun when Seattle's unemployed labor organized a self-help group—the Unemployed Citizens' League—in 1931. The UCL's first political accomplishment was its decisive role in the 1932 election of Dore as mayor, along with other "liberal" candidates. Then Dore soon turned on them in trying to attract business support through his economy measures—he could not concurrently adopt policies favoring the unemployed and attract tax-conscious business support, particularly after promising to soak the rich in his campaign utterances. After failing to win over support from the business community, and seeing the rise of Dave Beck and the Teamsters union to power, Dore courted Beck, and with his backing he defeated Mayor Charles Smith, whom the business community had put up when Dore sought and failed re-election in 1934. Soon after Dore's re-election in 1936, he cemented his alliance with Beck in the *P-I* strike. Concurrent with these developments in labor politics was the rise of radical unionism on the waterfront, which resulted in the successful rank and file challenge to the domination of the International Longshoremen's Association by Joseph Ryan. In Seattle the maritime unions had taken their current form from their origins among the locals of the UCL—radical, yet distinctly not significantly penetrated by the Communist Party. These rivalries were reaching a climax in 1937-1938.[2]

Turning first to the *Star* conflict that began on July 2, 1937, we can see the basic elements of the jurisdictional disputes and their exploitation, by management and politicians, of these divisions within the ranks of organized labor. Before this dispute broke out, the American Newspaper Guild had affiliated with the CIO. With that done, the Seattle Guild's jurisdictional claim over the Newsboys Union was upheld in late June by Judge James T. Ronald. Ronald's decision was reinforced July 10 when he restrained the AFL from interfering with *Star*'s deliveries to the Newsboys. Locally, the *Times* had already signed an agreement with the Teamsters covering all its circulation department employees. At the *P-I*, the Teamsters also were trying to bring advertising department workers into the fold. At the *Star*, only the drivers belonged to the Teamsters. With the pot at simmer, the *Star* management—knowing that 19 of its district circulation managers belonged to the Guild, and knowing that the Teamsters wanted to extend its jurisdiction over the department along the lines established at the *Times*, called the managers to a meeting on July 2. When Lew Shaw of the Teamsters was introduced, he announced that they would have to join the Teamsters. The Guild members refused, were discharged, and voted that night to strike the newspaper. An unfair labor charge also was filed with the Regional Labor Relations Board in which the Guild represented itself as a CIO affiliate.[3]

Picket lines were established by the Guild on July 3. The Teamsters also established pickets outside the press and mail rooms to prevent mailed editions from leaving the building, until the management finally agreed to let them handle the papers. On July 9, the Guild picket line was broken when Mayor Dore so ordered the police, aided by the then-infamous Teamsters' "goon squad". Dore's action had been agreed to the day before when *Star* business manager, Harry Marshall, met with Dore and Beck, getting Dore to agree to police protection. In gratitude, the *Star* printed on its front page: "[The *Star*] thanks Mayor John F. Dore and the Seattle police department and its friends in the ranks of organized labor [for permitting the newspaper to resume publication after 4 days being shut down]."[4]

With the picket line broken, the Guild members agreed to return to work in other departments until the NLRB decision; and, also, that the *Star* would bargain with the Guild for all its employees, except the printers and drivers. At the same, time Charles Hope, regional director of the NLRB, announced that the Teamsters had rejected a proposal to poll the affected staff to see whom they might want as their bargaining agent. The Central Labor Council then called the strike illegal and threatened retaliation—to which Dore lent his voice. The CLC also claimed that the Guild still belonged to the AFL. Finding this claim agreeable, the *Star* asserted that it was up to the AFL to settle jurisdiction. The normally conservative Typographers Union sided with the Guild and condemned Dore for "conducting a most un-unionlike campaign" against the Guild. In one of his outbursts in August, the mayor defended violence against *Star* pickets, warning, they would be "sent to jail, the hospital, or the morgue." Under this official protective cover two *Times* reporters reporting the strike also were beaten.[5]

Toward the end of July, NLRB examiner, Walter Wilbur, denied the Teamsters' union the right to intervene in the hearings because the Guild was in the CIO, not the AFL. In unison, both the *Star* and Teamsters protested. The strike lasted seven months, involving 60 strikers, 34 of whom returned to work, 11 had found other employment, while 15 had left the city. Back pay was awarded, and the Guild was recognized as the bargaining agent. The *Star*'s circulation reportedly fell from 110,000 to about 55,000, and its size was reduced by one-third. For Dave Beck this meant a temporary setback, inasmuch as his threats to picket business firms that withdrew their advertisements proved fruitless, and Mayor Dore lost face for his open favoritism. The presence and actions of the goon squads also dismayed much of the populace, adding high color to their fears of "labor racketeering". Compounding the frustration being experienced by Beck and Dore was the Teamsters ongoing contest with the International Longshoremen's and Warehousemen's Union (ILWU). The community's weariness with these seemingly pointless jurisdictional disputes also paved the way for the overwhelming victory of Arthur Langlie in the 1938 mayoral election.[6]

Because of its strategic location in the economy, the Teamsters' union was the ideal instrument of the AFL in contesting the CIO for jurisdiction. No one realized this more than Dave Beck. As noted above, he had patiently built up the Teamsters in the region throughout the 1920s, and he had developed alliances with other AFL unions by lending them critical support. He had also established close ties with the businesses he had organized by taking wages out of competition and stabilizing the terms of competition among these firms in the process. During the 1930s, this progression was continued, but it also became reinforced by the rise of industrial unionism after passage of the National Industrial Recovery Act. Employers who had successfully resisted the weak organizing attempts of the AFL now found it preferable to the portentous CIO with its emphasis on rank and file participation in policy and decision-making—that which astonished the AFL leadership so pointedly in the 1934 maritime strike. Referenda on these matters were anathema to the AFL leadership, destabilizing, in fact. It is not surprising that business leaders were at one with the AFL executives, local, state, and national, who claimed the CIO was, in Beck's words, using "communistic and subversive tactics." In WSFL president James Taylor's phrasing: "The C.I.O is working from within to disrupt the labor movement." Nowhere did these elements come into more dramatic focus than in the rivalry between the Teamsters and the ILWU.[7]

As described above, the initial confrontation between Beck

and Bridges was during the 1934 maritime strike when Beck acted unsuccessfully to mediate the dispute in favor of ILA president Joe Ryan. The Teamsters, as such, had remained at arm's distance, for the most part. The Teamsters even had played a crucial role, with the longshoremen, during the 1936 P-I strike. However, just as that strike was nearing its conclusion, and as the general election approached, the West Coast ILA started a ninety-eight day strike, after negotiations with the Waterfront Employers Association broke down. Mayor Dore, still ambivalent about Bridges, threatened the WEA with police action if they started any of the usual violence, once strikebreakers entered the stage. He offered the WEA no police protection.[8]

Toward the middle of this strike, Bridges announced, "The longshoremen's union is not going to stay on the waterfront. It is going inland." He intended to organize the warehousemen, seeing them unorganized and simply an extension of longshore work . . . ripe for organizing. Bernstein points to another factor—that Bridges wanted to prevent the employers from using railroads to move the cargo, as they had been able to do in the 1934 strike. Beck countered with his own organizing drive. With the ILA still in the AFL, Beck pleaded his case in Portland before AFL president, William Green, and predictably won out. Green ruled against Bridges's decision to "march inland", granting the Teamsters jurisdiction. Organizing by both factions continued until a truce was called in June 1937 to await Green's decision in October on the appeal from the ILA. However, in August, all but four Pacific Coast ILA locals had voted to affiliate with the CIO. The Seattle ILA Local 38-12 became ILWU Local 1-19. Three of these ILA locals were in Tacoma, Anacortes, and Port Angeles. They remained in the ILA until the 1950s, offering tactical opportunities to Beck and the AFL throughout the period.[9]

Comic relief was supplied during the AFL's Labor Day parade when permission was granted the new ILWU to march along with its former labor brethren. Peaceably they did it, but not without jeering Mayor Dore upon passing the reviewing stand: "We're CIO, Johnny, What do you think of that . . . " To which Dore pronounced Seattle to be "an American Federation of Labor town and I will help keep it so." At the following AFL convention, Dore added that no picketing would be allowed in Seattle without approval first from the Central Labor Council. He stuck by his word.[10]

At the time of the Labor Day parade, the Teamsters had established an embargo on the ports of Oakland and San Francisco, and Beck threatened to spread it over the entire coast if necessary, as he contested the ILWU for control of the warehousemen. He also told the ILWU to clean out the communists and return to the AFL. The immediate cause for dispute came from the invitation extended by the California Packers Association to the Teamsters after the company had fired its ILWU warehousemen.[11]

The problem with the Bay Area Teamsters was their historic indifference to organizing opportunities offered by long-haul truckers and warehousemen. Beck, despite his leadership capabilities and far-sighted opportunism, could not overcome the legacy of the past. The ILWU had gotten to the warehousemen first, had them in the fold before Beck's move. He called off the blockade at the end of September. In Seattle the story was different.[12]

Before continuing with the "war" over control of the warehousemen, it is well to place it in a larger, but relevant, setting, that within the city as a whole and on the Pacific Coast.

In mid-December 1937, labor jurisdictional strife took a more violent turn than picket line rough-stuff involving mere goon tactics—bombings in Seattle that were finding their parallel on a larger scale in Portland and other Oregon cities. The difference was that, in Oregon, state and local police joined together in tracking down the perpetrators, whereas no sustained investigation was undertaken in Seattle. The Oregon situation was to prove so embarassing to Dave Beck, that he was forced to take control in that state—Beck had assumed Teamster leadership on the Pacific Coast after Mike Casey's death in May 1937.[13]

The first Seattle bombing occurred in December at the Sound Wholesale Wood Company yard in the North End. Its new owner, John Damascus, had refused to stop selling to CIO truck drivers, despite the Teamsters' threat to picket his wood yard. Hardly had the police begun their investigation, when another bomb found its target on December 17, seriously damaging the Clean Well Dye Works on Rainier Avenue. Bombing of the latter operation illustrated the tie-in between employer associations and organized labor at the expense of both labor and small merchants. A third bombing came within the three-week span, tearing into Tom's Coffee Pot Cafe along East Marginal Way.[14]

The bombed cleaning and dyeing plant was a family business operated by Sol and Rachel Stalin. They had been regularly selling at rates below those pegged by the Cleaners and Dyers Association whose president was the former president of the Washington State Federation of Labor, William Short. Short and

Beck had joined together in eliminating the industrial unionists from control of the Central Labor Council and in ousting suspected Communists in the mid-1920s. They had remained close friends after Short resigned as president. Beck had been instrumental in establishing pricing and wage rates in the cleaning and dyeing business by collaboration with the association. That Short should wind up as its head is not surprising—he had been a long-time proponent of labor-business collaboration. The *Argus* commented that bombings and vandalism had been practiced for years against "cut price operators"; later, the industry was organized under Short's direction, and vandalism ceased. Approvingly, the *Argus* editors continued, cut price operators "fell into line".[15]

Reportedly, Seattle's prices for this work were the highest for any city of comparable size. Weekly dues paid to the association were 1% of retail volume, and 3% of wholesale volume. Operators who were not in "good standing" with the union would not have their goods picked up or delivered by the drivers, who were Teamsters. Altogether there were about 500 such operators in the city, most of whom depended upon the wholesale plants for their business. The Stalin's small plant was believed to be virtually the only holdout. It had first been bombed March 4, 1932, and it had been picketed intermittently ever since. The Stalins had been threatened with a note the week before: "You'd better play ball or else . . . ." Short, of course, denied that his association had any connection with the bombing. No sustained newspaper coverage took place, except by the weekly *Sunday News*, the organ of the Washington Commonwealth Federation, although the *Times* did report, on December 19 that the prosecuting attorney had "special investigators . . . running down a protection racket recently reported by Seattle merchants."[16]

The *Sunday News* reported that this price-wage fixing was common to associations in the ice, fuel, soft drinks, bakery, and other lines of business. The plumbing and heating business, for example, was controlled by a board composed of three contractors, three union officials, and a seventh man named by those six. Through this board, prices were controlled and only union labor was hired by the association members. Price cutters and hirers of non-union labor knew what to expect in terms of harassment and potential violence, if they did not conform to the rules.[17]

In his study of the Teamsters' union on the West Coast, J.B. Gillingham outlined the strategy of the union in negotiating agreements with the trade association of a given trade instead of negotiating business-by-business. Simplicity in both negotiating and enforcement were gained. The trade association would use its power to force non-compliant employers into line on pricing and labor standards, and entry into the field could be controlled so as to eliminate cut-throat competition which results when a trade becomes overcrowded. New entrants would have to join up or suffer from the combined force of the association and union. The trade association becomes, in this context, the enforcer of labor standards agreed to with the union, but the union also can be called upon to lend its hand as enforcer. Strikes in such fields become a rarity, as long as the union and trade association do not violate the agreement between themselves, but instead concentrate upon bringing non-conformers into line. Bear in mind also that trade associations traditionally have been dominated by the larger scale employers, who can, in turn, mobilize economic resources and political influence that small operators usually cannot command.[18]

Small merchants in these lines felt coerced and were joining together to defeat Dore in the upcoming primary election. Linkage of Dore to Short and Beck became obvious when Short was appointed head of Dore's campaign committee and Beck required active teamster participation in the campaign. To counter attacks on Beck and the associations, Short organized a committee of business leaders that included George Allen of the Seattle Brewing and Malting Company, Stanley Sayres of the Automobile Dealers Association, J.B. Fowler of the Washington Bakers Association, Nathan Eckstein of Schwabacher Brothers, and others.

Speaking at a meeting of the Washingtonians, Beck claimed his union was "doing the work that properly belongs to the Chamber of Commerce." Countering charges of "racketeering", Beck cited the milk business: "If we let milk come into the Seattle market without restriction every dairy in Seattle would be bankrupt in two weeks." He and Short frankly took pride in the price-fixing and industry regulation they had been instrumental in achieving. That these measures were necessary "to protect 'responsible' businesses and keep up wages" seemed socially as well as economically meritorious to Beck and his allies. Beck reminded listeners these goals had been the purpose of the NRA.[19]

The *Argus* editors commented on the recent history of these "labor-political setups", reporting that after Dore's 1936 election, businessmen were disturbed by Dore's announcement that he intended to pay off his election debt to Dave Beck. First, the business groups decided to fight this powerful combination, then they switched to "play along with the new labor-political setup", upon their assurance of labor peace, "and protection from the CIO sit-downers . . . ." Promised this kind of protection, they agreed to support Dore in his next election campaign. The editors continued: "Industry's investment in the labor-political combine has, employers for the most part agree, paid dividends in the past twelve months."[20]

While these local developments were unfolding in late 1937 and early 1938, Beck was leading a successful organizing drive in the open shop bastion of Los Angeles. Denied financial backing from the International Teamsters headquarters, Beck drew mainly upon the resources provided by Teamsters' unions in the Pacific Northwest, particularly those in Seattle and Portland. With the collaboration, in early 1937 of the International Longshoremen's Association (before Bridges took it into the CIO), by use of a secondary boycott of the targeted Pacific Freight Lines, and the tactical use of violence, Beck brought the PFL to its knees in June 1937. This was followed in November by a general master agreement between the Teamsters and the Motor Truckers Association of California. These victories in southern California helped Beck to overcome the opposition to his coastwise control by the Bay Area Teamsters, and paved the way for Beck's goal of forming a Western Conference of Teamsters.[21]

A temporary distraction was provided just before the Seattle primary election in February, by the roundup of Oregon Teamsters officials and thugs hired by them, as they tried to head off the CIO's organizing drive. Months before the roundup, in August, four wood truck drivers had been assaulted by two carloads of men. Not until February 5 were seven culprits charged. Four were Teamsters, two from the AFL Brewery Workers. Of them, two were ex-pugilists, and one a wrestler. Charges against other Teamsters and AFL officials quickly followed along with confessions. One related to an attempted bombing of two ships in the Portland harbor, others to window-breaking vandalism against bakeries, automobile firms, grocery stores, beatings, the burning of the Salem Box Manufacturing Company and the Copeland Lumber Company, burning of two trucks, and other acts of violence. State police became involved as the violence spread from Portland and Salem to Hood River and Dallas. Each day brought more arrests. The key figure became Al Rosser who, as head of the Joint Council of Drivers was the "right hand man to Dave Beck". With his arrest and indictment on the 10th, Teamster records also were seized, providing evidence that Rosser was also guilty of misappropriation of funds. Others testified to Rosser's role as far back as 1935 in engineering the "beer war bombings", and in more recent ones as well. In Rosser's own local, number 162, a short-lived rank and file revolt was nipped in the bud when Beck sent his own former Seattle boss, Harry Dail, from Los Angeles. Dail did what he was sent to do—the revolt was reported "dead" by the *Oregonian*. Reorganization followed. But how was all this to affect Seattle?[22]

While the *Sunday News* highlighted its February 5 edition with a front page banner article: "Portland Terrorism Should Sound Alarm To Seattle", followed with details in this and in subsequent issues, the *P-I* and *Times* gave little space and no serious follow-up to what the Oregon roundup might portend for Seattle, if trends noted above were to continue unabated. The *News* saw the same elements for terror at work in Seattle " . . . under the guise of fighting the C.I.O."[23]

"War" Over the Warehousemen

Workers were becoming susceptible to unionization, once federal protection was provided under the NRA. Consequently, union organizers were brimming with unusual confidence. Organizing of warehousemen in Seattle was born in 1934 of high expectations. That year, a federal AFL union was formed at the Fisher Flouring Mill. However, the company countered by creating a company union, the Plant Employees' Association. Fisher then fired seven union activists June 1, 1935. Strike action quickly followed in conjunction with a boycott of Fisher products. The strikers then applied for and received a charter from the International Longshoremen's Association, becoming its Local 38-117, formally named the Weighers, Warehousemen, and Cereal Workers Union. Joined by the Teamsters, the ILA successfully prosecuted the boycott, forcing Fisher to recognize the union, settling the dispute on January 23, 1936. Six other plants fell into line under leadership of the local's business agent, Hugh Bradshaw. These successes encouraged him to expand organizing to cover other warehouses in the city, just coinciding with Harry Bridges' strategy of organizing warehouses inland from the waterfront—those not yet under union jurisdiction. In Seattle the ILA now claimed about 3,000 members and stood ready to assist Bradshaw's own ILA local.[1]

A small delegation from two drug companies—McKesson

Stewart Holmes, and Blumauer Frank—was referred to Bradshaw by Claude O'Reilly, head of the Central Labor Council. Not only were they admitted to Local 38-117, but attempts to organize warehouse workers at these two plants and the West Coast Drug Company and about thirty other warehouses moved ahead. Hiring hall control by the union, as well as union recognition, were the objectives. At two manufacturing plants, Bemis Bag Company and West Coast Kalsomine Company, a minimum wage was demanded, along with elimination of wages based on piece work. Focus was upon these five plants. The union asked for preferential hiring of union-supplied workers, not for a closed shop. By September 1936, the union had secured pledges from most of the workers in these plants. Bradshaw next sought union recognition. The drug companies countered by forming the Drug Products Distributors Association. Bemis and West Coast Kalsomine then hired two lawyers, E.L. Skeel and Harry Henke, Jr., to represent them in the ensuing negotiations. Bradshaw hired Paul Coughlin, a former deputy prosecuting attorney and a member of the Houghton, Cluck, and Coughlin law firm (whose members were active in the public power movement) to represent the union. Coughlin filed claims with the regional National Labor Relations Board for union jurisdiction. The five companies rejected the union demands. On September 28, 1936, the union struck.

Longshore pickets immediately began picketing drug stores throughout the city. However, Beck had been organizing some wholesale and department store warehouses during the summer and had struck the warehouse of an auto supply firm in late August. Consequently, when the ILA local struck these five plants, Beck claimed jurisdiction over them as well. The stage was now set for the "War of the Warehousemen". However, a third element was soon added—a "citizens' committee". (Bear in mind that from 1934 to late October 1937 the ILA remained in the AFL.)

On September 29 the *Times* ran a "drug-scarcity" scare article, based on false information supplied by a spokesman for the Drug Distributors' Association. On the basis of this falsehood, the local druggists and pharmacists petitioned the Chamber of Commerce to intervene. The Chamber created a Citizens' Committee, chaired by Nathan Eckstein of the Schwabacher firm. Its manager, E.B. Fish, was head of the chamber's labor relations department. How this committee would interface with the companies and the two unions steadily unfolded.

The Teamsters, in October, obtained a federal charter to organize warehousmen away from the waterfront, and began seeking closed shop agreements, becoming Local 19-117 of the Teamsters Union by the end of the month. Bradshaw responded to the Teamster initiative by also seeking closed shop agreements, getting one with the West Coast Drug Company on October 9. While negotiations resumed with the other firms, the strikers tried to return to work, once given approval, but they found themselves locked out because the Teamsters Union had ordered the drivers to cease hauling until the companies signed with the new Teamsters warehouse local. As to the ILA warehouse local, it gained an agreement with the companies by mid-December, and filed it with the NLRB on December 29. Operations by the companies were expected to resume the first of the new year, 1937.

Teamster pickets, however, greeted the companies and the ILA warehousemen, intending to stop any trucks from running. McKesson and Blumauer Frank closed down on January 7. On March 7, Bemis and West Coast Drug shut down as a result of Teamster pressure. Workers at West Coast Kalsomine were coerced into joining the Teamsters, but then the longshoremen began picketing the plant. This firm then shut down completely. The Citizens' Committee now stepped into the picture to seek a compromise, inasmuch as the business of these corporations was being transferred to their divisions in other cities.

Bradshaw's offer to accept the verdict of a majority of the workers in the affected plants was rejected outright by the Teamsters leadership, which pointed to the jurisdiction just confirmed by the AFL headquarters in early February. The Citizens' Committee then offered its compromise proposal—reopening the plants; giving the Teamsters jurisdiction over the drug company warehousemen, granting the ILA jurisdiction over Bemis employees, letting the West Coast Kalsomine employees decide for themselves, and, last but not least, turning the final decision over to the AFL when it met in its October national convention. There was no doubt about the decision coming from the AFL leadership—it had already made that clear by its chartering of the Teamster Local 19-117. So, was this a compromise or a concession to Beck?

On the heels of the April 12 ruling of the Supreme Court, affirming the constitutionality of the National Labor Relations Act, the ILA's Pacific Coast District opened its annual meeting in Seattle. Led by Bridges, a special committee met with Mayor Dore and Eckstein of the Citizens' Committee concerning the warehousemen's dispute. On May 5, Dore announced that a meeting between Bridges and Beck was being arranged. Beck, however, left for San Francisco, where the Teamster local had been placed in receivership and Beck had been assigned responsibility for running the Bay Area Teamsters after it refused to authorize breaking the longshoremen's picket line at warehouses in the region. At the rump meeting, Bridges was told by Dore that he would stick with the Teamsters if he had to choose. Following the Dore-Bridges meeting, on May 8 the AFL officially set up offices in the Seattle Textile Tower to begin its campaign against the Committee for Industrial Organization. Ironically, the Teamsters Union, which was the AFL's tactical weapon being used against the CIO, was itself behaving as an industrial union.

On May 19, the AFL's president, William Green, sent telegrams to all the central labor councils on the Pacific Coast, instructing them to "unseat warehouse local unions . . . who refuse to recognize the jurisdiction of the Teamsters . . . over those employed in warehouses located inland." The CLC responded in quick time, voting to expel Local 38-117 by a vote of 156 to 67. This vote inspired those attending to break into a longshoremen's dance to attack and injure various leaders there in attendance. The next day, May 20, Bemis plant employees found their way blocked by Teamsters. About one hundred longshoremen then marched to the plant and chased off the Teamsters, but only until the afternoon, by which time Teamster reinforcements had been marshalled, being led by a sedan, which ran up then down the sidewalk, hitting and injuring some of the longshoremen. This violence was met by an order from Superior Court Judge Roscoe R. Smith, charging Teamster officials with coercion and conspiracy, and requiring the executives of Bemis and the West Coast Drug Company to show cause for not being enjoined from use of illegal activities.

Re-enter the Citizens' Committee. With no end of violence foreseen, and plant shutdowns expected to continue, the committee, after several meetings with the contesting parties, arranged a truce that embodied the same elements that were included in its April 7 proposal. However, a supplemental page was added by the Teamsters' attorney, George Vanderveer. It stated that, should the ILA sever its relationship to the AFL, jurisdiction would remain with the AFL—which was tantamount to giving jurisdiction to the Teamsters. On June 12, the very day that Bridges signed the truce, he introduced a resolution to have the Maritime Federation of the Pacific vote on whether to affiliate with the Committee for Industrial Organization. On June 14, 26,000 ballots were mailed to ILA members. The International Woodworkers of America followed suit from its convention in Portland. E.B. Fish, manager of the Chamber of Commerce's labor relations committee and member of the Citizens' Committee, responded to these events by resigning, and then setting up his own labor relations firm, advising Seattle businessmen to deal only with the AFL.

Jurisdiction Over the Cannery Workers: Racial Politics in the Labor Movement

Filipinos became a significant part of the Alaska cannery workers labor force in the late 1920s. They were normally recruited by Japanese, Caucasian, and Filipino labor contractors. Two of the best known were Pedro Santos and Pio DeCano. Beginning in 1914, Santos, apparently, became the first Filipino labor contractor, eventually becoming responsible for hiring about 500 workers for the New England Fish Company each season. Reportedly, DeCano had begun in 1926, taking over the operations of the deceased Valeriano Sarasal, assuming responsibility for supplying 600 workers for the canneries in southeast Alaska (at Sand Point, Drier Bay, Kake, Port San Juan, and Uganik). As a cannery operator himself, he employed about 70 workers directly. Although he was treated with respect in the Seattle Filipino community's newspapers, labor contractors in general were considered to be ruthless and so rapacious that workers returned to Seattle with but a small percentage of their gross earnings, having been fleeced by the contractors according to well-established procedures of which the company town offers the best model. To that model must be added the promotion of gambling and prostitution. The contractor kept the books. The first opportunity to end this kind of exploitation came in 1933, when the green light for unionization was turned on by passage of the National Industrial Recovery Act.[1]

Virgil Duyungan, who had graduated from Broadway High School in 1926 and had been working at the New Washington Hotel, took the initiative. Responding to the need for union protection of the cannery workers, he applied to the State Federation of Labor for a charter, obtaining one in June 1933 for the Cannery Workers and Farm Laborers' Union, Local 18257. By 1936, the local had 3,000 members of different nationalities, but Filipinos and Japanese predominated. Before 1936 no elections were held by the union. Its voice was the *Philippine-American*

Chronicle, succeeded in 1936 by the *Philippine-American Tribune*. An opposition group in the union, suspecting Duyungan of fraud, after he had raised union dues following the 1934 season, established its own newspaper, the *Philippine Advocate*. Its editor, Victorio Velasco, found suspicious Duyungan's insistence that union membership be required before sailing and in the absence of any wage agreement that was consistent with the freshly enacted NRA code for the cannery industry. These dissidents formed the Filipino Protective Laborers Association. Of the latter, the secretary of Local 18257 had written to AFL president William Green in April 1935 that the association was a company union controlled by "cannery labor agents".[2]

Harry Lundeberg, then president of the Maritime Federation of the Pacific, held a mediation meeting of the opposing factions on May 10, 1935, at which charges were made against Duyungan. Lundeberg "reprimanded" him for being paid off by the canneries. In August, he was charged with keeping over $4,500 in membership dues, and along with other officers, he was facing trial for grand larceny. In the words of the *Advocate* : "These men failed to give . . . Local 18257 funds donated by the various cannery operators . . . from January 1, to April 27, 1935, the day of their arrest . . . ." "Donated" seems to have been a euphemism for the fact that the canneries paid the money to the union in order to have their workers in good standing; otherwise the longshoremen would not let them pass through their picket line. Indications are that the charges could not be validated. The officers remained in charge through 1936.[3]

Under these pressures, an election was forced in September 1936. With about 500 of the 3,000 members voting, Duyungan defeated Vincente Navea by 113 votes. The *Tribune* saw the bloc of 85 to 90 votes cast by Japanese cannery workers as decisive. That Navea's strength lay among the Yakima farm workers, and less among the the cannery workers, also was a factor. Out of the bitter factionalism generated, it was no great surprise when Duyungan and two other officers were murdered. Baseda Patron, the killer, was shot in self-defense by Duyungan. The Maritime Federation of the Pacific claimed Patron was but a "cog in an organized plot [to] smash the principle of the hiring hall in the canning industry"—a suspicion to which Patron's dying words lent credence: "They were trying to cut into my hiring hall"—which his uncle operated. A funeral parade of more than 3,500 marched in honor of the three murder victims, from the union hall through downtown.[4]

The FPLA dissolved after the murders, and after the Central Labor Council negotiated an improved labor contract with the canneries. But, then, the AFL's district organizer, Leo Flynn, in cooperation with Clarence Arai, decided to establish racially autonomous locals for the cannery workers after accepting the claim that Local 18257, being dominated by Filipinos, discriminated against Japanese. The Alaska Cannery Workers, Local 20454, a federal union of Japanese cannery workers came into being under Arai's leadership. Arai, himself, was a lawyer who had been retained by labor contractors in the past. Local 20454 set up picket lines in late April 1937 to prevent Local 18257 members from sailing. Local 18257, nevertheless, concluded a contract with the Canned Salmon Industry on April 28—the CSI was under time-constraints, and could not withstand any delay. On May 1, Local 18257 members broke the lines and sailed for Alaska.[5]

When Flynn retaliated by trying to suspend Local 18257's charter, he was opposed by the Central Labor Council. But this was not the end of the matter, for this factionalism was occurring just at the time the split between the AFL and its Committee on Industrial Organization was reaching its breaking point. Local 18257 was urged to affiliate with the United Cannery, Agricultural, Packing, and Allied Workers of America, CIO. Members voted in favor of CIO affiliation, becoming Local 7. Then, faced with a re-chartered Local 18257, under John Ayamo, a classic AFL vs. CIO jurisdictional dispute developed. Local 7 came under heavy attack for being under "communist" control, and its members met with intimidation and harassment, some allegedly from the Seattle police. Local 7 then filed a formal complaint, charging unfair labor practices with the NLRB, and requested an election to see which union could act as bargaining agent. The canneries favored Local 18257 and had granted wage concessions and a closed shop in May 1937 to head off the dissidents. Two elections were held—the second under a U.S. Marshall's supervision—allegedly, after the first was tainted by Mayor Dore's injection of the police to harrass Local 7 members. The vote was close, but Local 7 won bargaining rights—1,560 voting for Local 7, and 1,307 for Local 18257. Local 20454 remained a dual, but ineffective union.[6]

26

City Politics, 1937

Seattle's internal politics of the year were played against a backdrop provided by the concurrent 1937 legislative session and the results of the November 1936 general election. Before turning to the city's politics, however, it is well to assess the effects of changing New Deal policies on the state and city, beginning in 1935. A look at the modifications also occurring in the State administration's attempts to deal with welfare in general and unemployment relief merit special attention. Seattle and King County, having the largest concentration of the state's population, received about one-third of the state's relief funds; their citizenry were, consequently, more affected than any part of the state.[1]

President Roosevelt and Harry Hopkins had become thoroughly discouraged by 1935 in their attempts to get cooperation of the states in the matter of unemployment relief. State matching funds never were forthcoming. In their concern to expedite employment projects, top federal priority was thereby assigned to funding of public works projects that did not depend upon matching funds from the states. Congress responded on April 5, 1935 with emergency relief legislation providing $4 billion for public works and $880 million for direct relief for the rest of the year. The Work Projects Administration became the centerpiece, to which were added projects of the Rural Electrification Administration, the National Youth Administration (NYA), and the Resettlement Administration. In Washington, effective implementation of the WPA was impeded during the first year by becoming entangled with the attempts of its state administrator, George Gannon, to create a highly personal and anti-Martin coalition through his control of all the patronage the WPA could give him, and spring him forth as the next governor. This attempt had not become transparent until late 1935. Hopkins dismissed him in April 1936, replacing him temporarily with a field representative who would begin depatronaging the program, until Don G. Abel of Hoquiam succeeded him before the general election.[2]

Washington benefited relatively well in rate of employment from all the work projects in comparison with other states, ranking eighth in 1936 and 1937, sixth in 1938, and fifth in 1939. For WPA funds alone, it ranked twenty-third in 1936, fifteenth in 1937, fourth in 1938, and sixteenth in 1939. By November 1935, and after much pressure from Hopkins, the WPA had become the largest employer of the unemployed in the state. However, Governor Martin and director Ernst of the Public Welfare Department, created in 1935 to carry out the new federal welfare program that required matching funds, acted as though the WPA and the other federal works programs would employ all of the employables, and that the counties would care for the unemployables, as a continuation of their poor law responsibilities. This expectation led them to refuse contributions to unemployment relief and instead divert funds to those social security programs for which the state would receive federal matching funds (the Social Security Act was passed in August 1935, establishing the social security program). Inspired by this thought, Ernst ordered the termination of relief to all employables on the relief rolls, beginning January 1936. Although employment in general picked up in 1936, each year, from March to June, there would be a "relief crisis" as a result of this policy.[3]

Governor Martin came out openly against the main thrust of New Deal policies after rejoicing in the defeat of the production-for-use initiative. Setting the tone, Martin, in his annual address, extolled the sales tax, finding it justifiable because it made everyone tax-conscious, thereby inducing the poor and destitute to expect less by way of government assistance. Anticipating improvement in the economy, he ruled out any increase in taxes—sufficient revenue obviously would flow from existing sources. In fact, a halt toward recovery occurred during 1937-1938, in large part due to the cutbacks in federally-funded public works projects. Martin could rely on his supporters in the legislature to back him up. Conservative Democrats in the Senate gained control of committee assignments by instituting a majority vote requirement instead of the former two-thirds vote, thereby depriving Lieutenant Governor Victor Meyers of effective control over committee assignments. In the House, also, the conservatives won control when they were able to elect a conservative from Spokane, Edward J. Reilly, as Speaker. Reilly had received WCF support after its candidate, Jurie B. Smith, lost in the first voting; the alternative seemed worse.[4]

Capitalizing on growing public resentment against the seemingly endless strikes into which bitter jurisdictional disputes only added seasoning, Governor Martin submitted a labor disputes bill that would empower a state tribunal to intervene in any dispute before or after a strike had begun, and to order a 30-day truce period. That this action drove the AFL leadership into the Martin opposition is not surprising. The State Federation of Labor thereby joined with the liberal-left forces in the House to frame an alternative measure that resembled the Wagner Act. So, while the Senate voted 35 to 9 in favor of Martin's bill, the House passed its own contrary bill by a vote of 77 to 22. The two cancelled each other out, in effect. Martin's would resurface as Initiative 130 in 1938, inspired by the Associated Farmers of Washington. It was an offspring of the Associated Farmers of California which, by then, was spreading its organization throughout the western states. Fayette Krause identifies this as "the first effort on the part of the state administration to modify a piece of New Deal legislation." The only significant liberal-left legislation to pass during the session was repeal of the Criminal Syndicalism Act of 1919.[5]

In the city election three council seats were open, with each of the three incumbents filing for re-election: Lockwood, James Scavotto, and Austin Griffiths. With Cincinnatan Lockwood as a focal target, the WCF encouraged Hugh DeLacy and Earl Gunther to file. The latter was a WCF veteran and one of its vice presidents. He also served as a delegate on the Central Labor Council, while DeLacy was a young newcomer, also on the CLC representing the Teachers Union. What gave DeLacy notoriety—and earned him support—was that he had been dismissed from his position as a teaching assistant in the English Department of the University of Washington when his filing came to the attention of President Lee Paul Sieg. Sieg, in 1935, had forced a WCF-founder, Richard G. Tyler, from the deanship of the College of Engineering, and he had demonstrated a firm hand against student political activism. Sieg's intentions seemed clear enough to many, bringing DeLacy labor support—though not immediately from the Teamsters. Since Eugene Dennett of the Inland

Boatmen's Union was campaign manager for both DeLacy and Gunther, this meant maritime union support, automatically alienating the Teamsters. In addition, Howard Costigan's radio time was given the fellow WCFers. William Norton, a former police officer and minister, and recipient of Teamster endorsement, also joined the race. Scavotto, also, earned Teamster support. In the primaries Lockwood, Scavotto, and Norton led, followed in order, by Cincinnatan William Whiteside, DeLacy, and Austin Griffiths.[6]

Focus of the campaign was only partly upon labor-related issues and the notorious alliance between Dore and Beck. The other big issue was Proposition A, a measure to refinance the street railway system. While Dore opposed it as a "swindle", and promised to come up with a plan of his own, the City Council had backed it. Characteristically, he pulled out all stops, charging that perhaps as many as four council members " . . . are owned body and soul by the Puget Sound Power and Light Company and Stone and Webster, and the enemies of the people." The WCF, through DeLacy, also opposed it as favoring the bondholders over the railway's wage earners. The CLC also opposed it on the same ground, and swung its support to DeLacy. The Teamsters gave DeLacy tacit backing in the runoff without naming him specifically. Proposition A had been converted into a labor issue in the process. (Proposition A will be discussed in chapter 29 in the context of J.D. Ross's proposed acquisition of PSP&L's property.)[7]

Dore led a last minute capacity rally of 6,000 at the Civic Auditorium, which Teamster union members were compelled to attend. Proposition A lost 53,501 to 39,069. The Council race found as winners: Norton, with 60,059 votes, Scavotto with 57,198, and DeLacy garnering 51,181. There were 7,626 more votes on Proposition A than there were for Council seats, a feature that Cincinnatus historian George Scott sees as the cause of Lockwood's loss—in Scott's words: "The distracting railway dispute".[8]

27

The 1938 City Election and the End to John F. Dore

In early December 1937, having become the hope of the Washington Commonwealth Federation and of the CIO locals, Lieutenant Governor Victor A. Meyers filed his candidacy for mayor. Not content with attacking the Dore-Beck combination for racketeering, Meyers lit into the "Seattle Model Labor Plan" that the Chamber of Commerce had hired the J. Walter Thompson Agency to draw up. This plan was intended to provide an alternative to the National Labor Relations Act in dealing with labor-management relations. He charged that the plan was the brainchild of Beck and a few wealthy industrialists who were promised support by Dore and the City's police department in implementing it. This serious tone of Meyers's campaign would soon deteriorate into one of flippancy, leading many voters who were inclined toward him to question whether he deserved their support.[1]

Despite his ailing health, for which he was hospitalized, Dore also had filed. His son, John, Jr., would be his personal spokesman throughout the campaign. His campaign head, as noted above, was William Short. Dore was supported by all the forces that Dave Beck could muster.

By December, the Cincinnatans were leaning toward Councilman Arthur B. Langlie for their candidate. After conducting a poll in November that showed him to be running "almost 100%"

ahead of potential-candidate Dore, and even more against Meyers, Langlie decided to run. That he chose Frank Jackson as his campaign manager was a measure of Langlie's priorities—Jackson had headed the 40-mill property tax limit campaign which was handicapping local government and the public schools in meeting their fiscal needs. But, although he and the Cincinnatans in general pressed against taxes, and sought by every means available to slash government expenses, Langlie and his advisers—chiefly Jackson and Hamley—saw the advantage of focusing upon the Dore-Beck "racketeering" combination.[2]

Knowing full-well the hostility of the CIO unions to Dore and Beck, Langlie, Hamley, and Jackson, particularly, abetted by Cincinnatus, even held meetings with Howard Costigan, executive secretary of the Washington Commonwealth Federation, Herman Ross of the CIO Industrial Union Council and other left-wing leaders to see about combining against Dore. Langlie was distrusted by them as a suspected "open-shopper", so these conferences bore no fruit. First priority became the mobilization of the Scandinavian vote in which Langlie had confidence—reports indicated they were anxious to work for his election. Arrangements also were made with the Municipal League to "spring" information later in the campaign, that Meyers had not paid taxes in the city for the last four years, thereby disqualifying him—but also to minimize the possibilty of another WCF candidate filing in Meyers's place.[3]

Langlie's blasts at labor racketeering and his extension of sympathy to the victimized small businessman, however, drew the fire of the *Argus*: "Candidate Langlie, rebuked by business men last week for his barrage of 'racket' talk, which was held to be injuring the city through outside press reports . . . [has changed the subject this week to city finances]." Although the *Argus* breathed some sigh of relief at Langlie's tactical switch, the editors fretfully asked in their pre-primaries issue, "What Will the Harvest Be?". Answering, they speculated that if Meyers should win, open labor war would follow because Beck would not take a CIO victory lying down. They were unhappy that Langlie would make Seattle "an open labor town and allow the [John L.] Lewis and Bridges elements to enter unhampered . . . undoing all of the progress that has been accomplished by civic bodies, the employers, and the Labor Temple in creating harmony and economic cooperation in Seattle."[4]

As to Dore, he had prepared by denying the Communist Party use of the Civic Auditorium on November 10, under the pretext that there might be violence of the sort that the American Legion was threatening—in the spring he had permitted its use by the party. This action was followed by his pronouncement for the AFL, and against the CIO, linking the latter with the Communist Party. These maneuvers split organized labor, and gave the middle class public a chance to end the turmoil which was leading many among them to unhappily supporting the AFL and its alleged racketeering practices, against the political uncertainties posed by the radical CIO.[5]

Other issues figured in the campaign, such as the city's financial crisis posed by a deficit of about $6 million, and the City's resort to issuing pay warrants that the Clearing House Association would not allow its members to cash. The state even refused to lend the city money to help out because to do so would appear to have been in response to WCF pressure. The WCF and Old Age Pension Union had been urging a special legislative session to deal with relief, and were staging a signature drive to dramatize the popular sentiment for such a session. By spring 100,000 signatures had been collected. Then there was the perennial street railway mess into which Mayor Dore had brought Teamster attorney George Vanderveer as the person to negotiate with Stone and Webster. Included was a 10% cut for Vanderveer from the savings expected, if he succeeded in negotiating a debt reduction. These issues, however, lacked the drama provided by labor-management relations. These were being played out in the bitter fight between the AFL and CIO. At this time their "war" over control of the warehousemen was reaching a crescendo, as was Beck's aggressive organizing drive to bring other crafts into the fold, such as the retail clerks.[6]

To deflect attention from charges linking him to labor racketeering, the Dore campaigners red-baited Meyers as a candidate of the "Communistic labor leaders". They even enlisted a strikebreaker and former state American Legion commander, Harry Lewis, in the anti-CIO attacks. Dore expressed pride in his labor record, and accused some of his opponents of threatening "to invite [the] CIO into Seattle. That means violence, riots. It means strikes. It means unemployment." As to Langlie's challenge, Short cried that he was "the candidate of the broken down open shoppers." Meyers's candidacy lost some luster when he declared that he intended to run for governor after he cleaned up the mess in Seattle. "Instead of making the mayor's office a millstone, I'd like to make it a stepping stone . . . " At least Meyers was no demagogue.[7]

With the labor vote clearly split between AFL and CIO factions there was no doubt that Langlie would win big, just by following in the wake of a fratricidal battle which had brought uneasiness to a public that traditionally had been relatively sympathetic to labor unions. That large scale employers had joined in alliances through the offices and bounding influence of Dave Beck in their joint effort to blunt the CIO drive seems to have passed notice. Organized labor as a whole was to suffer in the outcome. The primaries eliminated Dore for good, while Langlie emerged not only victorious, but with an open political field ahead of him. The vote count was: Langlie 51,175, Meyers 27,463, Dore 21,480, William Norton 10,457. Winners in the council race were incumbents Mildred Powell and John E. Carroll, WCF-supported candidates, Old Age Pension Union president James T. Sullivan, and Michael B. Smith, former mayor Edwin J. Brown, and Samuel J. Humes (son of turn-of-the-century mayor Tom Humes).[8]

The WCF basked in the defeat of Dore. At the same time the Communist Party also took credit for Dore's defeat and began broadcasting on radio stations KIRO and KEEN, sounding the theme that the finals were between the New Dealers and the reactionaries. Credibility was lent thereby to charges that the WCF was a Communist front. Also some of the more conservative pro-New Deal Democrats became unsettled by this left-wing endorsement of the New Deal, and certainly anti-New Deal Democrats, who operated under the aegis of Governor Martin, were further alienated from the national party leadership. It is safe to assume that the CP's promotion of the candidacies of Meyers, Sullivan, and Smith hurt their cause. Although Meyers did not receive the official endorsement of either the CP or the WCF, it was known that he was their choice. They preferred to market him as the "New Deal candidate". The WCF emerged blemished in the process, although its endorsement of Mildred Powell for her support of many of DeLacy's proposals did not affect her—she led everyone with over 84,000 votes. Langlie defeated Meyers 80,149 to 48,563. Sullivan and Smith ran last in the councilmanic race. The two WCF school board candidates also lost badly. And former King County commissioner, John C. Stevenson, lost by 19,000 votes to incumbent Port of Seattle commissioner Smith Wilson in that race.[9]

In the aftermath, Governor Martin was quick to congratulate Langlie on his victory. First, in an address at the University Christian Church urging voters not to send any more "no-good Democrats" to Olympia. He preferred "no-good Republicans" instead. Then, Martin promised, finally, to help in Seattle's financial crisis—indicating that he could have helped more all along. This promise was to emerge in June in the form of his support for the diversion of 2 mills from the higher education budget to the cities. Supporters of Initiative 129 (for implementing the 40-mill statute) endorsed Martin's proposal, thereby provoking the education establishment, the Grange, the Central Labor Council, and other organizations to start a counter-initiative campaign, number 135. For his part, a confident Mayor Langlie included the 2 mills in his budget.[10]

Before Langlie took office, though, the Governor's Social Security Board administrator, Charles F. Ernst, ordered a 20% cut in relief, effective April 1. As though inspired by ex-president Herbert Hoover, Ernst pontificated: "We are on the wrong track in our method of handling relief . . . Going to Olympia and asking for more money doesn't solve the problem. People must accept the responsibility of caring for their needy relatives. Citizens must help the needy in their communities." Ernst's edict meant the elimination of at least 12,000 Seattleites from the rolls, and about 20,000 in the county. Coming at the time of the 1937-1938 recession, in which cutbacks in public works funding played a crucial role, this action only hurt the unemployed and partially employed all the more. King County, along with other counties, was piling up a deficit that depreciated its credit rating, and the 40-mill property tax limit blocked its recourse to taxation as a remedy. Adding fuel to the fire was the fact that the King County Commission had become the only stronghold of the WCF. Conflict became inevitable between Ernst and King County Commissioner Tom Smith when Ernst refused to accept relief vouchers certified by the county. On May 20, King County relief admministrator, Kenneth Wadleigh, further added tension when he announced the cessation of all relief for able-bodied men and women, the assumption being that such persons were willfully without employment. The WCF charged that repeated cutbacks in state relief funding was due to Martin's desire to preserve what balance there was in order to claim that the state had no financial crisis, therefore, no special legislative session was justified. The WCF also charged that by these reductions Martin was endangering the receipt of federal matching funds. Smith threatened mandamus action to get the courts to rule in favor of the counties in certification matters, thereby making possible restoration of funding . . . and perhaps creating the financial crisis needed to justify a special session. These elements of controversy also played against the background of a bitter fight within the state Democratic Party, between the anti-New Deal faction of Martin's group and the pro-New Dealers.[11]

On the heels of organized labor's decisive political defeat, some employer groups decided to test the waters by threatening wage cuts and to use any success gained thereby to weaken the unions. They seemed to take their cue from Langlie's first major act as mayor, the elimination of the clause in the garbage contract that provided for payment of the prevailing wage scale to drivers and their helpers. The contract with the Diamond Tank Corporation was based on their low bid that included wages below scale. Given that low bid and its built-in premise, Diamond's president, Joseph Razore, insisted he could not pay the Teamster scale. Teamster head, Frank Brewster, threatened to call a strike, if wages were not brought up to scale. During the summer the City Council considered paying the difference in order to head off strike action, then deferred by appointing Councilman William Norton to seek a compromise. No strike took place—Langlie won. But, as the garbage contract dispute was playing out, the auto repair shops decided to cut wages and to abrogate the contract they had been induced to sign in July 1936 when Beck had decisively intervened. A 10-day strike followed, but the auto mechanics, led by the still-doughty James Duncan, won out. Also, shortly after signing a contract with the Alaska salmon packers in May, cannery workers were forced to accept a 7% cut. In July, wage cuts were warded off in the building trades and by the culinary workers. Rumors surfaced that Boeing was planning cuts for its mechanics. A compromise finally was agreed to in October.[12]

Broader in scale than attempted wage cuts by some employer groups was the action of Deputy County Prosecutor Henry Clay Agnew in his filing price-fixing conspiracy charges against the Teamsters union. A group of independent coal dealers, and the mines serving them, were allegedly being forced to charge prices fixed by the Teamsters. Triggering his attempted indictment was the beating in mid-June by a mob of about forty, of two drivers who had tried to pick up coal at the Harris Mining Company near Issaquah. When Prosecuting Attorney B. Gray Warner refused to issue the indictments against the Teamsters and other AFL officials, Agnew resigned. Warner contended that he needed facts first, and he questioned whether unions alone could be guilty of price-fixing since businesses, inescapably, would have to be party to such agreements. Warner charged Agnew as being inspired by the success of the recent Teamster prosecutions in Oregon. Agnew then laid his case before Governor Martin, hoping to get the governor to take some action in King County. Whether he decided to run against Warner in the fall election as a result of his conference with Martin is uncertain, but he did so, losing narrowly, then contesting the election.[13]

Langlie and Hamley still smarted about their being overridden when they attempted to reform the police department in 1936-1937. Although the five-year tenure given each chief was intended to free the incumbent from political manipulation, it became clear that Chief William Sears had been under Dore's thumb, at least in dealing with labor and the AFL-CIO jurisdictional disputes. Whether Dore was being cut in on payoffs can never be proven, but that he was unaware of the existence of graft is hard to believe. No scandals like those illuminated by Councilman Hamley's Efficiency Committee surfaced during Dore's tenure. However, before Dore died in April, while still in office, Hamley received a report from a dectective sergeant, Tim Carroll, that all kinds of graft and corruption were rampant in the department. About one hundred men were responsible, including Sears and "all the gold braid." But at least fifty men were "absolutely honest", and they had the courage to "correct conditions if given the opportunity." Carroll told Hamley that Sears was actually receiving graft from Chinese gambling establishments, "but not from any other source" . . . that Harvey Lou controls most of it . . . that Sears has a 25% interest in the largest one . . . that the money is collected by three officers who send it to a man named Zimmerman in Grays' Harbor County, where Sears goes once a month to collect.[14]

The above elements—relief, labor relations, and police department corruption—remained at the periphery of Mayor Langlie's administration. City finances became the central feature of his tenure; and settlement of the street railway systems' indebtedness and modernization of the system were essential in dealing with the City's financial crisis. However, before turning to Langlie's dealing with this financial crisis it is well to follow the course of relief politics to 1940.

28

The Politics of Unemployment and Relief, 1935-1940

With passage of the Social Security Act in August 1935, and implementation of the WPA in the state just two months later, Ernst reorganized the state's Emergency Relief Administration in order to implement the whole range of social security programs for which federal matching funds were available, such as aid to dependent children, old age assistance, direct relief, commodity production and distribution, self-help cooperatives, and food preservation and garden programs. These were the kind of programs that social workers had been trained to handle, Ernst among them. Not so with work relief since chronic unemployment on as massive a scale as the present had not been recognized, even by most economists of the period, let alone the nation's business leaders and politicians—the memory of 1893-1896 seemed to be suppressed by its survivors and non-existent for others. Because the states had not cooperated by providing matching funds during the FERA period, all work relief programs were transferred to federal jurisdiction, mainly to WPA. However, certification of those eligible for WPA employment was undertaken by Ernst's new administrative unit, the Department of Public Welfare.[1]

In Washington, WPA employment had reached 28,789 by

December 1, 1935 and 49,523 by March 15, 1936—the highest number until 1938, when attempts were made to stem the course of that recession. The state had been allotted $14,800,000 by WPA administrator Harry Hopkins. That this underpinned the gradual improvement in the economy was made clear when it was severely cut back late in 1937; a devastating recession then set in. However, the WPA never came close to employing all of the employables. An immediate stumbling block was that an applicant had to be already on relief on May 1, 1935, or after, but before November 1. This stricture led many of the needy who had resisted going on relief, to apply for relief in order to qualify for WPA jobs. Understandably this caused much bitterness. Yet, Washington benefited more than most states from the combined federal employment programs. Blumell reports that, "In average number employed per 10,000 population only three states and the District of Columbia benefited more than Washington." The following table from Ruth Chaskel's study of the WPA shows the average number employed by the WPA to the end of 1940.[2]

Monthly Report of Certified Persons Terminated From W.P.A. Projects May, 1938 to December, 1940

	Found Private Employment	Found Public or Private Employment	
	1938	1939	1940
January		590	262
February		531	188
March		899	499
April		1,074	673
May	1,140	1,347	797
June	1,244	1,196	900
July	1,450	1,846	882
August	2,134	1,654	760
September	2,403	707	645
October	1,201	612	566
November	885	436	422
December	430	190	341

Yet, despite clear evidence that WPA and the other federal work relief programs (National Youth Administration and Public Works Administration, for example), could not employ all who could work, Ernst, with Martin's wholehearted concurrence, spiritedly assumed the opposite. Both wishfully overestimated the strength of the economic revival. For his part, Ernst concentrated on social security, specifically child welfare and old age pensions. He even siphoned money from the State's $11,000,000 of direct relief funds that the 1935 legislature had provided, into social security programs—being attracted to them by the available federal matching funds. He aimed to have all of the employables off the relief rolls by July 1, 1936, and he pressured his home visitors to insist upon positive proof from relief recipients that they had exhausted all their possiblities for employment. He instructed his relief workers that the department was out of the relief business. During the 1935-1937 biennium, only $7,354,453 of this money was spent on direct relief. In the King County/Seattle/Tacoma area, migratory workers tended to concentrate because of the greater number of job opportunities there. This added to the tensions ever-present among the more permanent elements of the region's unemployed employables as they competed for scarce aid. That a large proportion of the migratory work force was non-Caucasion added a racial component to the tension. Governor Martin, for his part, wanting to attract outside investment, was bent upon avoiding taxes that would fall upon business. The other part of his program to entice investors was to quell labor disputes by requiring arbitration.[3]

Washington's share of federally funded public assistance under the Social Security Act (ADC, OAA, and Aid to the Blind) was as exceptional as its share of WPA funds. The state ranked twelfth nationally. During the 1937-1939 biennium, King County absorbed slightly more than 30% of state public assistance funds, which included 37% of the state's direct relief funds. Yet, with respect to old age assistance, only about one-half of the $10 million allotted for that purpose by the 1935 state legislature was spent, due probably to the absence of a strong pension lobby. The pension movement was weak and disorganized, but not for long. When the November 1936 general election saw the defeat of gubernatorial aspirant John C. Stevenson's pension plan (Initiative 115), the WCF's Howard Costigan conceived of the idea that a union of all the pension groups might strengthen the pension lobby. Those who were age 65 or over in 1930 numbered 101,503. By the end of the 1935-1937 biennium 30,268 were receiving OAA benefits—a sizeable potential voting bloc. A split among the Townsendites lent encouragement to forming such a union. An added incentive was the flagging fortunes of the WCF itself. Not only had Initiative 115 failed, but that of central concern to the WCF also had been resoundingly rejected—Initiative 119, "Production-for-Use". The WCF needed a new cause and took the lead, with Costigan doing the spade work between July and November, organizing locals statewide, though concentrated in the Puget Sound region. It is not surprising that the organizing committee of fifteen was dominated by Seattleites since fifteen locals had been organized in the city during July alone. Formation of the Washington Old Age Pension Union (WOAPU) occurred at Moose Hall in Seattle, November 6 and 7. There would be trying times ahead, before the union achieved its crowning objective in 1940, when voters approved its Initiative 141. Responsibility for creating such a political opportunity lay in the retrogression of the state administration in applying its harsh requirements in the matters of dependency, and its seemingly conscientious efforts to place the blame on employables for not finding work, while ignoring the lack of job opportunities. All this created a favorable climate of opinion for approval of the pension initiative.[4]

Just as the Workers' Alliance had become the bargaining agent for the unemployed in dealing with federal agencies, the WOAPU aimed to do the same for the elderly in dealing with the new Social Security Department which had replaced the Public Welfare Department by act of the legislature in 1937. To build up membership, WOAPU sent out questionnaires for the twofold purpose of establishing its recognition by the recipient, and to compile a list of prospects. Even before their convention, the King County commissioners had granted to the union the right to act as bargaining agent for the county's elderly. Thurston, Whatcom, Pierce, and Snohomish county commissioners followed suit. The act creating the new department had established $30 as the minimum amount to to be received by each applicant for old age assistance. The amount actually being received averaged about $22. However, in late September Ernst succumbed to pressure from the county commissioners, who had in turn had been under pressure from the union and affected individuals, to promise the full amount for those without resources.[5]

Although the amount paid to pensioners was of major concern, it was the definition of dependency that became the most controversial issue. Ernst shared with Governor Martin the view that the family was the primary social and economic unit, and its members must bear primary responsibility against reversals in any of their fortunes. Any able-bodied person could find employment in their view. That many did not only bore testimony to their incompetence or lack of will power. Together, they carried this interpretation, by 1940, to the extreme that any applicant must have exhausted all personal and family resources to qualify for assistance—in short, proof of destitution.[6]

The recession that began in August 1937 coincided with the unification of the pension forces. Cutbacks in federal work relief funds coincided with unemployment levels that approached those of 1932-1933. Already about three-fourths of the State's biennial total in relief funds was spent, and there was a year to go. This, combined with a falloff in revenues, the existence of a $4,000,000 deficit for King County, a comparable one for the city, and the refusal of Governor Martin to consider deficit spending to meet this unanticipated recession, led Ernst to announce on March 10, 1938 that no relief funds would be available to the unemployed after March 31. He reassured readers of this news, that the state would continue to provide funds for social security and for the unemployables. He admonished the rest to find employment in the private sector. Statewide, about 24,000 cases were dropped from the relief rolls on April 1. This affected about 68,000 persons, representing a sharp cut from the March figure of 122,664 who were on relief. The problem was not need, but funding—there were not enough funds to go around, so the rolls were cut to fit the State's pocketbook, since deficit spending was resisted by the State administration. In King County, this meant 4,500 cases or about 13,000 persons. This number could potentially be reduced for those who had been WPA-certified, if WPA funding were to be increased. However, WPA Administrator Don Abel reported a conundrum: although WPA funds were available, no projects had been lined up—the county's dilemma lay in its inability as "sponsor" to put up "its share of the expense." Ernst's control, in turn, of WPA certification by the county commissioners inhibited commissioners from bothering to line up projects.[7]

Responding to Ernst's announcement, telling the afflicted and affected that they could expect no help from the State administration, two mass meetings, each of different character, were held on March 31, 1938. One, a gathering of "500 Workers' Alliance members" in City Hall park was assured by County Commissioner Tom Smith that "no one in King County would be permitted to starve." The other group assembled at the Chamber of Commerce building to see about waging a campaign "to provide jobs for the needy." Smith also spoke to this assemblage, followed by fellow commissioner Jack Taylor who warned, "Unless this problem is met, radicals will step in to create disorder and chaos." He claimed 19% of the county's residents were on relief in February, a 6% increase over February

1937. The county commissioners countered Ernst by announcing they planned to issue relief vouchers. They did, but only Eba's grocery chainstores and Safeway honored them. The vouchers, though reduced in value from $1.85 per person per week to 50 cents, were supplemented with the issue of federal surplus food commodities. On April 1 the State closed the shelter for homeless men, the Blue Ox Lodge at First and Main Street. About 300 of them then marched to the County-City building, occupying the seventh floor, where they were allowed to stay overnight after assuring the commissioners that they would be orderly. Next morning, the commissioners and sheriff deputies "forcibly" reopened the shelter (according to the *P-I*), and began feeding about 1,000 men. No reference is ever made to the plight of women and children throughout these crises; their fate is only implied under "family" designations. Under this pressure, Ernst allowed the commissioners to divert hospital funds to relief—the State would pay the hospital bill later. Ernst's response to these counter-measures of the commissioners was to take over the administration of relief in King County. And he dropped 1,345 pensioners in King County from the OAA program on April 23, thereby helping the WOAPU build up its membership.[8]

These tensions augmented those already in play during the city's mayoral election then in progress. Ernst's announcements of cuts occurred just after the election. Governor Martin congratulated Arthur Langlie for his victory over Vic Meyers—by July he would proclaim what a pleasure it was to work with "that young man", and that the governor now would lend a hand in alleviating the City's financial crisis, implying that he could have done so before. Further indicative of the split in the party, several Democratic city and county office holders had openly supported Langlie. Responding to Martin's congratulations to Langlie upon his mayoral victory, and the governor's denouncement of the "no-good Democrats", the WCF blasted the Martin Democrats, claiming there was no longer a state Democratic Party, but a New Deal Party, instead. Two Martin Democrats in the House, John Sylvester and George N. Adams, quickly formed a "purge committee" to defeat "irresponsible radicals" in the November 1938 election. They listed 43 state representatives, including 21 from King and Pierce counties.[9]

As the relief crisis continued, and with a showdown looming among Democrats, the State Central Committee of the party, dominated by the Martin forces, decided to call a state convention in Tacoma. When it was held there in mid-July, bitter fights, both physical and verbal, broke out on the floor after the conservatives won the first round by abolishing the unit rule. The convention broke in two, with the state party chairman Elwood Caples and state party secretary Jack Dalton leaving with the records after announcing its adjournment. The rump continued under the chairmanship of George Yantis, adopting a liberal platform that included most of the WCF planks. The next week, Dalton presented a statewide radio address, "Communism and the Trojan Horse", alluding to the WCF, while lauding the achievements of the Martin administration, particularly in the area of social security—where, in fact, the state was pictured as a model to the rest of the nation.[10]

Although relief and pension issues inspired the Democratic Party convention, the main issue of the 1938 state election campaign, after the September primary, would become Initiative 130, the "right to work" measure. The intra-party strife had been spiced by a red-baiting campaign waged by the *Star*, beginning in January 1938. The *Star* charged the WCF as being a Communist front. The series on the WCF-CP connection was written by a pseudonymous "Max Swain", (which, Acena suggests, was not far off the mark). After the Democratic Party convention in July, the *Star* capped off its attempt to undermine the WCF on August 3 with a front page editorial, "A Job for the Democrats: Clean Out the Communists!". This was followed on August 6 by a reprint of an article that appeared in the February 1937 issue of *The Communist* authored by the CP's Northwest District Organizer, Morris Raport. In covering the 1936 general election in Washington, Raport implied that the WCF welcomed communists. Invited to respond for the WCF, Howard Costigan parried the questions asked by the *Star* by claiming that the only qualification for membership was, "we do not welcome any person or organization . . . who will not support the New Deal." Exchanges continued throughout the month, as the *Star* hammered away at WCF strength prior the September 13 primary election. As for the WCF, it stubbornly claimed to be the only true expression of New Deal policies in the party. For the *Star* this meant in part the NLRB and its intervention against the paper in its 1937-1938 Guild strike.[11]

Despite identification of the WCF with the CIO, the Central Labor Council, nevertheless, conferred a satisfactory, or better, rating upon all but one WCF-endorsed candidates in King County. What brought this AFL organization to swallow its pride was Initiative 130. Titled "Prevention of Labor Uprisings", it joined together the AFL and CIO in opposition. Sponsored by Women of Washington and Associated Farmers, it was part of a general "right-to-work" campaign being staged throughout the West by the Associated Farmers of California and its affiliates. WCF election successes in the primary can be credited largely to Initiative 130. James Taylor, president of the WSFL, asserted Initiative 130 "would wipe out unions" by requiring 30 days notice by employees of any one employer to negotiate a change in working conditions, even if there is an industry-wide union contract. Also, only those employees of that one organization would be allowed to vote, "although their actions would affect all the employers and employees in that particular industry." As if that were not sufficient, thirty days following a strike vote the county auditor would then be given a list provided by the employer noting those employees allowed to vote. Picketing and discussion about an ongoing controversy would not be permitted. This improbable coalition of AFL-CIO-WCF-Democratic Party carried over to the general election in November. That Governor Martin had earlier proposed a similar measure would not help him in his 1940 re-election campaign.[12]

A further measure of the internal divisions within the party is seen in the formation of the Democratic League under Martin-Democrat Jack Dalton. The League combined with the Washington Medical Association and the reactionary Pro-America organization against Warren Magnuson's re-election; Magnuson continued to enjoy WCF support, and had supported federally funded cancer research to the dismay of the WMA. The *Times* urged cross-over voting in general, as the campaign heated up. A record turnout followed in the primaries. November saw another record vote: 632,813 of a total of 808,159 registered voters. Initiative 130 lost, 295,431 to 268,848 votes, losing by large majorities in King, Pierce, and Snohomish counties, and narrowly in Spokane county. Only 17 counties voted "No". Cross-over voting did not affect the Congressional races—all were New Deal Democrats and won re-election. The WCF influenced the outcomes only where its membership was centered, with seven of its candidates winning Senate seats along with fifteen of the seventeen House candidates it endorsed.[13]

After the general election, relief and welfare resumed their critical position. With this resumption came the enhanced role of the Washington Old Age Pension Union. A measure of its significance would emerge in the 1940 general election when its pension initiative, Initiative 141, was adopted by the voters from all parties. The groundwork was laid after the 1938 general election.

In November, the state Supreme Court ruled, 6 to 3, against

Ernst and Martin in the case of Joanna Conant. She had been refused old age assistance when she attested to receiving help from her daughter and son-in-law. The court contended that she was the State's obligation. Responding to this court decision, in mid-December the federal Social Security Board notified the state that it would not receive matching funds for any new recipients. This was not the end of the matter, because Governor Martin then asked federal Social Security Board chairman, Arthur Altmeyer, for a more refined interpretation. He got what he wanted: " . . . all income from any source shall be taken into account . . . ." But this was not the end of the matter, either, for whether the income was provided voluntarily or involuntarily had not been addressed. When asked, Congressman Warren Magnuson indicated the state social security act could easily be amended to indicate that relatives could not be forced to make contributions. The 1939 state legislature had to act on this information and advice. It took its cue not from Magnuson, but from Altmeyer.[14]

Act, it did. Ignoring Magnuson's suggestion, and with conservatives firmly in the saddle, the legislature took the advice the governor offered in his annual address, in which he stated that the economy could not tolerate an increase in social security. Indicating his preference, he recommended a $13,000,000 reduction in social security funds. The legislature acted by setting $30 as the maximum for old age assistance and it made financial assistance from relatives mandatory. When the House insisted upon increasing the budget on social security and for schools, it had to concede to Martin by extending the sales tax to all retail items, including previously exempted food items. Also, gasoline and cigarette taxes were increased to meet the anticipated costs. The Senate failed to muster the two-thirds majority required to pass an initiative recomended by Martin to make the 40-mill property tax limit a constitutional amendment.[15]

Soon after the legislative session, on April 1, cuts were made simultaneously in relief funds and WPA jobs. In King County, March levels for relief expenditures were reduced to 57%: from $143,664 to $82,150 in April. In terms of cases this translated into elimination of 2,544 cases from the March figure of 11,523—the number of people dropped was about 11,376. WPA cuts numbered 614, representing a drop from 11,769 persons employed to 11,155—in December 1938 there had been 13,464 on the county WPA payroll. No state funds were available for April, so the county commissioners appropriated, as an emergency measure, $38,000 to be paid on the basis of $2.80 per person per month to those the commission had not eliminated from the rolls. Supplementation with surplus federal commodities and donations of clothing were added.[16]

A Citizens' Relief Council met at the Chamber of Commerce on April 12, then twice again to petition the governor for expanding WPA assistance and for relief funds. The Joint Council for Aid to Social Security sent speakers to more than 300 meetings held throughout the county. All to no avail. Raymond Chagnon, in his survey, reported that statewide, "Less than thirteen percent of the workers dismissed had found employment in private industry by November 1939. About one-half of those in private employment were earning less than the security wage previously earned by them on WPA. The remainder of the dismissed workers, 32.2 percent, had no private or WPA employment and were not receiving direct relief, except as they were able to obtain surplus commodities." In Seattle 11% found employment in private industry, averaging about $19.50 pay a week. For his part, Ernst refused to provide funds, informing the King County commissioners that it was their problem, adding that the whole social security program "was to help able bodied citizens to become self-supporting." Not until November did Ernst supply any funding, and this was only after the commissioners had spent $700,000 and had filed a mandamus action, which the state Supreme Court denied on February 2, 1940. By June, the federal Social Security Department reported that of the 123 largest cities in the nation Seattle was "by far the most seriously affected".[17]

An Epitaph for 1937-1939

In light of the defeat of all WCF-supported candidates in the 1938 City election, and their isolation in the legislature, the liberal-left had become almost powerless. Their narrow base in King and Pierce counties, combined with solidification of conservative policies at the state level, and, finally, revulsion over union jurisdictional fights undermined their credibility. That the deeper significance of the jurisdictional disputes escaped a growing number on the sidelines, did not help their cause. Albert Acena writes, in his study of the Washington Commonwealth Federation: "The left wing had not been in control of the legislature, the Seattle city council, or the Democratic Party . . . But the presence of the left wing—especially of the fellow-travelling left wing—in politics and in labor unions provided conservatives and reactionary anti-Communists with the target for their red-baiting efforts . . . [T]he conservatives never lost their grip . . . ."[18]

Respecting the 1939 legislative session, Acena adds, "Republicans and conservative Democrats were able to caucus before the session opened, and when the legislature convened on January 9 . . . the ineffectuality of the WCF and the liberal Democrats was demonstrated." They lost the Speaker fight, and, with it, any effect on committee assignments, and a rule change was made, requiring a 2/3 majority in the Rules Committee to bring a bill to vote. A similar result occurred in the Senate, continuing the procedures established in the 1937 session. The liberal-left succeeded only in contributing to the passage of a bill opening up the State's participation in the Federal Housing Act (matching money was the bait). They also got passed a free legal services bill. FHA participation for Seattle meant the possibility for demolishing the slums on Yesler Hill, erecting the Yesler Housing Project, and stimulating the construction trades.[19]

29

Financial Crisis: Taking the Street Railway Out of It

Although the City's deficit of about $6,000,000 had been growing steadily to that point since 1931, the plight of the Municipal Street Railway was only part of the problem, though a major one. Resolution of that system's financial burdens offered a part-way out of the emergency. How far, is another matter. But addressing its problems could not be done independently. Annual requests for its bond payments, its antiquated equipment, its steadily declining revenues, from a high of $16,347,000 in 1921 to a low of $3,673,000 in 1933, and only $4,370,000 in 1936, its bad management—all this affected the City's bond issues in general. The negative effect on City Light's bonds practically invited J.D. Ross's intervention.

A review of the diverse elements that now merged into essentially three propositions is in order. One proposition was Ross's proposal to resolve the street railway debt, but coupling it with acquisition of PSP&L's electrical properties in the city, even if it meant having to acquire not only all of the company's Seattle electrical properties, but those in western Washington, as well. On the latter, the State Grange would necessarily be involved as it formed public utility districts. Columbia Basin development and formation of public utility districts in eastern Washington, in turn, encountered opposition tactics from the company and its allies in eastern Washington and Portland. A third element was introduced in the 1935 legislative session by Senator Homer T. Bone's lobbyist, Kenneth Harlan, who framed a bill to amend the state constitution that would put the State into the power business. Its effect was to split the traditional Ross-Bone public ownership alliance.

The Lighting Department was one City department that had come to operate as a quasi-autonomous governmental unit. In repeatedly meeting and overcoming opposition to its growth it seemed finally to have achieved this enviable status. Its superintendent, J.D. Ross, was now more firmly entrenched than ever before—after the recall of the mayor who had fired him in 1931. However, City Light's bonds bore a higher interest rate than they should have because of the financial plight of the street railway, and they met with difficulty in their sale despite the admittedly sound condition and record of City Light in meeting its obligations while continuing to upgrade its plant and operations. Thus, in trying to improve the market for the department's own bonds, and in seeking federal aid for its Skagit project, as well as its downtown office building construction, Ross linked the resolution of the street railway's financial problems with those of the Lighting Department. What made possible the joining of their fates was the fact that each had to deal with the same party in resolving their difficulties—Puget Sound Power and Light and its parent holding company, Engineers Public Service Corporation, successors to Stone and Webster—but with many of the same officials carried over. County granges in western Washington also had to deal with PSP&L—as did Chelan County, where the company's Rock Island dam was located.

Somewhat ironically, this linkage of the City's street railway's financial obligations with the fate of City Light had been the objective of PSP&L from the time of its sale to the City in 1919. Culmination of the company's A.W. Leonard's efforts was seen, first, in his agreement with Mayor Bertha Landes to reduce the annual payments due the company and to spread them over a longer period. The qualifying factor lay in a clause which obligated the Lighting Department to reduce its charges to the street railway to half the existing rate, thereby hazarding the department's own financial standing, weakening it to a point favoring the takeover of the City's electrical utilities by PSP&L. The City Council rejected this agreement. The next high point in these efforts was reached when Mayor Frank Edwards fired Ross in March 1931. To what extent the company was involved in Edwards's action is moot, but that it would have benefited seems unquestionable.

Ross, for his part, wanted to buy out the company's holdings in Seattle, having made this clear as early as 1930. Since then, voters in eighteen counties had voted in 1936 to form public utility districts, responding to the legislation enacted under the Grange Power Initiative of 1930. In western Washington Puget Sound Power and Light operated most of the private utilities, intertying them into a single network. Inasmuch as the separation of the components ostensibly would pose enormous technical difficulties, Ross and investment banker Guy C. Myers, who was to provide the necessary financial assistance to City Light and the PUDs, attempted to produce a package for purchasing all of the company's electrical property holdings in western Washington at a "fair price". Ross and Myers were agreed that such an offer, if arrived at by "expert engineers" from federal departments, was far preferable to using long drawn out condemnation proceedings as the means to acquire the property. They assumed as their operating premise that PSP&L would choose to exit from the electrical utility business in western Washington, if simply offered a fair price for its total system. PSP&L's Frank McLaughlin tantalized them appropriately. Was the company really serious? Or was it stringing Ross and Myers along?

To effect such a purchase required the cooperation of the Mayor, City Council, and ultimately the electorate, as well as the company. But the Cincinnatus threesome—councilmen Langlie, Lockwood, and Hamley—had consistently opposed all proposals of Ross to acquire the company's holdings—the "merger" proposals, as they were called. All three chose to focus upon the street railway problem for its refinancing and rehabilitation. They, and other Council members, of necessity, had to be in communication with the company's president, Frank McLaughlin. What was said and agreed to is not a matter of record, but there are indications that a general strategy was agreed upon, insofar as any prospective merger was concerned. McLaughlin was anxious to resolve the bonded debt owed by the City to his company instead of having to annually grant unremunerative moratoria, and he saw no prospect for change in this ritual. Discounting the bonds was accepted as a premise from the start, and there seemed little disagreement as to the amount. But it became clear that McLaughlin did not favor the joining of any railway proposition with the buy-out of the company's electrical system. However, as long as no offer had yet been made, he consistently indicated the company would consider any serious tender. Mayor Dore could not resist complicating these negotiations, first by helping persuade the voters to reject a proposition—Proposition A—to settle the street railway debt in 1937 (to be followed by an unfulfilled promise to submit his own package), then by impounding the streetcar revenues in June 1937 so that operations and wages could be put on a cash basis. The bankers expected the next step would be outright default. This occasioned two lawsuits—one by PSP&L and the other by a lumber company that held warrants.[1]

Further confounding this picture was the status of the Grand Coulee dam—a high dam versus a low dam. There appeared to be competition for federal money between Coulee supporters and City Light for its Skagit project, as opposition mounted against giving ever more funds to Washington State which already seemed to have more than its share.

With the above factors in mind, it is well to tell the story as it unfolded.

The bond market was so depressed in 1932 that no money had been forthcoming from sale of City Light's bonds. Work on the Diablo Dam was halted. Machinery, wire, and equipment that had been paid for with warrants were stored at the Skagit site. And Ross adopted a spread-the-work policy to minimize layoffs. But even in the face of these cutbacks he reduced rates to less than cost for those who were on relief. In August 1932, he applied to the Reconstruction Finance Corporation for a loan of $7,500,000. In December, after the election of Franklin D. Roosevelt, the RFC approved a loan of $1,625,000, on condition that the City pay off the Lighting Department's warrants. But since these payments could be made only from revenues and bond sales, acceptance of the offer was postponed.

While waiting for the RFC to act, Ross met in November with Guy C. Myers for the first time. Myers sent a night letter: "Pleased to meet you and your committee [U]pon arrival we can hold commitment providing it is understood that regardless of what RFC does we will get our commitment less only additional bonds taken by RFC . . . ." The poor condition of the bond market in general actually was beginning to work in favor of Ross because in Myers he had found a way into the market, once Myers became convinced of the essentially sound condition of City Light. All Myers had to do was to convey that confidence to enough other investment bankers so that financing would be available. Since Myers saw their "greed" as part of their undoing, he had first to get members of any syndicate he would form to scale down their prospects in keeping with actual operational earnings.

Barely one week later Myers and his partner, Walter B. Smith, wired the City Council: "This is to inform you that we stand ready to make commitment for the purchase of $1,860,000 of Municipal Light and Power Utility Revenue Bonds of the City of Seattle; the money to be used in the retirement of outstanding warrants to be issued . . . [After RFC] has made satisfactory terms to you we will make formal commitment." Early in 1933, the RFC funds, though far less than requested, were made available, and advertisements for bids were published.[2]

To prepare Ruby Creek basin for the future Ruby Dam, Ross next applied to the Public Works Administration for funds to clear the basin, justifying it as a measure to control Skagit River flooding of the valley, and for unemployment relief. Interior Secretary Harold Ickes denied the application on the ground that the state already had more than its quota of federal funds committed to the Grand Coulee project. Ross then came under heavy attack from two long time opponents—Willis Batcheller and Ashley Holden—and a third who had not seemed previously so disposed—Rufus Woods, editor and publisher of the *Wenatchee World*. Ross, in being portrayed by them as hostile to Grand Coulee and Bonneville dams, explained self-satisfyingly that he was not, pointing out that he favored "co-relation" of the municipally owned utilities with Grand Coulee and Bonneville power ultimately into a single public power network.[3]

Batcheller, who had been heavily into the Quincy irrigation project as its chief engineer, operated through the Municipal League. Ashley Holden, who had previously been on the staff of the reactionary *Business Chronicle*—which had always bitterly opposed municipal ownership and Ross—came to his new position as executive secretary of the Columbia River Development League (CRDL) with his built-in bias, having replaced the league's original secretary, James O'Sullivan, who had been named secretary of the State's Columbia Basin Commission. That Ross became hyper-reactive is understandable. But he played into their hands, and alienated many in eastern Washington among whom he might have gained support—such as Rufus Woods. Underlying much of their antagonism also was a populist suspicion of eastern bankers to whom Ross was being driven after being denied federal funding for his primary concern—the Skagit. Woods and long time friends and co-workers for the Grand Coulee—O'Sullivan and William Clapp in particular—were comparably focused upon their project . . . and, in their own minds, competing for the same limited federal dollars.

That Ross failed to convince those favoring the Columbia Basin "program" when he focused upon power production and its distribution, is seen in a biting letter that Woods shot off to Ross in November 1934. Woods had been a long time promoter of the Grand Coulee Dam and all else it entailed for the Inland Empire, not the least of which was producing power to pump irrigating waters to that vast sage brush country. Woods wrote: "Everyone in this section of the country all over Eastern Washington read your statement to the city council as nothing more nor less than an attack on the dam . . . [The dam] . . . is a program for the whole Northwest . . . [It] is not merely a dam with a power plant." Woods downplayed Ross's fear of land speculation, pointing out that elsewhere land sales were required to be at pre-irrigation prices. That Ross also was reported to have charged that Portland, downstream on the navigable Columbia, would become the primary beneficiary from the arid lands being nurtured into productivity—this did not sit well either. Nor did Ross's remarks, that eastern Washington was getting a disproportionate amount of federal dollars, go down easily. Woods concluded: " . . . [T]he $5,000,000 which you got from the New York bankers tied you up to fight Grand Coulee Dam. That was what we understood early in the game. You are certainly running true to that report."[4]

Meanwhile, during the year, the Municipal League, which had consistently backed Ross's leadership previously, formed a City Light Committee in November 1933. The report that later emerged took on the name of the person who dominated its composition: "the Batcheller Report". In January 1934, the League decided to investigate the Lighting Department along three lines: engineering, financial, and public relations. Willis T. Batcheller had ghost-written much of recalled-Mayor Edwards's attacks on Ross. When the committee's report was issued in October 1934 and was published in four successive installments of the *Municipal News*, it is not surprising that it resubmitted the substance of the 1930 Lybrand, Ross Brothers, and Montgomery recommendations, plus the injection of the Grand Coulee, into the picture as justification for not proceeding with Ruby Dam construction. Completion of the Diablo Dam project was recommended, in part, because of the commitment already made in the wire, machinery, and equipment—for which Ross had been attacked by Batcheller (speaking through Edwards) in 1931 and 1932. Any work on Ruby should be postponed until the capacity of Grand Coulee had been exploited first, ran the argument: "The heavy inactive investment in the Seattle municipal power system has prevented the Seattle Light and Power customers from enjoying rate reductions such as those which have been experienced in Tacoma . . . [W]e are of the opinion that the development of further power resources . . . should be deferred by the City of Seattle until [Bonneville/Coulee power are no longer sufficient]." The report concluded by opposing the proposed merger. Cessation of work on Ruby Dam for three to five years was urged, and "Seattle should cooperate to find a market for Coulee Power and buy that power, if advantageous, in order to promote the development of the Columbia basin." Although Ross was invited to respond at a League meeting he never did. And when he was appointed to the Securities and Exchange Commission in 1935, the *News* objected to Ross taking only a leave of absence: "J.D. Ross continued this week his speaking career with respect to the purchase of Puget Sound property and propaganda on City Light. Must we tolerate the continued efforts of the City Light Superintendent along political lines, continuing City Light as a political football?" The tone was Batcheller's. Clearly, the Municipal League had turned a corner.[5]

Ross was then confronted by the Columbia River Development League (CRDL) and the Wenatchee Chamber of Commerce (PSP&L had built the first dam on the Columbia at Rock Island just downstream from Wenatchee) for presumably being opposed to the Grand Coulee. Ashley Holden had charged Ross with fearing that power from the Grand Coulee would compete with City Light. Ross responded, "Where did you ever find me opposing the Coulee or Bonneville projects? You have made that all up yourselves, I think, with the help of the Washington Water Power Company . . . Don't you think it would be better for all of us to try to work out the distribution of power and the cutting of the costs of distribution where . . . nine-tenths [of the costs] lie?" He reminded the publishers of the newspapers which ran the attack by Ashley Holden, that the 1933 legislative session had tried to put the State into the power business and thereby absorb the existing municipally owned utilities.[6]

Earlier, in the same October 1934 that saw the issuance of the Municipal League's report, Ross presented his plan for the purchase of PSP&L at a "fair price". Settlement of the street railway bond obligations was included in the package. Of the company's output, 43% was distributed in King County, including one-third in Seattle. He added: "A strong syndicate of New York bankers has agreed to undertake the issuance of utility revenue bonds in exchange for all securities against the company's properties . . . at a figure not to exceed ninety-nine million dollars . . . ." Ross no longer pursued federal money for dam construction per se, although he would continue seeking PWA funding to clear Ruby basin. An appraisal was in progress according to Ross. Once again Ross's presumed opposition to Grand Coulee was pictured, this time by Kenneth Harlan, the Northwest's former representative on the Federal Power Commission. He claimed Ross would try to block funding of Grand Coulee "because it would wreck" City Light's attempt to buy PSP&L— an attempt that would leave City Light with an obsolete plant, in Harlan's opinion.[7]

With the 1935 legislative session starting up, Harlan wired Senator Bone, January 26, from Olympia: "Will introduce constitutional amendment for power lines Columbia River development first of next week stop out look for passage good . . . ." On the 28th, Harlan wrote Bone and Schwellenbach, postulating "one great coordinated 'Pool' of Power" connecting Bonneville, Coulee, Skagit, and Cushman to balance power loads. He contended transmission lines could be built either by federal or state governments. To this, Harlan expected opposition from both private and public utilities: "Ross is determined . . . to operate Skagit and City Light independently; [Marshall] Dana and the Portland group are equally determined to operate . . . the Bonneville Plant independently . . . and the private power companies . . . are lending their support . . . to such plans." Harlan saw the private companies trying to "salvage all of their dead and obsolete property [by establishing a rate structure that would combine the total value of both the private and public systems, thereby forcing the public to underwrite the] Inflation [*sic*] and Overcapitalization [*sic*] of these private corporations." If this were to occur, no "yardstick" could be established. To counter this opposition, Harlan urged formation of a Columbia Valley Authority to pool the power. Meanwhile he would work toward creating a state authority by a state constitutional amendment.[8]

Concurrently, Ross's merger proposal had inspired Holden to move the CRDL headquarters from Spokane to Seattle from where he could lobby against it, even choosing to run for a seat on the City Council in the February 1935 primaries election on that single issue. In that race the Municipal League supported him and opposed incumbent Ross supporter, Frank Fitts. Leading into the election, Holden succeeded in getting a court order restraining City Light from spending funds on the merger proposal. Reporting to Woods, who was representing the Columbia Basin Commission in Washington, D.C., Holden wrote that since moving the CRDL office to Seattle four months ago " . . . we have accomplished a great deal in educating the public and enlisting support for the High Dam. The Seattle Chamber of Commerce has swung into line in fine shape and just last week the Seattle Municipal League 'cracked' down on Supt. J.D. Ross in a report . . . and [we] avail ourselves of cheap power from Grand Coulee." Two weeks earlier Holden had written Woods that Ross had told Columbia Basin Commission chairman, E.F. Banker, that he favored a high dam, but: "This does not sound very good to me. I believe that Ross is simply trying to lull our friends into a false sense of security . . . [H]is paid agents will exert their utmost influence to block any move . . . to aid in the development of the Grand Coulee."[9]

What seems significant in these shifting views on the high dam issue is that opposition to it from the private sector subsided as those leaders came to realize that power distribution was the crucial factor, not dam ownership. Presumably, this was part of Holden's message, although evidence shows that private utilities were recognizing this on their own. The private sector also was getting hungry for federally produced power, once it became clear that profits really lay in control of its distribution.

While the PWA application was being considered, Ross and Myers succeeded in selling $4,956,000 worth of bonds (the figure to which Woods had referred above) to complete the Diablo power installation and to complete the downtown office building. The investment bankers' disenchantment with financing private utilities was proving fortunate for Ross. They were now anxious to find trustworthy places for their money and, being leery of the private utilities sector, some were pleased to be alerted by Myers to the possibilities offered by City Light bonds.[10]

Implementation of the Grange's District Power Bill was, in the meanwhile, meeting with obstructions from the private power companies. Although the state Supreme Court, in December 1931, upheld a Superior Court ruling authorizing utility districts to buy electric power, the bill did not allow its sale. More legislation was needed. For this a new Bone Power Bill was passed by both houses and signed by Governor Martin in March 1933. But the private power lobby succeeded in attaching a referendum requirement to it, forcing it upon the 1934 general election ballot as Referendum 18. Voters did approve it 221,590 votes to 160,244 but that was about eighteen months later . . . further delaying any active PUD operation.[11]

With the Grand Coulee project moving ahead, there was growing concern over distribution of its electric power—the private companies wanted control, but so did the Grange on the public ownership side. The latter, during the 1933 legislative session, succeeded in getting House Joint Resolution Number 5 passed. It provided for the utility districts to contract with the Federal Government for power from the dam, and enabled the State to build transmission lines for distribution of power to public utilities at cost. And when the dam was finally paid for the Federal Government would deed it to the State. But a State agency would have to be established for this purpose, and it would take over complete control over public utilities in the state, including the existing municipals. Although the Grange, by this bill, had hoped to prevent a takeover of the dam by private utilities—as in the case of Muscle Shoals—the commission that would assume jurisdiction would be as susceptible to influence by the private utilities as had similar public bodies, normally. J.D. Ross was relieved when the Senate rejected this bill. But, by the end of the year the legislation would be revived as a constitutional amendment by the 1935 legislature. It is easy to see how Ross's opposition here could be misconstrued, and it was. Since passage of the Public Services Commission Act in 1911, exempting publicly owned utilities from regulation by the Commission, the private power companies had been trying to remove that exemption.[12]

Legal challenges were posed as well to formation of utility districts. Just as the Bone Power Bill was awaiting voter action in November 1934, the Washington Water Power Company, the Great Northern Railroad, and the Northern Pacific Railroad enjoined Lincoln County from putting on the county ballot a referendum authorizing formation of a Public Utility District (PUD). Concurrently, Holden was lobbying four of the railroads, through Great Northern's Luthene Gilman, for high dam support and for funding the CRDL. When the Superior Court judge ruled for the companies, the Grange appealed to the state Supreme Court which ruled the case was defective because the petitioners had not nominated any commissioners. This ruling came about one month before the election when other counties also were preparing to vote on PUD formation. Only Franklin County and part of Mason County succeeded in passing referenda, Clark County voters failed to do so by a mere 65 votes, and both Adams and Lincoln counties failed to nominate commissioners.[13]

Entering 1935, three elements were fusing: the March city election; the course of the "Bone Bill" in the legislature; and power transmission from Coulee/Bonneville. Ashley Holden's intrusion into the city election has been outlined above. Parallel with the events revolving around the city election, Ross was moving ahead toward his objective of proposing a purchase of PSP&L's city operations and resolution of the always-intrusive street railway problem. Opposition from the Cincinnatus threesome on the City Council took shape. In late March, they agreed to see about getting PSP&L to reduce its bonds to "Four or Five Million Dollars", at a lower rate of interest spread over a longer period of time, and to see about floating bonds for equipment, in conjunction with surveying Seattle businessmen to learn how many would buy them—partly with an eye to having as much of the work as possible done in the city. On March 28, the threesome asked Ross about reducing City Light rates on street lighting. To this proposal Ross innocently told them the "saving to the City would have to be made up by an increase in taxes", an obvious sore spot for the Cincinnatans. The following week, they met with "a disgruntled City Light employee . . . [who] is working with Batcheller on the latter's fight to have City Light audited"—something that was done annually by the State auditor. The effect of their move to isolate the street railway's debt was to contribute to sentiment against any merger of City Light and PSP&L.[14]

Moving ahead, in mid-April they met with Nathan Eckstein, chair of the State Planning Council, to learn from him the possibilities of federal help. Eckstein expressed optimism about their obtaining funds to refinance the street railway. They soon met with local RFC officials. Councilman Frank Laube, chair of the Council's Finance Committee, then met with McLaughlin in June to see about a reduction in the debt. Reportedly, a $3,000,000 reduction was offered. Hamley thought Laube was merely grandstanding in preparation for making a run for mayor but, in any case, it now had become publicly known that the company was prepared to make a deal toward that end.[15]

Meanwhile, Kenneth Harlan shepherded his constitutional amendment bill (the "Bone Bill") through the legislature. He reported to Bone on February 4, 1935 that the "power amendment" had just passed the House 91 to 2 as House Joint Resolution Number 10, but that Ross and Frank Fitts had fought futilely against it. He added that E.F. Banker, head of the state's Columbia Basin Commission, had also opposed the bill. HJR 10 would empower a State Power Authority in conjunction with the federal government and any subdivisions in the state "to produce, own, maintain and/or operate . . . generating plants within the state and/or . . . transmission and distribution lines."

The Senate approved the bill on February 26 by a 34 to 11 vote. The conflict within the public power ranks deepened as Ross, in early July, formed a "Home Rule Power League", behind which Harlan saw the "guiding genius" of Guy Myers. As to the Grange, Harlan added that when its state leaders—Helen Dahl, Fred Chamberlain, and Ervin King—met with the "Ross-Meyers [sic] group", they refused to go along, but are "standing pat" with us.[16]

Upon assuming his initial duties on the Securities and Exchange Commission, Ross cabled from Washington in late August 1935 that he would like to be given authority from the City Council to apply for a $13,000,000 grant to clear Ruby basin, build the dam to 1,500 feet, a substation in the city, a transmission line from Gorge, and other items. Federal funds would be divided into an outright grant of 45% of the total, and 55% as a loan to the City at 4% interest. Establishing their opposition to Ross's initiatives, the Cincinnatus minority of Langlie, Hamley, and Lockwood opposed Ross's request, wanting to study it first. When Ross then asked for an unpaid leave of absence from City Light to pursue these negotiations, Lockwood proposed that a business manager be appointed "in keeping with the Lybrand, Ross Bros., and Montgomery" proposal of 1930. To this suggestion, Hamley recorded that Ross was "bitterly opposed", wanting to remain in control of the department. Indeed, it was like waving a red flag at the bullish Ross.[17]

Protection of PSP&L's interests by the threesome was again in evidence when they opposed, on October 1, City Light's request for $2,500 to survey the company's property. Three days later, Hamley was urged by former Eminent Domain commissioner Ottway Pardee, Willis Batcheller, and one other man to oppose the prospective purchase. As a kind of insider joke, Hamley, with professed innocence, volunteered that Clarence Dill and state WPA administrator, George Gannon, were trying "to put the State in the general power business and then control that business. [T]hey admitted that this was probably true."[18]

During October, when the threesome met with local bankers concerning the suggestion made by Guy Myers to the City Council that they authorize an unbidded sale of $5,000,000 worth of City Light bonds, but with publicity about the sale, they learned of banker opposition. The Council did call for bids, however, and accepted one discounted to 96.5%. Of the total, $4,900,000 were in the form of refunding bonds. On the first day of sale, Myers reported to Ross that $4,000,000 had been taken up, commenting: "Remember this is retail and in the hands of the investor. Wait until we get the competition eliminated and we will show you a rate of interest that will certainly satisfy everybody." Proceeds from the sale made possible the refunding of $6,400,000 worth of 4 1/2%, 4 3/4%, and 5% bonds at a new rate of 4%. Another $1,287,000 worth of bonds were redeemed at maturity—a testimony to the Lighting Department's credit standing and to the persuasive powers of Guy C. Myers. These sales sustained work toward completion of Diablo's power plant, and progress on office building construction at Third and Madison. In his annual report for 1935 Ross portrayed an intertie of Seattle and Tacoma with the Federal plants on the Columbia. In this euphoric atmosphere even residential rates were lowered modestly.[19]

Myers, writing in early December 1935 from Seattle, exuberantly asked Ross to submit ten to fifteen names of persons whom Myers could add to his committee supporting "consolidation" and solving the street railway mess. He outlined his plan: " . . . [W]ith your presenting to the City the fact that you can make a saving of $2,500,000 a year [by eliminating duplication of facilities], balance the budget, and straighten up the street railway situation, there is nothing in the way that can stop you in being successful in your campaign." How long this optimism could be furbished remained to be seen. Were the private companies really serious about accepting a "fair price" and simply getting out of the electric utility business?[20]

When dealing with refinancing and rehabilitating the street railway, the Cincinnatan council members were receptive to the Myers and Ross initiatives. To the fanfare of the *Times* headline, "Car Line Loan Believed Near", Myers met in late May with Langlie, Scavotto, Isaac ("Ike") Commeaux (the City's chief accounting officer in whom all parties placed full confidence), Frank McLaughlin, and his legal counsel, Frank Holman, to learn (according to Hamley) what "the company would take for their street car bonds. This was settled at slightly below the $5,000,000 figure but it got mixed up in a discount of the bonds so we are not [sure of the price]. Both Langlie and Scavotto were well pleased with the meeting."[21]

Meanwhile, the private utilities business gradually was improving, causing some anxiety within City Light's ranks in its pursuit of its merger proposition. Ross's surrogates, Glen Smith and acting superintendent Willam McKeen, alerted Ross at his SEC office: "any rise in business makes it so much harder to put the purchase over." Time seemed to be running out. Advice had poured in during all of 1935 pressing for a special election on the merger issue. His protege, Robert W. Beck, wired Ross in November, favoring a ballot on February 15, 1936, preceding the City's primaries: "we believe further delay may prove fatal." Ross was being pressed also to name a "fair price", just as opposition to the merger continued accumulating. The *P-I* spoke its opposition, in line with all Hearst papers to oppose public ownership—an abrupt policy change, reportedly timed to delivery of the Supreme Court's TVA decision. Both mayoral race finalists, John Dore and Arthur Langlie, announced their opposition, causing Beck to advise Ross to lay off the campaign until after the election. The merger now seemed a lost cause, although it was resuscitated throughout the year. It had been tied loosely with the refinancing and rehabilitation of the street railway, with City Light agreeing to furnish the trolley lines. Separation of the two items now went ahead, finally to be concluded in 1940.[22]

Newly-elected Mayor John Dore proceeded to muddy the waters by injecting a promise to submit his own plan for refinancing and rehabilitating the street railway. This promise remained a threat on the periphery throughout the negotiations, and would persist until Dore was finally defeated in his re-election attempt in 1938. As to the main line of negotiations, Myers reported to Ross in late July that it was tough going trying to sell the street railway bonds because, in his opinion, General Motors wanted the street railway to be sold to a private company with which it could make a deal in selling its buses without competitive bidding. These would be gas buses. Dore favored gas buses, and ruled out trackless trolleys, despite the mounting evidence nationwide that trackless trolleys were making such profits that investment houses were entering a field they had been avoiding. During the remainder of 1936 Ross, Commeaux, and Myers, using a report by the Beeler Organization as a basis, worked up a plan to float 4 1/2% revenue bonds worth $11,400,000 with a ten-year maturity. Provision was made for trackless trolleys supplemented by gas buses as feeder lines.[23]

So swimmingly did events seem to be moving toward consummation of a deal with PSP&L for both its electrical operations and street car bonds that Myers continued to express his optimism to Ross in Washington. In June of 1936, the City Council had instructed Ross to arrive at a "maximum sum" to offer the company for its facilities. To this, McLaughlin promised "earnest consideration". That month also saw Ross's surrogate, Robert W. Beck, and Batcheller argue the merger proposition before the Municipal League. By then, other events took center stage: the Auto Mechanics strike followed by the *P-I* strike—the outcome of which was affected by the 1936 general election—and shutdown of the waterfront by the Waterfront Employers' Association lasting until February 1937.[24]

Heading into the November 1936 general election, after having lost the constitutional testing of the District Power Bill, the private utilities had stepped up their legal obstructions to the bill's implementation. They also had campaigned strenuously against HJR 10. The resident City Light management (Smith, McKeen, and Beck) laid blame upon Bone's surrogate, Kenneth Harlan. They accused Harlan of "working hard to stir up a fight between the Grange and City Light", and of collaborating with Batcheller. Contrary to Harlan's July 1935 report to Bone, they assured Ross that Grange leaders (headquarters were in Seattle) Ervin King, Fred Chamberlain, and Helen Dahl "are very much with us and against Kenneth." As it turned out, voters rejected the bill by more than 100,000 votes. But they simultaneously approved the formation of 15 more PUDs, bringing the total to 18 counties and 2 less-than-county-size PUDs on the books. More would soon be added. But it would take time to make fair price offers to the companies for their properties, and failing acceptance, condemnation proceedings would eat up more time. And, if the Columbia dams were completed before the Washington PUDs and other comparable operations in Washington and Oregon—where the main battle was fought—were ready to have power transmitted to them, who would get the power? The Washington Public Utilities Districts Association was sure that the Army Engineers were collaborating with the private utilities when it was learned that it had installed equipment at Bonneville that was capable only of short-distance transmission, primarily to the Portland region. These factors fed into the City's dealings with PSP&L.[25]

Having given up, for the time being, the idea of submitting a merger proposition to the city's voters, Ross's cohorts turned to the City Council's "Proposition A". This proposition provided for refinancing the street railway bonds. In early February 1937, electioneering on this issue heated up. Ross and Myers's strategy was to address the merger proposition after passage of Proposition A. Not only would these two be linked by the opposition, but the PUDs also would be attacked. The *Star* blared: "City Light Coercion Probe Today", and in a later edition of February 3: "City Light Coercion Hearing Set". George Mulkey, who was on leave from PSP&L to act as business agent for Local 77 of the Electrical Workers Union, charged City Light with coercing its employees to contribute to the PUD campaign. Ross denied this charge, and further insisted to Rodney Brink of the *Star* that the unnamed reporter who misquoted him be subpoenaed, saying the unions "are dissatisfied and are trying to oppose the power merger." Ross accused Mulkey of producing a pamphlet for the 1936 political campaign attacking PUDs, and he wrote a lengthy letter to the president of the International Brotherhood of Electrical Workers, M.H. Hedges, in which he accused the company of working with Mulkey in transferring all of PSP&L's electrical workers to Local 77 where Mulkey could then control its proceedings against both the merger and the PUDs. Concurrently, Dore came out against the purchase plan, calling it a "swindle". Myers attributed Dore's opposition to mayoral candidate Frank Fitts's support for it—Fitts also courted the labor vote, drawing his strength from the new CIO locals and the Washington Commonwealth Federation.[26]

In the face of this mounting opposition to Proposition A, its defeat was not surprising. The *P-I*'s headline trumpeted, "Dore Jubilant At Trolley Defeat", as it lost 53,501 to 39,069—and also at defeat of Cincinnatan David Lockwood, one of those whom Dore held in contempt for trying to clean up the city's politics, a task which Dore seemed to make impossible. The *P-I* called it a victory for organized labor, and contributed a front page editorial: "Mr. Mayor Dore, It's Up To You" to solve the street car problem. To this challenge, Dore urged the Board of Public Works to undertake a study and come up with a comprehensive rehabilitation plan.[27]

Dore began injecting now-Teamster attorney, George Vanderveer, into the merger/street railway picture. Ross wrote to Myers in early April that Vanderveer wants to hold off on the merger part of the deal until he and Dore can get the street railway matter settled first . . . "[After that] . . . they will be willing to talk business on OUR terms." When Vanderveer suggested to Ross that City Light force customers away from the company "as a prelude to negotiations", Ross asked Myers, "Isn't it apparent to you what they are driving for?" A week later, Robert Beck was informed that the Mayor and Vanderveer had decided against trackless trolleys, preferring gas buses instead, and they were waiting for the new Council to get seated before springing their plan. The Cincinnatans and Ross wanted trackless trolleys and gas buses only as feeder lines.[28]

Despite advice from Van Soelen that impounding street car fare receipts was illegal, Dore began doing so in June to meet the system's payroll after the Central Clearing House Association refused to cash City warrants. Dore then had Van Soelen file a law suit challenging the validity of the original purchase contract. Late in July, Myers wrote Ross: "I hope you are going to be able to get the Mayor to see the foolishness of having Van start a lawsuit on the railway bonds, which will upset the market on our Light Bonds, and raise the dickens with financing anything from the City of Seattle . . . It will still look as if the City of Seattle is trying to repudiate its bonds. They are already disturbed over the fact that the City is diverting funds from one account to another, as they are doing in the railway situation . . . There can be only one reason, and that is that somebody will make more out of doing it the wrong way . . . ."[29]

Also at issue here was the City's test case to determine which had precedence in revenue bond payments: interest and principal or other charges, including wages and salaries? The PUDs were awaiting court determination of this long standing issue, inasmuch as they were considering the issuance of revenue bonds. Myers wrote Dore in late August, complaining the suit was having a dismaying effect: "hampering" the sale of City bonds, complicating the PUDs predicament," . . . playing right into the hands of the power companies to the detriment of municipal ownership."[30]

When the City defaulted on its interest payments in September, out of self-defence and to save face, the PSP&L filed suit against the City. McLaughlin explained to R.W. Beck that he was avoiding Vanderveer, and for Beck to tell Myers not to take it seriously, that the company preferred working with Myers, not trusting Dore and Vanderveer. Beck, in reporting this information to Myers, said Vanderveer had speculated that Ross "has been taken in by you [and you are working for the company]."[31]

The next step in this scenario was Vanderveer's contracting with the City Council to give him 10% of any saving he could gain for the City in renegotiating the street railway bonds. That Vanderveer and Dore had a contingent deal is easily imagined and cannot be dismissed for lack of more concrete evidence. By now it was common knowledge that the company was indeed prepared to save the City money, while also benefiting its bondholders. For Vanderveer it was almost money in the bank.[32]

In the face of these developments, the earlier optimism of Myers, R.W. Beck, and Ross about a prospective purchase of the PSP&L's electrical properties was deflated, at least for Beck. Myers was in the middle of negotiations to put the State of Nebraska into the utility business by buying up the private utilities in that state (Myers's syndicate was handling the transaction).

He was using Beck as his engineering consultant in this venture, as well as working with the PUDs to arrive at a fair price to offer PSP&L for its properties in western Washington. Beck discouragingly wrote PUD attorney, Jack Cluck, in mid-October, that after having met with several of the "bankers and utility people [in Nebraska, I am now convinced] . . . these companies and the men that run them do not want to sell . . . [They resent Myers's pressure.] That is why one seldom gets past the front door in trying to arrange a purchase of a company." To Beck, it appeared that any fair price would be rejected locally, and that condemnation would have to be resorted to, if the merger were ever to take place, and if the PUDs, themselves, were ever to become operational. Locally, Myers was meeting with "procrastination" from the bankers, but he felt, "They cannot delay with us, because of my work with the investors, which is a club we can use to bring about quick and fair trades"—Myers had just emerged buoyantly after speaking with President Roosevelt about the TVA and Nebraska situations. If the Nebraska deal bore fruit, it would be considered a model for the PUDs to follow in their negotiations.[33]

Mayor Dore, as we have seen, was defeated in the February 1938 primary election. Neither he nor Vanderveer ever produced a plan for the street railway, but they had succeeded in pushing to the side Ross's merger proposal. By doing so, they strengthened the opposition of Councilmen Langlie and Hamley. And, with the former's election to the Mayor's office, Langlie could now pursue his own plan for refinancing and rehabilitating the street railway system while keeping a lid on the merger proposition. Concurrently, Jack Cluck was reported to have a draft of a comprehensive plan for the purchase of all PSP&L's electrical properties in western Washington.[34]

Setting the stage for Councilman Langlie's initiative as Mayor, the Council terminated Vanderveer's contract. While Ross and Myers remained optimistic about Council approval of the merger—Langlie had not spoken publicly against it—Langlie persuaded the Council to let him begin work on a modernization plan for the street railway. His starting point was the status left after negotiations with the company were terminated by the defeat of Proposition A in the 1937 city election. In fact, little more had to be done besides bringing the same parties together. This meant that Ross, now Administrator of the Bonneville Power Administration, and on leave from City Light, would have to lend Commeaux back to the City. Confidence in Langlie continued to be expressed through Beck to Myers (Ross also had taken Beck to the BPA): "[Langlie and Ross had had a good meeting, and] Langlie wants the Street Railway to go separately and wants Ike to come up here . . . and get started on it." Ross consented. As to Langlie's disposition by then, Beck sadly reported to Myers that the new mayor was against any merger of the two elements: the railway bonds and the purchase of PSP&L's Seattle electrical system.[35]

In late May, Mayor Langlie applied to the RFC for a loan of $11,500,000 to refinance and rehabilitate the street railway and sent Commeaux to Washington, D.C. to head up the negotiation team. He also contracted with the Beeler Organization to continue where it left off in 1937. Guy C. Myers was cut out of the proceedings, once the RFC merged into the process, but he expressed doubts that the RFC would complete the deal. However, by September 1938, the agency had tentatively agreed to lend $10 million, of which $4,300,000 would pay off the City's bonded debt of over $8 million, and the balance would be for new equipment. From this time on, negotiations would continue until they were consummated in August 1939. The debt of $8,336,000 was settled by payment of $3,250,000. The bonds were publicly burned in celebration. Rehabilitation would get quickly underway with trackless trolleys and gas buses as feeder lines to be the cornerstones of the system. The merger proposition would remain on hold as Myers and Beck (Ross died March 14, 1939) continued work toward establishing what Myers considered a fair price for all of PSP&L's western Washington electrical properties. Myers really believed that the private companies would choose to get out of the electrical utilities business for a price. Beck was less optimistic, particularly after Ross's death—Ross, sharing Meyers's optimism, had kept up Beck's spirits.[36]

30

City Elections, 1939 and 1940

The political excitement generated for the 1938 city election was followed by lassitude as the tensions in the labor movement subsided, now that the Dore-Beck combination had been sidelined. Tempering this slackening of tensions was confidence that the street railway mess of the past two decades finally was about to be resolved—it had been an unremitting source of political hostilities because of its repeated linkage with the fate of the Lighting Department's Skagit project, even extending to the broad issue of public ownership of utilities itself. And, not to be slighted, was the stimulus injected into the economy by war preparations.[1]

By the end of 1939, with war production in full swing, the effects were being felt. Symptomatic was the situation at the region's biggest manufacturing employer, the Boeing Airplane Company. The company was then employing about 6,000 workers and was gearing up to fill the rush of incoming orders. As noted above, the Aero Mechanics Union in 1940 had threatened a strike and forced the company to accept arbitration. The company was receiving invitations from San Francisco, Portland, and, allegedly, other cities to move its plant to their friendlier environs. Boeing management, striking a pose that would become familiar in the years ahead, declared: "The attitude of organized labor . . . must be weighed as one of the major factors by the company, in considering [these] overtures . . . Because of the difference between the wage rates which Boeing has paid and those of competitive factories, the company has remained in Seattle only with difficulty . . . [Its] market [is] a national or world market . . . This is what governs allowable production costs." Wartime pressures would force reconciliation of both parties, but it was the improving economy that brought them together in a truce that would last until 1947.[2]

It is uncertain whether the low interest registered for the February 28, 1939 primary was due to voter indifference or to the slighting of it by the three major daily newspapers. Both certainly were factors. The primary was focused on the council race, in which veteran incumbents, David Levine, Robert Harlin, and Frank Laube were being "challenged" by six political unknowns. Not on the primary ballot was an issue that would draw voters to the March 14 finals—a 3-mill school levy. Only 38,003 people voted, out of a total registration of 176,697—the smallest turnout since 1927. Not surprisingly, the incumbents led the vote count by wide margins. 80,001 voters turned out for the March 14 finals. Harlin's 50,584 led the pack, followed by Laube with 49,063 and Levine with 47,634. Far back in fourth position was Ross Kingston, with 26,949. As there were no real issues to enliven the council contest, name familiarity appeared decisive. It was the school levy that energized the voters sufficiently for its passage. The *Times* attributed the doubling of voter participation to this one issue.[3]

The 1940 primary election, similarly, elicited little newspaper interest. The *Times*, for example, carried a little squib in the lower right corner of its front page: "Go To Polls Tomorrow, Candidates Tell Voters". Mayor Langlie, riding a crest of popularity, was being opposed by four political unknowns. Up for reelection to the City Council were James Scavotto, William Norton, and Hugh DeLacy. Only the latter faced a close race for third place among the six finalists—DeLacy's margin was a mere 37 votes over those of Bob Jones of West Seattle. Indicative of how Langlie would run in the March finals was his victory margin—45,136 to those of Warren Cook's 4,576 votes. (Cook operated an automobile rental agency.)[4]

DeLacy, as president of the Washington Commonwealth Federation, was coming under fire for leading the WCF to endorse whatever line on foreign policy and the third term issue came from the Communist Party. The WCF had gone from posing as THE New Deal heart of the state's Democratic Party, to opposing President Roosevelt's foreign policy because it drew the United States into opposition to the Soviet Union. For this subservience, he attracted opposition not only from traditional conservatives, but also from the anti-communist liberal-left. To enliven the councilmanic contest, the *Times* ran a "Guest Guessers" for the "Third Spot" on the Council. Six days before the March 12 election, the *Times* concluded Jones was favored by a 4 to 1 majority over DeLacy. On the day before the election, the *Times* carried a story: "Election Tamperers Are Warned"—due to the tightness of the race for the third position between Jones and DeLacy. With the local economy surging to the impulse of war production, at a time when the WCF had convinced most people that it was a Communist-front, with DeLacy its leader, it is not surprising to find him losing by a wide margin to Jones: 56,686 to 36,512. That DeLacy captured as many votes as he did, is what seems more amazing. Still, the voter turnout of only 94,774 was the lowest since 1926. In this way did foreign policy energize a city election.[5]

Not so the general election in November 1940. Here, domestic issues dominated. The governor's race would be hotly contested, first within the Democratic Party, then even more so between the Republican nominee, Seattle's own Arthur B. Langlie, and former Senator Clarence C. Dill. Two critical initiative measures competed for attention—Initiative 139 which was aimed at undermining the formation of Public Utility Districts, and Initiative 141, an old age pension initiative sponsored by the Seattle-based Washington Old Age Pension Union. With the decline of the WCF's political influence, the WOAPU was becoming the voice of the radical left. Its initiative would draw support from across the political spectrum.

31

Prelude to the 1940 General Election

Politics of city and state would be uniquely affected by United States foreign policy as the Roosevelt administration responded to the European crisis on the heels of the Munich Conference in September 1938, settling the fate of Czechoslovakia as it became absorbed by Nazi Germany in March 1939. The portent for outright war seemed daily more real. Tied in with these events abroad was the matter among Democrats of who should succeed FDR. Or, failing to find a new leader who also was a liberal on domestic issues, and an anti-fascist who pursued a policy of collective security in foreign policy—should support be drummed up for a third term movement?

FDR, himself, was strongly committed to shoring up the forces bent on collective security—a "Popular Front" against fascism. And he lacked confidence in anyone else to continue that policy. This commitment led him to court a modest movement among liberal-New Deal organizations in the western states like the Washington and Oregon Commonwealth federations, Labor's Non-Partisan League (LNPL), and the California and Colorado Progressive federations. Though prolonged as a low-level strategy for about fourteen months, it was not terminated until January 1940. Prior to that date, early in summer 1939, the WCF's Tom Rabbitt organized a statewide "Draft Roosevelt For '40" button campaign—more than 50,000 were sold by mid-August. Orders from outside the state poured in. In the words of

WCF-historian, Albert Acena, "The WCF had never before undertaken an effort so enthusiastically which also generated a warm response in the Northwest and elsewhere in the country." The WCF leadership found itself not only riding a wave of New Deal support, but it was becoming convinced that it was actually leading it. Howard Costigan had even met with the President himself, coming away confident of putting together a "western federation" under his personal leadership . . . and, seemingly with FDR's backing to boot.[1]

Costigan gradually would be cut out of this short-lived movement by anti-WCF liberals who were concentrating on the defeat of Governor Martin. Among these liberals were WCF founders Mary and Burt Farquharson, Jack Cluck, Rolla Houghton, Fred Shorter, and Cyrus Woodward. And, from the Roosevelt administration in D.C. was Seattle's Norman Littell, working through Anna Roosevelt Boettiger and her husband, John, publisher of the *P-I.* The determining factor in the failure of the conference was need for support from the CIO's political arm, Labor's Non-Partisan League, whose real head was John L. Lewis. Lewis distrusted Costigan (potential head of a western liberal federation), was lukewarm toward a third term for FDR, and felt wounded for being bypassed in the early discussions. Lewis ordered the LNPL to withdraw its support. By then (late October, 1939), the WCF also was decidedly ambivalent about a third term—the Nazi-Soviet Non-Aggression Pact of August 23, followed by the German invasion of Poland on September 1, and two weeks later by the Soviet invasion of Poland, had forced the WCF to rethink its popular/democratic front stand against fascist aggression. On September 18, two days after the Soviet attack on Poland, a mass meeting sponsored by liberal-left leaders was held in the Senator Ballroom in downtown Seattle, at which all speakers urged amendment of the neutrality act to permit aid to the Allied forces. Pressure, nationwide, resulted finally in passage and signing on November 4, of the Neutrality Act so that arms could be sold to belligerents on a cash-and-carry basis. By the end of November the WCF became pacifist on the war, contending it was a foreign war—a position of the American Legion and the Veterans of Foreign Wars as well. When the Soviets invaded Finland on November 30, the WCF lost more of its key members—legislators Michael B. Smith, the Old Age Pension Union's president, James T. Sullivan, Paul Thomas, Edward Henry, and Jurie B. Smith, among them. Many CIO affiliates and the LNPL disaffiliated. While the Russo-Finnish war was being fought, so too was the city's election. As noted in the previous chapter, the electioneering tended to focus on the WCF and the re-election campaign of Councilman Hugh DeLacy, the WCF's president. By this time, the WCF's shifts in response to the changes in Soviet foreign policy had marked it convincingly as a Communist front in the eyes of the electorate. DeLacy was resoundingly defeated.[2]

While the liberal-left elements in the state's Democratic Party were mobilizing behind FDR for a third term, its anti-New Dealers on the right were seeking an alternative. Seattle's Stephen F. Chadwick whom Homer Bone had defeated in the 1932 Democratic senatorial primary, and who subsequently swung to Republican Wesley Jones in the runoff, was the state leader in this effort. He operated from his base as ex-National Commander of the American Legion (1937-1938), from which he had established influential contacts operating at the national level. He was thinking of another run, but was waiting until after the Democratic Party's national convention in June before deciding under which party label he would campaign. Whichever it was, the campaign would be isolationist in tone and hostile to the domestic policies of FDR. In the latter, he would find strong support among conservative Martin Democrats who dominated the legislature as they coalesced with Republicans to defeat social reform measures that carried more tax impositions.[3]

In preparation for the state Democratic Party convention in June, many of the WCF candidates were defeated by former WCFers, but the WCF could still claim a bloc of 80 to 90 votes, enough to have some effect. The King County delegation, with Mary Farquharson chairing the platform committee, brought in a platform that included endorsement of a third term. But at the state convention, DeLacy spoke out against a third term on the ground that FDR had violated the neutrality act that week by declaring for the Allies. FDR, earlier, on December 1, 1939, had placed an embargo on arms shipment to the Soviets. DeLacy would represent the First Congressional District at the national convention, and in that role he became the only delegation member not voting for the third term endorsement. Upon return from the Chicago convention, former mayor "Doc" Brown and County Prosecutor B. Gray Warner led a movement to oust DeLacy from the Democratic Party. DeLacy fended off these efforts, declaring that the WCF would continue to work within the Democratic Party, but would remain neutral on the presidential issue, and would still retain the right to act independently. However, DeLacy's and the WCF's performance inspired Jack

Cluck and Cyrus Woodward on June 18 to work for a Progressive Democratic Conference, to be held in the Civic Auditorium on August 24. This rally of some 1200 people bugled the presidential campaign in the state, and it effectively removed the WCF as the nominal voice of the New Deal. By then France had fallen to the Germans, and the "Battle of Britain" was at fever pitch, leading Congress to pass the Burke-Wadsworth bill establishing Selective Service. FDR signed the bill on September 16. Prior to this signing, DeLacy and Tom Rabbitt prepared to call an Independent Democratic convention on the day of the September primary. Sixty-three delegates attended, forty-two from Seattle. DeLacy was named their gubernatorial candidate. Endorsements of some Democrats were handed out, but as Albert Acena succinctly writes: "The WCF, straitjacketed by the CP line, was forced into a politically suicidal position: it professed to back certain Democrats, but it could not back the head of the Democratic ticket; it supported the New Deal, but it could not support the chief New Dealer."[4]

32

The 1940 General Election

We have seen how foreign policy and the third term issues split the liberal-left in the state's Democratic Party, thereby strengthening the anti-New Deal Democrats gathered under Governor Martin's wing. The WCF was no longer an influence in the party after the June national convention in which Hugh DeLacy distinguished himself and the WCF by not voting for a third term. The remaining members of the New Deal leaders in the party were left to find a candidate to defeat Martin, if he should seek a third term for himself. Martin had not supported the Grange's efforts to implement the public power district program, so this meant that a traditionally Republican-leaning organization—not expecting that party to support public ownership—would probably join in seeking an alternative to Martin. Grange following could be anticipated if someone could be found who was dependable on the PUDs issue. This factor underscored the need to attract rural support, and avoid the anti-Seattle/anti-urban stigma which the WCF had unavoidably fastened upon the party. For a brief time, Congressman Knute Hill loomed as a candidate, but he hedged in his bid. What galvanized this faction to action was the introduction of Initiative 139 into the campaign and Martin's declaration to run for a third term. The initiative was sponsored by the "Let the People Vote League", to which the Washington Taxpayers Association funnelled money. From Martin's own stronghold came the challenge from former Senator C.C. Dill, a known public power leader—AND he came from east of the Cascades.[1]

The state's Republican Party had depended upon its coalition with conservative Democrats—mainly from eastern Washington and Clark County—to restrain or stifle legislation that would carry tax burdens—welfare programs, unemployment remedies, common school and higher education support, chief among them. The Martin Democrats had attracted so much conservative support that would normally have gone to the Republicans that the latter were almost neutered, in effect. Mayor Arthur Langlie, however, had emerged as a potential state leader of a Republican revival. He keynoted the state party's June 1940 convention. The redoubtable Ashley Holden, once on the staff of the reactionary *Business Chronicle,* now political editor of the *Spokane Spokesman-Review,* had been actively drumming up Langlie support there, and in eastern Washington generally. So successful was his spadework that on July 9 a "caravan" representing every urban center in eastern Washington journeyed to Seattle to present Langlie with a petition carrying 25,000 signatures, urging him to declare for the party's nomination. Despite reservations expressed by Martin-Republicans that his entry would mean Martin's loss to Dill, followed by Langlie's defeat by Dill, if FDR carried the state by a big margin, Langlie, nonetheless, declared his entry on July 13.[2]

Special color early in the campaign was lent by the Initiative 141 petition drive. Spearheaded by the Washington Old Age Pension Union (WOAPU), it received unprecedentedly wide support during the spring signature campaign. So successful was it that Martin's opening speech brought a promise that he would seek to raise the state pension to the federal maximum of $40. Would voters take him seriously in the face of his record? Langlie also jumped on the pension bandwagon with a leaflet in which he advocated raising "the state contribution from $30 to $40 and then get federal matching dollars." He also promised to eliminate the "preferred claim clause" which required a pensioner to "assign his property to the state", and he added that he would end "unwarranted snooping and investigation of aged people . . . in the administration of the old age pension act." As for the WOAPU, its leaders hoped to use the initiative to unite them and others in a way that no other issue had been able to do: "Any decent citizen cannot help to go along with us. The opportunities are tremendous—even with Republicans . . . Let us cooperate with the Townsend forces." They hoped to "switch the national administration toward concern about European politics rather than American problems . . . ." Along this line, the WOAPU's William Pennock, seeking re-election to the state House of Representatives, declared in a leaflet: "Vote for those candidates who say clearly and fearlessly: NO WAR! NO DICTATORSHIP! NO CONSCRIPTION! Peace, Democracy, Pensions are American's Best Defense!". The WOAPU clearly was picking up the cudgels for the WCF.[3]

Martin's tactic was to link Dill with the radicals and to encourage cross-over voting that had served him so well in the 1936 campaign against John C. Stevenson. He earned the backing of Dave Beck, for what it was worth at this time. To no avail, as he lost to Dill by a vote of 186,008 to 114,484. Dill took King County, but Martin won in Seattle, due in part to cross-over voting, since the downtown establishment feared Langlie could not beat Dill. Martin endorsed Dill in the finals. In Seattle, the Teamsters, having no stomach for Langlie, came out for Dill, staging an overflow gathering of about 10,000 at the Civic Auditorium on October 30, at which teamster attendance was compulsory—a feature that Langlie was to use to great advantage. Langlie later observed that he did not run against Dill, but against Dave Beck. The Central Labor Council withheld any endorsement, and "its" two City Councilmen, Harlin and Levine, were known to be active for Langlie. Former WCFers—Professor Richard Tyler, Jack Cluck, legislators Jurie B. Smith and Mike Smith, John Fox (head of Masters, Mates and Pilots Union, CIO), and Howard Costigan organized a Progressives for Roosevelt Committee, endorsing, of course, the Democratic slate.[4]

The two big initiatives, 139 and 141, further enlivened the campaign. Initiative 139 was written by the private power companies to obstruct the Public Utility Districts from issuing bonds without a vote of at least 50% of the vote cast in the last election. Such elections would occur in off-years, not in the general election, so such bond issues were sure to fail. Langlie, knowing rural preference for the PUDs, and that Dill depended upon this rural vote—along with himself—he chose to oppose 139. Responding to complaints of fraudulent financing, the Federal Power Commission held hearings in Seattle in October, the month before the election. Newspaper coverage displayed Puget Sound Power and Light Company contributions in September, alone, to be $17,500 to the Washington Taxpayers Association, which the WTA transmitted to the Let The People Vote League, sponsors of the initiative. It would be revealed that $670,000 had been spent by PSP&L to fight the condemnation suit of Whatcom County, and that it had been illegally charged to operating expenses. Hearings extended to Oregon and California, revealing that, from 1935 to 1940, $790,653 had been spent on elections by the five largest utilities in Washington and Oregon. An additional $246,863 had been also allocated for political purposes. About half of this million had been charged to operating expenses, for which the consumer was charged. This was not only flagrantly illegal, but it certainly hurt the political cause of the companies. The publicity, coming just before the election, practically insured its defeat. The vote was 362,508 against 139 to 253,318 for it.[5]

Picking up on the later stage of the Initiative 141 campaign, Langlie came out against it, agreeing with the original sponsors of pension legislation in the 1920s and 1930s, the Eagles. The fraternal organization contended that no provision had been made in the initiative for its funding. Langlie indicated he would apply for federal matching money until the initiative could be implemented by the legislature. The Washington State Federation of Labor also opposed it. Dill was only lukewarm toward it. But the State Grange, the Democratic Party, the CIO, and others, endorsed it. That voters flocked to its support in the face of such strong opposition testifies to the frustrations to which the Martin administration had contributed with its stubborn resistance to amelioration of the fate of older citizens. Martin's last annual message conceded its absolute futility in dealing with pension and relief issues by placing responsibility upon the individual and family unit for their economic plight—acceptance of the poor law mentality in dealing with the system's failure. The 100,000 favorable vote margin—358,009 to 258,819—testifies to 141's broad appeal, at least to those in their waning years.[6]

Langlie portrayed Dill as a radical, to which Dill expressly laid claim at a public gathering in the Workers Alliance Hall in Seattle. Dill linked Langlie with the private utilities. Langlie played upon the Beck connection to advantage because Beck's name had become synonymous with labor racketeering for many voters. Oddly, Dill stressed what was Langlie's demonstrable long-suit—efficiency in government, when Dill had no comparable record to show for himself. Given the wide popularity of President Roosevelt who defeated Wendell Willkie by

140,022 votes (462,145 to 322,123), it is surprising that Dill lost to Langlie. But lose he did, though only by 5,816 votes (392,522 to 386,706). Langlie was the lone Republican to win a major office in the state, and as George Scott points out, Langlie was the only Republican who could have won. In Seattle, Dill ran slightly ahead of Langlie (84,799 to 82,283 votes), and by a larger margin in King County (121,013 to 114,296 votes). Dill also led in other urban counties—Pierce County (44,870 to 38,726), in Snohomish County (21,412 to 18,458), and in Spokane County (39,101 to 38,393).[7]

Summary and Conclusions

When one is reading and writing about the period between the two world wars while living in the 1980s, there is a ring of consonance. Scale creates an illusion that the periods are radically different. Yet, the present global integration of economies, political structures, and cultures only continues what was in process before World War II. Attitudes toward resolution of comparable economic, social, and political problems appear least modified at the level where decisions are made and given extended social effect. These attitudes seem the more constant factor amidst turbulent change. In the 1930s, a permanent underclass was in the making. Now it has been made and is being extended internally within the United States, though its composition differs from the one taking shape before the second war threw it a lifeline. Globally, there has always been an underclass, irrespective of national boundaries. Now the United States' version of a permanent underclass is merging with that elsewhere. Feeble attempts in the Thirties to deal with unprecedented unemployment and relief problems only resigned the policy makers to search despairingly for a rationale that would not burden taxpayers because, allegedly, entrepreneurs would be deprived of requisite investment incentives. Policy makers returned to attitudes shaped by the very archaic poor laws which they thought they had displaced. Having found the poor laws deficient, with their roots in county level administration, state and federal administrations assumed greater responsibility for dealing with these Great Depression problems. Meeting resistance from the influential taxpayer lobbies, but feeling relatively comfortable in naysaying the liberal-left, administrators and political leaders came full circle in assessing responsibility for unemployment—not the system, but the jobless or underemployed individual was to blame. He or she would have to find their way relatively unaided. At the onset of the Great Depression and toward its end—before war preparations provided the essential jobs—this defeatist attitude governed. In between lay state and federal failure.

Within the state, the contest for control of the Democratic Party between the Martin Democrats and New Deal Democrats seriously compromised provision for unemployment, relief, and old age pensions. Martin Democrats felt more comfortable with the assumptions of the poor law mentality that had gripped the Hoover administration in facing the down-sliding economy and its social consequences. Underscoring this intra-party rivalry for party control was Governor Martin's declaration to mayor-elect Arthur B. Langlie, in early 1938, that Langlie could expect state fiscal aid for Seattle, now that the Washington Commonwealth Federation's mayoral candidate had been roundly beaten. However, it was the federal government that came to Seattle's rescue, not the state. Langlie negotiated with the Reconstruction Finance Corporation to support the refunding of the street railway debt and the system's rehabilitation. Add to this the revival of the construction trades by implementation of the Yesler Housing Project, under Jesse Epstein's leadership in seeking National Housing Act funds for not only the city but for the state as a whole. Federal money continued as the chief source of relief and old age pension funds. Then came the boost from war production from 1939 on, pulling the state and nation out of the 1937-1938 recession which had been prompted by a sharp reduction of federal funding.

Publicly funded education suffered all through the period from underfunding, becoming even more afflicted when the taxpaying lobbies succeeded in limiting the property tax to 40 mills in 1932 without a compensating public school funding source to take its place. In the 1920s, even if the taxpayer lobbies had decided to adequately provide for public education, Governor Roland Hartley probably would have overridden them. It never came to that. Instead, in Seattle, the lobby coalesced tax-conscious forces into a Tax Reduction League in 1921, primarily to fight proper school funding—just at education's critical juncture, when public education was being redefined in light of the war experience and when dramatic shifts in technology were decisively affecting the economic and social structure of the nation, and with it, the new educational requirements imposed upon the work force. Until publicly funded education is considered an investment in the nation's future, under-achievement will characterize the product of the system.

Throughout the period, social amenities in the form of parks, playgrounds, boulevards, the fine arts and live theater suffered equally from niggardly funding, both public and private. Ironically, the city's parks and playgrounds finally benefited during the period after 1933, following a period since 1920, when they had been allowed to steadily deteriorate. Federal funding in the shape of the WPA and the CCC performed the resuscitation rites. Only a tiny circle among the social elite kept the fine arts alive. Others among them seemed bent solely in the direction of business success, concentrating upon tax avoidance while quieting their consciences about the kind of support that the business elite in major metropolitan centers was expected to provide. Nellie Cornish's experience is but a case in point.

Organized labor became neutered by the early 1920s, partly from conservative forces within the AFL, partly by the success of the open shop movement, heralded by business groups as the "American Plan". Before U.S. entry into the Great War, organized labor was becoming a political force in an increasingly effective pluralistic society, under the prod known popularly as the "progressive movement". Organized labor became alienated from this pre-war reform coalition. During and after the war it became, by stages, politically neutralized, losing uneasy allies from among the middle class, as typified by Municipal League membership. Not until 1934 did the AFL revive as an active force, goaded by organizing drives, generated largely from outside its ranks, among the unorganized. Only the Teamsters had shown any organizing initiative during the 1920s. In Seattle, they became the catalyst for unionization in the 1930s, striking fear among many employers and the general public in the process. But, not until the Great Maritime Strike of 1934 revealed a class conscious alternative to the Teamsters' organizing drives, did employers line up with the Teamster-generated AFL locals. Under Dave Beck's guidance, industries and trades were successively organized by agreement with individual trade associations to limit business entry into a particular line, control output, prices, and the like, all under a "dictator"—to use the term applied by the Chamber of Commerce's Alfred Lundin. Lundin, in outlining the threat to open shop conditions in 1936, had pointed to the "communist" threat, but having ritualistically issued that epithet, he passed quickly, fearfully, and lengthily to detailing Beck's operations and apparent goals: taking the freedom out of business enterprise. In the process, from 1934 until then, organized labor had become reactivated politically. Beck had Mayor John Dore in his pocket, while the maritime union radicals joined with the liberal-left in spearheading a statewide campaign to deal with unemployment and relief. Organized labor had regained political influence with a vengeance, but of divergent character. The community's weariness with the civil disruptions, caused by labor's attempts to right the imbalance forged by the open shop movement of the early 1920s, encouraged employer groups to re-establish their dominance in 1938 with Initiative 130—a "right-to-work" initiative. Its temporary effect was to draw the two wings of the labor movement together, thereby assuring the initiative's rejection by the state's voters.

These civil disruptions, combined with growing public awareness of civic corruption during the mayoral regimes of Charles Smith and John Dore, led to a clean government backlash. The "clean government crowd" joined against both police corruption and the seemingly pointless jurisdictional strife within organized labor. Spearheaded by the New Order of Cincinnatus, these constituencies in the Council of Churches, the Municipal League, the PTA, and Federation of Women's Clubs, elected Cincinnatus-backed candidates to the City Council in the mid-Thirties, and one of them—Arthur Langlie—to the mayorship in 1938. Mayor Langlie's singular achievement— as noted above—was resolution of the perennial Municipal Street Railway mess as he dealt with the City's debt crisis. The street railway and the status of the Lighting Department, as we witnessed in the main text, poisoned city politics throughout the period. Its importance is too critical not to comment upon at this juncture.

In the city, the public ownership battle had focused upon the Skagit power project of the Lighting Department and its linkage with the financial status of the Municipal Street Railway. In 1917 the department's J.D. Ross had pulled Puget Sound Traction, Power, and Light's Skagit license away from the Forest Service upon learning of the company's failure to demonstrate proof of its development commitment. Losing the Skagit power site, while disappointing, only drove the company to exploit its other resources and assets. Among the latter was its decrepit street railway system. Though a dubious asset in its present condition, the company found that it could use the wartime emergency to unload the system on the City. It did so at a price considered by most observers to be at least twice its real value, $15,000,000. Strong suspicions of fraud and bribery surrounded the transaction. These doubts were never allayed, as convincing circumstantial evidence surfaced time and again. Bond payments, however, could only be made from the railway's revenue, not from the general fund. Wrangling on this issue continued throughout the 1920s, because the Puget Sound Power and Light's Boston parent, Stone and Webster, felt the City would be forced to tap its general fund ultimately to avoid default. Should this happen, the City's credit standing would be threatened, impairing its ability to market all of its bonds in the future. But, while the bond payments were important to the company, its real concern was the City's Skagit project. The company wanted to regain the Skagit and, by doing so, terminate the City's Lighting Department. With only Tacoma then remaining a bastion of municipal ownership, Stone and Webster would have practically a monopoly on electrical power in western Washington. The City's railway debt became the mechanism through which the company sought to acquire the City's electrical properties.

PSP&L, early, withstood charges of fraud and bribery in the street railway transaction. And through its allies in the Chamber of Commerce and the *Seattle Times*, and by its covert (until the FTC investigations beginning in 1928) control of the Voters Information League, it sustained a steady attack on City Light's Skagit project. Against this tattoo in the background a city charter-city manager fight ran for almost three years, beginning as a second effort by the Municipal League to get voter approval of its city manager amendment in 1925. Enough voters had been confused about the two issues because promoters of charter revision created the impression that there was little difference in their respective objectives—fifteen freeholders simply would be elected to write a new City charter, whose character was yet to be defined. "Trust me" was its promoters' tactic. We have seen the elitist document that emerged, and its resounding defeat. Instrumental in its defeat was the role played by J.D. Ross. But Ross also had mobilized opposition to the city manager plan, just as he had in 1914, seeing the hand of the "power trust" in all instances. The city manager plan's intention seemed to him the dilution of his control of the Lighting Department and the end of "Your City Light". Regardless of the validity of his suspicions—

and there were grounds for them, which many voters shared—the fact that the Freeholders' chairman was a PSP&L attorney and the group appeared to be stacked with the company's advocates, certainly persuaded voters to reject the proposed charter, whether or not the company was more directly involved.

While the charter fight was going on, Councilwoman Bertha K. Landes was elected mayor, supplanting Edwin "Doc" Brown, who had become tarnished with corruption, and whose devotion to the City's Skagit project had become seriously questioned. Landes was an unmistakeable proponent of City Light—as well as the Municipal League's city manager plan, causing Ross to have reservations about her. She had given signs as Acting Mayor that she would clean house in the police department. But, in trying to resolve the street railway's bonding obligations, she had been roped in to a deal with PSP&L's Alton W. Leonard that linked its resolution to the rate charged by the Lighting Department to the street railway, lowering it to the point that might hazard the financial condition of the department. Their agreement was rejected by the City Council. The company's role in Landes's defeat by Frank Edwards, though unclear, was felt by many voters at the time to be decisive. When Mayor Edwards fired Ross in 1931, he was recalled because enough voters felt the company was behind the firing. Contributing more immediately to that suspicion than the whole train of events just outlined, were the widely publicized Federal Trade Commission hearings into the propaganda campaigns waged by the private utilities nationwide, and to the role of the company in trying to defeat the Grange District Power initiative in 1930. At this juncture Stone and Webster underwent reorganization and Frank McLaughlin replaced A.W. Leonard as head of PSP&L.

The 1920s witnessed the acquisition of water power sites and existing electrical properties statewide by the utility holding companies, and tying them into a power grid. Outside of Tacoma and Seattle electrical rates were variable but uniformly higher by far than those charged by the two big municipals. The latter rates served as a yardstick, embarassing the private utilities. The State Grange, striving for more electrical power and cheaper rates for its various rural/county constituencies, joined with the public power leaders in the two cities to pass a power bill that would allow formation of public utility districts, and permit the sale by the municipals of electrical power outside their corporate limits. Though failing to get legislation passed in 1923, and being thwarted through the initiative route in 1924, the Grange finally won voter approval in 1930 for its district power bill (after the legislature had again refused to pass such a bill). By this success the public power forces in the state joined against a common enemy throughout the 1930s. PSP&L was fought tooth and nail by both the Grange and the municipals.

In Seattle this struggle first took shape in 1934, when Ross proposed that the City acquire PSP&L's Seattle electrical properties. The timing was propitious because the company was in a weakened condition, as were private utilities nationwide. Soon, however, PSP&L's condition improved to the point that Stone and Webster was no longer tempted to sell. Meanwhile the private utilities were waging legal battles and going to court to prevent the Public Utility Districts from being formed. Failing in the courts, their strategy then aimed to obstruct takeover of their electrical properties by either negotiation, condemnation, or by a combination of each. Ross's merger proposal was defeated, along with a proposition in 1937 for resolution of the street railway's debt. During the course of this merger fight the public power forces became divided. Senator Homer T. Bone had one of his state lobbyists, Kenneth Harlan, frame a bill for the legislature that would put the state in the power business. In opposing every previous attempt to place municipal utilities under control of a state power commission, Ross and his lobbyists fought this proposal. Its defeat split Bone and Ross. And, as the Grange leaders tended to favor the bill, their future collaboration with Ross was compromised as well. Grange leaders wanted both rural electrification and irrigation. Private utilities were their opponents—the same as City Light's. Ambivalence prevailed among the Grange leaders as the 1940s decade began.

When Arthur Langlie became mayor in 1938 he bypassed Ross—who (in cooperation with financier Guy Myers) had a joint merger-street railway package in hand. Langlie, instead, worked directly with PSP&L's Frank McLaughlin and the Reconstruction Finance Corporation for the street railway's refinancing and rebuilding. Ross, by this time, was the Bonneville Power Administration's Administrator, though still acting as superintendent of the Lighting Department. Ironically, he and Myers were coming under fire from the Grange leaders for taking seriously the idea that the private power companies wanted to establish a "fair price" by negotiation without the goad of condemnation hanging over their heads. No such price could be determined without access to the company's books, and access was consistently denied.

Ross's merger proposal peculiarly became entangled with the Grand Coulee high dam-low dam controversy. Ross, in promoting the Skagit project, found himself competing with the promoters of the Columbia Basin project for the same federal dollars. The latter were convinced that Ross opposed their project, in particular the high dam. The Seattle Chamber of Commerce, along with its brother chambers in the region, also opposed the high dam, lining up behind Spokane's Washington Water Power Company, which was pushing for its own dam at Kettle Falls. These opponents, in their ideological commitment to fight any publicly funded/owned enterprise, had not realized that ownership of the power to be generated was not the critical issue. Its distribution was, however. Primed probably by Willis T. Batcheller, who was a long-time opponent of Ross, Ashley Holden, as director of the Columbia River Development League, saw as his first priority the twofold task of persuading the Seattle Chamber of Commerce to support the high dam proposal while simultaneously mustering opposition to Ross's merger proposal in early 1935. In succeeding, Holden got the chamber to direct its energies toward support for the high dam, and to focus on power distribution. PSP&L and the other private utilities acted accordingly by using every measure possible to thwart implementation of the PUD operations, and their purchase of the companies' properties. The private utilities also aimed to blunt activation of the public preference clause in the BPA's charter. How these elements interplay during the 1940s decade will be the subject of the following volume.

In referring above to the state of the economy in the 1930s, to the volatility of the labor movement, to the public power issues—as reflected in City Light's contest with Puget Sound Power and Light and in the Grange's struggle to establish Public Utility Districts—no mention was made of the fascination "production-for-use" held for the liberal-left. In a real sense, the idea synthesized elements from all of the above. Born of the despair portrayed by idle factories and docks, boarded-up shops and stores, mortgage foreclosures, bank failures, proliferating lines of unemployed, the notion took root that if a parallel non-profit economy could be established by reactivating all that lay idle, that of the profit sector itself would be invigorated. Finding expression in Upton Sinclair's EPIC platform and briefly in Technocracy propaganda, the idea transfixed liberal-left organizations, beginning with the self-help-oriented Unemployed Citizens' League, through its political offshoots. These offshoots, successively, were the Commonwealth Builders and the Washington Commonwealth Federation. "Production-for-Use" emerged as Initiative 119 in 1936. It was resoundingly defeated, probably because, finally, it seemed so fanciful by 1936. That it endured beyond 1933, though, seems puzzling. It seems to the author, that political leaders of the liberal-left readily used "production-for-use" mainly as one effective means of pointing out the shortcomings of the capitalist economy. Evidence of its failure was everywhere. Yet there was no possibility this parallel economy could exist self-contained, and no serious attempt seems to have been made to explore the issue in this vein. It remained visionary and propagandistic in character until rejected. After that, little was ever seriously heard of the idea again.

Conservation as a movement bore internal contradictions. One group wanted to prevent private monopolization of water, forest, and other natural resources, while saving them for exploitation ostensibly through the protective management of governmental agencies. Efforts took the form of having state and federal agencies reserve water power sites for public development, setting aside more forest land under U.S. Forest Service control, including National Monuments within them, and establishing national parks. Commercial, mineral, agricultural, and industrial exploitation within these public confines was contemplated. And, as the Hetch Hetchy reservoir demonstrated in Yosemite, national parks would not be immune to such pressures. Gifford Pinchot provided the intellectual and political rationale for this line of conservationist thought—that all natural resources ultimately were candidates for development if persuasive justification could be adduced. Somehow, this self-restraint on the part of the Forest Service technocrats was to be observed, while preventing private monopolization of water power sites.

In implementing these principles, the Forest Service confronted a second group of conservationists, those who initially focused narrowly on "wilderness" values, and later, on more encompassing ecological values, by which humans are viewed as but one element in the larger matrix of earthly habitat. These two confronted one another locally in the Olympic National Park controversy. The Forest Service program, for the first time, was articulated for public consumption, and it was found wanting. Even within the service its operational premises came into question, most critically in the matter of sustained yield policy, when its plans were revealed for cutting all merchantable timber on the peninsula in order to implement this policy. As it turned out, sustained yield for the region was predicated on an unarticulated premise—that the service would be able to come to some agreement with private owners of timbered land for implementing its program—this in face of the acknowledged severe overcutting of private lands. Having no authority over private lands, the service cannot compel conformity to a sustained yield policy.

Disenchantment with the Forest Service, on the part of the environmentalists, spread to other federal agencies, as well as state administration, by the late 1950s. Conservation, as a program of the Mountaineers and the State Federation of Women's Clubs receded, but other local groups filled the void. Interest revived in earlier targets—the Glacier Peak area, that of the North Cascades, the region lying between Stevens and Snoqualmie passes, and the Mt. Baker-Mt. Shuksan complex. Public sensitivity was sharpened about the extent to which resource exploitation had gone, practically unabated, in but one generation, and the ecological consequences were more dramatically portrayed. These local groups—the North Cascades Conservation Council and the Alpine Lakes Protection Society, in particular—developed a statewide constituency for direct action. The Mountaineers finally established a publication program to articulate these views. In tandem, a nationwide conservation network coalesced including the Sierra Club, the Wilderness Society, the Audubon Society and other organizations for lobbying purposes. To this the Olympic National Park controversy had contributed decisively in forming the lines of future controversy. These developments are the subject of the following volume.

Endnotes

Chapter 1

Labor in Turmoil

The *Union Record*: Target of Left and Right

1. For general background as well as detailed coverage see: Mary Joan O'Connell," The Seattle Union Record, 1918-1928: A Pioneer Labor Daily" (Unpublished Master's Thesis, University of Washington, 1964), chapter 9; and Jonathan Dembo, "A History of the Washington Labor Movement, 1885-1935 (Unpublished Ph.D. Dissertation, University of Washington, 1978), chapter 7. Dembo's dissertation has been published as *Unions and Politics in Washington State, 1885-1935* (New York: Garland Publishing Company, 1983); however, citations herein are to Dembo's unpublished dissertation.

2. O'Connell, *ibid.*, pp. 177-8, 186; Dembo, *ibid.*, pp. 303-04, and 316-18 for the financial aftermath of the "labor-capitalist" fight. Added to Ault's woes was the regaining of control by some corner owners of the Newsboys' Union, and control over the corners with it. Ault refused to sign new corner contracts, choosing first to appeal to the United States Department of Labor: Ault to Dept. of Labor, 13 Nov., 1920, File 4-13, Part 2 of Ault Papers.

3. O'Connell, *ibid.*, pp. 179-85; Dembo, *ibid.*, p. 298.

4. O'Connell, *ibid.*, pp. 182-4. The *UR* was incorporated with a capital stock of $600,000, including $500,000 of preferred stock which remained largely unsold, thereby hampering expansion: Ault to J.W. Kelly, 3 Nov. 1920, File 4-13, Part 1, Ault Papers.

5. O'Connell, *ibid.*, pp. 184-7; Dembo, *ibid.*, pp. 302-04; *P-I*, 6 Nov., 1921 carried an advertisement announcing the merger of these theaters

under the Workers Union Theaters. Also Ault to C.A. Mann, fiscal agent of the theaters, 5 Jan., 1921, congratulating Mann on his financial and educational success: File 4-14, Part 1, Ault Papers. By mid-1922, however, Ault reported, "with exception of one or two grocery stores, there is not a single successful [Rochdale type of] cooperative . . . in the city." He reported success for the Mutual Laundry, the savings bank, and—generously—the *UR* itself: Memo, 5 July, 1922, File 4-20, Part 1, Ault .

6. O'Connell, *ibid.*, pp. 184-85; Dembo, *ibid.* pp. 304-06; Seattle Chamber of Commerce, *Minutes*, 7 June 1921. The *Tacoma Labor Advocate* also attacked Ault as a labor- capitalist; see Shimmons to Ault, 12 Nov. and 3 Dec., 1921, File 4-5. Part 1, Ault Papers.

7. O'Connell, *ibid.* pp. 183-86; Dembo, *ibid.*, pp. 308-15. Duncan, however, remained as secretary of the SCLC after Local 79 of the Machinists' Union recalled him because the Auto Mechanics, Local 289 appointed him its representative. (Dembo, *ibid.*, p. 310).

8. O'Connell, *ibid.*, p. 192; Dembo, *ibid.*, pp. 313-15.

9. O'Connell, *ibid.*, p. 195; Dembo, *ibid.*, p. 315; *UR*, 2 Apr., 1921. Ault to O'Connor and Chamberlain, 25 May 1921, File 4-14, Part 1, Ault Papers.

10. Ault to Haas, 11 Oct., 1921, File 4-15, Part 1, Ault Papers. See also chapter 22, "Dave Beck and the Rise of the Teamsters".

11. O'Connell, *ibid.*, pp. 198-204; Dembo, *ibid.*, pp. 318-23; Ault to Carpenters Union, Local 131, 31 May 1921, File 4-14, Part 1, Ault Papers.

12. O'Connell, *ibid.*, Chapter 10, "Toward Bankruptcy"; Ault to Baldwin, 29 Oct., 1923, and to Haas, 17 July 1923, File 4-20, Part 1, Ault, Papers.

Unemployment, 1921-1922

1. Seattle Chamber of Commerce, *Minutes*, 7 and 14 Dec., 1920; *UR*, 9 May 1921. The *UR* reported 3,000 men with 10,000 dependents were unemployed. An average of 5 children a day visited the Unemployed Association asking for shoes to go to school.

2. *UR*, 4, 5 and 31 Mar, 7 Apr., 1921; 8 Apr., 1922.

3. *UR*, 16 Mar., 1921.

4. Chamber of Commerce, *Minutes*, 18 Oct., 1921; *Municipal News* 19 Nov., 1921.

5. *UR*, 10 and 14 Oct., 1921.

6. *UR*, 9 and 23 Jan., 23 Apr., 1922. The *UR* reported on 10 February 1922 that the Mayor's committee will act on a request to use vacant public buildings to house the jobless and homeless.

Employer Insurgency and Strikes, 1921-1922

1. *UR*, 17 Mar., 1921.

2. *UR*, 16 and 19 Mar., 1921.

3. *UR*, 6 May 1921.

4. *UR*, 4 Mar., 11 Oct., 1921; District 10 of the UMW to Short, 1 Nov., 1921, urging Short to postpone any demonstrations until after the relief caravans arrived so that the operators' request for National Guard protection would not be justified: Box 3 WSFL, Records. In this box are

many handwritten letters from local relief committees. On 3 April 1921 the SCLC sent letters to all locals for contributions; Box 15, WSFL, Records.

5. *UR*, 21 Apr., 14 Sept., 1921; Chamber of Commerce, *Minutes* 18 Aug., 1921. John McIntosh, manager of the Federated Industries, issued a mimeographed letter on 5 December 1921, urging businesses, "as a believer in the American Plan of employment, . . . [it is necessary to give] at least a part of your business to these . . . open shop coal companies . . . " Pacific Coast Coal Company, Records. In another letter of 13 Dec., 1921 McIntosh wrote: "90% of the strikers are foreigners . . . 90% of those who have taken the places of strikers are American citizens." PCC, Records.

6. *UR*, 18 Mar., 1922; WSFL, *Proceedings*, 1922, pp. 5-7.

7. *UR*, 1 and 3 Sept., 1921, 20 Feb., 1922. In its report to stockholders, 11 Mar., 1922, the PCC officers wrote: "With production now about two-thirds normal and the wage scale 25% below that formerly paid, the favorable outcome of our program seems in sight . . . " Later in the year, however, the local operators informed president William Barnum that turnover had been "unusually high", new men making up 91% of the work force, thereby entailing high costs of recruiting, training, and damage to tools and equipment, amounting to about $222,000 for the year: Box 20, PCC Records.

8. *UR*, 9 and 19 Mar., 1921.

9. *UR*, 10 May 1921; *Minutes* , 20 Jan., 13 Feb., 24 Apr., 29 May, 10 July, 30 Oct., 27 Nov., 1921; 15 Jan., 5 Feb., 14 and 28 May, 25 June, 31 Dec., 1922. *Minutes* of 25 Mar., 1923 indicate that a three year contract recommended by a local arbitration board would be voted upon, but later 1923 minutes make no reference to voting results: Seattle Typographers Union, Local 202, Records.

10. *UR*, 1 and 30 Apr., 1921, 23 Mar., 1922; Ault to K. Sasaki, 30 July 1921, File 4-15; Ault to Japanese Hotel Keepers Association, 23 May 1922, File 4-17, Part 1, Ault, Papers.

11. Chamber of Commerce, *Minutes*, 21 Sept. 1921; on Waterhouse, *UR*, 20 and 25 Feb., 21 Mar., 1922.

12. *UR*, 10 June, 5 and 10 Oct., 1921; Donald Garnel, *The Rise of Teamster Power in the West* (Berkeley: University of California Press, 1972), pp. 12-12, 59-60, 80-91; Dembo, *ibid.*, pp. 435-42. See chapter 22, "The Rise of Dave Beck and the Teamsters".

13. Garnel, *op. cit.*; Dembo, *op. cit.*

14. Garnel, *op. cit.*; Dembo, *op. cit.*

15. *UR*, 12, 17, 19, 24, and 28 Oct., 1921.

16. *UR*, 10 Mar., 1922.

17. *UR*, 20 May and 30 Aug., 1921; William Thomas White, "A History of the Railroad Workers in the Pacific Northwest, 1883-1934" (Unpublished Ph.D. Dissertation, University of Washington, 1981), Chapter 7 gives the general background; on the 1922 strike see his pp. 240-61. White writes (p.241): "[the RLB in April declared an] absolute wage reduction in response to the declining cost of living, [and to end] rules, working conditions, and agreements instituted by the [wartime] Railroad Administration."

18. White, *op. cit.*

19. White, *op. cit.* (quotation is from p. 240).

20. *UR*, 27 Sept. and 14 Oct., 1921; White, *ibid.*, pp. 240-41.

21. *UR*, 18 Oct., 1921; Irving Bernstein, *The Lean Years: A History of the American Worker, 1920-1933* (Baltimore: Penguin Books, 1966), pp. 211-12. In the *P-I*, 1 Nov., 1922, Hearst was reported to have denounced the RLB ruling on September 11 for refusing to authorize a living wage, and on November 1, that the Labor Department had promoted the idea of a living wage as contributing to the national welfare; but that the RLB ruled the notion to be "impracticable". The Chamber of Commerce *Minutes* of 25 July 1922 record that body as claiming the shopmens' strike to be "against the Government and against the public."

22. *UR*, 15, 18, and 20 Oct., 1921; Bernstein, *ibid.*, considers the shopmens' strike to have been the "greatest strike of the decade"; that "Wilkerson found a legal basis for his decision by finding that the unions had violated the Sherman Act . . . [putting under its coverage] every sort of act which was part of an alleged unlawful conspiracy to restrain interstate commerce." The U.S. Supreme Court ruled in the *United States vs. Brims* that a "collective bargaining agreement [was] illegal under the Sherman Act."

23. White, *op. cit.*

24. Bernstein, *op. cit.*; White. *op. cit.*

The Great Maritime Strike of 1921

1. Darrell H. Smith and Paul V. Betters, *The United States Shipping Board: Its History, Activities, and Organization* (Washington, D.C.: Brookings Institute, 1931), pp. 48-64 for background on Shipping Board; also the Shipping Board *Annual Report*, 1925 and 1926.

2. Smith and Betters, *Ibid.*, pp. 82-3 concerning "Labor Problems". In 1921, the Board released shipyard employers from adhering to existing wage scales. A 10% cut followed, then a 15% cut, which led to the general maritime strike. The *UR* reported the possibility of a strike in the face of a threatened 20% to 30% reduction by the American Shipowners' Association: *UR*, 20 Apr., 1921, and 2 May 1921, indicating the fear of the International Seamens' Union that pre-war conditions were being sought by the employers, and that they were evading the rules set out in the 1915 Seamens' Act. The *UR* pointed to the irony of having to force a government agency to obey the law. Kenneth Kerr of the *Railway and Marine News* (abbreviated RMN hereafter) claimed these cuts were justified because of foreign competition, that wages still remained above foreign levels, and currently were better than steel workers (with their 20% cut) and textile workers (with their 22.5% cut): *RMN*, XIX:6 (June 1921). Bruce Nelson, in *Workers on the Waterfront: Seamen, Longshoremen, and Unionism in the 1930s* (Urbana: University of Illinois Press, 1988) explores the seamens' sub-culture, out of which springs a persistent "syndicalist mood", from the late 19th century to the 1930s, and the impact of the Seamens' Act in ameliorating working conditions: chapters 1 and 2.

3. *UR*, 2 May 1921.

4. *UR*, 19 Apr., 1921; the secretary of Local 38-12 claimed this shipping diversion was intended to break the union.

5. *UR*, 30 Apr., 1921; more than 100 men reportedly stood on the docks and were refused jobs as the Commissioners indicated they would hire only "from the preferred list". On 6 May 1921, Traffic Manager Muirhead announced new regulations, calling for a board of governers consisting of three elected by the workers and three elected by the commissioners.

6. *UR*, 2 May 1921; President Harding's plans to appoint an arbitration board was greeted cooly by the shipowners. Bruce Nelson points out that the Seamens' Act was a "dead letter" between 1921 and 1934, *ibid.*, p. 45.

7. *UR*, 6 May 1921; *RMN*, XIX:6 (June 1921); Kenneth Kerr considered the strike to be one "against the government".

8. *UR*, 2 May 1921.

9. *UR*, 11 and 13 June 1921.

10. *UR*, 18 May, 8 and 9 June 1921.

11. *UR*, 10 June 1921.

12. U.S. Shipping Board, *Annual Report*, 1921-1922, pp. 22-3; *UR*, 11 and 19 May 1921, 14 June 1921.

13. Joseph S. Jackson, "The Colored Marine Employees Benevolent Association of the Pacific, 1921-1934" (Unpublished Master's Thesis, University of Washington, 1939), p. 90.

14. U.S. Shipping Board, *Annual Report*, 1922, pp. 23-4; Frank Foisie, *Decasualizing Longshore Labor and the Seattle Experience* (Seattle: Waterfront Employers of Seattle, 1934), pp. 10 ff; Foisie, "Stabilizing Seattle's Longshore Labor", National Conference of Social Work, *Proceedings*, 1925, pp. 302-07. In 1927 Foisie saw "port days" as the critical area in which labor costs could be sharply reduced; hence, "Group action by cooperation among employers of a port is essential [for substantial reductions]". See also *RMN*, XXIV:5 (May 1927), pp. 9-10. According to Bruce Nelson, "Careful estimates in 1924 and 1937 found that wages constituted [12% of operating costs in 1924 and 14% in 1937]", *ibid.*, p. 70; Nelson contradicts Foisie about the ineffectiveness of the employers in combating worker organization, contending that employers "exercized nearly complete dominance in maritime relations between 1921 and 1934" (p. 68). Indeed, the evidence points overwhelmingly to this dominance as the chief reason for the 1934 strike. For the British response, much earlier, to decasualization see Gareth S. Jones, *Outcast London: A Study in the Relationship Between Classes in Victorian Society* (New York: Pantheon Books, 1984), pp. 318-19, 327-29.

15. Chamber of Commerce, *Minutes*, 10 and 17 May 1921; *UR*, 12 and 16 May 1921.

16. Nelson, *ibid.*, pp. 60-1. Nelson observes that ties between lumber workers and waterfront workers were close, with the same worker floating from one to the other; "more than half of the Pacific Coast seamen were employed in the steam schooner trade whose source was the lumber industry [of the coastal states]". He argues that it was the "syndicalist mood", not necessarily any particular syndicalist organization that pervaded the waterfront worker's attitudes toward the mainstream culture from which he was segregated in almost every way. This segregation is

what underlay direct action as a common tactic: wildcat strikes, slow-downs, "job actions", pp. 62-5; also pp. 42-3. On their affililiation with the Unemployed Citizens' League see *The Unemployed Citizen*, 3 Feb., 1933.

The Labor Movement in Transition: Near Stagnation

1. David Montgomery, in his *The Fall of the House of Labor: the Workplace, the State, and American Labor Activism, 1865-1925* (New York: Cambridge University Press, 1987), describes in detail this process of structural changes in the character of the workforce in relation to technological changes, and how the labor movement and government reacted. Also instructive is Gabriel Kolko, *Main Currents in Modern American History* (New York: Pantheon Books, 1984), pp. 101-05.

2. Montgomery, *ibid.*, p. 407.

3. Montgomery, *ibid.*, pp. 399, 406 (quotation is from p. 399); Robert E. Ficken, *The Forested Land: A History of the Lumbering Industry in Western Washington* (Seattle: University of Washington Press, 1987), pp. 162-63; Bruce Nelson, *ibid.*, pp. 70-4.

4. Dembo, *ibid.*, chapter 9, "The Conservatives Counterattack . . . " covers the subject in detail, although I have added some detail, as noted below. Short, to C.P. Taylor, 15 Aug., 1923, Box 42, WSFL, Records.

5. Short to Bone, 25 Sept., 1923; Short to D. D'Allessandro, 25 Oct.,1923; Short to H.W. Bullock, 5 Mar., 1925, in Longview, concerning the 8-hour day, in which Short advised that exceptions must be fought by the men themselves, through organization, at which time the Federation would "be able" to help. Also a similar letter, 17 Mar., 1925, to C.D. Long of Kelso. Short to Cotterill, 3 Feb., 1925. All in Box 42, WSFL, Records. Short was castigated by Grange president, A.S. Goss, 20 Aug., 1925, for not taking seriously his representation on the State Chamber of Commerce, leaving the defense of labor to Goss and "Scollard"; in Box 26, WSFL, Records. See also Dembo, *ibid.*, pp. 459-61, 500.

6. 6 Sept., 1933, report of the ["Committee for Promoting an Organizing Campaign"]; in the upper left corner is pencilled": "Original sent to Pres. Green Oct. 9, 1933".

Chapter 2
Politics in General

The Legislature and the City

1. See: Douglas R. Pullen, "The Administration of Washington State Governor Louis F. Hart, 1919-1925" (Unpublished Ph.D. Dissertation, University of Washington, 1974), chapter VI for general background on 1921 legislative session; John A. Rademaker, "The Ecological Position of the Japanese Farmers in the State of Washington" (Unpublished Ph.D. Dissertation, University of Washington, 1939), chapter 11 for general background leading to and on the Anti-Alien Land Acts of 1921 and 1923; S. Frank Miyamoto, *Social Solidarity Among the Japanese in Seattle* (Seattle: University of Washington Publication in the Social Sciences, Vol. II, No. 2, pp. 57-130), pp. 66, 85, and 114; John I. Nishinori, "Japanese Farms in Washington (Unpublished Master's Thesis, University of Washington,

1926), pp. 10 and 14. For a contemporary pamphlet by a traditional defender of minority rights see U.G. Murphy, "The Anti-Japanese Agitation", representing the view of the Council of Churches. See also, chapter 8, "Seattle and its Agricultural Hinterland".

In 1924 both Senators Dill and Jones favored exclusion; the state American Legion commander, Hinton Jones, and the WSFL's Short joined in a telegram: "The Pacific Coast . . . is encouraged at the prospect of a federal law ending threat of Japanese domination . . . ": *P-I,* 8 Apr., 1924.

In addition to the above sources, see specifically: Chamber of Commerce, *Minutes*, 24 Aug., 1920 for its response to complaints from Tokyo about anti-Japanese agitation; and 1 Mar., 1921 concerning its opposition to the bill (the act would have "no vital force" because the state constitution already defines the rights of aliens to real property, and the act would infringe on federal jurisdiction). On Beeler, see *UR,* 9 Mar. 1921; on Tindall see *P-I*, 31 July 1922. The *P-I,* for 28 Apr., 1923 reports on the first escheat case issuing from enforcement of the act; there were about 100 cases in line.

2. Pullen, *ibid.* chapter IV for general background, especially pp. 128-30; Yung-Ping Chen, "A Historical Study of the General Property Tax in the State of Washington" (Unpublished Master's Thesis, University of Washington, 1957), chapter I, and pp. 21-34 for historical antecedents prior to voter approval of the 40-mill property tax limit in 1932.

3. Pullen, *ibid.*, chapter II, especially pp. 132-37.

4. Pullen, *ibid.*, pp. 138-46

5. Pullen, *ibid*, pp. 146-56. On the poll tax see *UR,* 16, 18, 21 Mar., 1921; *Municipal News,* 26 Mar., 1921 (the League also favored it because it provided relief for the small home owner). The *UR,* for 25 Jan., 1923, reported that at the Peace Officers' convention in Bellingham, a resolution was approved, urging its repeal.

6. Pullen, *ibid.*, pp. 146-56.

7. Marsh's form letter of 3 Feb. 1921, Box 1, Accession 731, WEA Records. In the 1920 special legislative session the WEA had joined with the Washington State Teachers League to pass the "20-20" law for "financial relief of the common schools". Soon thereafter the two organizations merged. In its "Revised Constitution and Bulletin" it concluded that its past political neutrality was a failed policy in not keeping up "with our industrial and economic development". It focused on getting "equal education opportunity for each child [based on] a just system of taxation and an equitable plan of distribution". The "30-10" plan became its first political objective; local levies of up to 15 mills would be allowed under it without recourse to popular vote, and up to 20 mills would be permitted by popular vote. Not lost sight of in the document was the goal of seeking teacher tenure, a fight which was yet to be won at the end of our period. Box 1 WEA, Records. On the reorganization see Ardath I. Champlin, "The Washington Education Association, 1889-1964 (Unpublished Ph.D. Dissertation, University of Utah, 1967), pp. 50-3.

8. Pullen, *ibid.*, chapter VI; William O. Sparks, "J.D. Ross and Seattle City Light, 1917-1932" (Unpublished Master's Thesis, 1964), pp. 77-8. A bill to give the Legislature control over city budgets was killed by filibus-

ter; and the attempt to deny Ports power to raise taxes was barely defeated. *UR*, 10-12 and 16 Mar., 1921.

9. Morris L. Cooke, ed., *Giant Power: Large Scale Electrical Development as a Social Factor (Annals* of the American Academy of Political and Social Science, Vol. CXVIII, March 1925); Edward B. Logan, ed., *Lobbying (Annals* . . . Vol., CXVIV, July 1929), pp. 24-32 on utilities lobbying.

10. *Times*, 31 Dec., 1923; *P-I* 1 May, 1922.

11. U.S. Federal Trade Commission [Hearings on utility corporations' propaganda , Pt. 71-A]; Wesley A. Dick, "Visions of Abundance: the Public Power Crusade in the Pacific Northwest in the Era of J.D. Ross and the New Deal" (Unpublished Ph.D., University of Washington, 1973), pp. 66-7.

12. Dick, *ibid.*, pp. 66-9; Sparks, *ibid.*, pp. 81-3.

13. *Municipal News*, 26 Mar., 2,12, and 16 Apr., 1921; *UR*, 8 Mar., 1921; *P-I*, 31 Oct., 1922. In a letter to the editor in the *Star*, 4 Sept., 1922, Ross pointed out that the Skagit development would have been prevented by the "certificate of necessity requirement" and urged defeat of Referendum 12.

14. *UR*, 4 and 7 Mar., 1921.

Electric Power, Public Ownership, and the Federal Power Act of 1920

1. David E. Nye, *Electrifying America: Social Meanings of a New Technology, 1880-1940* (Cambridge, MA: MIT Press, 1990), pp. 92-3, 132-34; Richard C. Berner, *Seattle, 1900-1920: From Boomtown, Urban Turbulence, to Restoration* (Seattle: Charles Press, 1991), chapters 5 and 18.

2. Nye, *ibid.*, p. 169 for Cochran quotation; pp. 170-73 (quotation is from p. 173); Alfred D. Chandler, Jr. *The Visible Hand: the Managerial Revolution in American Business* (Cambridge, MA: Harvard University Press, 1977), pp. 426-31.

3. The legislative history of this legislation is detailed in Judson King, *The Conservation Fight: From Theodore Roosevelt to the Tennessee Valley Authority* (Washington, D.C.: Public Affairs Press, 1959), chapter VI; Morris L. Cooke, ed., *Giant Power . . . op. cit.*

4. See Harold T. Pinkett, *Gifford Pinchot: Private and Public Forester* (Urbana: University of Illinois Press, 1978), chapter XI; Roderick Nash, *Wilderness and the American Mind* (New Haven: Yale University Press, 1973), chapter 10 on Hetch Hetchy; Harold K. Steen, *The U.S. Forest Service: a History* (Seattle: University of Washington Press, 1976), pp. 74, 115-22; Ben F. Twight, *Organizational Values and Political Power: the Forest Service Versus the Olympic National Park* (University Park: Pennsylvania State University Press, 1983), Part I. See also chapter 15, "Conservation and Mountain Recreation Between the Wars".

5. Nash, *ibid.*, chapters 11 and 12.

"Electrifying America" . . . and Seattle

1. Nye, *ibid.*, pp. 259-62

2. Nye, *ibid.*, pp. 260-77; Stephen Fox, *The Image Makers: a History of*

American Advertising and its Creators (New York: Vintage Press, 1985), chapter 3 for the general transformation of advertising in the 1920s.

3. File 124, Seattle Lighting Department, Records.

The Public Ownership Fight: PSP&L Links Street Railway Rescue With Acquisition of City Light

1. Ross persuaded Caldwell to oppose the dam, and he soon rejected his own proposal for a tunnel under the lake to supply power temporarily (the Chamber of Commerce approved the tunnel idea): Ross to Caldwell, 6 Dec. 1920 and 22 Apr., 1922, File 11-22; *Times*, 25 July, 1920 and *Star*, 4 Dec. 1920. Over Erickson's objections, Ross had earlier opposed continuation of sealing operations as well. Ross to Fitzgerald, 3 Jan., 1920, File 11-17, Seattle Lighting Department, Records (hereafter cited as SLD, Records).

2. Ross to Caldwell, 6 Nov., 1920, File 11-22, SLD, Records.

3. Copy of Caldwell to Comptroller H. Carroll, 28 Jan., 1921; Caldwell insisted that the contract specified railway revenues as the only source, and that for the City to guarantee payment from the general fund would simply be a "present" to the company: Box 100, PSP&L, Records; *Municipal News*, 15 Jan., 1921. The *Times*, 13 Feb., 1921 editorial agreed with the grand jury, that Stone and Webster had "buncoed" the City Council in its sale of the street railway (no admission of the newspaper's own role in the buncoeing is noted; see Berner, *ibid.*, pp. 264-68).

4. Pratt to Leonard, 12 Jan., 1921; Leonard to Pratt, 23 Apr., 1921, Box 100, PSP&L, Records.

5. Pratt to Leonard, 12, 22, and 31 Jan., 1921; Leonard to Pratt, 1 Feb., 1921; Howe to Pratt, 3 Feb., 1921; Leonard to Pratt, 7 Feb., 1921, Box 100, PSP&L, Records; Chamber of Commerce, *Minutes*, 19 Oct., 1920.

6. Pratt to Leonard, 7 and 10 Feb., 1921, Box 100, PSP&L, Records.

7. Leonard to Pratt, 3 May 1921, Box 100, PSP&L, Records.

8. Ross to Chamber of Commerce, 18 June, 1921, File 11-23, SLD, Records.

9. Chamber of Commerce, *Minutes*, 8 and 19 July 1921.

10. *Municipal News*, 16, 23, and 30 July 1921.

11. *Municipal News*, 29 Oct., 1921; *Times*, 24 and 25 Oct. 1921.

12. *UR*, 11 and 17 Apr., 2 May, 1922; *Star*,1 May 1922; *Times*, 2 May 1922. On Ford: *UR* and *P-I*, 15 May 1922; *Times*, 16 May, 1922; the *Star*, 14 June 1922, charged the Ford motion was a "smoke screen" to allow the "co." to take over at the "crucial moment" when Ford would choose Muscle Shoals over the Skagit.

13. Fitzgerald's flier is in the PSP&L Records for 21 Feb., 1922, Box 100. The *P-I*'s City Hall reporter, the respected Carl Cooper, told Frederick Hamley, Arthur Langlie, and David Lockwood that, "he always regarded Cecil Fitzgerald as being much more involved in the [street railway] transaction than was Mayor Ole Hanson, who got the blame".: Hamley *Diary*, 21 Aug., 1935.

14. *P-I*, 12, 29, and 31 July 1922. The *Municipal News*, 5 August 1922, questioned the reason for the *P-I* "attack", alleging that it was Dimock's

support of the Skagit project that inspired Brown to replace him with Blackwell who had been "a severe critic" of it and had been pressing for its delay until a "business survey" could be conducted.

15. *Times*, 27 Sept., 1922.

City Politics, 1921-1922

1. Chamber of Commerce, *Minutes*, 25 Feb., 1921.

2. Voters Information League, *Bulletin 2* (March 1921) and *Bulletin 6* (July 1921); Chamber of Commerce, *Minutes*, 12 Oct., 1920 and 10 May 1922; *P-I*, 13 July 1922.

3. SLD, *Scrapbooks*, 12 and 13 July 1922; VIL, *Bulletin 8* (Sept. 1921). Ebenezer Shorrock, banker, and Board member since 1920, led the conservative opposition to Cooper. According to Bryce Nelson: "after the 1920 election, the Board majority walked hand-in-glove with the tax-cutting groups". (p. 147): Nelson, *Good Schools: the Development of Good Schooling in Seattle, 1901-1930* (Seattle: University of Washington Press, 1988), chapter 9. Nelson reports that after the general strike construction contracts were awarded only to open shop firms. When Socialist Board member Richard Winsor ran for re-election in December 1920, he antagonized Shorrock and other members for casting suspicion of fraud and graft in the granting of these contracts; he was defeated by Carl Croson, who ran on an Americanism platform, *ibid.*, pp. 144-45.

4. *Municipal News*, 8 Jan, 12 Mar., 1921. In Seattle, high school teachers were paid a minimum of $1,800 and a maximum of $2,400 annual salary, compared to Tacoma's $1,500/$2,220 and Spokane's $1,500/$2,150: *Municipal News*, 8 July 1922. The Chamber of Commerce found these costs "comparatively high", and it recommended that a school survey commission be appointed to come up with an "adequate, economical and efficient proposal for the future conduct of the schools system":, *Minutes*, 19 July 1921.

5. *UR*, 12 Sept. 1921.

6. Chamber of Commerce, *Minutes*, 24 Jan., 1922.

7. *UR*, 8, 9 and 11 Feb., and 18 Mar., 1922.

8. *UR*, 6 Feb., and 8 Mar., 1922.

9. *UR*, 8, 10, and 15 Mar., 1922.

10. *UR*, 11 and 14 Mar., 1922.

11. On Meiers's actions see chapter 2 below, "City Politics: City Managers vs. Charter Revisionists".

12. *Municipal News*, 2 and 11 July, 1921, 22 Jan., and 4 Feb., 1922.

13. *Municipal News*, 4 and 11 Mar., 8 and 22 Apr., 1922.

14. *P-I*, 13 May 1922.

15. *UR*, 17 Mar., 11 Apr., 2 May, 1922; *Municipal News*, 18 and 25 Mar., 1922, and 29 Dec., 1923; Chamber of Commerce, *Minutes*, 9 May 1922.

16. *UR*, 3 May 1922. On Miracle see *UR*, 10 Apr., 1922.

17. Leonard to Pratt, 3 Jan., 1921, in which Leonard reported that he will be seeing Blethen soon to explain to him the "the street railway

situation . . . is not such a serious matter from a public standpoint as the lighting department". Also, Howe to Pratt, 14 Feb., 1921; Leonard to Pratt 14 Feb., 1921, Box 100, PSP&L, Records.

18. A memorandum from Mr. Torrance to Norwood Brockett, 12 Oct., 1928, recounts the chronology of the litigation surrounding the street railway purchase; Box 100, PSP&L, Records. The CHA's role varied over time: In 1923 it informed Council Finance Committee chair, E.L. Blaine, that if it were to authorize the cashing of warrants, its position would be that of underwriter—which it wished to avoid. See copy of CHA to Blaine 11 and 14 June 1923 in Box 100 of PSP&L, Records. In 1925 its neutrality can be questioned as when CHA secretary, J.W. Spangler authorized cashing warrants in 1925. A pencilled note signed "JWB" read, "Why not see Spangler sometime and ask him why?" This was accompanied by another note signed "BWB", reporting that "Spangler thought he was doing the right thing . . . He felt he was taking a crack at the city. He now sees our point of view and says it won't happen again": copy dated 12 Dec., 1925, in Box 100.

19. Leonard to Pratt, 12 Mar, 1921; H.G. Bradlee, 23 Jan., 1922; Leonard to Bradlee, 27 Jan., 1922; Howe to Pratt, 8 Mar., 30 Oct., 1922: Box 100, PSP&L, Records.

20. *P-I*, 13 May 1922; *Municipal News*, 2 and 9 Dec., 1922.

21. A memorandum by Leonard dated 26 May 1922; Pratt to Howe, 4 May 1922; Howe to Pratt, 30 Oct., 1922, Box 100, PSP&L, Records.

Voters Reject Handiwork of 1921 Legislature

1. *Times*, and *P-I*, 8 Nov., 1922.

2. *Op. cit.*

3. Marsh to Roy Knight, Superintendent of Woodland Schools, 31 Oct., 1922; Showalter to Marsh, 10 Nov., 1922; Marsh to A.C. Kellogg, Superintendent of Schools, Grandview, 24 Nov., 1922, Box 1, Accession 731, WEA, Records; *Municipal News*, 28 Oct., 1922; *P-I*, 5 Nov. 1922 reported Mrs. Malstrom, accusing the big corporations, working through the State Federation of Taxpayers, as opposing efforts to distribute costs more equitably, as that would mean taxing property in their districts, which happen to be the richer ones. Early in the campaign the Seattle Chamber of Commerce welcomed the "new attitude among teachers in endeavoring to cooperate with business men . . . and the desire [of the Seattle business community] to eliminate waste . . . in the guise of benefit to children . . . " Complaint was registered about the comparatively high school salaries, however. The Chamber preferred to substitute a centralized school administration in place of the "seven-headed" one: Chamber of Commerce, *Minutes*, 9 May 1922. Earlier, on motion of Nathan Eckstein, it also opposed the bill, except for one item. *ibid.*, 25 Feb., 1921.

The Legislature and the City, 1923

1. *P-I*, 24 and 25 Jan., 1923.

2. U.S. Federal Trade Commission, *Hearings [on electrical utilities*

propaganda], 1930; those relating to Stone and Webster in the state are on pp. 141, 145, 156-60. Wesley A. Dick, *ibid.*,pp. 66-7; *P-I*, 11 and 25 Jan., 1923. *Star*, 30 Jan, 1923.

3. Terry Slatten, *Homer T. Bone: Public Power and Washington State Progressive Politics in the Mid-1920s* (Unpublished Master's Thesis, Western Washington University, 198?), pp. 93-100, and 174. *P-I*,3 Mar., 1923.

4. Pullen *ibid.*, pp. 308-09; Sparks, *ibid.*, pp. 81-7; *P-I , 13 June, 23 Nov., and 5 Dec., 1923; Star*, 3 Dec., 1923 gives Ross credit for victory in Aberdeen. Ross reports of 16 June 1923 in File 12-2 and 10 Mar., 1924 in File 12-4; on Tacoma intertie: Ross to Llewellyn Evans, 10 Jan., 1922, and Ross to Mayor Caldwell 24 Mar., 1922, both in File 11-25; Ross to Ira Davisson, 4 May 1922; Ross to City Council 9 Aug., 1922 in which Ross contended that PSP&L "did not guarantee to furnish a single kilowatt hour",, all in File 11-29. On Referendum 12 Ross wrote to E.T. Mathes of Bellingham on 1 Nov., 1922 that City Light "would like to sell power all along its Skagit lines, including Bellingham; File 11-36, SLD, Records.

5. For coverage of the Bone Bill see: Sparks, *ibid.*,, pp. 80-93; Pullen, *ibid.*, pp. 309-11; Robert L. Cole, "The Democratic Party in Washington State, 1919-1933: Barometer of Social Change" (Unpublished Ph.D. Dissertation, University of Washington, 1972), pp. 121-23; Dick, *ibid.*, chapter IV and pp. 118-28 on 1924 election; Slatten, *ibid.*, chapter IV; Hamilton Cravens, "A History of the Washington Farmer-Labor Party, 1918-1924" (Unpublished Master's Thesis, University of Washington, 1962), pp. 188-93; *P-I* and *Times*, 17 Feb., 1923; the *P-I*, on 21 March 1923 reported Reed as saying opposition to the Bone Bill was based on "resentment in smaller counties against the increasing amount of property taxes taken off the tax rolls by Seattle's expansion of her municipally-owned utility."

6. Ficken, *Reed*, pp. 88-90; Seattle Lighting Department *Scrapbooks*, 17 Feb. 1923; Pullen, *ibid.*, pp. 311-16.

7. Sparks, *ibid.*, pp. 81-7; Pullen, *ibid.*, pp. 316-19.

8. *P-I*, 5 Jan., 1923, 2 and 7 Jan., 1924; *Star*, 21 Jan., 1923.

9. Robert E. Ficken, *Lumber and Politics: the Career of Mark E. Reed* (Seattle: University of Washington Press, 1979), pp. 88-91; Pullen, *ibid.*,pp. 295-96; Slatten *ibid.*, pp. 166-204; *P-I*, 4 and 5 Apr., 1924.

10. Ficken, *op. cit.*; Pullen, *op. cit.*

11. Slatten, *ibid.*, pp. 123-25; *P-I*, 18 Nov., 1925.

12. Slatten, *ibid.*, pp. 146-49; *Times*, 26 Jan. 1924; *Star*, 2, 24 and 31 Jan. 1924.

13. Sparks, *ibid.*, p. 88; Ross wrote to all Division heads, 24 Aug., 1924, asking for $300 more for a circular on the Bone Bill, "to get into every home in the State . . . I think our boys would willingly help": File 12-5, SLD, Records. *P-I*, 19 Nov., 1923; *Washington Democrat*, 2:3, March 1924. Bone complained to President Short of the State Federation Labor, 19 Sept., 1924, that Pieter Prins, owner and editor of the *Washington Co-operator*, had been claiming to be the Federation's voice, but he had been editorializing in favor of Stone and Webster in exchange for their advertising: Box 13 WSFL, Records.

14. Sparks, *ibid.*, pp. 85-95; Slatten, *ibid.*, pp. 236-51 in which Slatten reports that Locals 46 and 944 of the International Brotherhood of Electri-

cal Workers were "Stone and Webster locals", and they attacked the Bone Bill; as to Short, Slatten (pp. 342-43, 355-57) contends he divided the "progressive forces" in the 1924 election, isolating himself from progressive politics in the state". *Times*, 16 Sept.,15 Oct., 1924; *P-I*, 16, 17, and 25 Sept., 16 Oct., 1924; *Star*,17 and 25 Sept., 1924.

15. Dick, *ibid.*, p. 79.

16. Slatten, *ibid.*, pp. 229-31; *P-I* and *Times*, 17 Sept., 1924; *Municipal News*, 25 Oct., 1924.

17. Dick, *ibid.*, pp. 66-8; U.S. Federal Trade Commission, *Hearings, op. cit.*; *P-I*, 10 Jan,. 1924.

18. Dick, *op. cit.*; Sparks, *op. cit.*; Slatten, *op. cit.*; *P-I*, 30 Dec., 1923; *Star*, 31 Jan., 1923.

19. Ficken, *ibid.*, p. 98; *P-I*, 2 and 13 Nov., 1924; Ross to Carl Thompson, 26 Jan. 1925, File 12-7, SLD, Records.

20. See chapter 3, "The Republican Party in Disarray".

The Street Railway: Charges of Fraud

1. Copy of Emil V. Minich affidavit, from Homer T. Bone Papers in University of Puget Sound Library; lent by Terry Slatten, Bone's biographer. See Slatten, *ibid.*, pp. 362-66; *P-I* , 22 Oct.,1924. The newspapers gave full front page coverage to the hearings.

2. Minich *Affidavit*; *P-I*, 22 Oct., 1924.

3. *P-I*, 18 Oct., 1924; *Times*, 21 Oct., 1924.

4. *P-I*, 22 Oct., 1924; *Star*, 22 Oct., 1924.

5. *P-I*, 2 Oct., 1924.

6. *P-I* and *Times*, 22 Oct., 1924.

7. *P-I*, 23 and 24 Oct., 1924. After the dust had settled, Leonard summarized the proceedings for Pratt: The Efficiency Committee had not intended, at first, to raise the street railway purchase issue "as I understand it". It was Minich who got Nichols going on it, because Brown had discharged Minich after paying him "several thousand dollars for conducting some sort of an investigation that had to do with the street railway sale, after Brown found out that Minich's information was not reliable and could not be substantiated". Nichols then tried "to connect Brown up with the Company and if possible create, also, sentiment against the Company which might be helpful in the interests of the Bone Bill, as Nichols was Secretary of the Bone Bill campaign.": Leonard to Pratt, 14 Nov., 1924, Box 100, PSP&L Records.

8. *Times*, 27 Oct., 1924.

9. *Star*, 13 Sept., and 31 Oct., 1924; Carl Cooper reported that Brown claimed to have appointed Bolton to aid him in the investigation, and denied the charge that "Bolton will do what I tell him": *P-I*, 30 Oct., 1924.

10. *Times*, 21 Oct., 1924; *P-I*, 30 Oct., 1924.

11. *Times*, and *Star*, 23 Oct., 1924.

City Politics: City Managers vs. Charter Revisionists, 1923-1926: Who Won, Lost?

1. *Municipal News*, 24 Feb., 1923; a summary of it appears in 3 March 1923 issue. Extensive coverage is provided by Sparks, *ibid.*, chapter V;

also Lee F. Pendergrass, "Urban Reform and Voluntary Association: a Case Study of the Seattle Municipal League" (Unpublished Ph.D. Dissertation, University of Washington, 1972), pp. 108-18.

2. *Municipal News*, 5 and 12 Jan., 1924.

3. *Municipal News*, 26 Jan., 2,16, Feb., 1 Mar., 1924. Brown was reelected, defeating Lundin 40,740 to 35,742 votes.

4. *Municipal News*, 14 and 28 June, 18 Oct., 1924. On June 23, Landes complained to Chief Severyns: "Either there is collaboration between the police force and criminals, or else the police department is so inefficient that law violators neither fear nor respect its power . . . Now if a statement by you that there are one hundred men on the police force who should not be there is true then . . . one hundred men should be removed . . . " She ordered them removed. On June 25, she pressed him further: "fraternizing [of police] with the lawless is consistently tearing down the morale of your own department". Finding his excuse, laying blame on the Civil Service Commission, to be "untenable", she fired him: File 1-7 Bertha Landes, Papers.

5. *Star*, *P-I*, and *Times*, 1 and 3 Dec., 1925.

6. *Star*, 2 Mar. and *Times*, 3 Mar., 1924.

7. *Times*, 21 Sept.,1925; *Municipal News*, 5 July, 20 Sept., 4 Oct., 1924, 24 Jan., 14 Mar., 9 May, 1925.

8. *Times*, 21 and 22 Sept., 1925; *P-I*, 2 Sept., 1925.

9. *Times*, 29 Sept., 1925.

10. *P-I*, 29 and 30 Sept., 1925; *Times*, 29 Sept., 1925.

11. *P-I*, 25 July, 6 Oct., 1925; *Star*, 15 Oct., 1925.

12. *Times*, 5,11,18, and 19 Oct., 1925; *P-I*, 6 Oct., 1925; *Star*, 20 Oct., 1925; *UR*, 20 Oct., 1925.

13. Ross to City Council, 13 Oct., 1925; Ross to City Light Patrons Club, 20 Nov., 1925, File 12-23, SLC, Records; *Times*, 5,9, and 11 Oct., 1925; *P-I*, 6 Oct., 1925; *Star*, 14 and 20 Oct., 1925; *UR*, 20 Oct., 1925.

14. *P-I*, 27 Oct., 3 and 16 Nov., 5 Dec., 1925; *Municipal News*, 31 Oct., 1925; *Times*, 2 Dec., 1925.

15. *P-I*, 16 Nov., 1925; *Times*, 18 Nov., 1925; *Municipal News*, 14 Nov., and 12 Dec., 1925. In Council E.L. Blaine introduced "business manager" as a substitute term for "city manager", under whom the functions of the Board of Public Works would fall; his measure was voted down, but it was not the last attempt to inject the "business manger" concept into the debate. The term would become central, ultimately, to the proposed revised charter; *Times*, *P-I*, *Star*, 1 Dec., 1925.

16. *P-I*, 5 and 6 Nov., 1925.

17. *Municipal News*, 5 and 19 Dec., 1925; *Argus*, 5 Dec., 1925.

18. *Municipal News*, 9 Jan., 1926.

Prohibition Mixes in: the Olmstead Trial and "Doc" Brown

1. The main published sources for this chapter are: Norman H. Clark, "Roy Olmstead, A Rumrunning King of Puget Sound", *Pacific Northwest Quarterly* (hereafter abbreviated PNQ), 54:3 (July, 1963), pp. 89-103; Clark, *The Dry Years: Prohibition and Social Change in Washington*

(Seattle: University of Washington Press, 1965), chapter 11; and Mabel W. Willebrandt, *The Inside of Prohibition* (Indianapolis: Bobbs-Merrill, 1929), chapter XVIII. Mayor Brown, in his 1926 *Annual Message*, defended Chief Severyns and the police department, pointing to his closing of "Japanese soft-drink bootlegging parlors, and over 100 blind-pig joints . . . that had never been closed since the state prohibition law went into effect January 1915 [*sic*]" (Jan. 1916 is the correct date). Note the absence of any reference to any uptown clubs.

2. Clark, *Dry Years . . .*, pp. 161-65; Clark, "Roy Olmstead . . . ", pp. 89-93; *P-I*, 2,3,4,8,17,18 Apr., 1924. The *P-I* ran a series of eight articles on prohibition enforcement and rumrunning operations in March and April 1924, converting to common knowledge what the police department found too elusive. In its April 8 issue, the *P-I* reported: " . . . an inner ring of dealers in illicit liquor has been striving . . . [for] a realignment of the police forces as would give their traffic the maximum of protection. Olmstead was said to have been their choice for an "invisible chief". The U.S. Navy Chaplain told the Municipal League that Seattle is looked upon by the Navy as a "wide open town": *Municipal News*, 6 Sept., 1924.

3. Clark, "Roy Olmstead . . . ", pp. 94-5.

4. Clark, *ibid.*, pp. 96-9; Willebrandt, *ibid.*, chapter XVIII; *P-I*, 1 and 2 Feb., 1926. The "Book of Jobs" was a 775 page typescript of the wiretap evidence.

5. *P-I*, 3 Feb., 1926.

6. *P-I*, 9,17, and 20 Feb., 1926; *P-I*, 2 and 3 Feb., 1926; Clark, "Roy Olmstead . . . ", p. 100. Olmstead converted to Christian Science while in prison, and after release from McNeil Island in 1931 he returned frequently for religious work among the prisoners: *ibid.*, p. 103.

7. *P-I*, 2,3,16,24, and 27 Feb., 1926. One of Landes's joint campaign managers was Dick Faris, who would manage Frank Edwards's campaign against her in 1928; he had resigned as chief clerk in the county auditors office. Also, Doris H. Pieroth, "Bertha Knight Landes: the Woman Who Was Mayor", *PNQ* 75:3 (July, 1984), p. 122. The *P-I*'s 24 February issue hailed Landes's primary victory as a "Victory For City Manager"—in the contest between the advocates of the Municipal League's city manger form of government and those who wanted to revise the City charter. This topic will be concluded in the following section.

8. *P-I*, 2,3,5,7, and 10 Mar., 1926.

Landes Challenges Brown; Charter Fight Continues

1. *Municipal News*, 14 and 28 June 1924; File 1-7 Bertha Landes , Papers. While other Council members vascillated on the city manager proposal, Landes always supported it, perhaps earning Ross's ambivalence about her in the process. See Sparks, *ibid.*, chapter V.

2. *Municipal News*, 30 Jan., 6 and 27 Feb., 1926.

3. *Argus*, 16 and 30 Jan., 6 and 13 Feb., 1926; *Municipal News*, 27 Feb., 1926.

4. *Star*, 2 Mar., 1926. See also above, "The Street Railway: Charges of Fraud".

5. SLD. *Scrapbook*, 6 Mar., 1926; *Times*, 3-5 Mar., 1926.

6. Ross to James Bushnell, 27 Feb. 1926, in which Ross explains that the League's plan would take all control of construction from the Lighting Department, costing about 30% more for the same work. "We do a great deal of our own construction work by permission of the Board [of Public Works]". By centralizing these activities, work would be turned over to "people who have no obligation to make good." File 13-7, SLD, Records. Sparks, *ibid.*, pp. 162-63, refers to the Erickson feuding; also Pendergrass, *ibid.*, pp. 119-21.

7. William J. Dickson, "Labor in Municipal Politics: a Study of Labor's Political Activities in Seattle" (Unpublished Master's Thesis, University of Washington, 1928), pp. 59-62, 67; Sparks, *ibid.*, pp.142-48; *Municipal News*, 13 Mar., and 19 June 1926; *P-I*, 9-13,16 Mar., 1926; *Times*, 7-9 Mar., 1926.

8. *Times*, 10 Mar., 1926.

9. *Argus*, 16 and 30 Jan., 1926; its editor pronounced enthusiasm at the "nominal" salary for Council members, 20 Mar., 1926; *Municipal News*, 20 Mar., 17 Apr., 15 May, 1926; *Times*, 2-6,9, and 13 May 1926.

10. *Municipal News*, 19 June and 17 July 1926.

11. On formation of the City Light Patrons' Club see *Star*, and *P-I*, 3 Oct., 1925; SLD, *Scrapbooks*, 26 Oct., 1926; Sparks, *ibid.*, pp. 142-48.

12. *P-I*, 7 and 27 Oct., 1926.

13. SLD, *Scrapbooks*, 25 Oct., to 3 Nov., 1926.

14. Sparks, *ibid.*, pp. 153-54. On its editorial page the *Times* ran its "Platform", which included as number 1: "Protection of our educational institutions" (in light of the firing of UW president Henry Suzzallo). Number 3 was: "Revise the city charter according to the Freehoders' Plan", 26,28, and 31 Oct., 1 Nov.,1926; *P-I*, 1 and 2 Nov., 1926.

15. Sparks, *ibid.*, pp. 153-56; *Times*, 3 Nov., 1926; *Municipal News*, 6 Nov., 1926.

Mayor Bertha Landes Begins

1. *P-I*, 29 May, 8 June 1926; *Times*, 7 June 1926; *Argus*, 22 May, 5 June, 4 Sept. 1926; Seattle Mayor, *Annual Report*, 6 June 1927. Landes established a police school, requiring attendance by all officers appointed since 1925. Instructors included University Law School Dean, Alfred Schweppe, staffs of the Corporation Counsel and Prosecuting Attorney's offices, and "other" lawyers.

2. *Argus*, 30 Oct. and 6 Nov. 1926.

3. *Argus*, 23, 30 Apr., 1 Oct. 1927; 28 Jan. 1928.

4. *Argus*, 9 July 1927.

Landes Takes Her Turn at Resolving the Street Railway Crisis

1. See above, "City Politics, 1921-1922" for background.

2. *Star*, 9 Dec. 1926.

3. *P-I*, 10 and 14 Dec. 1926.

4. *Times*, 3 and 6 Jan. 1927; *P-I*, 7 Jan. 1927. To deal with the intake problem, by which sand and gravel were entering, Morse got Ross to

agree that the Engineering Department would take charge: *P-I*, 10 Nov. 1927.

5. *P-I*, 8 Jan. 1927; *Star*, 7 Jan. 1927.

6. *Star*, 7 Jan. 1927; *Times*, 8 and 13 Jan. 1927; *P-I*, 25 Jan. 1927.

7. Leonard to Pratt, 29 Dec. 1926, Box 100; Leonard to Landes, 21 Jan. 1927; correspondence between Leonard and Hagan, 16 Dec. 1926, Box 122; Pratt to Leonard 16 Dec. 1926; memorandum, Brockett to Pratt, 31 Dec. 1926, Box 100, PSP&L, Records.

8. Leonard to [Pratt] 6 and 13 Dec. 1926, Box 100, PSP&L, Records.

9. *Times*, 3 Feb. 1927; *Star*, 4 Feb. 1927.

10. Leonard to Landes, 3 Feb. 1927, Box 100, PSP&L, Records. *Times*, 1 Feb. 1927.

11. *Times*, 28 July 1927; *P-I*, 29 July 1927

12. Leonard to Pratt, 12 Jan. and 10 and 28 Feb. 1927; Leonard to [Pratt] 15 Jan. 1928, in which Leonard explains that the *Times* and business leaders have been urging Von Herberg to drop his suit to halt a drop in the value of securities held by the company's bondholders. *Argus*, 27 Nov., 1926 and 15 Jan. 1927; SLD, *Scrapbooks*, 5 to 8 Feb. 1927; *Star*, 8 Feb. 1927; *P-I*, 9 Feb. 1927; *Times*, 11 Feb.1927. Erickson renewed his earlier suggestion (when he was advocating a 3-cent carfare) that the general fund be tapped by the Municipal Street Railway. In its 16 July 1927 issue, Harry Chadwick saw such usage of the general fund as inviting "labor troubles", and recommended making the best of a bad contract.

13. Leonard to Pratt, 10 Feb. 1927; Box 100, PSP&L, Records.

14. *Star*, 25 Feb. 1927; *P-I*, 26 Feb. 1927; *Times* 1 Mar. 1927.

15. *P-I*, 1 and 11 Mar. 1927; *Star*, 11 Mar. 1927.

16. *P-I*, 8 Mar. and 21 Apr. 1927.

17. *P-I*, 21 May 1927; Leonard to Pratt, 16 Feb. 1926, Box 100, PSP&L, Records. Leonard was responding to inquiries Pratt was getting from "Our bankers [who] are considering purchase of our City of Seattle bonds. They want to know what is physical condition of the street railway property."

18. *P-I*, 12 and 15 Nov. 1928.

19. *Times*, 27 Nov. 1927; 12 Jan. 1928; *Star*, 30 Dec. 1927 and 29 Jan. 1929.

20. *P-I*, 9 June, 29 July and 13 Aug. 1927; *Star*, 13 Aug. 1927; *Times*, 28 July 1927; *Argus*, 6 Aug. 1927.

21. *P-I*, 20 Dec. 1927; *Star*, 1 Sept. 1927.

22. *P-I*, 6,7, and 22 Oct. and 6,8, and 10 Nov. 1927. On Dean Witter, *P-I*, 22 Oct. 1927; *Times*, 24 Oct. 1927.

23. *P-I*, 8,9,11, and 15 Nov., 2 and 7 Dec. 1927; *Star*, 30 Nov. and 27 Dec. 1927; *Times*, 30 Nov. 1927.

Mayoral Politics, 1928: Foul Play?

1. *P-I*, 10 Dec. 1927 and 20 Jan. 1928; *Star*, 8 Dec. 1927.

2. *Argus*, 5 Nov. 1927 and 7 Jan. 1928.

3. *P-I*, 31 Dec. 1927 and 6,11, and 17 Jan. 1928; Dickson, *Labor in Politics . . .* ", p. 68.

4. *P-I*, 8 Feb. 1928.

5. *P-I*, 21 and 26 Feb. 1928.

6. *P-I*, 26 Feb. 1928. Landes attributed her initial political base to be in the womens' clubs, and that she felt particularly obligated to them in making good by exemplary behavior in public office, proving women can do a better job than men by being more isolated from the temptations offered by graft and corruption: "If the time ever comes when many women sink to the depths of political corruption, then we may indeed fear for the future of both government and society.": Landes, "Does Politics make [*sic*] Women Crooked?", *Collier's*, 16 Mar. 1929, pp. 24,36, and 38.

7. *Times*, 3 Mar. 1928. This election campaign is covered in Doris Pieroth, "Bertha Knight Landes: The Woman Who Was Mayor", *PNQ*, 75:3 (July, 1984), pp. 122-26.

8. Memorandum by Brockett, Box 100, PSP&L, Records.

9. *P-I*, 27 and 29, Feb. 1928.

10. *P-I*, 29 Feb. and 4 Mar. 1928; *Argus*, 25 Feb. and 3 Mar. 1928.

11. *P-I*, 1,3 and 4 Mar. 1928.

12. *P-I*, 3 Mar. 1928; *Star*, 5 Mar. 1928.

13. *Star*, 5 Mar. 1928. In its front page editorial the editor speculated that many will admit they oppose Landes because she is a woman. *P-I*, 6 Mar. 1928.

14. *P-I*, 6 Mar. 1928.

15. *P-I*, 5,6,9 and 10 Mar. 1928; *Star*, 9 Mar. 1928; *Times*, 6 Mar. 1928. In the lead article in the 4 March issue of the *Times*'s "National Weekly" section appeared an article by Isabel Stephen, "Is America Becoming Woman-Ruled?". A flier in Nellie Fick's *Scrapbook* contains a notation: "Edwards has Billion dollar Power Co [sic] behind him . . . to fight City Light."

16. *P-I*, 11 and 12 Mar. 1928.

17. *P-I*, 12 and 13 Mar. 1928.

18. *P-I*, 12 Mar. 1928.

19. *P-I*, 13 Mar. 1928.

20. *P-I*, 14 Mar. 1928.

21. Julia Budlong, "What Happened in Seattle?", *The Nation*, 29. Aug. 1928, pp. 197-98.

22. Copy in Box 16, Willis T. Batcheller, Papers, "1928 Campaign".

23. Box 16, Batcheller, Papers.

24. *Civil Service Journal*, Sept. 1927 and March 1928.

25. Dickson, *ibid.*, pp. 68-74.

26. *Star*, 14 Apr. 1928.

27. *P-I*, 29 and 30 Mar. and 16 Aug. 1928.

28. Ross to McDonald, 7 Mar. 1930, File 20-13, SLD, Records. The author's own judgment is that Ross was so alienated by Landes's unmovable support of the city manager plan of government, by which he felt threatened, and by her backfired deal with Leonard, that he turned to Edwards for support of City Light despite the warnings all around that the power trust was behind Edwards . . . whether or not that was true.

Mayor Frank Edwards Begins

1. *P-I*, 5 June 1928; *Times*, 2 July 1928.

2. *P-I*, 3,6,12,23 and 25 June 1928; Its front page "blunder" editorial of June 3 ran under: "Barkhuff is Not Competent to Fill City's Biggest Job". *Star*, 25 June 1928; *Times*, 2 and 8 Aug. 1928.

3. *P-I*, 6 June 1928.

4. *Times*, 1 Apr. 1928.

5. Seattle, *Yearbook*, 4 June 1928 (Annual Report of Mayor); *P-I*, 26 May 1928.

6. *P-I*, 19 and 20 Oct. 1928; *Times*, 16 and 21 Nov. 1928.

7. *P-I*, 16 Nov. 1928.

8. *P-I* and *Times*, 6 Jan. 1929.

9. *P-I*, 12 and 17 Jan. 1929; *Star*, 7 Jan. 1929.

10. *Times*, 21 Jan. and 10 Mar. 1929; *P-I*, 5 Feb. and 12 Mar. 1929; *Star*, 23 and 24 Jan. 1929.

11. *Star*, 16 May and 27 June 1929; *Times*, 2 July 1929.

12. A. Gordon to G.C. Tenney of *Electrical West*, 5 Nov. 1928, Box 100, PSP&L, Records.

13. Leonard to H.H. Hunt, Boston, 3 Dec. 1928, Box 100, PSP&L, Records.

14. Leonard to Hunt, *op. cit.*; *P-I*, 6,9 and 16 Feb. 1929.

Erickson vs. Ross: Who's in Control?

1. *Times*, 14-16 Aug. 1928. The best published source on the Skagit project is by Paul C. Pitzer, *Building the Skagit: a Century of Upper Skagit Valley History, 1870-1970* (Portland, The Galley Press, 1978).

2. *P-I*, 1 Dec. 1928.

3. *P-I*, 2 Jan. 1929; *Star*, 2 Jan. 1929; in front page editorial of 28 December 1928, the newspaper noted that Ross's opponents had refused to authorize the powerhouse funding after the final rejection of the Hanging Rock damsite.

4. On Ross-Erickson feud see above, "Landes Challenges Brown . . . "; also Sparks, *ibid.*, pp. 161-62; *P-I*, 10 Feb. 1929; *Star*, 8 Feb. 1929; *Times*, 15 Feb. 1929; Pendergrass, *ibid.*, pp. 119-21.

5. *P-I* and *Times*, 5 Jan. 1929; *Star* and *Times*, 5 Dec. 1928.

6. *P-I*, 29 Dec 1928.

7. *Star*, 19 Feb. 1929; *Journal of Commerce*, 8 Mar. 1929.

8. *Times*, 22 and 24 Mar. 1929.

9. *P-I*, 28-30 Mar.and 1 Apr. 1929.

10. *P-I*, 1 Apr. 1929.

11. *Star*, 2 and 5 Apr. 1929; *Times*, 19 Apr. 1929; *P-I*, 17 Apr. 1929.

12. *Star*, 18 and 30 Apr. 1929; *P-I*, 16,17 and 19 Apr. 1929; *Times*, 19 Apr. 1929.

13. *P-I*, 20 Mar., 1 and 22 May, and 5 June 1929; *Times*, 17 Feb., 19 Mar., 8 May 1929; *Star*, 1 and 8 May 1929.

14. *Times*, 18 and 30 Apr. 1929; *P-I*, 20 Aug. 1929.

15. *P-I*, 15 and 16 May 1929. At a King Conty Democratic Club meet-

ing each chided the other over raising the issue of who should have the monopoly over electrical power in the city, 3 July 1929.

16. *Star*, 24 May, 1 June 1929; *P-I*, 29 May 1929.

17. *Times*, 3 June 1929; *Star*, 4 June 1929.

18. *P-I*, 31 July, 15 and 30 Aug., 6 Sept., and 1 Oct. 1929; *Times*, 20 Sept. 1929.

19. *P-I*, 30 Sept. 1929 and 7 Jan. 1930; *Times*, 21,30 and 31 Jan 1930; *Star*, 30 and 31 Jan. 1930.

20. *Times*, 17 Oct., 10 Dec. 1929; 9 Jan. 1930; *P-I*, 19 Oct., 5 Dec. 1929.

Edwards Re-elected, Seeks Government Reorganization; Confronts Ross Machine

1. *Star*, 22 Feb. 1930; *P-I*, 5 Mar. 1930; *Times*, 12 Mar. 1930.

2. *Star*, 15 Mar. and 3 Apr. 1930; *P-I*, 8 Apr. 1930.

3. *Times*, 1 June 1930.

4. *P-I*, 20 Apr. 1930; *Times*, 16 May, 6 and 12 June 1930; *Star*, 5 Mar. 1930.

5. *Star*, 2 June 1930; *P-I*, 3 June and 11 July 1930; *Times*, 29 July 1930.

6. *Times*, 3 June 1930.

7. *Times*, 22 and 29 July and 20 Oct. 1930; *P-I*, 22 July and 16 Aug. 1930; *Municipal News*, 22 Nov. 1930.

8. *P-I*, 22 July 1930.

9. *Times, P-I , and Star*, 28 Aug. 1930; *Star*, 17 Nov. 1930; *Journal of Commerce*, 23 Oct. 1930.

10. *Times*, 20 Oct. 1930; *Municipal News*, 22 Nov. 1930.

11. Copy of Report of Transit Committee to Edwards, 31 Oct. 1930, Box 100, PSP&L, Records.

12. Leonard to D.C. Barnes, 23 Jan. 1931; Barnes to Boston office, 4 Feb. 1931; see also memorandum of 3 Feb. 1931, Box 100, PSP&L, Records; *Star* and *P-I*, 14 Jan. 1931.

13. *P-I*, 5 Jan. 1931; *Star*, 3,6 and 13 Jan. 1931; the latter carried a front page editorial: "Hands Off City Light". *Times*, 13 Jan. 1931. On construction by Lighting Department see Ross to Mark Matthews of Charter Revision Committee, 6 Apr. 1926, File 13-12, SLD, Records.

14. *Star*, 3 Jan. 1931.

15. *Star*, 26 Jan., 3 and 6 Feb. 1931; *Times*, 2 Feb. 1931. State Grange Master, A.S. Goss, got included in Senate Bill 24 the tax on municipal utilities in exchange for allowing the latter to sell power outside their corporate jurisdictions.

16. *Star*, 3-6 and 16 Feb. 1931; Sparks, *ibid.*, pp. 157-67.

17. Sparks, *op. cit.*; *Times*, 4 Mar. 1931; *Argus* editor Harry Chadwick commented: " Mr. Ross is an engineer of ability. He knows his stuff, and knows it thoroughly. Mr. Thomson is an able engineer. But he is very opinionated . . . ": 7 Mar 1931.

18. Sparks, *op. cit.*; *Times*, 9 Mar. 1931; *P-I*, 10,11 and 24 Mar. 1931; *Star*, 10 and 22 Mar. and 1 Apr. 1931.

19. Sparks, *ibid.*, pp. 167-81; *Argus*, 14 Mar. 1931.

20. Sparks, *op. cit.*

21. Sparks, *op. cit.*

Chapter 3
Political Parties at the State Level

The Republican Party in Disarray, 1924-1932

1. For general coverage see: Ficken, *Lumber and Politics . . .* , chapter 4; Albert F. Gunns, "Roland Hill Hartley and the Politics of Washington State" (Unpublished Master's Thesis, University of Washington, 1963), chapters IV-VIII.

2. Gunns, *ibid.*, pp. 73-86; Ficken, *ibid.*, pp. 100-02.

3. Gunns, *ibid.*, pp. 86-103 (quotation is from p. 98); Ficken, *ibid.*, p. 103.

4. Gunns, *ibid.*, pp. 104-12; Ficken, *ibid.*, pp. 104-07.

5. Gunns, *ibid* , pp. 113-33; Ficken, *ibid.*,pp. 108-20. The *Argus*, 29 May 1926, quotes Reed: "The whole timber controversy was a smoke screen raised by the governor to hide destructive designs on the educational system and reclamation policy of the state." At this juncture the *Argus* supported Hartley's policies, but, by September the paper opposed him as a dictator.

6. Gunns, *ibid.*, p. 63 and chapter V; Ficken, *ibid.*, pp. 120-22; Charles M. Gates, *The First Century at the University of Washington, 1861-1961* (Seattle: University of Washington Press, 1961), pp. 165-72; Donald T. Williams, Jr., "The Remarkable Dr. Henry Suzzallo: a Biography", (Unpublished manuscript in UW Archives), chapter 10.

7. Gunns, *ibid.*, chapter V, (quotation is from p. 148); Gates, *ibid.*, pp. 165-72; Williams *ibid.*, chapter 10.

8. Gunns, *ibid.*, pp. 154-60; Gates, *ibid.*, pp. 165-72; Williams, *ibid.*, chapter 10.

9. Gunns, *ibid.*, pp. 161, 177-87 (quotation is from p. 183); Ficken, *ibid.*, pp. 121-22; Gates, *ibid.*, pp. 165-72; Williams, *ibid.*, chapter 10.

10. Gunns, *ibid.*, pp. 188-207.

11. Gunns, *ibid.*, pp. 206-16.

12. Gunns, *ibid.* , pp. 215-18; Cole, *ibid.*, pp. 198-213.

The State Democratic Party After 1924

1. Cole, *ibid.*, pp. 125-27, 140, 156; William Stuart Forth, "Wesley L. Jones: a Political Biography (Unpublished Ph.D. Dissertation), University of Washington, 1962), pp. 649-64 (Jones largely divorced himself from the disputes generated by Hartley); Norman Clark, *The Dry Years . . .* ,pp. 191-205 for the general background, with special emphasis on the relationship of prohibition to local and state politics of the period. See also Fayette F. Krause, "Democratic Party Politics in the State of Washington During the New Deal, 1932-1940" (Unpublished Ph.D. Dissertation, University of Washington, 1971), chapters I and II.

2. Cole, *ibid.* , pp. 153, 140-42, 146-50; Clark, *ibid.*, pp. 192-93; Thomas Stimson Bayley, *The Stimson Family* (Seattle: [T.S. Bayley], 1976), pp. 71-3.

3. Cole, *ibid.*, pp. 150-67; Clark, *ibid.*, pp. 196-97; Forth, *ibid.*, pp. 654-64.

4. Cole, *ibid.*, chapter 5; Clark, *ibid.*, pp. 199-203.

The 1930 Election: Repeal and Public Power

1. Cole, *ibid.*, pp. 234, 236-37; Clark, *ibid.*, pp. 210-17 (quotation is from p. 213); Forth, *ibid.*, pp. 664-70.

2. Cole, *ibid.*, pp. 235-39.

3. Cole, *ibid.*, pp. 239-45; Cole notes that Mr. Riley worked for Graybar Electric. Clark, *ibid.*, pp. 209-10. Edith Riley, writing to the party's women's division chief, Mary Dewson, 23 Oct. 1931, in response to Dewson's questionnaire, reported that many of the "irregular democrats" are now usurping power, and are pressing for adoption of the Grange Bill (quotation is from this letter, File 1-26). See also copy of Bullitt letter to FDR, and Riley's letter of 11 Jan. 1929 to FDR's inquiry about strategy, File 1-31, Edith Dolan Riley, Papers. Krause, *ibid.*, pp. 30-41.

4. Cole, *ibid.*, pp. 247-52; *Grange News*, 10 June 1939; George T. Melton, "The State Grange and the Development of Water Power Resources in Washington" (Unpublished Master's Thesis, University of Washington, 1954), pp. 58-68; *P-I.*, 3,19,29-31 Jan., 2 Oct., 1929; *ibid.*, 1 Feb. 1929.

5. Cole, *ibid.*, pp. 247-52; Melton *ibid.*, pp. 58-78; Elliott Marple, "The Movement for Public Ownership of Power in Washington", *Journal of Land and Public Utilities Economics*, VII (Feb., 1931), pp. 65-6.

Heading into the 1932 Election

1. Cole, *ibid.*, pp. 261-70.

2. Cole, *ibid.*, pp. 217-79, footnote 70, pp. 283-84, 286-87. Archival documentation of Chadwick's and Bone's campaign may be found in the Stephen F. Chadwick, Papers, and the Saul Haas, Papers, both in the UW Libraries' Manuscript Collection.

3. Cole, *ibid.*, pp. 282-88.

4. Cole, *ibid.*, pp. 288-96; Gunns, *ibid.*, pp. 219-20; Forth, *ibid.*, pp. 751-65, 775,90. Jones, though a Hoover loyalist, sometimes broke ranks and voted for measures to remedy unemployment and for more equitable taxation. Forth portrays Jones as an advocate of the "little man" (pp. 738-41).

Chapter 4

The Waterborne Commerce of the City in the 1920s

1. The *San Francisco Examiner*, 22 Nov. 1917, p. 1 has a feature article pointing to the rise of Seattle to fourth place (from 22d place in 1912) in the volume of the nation's waterborne commerce, exceeding San Francisco's by about $90 million during fiscal 1916/17: "[Seattle] has been leading San Francisco and other principal California ports in recent years." Part of the Bay city's decline was attributed to compulsory pilotage and to higher dock charges. Port of Seattle *Yearbook*, 1930: Padraic Burke, *The History of the Port of Seattle* (Seattle: Port of Seattle, 1976), pp. 70-71; *Railway and Marine News* (RMN), XVIII:12 (Dec. 1920), XIX:3 (Mar., 1921), XIX:10 (Oct., 1922), XX:9 (Sept., 1922), XX:11 (Nov., 1922), XXI:1 (Jan., 1923); Cotterill speech on Port of Seattle, File 14-3, Cotterill, Papers; *Journal of Commerce*, "Annual Review", Jan., 1927; *Municipal News*, 17

Mar. and 21 Apr., 1923; Chamber of Commerce, *Minutes*, 13 Feb. 1923; *P-I*, 29 Apr. and 7 May 1923.

2. Port of Seattle, *ibid.*; *RMN*, XXIV:5 (May 1927), XXV:8 (Aug., 1928); copy of 20 page report by Otto Rupp and R.M. Semmes to Tax Advisory Commission of Washington, File 7-15, Cotterill, Papers.

3. Seattle Port Warden, *Annual Report*[s] are the source for the following account of waterborne commerce.

4. Port Warden, *ibid.*; Chamber of Commerce, *Seattle, an Industrial, Commercial, and Investment Opportunity* (Seattle: Chamber of Commerce, 1927).

5. Port of Seattle, *Yearbook*, 1932; *RMN*, XXIV:9 (Sept., 1927); *Star*, 1 June 1926.

6. Port Warden, *ibid.*

7. Port Warden, *ibid.*

8. Portland Public Docks Commission, *Annual Report[s]*, 1921, 1929, 1931, 1940. (TABLE 5)

9. Port of Seattle, *Yearbook*, 1937. (TABLE 5)

10. Port of Seattle, *Yearbook*[s], 1921 and 1924.

11. Port of Seattle, *Yearbook*[s], 1928 and 1930.

12. Port of Seattle, *Yearbook*, 1937.

13. Port of Seattle, *Yearbook*, 1928.

Chapter 5
Manufacturing, 1919,1929,1939

1. U.S. *Census of Manufactures*, 1920 and 1930; Dun and Bradstreet, *Seattle* (Seattle: Seattle Lighting Department, 1948), pp. 14 and 24.

2. U.S. *Census of Manufactures*, 1920 and 1930; *Journal of Commerce*, 9 Jan., 1924) and its "Annual Review" in January 1927; Seattle Chamber of Commerce, *Seattle's Industrial Expansion* (Seattle: Chamber of Commerce, 1927); *Times*, 2 July 1928.

Chapter 6
Manufacturing in Seattle's Hinterland

1. Seattle City Council, *Petitions* 81561 (6/20/1921) and 81785 (7/11/1921) in City Archives; Chamber of Commerce, *Minutes*,4 and 18 Oct., 22 Nov., and 6 Dec. 1921, 9 May 1922; *Town Crier*, 31:4 (Apr., 1936), pp. 12-13, 15. The *Vanguard*,14 Apr. 1933, reported that Boeing threatened to leave the state if the proposed unemployment insurance bill were passed by the state legislature. Reed R. Hansen provides a summary of Boeing's corporate history in his "Collective Bargaining Between the Boeing Airplane Company and the Aero Mechanics Union (Unpublished Master's Thesis, University of Washington, 1951), pp. 12-16. During the 1920s, Boeing was kept afloat partly from U.S Army orders. In 1927, government contracts led to formation of the Boeing Air Transport Company, the longest route in the country, Chicago to San Francisco. In 1928, it purchased the Pacific Air Transport Company, extending its route to Los Angeles. Then, with the financial backing of the National City Bank, it

formed a holding company, the United Aircraft and Transportation Corporation, a vertically and horizontally integrated operation whose extent brought it under scrutiny of the Anti-Trust Division of the Justice Department. It was required, in 1934, to separate its transportation system from its equipment manufacturing companies. The United Airlines was but one entity that sprang from the holding company. Responding to a temporary economic upswing in 1937 Boeing completed an assembly plant that proved inadequate in meeting new orders from Pan American, Transcontinental, and Western Air. Another plant, double the size of the previous one was then planned; the company then had about 2,000 employees. Chamber of Commerce, *Minutes*, 23 Feb., 30 Mar., and 12 Oct., 1937.

2. See City Council, *Petitions*, 93472 (5/5/1922), 83827 (5/23/1922), 89444 (5/12/1923), 93396 (3/10/1924), 118776 (10/12/1928).

3. Harold Mansfield, *Vision: the Story of Boeing* (New York: Popular Library Paperback, 1966), p. 20; Charles M. Gates, *The First Century at the University of Washington, 1861-1961* (Seattle: University of Washington Press, 1961), p. 151.

4. Statistical information supplied by Boeing Historical Services Division, courtesy of Paul Spitzer; Port of Seattle, *Yearbook*[s], 1932 and 1933.

5. Hansen *ibid.*, pp. 24-9; *Town Crier*, 31:4 (Apr., 1936), pp. 12-13, 15; *Vanguard*, 14 Apr., 1933.

Chapter 7

Other Lines of Economic Activity

1. U.S. Bureau of Labor Statistics, *Building Construction in the United States, 1921-1940.*

2. Marilyn Druck Robinson, *Washington State Statistical Abstract* (Seattle: University of Washington Press, 1952), p. 75.

3. *Journal of Commerce*, "Annual Business Review", January 1927; in its 28 Jan., 1928 issue it reported "Regrade" sales at a record high, second in "investment buying", quoting Poor; on seawall, 3 Jan. 1933.

4. *Journal of Commerce*, "Annual Review[s]", Januaries for, 1925-1927, 1929.

5. *Times*, 31 Aug. and 28 Dec. 1930.

6. Neal O. Hines, *Denny's Knoll: a History of the Metropolitan Tract of the University of Washington* (Seattle: University of Washington Press, 1980), pp. 150-60.

7. Hines, *ibid.*, pp. 160-73 (quotation is from p. 167).

8. Hines, *ibid.*, pp. 179-85 (quotation is from p. 185); Chamber of Commerce, *Minutes*, 9 June and 25 July 1922

9. Seattle Housing Authority (SHA), *Real Property Survey, 1939-1940* (W.P.A. Project 3272, Seattle, 1942, 2 vols.), vol. 1, p. 5. The Chamber of Commerce recorded in its *Minutes*, 12 Oct., 1937, that Seattle had a shortage of modern houses, and that it was "lagging behind other cities on this Coast on all types of construction, particularly houses". The 11,888 figure probably should be corrected to be 12,635.

10. SHA, vol. 2, p. 4, plate 12 showing "Race of Household".

11. SHA, *Annual Report*, Jan. 1941; SHA, *Survey*, vol. 1, p. 1.

12. SHA, *ibid.*; Roger Sale, *Seattle Past to Present* (Seattle: University of Washington Press, 1976), pp. 163-6; clipping dated 7 Nov.1939 in Epstein *Scrapbook;* author's interview with Epstein, 5 Apr. 1989.

13. SHA, *ibid.* It is uncertain whether Langlie appointed Epstein to the chairmanship because of his unique expertise or because he was Jewish. Langlie conceded to Epstein that there was no member of "your race" in his administration, so he might as well be the first. Interview with author, 5 Apr. 1989.

14. Jesse Epstein, *Scrapbook,* and interview with the author, 5 Apr. 1989.

15. Sale, *op. cit.*; SHA, *ibid.*; author's interview. Altogether, about 500 persons were employed in the survey. They were hired "regardless of color". Completed in 1941, Yesler Terrace comprised 690 homes, divided among 84 residential structures of varying sizes, distributed at different angles in quasi ranch-style buildings of only two stories in height. Constructed of wood frame materials, they were built to last, unlike their demolished predecessors—sturdily they stand today as respectable structures, a source of civic pride to many. Landscaped to accent the spectacular views of Mt. Rainier to the southeast, the industrial district to the south, the harbor and Olympic Mountain Range to the west, it is a model of public low-cost housing. As national defense spending picked up from 1939 on, other public housing followed in tandem during the war—permanent housing at Sand Point for Naval personnel; defense worker housing at Holly Park, Rainier Vista, and High Point. After the war, the permanent housing reverted to the SHA with the status of "permanent low-cost housing".

Chapter 8
Seattle and Its Agricultural Hinterland

1. See chapter 4, "Waterborne Commerce . . . "

2. John A. Rademaker, "The Ecological Position of the Japanese Farmers in the State of Washington" (Unpublished Ph.D. Dissertation, University of Washington, 1939), p. 229 for the 1930 figures. See his chart 10 on the timing of the seasons; pp. 60-62 for the symbiotic realtionships; pp. 24-6 on the competition-political opportunism factors; p. 38-55, 74-9 and 92 for results of the Anti-Alien Land Acts; pp. 80-81 on failure of the white farmers; p. 90 on migration to the cities; pp. 96-7 on reduction of anti-Japanese sentiment; and p. 97 on the introduction of Filipinos.

3. Rademaker, *ibid.*, pp. 88-97 (quotation is from footnote 74 on p. 96).

4. H. Brett Melendy, *Asians in America: Filipinos, Koreans, and East Indians* (Boston: Twayne Publishers, 1977), pp. 33-4,37, 41; Sebastian Abella, "Migration of Filipinos to the Pacific Northwest", in *Filipino Forum*, 15 and 30 May 1929. The Polk, *City Directory*, 1920 reported: "Seattle's hinterland produces more than $600,000,000 in farm products and livestock each year".

5. *Philippine-American Chronicle*, II:6 15 Mar. 1935; IV:1 14 Jan. 1936, reporting that Bellevue farm workers earned $.17 an hour on average; *Philippine-American Tribune*, VI:7 24 Apr. 1937.

Chapter 9
Women in the Work Force

1. Mary V. Dempsey, *The Occupational Progress of Women, 1910 to 1930* (Washington: U.S. Labor Department, Womens' Bureau, Bulletin No. 104, 1933), pp. 1-3; Elyce J. Rotella, *From Home to Office: U.S. Women at Work, 1870-1930* (Ann Arbor: University Microfilms International Research Press, Studies in American History and Culture, No. 25, 1981), pp. 61-70, and p. 35 on telephone operators. For background on women in the Seattle work force before 1921 see Maurine Weiner Greenwald, "Working-Class Feminism and the Family Wage Ideal: the Seattle Debate on Married Women's Right to Work, 1914-1920", *Journal of American History*, 76:1 (June, 1989), pp. 118-49. The number of women in the city's work force expanded from 4,774 in 1900 to 33,114 by 1920, in which married women numbered 881 in 1900 and 8,203 by 1920 (p. 124); David E. Nye, *Electrifying America: Social Meanings of a New Technology, 1880-1940* (Cambridge, MA: MIT Press, 1990), pp. 266-81 (quotation is from p. 124); Margaret A. Hall, "A History of Women Faculty at the University of Washington, 1896-1970" (Unpublished Ph.D. Dissertation, University of Washington, 1984), pp. 113-14.

2. Dempsey, *ibid.*, pp. 4-5.

3. Rotella, *ibid.*, pp. 17, 21-6; Bryce E. Nelson, *Good Schools: the Seattle Public Schools, 1901-1930* (Seattle: University of Washington Press, 1988), p. 48, footnote 3.

4. U.S. Census Bureau, *Population Census: the Labor Force, 1940* (Washington: Government Printing Office, 1940).

5. Dempsey, *ibid.*, p. 7.

Chapter 10
The Economy in the 1930s

1. Wytze Gorter and George H. Hildebrand, *The Pacific Coast Maritime Shipping Industry, 1930-1948* (Berkeley: University of California Press, 1954, 2 vols.), vol. 1, chapter II, vol. 2, chapter XII; Port of Seattle, *Yearbook*, 1937.

2. Gorter and Hildebrand, *ibid.*, vol. 2, chapter XII; Port of Seattle, *ibid.*, 1929.

3. Port of Seattle, *ibid.*, 1931-1937.

4. Port of Seattle, *ibid.*, 1937.

5. Port of Seattle, *ibid.*,1932, 1937.

Chapter 11
General Characteristics

1. Calvin F. Schmid, *Social Trends in Seattle* (Seattle: University of Washington Press, 1944), p. 5.

2. Schmid, *ibid.*, pp. 75,80; Richard White, "Poor Men on Poor Lands: the Back-to-the-Land Movement of the Early Twentieth Century", in Thomas G. Edwards and Carlos A. Schwantes, editors, *Experiences in the Promised Land: Essays in Pacific Northwest History* (Seattle: University of Washington Press, 1986), pp. 291,293.

3. Schmid, *ibid.*, pp. 81-5.

4. Schmid, *ibid.*, pp. 99-103.

5. Schmid, *ibid.*, chart 20 on p. 102; there are also maps for each ethnic group on pp. 103-29; Seattle Housing Authority, *Real Property Survey . . .* vol. 1.

6. Schmid, *ibid.*, pp. 117,123, and chart 39 on p. 119

7. Schmid, *ibid.*, p. 123 and chart 40 on p. 121.

Chapter 12
Seattle's Non-Caucasian Population: General

1. Schmid, *ibid.*, chapter V. See chapter 8, "Seattle and its Agricultural Hinterland" for coverage of Japanese and Filipinos, and chapter 25, section on "Jurisdiction Over the Cannery Workers . . . ".

2. Schmid, *ibid.*, chapter V.

3. Copy of enclosed letter addressed to Frank S. Bayley dated 7 May 1929 (enclosed with a 17 May letter by Charles F. Ernst), File 1-17, Charles F. Ernst, Papers.

4. The *Philippine Advocate*, I:3, May 1935. See also Horace R. Cayton, *Long Old Road: an Autobiography* (Seattle: University of Washington Press, 1970 paperback edition), chapter 5, covering Cayton's period as a King County deputy sheriff. See also the *Star* for a series of articles by "Capt. G." on vice and gambling operations, December 1936.

5. S. Frank Miyamoto, *Social Solidarity . . .* , p. 63

6. Miyamoto, *ibid.*, pp. 71-3. Unfortunately, there are no comparable statistics for other non-white ethnic groups.

7. Miyamoto, *ibid.*, p. 73. This census was compiled by the North American Japanese Association.

8. Miyamoto, *ibid.*, p.63

9. Miyamoto, *ibid.*, p. 68. James Sakamoto to Sam Fujita, 8 Oct. 1938. Clarence Arai of Seattle made several trips to San Francisco and Los Angeles in 1928 and 1929, succeeding in getting an agreement for an organizational meeting in Seattle in 1930 that brought together "citizens leagues" that had been formed in many communities in the coastal states between August 1929 and September 1930: File 11-1 James Sakamoto, Papers.

Chapter 13
African Americans in the City

1. Schmid, *ibid.*, pp. 137-41; Esther Hall Mumford, *Seattle's Black Victorians, 1852-1901* (Seattle: Ananse Press, 1980), pp. 30-67; Robert Bedford Pitts, "Organized Labor and the Negro" (Unpublished Master's Thesis, University of Washington, 1941), p. 42; Horace R. Cayton *Long Old Road: an Autobiography* (Seattle: University of Washington Press, Pa-

perback Edition, 1970); Joseph Sylvester Jackson, "The Colored Marine Employees Benevolent Association of the Pacific Coast, 1921-1934" (Unpublished Master's Thesis, University of Washington, 1939), p. 84.

2. The *Northwest Enterprise* for dates as noted in text. Founding and development of the Negro Repertory Theater is covered in chapter 15, the section on "The Seattle Repertory Playhouse".

3. *Northwest Enterprise* for dates as noted in text; Urban League, *First Annual Report,* 1 Nov. 1930/31 Oct. 1931; Jackson to E.K. Jones, executive secretary, National Urban League, 4 Jan. 1933; John F. Hall, exec. secty., Community Fund to Jackson, 26 Jan. 1931; "Placements" listing , 31 May 1931, all on microfilm in Seattle Urban League, Records.

4. *Northwest Enterprise,* 11 Aug.,15 Sept., 27 Oct., 3 and 10 Nov. 1932.

5. Urban League By-Laws, dated 23 Apr. 1936; *Northwest Enterprise,* 8 Sept. 1932.

6. *Northwest Enterprise,* 8 Dec. 1932, 9 Feb., 27 Apr., 1933, 5 and 19 Apr., and 15 June 1934.

7. Cayton, *ibid.,* chapters 5 and 6; Juana Racquel Royster Horn, "The Academic and Extracurricular Undergraduate Experiences of Three Black Women at the University of Washington, 1935-1941" (Unpublished Ph.D. Dissertation, University of Washington, 1980), chapters 5-7 particularly. Earlier chapters describe the Seattle social environment in which the three daughters of Mr. and Mrs. Edward A. Pitter lived at 24th Avenue and E. Pine Street. Their home served as a social and political center within the Black community. Mrs. Pitter, in particular, was a battler for equal rights. She and Mr. Pitter, performed leadership roles in inspiring Blacks to move into the Democratic Party, though it would have to be on a segregated basis—State and King County "Colored Democratic Club[s]" (cf. pp. 66-8).

8. Pitts, *ibid.,* pp. 21, 32-3, and 36.

9. Pitts, *ibid.,* pp. 46-9.

10. Pitts, *ibid.,* pp. 59-65.

11. Pitts, *ibid.,* chapter 6.

12. Pitts, *ibid.,* chapter 7.

13. Pitts, *ibid.,* chapter 8.

14. Pitts, *ibid.,* pp. 91-2,95-7.

15. U.S. Census Bureau, *Population: Labor Force, 1940* (Washington: Government Printing Office, 1940). Of the 104,058 males employed in the city in 1940 on non-public projects, 99,923 were White, 909 Negroes, 3,226 of other races. Main lines of Black employment included: 24 musicians and music teachers, 54 in clerical, sales, and kindred work, 54 as craftsmen, foremen, and kindred work, 10 as carpenters, 17 as mechanics and repair men, 76 as operatives and kindred workers 18 as chauffeurs, truck drivers, and delivery men, 16 as sailors and deck hands, 18 as domestic service workers, 20 as protective service workers, 459 as service workers, except domestic and protective. In the latter category were 230 "charwomen [*sic*], janitors, and porters, 56 cooks, 74 waiters and bartenders, 18 servants. Under "Laborers, except farm and mine", were listed

141 Blacks among which seemed to be 22 in construction, 13 in manufacturing, and 53 in non-manufacturing, including 20 on railroads and 16 in communications and utilities. 34 longshoremen were noted.

Of the 43,894 women who were gainfully employed in Seattle in 1940 there were 356 "Negroes". Of this number 204 were employed as domestic service workers, and 90 as "service workers, except domestic and protective". Of this latter number 19 were listed as "charwomen, janitors and porters", 27 as servants, and 14 as waitresses and bartenders.

Chapter 14
Education

The Public School System in the 1920s

1. Seattle Public Schools, *Triennial Report[s]*, 1921/24,1924/27,1927/30; Nancy Rockafeller, "In Gauze We Trust: Public Health and Spanish Influenza on the Home Front, Seattle, 1918-1919", *PNQ* (July, 1986), pp. 104-13. See also "City Politics, 1921-22", and "Voters Reject Handiwork of 1921 Legislature", in chapter 2 above.

2. "Higher Standards of Qualifications for Teaching", *Washington Education Journal* (hereafter, WEJ), I:1 (Sept., 1921), pp.7-8, (Mar., 1922), p. 222; Washington Federation of Labor, *Proceedings*, 1921.

3. *Triennial Report[s]*, 1921/24-1927/30. On Tripp, *et al*, see "Mayoral Politics, 1928: Foul Play?", in chapter 2.

4. *Triennial Report[s]*, 1921/24, 1924/27.

5. *Triennial Report[s]*, *op. cit.*

6. *Triennial Report*, 1927/30.

7. *Triennial Report*, 1927/30.

8. Bryce E. Nelson, *Good Schools: the Seattle Public School System, 1901-1930* (Seattle: University of Washington Press, 1988), chapter 6 and pp. 157-8, 171.

9. Nelson, *ibid.*, pp. 158-63,167-8; *Triennial Report[s]*, 1924/27,1927/30.

10. Nelson, *ibid.*, pp. 166-9.

The Public School System in the 1930s

1. Dietrich Schmitz's response to a Stanford University questionnaire, 31 July 1936, File 1-4; State Auditor report in File 3-19; Schmitz to McClure concerning State's obligation, 28 Dec. 1931, Dietrich Schmitz, Papers. On pay cuts see *P-I*, 3 Feb. 1935. Seattle School District No. 1, *[Annual Report]*, 1930-31. The Child Welfare Board of the Unemployed Citizens' League took credit for winning a 5-cent hot lunch dish, and milk "for every child who needs one", plus free transportation: *Voice of Action*, 23 Oct. 1933.

2. Seattle Teachers League, *Bulletin*, vol. 2, no. 9 (4 June 1934), vol. 3, no. 7 (31 Jan. 1935), File 3-31, Schmitz, Papers. The "Yellow-Dog Contract" clause read: "No person will be employed hereafter or continued in the employ of the District, as a teacher, while a member of the Ameri-

can Federation of Teachers or any local thereof". Teachers were also required to sign a loyalty oath that the Legislature passed in 1931: File 3-31, Schmitz, Papers. See Jonathan Dembo, "A History of the Washington State Labor Movement . . . " pp. 496-8 on the contract and its validation by the Supreme Court. On the loyalty oath see Gunns, "Civil Liberties and Crisis . . . " pp. 157-8. Marsh to Reynolds, 24 Jan. 1938, Box 1, WEA, Records. The Seattle Classroom Teachers Association sought to reintroduce legislation in 1937, setting up a retirement fund: File 3-21, Schmitz, Papers. Copy of AFT, Local 200 letter of [Dec.] 1939 in File 1-13, Schmitz, Papers. Further, on the legislative front, when a retirement bill was passed Senator Mary Farquharson complained that it provided even less than Social Security; *P-I*, 27 Dec.1939; File 3-25, Schmitz, Papers. Marsh of the WEA was encouraged after passage of the "Showalter Equalization Bill" to press further for tenure legislation: Marsh to Ethel Johnson,, principal of East Seattle High School, Mercer Island, 5 Feb. 1935, Box 1, Accession 731, WEA, Records. Washington was but one of eight states not granting tenure: *WEJ*, XV:7 (Apr.1936).

3. Schmitz to Moody's Investor Services, 25 Oct. 1937, File 5-6, "School Facts", File 1-6, Schmitz, Papers. Seattle School District, *[Annual Report]*, 1931-32 and 1937-38.

4. Seattle School District. *[Annual Report]*, 1931-32 and 1937-38. *Minutes*, 9 and 16 Sept. 1932, Seattle Public Schools Archives.

5. *WEJ*, XIV:3 (Dec., 1934), p. 72. James Wheeler, who headed up the Citizens' Legislation League, recounted to Adam Schantz, chairman of the National Committee of the National Real Estate Boards, on 5 Dec. 1934, that, although the margin of victory was smaller than that which won the 40-mill property tax limitation, it was due to the publicity given the big contribution of the Northern Pacific Railway. It would get a bigger tax break by far than the small home owner to whom the league appealed. He concluded that in 1932, the opposition was the "education group", but in 1934 it was "all of the tax spenders": also on Community Tax Bureau in 1934, Box 134 "Seattle Real Estate" file, West and Wheeler Real Estate Company, Records. Also, *Municipal News*, 3 Nov. 1934

6. File 14-42, Stephen F. Chadwick, Papers; for American Legion's involvement in public schools see also File 2-2.

7. McClure's report to the Board, 11 Mar. 1938, File 1-10; Schmitz to Kizer, 1 Oct. 1937; Kizer to Schmitz, 29 Oct. 1937, File 1-8, Schmitz, Papers; Washington State Federation of Teachers to Kizer, 17 Jan. 1938, File 20-6, Elmer Miller, Papers. *Minutes*, 10 Aug., 13 and 27 Oct., 15 Dec. 1939 and 21 June 1940, Seattle Public Schools Archives. Edison started in 1919 under a federal grant implementing the "Smith-Hughes law" to provide vocational training for students who, for economic reasons, had dropped out of school but had not yet fulfilled the age requirement—Part-Time schooling was provided.

8. On policy see the District [*Annual Report*], 1937-38. On the milk prices issue see Holmes' report in File 1-4, Schmitz, Papers; on UCL see *Vanguard*, January 1932.

9. Calvin Schmid, *Social Trends . . .*, pp. 160, 161, charts 54 and 55.

Funding of Common Schools in the State

1. William E. Torget, "Financing the Common Schools in the State of Washington" (Unpublished Master's Thesis, University of Washington, 1954), pp. 25-9,32. In a footnote on p. 109 Torget lists all the sources making up the State common schools' "permanent fund". The principal sources listed are: appropriations and donations by the state, donations and bequests by individuals for common schools, proceeds of lands and other property for which grants are not specified, and proceeds from the sale of timber, stone, minerals, or other property from school or state lands.

2. Torget, *ibid.* table on p. 34.

3. Torget, *ibid.*, table on p. 34, pp. 54-60, and table on p. 69.

4. Torget, *ibid.*, pp. 45-57. The other tax sources are motor vehicle licence fees and taxes, cigarette tax, public utility tax, a compensating tax, liquor tax, insurance premium tax, inheritance and escheats tax, pinball and slot machine tax, beer and wine tax, horse racing tax, conveyance tax, corporation licence tax, gift tax, and tax on liquor board profits.

5. Torget, *ibid.*, table on p. 78, and discussion on pp. 77-9.

6. Torget, *ibid.*, pp. 107-110 (quotation is from p. 110).

7. Torget, *ibid.*, pp. 112-27.

The University of Washington and the City

1. Charles M. Gates, *The First Century at the University of Washington, 1861-1961* (Seattle: University of Washington Press, 1961),pp. 156-7,163-5.

2. Gates, *ibid.*, pp. 156-9. Gates comments on the effects brought on by the combination of financial stress and rising enrollments: "They suggest also a second phase in the history of the Graduate School and professional programs when the growing number of graduates produced strong temptations to appoint them locally rather than bring graduates from other institutions . . . [fostering] a new provincialism" (p. 157). Margaret A. Hall, "A History of Women Faculty at the University of Washington, 1896-1970" (Unpublished Ph.D. Dissertation, University of Washington, 1984), pp. 164-8; Douglas R. Pullen, "The Administration of Washington State Governor Louis F. Hart, 1919-1925" (Unpublished Ph.D. Dissertation, University of Washington, 1974), chapter 3, esp. pp. 93ff; Donald T. Williams, Jr., "The Remarkable Dr. Henry Suzzallo: a Biography" (Unpublished manuscript in the University Archives), chapter 9.

3. Gates, *ibid.*, pp. 158-59.

4. Henry Schmitz, *The Long Road Travelled: an Account of Forestry at the University of Washington* (Seattle: University of Washington Press, 1973),pp. 35,37,41-2,48-9.

5. Robert R. Stickney, *Flagship: a History of Fisheries at the University of Washington* (Dubuque, IA: Kendall-Hunt Publishing Co., 1989), chapter 1.

6. Gates, *ibid.*, p. 159.

7. Gates, *ibid.*, pp. 174-6 (quotation is from p. 175).

8. Albert F. Gunns, "Civil Liberties and Crisis . . . " pp. 156-7 on the Stern case; on ROTC protests see *Union Record*, 16 and 29 Mar., 1921; on

fees see 27 and 30 Sept. 1921 and 9 Jan. 1922 issues; on Stern case see *Vanguard,* Oct. and Nov. 1930 issues in which Stern is quoted as blaming the clergy for his "scientific approach" to religion; the Padelford and Spencer quotations are in its November issue.

The University of Washington During the Depression Years

1. Gates, *ibid.,* pp. 176-9; Schmitz, *ibid.,* pp. 55-7.
2. Gates, *ibid.,* pp. 179-80; Hall, *ibid.,* pp. 172-5.
3. Gates, *ibid.,* pp. 180-83.
4. Gates, *ibid.,* pp. 183-7.
5. Gates, *ibid.,* pp. 188-9; Hall, *ibid.,* pp. 169-75 (quotations are from pp. 172 and 173).
6. Gates, *ibid.,* pp. 189-91.

Chapter 15

The Cultural Scene Between the Two Wars

Introduction

1. This observation is derived from the following sources: Ellen Van Volkenburg Browne and Edward Nordhoff Beck, editors, *Miss Aunt Nellie: the Autobiography of Nellie C. Cornish* (Seattle: University of Washington Press, 1964); William Cumming, *Sketchbook: a Memoir of the 30s and the Northwest School* (Seattle: University of Washington Press, 1984); Anne Calhoun, *A Seattle Heritage: the Seattle Fine Arts Society* (Seattle: Lowman and Hanford, 1942); Nancy Wilson Ross, *Farthest Reach: Oregon and Washington* (New York: A.A. Knopf, 1941); Seattle Art Museum, Records (hereafter referred to as SAM, Records; Florence Bean James, "Fists Upon a Star", a draft manuscript autobiography in her Papers.
2. Calhoun, *ibid.,* pp. 77-8.
3. Kenneth Callahan review, copy in Box 24, SAM, Records; Cumming, *ibid.,* pp. 24-6,29,38-44,54-63,68-84.

The Cornish School

1. Browne and Beck, *ibid.,* pp. 155-60, 169-70,212-14,260; Ross, *ibid.,* pp. 181-2.
2. Browne and Beck, *ibid.,* pp. 205-06,209-10,269-70, and for hiring Tobey, pp. 134-5; Cumming, *ibid.,* 112-18.
3. Browne and Beck, *ibid.,* pp. 147-56, 161-3,173-4, in which Miss Cornish tells of the difficulties in getting the local wealthy to contribute to the city's chief cultural institution.
4. Browne and Beck, *ibid.,* pp. 162-3,171-4,205,218-22.

The Fine Arts Scene, Founding of the Seattle Art Museum, and Beginnings of the "Northwest School"

1. Calhoun, *ibid.,* pp. 64-7; Callahan review in 1938, Box 24; and File 35-42, SAM, Records.
2. *Minutes,* 14 Jan. 1926, 27 Oct. 1927, 10 Nov., 6 Dec. 1927; Secretary's

report, 6 Jan. 1927; Carl Gould recommendation, 19 Apr. 1927, all in File 34-3, SAM, Records. Paid membership was 237 in 1920, 551 in 1921, 632 in 1923, 523 in 1926, 1,721 in 1927, 2,691 in 1928: File 35-40, SAM, Records.

3. Calhoun, *ibid.*, pp. 68-82,92-8; *Minutes*, 6 Jan. 1927; *Washington Alumnus*, 17:7 (April, 1926), p. 6.

4. *Bulletin*, I:1 (Dec., 1927), File 35-42; Secretary's report, 19 Dec. 1927, File 34-3; *Minutes*, 9 May, and 9 and 16 July, 13 Aug., 11 and 18 Sept. 1928, in File 34-4; prospectus is in File 31-1, SAM, Records.

5. The following account is derived from Martha Kingsbury, *The Art of the Thirties: the Pacific Northwest* (Seattle: University of Washington Press, 1972), her essay, "Four Artists in the Northwest Tradition", in Charles Cowles, *Northwest Traditions* (Seattle: Seattle Art Museum, 1978), pp. 9-60, an introduction by Betty Bowen to *Tobey's 80: a Retrospective* (Seattle: for SAM by University of Washington Press, 1970), Cumming, *ibid.*; Ross, *ibid.*, pp. 177-85. An excellent biographical sketch of Graves is in Frederick S. Wight, John Baur, and Duncan Phillips, *Morris Graves* (Berkeley: University of California Press, 1956). File 1-1, SAM, Records, has Fuller's memorandum on the core collection and program.

6. Callahan article in *Town Crier*, 28:50, pp. 34-5.

7. Kingsbury, *Northwest Traditions* . . . p. 11.

8. Kingsbury, *Art of the Thirties* pp. 9-18, and in *Northwest Traditions* . . . p. 9ff.

9. Bowen, *op. cit.*; Cumming, *ibid.*, pp. 21-6,122-44; Kingsbury, *Art of the Thirties, op. cit.*

10. Cumming, *ibid.*, pp. 80-81 on Graves's "stealing" of Tobey's "white writing" technique, and the "The People", pp. 147-212; Wight, *et al*, *Graves*, pp. 10ff for interaction of the artists upon one another; Kingsbury, *Art of the Thirties, op. cit.*

11. Cumming, *ibid.*, pp. 147-52; Kingsbury, *ibid.*

The Seattle Repertory Playhouse

1. On the "Negro Theater" see Evamarii A. Johnson, "A Production History of the Seattle Federal Theatre Project's Negro Repertory Company: 1935-1939" (Unpublished Ph.D. Dissertation, University of Washington, 1981), pp. 14-20.

2. *Town Crier*, 28:50 (Dec., 1933), p. 15.

3. Florence Bean James, "Fists Upon a Star", Box 1, James, Papers; see statement of Burton James [1938?] in Box 38, Seattle Repertory Playhouse, Records.

4. James, "Fists". Peer would be given the SRP's 100th production in December 1940. By then a total audience of 20,000 had seen it: Box 62, SRP, Records. The *Times*, in an editorial of 20 Sept. 1931, wrote under "Our Playhouse": "The playhouse has assumed a surprising stature in things civic in Seattle . . . Its program reveals it as continuing its avowed course of presenting the finest in the drama of all lands and of all times.".

5. Johnson, *ibid.*, pp. 1-5,12-34; James, "Fists"; Guy Williams, "Seattle's Negro Theare", *Federal Theatre*, 2:1 pp. 7-9; Heloise Wardall to Tobey, 12 Jan. 1933, File 5-9, Mark Tobey, Papers. James, in her "Fists", writes: "The

success of the negro group was creating friction with the white group, who were doing vaudeville acts in the parks . . . [who claimed they] were denied opportunities that negro amateurs were getting". T'was ever thus!

6. On the WST see Gloria A. Hewitt, "A History of the Washington State Theatre, 1931 to 1941" (Unpublished Master's Thesis, University of Washington, 1964). For its productions see Box 57, SRP, Records; James, "Fists".

7. Burton James's statement [1938?], Box 38, SRP, Records; "History" file in Box 38, SRP, Records.

8. Glenn Hughes memorandum to President Charles E. Odegaard, 1961, gives his version of relations with the SRP: with inventory to Drama School, Records, UW Archives; James, "Fists"; F.M. Padelford to Hughes, 25 Feb. 1930, explaining his and Griffiths' opposition to any "University Theater", File 119-3, Accession 71-34, UW President, Records, UW Archives.

9. Griffiths to Winkenwerder, 28 Apr. 1933; Hughes to Sieg, 26 Oct. 1937, and Hughes to Fitz, 25 Oct., 1937, UW President, Records.

10. Johnson, *ibid.*, p. 15; Margaret Hall, *ibid.*, pp. 198-204 on the James case; Jane Sanders, *Cold War on the Campus: Academic Freedom at the University of Washington, 1946-64* (Seattle: University of Washington Press, 1979), p. 192, footnote 10. See also Hughes Memorandum to Odegaard, *ibid. Minutes*, 6 May and 21 July, 1933, Board of Regents, Records. Hughes writes about the Penthouse as the "first ever constructed for presentation of drawing room plays in arena style". Hughes contended that the University of Washington, represents the "only instance of a college theatre operating on a professional schedule [with two playhouses acting on that schedule]": Box 38, SRP, Records.

11. James, "Fists".

The Seattle Symphony and Other Musical Groups

1. Edward Sheppard and Emily Johnson, "Forty Years of Symphony in Seattle, 1903-1940", *PNQ* (January 1944), pp. 23-4; Esther W. Campbell, *Bagpipes in the Woodwind Section: a History of the Seattle Symphony Orchestra and its Women's Association* (Seattle: Seattle Women's Association, 1978), p. 13; Browne and Beck, *ibid.* pp. 135-7; *Minutes*, 18 Jan. and 1 Feb. 1921, Chamber of Commerce, Minute Books.

2. Campbell, *ibid.*, pp. 15-20; Sheppard and Johnson, *ibid.*, p. 25; Browne and Beck, *ibid.*, p. 159; Cecilia Schultz, *Scrapbooks*, on the 1927-28 season. The *P-I*'s Everhardt Armstrong pleaded for some Brahms, Beethoven, and Schubert—as for Bruckner, his is but a "mere name to us". He claimed only one Brahms symphony had ever been given in Seattle.

3. Campbell, *ibid.*, pp. 21-7; *Town Crier*, 31:3 (March 1936), p. 11.

4. Campbell, *ibid.*, chapter 5 and pp. 32-5.

5. Schultz, *ibid.*; the latter quotation is from a clipping from the *Washington Business Woman*, June 1935, p. 39.6.

6. Schultz, *ibid.*

Parks, Playgrounds, and Boulevards Between the Wars

1. Seattle Superintendent of Parks, *Annual Report*, 1922.

2. Superintendent, *ibid.* According to the 1933 *Report*, the Auto Camp was closed in 1928, and reopened in 1933 to accomodate increasing numbers of people who seemed to have become "gypsies". This was during the worst years of the Depression.

3. Superintendent, *ibid.*, 1930.

4. Superintendent, *ibid.*, years 1930-1933.

5. Superintendent, *ibid.*, years 1934 and 1935. The Auto Camp was discontinued, impliedly, because of pressure from operators of commercial camps and cabins outside the city.

Catherine Joy Johnson, "The Olmsted Designs for the Washington Park Arboretum", *Washington Park Arboretum Bulletin*, 52:1 (Spring 1989), pp. 14-17.

6. Superintendent, *ibid.*, years 1930-1940.

Conservation and Mountain Recreation Between the Wars

1. The Mountaineers, *Minutes*, 5 Jan. 1922 for Lake Crescent dam; 5 Nov. 1925 for Lake Chelan dam. At its 9 Dec. 1926 meeting the National Parks Committee was authorized to lobby for a comprehensive survey of wilderness areas in the state for their "preservation in perpetuity". See 8 Sept. 1927 for Mt. Baker-Mt. Shuksan; 6 Sept. 1928 for a Glacier Peak National Park; and 4 Apr. 1929 for Northern Pacific timber sale. Mountaineers, Records.

2. *Minutes*, 23 Feb. 1922, 5 May 1927, Mountaineers, Records.

3. *Minutes*, 4 Nov. 1920, Mountaineers, Records. The club pressed to eliminate sheep grazing in Grand Park and appeared to have won out, *Minutes*, 3 Feb. and 7 Apr. 1921. At its 8 Sept. 1927 meeting the club passed a resolution to limit grazing at the head of the Whitechuck and Sauk rivers trails, and complained about overgrazing at White Pass, just south of Glacier Peak. On park service controversy see File 2-9, Asahel Curtis, Papers, and Mountaineers, *Bulletin*, January, February and March 1923 (the author has been unable to find a copy of the pamphlet). Paul Harper and Dr. H.J. Whitacre defended the Company whose president, Everett Griggs, of the St. Paul and Tacoma Lumber Company, spoke at the 3 December 1922 meeting. On the tramway see *Minutes*,3 Nov. 1927 and 7 June 1928; on wilderness set asides, 6 Sept. 1928; on the golf course, 8 Jan. 1931.

4. Carbon copy, [December 1922] Superintendent Peters to George Goodwin, chief civil engineer of the National Park Service, File 2-8, and copy of letter from Bert Burrell to Horace Albright, 27 Aug. 1925, File 2-39, Curtis, Papers.

5. Hanson to Meany, File 32-1, Part 2, Edmond S. Meany, Papers; *Minutes*, 23 Feb. 1922, Mountaineers, Records.

6. Esther Stark Maltby, *Scrapbooks*, 16 Oct. 1927, 5 Jan. 1928; *Minutes*, 11 and 12 Jan. 1928, Federation of Women's Clubs of Washington, Records. Maltby later recorded the sequence of events for the Federation. She

noted that George Long would never have agreed to the original sale if he had known the women could have carried it out. File 14-9 Federation of Women's Clubs, Records.

7. Ben Whitfield Twight, *Organizational Values and Political Power: the Forest Service Versus the Olympic National Park* (University Park, PA: Pennsylvania State University, 1983), pp. 40-57. Facsimile copies of Twight's source materials are in the UW Libraries Manuscript Collection. He points out that the Forest Service was planning to cut inside the Monument anyway. Elmo Richardson, "Olympic National Park: 20 Years of Controversy", *Forest History*, 12:1 (April, 1968), pp. 7-8.

8. Twight, *ibid.*,pp. 64-7. Twight's dissertation,"The Tenacity of Value Commitment: the Forest Service and the Olympic National Park" (Unpublished Ph.D. Dissertation, University of Washington, 1971), defines in his footnote on p. 87, the USFS operational categories: "certainty" relates to unchanging technology, consumption patterns, production techniques, and social values; "closed economy" refers to the peninsula as being engaged only in timber production on a continuing basis pointed toward self-sufficiency; "scientific elitism" refers to planned use by foresters employing scientific methods; and "telic forestry" refers to development of permanent forest-based communities. Richardson, *op. cit.*

9. Twight, *Organizational Values . . .* , pp. 58-61. Dean Hugo Winkenwerder of the UW's School of Forestry objected to the Mountaineers' advocacy of national park status, further urging return of the Monument to Forest Service jurisdiction. See Ross Tiffany to Irving Clark, 21 Nov. 1934, File 3-5, Accession 273, Clark, Papers. Earlier, Clark was instructed by the trustees to investigate national park status for Mt. Baker: *Minutes*, 8 Mar. 1934, Mountaineers, Records.

10. Twight, *ibid.*, pp. 61-9; Richardson, *op. cit.*; Harold K. Steen, *The U.S. Forest Service: a History* (Seattle: University of Washington Press, 1976), pp. 199-204, 210-11; *Minutes*, 8 Mar., 7 and 9 June 1934, Mountaineers, Records.

11. Twight, *ibid.*, pp. 69-73. The Forest Service's Ira J. Mason reported that "Mills have been installed with no consideration of permanent timber supplies, but only as to a supply adequate to depreciate them . . . If cuts had been held down to 400 to 500 million feet annually . . . the industry would have been maintained on a permanent basis . . . [This] will result in abandoned mills and the decay of settlements". Hemlock had been cut to get fir, and left to waste. Measures were being taken to see if hemlock could be pulped. A colleague, Frank Heintzelman, proposed that "iron-clad" agreements with private owners would be needed to establish a basis of permanency. Irving Clark, as the Mountaineers' chief lobbyist, was told by Wallgren that the first bill would have passed, if the states' two senators had endorsed the bill: File 6-12, Accession 273, notebook entry for 10 July 1935, Clark, Papers. The club also opposed logging of the Quinault Indian Reservation, *Minutes*, 5 Nov. 1936. On the State Planning Council see copy of its resolution of 10 July 1934; Tomlinson to Clark, 9 Nov. 1934; and copy of Tiffany to FDR, 2 July 1935, File 2-32; and mimeograph copy of proceedings of Council meeting of 22 June

1934, File 6-12, and in same file the Curtis statement of 28 July 1934, Clark, Papers. A copy of the Mountaineers statement to the Council, dated 27 Aug. 1936 is also in File 6-12. See also Mountaineers, *Bulletin*, November 1935.

12. Twight, *ibid.*, pp. 81-93. See also House of Representatives, Public Lands Committee, *Hearings*,on H.R. 10024 for testimony of Kizer and Governor Martin.

13. Richardson, *ibid.*, pp. 11-13; File 1-12, Preston Macy, Papers; Notebook entry of 28 Apr. 1938, File 6-12, Clark, Papers.

14. Twight, *ibid.*, pp. 97-104; Richardson *ibid.*, pp. 11-14.

15. *Minutes*, 12 Oct. 1937, Chamber of Commerce, Minute Books; its resolution opposing creation of a "Cascades Ice Peaks Park" read: "The area is now kept in its primitive state . . . No roads will be built into this area unless the Forest Service deems them absolutely essential". For instructions to its Public Affairs Committee see *Minutes*, 12 Oct. 1939, Mountaineers, Records.

16. C.J. Conover, "Forest Service Program on Cascade Crest Trail—1937", *The Mountaineer*, 30:1 (!5 Dec. 1937), p. 25; Madelene Ryder, "The Third Decade", *ibid.*, pp. 16-18; Joseph T. Hazard, "Our Second Ten Years", *ibid.*, pp. 13-16.

17. George MacGowan, "Five Years of Climbing Courses", *The Mountaineer*, 32:1 (15 Dec. 1939), pp. 5-8.

18. Ryder, *op. cit.*; Hazard, *op. cit.*; *Minutes*, 3 Dec. 1931 and 9 Feb. 1939, Mountaineers, Records. In 1938 the club agreed to help form a ski patrol, once the [First Aid Ski] patrol had been set up: *Minutes*, 13 Oct. 1938. Beginning in 1933 an annual patrol race of 18 miles length was held between Snoqualmie and Stampede passes: Don Blair to Bestor Robinson of the Sierra Club, 17 Oct. 1935, reporting on trail marking and the race: Mountaineers, Ski Mountaineering Committee Records. The Chamber of Commerce, through the lobbying of trustee Darwin Meisnest, was instrumental in getting the Olympic Games tryouts, assisted by its Tacoma counterpart: *Minutes*, 11 Dec. 1934, Chamber of Commerce, Minute Books. The author has added some personal memories.

Chapter 16

Civil Liberties Between the Wars

1. Albert F. Gunns, "Civil Liberties and Crisis: The Status of Civil Liberties in the Pacific Northwest, 1917-1940" (Unpublished Ph.D. Dissertation, University of Washington, 1971), pp.120-22, 173-5; Norman Clark, *The Dry Years . . .*, pp. 151-3,184,197. On Judge Neterer see *Times*, 6 Apr. 1921, and *Union Record*, 21 Feb. 1921. The *UR* reported on 23 Jan. 1922, that the City's dry squad felt impeded in conducting "booze raids" because the courts were requiring search warrants; also, that there were only 12 enforcement officers in western Washington. See also, chapter 17 below, "Mayor Edwards and the Radicals".

2. Jonathan Dembo, "The Washington State Labor Movement . . . ", pp. 432-3,495-7.

3. Dembo, *ibid.*, pp. 243-6 (quotation is from p. 245).

4. Gunns, *ibid.*, pp. 125-9. See also chapter 17.

5. Gunns, *ibid.*, pp. 129-30,140-52; deportation figures are on p. 139, footnote 62. Wolck was actually not deported because the steamship company that was to transport him went bankrupt. (pp. 148-9).

6. Gunns, *ibid.*, pp. 156-8,205. Accounts provided the author by two of the student participants, Miner Baker and Hu Blonk, merit special attention. Baker was elected student body president in April 1935, just as the anti-militarism protest was at its height. He became the economist for the First National Bank. Blonk, after a career in the Reclamation Service ended with his resignation for criticizing the role of the Idaho Power Company in the Hells Canyon Dam controversy, joined the *Wenatchee World* as its managing editor in 1955. Baker portrays Winkenwerder as a "kind and sympathetic man caught in the middle [who] selected 'indefinite' instead of 'six months' because it sounded more severe but would permit almost immediate reinstatement". Blonk, reminiscing in the *World*, found the president fearful of "public reaction, or more specifically that of the Legislature and downtown newspapers". Blonk continues: "[The leaders responded,] that any institution of higher learning that wouldn't allow freedom of speech . . . shouldn't be entitled to appropriations". Improvised formation of club organization is derived from Blonk's account.

7. Gunns, *ibid.*, pp. 205-09; *P-I*, 3 Mar. 1934; *Vanguard*, 26 May, 2 and 9 June 1934; *Voice of Action*, 31 May and 7 June 1934.

8. James Wechsler, *Revolt on Campus* (Seattle: University of Washington Press, American Library Edition, 1973). Wechsler wrote this in 1935 as a Columbia University activist; some of his facts about the UW are not validated by the author. His coverage of the University of Pittsburg is on pp. 200-06; on the UW, pp. 187-8; for his nationwide coverage see pp. 149ff. *University of Washington Daily*, 5 Oct. 1934 has the text of Sieg's speech.

9. On protests and suppression at UCLA and Berkeley see Wechsler, *ibid.*, pp. 268-86; *Daily*, 30 and 31 Oct., 1,7,8,13-15 Nov. 1934. As of 8 November, no independents had joined the Pathfinders. The latter planned chapters elsewhere in the state, then would proceed down the coast before expanding eastward. In response to the California demonstrations, the Pathfinders declared they "Will Oppose Radical Demonstrations". *P-I*, 8 Nov. 1934.

10. *Daily*, 2,3,11 and 12 Apr. 1935; *P-I*, 11 and 13 Apr. 1935. The participation of nearby Roosevelt High School students on the day before their spring holiday was being investigated by School Superintendent Worth McClure; estimates of their number ranged from 150 to 190.

11. Margaret A. Hall, "History of Women Faculty . . . "pp. 219-23 (p. 223 for first quotation, p. 221 for second).

12. Hall, *ibid.*, pp. 221-5; *Argus*, 19 Dec. 1931; *Times*, 16 Sept. 1931. I am indebted to City Archivist Scott Cline for information on the City Council tabling action.

13. Hall, *ibid.*, pp. 226-44 and p. 238 on McMahon.

14. *P-I*, 14 Jan. 1938; *Times*, 5 Jan. 1938: "Discharge of Mrs. Miller . . . Stirs Controversy"; on King County action, 7 and 8 Feb. 1938. Samuel Walker, *In Defense of American Liberties: a History of the ACLU* (New York: Oxford University Press, 1990), p. 55. Walker records the tireless efforts of the ACLU's attempts throughout the 1920s and 1930s to gain court recognition of the Bill of Rights, beginning with First Amendment protections for freedom of speech and assembly, and incorporating due process requirements into these first ten amendments: chapters 3-6.

15. Gunns, *ibid.*, pp. 90-91,98-113 (quotation is from p. 113), 215.

16. Gunns, *ibid.*, pp. 125,214-19.

17. Gunns, *ibid.*, pp. 223-7.

18. Gunns, *ibid.*, pp. 228,243-50; Gunns, "Ray Becker, the Last Centralia Prisoner", *PNQ* 59:2 (April, 1968), pp. 88-99.

Chapter 17

Mayor Edwards and the Radicals

1. An excellent introduction to the Seattle scene is provided by William H. Mullins, "San Francisco and Seattle During the Hoover Years of the Great Depression: 1929-1933" (Unpublished Ph.D. Dissertation, University of Washington, 1975), chapters 1 and 2. See also Mullins, *The Depression and the Urban West Coast, 1929-1933: Los Angeles, San Francisco, Seattle and Portland* (Bloomington: Indiana University Press, 1991), pp. 38-40,76-7,127-8. See also chapter 19 below, "The Unemployed Citizens' League".

2. Mullins, *ibid.*, pp. 29-30; Gunns, "Civil Liberties and Crisis . . . ", pp. 125-26, 145-49 concerning raid and mass arrest.; *Times*, 27 Feb., and 1 Mar. 1930. Its 27 February headline ran: "Reds Routed on Yesler!" "Police Battle 300 Radicals", accompanied by photos captioned: "Fighting Officers Disperse Communists". *Vanguard*, Feb., 1930; its March edition reported that: "More than five thousand workers had a demonstration . . . [It was called by the Communist Party in reaction to the] unemployment situation'". On 4 May 15 men and 2 women were arrested, but their cases were dismissed by Judge Gordon, *Vanguard*, May-June, 1930.

3. *Vanguard*, May-June, 1930.

4. *Seattle Review*, 19 June 1931 (copy is in Box 16,. Willis T. Batcheller. Papers, "Edwards Recall").

5. *Fair Play*, 10 July 1931, *Op. cit.*, Batcheller, Papers.

6. On national Unemployed Councils see Harvey Klehr, *The Heyday of American Communism: the Depression Decade* (New York: Basic Books, 1984), chapter 3. On the Seattle Unemployed Councils and their takeover by the Unemployed Citizens' League see John A. Hogan, "The Decline of Self-Help and Growth of Radicalism Among Seattle's Unemployed" (Unpublished Master's Thesis, University of Washington, 1934).

7. Seattle, *Yearbook*, 4 June 1928; Washington State Federation of Labor, *Proceedings*, 1931.

8. Mullins, "San Francisco and Seattle ", pp. 28-31. Pointing to the most publicized effort in Seattle, Mullins writes: " Although the city's

problems appeared to be worsening, one of the primary responses, public or private, was a dose of ballyhoo" (p. 26).

9. Mullins, *ibid.*, pp. 43-4. *Vanguard*, July-Aug. 1930.

10. Washington State Federation of Labor, *Proceedings*, 1932, p. 21; *Vanguard*, Feb., May-June, 1930, July 1931.

11. *Vanguard*, Feb., 1930.

12. Mullins *ibid.*, pp. 43-7.

13. Vanguard, Feb., Oct., 1930; Jan., Feb., 1931. On the CPLA, led by A.J. Muste, see Klehr, *ibid.*, pp. 15-16 and Irving Bernstein, *A History of the American Worker, 1933-1941: the Turbulent Years* (Boston: Houghton Mifflin, 1970), p. 221.

14. Seattle Port Warden, *Annual Report[s]*, 1930-32.

Chapter 18

Edwards Is Recalled

1. Sparks, *ibid.*, p. 167. For Sparks's overall coverage of the recall election see pp. 164-84. Viewed from afar, see Robert Hill, "Power Politics in Seattle", *The Nation.*, vol. CXXXIX (2 March 1932), pp. 254-56. Hill concluded that Ross now "holds the upper hand in Seattle politics".

2. *Journal of Commerce*, 18 Mar. 1931; *P-I*, 26 May 1931; Hill, *op. cit.*

3. Sparks, *ibid.*, p. 170.

4. Sparks, *ibid.*, pp. 171-74; *Star.*, 24 and 26 Mar., 2 Apr. 1931; *P-I*, 24 Mar., 25,29, and 31 Apr. 1931. Edwards was quoted by the *P-I* as being entirely "innocent" of Ross's record before becoming mayor. *Times*, 23 Mar. 1931.

5. Sparks, *ibid.*, pp. 174-77.

6. *Star*, 16 June 1931; *P-I*, 3 July 1931. The Supreme Court divided 4 to 4, thereby leaving Judge Ronald's decision intact.

7. Sparks, *ibid.*, p. 177; *Star.*, 13 and 30 Apr. 1931.

8. *Argus*, 11 July 1931.

9. *Times*, 29 Apr. 1931.

10. *Star*, 14 May 1931; *Times*, 20 May 1931.

11. Copy of the bulletin is in File 87-8, SLD, Records.

12. Sparks, *ibid.*, pp. 178-84.

13. Sparks, *ibid.*, p. 180.

Chapter 19

Politics of Unemployment and Relief, 1931-1935

The Unemployed Citizens' League

1. Allen R. Potter, et al, *Occupational Characteristics of Unemployed Persons in Cities of 11,000 or More Persons, State of Washington* (Olympia: Washington Employment Relief Administration, 1935), p. vii.

2. William S. Hopkins, *Seasonal Unemployment in the State of Washington* (Seattle: University of Washington Publications in the Social Sciences, vol. 8, no. 3, pp. 81-168, Dec., 1936), p. 109.

3. Hopkins, *ibid.*, pp. 110-18, 123-46; Potter, *ibid.*, p. 23 for quotation.

4. Potter, *ibid.*, pp. 2-7.

5. Potter, *ibid.*, pp. 9-10.

6. Potter, *ibid.*, pp. 10-12.

7. Hogan, *ibid*; Bruce D. Blumell, "The Development of Public Assistance in the State of Washington During the Great Depression" (Unpublished Ph.D. Dissertation, University of Washington, 1973), pp. 36-51: (Note: Though published in 1983 by the Garland Press, citations are to the unpublished version; this note applies also to the Gunns and Dembo dissertations cited below). Arthur Hillman, *The Unemployed Citizens' League of Seattle* (Seattle: University of Washington Publications in the Social Sciences, vol. 5, no. 3, pp. 181-270, 1934), pp. 185-91; Gunns, *ibid.*, pp. 123-25; Dembo pp. 550-51 and 569-70; Tom Jones Perry, "Republic of the Penniless", *Atlantic*, vol. 150 (Oct., 1932), pp. 449-57. On the Conference for Progressive Political Action see Roy Rosenzweig, "Radicals and the Jobless: the Musteites and the Unemployed Leagues", *Labor History*, 16:1, pp. 52-77. The CPLA started up in 1929 to find a course between the AFL and the CP's dual unionism (Trade Union Unity League). By 1931, it revised its position to left of the Socialist Party, denouncing it for gradualism. A.J. Muste emerged as the leader, and the unemployed were seen as the possible mass organizational base. The Seattle UCL leaders took their lead from Muste. On the Unemployed Leagues of the CP see Klehr, *ibid.*, pp. 49-68; Bernstein, *The Lean Years . . .*, p. 428.

8. Hogan, *ibid.*, pp. v-vi.

9. Hogan, *ibid.*, chapter 1. Rivalry between the rival radical factions is reflected in the succession of newspapers by them until the Communists drove Wells, Brannin, and the other socialists from the UCL leadership; Brannin was a member of the executive committee of the CPLA. A biographical sketch of Brannin appears in his *Dissenting Opinion: Carl Brannin's Letters to the Editor, 1933-1976* (Dallas: Carl Brannin, 1977). The *Vanguard* began monthly publication under auspices of the Seattle Labor College from January 1930 until 25 November 1932, when it became the *Unemployed Citizen*, but only until 24 February 1933. Brannin, discouraged, returned to Texas after a long sojourn, leaving Wells as editor until May, when he retired. Sponsorship passed from the College to the "Vanguards", who began publishing the *Voice of Action* on 25 March 1933 as open rival to the *Vanguard*, with the aim of establishing a mass base of its own for political action by advocating direct action techniques in the form of mass protests. Unlike the *Vanguard*, which separated news from opinion, the *Voice* made no distinction, coloring the news with opinion. The *Voice* became the only radical publication by the end of the year. Details behind this outline may be found in Ronald M. Leistra, "Seattle's Radical Press, 1930-1934 (Unpublished Master's Thesis, University of Washington, 1964). The *Voice*, in its 3 April 1934 issue, reported: "A year ago following the ousting of [Phil] Pearl and Wells from the leadership [of the UCL] members of the Communist Party were elected into the leadership of the organization and the program for the [UCL]". As the CP began seeking alliances on the liberal-left, in particular with the Commonwealth Builders, Inc., the *Voice* was soon replaced by the *Washington*

Commonwealth Builder on 23 August 1934; its name was changed to *Washington Commonwealth,* then *Commonwealth News* 19 October 1935. Under that name it continued until 15 November 1936, after which its name became the *Sunday News,* continuing from 26 November 1936 to 10 September 1938. Then its name was changed to *Washington New Dealer* (when it responded to the Comintern's change of line from opposition to the New Deal to support a popular front against fascism); under this name it continued until 21 January 1943, when it became the *New World.*

10. See Sarah Ellen Sharbach, "Louise Olivereau and the Seattle Radical Community, 1917-1923" (Unpublished Master's Thesis, University of Washington, 1986) pp. 136-45 for background on the Seattle Labor College (quotation is from p. 144).

11. Hogan, *ibid.,* pp. 1-5 (quotation is from p. 5).

12. Hogan, *ibid.,* pp. 6-20-.

13. Hogan, *ibid.* pp. 13-15.

14. File 1-9, Bertha K. Landes, Papers

The Unemployed Citizens' League Becomes Politicized

1. Hogan, *ibid.,* pp. 17-27; Hillman, *ibid.,* pp. 198-202 (quotation is from p. 199); Blumell, *ibid.,* pp. 40-2, 46-50; Krause, *ibid.,* pp. 59-60. See also Murray Morgan, *Skid Road: An Informal Portrait of Seattle* (Seattle: University of Washington Press, 4th printing, 1991), pp. 232-33, 237-38.

2. Hogan, *ibid.,* pp. 20-2; Hillman, *ibid.,* pp. 207-10. The *Argus* issue of 12 May 1900 carried a note on the character of the rising John F. Dore: he slugged the opposing attorney, Ellis Bruler, in Judge T.H. Cann's court.

3. *Vanguard,* Dec. 1931. The Edwards campaign literature and Batcheller's drafts are well represented in Box 16 in the Batcheller Papers.

4. *Times,* 25 Feb. 1932; *Argus,* 16 and 23 Jan. and 13 Feb. 1932; Hillman, *ibid.,* pp. 207-09.

5. Washington State Federation of Labor, *Proceedings,* 1932, p. 21; Hillman, *op. cit.;* Hogan, *ibid.,* pp. 21-3; *Vanguard,* Apr., 1932.

6. *Vanguard,* Jan. 1932; in its March and June issues the editors urged an "independent labor party". In its June 1932 issue the editors charged: "The Communists, as usual, are practicing their disruptive tactics within the [UCL], accusing the party with trying to break up the UCL". Hogan, *ibid.,* pp. 24-7,61-72; Hillman, *ibid.,* pp. 204-05; Blumell, *ibid.,* pp. 51-2. UCL chairman and local CP leader, William Dobbins, had led a protest of about 4,000 and occupancy of the County-City Building in mid-February 1933. The CP leadership, disappointed in his leadership, announced Dobbins's "resignation" from the UCL chairmanship, declaring: "A year ago following the ousting of Pearl, Wells, Griffin, Smith, and Hyde from leadership of the organization and the program proposed by the [CP] through its members was accepted as the new program of the [UCL]". Dobbins confessed to his failure to expand the demonstration, for having dealt with the opposition, and for not drawing in more of the unemployed into the "struggle for more relief". Typed copy of: "[To]

members of the Unemployed Citizens' League", issued by the Communist Party, District 12, Seattle, 28 March, 1934, in Box 8 of the Eugene V. Dennett, Papers.

7. Hogan, *ibid.*, pp. 22-3; *Vanguard*, April and May, 1932.

8. *P-I*, 20 Mar. 1932; *Municipal News*, 19 Mar. and 2 Apr. 1932.

9. Hillman, *ibid.*, pp. 210-11; *P-I*, 1,3,15,19,21, and 23 July 1932.

10. *P-I*, 27 Sept. and 28 Oct. 1932.

11. *P-I*, 1 and 2 July 1932.

12. *P-I*, 2 July 1932; Hogan, *ibid.*, pp. 25-7.

13. *P-I*, 3-7 July 1932.

14. Hogan, *ibid.*, pp. 26 and 40-2.

15. Hogan, *ibid.*, pp. 22-5, 34-8.

16. Hogan, *ibid.*, pp. 25-7, 43-6, 68-72; *P-I*, 16 Aug. 1932.

17. *P-I*, 25 Aug. 1932; *Vanguard*, 9 Sept. 1932.

18. *Vanguard*, 14 and 21 Oct. 1932; *Unemployed Citizen*, 25 Nov. and 30 Dec. 1932; *P-I*, 19 July 1932.

Hooverville and the Unemployed Citizens' League

1. Donald Francis Roy, "Hooverville: a Study of a Community of Homeless Men in Seattle" (Unpublished Master's Thesis, University of Washington, 1935). The Washington Emergency Relief administration hired Roy in January 1934 to study this community. In pages 1-20 Roy describes the improvised living conditions. Survival techniques are described in pages 80-6. Calvin F. Schmid incorporated an account by Jesse Jackson, the "mayor" of Hooverville in his *Social Trends in Seattle*, pp. 286-93: "The Story of Seattle's Hooverville". In Jackson's account governance and interaction of the community's governing apparatus with the City's is also outlined. See also Morgan, *ibid.*, pp. 224-32.

2. Roy, *ibid.*, pp. 56,60 (for quotation), tables on pp. 63-9.

3. Roy, *ibid.*, pp. 39-43, 57-9.

4. Roy, *ibid.*, p. 93; Jackson, *op. cit.*

Poor Law Mentality Greets the Great Depression

1. Blumell, *ibid.*, chapter 1; Mildred E. Buck and staff, *Public Welfare in Washington: a State-Wide Study of Problems of Public Welfare Administration* (Olympia: State Printer, 1934), chapter I.

2. Blumell, *ibid*, pp. 19-25, 31-2; Buck, *ibid.*, chapter IV.

3. Blumell, *ibid.*, chapter 1 (quotation is from p. 15); Buck, *ibid.*, pp. 88-96.

4. Buck, *ibid.*, pp. 104-05.

5. Blumell, *ibid.*, pp. 33-4, 60-1.

Politics of Unemployment and Relief, 1932-1935

1. Blumell, *ibid.*, pp. 61-9; Hogan, *ibid.*,pp. 33-9; Hillman, *ibid.*, pp. 216-27; *Municipal News*, 8 Oct. 1932; *Vanguard*, 14 Oct. 1932. The *Vanguard*, of 18 Nov. 1932 reported that 2,000 cords of wood per week were needed by about 3,500 families, but the *Unemployed Citizen*, of 2 Dec. 1932 reported the conflict between volunteers and the paid managers over

distribution of gas, oil, etc., when the latter insisted on control of distribution. When the new commissioners took office the UCL volunteers were given modified control under County supervision: *Unemployed Citizen*, 6 and 13 Jan. 1933. Ernst reported to Joanna Colcord of the Russell Sage Foundation that the new County Commissioners had "made an issue of the fact that the County Commissioners had taken the commissaries away from the unemployed . . . ", Ernst to Colcord, 11 Nov. 1932, File 1-17, Charles F. Ernst, Papers. Mayor Dore added his dash of color to the November election by attacking Stevenson and Marion Zioncheck, under auspices of the City-County Home Defense League, and using the radio: "if [Stevenson] should be elected . . . I would declare a public emergency existed, and that I would arm householders to protect the lives of themselves and family . . . I would say to you in all sincerity, if this man were elected . . . this city would run with blood inside four months . . . He believes that the crosses should be torn from the churches, and that it would be a crime to mention the name of God in this country . . . Commissaries will be turned back to the agitators, to anarchists and Russian agents".: Hillman *ibid.*, p. 223.

2. *Municipal News*, 10 Dec. 1932; *P-I*, 16 Nov. 1932.

3. Blumell, *ibid.*, pp. 69-78; *Municipal News*, 20 Apr. 1932 and 21 Jan. 1933.

4. Blumell, *ibid.*, pp. 69-78; *Unemployed Citizen*, 27 Jan. and 3 Feb. 1933; Warren Magnuson, as legal counsel to WERA, urged a broad construction in cases of doubt, because the purpose of the program was to give employment and unemployment relief, and that the funds were intended for local work projects, not those of the State.: Magnuson to WERA Commission chair, Frank Baker, 21 Jan. 1933, File 1-20, Warren G. Magnuson, Papers. Ernst wrote to Colcord, 27 Apr. 1932: "Altogether we are having a beautiful time—absolutely no improvement in employment means that the work load grows heavier . . . The big thing is to win the voters over to the idea of the $2,000,000 bond issue for work relief".: Ernst to Colcord,, File 1-17, Ernst, Papers.

5. Blumell, *ibid.*, pp. 86-105. Blumell records that in canvassing for CWB members Ernst ignored labor organizations, pp. 80, 101-03; on UCL confrontations see pp. 86-9, 98-100; on "forced labor" see pp. 100-01. *Vanguard*, 17 Mar., 10 and 21 Apr. 1933; *Unemployed Citizen*, 3 Feb. 1933; *P-I*, 1 Mar. 1933; Shannon *Diary*, p. 51, File 1-1, William D. Shannon, Papers, part 1. Shannon later served 16 years in the State legislature. Shannon reported to the Municipal League that the "relief burden is steadily lightening . . . and thousands of names have been taken from the relief rolls in recent weeks . . . a definite indication of rehabilitation". On 1 May 69,700 persons were on the rolls; by 16 June the number had been reduced to 61,400: *Municipal News*, 3 and 24 June 1933. Frank Baker, in responding to an article in the *Atlantic* on the dole, wrote: "The least expensive way is the dole, but retaining character requires work compensating for relief. Therefore Welfare Boards are asked to find work opportunities for those who desire work [and since 85% want to work,

when they do work it should not be made to appear to the public that they are being forced to do so]. This breaks down morale." Minutes of the Public Welfare Board, 23 May 1933, in WERA subgroup of Warren G. Magnuson, Papers, accession 3181-1.

6. Hillman, *ibid.*, pp. 228-29; Ernst to Colcord, 23 Aug. 1932, File 1-17, Ernst, Papers, in which Ernst reported: "The fight here . . . seems to be between this group led by the I.W.W.s and the group led by the so called communists to whom the former crowd refers [to] as the 'Comicals'". *Unemployed Citizen* , 6 jan. 1933.

7. Hogan, *ibid.*, pp. 77-80; Blumell, *ibid.*, pp. 98-9. *Unemployed Citizen*, 10 and 17 Feb. 1933.

8. Hogan, *ibid.*, pp. 81-6; *Unemployed Citizen*, 25 Nov., 9 Dec. 1932, 13 Jan., 3 and 10 Feb. 1933; *Vanguard*, 3 Mar. 1933; *Star*, 1 and 2 Mar. 1933.

9. *P-I*, 2 and 3 Mar. 1933; *Times*, 1 Mar. 1933.

10. *Vanguard*, 17 and 31 Mar., 7 Apr. 1933; *Voice of Action*, 25 Mar., 3 Apr. 1933.

11. Blumell, *ibid.*, pp. 108-09.

12. *Voice of Action*, Apr. and 24 May 1933; *Vanguard*, 3 Mar. 1933.

13. Blumell, *ibid.*, pp. 113-15, 119-36, 143-47, 166-67.

14. Blumell, *ibid.*, pp. 115-16, 166-67; *Municipal News*, 5, 12, and 19 May, 2 June, 1934; *P-I*, 18 Feb. 1934; *Vanguard*, 15 Sept. 1933; *Voice of Action*, 8, 15, 22, and 29 Jan., 27 Feb., 27 Mar. 1934.

15. Blumell, *ibid.*, pp. 158-59.

16. Blumell, *ibid.*, p. 177.

17. Blumell, *ibid.*, pp. 179-208.

Political Realignments, 1932-1935: an Overview

1. See chapter 3, above, "Political Parties at the State Level". Fayette Krause, "Democratic Party . . . During New Deal . . . , chapters 1 and 2; Robert Cole, "Democratic Party . . . 1919-1933", pp. 1-28; William E. Leuchtenburg, *Franklin D. Roosevelt and the New Deal, 1932-1940* (New York: Harper Torchbooks, 1963), pp. 315-16; correspondence between Stephen F. Chadwick and Theodore Carlson and Edward Seay, 1939-40,concerning anti-New Deal strategy within the Democratic Party: Stephen F. Chadwick, Papers.

2. Krause, *ibid.*, pp. 10-35; Gunns, "Hartley", pp. 225-30; George C. Scott, "The New Order of Cincinnatus' (Unpublished Master's Thesis, University of Washington, 1966), chapter 1.

3. Scott, *ibid.*, provides the details; see also his "The New Order of Cincinnatus: Municipal Politics in Seattle During the 1930s", *PNQ*, 64:4 (October, 1973), pp. 137-46.

4. Albert A. Acena, "The Washington Commonwealth Federation: Reform Politics and the Popular Front" (Unpublished Ph.D. Dissertation, University of Washington, 1975), chapter I.

5. Acena, *ibid.*, pp. 5-6, 46-9, chapter II; for the national setting see Klehr, *ibid.*, pp. 197-206.

6. Frederick G. Hamley, File 18-1, Hamley, Papers.

7. Scott, *ibid.*, (thesis), pp. 47-9.

8. Quotations are from "Electric Fist", publication of the NOOC, 7 Dec. 1933 and 17 Sept. 1934 issues, File 18-20 and *Diary*, Hamley, Papers.

9. Scott, *ibid.*, pp. 16-20, and *PNQ* article, p. 138; Files 18-1,18-20,22, and 23, Hamley, Papers.

Chapter 20

Labor Movement Revives, Becomes a Political Force Again

The Great Maritime Strike of 1934—A Watershed—From Dore to Smith

1. The three main published sources used for this narrative are: Irving Bernstein, *A History of the American Worker, 1933-1941: the Turbulent Years* (Boston: Houghton Mifflin, 1970), pp. 252-98; Charles P. Larrowe, *Harry Bridges: the Rise and Fall of Radical Labor in the United States* (New York: Lawrence Hill, 1972); and Bruce Nelson, *Workers on the Waterfront* . . . , chapters 3-5. Nelson is the only writer known to me who traces the sub-culture of the waterfront worker, largely segregated from the mainstream, acutely exploited under dictatorial conditions, inclined toward direct action in the absence of political alternatives, all this inculcating a "syndicalist mood", which might from time to time make him susceptible to IWW and Marxist preachings. Their recruitment into the Maritime Workers Industrial Union is explored in detail. Focus is upon San Francisco, though not to the neglect of other ports. The two main unpublished sources used are: George M. Jones, "Longshore Unionism on Puget Sound: a Seattle-Tacoma Comparison" (Unpublished Master's Thesis, University of Washington, 1957), pp. 77-90 for the strike's chronology; but he covers the century to 1956. The other main unpublished source is Dembo's dissertation "A History of the Washington State Labor Movement . . . " With respect to development and implementation of the NRA codes in Seattle, Chamber of Commerce president Cassius Gates claimed credit for the chamber in its "Blue Eagle" campaign, in which a "military" organization was set up, headed by "general" William O. McKay and "lieutenant-general", Mrs. David Ragan of the Federation of Womens' Clubs. 5,000 volunteers canvassed the community. Gates wrote: "The very great importance of trade associations and organizations of business under the New Deal became apparent. It was through these groups, local, regional, and national, that the new codes of fair competition were to be prepared and presented to the President": Chamber of Commerce, *Annual Report*, 1933-34.

2. Bernstein, *ibid.*, pp. 30-6, 172-77; Vernon H. Jensen, *Lumber and Labor* (New York: Farrar and Rinehart, 1945), chapter 8; Robert E. Ficken, *This Forested Land: a History of Lumbering in Western Washington* (Seattle: University of Washington Press, 1987), p. 213; *P-I*, 1,5,and 8 Mar. 1934.

3. *P-I*, 21 and 27 Feb., 14 Mar. 1934; Dore accused the police and fire departments with "making the most noise . . . They have less work to do

and more time to agitate": *P-I*, 2 Mar. 1934; *Argus*, 13 Mar. 1934, p. 6; *Voice of Action*, 29 Jan., 20 and 27 Feb., 6 Mar. 1934 for coverage of the Communist Party candidates, who "tripled their vote" over that in 1932.

4. Larrowe, *ibid.*, pp. 16-7; Nelson, *ibid.*,pp. 118-26 on the MWIU; Jones *ibid.*, pp. 72-8 for antecedents of the strike; he provides a careful chronicle of the stages in the strike's course. *Argus*, 2 and 9 June 1934; *Voice . . .* ,14 June 1934; the *Voice* charged that recognition of the ILA by the employers was done to head off the MWIU, 2 Oct. 1933.

5. Larrowe, *ibid.*, pp. 18,22-3; Bernstein, *ibid.*, pp. 260-61; Jones, *ibid.*, pp. 76-8.

6. Larrowe, *ibid., pp. 23-7; Nelson, ibid.*, pp. 125-26; Bernstein, *ibid.*, pp. 260-62; *Voice*, 25 Dec. 1933.

7. Larrowe, *ibid.*, pp. 28-9; Nelson, *ibid*,, pp. 124-26; Bernstein, *ibid.*, p. 261; *Voice*, 5 and 27 Feb. 1934.

8. Larrowe, *ibid.*, pp. 23-4; Bernstein *ibid.*, 262-64; Nelson, *ibid.*, p. 128.

9. Larrowe, *ibid.*, pp. 24-7; Jones, *ibid.*, pp. 77-9; Bernstein, pp. 262-64.

10. Larrowe, *ibid.*, pp.27-8; Jones, *ibid.*, pp. 79-80; Bernstein, *ibid.*, pp. 262-64.

11. Bernstein, *ibid.*, pp. 262-63.

12. Nelson, *ibid.*, p. 129; Jones, *ibid.*, pp. 81-3; *Argus*, 12 and 19 May 1934; *Times*, 10 and 12 May 1934, reporting that Dewey Bennett of the ILA said 500 pickets would be brought in from Tacoma, and 200 from Everett so as to concentrate forces in Seattle. *University of Washington Daily*, 11 and 15 May 1934 reported the administration was concerned about its legal obligations to students under age 21.

13. Jones, *ibid.*, pp. 83-4; *Times*, 15 and 18 May 1934.

14. Jones, *ibid.*, p. 83; *Times*, 15-17 May 1934, reporting closure of the Fisher Flouring Mill and cancellation of seaborne shipments; *Times*, 25 and 29 May concerning Beck as Martin's emissary; 28 May, 9 June concerning Ryan truce offer on basis of port-by-port negotiations, and seconding Dewey Bennett.

15. Bernstein, *ibid.*, pp. 265-68.

16. Bernstein, *ibid.*, pp. 265-68; Nelson, *ibid.*, p. 144.

17. Larrowe, *ibid.*, pp. 50-54.

18. *Times*, 17 May 1934.

19. Larrowe, *ibid.*, pp. 53-6.

20. Larrowe, *ibid.*, pp. 55-9.

21. Jones, *ibid.*, pp. 83-90; *Argus*, 16 and 30 June 1934; *P-I*, 15 June 1934.

22. *Argus*, 30 June 1934; *P-I*, 16 June 1934, reporting the Chamber of Commerce's claim that 25,000 people have been thrown out of work by the strike; *Times*, 22 June 1934; *Municipal News*, 30 June 1934.

23. Larrowe, *ibid.*, chapter 3; Bernstein, *ibid.*, pp. 272-83; *P-I*, 9 July 1934.

24. *P-I*, 2 July 1934; *Argus*, 2,3, and 7 July 1934.

25. *Argus*, 7 July 1934; *Times*, 10 July 1934.

26. *Times*, 1,3,6-8,10 July 1934. Its headline of the 10th ran: "Seattle's Red Terrorism Blamed To Outside Agitation".

27. Larrowe, *ibid.*,pp. 62-80; *Argus*, 21 and 28 July 1934; *P-I*, 13 July 1934. Police Chief George Howard resigned when Smith had gone "over Chief Howard's head and took personal command . . . to protect pro-union workers . . . and it was the mayor himself who issued orders to move pickets back off the pier": *P-I*, 20 July 1934. See also 17-19 and 21 July 1934 issues for the following: On the 17th the City council voted 4 to 4 refusing to authorize hiring 90 emergency police by the mayor; concerning a possible sympathy strike, the Machinists Local 79 voted against it by a margin of 5 votes, while the Boilermakers, Local 104, voted for it by a 222 to 48 vote; on the 18th, a meeting of 3,000 heard pro- and con-speakers at the Civic Auditorium; by the 21st, the police had established control of the docks for the first time in two months. The *Times*, 18 July issue, also contained one of a series by Matthew Woll, Third Vice President of the AFL: "Is Red Russia Striking at American Industry?"; it was reprinted as a series from *Liberty Magazine*, and was run parallel to strike coverage. See also *Times*, 19 and 20 July 1934. Note should be taken of the promotion of Captain George Comstock to Chief for his handling of the Smith Cove operation. Comstock in 1916 gained fame for his part in selling contraband liquor collected by his "Dry Squad".

28. Larrowe, *ibid.*, pp. 80-93; *P-I*, 25-31 July 1934.

29. Larrowe, *ibid.*, pp. 90-3; Bernstein, *ibid.*, pp. 291-97; *P-I*, 1 Aug. 1934. Two persons were killed during the Seattle phase of the strike: First was Shelby Daffron, on July 1 at the Standard Oil dock at Wells Point in a "pitched battle" between strikers and company guards; the sheriff arrested one of the guards. The second was Steve Watson, a special sheriff deputy, on July 9; the *P-I*, (11 July) noted that he had "been used for special work by the citizens' emergency committee, and unlike six other deputies attacked at the same time, he carried no gun". During this period the *P-I* ran a series of articles by Robert Matthews outlining the "Red Army" being formed in the country, "daily gaining recruits". Cf. *P-I*, 11 July 1934.

Maritime Unions Become Reconciled to Blacks as Fellow Unionists

1. Bruce Nelson, *Waterfront Worker* . . . pp. 48-9,84-5; Joseph S. Jackson, "Colored Marine Employees . . . ", *op. cit.*; Robert B. Pitts, "Organized Labor and the Negro", pp. 38-47,51-2.

2. Pitts, *ibid.*, pp. 20-27,51-2.

3. Pitts, *ibid.*, pp. 46-50; *Northwest Enterprise*, 17 May 1934.

4. *Northwest Enterprise*, 17 May 1934. These deaths were not reported by the three dailies. Pitts, *ibid.*, pp. 54-8.

Chapter 21

Mayor Smith Faces the Clean Government Crowd

1. This outline is derived from George W. Scott's master's thesis on Cincinnatus, chapter III. Frederick Hamley's *Diary* provides a running

account of his, Langlie, and Lockwood's councilmanic careers and about Cincinnatus. The *P-I,* concluded its 13 March 1935 issue: "Citizens . . . voiced in emphatic terms their demand for . . . continuance of sound business management of school and port affairs [and a] new deal in the city council".

2. Scott, *ibid.,*pp. 69-70.

3. Scott, *ibid.* pp. 76-9; Hamley, *Diary,* 25-27,30 Apr., 13,27-9 May 1935.

4. Scott, *ibid.,* pp. 74-9; on Landes/Powell, see Hamley, *Diary,* 3 June 1935; *Municipal News,* 8 June1935.

5. Scott, *ibid.,* pp. 79-81; Hamley, *Diary,* 11 Apr., 24 June 1935; *P-I,* 1 June 1935.

6. *Philippine-American Chronicle,* 15 Sept. 1934; in its 1 Feb. 1935 issue was reported: "Chinese Gambling Dens Operate Lavishly in the Eyes of the Law".

7. Scott, *ibid.,* pp. 81-2; Hamley, *Diary,* 24 June 1935. Hamley, Powell, and Lockwood conducted regular "slumming" expeditions into the vice areas throughout this period, which are recorded in the diary.

8. Scott, *ibid.,* pp. 81-5; Hamley, *Diary,* 10 July. A transcript of the Council's investigation is in Box 4 of the Ralph B. Potts, Papers. Julius Baldwin reported to the Municipal League that "all drives to clean up the city were aimed at the small houses of gambling but . . . the bigger gamblers had been permitted to operate practically unmolested". *Municipal News,* 4 June 1935.

9. Hamley, *Diary,* 17 July 1935.

10. Scott, *ibid.,* pp. 85-8; Hamley records the futility of it all in his entries of 6 and 7 Nov. 1935, when an attempt was made to revoke the licences of Green's Cigar Store and the Turf, when clear evidence had shown gambling there. Council was 5 to 4 against, Harlin and Scavotto defending the operations. (Dore was Green's attorney, and Charles Moriarty, the Turf's). In talking with Magnuson and former Zioncheck staffer, Ed Henry, Hamley was discouraged from seeking a "clean town". The Municipal League praised the investigation and was flabergasted that the 35 to 40 officers who had testified to ignorance of any vice operations in the afflicted area were not being prosecuted for perjury, *Municipal News,* 26 Oct. 1935.

11. The election is covered by Scott, *ibid.,* pp. 101-18. On the WCF in the election, which pitted "Commonwealth versus Cincinnatus" see Acena, *ibid.,* pp. 105-07.

12. Scott, *ibid.,* pp. 111-18.

13. Scott, *ibid,* pp. 117-18.

Chapter 22

The Rise of Dave Beck and the Teamsters

1. This outline is derived from Donald Garnel's *Rise of Teamster Power in the West . . . ,* pp. 5,6,10, 51-3,and 59; Dembo, *ibid.,* pp. 435-37; Dembo, "Dave Beck and the Transportation Revolution in the Pacific Northwest, 1917-41", in Thomas G. Edwards and Carlos A. Schwantes,

editors, *Experiences in the Promised Land . . .*, pp. 339-52; J.B. Gillingham, *The Teamsters Union in the West* (Berkeley: Institute of Industrial Relations, University of California, 1956). Murray Morgan has a brief biographical sketch of Beck in *Skid Road*, pp. 220-24.

2. Garnel, *ibid.*, pp. 11,12,59 and 60.

3. Garnel, *ibid.*, pp. 80-91; Dembo, "History . . . ", pp. 437-8.

4. Dembo, *ibid.*, pp. 438-42.

5. Washington State Federation of Labor, *Proceedings*, 1925 and 1926; *Vanguard*, Jan. April-May, Oct. 1931; *Labor News*, 8 and 15 May 1925; Polk, *City Directory*, 1923-35. President Short, writing to Harvey O'Connor on 26 Jan. 1926, reported on the general situation in the city and state: "We are facing a very bad situation in Seattle and probably . . . we will have the Laundry industry of Seattle tied up as the Laundry owners this morning cancelled their agreement and have declared for the open shop . . . ": Box 43, WSFL, Records.

6. Dembo, *ibid.*, pp. 600-05; *Argus*, 26 June 1937; WSFL outgoing letters, 12 Sept. 1934, Box 44, and letter 15 Nov. 1933 reporting expulsion of the Brewery Workers from the SCLC for claiming jurisdiction over all trades in the industry, Box 15, WSFL, Records; J.B. Gillingham, *ibid.*, pp. 41-54, covers this dispute thoroughly; a good summary, placed in the national setting, is made in Walter Galenson, *The CIO Challenge to the AFL: a History of the American Labor Movement, 1935-1941* (Cambridge, MA: Harvard University Press, 1960), pp. 488-90.

7. *Argus*, 19 June 1937; on Produce Merchants' Association, 31 Aug. 1935 issue; in its 25 July 1936 issue, looking at a possible *P-I* strike, the editors commented on Beck's boast that the Teamsters would give full support: "[this is what the Teamsters have been doing for] almost every local labor controversy in the past two years". As tensions over *P-I* labor policies intensified, Beck was charged with looking upon Guild recognition as an "opportunity to test the power of a united front of all unions". In its 22 August issue Beck was accused of engineering the strike. The *P-I* strike is covered below.

8. The *Argus* issue of 20 June 1936 compared Beck's local power with that of Bridges' in San Francisco: "His power had been asserted in the stevedoring, milk, beer, laundry, dry cleaning, and other fields prior to his taking charge of the mechanics' strike last week". The *Argus* for 10 Apr. 1937 commented: "certain it is that Dave Beck has warm friends among Seattle bankers and industrialists, some of whom were publicly denouncing the head of the teamsters' union only a year ago . . . [T]he value of Dave Beck's consolidating his position with employers is apparent". See also Galenson *ibid.*, pp. 474-7. In Bulletin No. 5, 7 April 1936 President Alfred Lundin of the Industrial Council of Washington's Seattle Division wrote: "Communism and the industrial racketeer are about to make this city their own". In what followed not a further word was said about "Communism"; instead, he presented a listing of what Beck had been up to. Lundin continued: "[F]ive men are building a machine to that end, and using their great weapon on organizing labor . . . All industries are to be organized . . . a closed shop [is to be] forced upon

employers . . . Prices, output and employment are to be controlled and fixed in each industry, an administrator appointed . . . The employer is to be forced to give to the dictator each month a certified copy of all business he has done, his price schedule, and he will be assessed a percentage of his gross income . . . The following industries are already organized and closed. Milk and meat, the cleaners, dyers and launderers, and the brewers have each their dictators. Five others are in the process of organization, and if successfully completed, your fish, fuel, lumber, and engravers and automobile dealers will all be in line". He then refers to the past acts of violence accompanying these organizing drives. Continuing: "In addition to the above five industries, actual organization work is going on in the metal trades, among the building employees . . . in the milling and fertilizer industry, among clerks, and in a number of others": typed copy in Box 8 of the Eugene V. Dennett, Papers. See also Morgan, *ibid.*, pp.247-49.

9. Dembo, *ibid.*, pp. 607-08; Hamley recorded in his diary for 27 Nov. 1935 that Beck had spoken to the Cincinnatans about craft vs. industrial unions, defending himself against racketeering charges, and concluded: "that communism has no place in organized labor".

10. See above: "The Unemployed Citizens' League"; "The Unemployed Citizens' League Becomes Politicized", and "The Great Maritime Strike of 1934".

11. William E. Ames and Roger A. Simpson, *Unionism or Hearst: The Seattle Post-Intelligencer Strike of 1936* (Seattle: Pacific Northwest Labor History Association, 1978), pp. 147-53.

Chapter 23

The 1936 *P-I* Strike: Teamsters and Maritime Unions in Uneasy Embrace

1. This outline is derived from Bernstein, *ibid.*,pp. 128-37; Ames and Simpson, *ibid.*, pp. 12-16; Morgan, *ibid.*, pp. 249-53, 256-60.

2. Box 26, Seattle Typographers Union, Local 202, Records; *Labor News*, 13 June 1924 sees the *P-I* as the "opening wedge" to establishing the open shop; interestingly, Frank Fitts was the *P-I*'s tough negotiator—later he joined the "Ross machine", leading the recall of Mayor Edwards and becoming a city councilman. See also *Labor News*, 6 Feb. 1925; *Union Record*, 2 and 7 Mar. 1925.

3. *Vanguard*, 19 May, 2 and 9 June 1933; *Voice of Action*, 16 and 24 May 1933; Washington State Federation of Labor, *Proceedings*, 1933.

4. Ames and Simpson, *ibid.*, pp. 16-22.

5. Ames and Simpson, *ibid.*, pp. 23-6.

6. Ames and Simpson *ibid.*, pp. 27-56.

7. Ames and Simpson, *ibid.*, pp. 60-63; *Time*, 28:25 (31 August 1936), pp. 25-6, reported: "Under Labor Boss Dave Beck, moving force of Seattle's Central Labor Council, a cordon of demonstrators from the American Federation of Teachers . . . the Teamsters', Lumbermen's, and Longshoremen's Unions tied up the plant tight . . . Open to [Hearst's]

almost daily diatribes against his absent employees were the columns of the leading afternoon newspaper, which fought him tooth and nail since he invaded Seattle in 1921 . . . [T]o Publisher Blethen, the strike marked 'the most shameful page in Seattle's history' [as he accused Beck of suspending the constitution.] Seattle is now the plaything of a dictator".

8. Ames and Simpson, *ibid.*, pp. 63-5;

9. The *Times*, front page column head for 17 Aug. 1936, ran: "Action By Dave Beck In Scuttling Leading Industry Crystallizes Public Sentiment . . . Union 'Boss' Seeks Only To Still Voice Of His Opposition". The *P-I*'s accusation of Beck's "reign of terror" was also carried, along with the Guild's own statement. The *Argus*'s "Stroller" complained in its 10 Aug. 1936 issue that Seattle had been losing industry to its "neighboring Northwest cities . . . No sane industrialist would seriously consider this moribund town as a safe risk for investment . . . It is the work the Communist party has long urged—tearing down industry".

10. Ames and Simpson, *ibid.*, pp. 86-90, chapter VIII.

11. Ames and Simpson, *ibid.*,pp. 148-53. The Stroller concluded that the Guild has affiliated with the CIO because they want "democracy in the labor movement", and they refuse to be intimidated by Beck, *Argus*, 19 June 1937.

Chapter 24

Governor Martin's Unwanted Left-Wing

1. Acena, *ibid.*, pp. 44-9; Krause, *ibid.*, pp. 128-35; Blumell, *ibid.*, pp. 373-75, 467-74. See also below, "The Politics of Unemployment and Relief, 1935-1940.

2. Acena, *ibid.*, pp. 46-9; Krause, *ibid.*, pp. 37-44.

3. Acena, *ibid.*, pp. 49-50.

4. Acena, *ibid.*, pp. 50-53.

5. Acena, *ibid.*, pp. 54-68; Krause, *ibid.*, pp. 112-28.

6. Acena, *ibid.*, pp. 71-3, 85.

7. Acena, *ibid.*, pp. 54-6,69-81,146-48; Klehr, *ibid.*, chapter 10, pp. 252-57.

8. Acena *ibid.*, pp. 94-8; Krause, *ibid.*, pp. 128-35.

9. Acena, *ibid.*, pp. 104-09; Krause, *ibid.*, pp. 84-5.

10. Acena, *ibid.*, pp. 107-15.

11. Acena, *ibid.*, pp. 117-21; Krause, *ibid.*, pp. 142-47,191-93.

12. Acena, *ibid.*, pp. 121-27; Krause, *ibid.*, pp. 147-51.

13. Krause, *ibid.*, pp. 153-54.

14. Acena, *ibid.*,pp. 130-33.

15. Acena, *ibid.*, pp. 133-34; Krause, *ibid.*, pp. 159-60.

Chapter 25

City Politics and the New Unionism, 1936-1938

Dore, Beck, and the New Unionism

1. For general background see: Bernstein, *ibid.*, chapter 14, esp. pp.

683-86; Galenson, *ibid.*, chapter 1; Philip Taft, *The A.F.of L. From the Death of Gompers to the Merger* (New York: Harper Brothers, 1959), chapters 5-7. See also Morgan, *ibid.*, pp. 253-56.

2. See chapters above on the UCL, the rise of Beck and the Teamsters, the 1934 maritime strike, and the *P-I* strike; also Acena, *ibid.*, pp. 186-87.

3. Ames and Simpson, *ibid.*, pp. 145-48; *Sunday News*, 26 June and 10 July 1937; *Star*, 3 and 9 July 1937.

4. *Star*, 3 and 9 July 1937; *Sunday News*, 31 July 1937.

5. *Star*, 12 July 1937; *Sunday News*, 14,21, and 28 Aug. 1937 (quotation is from 21 Aug. issue).

6. *Star*, 10,12, and 29 July 1937; *New Republic* 94:59 (23 Feb. 1938); *Argus*, 12 Feb. 1938; *Sunday News*, 24,25, and 31 July 1937; in the latter issue, reporting that at the NLRB hearings Harry Marshall admitted to having visited Dore, Beck, and Charles Doyle (secretary of the Central Labor Council) on the day before the paper reopened and got Dore to promise to use police to disperse the pickets.

7. See Bruce Nelson, *ibid.*, chapter 8; *Star*, 13 July 1937. Consistent with *Star* actions at this time, Dore called out the police to break picket lines around several fur plants; 6 had reopened with non-union employees, who then were signed up by a federal AFL union instead of the competing CIO Fur Workers. The NLRB had been asked to intervene: *Sunday News*, 7 and 14 Aug. 1937.

8. For general background on the local scene see Jones, *ibid.*, pp. 90-94; and for Teamster-ILA rivalry, pp. 95-8; Larrowe, *ibid.*, pp. 119-28; Betty V.H. Schneider, *Industrial Relations in the West Coast Maritme Industry* (Berkeley: Institute of Industrial Relations, University of California, 1958), pp. 44-8 on 1936-37 strike. Schneider writes: "The 1936-1937 strike was an important turning point in West Coast maritime industrial relations . . . The employers were unable to recapture their former position relative to the workforce" (p. 46).

9. Bernstein, *ibid.*, p. 582; Larrowe, *ibid.*, 119-23; Gillingham *ibid.*, pp. 55-61; Nelson, *ibid.*, pp. 219-21.

10. Larrowe, *ibid.*, p. 120; Jones, *ibid.*, pp. 94-5 and p. 98 for the quotation.

11. Galenson, *ibid.*, pp. 475-77; Gillingham, *ibid.*, pp. 59-60; *Star*, 4 Sept. 1937.

12. Garnel, *ibid.*, pp. 48-51, 56-7.

13. Garnel, *ibid.*, pp. 130-38, esp., 136-38.

14. *Times* and *P-I*, 17-19 Dec. 1937; *Sunday News*, 24 and 31 Dec. 1937.

15. *Times* and *P-I*, 18 Dec. 1937; *Sunday News*, 24 Dec. 1937.

16. *Sunday News*, 19 Feb. 1938; *Times*, 19 Dec. 1937; *Argus*, 25 Dec. 1937; *P-I*, 18 and 19 Dec. 1937.

17. *Sunday News*, 15 Jan. and 16 Apr. 1938; *Argus*, 19 Mar. 1938.

18. Gillingham, *ibid.*, pp. 12-13; Galenson, *ibid.*, pp. 466-67.

19. *Argus*, 29 Jan. 1938; *Sunday News*, 15 and 29 Jan. 1938.

20. *Argus*, 1 Jan. 1938.

21. Garnel, *ibid.*, pp. 153-62, 169-72.

22. *Portland Oregonian*, 6-10, 15-21 Feb. 1938.
23. *Sunday News*, 5 Feb. 1938; *P-I*, 10 Feb. 1938; *Times*, 10-12 Feb. 1938.

"War" Over the Warehousemen

1. Herbert Clay Prouty, "Seattle's A.F. of L.-C.I.O. War of the Warehousemen" (Unpublished Master's Thesis, University of Washington, 1938). Prouty's thesis is the basis for this entire chapter. Due to the contemporaneity of his study he had direct access to the key participants, many of whom he interviewed, to the propaganda, to witnessing the NLRB hearings, and to the full range of newspaper coverage.

National coverage appeared in popular magazines: *Time*, 20 Sept. 1937; *Life*, article 25 Oct. 1937, "Life On The American Newsfront: Labor Leader Dave Beck Is The Boss Of Seattle", containing a full-page spread of Beck's face opposite the narrative page that carried photographs of Clarence Blethen, Eugene V. Dennett (head of the Seattle Labor Unity Council and of the local Inlandboatmens' Union), Hugh DeLacy, the WCF's Howard Costigan, George Vanderveer conferring with Beck, and one of Beck shaking hands with the *P-I*'s John Boettiger in the presence of Mayor Dore, all topped with a picture of Beck's secretary Ann Watkins. The *Saturday Evening Post* of 14 May 1938 carried a story by George Creel, "Closed During Altercations: The Unions Fight for the West Coast, With the Public in Between"—Creel had been a mediator in the 1934 maritime strike. He characterized Beck as running a "little NRA with rules as hard and fast as any ever imposed by General Johnson [former head of the NRA]".

Supplemental accounts may be found in Nelson, *ibid.*, 219-21; Larrowe, *ibid.*, 119-23; Gillingham, *ibid.*, pp. 56-64.

Jurisdiction Over the Cannery Workers: Racial Politics in the Labor Movement

1. Jack Masson and Donald Guimary, "Asian Labor Contractors in the Alaskan Canned Salmon Industry", *Labor History*, 22:3 (Summer, 1981), pp. 337-97; *Philippine-American Tribune*, V:8 (27 May 1936); *Philippine Advocate*, I:6,7 (Aug. and Sept. 1935); Fred Cordova, *Filipinos: Forgotten Asian Americans* (Seattle: Demonstration Project for Asian Americans, 1983), pp. 57-71.

2. Cordova, *ibid.*, pp. 72-81; *Philippine-American Tribune*, V:12 (23 Sept. 1936), V:15 (9 Dec. 1936); *International Examiner* May and June 1977, parts 4 and 5 of a series by Gene Viernes on Local 7 of the ILWU; *Philippine Advocate*, I:2,3,7 (Apr., May, Sept. 1935); *Philippine-American Chronicle*,I:6 (1 Dec. 1934); *Vanguard*, 21 Apr. 1933, reported that a 50% wage cut inspired the young Filipinos (ages 20-30) to form the union.

3. *Philippine Advocate*, I:6,7 (Aug. and Sept. 1935); *Philippine-American Tribune*, V:12,13 (23 and 30 Sept. 1936). The *Tribune* never reported the misdoings of Duyungan.

4. Cordova, *ibid.*, pp. 78-9; *International Examiner*, (Viernes articles); *Philippine-American Tribune*, V:12,13, 15 carries story on the murder. *Star*,

4 Dec. 1936. Statement in File 7-10 of the Cannery Workers and Farm Laborers'Union, Local 7, Records, dated 5 Dec. 1936, (hereafter, "Local 7" Records), accused the press of misleading the public by picturing the dispute as a "labor war", when it really was labor vs. employers over control of the hiring halls, the employers wanting to perpetuate the labor contractor system: *Minutes*, 9 Dec. 1936, King County Central Labor Council, Records.

5. *International Examiner*, (Viernes articles); S. Frank Miyamoto, *Social Solidarity . . .*, p. 80; File 8-25, Local 7, Records; *Northwest Enterprise*, 23 Aug. 1934, reported Arai to be planning to run as Republican for Congress; *Minutes*, 21 Apr. 1937, KCCLC, Records.

6. Cordova, *ibid.*, pp. 78-80; Antonio Rodrigo, acting secretary to Flynn, 11 Sept. 1937, asking for revocation of 20454's charter and repudiation of public statements made by AFL officials "insulting the intelligence of the membership and integrity [of the union]". Also, Superior Court hearings transcript, both in File 8-25, Local 7, Records. *Cosmopolitan Weekly,*, VI:8,9 (4 and 15 May 1937); *International Examiner*, (Viernes article, no. 5); *Cosmopolitan Courier*, VII:3 (Mar. 1938); Files 12a-3 and 12a-7, Victorio Velasco, Papers.

Chapter 26
City Politics, 1937

1. Blumell, *ibid.*, p. 147.

2. Blumell, *ibid.*, pp. 231-2; on Gannon see pp. 256-61; for effects of federal projects on state see pp. 287-8; Krause, *ibid.*, pp. 136-8.

3. Blumell, *ibid.*, pp. 278-82, 306-09.

4. Krause, *ibid.*, pp. 161-3; Acena, *ibid.*, chapter IV covers the WCF's role in 1936-37; pp. 149-52 summarizes the WCF's effectiveness in the legislature, and pp. 162-81 relate to the 1937 election campaign.

5. Krause, *ibid.*, pp. 164-70 (quotation is from p. 167); Acena, *ibid.*, pp. 150-62.

6. Acena, *ibid.*, pp. 162-81 (on Sieg-DeLacy, pp. 165-9); Scott, *ibid.*, pp. 139-47.

7. Acena, *ibid.*, pp. 174-81; Scott, *ibid.*, pp. 140-7 (quotation is from p.141). Proposition A is discussed in chapter 29,below, "Financial Crisis: Taking the Street Railway Out of it", placing it in the context of City Light's proposal to purchase the city electric properties of PSP&L.

8. Acena, *ibid.*, pp. 174-81; Scott, *ibid.*, pp. 140-7. Councilman Hamley recorded in his diary for 16 March 1937 that with Dore elected, and with only 4 sure votes, it is clear that "we" will have to avoid bills on finances and law enforcement if we expect to "accomplish anything constructive this year . . . We decided that we would not do anything to hinder rehiring of the sixty-one policemen and the reopening of three precinct stations as provided in an initiative Charter Amendment adopted by a slim margin of votes last Tuesday". He also signed off on taking an active part in police chief selection except to oppose Norton if Dore nominated him: Hamley, Papers.

Chapter 27

The 1938 City Election and the End to John F. Dore

1. Two studies combine for the most comprehensive coverage of the 1938 city election. These are Albert Acena's dissertation on the WCF, chapter VI; and George Scott's thesis on Cincinnatus, chapter IV. The narrative which follows depends primarily upon their studies. The most comprehensive manuscript source is the diary of Frederick G. Hamley, and in his subject series, "Langlie's 1938 Mayoral Campaign". On the "Model Labor Plan" see *Sunday News*, 4 Dec. 1937. On 11 Dec. 1937 the *News* reported, "Anti-Dore Clubs Growing Rapidly" . . . at least in all but 4 legislative districts, and the meetings are "packed". In its 15 Jan., 1938 issue it reported the finding of evidence linking Beck with business associations, involving percentage payoffs, "dues collections", and price schedules.

2. Scott, *ibid.*, pp. 155-62; File 2-7, "Langlie campaign", Hamley, Papers.

3. Scott, *ibid.*, pp. 150-51; Acena, *ibid.*, p. 212; On 13 Jan. 1938 Hamley reported a meeting with Alfred Lundin, Ed Cox of Washington Mutual Savings Bank, and Jackson, agreeing to get out the Scandinavian vote, and using the Municipal League as noted, File 2-7, Hamley, Papers.

4. Scott, *ibid.*, pp. 155-6, 161; *Argus*, 5 and 19 Feb. 1938.

5. Scott, *ibid.*, p. 158; Acena, *ibid.*, p. 212.

6. Scott, *ibid.*, pp. 154-63; Acena, *ibid.*, pp. 214-15 notes the brief walkout of 600 longshoremen in early January, and its mediated settlement by Maritime Commissioner Joseph Kennedy and John Boettiger amid charges by Beck and Dore that CIO meant strikes, while the AFL meant labor peace. *Argus*, for 8 Jan. 1938 reported that the Central Clearing House Association forbids its member banks from cashing pay warrants, and notified Councilman Laube that the State Finance Board had refused to make further investments in the City's general warrant fund.

7. Scott, *ibid.*, pp. 160-2; Acena, *ibid.*, pp. 220-21; *Star*, 21 Feb. 1938.

8. Scott, *ibid.*, pp. 160-2; Acena, *ibid.*, pp. 223-5.

9. Scott, *ibid.*, pp. 231-2; Krause, *ibid.*, pp. 225-32. Former activist in the UCL, Selden Menefee, wrote in the *Nation* (26 Mar. 1938), "The real significance of the elections . . . was that they were a milestone in the decline of Dave Beck". His article bore the title, "The Decline of Dave Beck". Wishful thinking.

10. Acena, *ibid.*, pp. 231-2; Krause, *ibid.*, pp. 179-81; *Argus*, 12 Mar. 1938; *Sunday News*, 11 June 1938.

11. Acena, *ibid.*, pp. 232-3; and for party split, pp. 236-45; Krause, *ibid.*, pp. 183-6; Blumell, *ibid.*, pp. 421-3; *Argus*, 4 June 1938.

12. *Argus*, 21 May, 23 July, 22 Oct. 1938; *Sunday News*, 11 and 18 June 1938.

13. *Argus*, 18 June 1938.

14. Hamley, *Diary*, 14 Mar 1938; Langlie to Sears, 8 Apr. 1939, Part 3, File 2-1, Arthur B. Langlie, Papers.

Chapter 28

The Politics of Unemployment and Relief, 1935-1940

1. Blumell, *ibid.*, 284-9; Krause, *ibid.*, pp. 172-3; Arthur G. Lindsay, "The Washington State Old Age Pension Union: a Political Presure Group" (Unpublished Master's Thesis, University of Washington, 1940), pp. 28-35.

2. Ruth Chaskel, "The Administration of the Work Projects Administration in the State of Washington" (Unpublished Master's Thesis, University of Washington, 1942), p. 199; Blumell, *ibid.*, pp. 257-9, 279-83 (quotation is from p. 280)

3. Blumell, *ibid.*, pp. 288-9, 301, 307-10, 370-72, and 417-18.

4. Blumell, *ibid.*, pp. 337, 354-60, 370-72, 417, and 426-6; Lindsay, *ibid.*, pp. 28-35, 40-44.

5. Acena, *ibid.*, pp. 189-93; Lindsay, *ibid.*, pp. 53-9.

6. Blumell, *ibid.*, pp. 336-9, 373-5.

7. Blumell, *ibid.*, pp. 420-25; Krause, *ibid.*, pp. 184-9; *P-I*, 2 Apr. 1938.

8. *P-I*, 1 and 2 Apr. 1938; Blumell, *ibid.*, pp. 423-6; Krause, *ibid.*, pp. 189-90.

9. Krause, *ibid.*, pp. 181-3 (quotation is from p. 182); Acena, *ibid.*, pp. 235-45.

10. Krause, *ibid.*, pp. 181-4, 190-91; Acena, *ibid.*, pp. 235-45; Blumell, *ibid.*, 359-60 on social security program.

11. Acena, *ibid.*, pp. 246-70; Krause, *ibid.*, pp. 196-206.

12. Acena, *ibid.* pp. 255-7, 262-70; Krause, *ibid.*, pp. 196-202; Washington Federation of Labor, *Proceedings*,1938; *Labor News*, 2 Sept. 1938; Klehr, *ibid.*, pp. 253-7.

13. Acena, *ibid.*, pp. 262-70; Krause, *ibid.*, pp. 265-8; Letter to all affiliates, 2 Dec. 1938, Box 44, WSFL, Records.

14. Blumell, *ibid.*, pp. 434-5; Krause, *ibid.*, pp. 202-06; *P-I*, 3 Apr. 1938.

15. Krause, *ibid.*, pp. 219-29; Blumell, *ibid.*, pp. 436-40; Acena, *ibid.*, pp. 275-80.

16. Raymond R. Chagnon, "Survey of One Hundred Eighteen Employable Families Affected by the Reduction of Relief Funds in Zone 4, King County, Washington, April 1, 1939" (Unpublished Master's Thesis, University of Washington, 1942), pp. 1-5.

17. Chagnon, *ibid.*, pp. 6-8; Krause, *ibid.* , pp. 226-7; Blumell, *ibid.*, pp. 449-54 (quotation is from p. 451).

18. Acena, *ibid.*, p. 280; Krause, *ibid.*, pp. 206-07.

19. Acena, *ibid.*, pp. 275-80 (quotation is from p. 275); Krause, *ibid.*, pp. 220-24.

Chapter 29

Financial Crisis: Taking the Street Railway Out of It

1. See the above chapters 2 and 17 for background; they are: "The Public Ownership Fight . . . "; "Mayor Landes Begins"; and "Mayor

Edwards and the Radicals". Ross's merger proposal of 44 pages was addressed to Mayor Smith, 3 October 1934. See also: Miner Baker, "The Proposed City Light Merger: A Study of Public Opinion" (Unpublished Master's Thesis, University of Washington, 1938), chapter II. Seattle Lighting Department, *Annual Report, 1935*, pp. 74-75. Baker provides an excellent contemporary background discussion of Ross's merger proposal. It follows Ross's 1929 suggestion that the company's property be acquired through condemnation; and his October 1934 proposal (when the company's worth was near its lowest point), that purchase of all its electrical properties in western Washington and that of its Rock Island dam ought to be considered. His discussion of the propaganda organization and techniques of each side as they tried to affect public opinion is indispensable as a point of departure. Public opinion was running 6 to 1 against the merger as of January 1936 (p. 36). The author's own discussion supplies information from archival sources that were not accessible to Baker, and the interpretation differs accordingly.

See also: Leslie Blanchard, *Street Railway Era in Seattle . . .*, pp. 130-31; Beeler Organization to Arthur Langlie, 24 Mar., 1938, Box 1, and copy of Van Soelen to Paul Harper, 18 Mar., 1938, Arthur B. Langlie *Papers*, Part 3, File 1-19; Frank McLaughlin to Donald Barnes, 15 Apr., 1938, PSP&L *Records*, Box 101; Hartley Rogers, "Analysis", pp. 26-7, Seattle Lighting Department *Records*, File 124-14.

On 23 July 1934, the Securities and Exchange Commission ordered the Engineers Public Service Company to divest itself of its interest in Puget Sound Power and Light Company within one year. The company owned practically all the common stock, thereby controlling the voting power affecting PSP&L. The preferred stock was largely owned locally, but it carried no voting rights. Donald Barnes headed the EPSC, Houghton, Cluck and Coughlin to Homer Bone, 14 Sept., 1942, Homer T. Bone *Papers* Accession 3456-2, File 1-4 , UW Mss.

2. Lighting Dept., *Annual Report, 1932*, pp. 6-7; Myers to Ross, 17, 23 Nov., 1932; copy of RFC to Mayor Dore, 16 Dec., 1932; Myers to City Council and Myers to Ross 9 Jan., 16 Feb., and 14 and 23 Mar., 1933, Lighting Dept. *Records*, File 74-12.

3. Lighting Dept., *Annual Report, 1933 and 1934*. An undated (pencilled: "Co. 1936") recommendation of 48 pages was written by Ross: "Correlation of the Federal Power Plants at Bonneville and Coulee With Municipal Plant of Seattle . . . and the Municipal Plants of Tacoma and Other Cities"

4. Woods to Ross, 27 Nov., 1934 (responding to Ross's letter of 29 Oct.), Rufus Woods *Papers*, at *Wenatchee World* office. Woods wrote Batcheller on 6 Dec., 1934: "I just hesitate in my mad career to note that you gave both barrels to the Mt. Baker Improvement Club last night. Ross has been carrying on a definite program of opposition to Grand Coulee now for some time".

5. Municipal League, City Light Committee, [Report, October 1934], Willis Batcheller *Papers*, Municipal League subgroup, Box 15; *Municipal News*, 2 Feb., through 13 Apr., 1935 for its series of articles; also 31 Aug., 1935, and a two-part article by Batcheller, "City Light—The Bond Bro-

kers' Darling", 13 and 27 June 1936. For Batcheller's connection to the Edwards campaign see Batcheller *Papers*, Box 16. Nelson Anderson had been the League's chair of its City Light Committee; its original report favored City Light. A sub-committee was then formed with Batcheller in control. Batcheller wrote that over the next three months, meetings were held, "and violent attempts were made to eliminate the basic data . . . so as to render the report merely one of opinion". Municipal League *Records'* Accession 472, Box 2. See also Lighting Dept. *Records*, Files 45-22 and 46-7 for internal reaction to League's report.

6. George Sundborg, *Hail Columbia: the 30-Year Struggle for the Grand Coulee Dam* (New York: Macmillan, 1954), pp. 281-83 (first quotation is from p. 281, the second from p. 283). See his chapter 28 for coverage of the high/low dam issue; the high dam received Congressional approval and final authorization from Interior Secretary Harold Ickes on 6 June 1935. His book is based mainly on the James O'Sullivan papers at Gonzaga University. Ross to Myers, 2o Nov., 1934 concerning Holden's accusation that Ross was opposed to a high dam, File 73-23, Guy C. Myers *Papers;* copy of Holden letter of 22 Oct., 1934 in Woods *Papers*: "[Ross is] so drunk with power that he is worse than a fanatic. He really intends to put over his deal to purchase the properties of the [PSP&L] and absurd as it may seem, he has the backing of the City Council and almost enough fanatical voters to put the deal over . . . He really believes that the Coulee development is responsible for Skagit not getting a federal loan [sic] When in reality the Skagit Project is so shady that it could not meet the Governmental requirements for a loan . . . " Woods had been fearful that the congressional delgation from western Washington was willing to sacrifice the high dam to their own regional projects. In a memorandum to himself he also complained that his friend, Governor Martin, had not yet come out for it, and that Columbia Basin Commission chair, E.F. Banker, was a Ross backer, 5 Feb., 1935; also Woods to Congressman Martin Smith, 25 Apr.,1935. State Grange Master Ervin King expressed surprise that Woods found Senators Bone and Schwellenbach "apathetic" on the question; but he promised to write them anyway: King to Woods, 15 Feb., 1935. As to Banker, Kenneth Harlan accused him in Wenatchee of being "an enemy of complete high dam development": Holden to Woods, 31 May 1935. In a letter of 1 July 1935 to Batcheller, O'Sullivan and six others, Woods continued to express worry about what effect Ross's merger proposal would have on Grand Coulee if it were to go through. Ted Little, secretary to US Fisheries Commissioner Frank Bell, tried to deflect Woods's attacks on Ross by citing to him that Ross had "reassured me that he is for the completion of the High Dam, lock, stock, and barrel . . . ": Little to Woods, 24 Sept., 1935. To this, Woods retorted that Ross must be kept on the "defensive": 2 Oct. 1935. All citations are to the Rufus Woods *Papers* in the *Wenatchee World* office.

7. Lighting Dept., *Annual Report*, 1934; *P-I*, 19 Feb., 1935.

8. Harlan to Bone 26 Jan., 1935; Harlan to Bone and Schwellenbach 28 Jan., 1935, File 18-1 and 31 July 1935 Homer T. Bone *Papers*, File 18-8 at University of Puget Sound Library.

9. *Municipal News*, 16 Feb., 1935; Holden to Woods, 11 Feb., 1935; 16

Jan., 1935; Manly Haynes, CRDL Finance Committee chair, to Woods, 9 Mar., 1935; Holden to Woods, 9 Mar., 1935, explaining his securing a permanent restraining order to prevent Ross from spending City funds to promote the merger proposal; Holden to Woods, 27 Jan., 1935 speculating on a Ross ruse, and his own plan to run for City Council; and Holden to Woods, 14 Feb., 1935 reporting that Ross will be in D.C., and will "consult with financial men in New York . . . Suggest you watch his movements and inform us about his efforts Stop Suspect he will contact Bone and in New York will attempt to to secure new proposition for purchase": Woods *Papers*. See also William McKeen to Ross , 12 Dec., 1935, reporting that Harlan is claiming Bone's support in his efforts to form a PUD in King County outside Seattle. Beck wrote Ross two days later, speculating that Bone seemed to have his eyes on a Supreme Court appointment, and might be courting EBASCO support., Lighting Dept. *Records*, File 47-2.

The Seattle Chamber of Commerce's D.C. lobbyist, Mr. Underwood, reported that Elwood Mead expected the administration would choose the high dam, that the administration would probably fund public works to win the election, and that "we might be left out on a limb with neither the high dam nor the low dam". The chamber then submitted a resolution to its National Affairs Committee to consider the high dam proposal. Mead discouraged sending anyone to D.C. at this time: "it would do more harm than good". Seattle Chamber of Commerce *Minutes*, 13 and 20 Nov., 1934 and 16 Apr., 1935. This evidence suggests the chamber was already prepared to accept the high dam even before Holden arrived in Seattle. The author suspects that Batcheller was the brain behind Holden, pushing not only for the high dam, but especially for identifying control over transmission as being more crucial than who did the power generation—Batcheller, not Holden, was the engineer.

10. Lighting Dept., *Annual Report, 1934* p. 66.

11. George T. Melton, "The State Grange and the Development of Water Power Resources in Washington" (Unpublished Master's Thesis, University of Washington, 1954), pp. 87-103. Melton chronicles the development of the PUD's; archival sources collected since his excellent study make possible a more definitive work.

12. Melton, ibid., pp. 94-103; *Grange News*, 5 Oct., 1934. At this time, there was also a move afoot, spearheaded by Bone, to create a Columbia Valley Authority; at the Washington state level, Bone's lobbyist, Kenneth Harlan, was preparing a constitutional amendment that would put the state in the power business. These elements are developed in the text. As to a CVA, Bone, Woods, and O'Sullivan were opposed, fearing Washington would be under-represented on it. See: Woods to C.C. Dill, 26 Oct.,1933; Woods to O'Sullivan and Holden from D.C., 18 Jan., 1935. In a memorandum to himself, Woods noted: "Then it will be an open river at the expense of the Grand Coulee and a steady development as a result . . . The high dam will be delayed indefinitely": Woods *Papers*. On 5 Oct., 1934 Glen Smith had written Ross that Saul Haas (Customs District head and Bone's state political manager) had called asking in what particular

the "Bone Bill" would restrict Seattle from purchasing PSP&L's system. Smith replied that Section 3 included the restrictive language, and that "no one was branding Bone as a representative of the power trust": Lighting Dept. *Records*, File 46-1. On the strategic issue of control over transmission, Kinsey Robinson of the Washington Water Power Company, an EBASCO subsidiary, argued before the Senate Appropriations Committee about the 1940 BPA budget that the private companies had lines capable of conveying the energy output of the dams, further contending "that the only transmission lines that should be built were those tieing together existing lines of the private companies": Bone *Papers* File 1-10, UW Mss. On the role of the State Public Service Commission see Berner, *Seattle, 1900-1920: From Boomtown, Urban Turbulence, to Restoration* (Seattle: Charles Press, 1991), pp. 116, 123-24.

13. Melton, ibid., pp. 96-103; Holden to Woods, 16 Jan., 1935, Woods *Papers*.

14. Frederick G. Hamley *Diary*, 27 and 28 Mar., 5 and 18 Apr., 18 June, and 22 July 1935: Hamley *Papers*.

15. Hamley *Diary*, 18 June 1935.

16. Harlan to "Homer" 4 Feb., 1935, File 18-2; Harlan to Bone 8 July 1935, File 18-8; and 31 July 1935, commenting: "The company naturally wants to unload this obsolete property at this time . . . Ten or fifteen years ago it would have been fine but not now". The split in the public power ranks is illustrated in a letter from Smith and McKeen to Ross 19 Feb., 1935: referring to a *P-I* quotation from Harlan that Ross and Frank Bell oppose the Coulee "It seems to us that Kenneth should be known for what he is as soon as possible and maybe this incident will help show him in his true light". Harlan later denied the accuracy of the quotation, but the suspicion endured. Lighting Dept. *Records* File 46-5.

17. Hamley *Diary* 28 Aug., and 5 Sept., 1935.

18. Hamley *Diary* 9 and 23 Sept., and 4 Oct., 1935.

19. Hamley *Diary* 17, 18, and 28 Oct., 1935; Myers to Ross, 31 Oct., 1935, Lighting Dept. *Records* File 74-14; and *Annual Report*. 1935.

20. Lighting Dept., *Annual Report, 1935*; Myers to Ross, 10 Dec., 1935, File 74-14; 25 May 1936, File 74-15; and 26 May 1936, File 74-16, Lighting Dept., *Records*.

21. Myers to Ross, "June 1936", 24 June and 25 July 1936, Lighting Dept. *Records*, File 74-16; *Municipal News*, 5 Dec., 1936; Hamley *Diary*, 20 Aug., 3 Sept., and 19 Dec., 1935; 29 Feb., 13, 17, and 23 Apr., 1936; *Municipal News*, 31 Aug., 1935 and 15 Aug., 1936. Mayor Charles Smith noted in his annual message of 3 June 1935 that of the 91,585 wage earners in the city, only 27,144 used the streetcars to go to and from work; and that for cities with populations of more than 300,000, Seattle's per capita tax was the lowest.

22. Smith and McKeen wrote Ross 20 Apr., 1934 that Councilman Ralph Nichols "thinks that the coming year is the psychological time to take over the Company's holdings . . . Power company securities . . . are looking worse than ever . . . " On whether a special election should be staged, and growing opposition to the merger, see letters and wires to

Ross 21,22, and 27 Nov., 1935, 23 and 30 Jan., 15, 17-21, and 29 Feb., 2, 4, and 11 Mar., 1936, Lighting Dept., *Records*, Files 45-18, 46-22, 47-3, 47-5, 47-6, and 47-7.

23. Myers to Ross, 29 June, 25 and 29 July, 10 Aug., 1936, Lighting Dept., *Records*, File 74-16; *Annual Report, 1935*, p. 74. Beck's and Batcheller's debates were reported in the *Municipal News*, 9 May, 6, 13, and 27 June 1936.

24. Melton, ibid., pp. 112-23. Ross was appointed BPA administrator in October 1937. The Bonneville Dam was the promotion of Portland interests which were aligned with the Army Corps of Engineers; their project competed with the Coulee project before being scotched by Senator Dill's direct meeting with President Roosevelt. Dill suggested a Bonneville-Coulee intertie. See Sundborg, ibid., pp. 246-48. One of Ross's priorities (uniform/postage stamp rates being topmost) became such an intertie. See Gus Norwood, *Columbia River Power for the People: A History of Policies of the Bonneville Power Administration* (Portland: Bonneville Power Administration, [1982]), chapter 11 on postage stamp rate policy. See also Wesley A. Dick, "Visions of Abundance . . . ", chapter VIII for coverage of the issue in Oregon.

25. Ross to Rodney Brink, *Star* editor, 3 Feb., 1937, and to Hedges, 4 Feb., 1937, File 36-9; Ross position paper, "Disposition of Public Power", 2 Feb., 1937, in File 36-9; Ross to Council Efficiency Committee, 12 Feb., 1937 in File 36-12; and Myers in Seattle to Ross in D.C., 4 Feb., 1937 in File 74-15. In the 1936 annual report, Ross recommended a price of $37,370,000. The City Council appointed a committee to confer with PSP&L, Lighting Dept., *Records*. In the campaign on the "Bone Power Bill" the private companies opposed it outright. In Seattle the pamphlet was promoted by PSP&L's own Mulkey. He also accused Ross of opposing the bill. Ross and his City Light surrogates did oppose the bill but tried to avoid opposing it too openly for fear of splitting public power ranks.. See Files 47-21,22, and 23 in Lighting Dept., *Records*.

For the subsequent critical importance of the condemnation/negotiation issue it is helpful to see how it was developing at this stage. It was argued thoroughly between Guy Myers and Jack Cluck, attorney for the PUDs. Myers to Cluck, 20 Apr., 1938, in which Myers contended: "Condemnation is easy enough to start, but expensive and long drawn out, and the price undetermined until the final decision is made. The history of the purchase of water works has been that in 90% of the cases they paid more . . . by condemnation than . . . through negotiation"; File 4-5; Cluck argued, 4 Oct., 17 Nov., and 28 Dec., 1938, that no progress was being made with negotiations because the companies would not open their books for the determination of a fair price. Condemnation was needed to spur negotiations: File 4-9. Cluck expressed his frustration 2 Apr., 1939: "It is too much to expect the districts to rely upon statements of any of the companies made orally and under circumstances which admit of no proof." To this, Myers replied: " . . . in my opinion Mr. Barnes [of Stone and Webster] is sincere and honest in his efforts", to which Myers attached a Barnes letter in which Barnes coyly said no purchase offer had been received, and that he would not negotiate with a "gun at our head"—meaning condemnation: 13 Apr., 1939, File 4-16, all in Houghton, Cluck, and Coughlin *Records*. Note: Not until late 1940 were the private firms required to open their books.

26. *P-I*, 10 Mar., 1937; *Star*, 3 Feb., 1937.

27. Ross to Myers, 12 Apr., 1937, Myers *Papers*, File 73-23.

28. Blanchard, ibid., pp. 130-31; R.W. Beck to Myers 19 Apr., 1937, Myers *Papers*, File 73-23; Myers to Cluck, 4 Oct., 1937, Houghton, Cluck, and Coughlin *Records* (Hereafter cited HCC *Records*), File 4-1. For an extended discussion of this issue see Fayette Krause, "Democratic Party in Washington . . . ", pp. 211-38.

In a BPA *Special Bulletin # 4* the public preferance clause was restated: "[The Administrator] is also directed to reserve 50% of the energy available at the dam for public agencies and cooperatives until Jan. 1, 1941", in HCC *Records*, File 13-8. Gus Norwood notes that one of the unintended effects of the preferance clause was the availability of "residual" energy which provided the private companies with low rates, enabling them "to avoid installing power plants, to reduce rates, strengthen their systems, and stop further sell outs of private power companies to public agencies". Norwood, ibid., p. 76.

29. Blanchard, ibid., pp. 130-31.

30. Myers to Cluck, 25 Aug., 1937; and copy of Myers's letter to Mayor Dore of 27 Aug., 1937; and Cluck to Myers, 28 Aug., 1937, File 3-25; and Myers to Cluck, 1 and 18 Sept., 1937, File 3-26, HCC *Records*.

31. Myers to Ross, 23 July 1937, Lighting Dept., *Records*, File 74-17.

32. Beck to Myers, 31 July 1937, Myers *Papers*, File 73-23. Beck wrote to Cluck on 8 Sept., 1937 about the "great wrong that [Dore and Vanderveer] have done". HCC *Records*, Box 1. See also copy of Myers letter to Vanderveer, 24 Dec., 1937, in which Myers castigates Vanderveer for making his compensation contingent upon "your success in getting [PSP&L] to accept a further discount upon its bonds", thereby discouraging the company from coming to terms. Lighting Dept., *Records*, File 74-18.

33. Beck to Cluck, 19 Oct., 1937, HCC *Records*, Box 1; Myers to Ross, 17 Jan., 1938, Lighting Dept., *Records*, File 74-19; copy of letter, Ross to Senator George Norris, 18 Feb., 1938, HCC *Records*, File 13-10. For general background of Ross's appointment see Dick, "Visions of Abundance . . . ", chapter IX.

34. See City Hall *P-I* reporter Carl Cooper's account, 6 Mar., 1938. Myers to Ross, 1 Mar., 1938, Lighting Dept., *Records*, File 74-19.

35. See Cooper's account, *P-I*, 22 Mar., 1938; Beck to Myers 6 Mar., 1938, File 73-23; and 10 and 27 Mar., 1938, File 73-32, Myers *Papers*; Hamley *Diary*, 10 18, 19, 21 and 23 Mar., 1938.

36. For general discussion see Blanchard, *ibid.*, pp. 131-33. *Argus*, 21 May, 23 July, 3 and 10 Sept. 3 and 17 Dec., 1938; [P-I], 23 and 26 Aug., 3 and 10 Sept., 1939; Frank McLaughlin to Barnes, 15 and 25 Apr., 1938; and "Original file", from 4 to 23 Aug., 1939, PSP&L *Records*, Box 101; McLaughlin has an undated summary (ca. 20 Jan., 1941) of the period

1929 to 1937 in Box 102. Myers to Ross, 19 Apr., 1938 and 29 June 1938 about the RFC cutting out the investment bankers; copy, Van Soelen to RFC 22 May, 1939, and Van Soelen to Langlie, 16 Aug., 1939 Langlie *Papers*, Part 3, File 1-19.

Chapter 30

City Elections, 1939 and 1940

1. See chapter 2, section, "The Public Ownership Fight: PSP&L Links Street Railway Rescue With Acquisition of City Light", and chapters 27 and 29 for background.

2. *Times*, 18 Feb. 1940; Gillingham, *ibid.*, pp. 66-75 covers the Boeing-union confrontation, and Teamsters and the Aero Mechanics Union, Local 751 for jurisdiction within the Boeing plant. His account is derived in part from Reed Hansen, "Collective Bargaining Between the Boeing Airplane Company and the Aero Mechanics Union" (Unpublished Master's Thesis, University of Washington, 1951), pp. 26-29. See also chapter 5 above, "Seattle and its Manufacturing Hinterland".

3. *Times*, 26 Feb., 1 and 15 Mar. 1939.

4. *Times*, 26 and 27 Feb., 4 and 6 Mar. 1939.

5. Krause, *ibid.*, pp. 251-2; Acena, *ibid.*, pp. 321-5; *Times*, 11-13 Mar. 1940.

Chapter 31

Prelude to the 1940 General Election

1. Acena, *ibid.*, chapter VIII (quotation is from p. 303); Krause, *ibid.*, pp.239-45.

2. Acena, *ibid.*, pp. 308-14, 325-29; Krause, *ibid.*, pp. 242-57. Littell was an Assistant Attorney General. What caused the WCF to lose its credibility? Its public medium, the *Washington New Dealer*, provides most of the reasons. During the week after the signing of the non-agression pact, it was mum, as though waiting for instructions. Which, in fact, it was—in its August 31 issue it announced that a speaker for the CP would explain. But, then came the German invasion of Poland the next day. The weekly, in its September 7 edition, carried no editorial comment, but Costigan had a piece on the front page headed, "Peace Action Now Vital". Then, on September 16—the day when the Soviets invaded Poland—the WCF's executive board issued its first policy statement: "To develop the strongest possible peace movement, to end plans of world conquest by fascist aggression, the United States should take the lead in inviting to a world peace conference all neutral, non-aggressive power[s]"; and it urged a special session of Congress to amend the Neutrality Act to single out Germany and Japan for embargo. At a September meeting of the Workers' Alliance, Costigan, when asked about the Soviet action, indicated that the Alliance would soon know whether it was for defensive or offensive reasons. A mass peace meeting followed on September 18 in which the WCF was not formally involved, but at which Costigan

spoke in favor of supporting France and Britain. Support for a third term still was undiminished. Then came an announcement from the CPUSA on September 19 that the war was an imperialist war; that: "The previous alignment into democratic and fascist camps loses its former meaning". Continuing, it opposed amending the Neutrality Act in order to prevent the nation's being dragged into the war. With this line hanging out, the WCF was forced to reconsider its own interpretation. Following soon upon John L. Lewis's withdrawal of the LNPL's potential participation in any western progressive conference—one was still on the backburner in Costigan's mind (though not in that of other WCF leaders)—Congress, at the President's prompting (September 21) to repeal the arms embargo, amended the Neutrality Act to allow belligerents to buy arms on a cash and carry basis. When the Soviets invaded Finland on November 30, Costigan wrote: "[Y]ou must admit, if you love peace, that the greatest danger to America's welfare is not Hitler but involment in a foreign war". This approximated the isolationist opposition to FDR's foreign policy—the very forces for the most part, that also opposed FDR's domestic reforms, for which the WCF considered itself to be the leading oracle. At its annual convention in January 1940 the WCF resolved that the government should "[A]bandon all policies involving our nation to any degree on either side in the armed struggle of European empires". Of course, this directly affected Seattle's politics, giving life to an otherwise dull election—Hugh DeLacy, president of the WCF and a City Councilman, would be the prime target in his re-election bid, as noted above.

3. Krause, *ibid.*, pp. 240-42, 265-6; William E. Leuchtenburg, *Franklin D. Roosevelt . . .* , pp. 310-11; see correspondence between Stephen F. Chadwick and Theodore Carlson and Ed Seay, 1940 in the Chadwick, Papers.

4. Acena, *ibid.*, pp. 338-62 (quotation is from p. 362); Krause, *ibid.*, pp. 257-61.

Chapter 32

The 1940 General Election

1. Krause, *ibid.*, pp. 232-3, 238, 257-61; Acena, *ibid.*, pp. 353-4; George W. Scott, "Arthur B. Langlie: Republican Governor in a Democratic Age" (Unpublished Ph.D. Dissertation, University of Washington, 1971), pp. 69-70; Melton, *The State Grange . . .* , pp. 139-41, 159,61.

2. Scott, *ibid.*, pp. 65-7; Krause, *ibid.*, pp. 261-2.

3. Scott, *ibid.*, pp. 70-72; Krause, *ibid.*, pp. 262-3, 269-71; Acena, *ibid.*, pp. 360-61. Both the Pennock and Langlie leaflets are in File 8-5, Washington Pension Union, Records. On the catalytic function of Initiative 141, *Minutes*, 2 May, 1940, File 3-17, WPU, Records; also, *Minutes*, for 4 May 1940 in File 3-17; its *Minutes*, for 3 Aug. 1940 read: "Suggest use of [the Townsends] re keeping our boys out of war except at home".

4. Krause, *ibid.*, pp. 260-68, 275-8; Scott, *ibid.*, pp. 71-3; Acena, *ibid.*, pp. 360-66.

5. Krause, *ibid.*, pp. 272-8; Scott, *ibid.*, pp. 74-80; Melton, *ibid.*, pp.

139-41, 156, 159-61. The FPC hearings. at the prompting of Senator Bone, began in Seattle on October 14. Indicative of the recent swing of the Municipal League into opposition to public ownership, was its endorsement of Initiative 139. When the Grange requested permission to speak before the League the latter responded that the debate must "be kept on a dignified and intelligent plane" (quotation is from Melton, p. 140).

6. Krause. *ibid.*, pp. 270-72, 277; Scott, *ibid.*, p. 75.

7. Krause, *ibid.*, pp. 276-8; Scott, *ibid.*, pp. 76-9; Calvin F. Schmid, *Social Trends in Seattle* pp. 263, 265; Washington Secretary of State, *Abstract of Votes* for the 1940 election.

Bibliography

Archival Sources

Museum of History and Industry, Seattle

Ladies Musical Club. Records

Seattle City Comptroller's Office

City Archives. Comptroller's Records

Seattle Public Libraries

Seattle Chamber of Commerce. Minute Books
Seattle Commercial Club. Minute Books

University of Puget Sound

Homer T. Bone. Papers

Wenatchee World Office

Rufus Woods. Papers.

University of Washington Libraries University Archives andManuscripts Division

American Civil Liberties Union. Records.
American Institute of Architects. Seattle Chapter Records
Nettie Asberry. Papers.
Harry E.P. Ault. Papers
Willis T. Batcheller. Papers.
Broussais Beck. Papers

Robert W. Beck. Papers.
Homer T. Bone. Papers.
Robert E. Burke. Collection relating to Washington Commonwealth Federation.
Cannery Workers and Farm Laborers' Union, Local 7. Records
Carpenters and Joiners of America, Local 131. Records.
Stephen F. Chadwick. Papers.
Stephen J. Chadwick. Papers.
Irving Clark. Papers.
Cornish School. Records and Scrapbooks
George F. Cotterill. Papers
Asahel Curtis. Papers.
Hugh DeLacy. Papers.
Eugene V. Dennett. Papers.
Jessie Epstein. Papers
Charles F. Ernst. Papers.
Mary Farquharson. Papers.
Nellie Fick. Scrapbooks
Frank Fitts. Papers
Saul Haas. Papers.
Frederick G. Hamley. Papers.
Houghton, Cluck, and Coughlin, law firm. Records.
Inland Boatmen's Union. Records.
Florence Bean James. Papers.
Wesley L. Jones. Papers.
King County Central Labor Council. Records. (includes those of Seattle Central Labor Council)
Roy Kinnear. Papers
Bertha Knight Landes. Papers.
Arthur B. Langlie. Papers.
Mark Litchman. Papers.
Preston Macy. Papers.
Warren G. Magnuson. Papers.
Esther Stark Maltby, Scrapbooks
Marine Engineers Benevolent Association. Records.
Mark A. Matthews. Papers and Scrapbooks
Edmond S. Meany. Papers.
Elmer Miller. Papers.
The Mountaineers. Records.
Municipal League. Records.
Guy C. Myers. Papers.
Pacific Coast Coal Company. Records
Parents-Teachers Association, Seattle. Records
Edward A. Pitter. Papers.
Ralph B. Potts. Papers.
Puget Sound Power and Light Company. Records
Edith Dolan Riley. Papers.
James Sakamoto. Papers.

Dietrich Schmitz. Papers.
Seattle Art Museum. Records
Seattle Federation of Teachers. Records.
Seattle Lighting Department. Records and Scrapbooks
Seattle Repertory Playhouse. Records.
Seattle Urban League. Records.
William D. Shannon. Papers.
Constance Pitter Thomas. Papers.
Mark Tobey. Papers.
Typographical Union, International, Local 99 and 202. Records
University of Washington Board of Regents. Records.
University of Washington Drama School. Records.
University of Washington English Department. Records.
University of Washington President. Records.
Victorio Velasco. Papers.
Washington Education Association. Records.
Washington Pension Union. Records.
Washington State Federation of Labor. Records
Washington State Federation of Women's Clubs. Records
Washington State Theatre. Records.
Hulet Wells. Papers
West and Wheeler Real Estate Company. Records.
Donald T. Williams, Jr., "The Remarkable Dr. Henry Suzzallo: A Biography," (Unpublished manuscript, University of Washington Libraries. University Archives.)

University of Washington Libraries Special Collections Division

Pike Place Public Market. Scrapbboks
Donald Sherwood, "Description and History of Seattle Parks". (Unpublished manuscript)
Seattle Lighting Department. Scrapbooks
Cecilia Shultz. Scrapbooks

Newspapers

The Argus
Commonwealth News
Cosmopolitan Courier (in Victorio Velasco Papers)
Cosmopolitan Weekly (in Victorio Velasco Papers)
Electric Fist (in Frederick Hamley Papers)
Filipino Forum
The International Examiner (in Victorio Velasco Papers)
The Northwest Enterprise
The Philippine Advocate
The Philippine-American Chronicle
The Philippine-American Tribune
Railway and Marine News

Seattle Journal of Commerce
Seattle Municipal News
Seattle Post-Intelligencer
Seattle Star
Seattle Sun
Seattle Times
Seattle Union Record
The Sunday News
The Town Crier
The Unemployed Citizen
University of Washington Daily
The Vanguard
The Voice of Action
The Washington Commonwealth Builder
The Washington New Dealer

Books and Government Documents

Ames, William E. and Simpson, Roger A. *Unionism or Hearst: the Seattle Post-Intelligencer Strike of 1936*, Seattle: Pacific Northwest Labor History Association, 1978.

Bayley, Thomas Stimson. *The Stimson Family*, Seattle: [T.S. Bayley], 1976.

Berner, Richard C. *Seattle, 1900-1920: From Boomtown, Urban Turbulence, to Restoration*, Seattle: Charles Press, 1991.

Bernstein, Irving. *A History of the American Worker, 1933-1941: the Turbulent Years*, Boston: Houghton Mifflin, 1970.

Bernstein, Irving. *The Lean Years: A History of the American Worker, 1920-1933*, Baltimore: Penguin Books, 1966.

Blanchard, Leslie. *The Street Railway Era in Seattle: A Chronicle of Six Decades*, Forty Fort, Pennsylvania: Harold E. Cox, 1968.

Blumell, Bruce D. *The Development of Public Assistance in the State of Washington During the Great Depression*, New York: Garland Publishing Co., 1983.

Browne, Ellen V. and Edward N. Beck, editors. *Miss Aunt Nellie: The Autobiography of Nellie C. Cornish.*, Seattle: University of Washington Press, 1964.

Buck, Mildred E. and Staff. *Public Welfare in Washington: a State-Wide Study of Problems of Public Welfare Administration*, Olympia: State Printer, 1934.

Burke, Padraic. *The History of the Port of Seattle*, Seattle: Port of Seattle, 1976.

Calhoun, Anne, *A Seattle Heritage: the Seattle Fine Arts Society*, Seattle: Lowman and Hanford, 1942.

Campbell, Esther W. *Bagpipes in the Woodwind Section: A History of the Seattle Symphony Orchestra and its Women's Association*, Seattle: Seattle Symphony Women's Association, 1978.

Cayton, Horace R. *Long Old Road: An Autobiography*, Seattle: University of Washington Press, 1964.

Chandler, Alfred D., Jr. *The Visible Hand: the Managerial Revolution in American Business*, Cambridge, MA: Harvard University Press, 1977.

Clark, Norman H. *The Dry Years: Prohibition and Social Change in Washington*, Seattle: University of Washington Press, 1965.

Clark, Norman H. *Washington: a Bicentennial History*, New York: W.W. Norton and Co., and Nashville: American Association for State and Local History, 1976.

Cochran, Thomas C. and William Miller. *The Age of Enterprise: A Social History of Industrial America*, New York: Harper Torchbooks, 1961.

Cooke, Morris L., editor. *Giant Power: Large Scale Electrical Development as a Social Factor*, *Annals* of the American Academy of Political and Social Science, vol. CXVIII, March, 1925.

Cordova, Fred. *Filipinos: Forgotten Asian Americans, a Pictorial Essay, 1763 circa 1963*, [Seattle]: Demonstration Project for Asian Americans, 1983.

Cowles, Charles. *Northwest Traditions*, Seattle: Seattle Art Museum, 1978.

Cumming, William, *Sketchbook: a Memoir of the 30s and the Northwest School*, Seattle: University of Washington Press, 1984.

Daniels, Roger. *Asian America: Chinese and Japanese in the United States Since 1850*, (Seattle: University of Washington Press, 1988)

Daniels, Roger.*The Politics of Prejudice: The Anti-Japanese Movement in California and the Struggle for Japanese Exclusion*, New York: Atheneum, 1972.

Dembo, Jonathan. *Unions and Politics in Washington State, 1885-1935*, Modern American History Series. New York: Garland Publishing Company, 1983.

Dempsey, Mary V. *The Occupational Progress of Women, 1910 to 1930*, Washington: U.S. Labor Department, Womens' Bureau, Bulletin No. 104, 1933.

Devine, Jean. *From Settlement House to Neighborhood House, 1906-1976*, Seattle: Neighborhood House, 1976.

Draper, Theodore. *The Roots of American Communism*, New York: Viking Press, 1957.

Dun and Bradstreet. *Seattle*, Seattle Lighting Department, 1948

Edwards, Thomas G. and Carlos A. Schwantes, editors. *Experiences in the Promised Land: Essays in Pacific Northwest History*, Seattle: University of Washington Press, 1986.

Ficken, Robert E. and LeWarne, Charles P. *Washington: a Centennial History* , Seattle: University of Washington Press, 1988.

Ficken, Robert E. *Lumber and Politics: The Career of Mark E. Reed*, Seattle: University of Washington Press, 1979.

Ficken, Robert E. *The Forested Land: A History of Lumbering in Western Washington*, Seattle: University of Washington Press, 1987.

Foisie, Frank. *Decasualizing Longshore Labor and the Seattle Experience*, Seattle: Waterfront Employers of Seattle, 1934.

Fox, Stephen. *The Image Makers: a History of American Advertising, and its Creators*, New York: Vintage Press, 1985.

Friedheim, Robert L. *The Seattle General Strike*, Seattle: University of Washington Press, 1964.

Frykman, George A. *Creating the People's University: Washington State University, 1890-1990*, Pullman, Washington State University Press, 1990.

Galenson, Walter. *The CIO Challenge to the AFL: a History of the American Labor Movement, 1935-1941*, Cambridge, MA: Harvard University Press, 1960.

Garnel, Donald. *The Rise of Teamster Power in the West*, Berkeley: University of California Press, 1972.

Gates, Charles M. *The First Century at the University of Washington, 1861-1961*. Seattle: University of Washington Press, 1961.

Gault, Lila. *The House Next Door: Seattle's Neighborhood Architecture*, Seattle: Pacific Search Press, 1981.

Gillingham, J.B. *The Teamsters Union in the West*, Berkeley: Institute of Industrial Relations, University of California, 1956.

Goldblatt, Louis, editor. *Men and Machines: a Story About Longshoring on the West Coast Waterfront*, [San Francisco]: International Longshoremen's and Warehousemen's Union and the Pacific Maritime Association, 1963.

Gorter, Wytze and Hildebrand, George H. *The Pacific Coast Maritime Shipping Industry, 1930-1948* , Berkeley: University of California Press, 1954, 2 vols.

Gunns, Albert F. *Civil Liberties in Crisis: The Pacific Northwest, 1917-1940*, New York: Garland Publishing Company, 1983.

Hawley, Lowell S., and Ralph B. Potts. *Counsel for the Damned: A Biography of George Francis Vanderveer* , Philadelphia: J. B. Lippencott, 1953.

Hillman, Arthur, *The Unemployed Citizens' League of Seattle*, Seattle: University of Washington Publications in the Social Sciences,vol. 5, no. 3, pp. 181-270, 1934.

Hines, Neal O. *Denny's Knoll: A History of the Metropolitan Tract of the University of Washington*, Seattle: University of Washington Press, 1980.

Hopkins, William S. *Seasonal Unemployment in the State of Washington*, Seattle: University of Washington Publications in the Social Sciences, vol. 8, no. 3, pp. 81-168, Dec. 1936.

Jensen, Vernon H. *Lumber and Labor*, New York: Farrar and Rinehart, 1945.

Jones, Gareth S. *Outcast London: a Study in the Relationship Between Classes in Victorian Society*, New York: Pantheon Books, 1984.

King, Judson. *The Conservation Fight: From Theodore Roosevelt to the Tennessee Valley Authority*, Washington: Public Affairs Press, 1959.

Kingsbury, Martha, *The Art of the Thirties: the Pacific Northwest*, Seattle: University of Washington Press, 1972.

Klehr, Harvey. *The Heyday of American Communism: the Depression Decade*, New York: Basic Books, 1984.

Kolko, Gabriel. *Main Currents in Modern American History*, New York: Pantheon Books, 1984.

Larrowe, Charles P. *Harry Bridges: the Rise and Fall of Radical Labor in the United States*, New York: Lawrence Hill, 1972.

Leuchtenburg, William E. *Franklin D. Roosevelt and the New Deal, 1932-1940*, New York: Harper Row Torchbooks, 1963.

Lind, Andrew W. *A Study of Mobility of Population in Seattle*, University of

Washington Publications in the Social Sciences, volume 3 number 1. Seattle: University of Washington Press, 1925.

Logan, Edward B., editor. *Lobbying, Annals* of the American Academy of Political and Social Science, vol. CXVIV, July, 1929.

MacDonald, Norbert. *Distant Neighbors: A Comparative History of Seattle and Vancouver*, Lincoln: University of Nebraska Press, 1984.

Mansfield, Harold. *Vision: the Story of Boeing*, New York: Popular Library Books, 1966.

McWilliams, Carey. *PREJUDICE Japanese-Americans: Symbol of Racial Intolerance*, Boston: Little, Brown and Company, 1944.

McWilliams, Mary. *Seattle Water Department History, 1854-1954: Operational Data and Memoranda*. Seattle: Water Department, 1955.

Melendy, H. Brett. *Asians in America: Filipinos, Koreans, and East Indians*, Boston: Twayne Publishers, 1977.

Miyamoto, Shotaro Frank. *Social Solidarity Among the Japanese in Seattle*, University of Washington Studies in the Social Sciences, volume 11 number 2. Seattle: University of Washington Press, 1939.

Montgomery, David. *The Fall of the House of Labor: the Workplace, the State, and American Labor Activism, 1865-1925*. Cambridge: University, paperback edition, 1989.

Morgan, Murray. *Skid Road: An Informal Portrait of Seattle*, Seattle: University of Washington Press, 1982.

Mumford, Esther Hall. *Seattle's Black Victorians, 1852-1901*, Seattle: Ananse Press, 1980.

Mullins, William H. *The Depression and the Urban West Coast, 1929-1933: Los Angeles, San Francisco, Seattle, and Portland*, Bloomington: Indiana University Press, 1991.

Murray, Robert K. *Red Scare: A Study in National Hysteria, 1918-1920*, Minneapolis: University of Minnesota Press, 1955.

Nash, Roderick. *Wilderness and the American Mind*, New Haven: Yale University Press, 1973.

Nelson, Bruce. *Workers on the Waterfront: Seamen, Longshoremen, and Unionism in the 1930s*, Urbana: University of Illinois Press, 1988.

Nelson, Bryce E. *Good Schools: the Seattle Public School System, 1901-1930*, Seattle: University of Washington Press, 1988.

Norwood, Gus. *Columbia River Power for the People: a History of the Bonneville Power Administration*, Portland: Bonneville Power Administration, [1982].

Norwood, Gus. *Washington Grangers Celebrate a Century*, Seattle: Washington State Grange, 1988.

Nye, David E. *Electrifying America: Social Meanings of a New Technology, 1880-1940*, Cambridge, MA: MIT Press, 1990.

O'Connor, Harvey. *Revolution in Seattle: A Memoir*, New York: Monthly Review Press, 1964.

Pinkett, Harold T. *Gifford Pinchot: Private and Public Forester*, Urbana: University of Illinois Press, 1978.

Pitzer, Paul C. *Building the Skagit: a Century of Upper Skagit Valley History, 1870-1970*, Portland: The Galley Press, 1978.

Polk. *City Director[ies]*, 1923-35.

Port of Seattle. *Yearbook*, Seattle: Port of Seattle, [1920s and 1930s].
Portland Public Docks Commission. *Annual Report[s]*, 1921, 1929, 1931, 1940.
Potter, Allen R. *Occupational Characeristics of Unemployed Persons in Cities of 11,000 or More Persons, State of Washington*, Olympia: Washington Employment Relief Administration, 1935.
Reichauer, Haru Matsukata. *Samurai and Silk: A Japanese and American Heritage*, Cambridge: Harvard University Press, 1986.
Robinson, Marilyn Druck. *Washington State Statistical Abstract*, Seattle: University of Washington Press, 1952.
Ross, Nancy Wilson. *Farthest Reach: Oregon and Washington*, New York: A.A. Knopf, 1941.
Rotella, Elyce J. *From Home to Office: U.S. Women at Work, 1870-1930*, Ann Arbor: University Microfilms International Research Press, Studies in American History abd Culture, No. 25, 1981.
Sales, Roger. *Seattle: Past to Present*, Seattle: University of Washington Press, 1976.
Sanders, Jane. *Cold War on the Campus: Academic Freedom at the University of Washington, 1946-64*, Seattle: University of Washington Press, 1979.
Schmid, Calvin F. and Wayne W. McVey, Jr. *Growth and Distribution of Minority Races in Seattle, Washington*, Seattle: Seattle Public Schools, 1964.
Schmid, Calvin F. and Stanton E. Schmid. *Growth of Cities and Towns: State of Washington*, Olympia: Washington State Planning and Community Affairs Agency, 1969.
Schmid, Calvin F. *Social Trends in Seattle*, University of Washington Studies in the Social Sciences, volume 14. Seattle: University of Washington Press, 1944.
Schmitz, Henry. *The Long Road Travelled: an Account of Forestry at the University of Washington*, Seattle: University of Washington Press, 1977.
Schneider, Betty V.H. *Industrial Relations in the West Coast Maritime Industry*, Berkeley: Institute of Industrial Relations, University of California, 1958.
Schwantes, Carlos A. *Radical Heritage: Labor, Socialism, and Reform in Washington and British Columbia, 1885-1917*, Seattle: University of Washington Press, 1979.
Seattle Chamber of Commerce. *Profitism, Slackism, and You*, Seattle: Chamber of Commerce, 1920.
Seattle Chamber of Commerce. Seattle's Industrial Expansion, Seattle: Chamber of Commerce, 1927.
Seattle Housing Authority. *Real Property Survey, 1939-1940*, Seattle: WPA Project 3272, 1942, 2 vols.
Seattle Lighting Department, *Annual Reports*, 1920s and 1930s.
Seattle Mayor. *Annual Report[s]/Yearbook[s]*, 1927, 1928.
Seattle Park Department. *Annual Report*[s], Seattle: Seattle Park Department, [1920s and 1930s]
Seattle Port Warden. *Annual Report*[s], Seattle: Seattle Port Warden, [1920s and 1930s].

Seattle Public Schools. *Triennial Report[s]*, Seattle: Public Schools, 1921/24, 1924/27, 1927/30.
Smith, Darrell H. and Betters, Paul V. *The United States Shipping Board: Its History, Activities, and Organization*, Washington: The Brookings Institute, 1931.
Steen, Harold K. *The U.S. Forest Service: a History*, Seattle: University of Washington Press, 1976.
Stickney, Robert R. *Flagship: a History of Fisheries at the University of Washington*, Dubuque: Kendall-Hunt Publishing Co., 1989.
Sundborg, George. *Hail Columbia: the 30-Year Fight for the Grand Coulee Dam*, New York: Macmillan, 1954.
Taft, Philip. *The A.F. of L. From the Death of Gompers to the Merger*, New York: Harper Brothers, 1959.
Taft, Philip. *The AFL in the Time of Gompers*, New York: Harper and Row, 1957.
[Tobey, Mark]. *Tobey's 80: a Retrospective*, Seattle: for the Seattle Art Museum by the University of Washington Press, 1970.
Twight, Ben W. *Organizational Values and Political Power: The Forest Service Versus the Olympic National Park*, University Park, Pennsylvania: Pennsylvania State University Press, 1983.
United States Bureau of Labor Statistics. *Building Construction in the United States, 1921-1940*, Washington: Government Printing Office, 1940.
United States Census Bureau, *Population Census: the Labor Force, 1940*, Washington: Government Printing Office, 1940.
United States Census Bureau. *United States Census*, Washington, D.C.: Government Printing Office, 1920, 1930, 1940.
United States Federal Trade Commission. *[Hearings on the Utility Corporations' Propaganda]*, Part 71-A, Washington: Government Printing Office, 1930.
United States Shipping Board. *Annual Report, 1922*, Washington: U.S. Shipping Board, 1922.
Walker, Samuel. *In Defense of American Liberties: a History of the ACLU*, New York: Oxford University Press, 1990.
Washington State Federation of Labor. *Proceedings*, Seattle: Washington State Federation of Labor, [1920sand 1930s]
Wechsler, James. *Revolt on Campus*, Seattle: University of Washington Press, American Library Edition, 1973.
Wight, Frederick, Baur, John, and Phillips, Duncan. *Morris Graves*, Berkeley: University of California Press, 1956.
Willebrandt, Mabel W. *The Inside of Prohibition*, Indianapolis: Bobbs-Merrill, 1929.
Woodbridge, Sally B. and Roger Montgomery. *A Guide to Architecture in Washington State: An Environmental Perspective*, Seattle: University of Washington Press, 1980.

Articles

Abella, Sebastian. "Migration of Filipinos to the Pacific Northwest". *Filipino Forum* , 15 and 30 May 1929.

Blair, Karen. "The Seattle Ladies Musical Club, 1890-1930, in Thomas G. Edwards and Carlos A. Schwantes. *Experiences in the Promised Land: Essays in Pacific Northwest History,* Seattle: University of Washington Press, 1986

Budlong, Julia. "What Happened in Seattle?". *Nation,*29 Aug. 1928, pp. 197-98.

Burke, Padraic. "Struggle for Public Ownership: Early History of the Port of Seattle." *PNQ,* 68:3 (April 1977): pp. 60-71.

Byler, Charles. "Austin E. Griffiths: Seattle Progressive Reformer." *PNQ,* 76:1 (January 1985): pp. 22-32..

Clark, Norman H. "Roy Olmstead, a Rumrunning King of Puget Sound". *PNQ,* 54:3 (July, 1963), pp. 89-103.

Conover, C.J. "The Forest Service Program on Cascade Crest Trail - 1937". *The Mountaineer,* 30:1 (15 Dec., 1937), pp. 19-25.

Cravens, Hamilton. "The Emergence of the Farmer-Labor Party in Washington Politics, 1919-20." *PNQ,* 57:4 (October 1968): pp. 148-157.

Creel, George. "Closed During Altercations: the Unions Fight for the West Coast", *Saturday Evening Post,* 14 May 1938.

Dembo, Jonathan. "Dave Beck and the Transportation Revolution in the Pacific Northwest, 1917-1941", in Thomas Edwards and Carlos A. Schwantes , editors, *Experiences in the Promised Land . . .* ", pp. 339-52.

Dimock, Arthur H. "Preparing the Groundwork for a City: The Regrading of Seattle, Washington." Paper Number 1669, American Society of Civil Engineers. *Transactions*: 1928.

Douglas, Paul. "Seattle Municipal Railway System." *Journal of Political Economy,* 29 (June 1921): pp. 455-477.

Foisie, Frank. "Stabilizing Seattle's Longshore Labor". In National Conference of Social Work, *Proceedings,* 1925, pp. 302-07.

Friedheim, Robert L., and Robin Friedheim. "The Seattle Labor Movement, 1919-1920." *PNQ,* 55:4 (October 1964): pp. 146-169.

Greenwald, Maurine Weiner. "Working-Class Feminism and the Family Wage Ideal: The Seattle Debate on Married Women's Right to Work, 1914-1920." *Journal of American History* 76:1 (June 1989): pp. 118-149.

Gunns, Albert F. "Ray Becker, the Last Centralia Prisoner", *PNQ,* 59:2 (April, 1968), pp. 88-99.

Hazard, Joseph. "Our Second Ten Years", *The Mountaineer,* 30:1 (15 Dec., 1937), pp. 13-16.

Hill, Robert. "Power Politics in Seattle", *Nation,* vol. CXXXIX (2 March, 1932), pp. 254-56.

Jackson, Jesse. "The Story of Seattle's Hooverville", in Calvin F. Schmid, *Social Trends in Seattle,* pp. 286-93.

Johnson, Catherine Joy, "The Olmsted Designs for the Washington Park Arboretum", *Washington Park Arboretum Bulletin,* 52:1 (Spring 1989), pp. 14-17.

Landes, Bertha K. "Does Politics [M]ake Women Crooked?", *Colliers,* 16 March 1929.

MacDonald, William. "The Seattle Strike and Afterwards." *The Nation,* 108:2804 (29 March 1919): pp. 469-470.

MacGowan, George. "Five Years of Climbing Courses", *The Mountaineer*, 32:1 (15 Dec., 1939), pp. 5-8.

Marple, Elliott. "The Movement for Public Ownership in Washington." *Journal of Land and Public Utility Economics*, 2 (February 1931): pp. 61-66.

Masson, Jack and Guimary, Donald. "Asian Labor Contractors in the Alaskan Canned Salmon Industry", *Labor History*, 22:3 (Summer, 1981), pp. 337-97.

Menefee, Selden. "The Decline of Dave Beck", *Nation* (26 March 1938).

Murray Keith A. "The Charles Niederhauser Case: Patriotism in the Seattle Schools." *PNQ*, 74:1 (January 1983): pp. 11-17.

Nelson, Bryce E. "Frank B. Cooper: Seattle's Progressive School Superintendent, 1901-1922." *PNQ*, 74:4 (October 1983): pp. 167-177.

Nelson, L. A. "Thirty Years in Retrospect: The First Decade in Mountaineer Annals." *The Mountaineer*, 30:1 (December 1937): pp. 9-12.

Pendergrass, Lee F. "The Formation of a Municipal Reform Movement: The Municipal League of Seattle." *PNQ*, 66:1 (January 1975): pp. 13-25.

Perry, Tom Jones. "Republic of the Penniless", *Atlantic*, vol. 150 (Oct., 1932), pp. 449-57.

Peterson, Richard B. "A Rational Employment System for the West Coast Longshore Industry." *University of Washington Business Review*, 26:3 (Spring 1967): 50-56.

Pieroth, Doris H. "The Woman Who Was Mayor". *PNQ*, 75:3 (July, 1984), pp. 117-27. Also in Edwards and Schwantes, *Experiences in the Promised Land . . .*, pp. 304-22.

Richardson, Elmo. "Olympic National Park: 20 Years of Controversy". *Forest History*, 12:1 (April, 1968), pp. 7-12.

Rockafeller, Nancy. "'In Gauze We Trust': Public Health and Spanish Influenza on the Home Front, 1918-1919." *PNQ*, 77:3 (July 1986): pp. 2-11.

Rosenzweig, Roy. "Radicals and the Jobless: the Musteites and the Unemployed Leagues", *Labor History*, 16:1 (Winter, 1975), pp. 52-77.

Ryder, Madelene. "The Third Decade", *The Mountaineer*, 30:1 (15 Dec., 1937), pp. 16-18.

Schwantes, Carlos A. "Farmer-Labor Insurgency in Washington State: William Bouck, the Grange, and the Western Progressive Farmers." *PNQ*, 76:1 (January 1985): pp. 2-11.

Scott, George W. "The New Order of Cincinnatus: Municipal Politics in Seattle During the 1930s", *PNQ*, 64:4 (Oct., 1973), pp. 137-46.

Soden, Dale. "Mark Allison Matthews: Seattle's Minister Rediscovered." *PNQ*, 74:2 (April 1983): pp. 50-58.

Stephen, Isabel. "Is America Becoming Woman-Ruled?", *Seattle Times*, 6 March 1928.

Tarbill, Von V. "Mountain-Moving in Seattle." *Harvard Business Review* (July 1930): pp. 482-489.

Viernes, Gene. "[Filipino Migration to the Pacific Northwest]", a series of articles in *The International Examiner*, April, May and September, 1935.

Voters Information League. "*Bulletins*", [1920s].

White, Richard. "Poor Men on Poor Lands: the Back-to-the-Land Movement of the Early Twentieth Century". In Thomas G. Edwards and Carlos A. Schwantes, editors, *Experiences in the Promised Land* . . . pp. 287-303.

Williams, Guy. "Seattle's Negro Theatre". *Federal Theatre,* 2:1, pp. 7-9.

Theses and Dissertations

Acena, Albert A. "The Washington Commonwealth Federation: Reform Politics and the Popular Front". Unpublished Ph.D. Dissertation, University of Washington, 1975.

Baker, Miner. "The Proposed City Light Merger: a Study of Public Opinion". Unpublished Master's Thesis, University of Washington, 1938.

Blumell, Bruce D. "The Development of Public Assistance in the State of Washington During the Great Depression". Unpublished Ph.D. Dissertation, University of Washington, 1973.

Chagnon, Raymond R. "Survey of One Hundred Eighteen Employable Families Affected by the Reduction of Relief Funds in Zone 4, King County, Washington, April 1, 1939". Unpublished Master's Thesis, 1942.

Champlin, Ardath I. "The Washington Education Association, 1889-1964". Unpublished Ph.D. Dissertation,University of Utah, 1967.

Chaskel, Ruth. "The Administration of the Work Projects Administration in the State of Washington". Unpublished Master's Thesis, University of Washington, 1942.

Chen, Yung-Ping. "A Historical Study of the General Property Tax in the State of Washington". Unpublished Master's Thesis, University of Washington, 1957.

Cole, Robert L. "The Democratic Party in Washington State, 1919-1933: Barometer of Social Change." Unpublished Ph.D. Dissertation, University of Washington, 1972.

Cravens, Hamilton. "A History of the Washington Farmer-Labor Party, 1918-1924." Unpublished Master's Thesis, University of Washington, 1962.

Dawson, Jan C. "A Social Gospel Portrait: The Life of Sydney Dix Strong, 1860-1938. Unpublished Master's Thesis, University of Washington, 1972.

De Shazo, Melvin. "Radical Tendencies in the Seattle Labor Movement as Reflected in the Proceedings of its Central Body." Unpublished Master's Thesis, University of Washington, 1925.

Dembo, Jonathan. "A History of the Washington State Labor Movement, 1885-1935." Unpublished Ph.D. Dissertation, University of Washington, 1978. (See entry above for its published version.)

Dick Wesley A. "The Genesis of Seattle City Light." Unpublished Master's Thesis, University of Washington, 1965.

Dick, Wesley A. "Visions of Abundance: the Public Power Crusade in the Era of J.D. Ross and the New Deal". Unpublished Ph.D. Dissertation, University of Washington, 1973.

Dickson, William J. "Labor in Municipal Politics: a Study of Labor's Political Activities in Seattle". Unpublished Master's Thesis, University of Washington, 1928.

Forth, William Stuart. "Wesley L. Jones: a Political Biography". Unpublished Ph.D. Dissertation, University of Washington, 1962.

Gramm, Warren S. "Employer Association Development in Seattle and Vicinity." Unpublished Master's Thesis, University of Washington, 1948.

Gunns, Albert F. "Civil Liberties and Crisis: The Status of Civil Liberties in the Pacific Northwest, 1917-1940." Unpublished Ph.D. Dissertation, University of Washington, 1971. (See entry above for its published version.)

Gunns, Albert F. "Roland Hill Hartley and the Politics of Washington State". Unpublished Master's Thesis, University of Washington, 1963.

Hall, Margaret A. "A History of Women Faculty at the University of Washington, 1896-1970." Unpublished Ph.D. Dissertation, University of Washington, 1984.

Hall, Margaret A. "Henry Suzzallo and the Washington State Council of Defense." Unpublished Master's Thesis, University of Washington, 1975.

Hansen, Reed R. "Collective Bargaining Between the Boeing Airplane Company and the Aero Mechanics Union". Unpublished Master's Thesis, University of Washington, 1951.

Hewitt, Gloria A. "A History of the Washington State Theatre, 1931 to 1941". Unpublished Master's Thesis, 1964.

Hoffland, Laura F. "Seattle as a Metropolis: the Integration of the Puget Sound Region through the Dominance of Seattle." Unpublished Master's Thesis, University of Washington, 1933

Hogan, John A. "The Decline of Self-Help and Growth of Radicalism Among Seattle's Unemployed". Unpublished Master's Thesis, University of Washington, 1934.

Horn, Juana Racquel Royster. "The Academic and Extracurricular Undergraduate Experinces of Three Black Women at the University of Washington, 1935-1941". Unpublished Ph.D. Dissertation, University of Washington, 1980.

Jackson, Joseph Sylvester. "The Colored Marine Employees Benevolent Association of the Pacific, 1921-1934." Unpublished Master's Thesis, University of Washington, 1939.

Johnson, Evamarii A. "A Production History of the Seattle Federal Theatre Project's Negro Repertory Compnay: 1935-1939". Unpublished Ph.D. Dissertation, University of Washington, 1981.

Jones, George Michael. "Longshore Unionism on Puget Sound: Seattle-Tacoma Comparison." Unpublished Master's Thesis, University of Washington, 1957.

Kimmons, Neil C. "The Historical Development of Seattle as a Metropolitan Area." Unpublished Master's Thesis, University of Washington, 1942.

Krause, Fayette F. "Democratic Party Politics in the State of Washington During the New Deal, 1932-1940". Unpublished Ph.D. Dissertation, University of Washington, 1971.

Lechner, Anna Bell. "The Seattle Municipal Street Railway." Unpublished Master's Thesis, University of Washington, 1936.

Leistra, Ronald M. "Seattle's Radical Press, 1930-1934". Unpublished Master's Thesis, University of Washington, 1964.

Lindsay, Arthur G. "The Washington State Old Age Pension Union: a Political Pressure Group". Unpublished Master's Thesis, University of Washington, 1940.

Melton, George T. "The State Grange and the Development of Water Power Resources in Washington". Unpublished Master's Thesis, University of Washington, 1954.

Moe, Ole K. "An Analytical Study of the Foreign Trade Through the Port of Seattle." Unpublished Master's Thesis, University of Washington, 1932.

Mullins, William H. "San Francisco and Seattle During the Hoover Years of the Great Depression: 1929-1933". Unpublished Ph.D. Dissertation, University of Washington, 1975.

Murayama, Yuzo. "The Economic History of Japanese Immigration to the Pacific Northwest: 1890-1920." Unpublished Ph.D. Dissertation, University of Washington, 1982.

Nelson, Bryce E. "Good Schools: The Development of Public Schooling in Seattle, 1901-1922." Unpublished Ph.D. Dissertation, University of Washington, 1981.

Nishinori, John I. "Japanese Farms in Washington." Unpublished Master's Thesis, University of Washington, 1926.

O'Connell, Mary Joan. "The Seattle Union Record, 1918-1928: A Pioneer Labor Daily." Unpublished Master's Thesis, University of Washington, 1964.

Ogle, Stephanie Francine. "Anna Louise Strong: Progressive and Propagandist." Unpublished Ph.D. Dissertation, University of Washington, 1981.

Pendergrass, Lee Forrest. "Urban Reform and Voluntary Association: A Case Study of the Seattle Municipal League." Unpublished Ph.D. Dissertation, University of Washington, 1972.

Pitts, Robert Bedford. "Organized Labor and the Negro". Unpublished Master's Thesis, University of Washington, 1941.

Prouty, Herbert Clay. "Seattle's A.F.of L.-C.I.O. War of the Warehousemen". Unpublished Master's Thesis, University of Washington, 1938.

Pullen, Douglas R. "The Administration of Washington State Governor Louis F. Hart, 1919-1925." Unpublished Ph.D. Dissertation, University of Washington, 1974.

Purdy, Harry. "Development and Cost of Municipal Operation of the Seattle Street Railways." Unpublished Master's Thesis, University of Washington, 1928.

Rademaker, John A. "The Ecological Position of the Japanese Farmers in the State of Washington." Unpublished Ph.D. Dissertation, University of Washington, 1939.

Roy, Donald Francis. "Hooverville: a Study of a Community of Homeless Men in Seattle". Unpublished Master's Thesis, University of Washington, 1935.

Scott, George W. "Arthur B. Langlie: Republican Governor in a Democratic Age". Unpublished Ph.D. Dissertation, University of Washington, 1971.

Scott, George W. "The New Order of Cincinnatus". Unpublished Master's Thesis, University of Washington, 1966.

Sharbach, Sarah Ellen. "Louise Olivereau and the Seattle Radical Community, 1917-1923." Unpublished Master's Thesis, University of Washington, 1986.

Slatten, Terry. "Homer T. Bone: Public Power and Washington State Progressive Politics in the Mid-1920s". Unpublished Master's Thesis, Western Washington University, 1987.

Soden, Dale E. "Mark Allison Matthews: Seattle's Southern Preacher." Unpublished Ph.D. Dissertation, University of Washington, 1980.

Sparks, William O. "J. D. Ross and Seattle City Light, 1917-1932." Unpublished Master's Thesis, University of Washington, 1964.

Thompson, Margaret Jane. "Development and Comparison of Industrial Relationships in Seattle." Unpublished Master's Thesis, University of Washington, 1929.

Torget, William E. "Financing the Common Schools in the State of Washington". Unpublished Master's Thesis, University of Washington, 1954.

Tripp, Joseph F. "Progressive Labor Laws in Washington, 1900-1925." Unpublished Ph.D. Dissertation, University of Washington, 1973.

Twight, Ben Whitfield. "The Tenacity of Value Commitment: the Forest Service and the Olympic National Park". Unpublished Ph.D. Dissertation, University of Washington, 1971.

Westine, Carl G. "The Seattle Teamsters." Unpublished Master's Thesis, University of Washington, 1937.

White, William Thomas."A History of Railroad Workers in the Pacific Northwest." Unpublished Ph.D. Dissertation, University of Washington, 1981.

Winslow, Barbara. "The Decline of Socialism in Washington, 1910-1925." Unpublished Master's Thesis, University of Washington,

Index

A

B

C

D

E

F

G

H

I

J

K

L

M

N

O

P

R

S

T

U

V

W

Y

Z

Richard C. Berner. Born, Seattle 1920; educated in Seattle public schools; graduated from Garfield High School, 1939. B.A. in Economics, University of Washington, 1947; M.A. in History, University of California, Berkeley, 1950; M.L.S., University of California, Berkeley, 1955. Founder of University of Washington's Manuscript Collection and University Archives Program, 1958. Author, *Archival Theory and Practice in the United States: a Historical Analysis* (University of Washington Press, 1983), which earned the Waldo Gifford Leland prize of the Society of American Archivists, 1984; a manual on archival practice and articles on archives for various journals; historical articles for *Pacific Northwest Quarterly*. Originator of the State Historical Records Survey (1977-1980)—the nation's first state survey since the federal historical records survey of the late 1930s. Author of volume 1 of Seattle's 20th century history, *Seattle, 1900-1920: From Boomtown, Urban Turbulence, to Restoration*.